CENSUS OF INDIA 1911

Census of India 1871-1951, 9 Sets In 384 Bindings (9788121258876) Rs. 700000

Census of India 1911, 23 Vols. In 41 Bindings (9788121271271) Rs. 69000

1. India - Report (9788121275071) Rs. 2475 (Vol. I, Pt. 1)
2. India - Tables (9788121275057) Rs. 2225 (Vol. I, Pt. 2)
3. Andaman and Nicobar Islands - Report & Tables (9788121275033) Rs. 900 (Vol. II, Pt. 1 & 2)
4. Assam - Report (9788121275019) Rs. 1000 (Vol. III, Pt. 1)
5. Assam - Tables (9788121274999) Rs. 1300 (Vol. III, Pt. 2)
6. Baluchistan - Report & Tables (9788121274975) Rs. 950 (Vol. IV, Pt. 1 & 2)
7. Bengal, Bihar And Orissa And Sikkim - Report (9788121274951) Rs. 3100 (Vol. V, Pt. 1)
8. Bengal - Tables (9788121274937) Rs. 2250 (Vol. V, Pt. 2)
9. Bihar And Orissa - Tables and Bengal And Sikkim - Chapter I of Administrative Volume (9788121274913) Rs. 1800 (Vol. V, Pt. 3 & 4)
10. City of Calcutta - Report and Tables and Administrative (9788121274876) Rs. 1300 (Vol. VI, Pt. 1 & 2 & 3)
11. Bombay - Report (9788121274814) Rs. 1950 (Vol. VII, Pt. 1)
12. Bombay - Imperial Tables and Administrative Report (9788121274791) Rs. 3300 (Vol. VII, Pt. 2 & 3)
13. Bombay (Town And Island) - Report And Tables (9788121274753) Rs. 1250 (Vol. VIII, Pt. 1 & 2)
14. Burma - Report (9788121274739) Rs. 2250 (Vol. IX, Pt. 1)
15. Burma - Tables (9788121274715) Rs. 1480 (Vol. IX, Pt. 2)
16. Central Provinces And Berar - Report (9788121274692) Rs. 1475 (Vol. X, Pt. 1)
17. Central Provinces And Berar - Tables (9788121274678) Rs. 1900 (Vol. X, Pt. 2)
18. Coorg - Report And Tables Madras - Report (9788121274630) Rs. 1740 (Vol. XI & Vol. XII, Pt. 1)
19. Madras - Imperial And Provincial Tables (9788121274616) Rs. 1500 (Vol. XII, Pt. 2)
20. Madras - Administrative Report and city of Madras (9788121274593) Rs. 630 (Vol. XII, Pt. 3 & 4)
21. North - West Frontier Province - Report & Tables (9788121274579) Rs. 2150 (Vol. XIII, Pt. 1 & 2)
22. Punjab - Report (9788121274555) Rs. 3000 (Vol. XIV, Pt. 1)
23. Punjab - Tables (9788121274531) Rs. 2200 (Vol. XIV, Pt. 2)
24. Punjab - Appendices To The - Imperial Tables (9788121274517) Rs. 950 (Vol. XIV, Pt. 3)
25. United Provinces of Agra And Oudh - Report (9788121274494) Rs. 2225 (Vol. XV, Pt. 1)
26. United Provinces of Agra And Oudh - Tables (9788121274470) Rs. 4000 (Vol. XV, Pt. 2)
27. United Provinces of Agra And Oudh - Provincial Tables And Appendices (9788121274456) Rs. 570 (Vol. XV, Pt. 3)
28. Baroda - Report (9788121274432) Rs. 2000 (Vol. XVI, Pt. 1)
29. Baroda State - The Imperial Tables (9788121274418) Rs. 850 (Vol. XVI, Pt. 2)
30. Central India Agency - Report And Tables (9788121274395) Rs. 1470 (Vol. XVII)
31. Cochin - Report And Imperial Tables (9788121274371) Rs. 1150 (Vol. XVIII, Pt. 1 & 2)
32. Hyderabad State - Report (9788121274357) Rs. 890 (Vol. XIX, Pt. 1)
33. Hyderabad State - Imperial And Provincial Tables (9788121274333) Rs. 1750 (Vol. XIX, Pt. 2)
34. Kashmir - Report (9788121274319) Rs. 950 (Vol. XX, Pt. 1)
35. Kashmir - Tables (9788121274296) Rs. 1170 (Vol. XX, Pt. 2)
36. Mysore - Report (9788121274272) Rs. 1200 (Vol. XXI, Pt. 1)
37. Mysore - Tables (9788121274258) Rs. 1500 (Vol. XXI, Pt. 2)
38. Rajputana And Ajmer-Merwara - Report (9788121274234) Rs. 1470 (Vol. XXII, Pt. 1)
39. Rajputana And Ajmer-Merwara - Tables (9788121274210) Rs. 1700 (Vol. XXII, Pt. 2)
40. Travancore - Report (9788121274197) Rs. 1870 (Vol. XXIII, Pt. 1)
41. Travancore - Imperial Tables (9788121274173) Rs. 870 (Vol. XXIII, Pt. 2)

CENSUS OF INDIA, 1911

VOLUME - IV

BALUCHISTAN

PART I - REPORT
PART II - TABLES

DENYS BRAY

GYAN

Published by

GYAN

Gyan Publishing House
5, Ansari Road
Daryaganj, New Delhi-110002
Phone: 011-47034999, 9811692060
E-mail: books@gyanbooks.com

Distribution Network
gyanbooks.com
India, USA, Canada, UK, Australia

ISBN: 978-81-212-7127-1 (Set) 23 Vols. In 41 Bindings

ISBN: 978-81-212-7497-5 (PB) Vol. IV, Pt. I, II

First Published, 1913

2nd Impression 2024

Printed at: Gyan Press, Delhi.

CENSUS OF INDIA 1911

CENSUS OF INDIA, 1911

VOLUME IV

BALUCHISTAN

Part I—REPORT

Agents for the Sale of Books published by the Superintendent of Government Printing, India, Calcutta.

IN THE UNITED KINGDOM.

Messrs. CONSTABLE & Co., 10, Orange Street, Leicester Square, London, W.C.
Messrs. KEGAN PAUL, TRENCH, TRÜBNER & Co., 68-74, Carter Lane, E.C.
Mr. BERNARD QUARITCH, 11, Grafton Street, New Bond Street, London, W.
Messrs. P. S. KING & SON, 2 and 4, Great Smith Street, Westminster, London, S.W.
Messrs. H. S. KING & Co., 65, Cornhill, and 9, Pall Mall, London.
Messrs. GRINDLAY & Co., 54, Parliament Street, London, S.W.
Mr. T. FISHER UNWIN, 1, Adelphi Terrace, London, W.C.
Messrs. W. THACKER & Co., 2, Creed Lane, London, E.C.
Messrs. LUZAC & Co., 46, Great Russell Street, London, W.C.
Mr. B. H. BLACKWELL, 50 and 51, Broad Street, Oxford.
Messrs. DEIGHTON, BELL & Co., Cambridge.
Messrs. OLIVER & BOYD, Tweeddale Court, Edinburgh.
Messrs. E. PONSONBY, Ld., 116, Grafton Street, Dublin.

ON THE CONTINENT.

Mr. OTTO HARRASSOWITZ, Leipzig.
Mr. KARL W. HIERSEMANN, Leipzig.
Messrs. R. FRIEDLANDER & SOHN, Berlin, W. N., Carlstrasse, 11.
Mr. ERNEST LEROUX, 28, Rue Bonaparte, Paris, France.
Mr. MARTINUS NIJHOFF, The Hague, Holland.

IN INDIA AND CEYLON.

Messrs. THACKER, SPINK & Co., Calcutta and Simla.
Messrs. NEWMAN & Co., Calcutta.
Messrs. R. CAMBRAY & Co., Calcutta.
Messrs. S. K. LAHIRI & Co., Calcutta.
Messrs. B. BANERJEE & Co., Calcutta.

IN INDIA AND CEYLON—*contd.*

THE CALCUTTA SCHOOL BOOK AND USEFUL LITERATURE SOCIETY, 309, Bow Bazar Street, Calcutta.
Messrs. BUTTERWORTH & Co. (INDIA), LD., Calcutta.
THE WELDON LIBRARY, 18-5, Chowringhee, Calcutta.
MESSRS. M. C. SIRCAR & SONS, 75, Harrison Road, Calcutta.
Messrs. HIGGINBOTHAM & Co., Madras.
Messrs. V. KALYANARAMA IYER & Co., Madras.
Messrs. G. A. NATESAN & Co., Madras.
Messrs. S. MURTHY & Co., Madras.
Messrs. THOMPSON & Co., Madras.
Messrs. TEMPLE & Co., Madras.
Messrs. COMBRIDGE & Co., Madras.
Messrs. P. R. RAMA IYER & Co., Madras.
Messrs. THACKER & Co., LD., Bombay.
Messrs. A. J. COMBRIDGE & Co., Bombay.
Messrs. D. B. TARAPOREVALA, SONS & Co., Bombay.
Mrs. RADHABAI ATMARAM SAGOON, Bombay.
Mr. SUNDAR PANDURANG, Bombay.
Messrs. GOPAL NARAYAN & Co., Bombay.
Messrs. RAM CHANDRA GOVIND & SON, Kalbadevi, Bombay.
Mr. N. B. MATHUR, Superintendent, Nazir-Kanun Hind Press, Allahabad.
RAI SAHIB M. GULAB SINGH & SONS, Mufid-i-Am Press, Lahore and Calcutta.
SUPERINTENDENT, AMERICAN BAPTIST MISSION PRESS, Rangoon.
Messrs. A. CHAND & Co., Punjab.
Babu S. C. TALUKDAR, Proprietor, Students and Company, Cooch Behar.
Messrs. A. M. & J. FERGUSON, Colombo, Ceylon.
Manager, Educational Book Depôts, Nagpur and Jubbulpur.*
Manager of the Imperial Book Depôt, 63, Chandney Chauk Street, Delhi.*
Manager, *East Coast News*, Vizagapatam.*
Manager, "The Agra Medical Hall and Co-operative Association, Limited" (Successors to A. JOHN & Co., Agra).*
Superintendent, Basel Mission Book and Tract Depository, Mangalore.*
Messrs. P. VARADACHARY & Co., Madras.*
Mr. H. LIDDELL, Printer, etc., 7, South Road, Allahabad.*
Messrs. D. C. ANAND & SONS, Peshawar.*

N.B.—[Those marked with an asterisk (*) are agents for sale of Legislative Department publications only.]

CENSUS OF INDIA, 1911

VOLUME IV

BALUCHISTAN

Part I—REPORT
Part II—TABLES

BY

DENYS BRAY, I.C.S.

CALCUTTA
SUPERINTENDENT GOVERNMENT PRINTING, INDIA
1913

PART I.

CONTENTS.

MAPS.

SUBSIDIARY TABLES.

PAGE.

NOTE.

This Report is unfortunately belated owing to the necessity of making special type for the transliteration of several vernacular words.

BALŪCHISTĀN
SHEWING
RACIAL DISTRIBUTION.

(N.B.—The racial boundaries are very approximate only.)

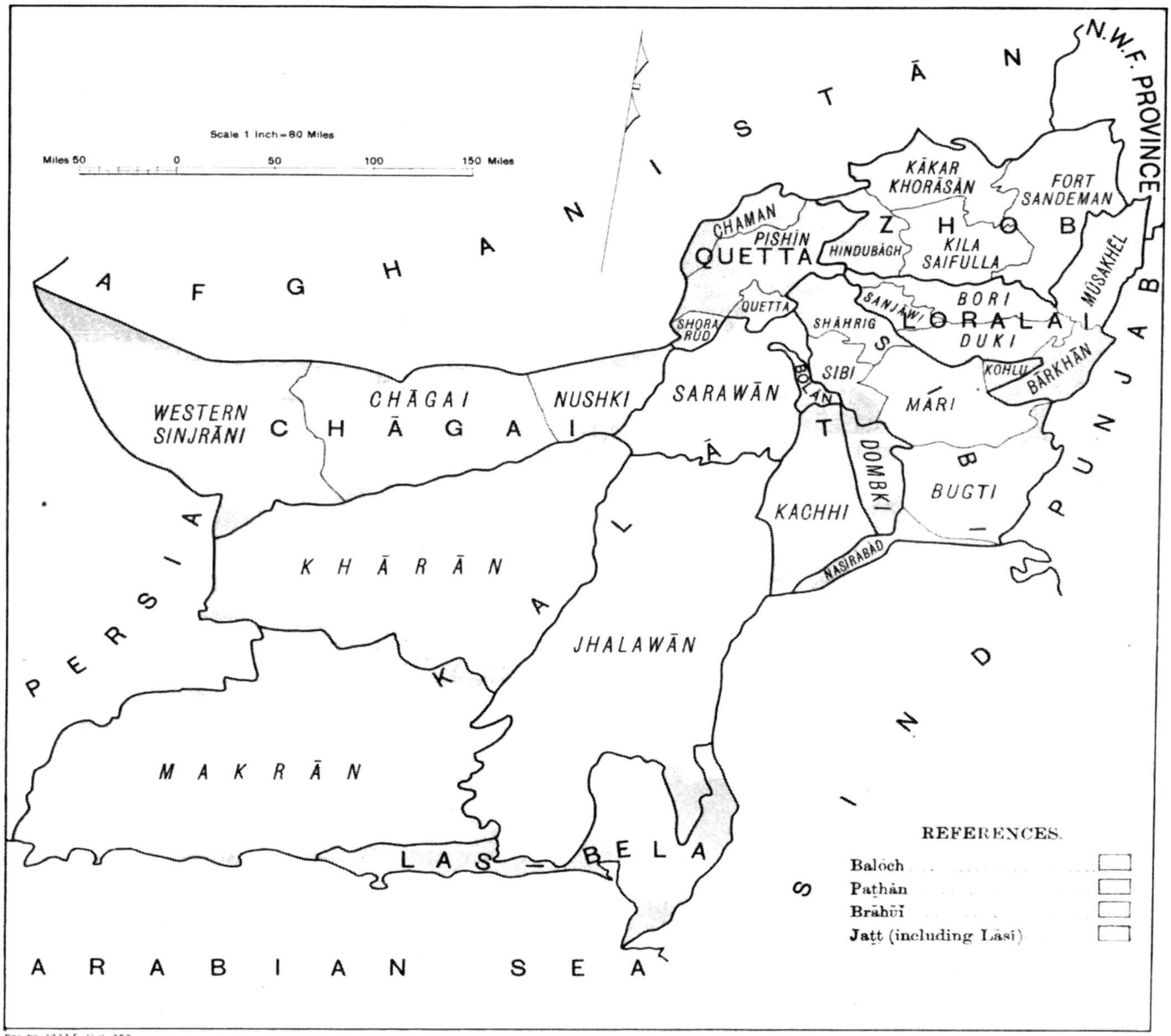

Reg. No. 3773 E. 11 H. 750

INTRODUCTION

1. So ends another census of Balūchistān—nominally the third in the series, yet the first to come home to every family in the length and breadth of the country. Not that Balūchistān is even now qualified to take its place among the ordered ranks of censused provinces of India. The latest joined recruit in the Indian Empire, it still has the awkward squad almost entirely to itself. A synchronous census, a census conducted on the precise lines of the standard schedule of India—these are still impracticable outside the few alien settlements dotted up and down the country. And the reasons lie on the surface. With but a dozen British officers and a proportionately small number of native officials to rule over this huge and mountainous area, a synchronous census is clearly a physical impossibility. Yet only half the difficulties have been stated. People the mountains with frontier tribesmen cleaving to the turbulent traditions of their forefathers, still broken in but imperfectly to the mysterious ways of British rule, suspicious of every symptom of innovation and reform, jealous to the verge of fanaticism of any enquiries touching their womenfolk—and an attempt to foist upon them in these early days of our administration a census framed on the searchingly inquisitive lines of the Indian schedule would not merely be foredoomed to failure, it would be a political blunder. **A regular synchronous census impracticable.**

2. And so, at first sight, we seem to have made little advance in our general methods of enumeration since the first census of 1891. Of that census there is, unfortunately enough, little to tell, for the very simple reason that nothing was left on written record except the bare facts that the operations extended over 20,568 square miles and that 171,752 souls were enumerated, with a few meagre details regarding the composition of the area and the distribution of the population. How the census was taken, has to be pieced together with the help of living memory from a few contemporary references in official documents. It appears that Quetta itself and three other garrison towns, together with the line of railway, were subjected to a synchronous but sketchy census, while the indigenous tribesmen were numbered on rough-and-ready methods. But the operations, such as they were—even in the Quetta Cantonment males and females were not distinguished—were confined to a very small part of the province. The Kalāt and Las Bēla states were left discreetly alone, and a census of Balūchistān which ignores the existence of the Brāhūī country is obviously shorn of most of its interest. **The census of 1891.**

3. The records of the second census of the country, on the other hand, are complete. The scheme of operations was somewhat complicated: civil headquarters, garrison towns and railway limits were censused by regular methods; the tribesmen in the districts were enumerated non-synchronously on a simple family schedule; the population of the native states was estimated still more roughly on a tribal basis. The operations covered an area of 82,950 square miles, and yielded a population of 810,746 souls all told. 51,688 square miles were left absolutely untouched. The results were admittedly rough: the estimated population, more especially in Jhalawān, was generally felt to be pitched too high; even in the district areas none but the barest details were recorded, and of the entries contained in the standard schedule those regarding age, marriage, subsidiary occupation, means of subsistence of dependants, birthplace, language, literacy, knowledge of English, and infirmities, were omitted altogether. But the census was a notable achievement for all that, and not the least notable feature of it was Mr. Hughes Buller's masterly report. Without the pioneer work done at the last census, the advance made at the census now concluded would have been impossible. And if I am able to go beyond Mr. Hughes Buller's conclusions, this is only because, standing on his shoulders, I am able to take a wider view of what before his time was in many ways an unknown land. **The census of 1901.**

4. As before, the census of municipalities, cantonments, railway limits and other settlements of aliens was taken on the census night (the night of the 10th March 1911) on the standard schedule. Nothing in this enumeration—and **The census of 1911.**

the same remark applies to the subsequent slip-work and tabulation of results as a whole—calls for comment. The operations were conducted on conventional lines, and have none of that imposing dignity of numbers which invests similar operations in other provinces.

The non-synchronous tribal census.

5. But the enumeration of the indigenous population proceeded non-synchronously on lines peculiar to itself. In the districts it was done by the village accountants, assisted here and there by the village schoolmaster or a levy clerk. Their work, which kept most of them busy for about three months, was scrutinised periodically by the district officials, who were however too heavily burdened with their ordinary duties to have much time to spare. Elsewhere, unfortunately, there was little or no staff available for the enumeration, and we had to engage special men to undertake it. The first essential we asked for in the enumerators was a knowledge of the tribesmen whom they were to enumerate; we found to our cost that this was too often coupled with a knowledge of very little else. But though the enumerators in the native states were poor stuff to begin with, they steadily improved as the operations developed, thanks to careful and patient training. That their eventual output of work was surprisingly good, was due in no small measure to the effective check of the state officials and the representatives supplied, but not paid, by the tribal chiefs, who responded admirably to the moral pressure brought to bear on them.

Necessity for a special schedule.

6. But if it was essential to humour the tribesmen by placing their enumeration in the hands of old acquaintances, it was at least as essential to enumerate them on a schedule that contained nothing to wound their very vulnerable susceptibilities. The crux of the problem lay of course in the enumeration of the women. While any question regarding their womenfolk is resented by the tribesmen, questions trespassing on the marriage state are resented in the extreme. All idea of adopting the apparently inoffensive division of the sex into 'married, unmarried or widowed' had necessarily to be abandoned. But so closely is the question of age interwoven with the delicate question of civil condition, that the recording of the one is as impossible as the recording of the other, and the most that could be done was to divide the womenfolk into those over and those under the age of puberty. And as it was palpably out of the question to enumerate the female portion of the population by individuals, it was felt advisable to give up an attempt at an individual census altogether, and to enumerate the whole tribal population on a household basis instead. The requisite schedule was not easy to devise. The original draft, modelled in the light of personal experience of Balūchistān on the schedule used at the last census in the Marī and Bugṭī country, was recast not once but several times in the course of discussion with the chiefs and tribesmen assembled at Sibī in the early spring of 1910 for the great half-yearly session of the Shāhī Jirga. In the end a schedule was evolved for the whole country which managed to pass muster before such very different and exacting critics as His Highness the Khān of Kalāt, the Jām of Las Bēla, the chiefs and the tribesmen on the one hand, and on the other the district officers, the Local Government and the Census Commissioner. Its final form was this:—

Serial No.	Name of householder.	House or tent or both.	Tribe.				Religion.		Occupation.		Language.		Members of the Household.								Remarks.
													Family.				Servile Dependants.				
													Males.		Females.		Males.		Females.		
			Race and tribe.	Clan.	Section.	Subsection.	Religion.	Sect.	Main.	Subsidiary.	Home language.	Outside language.	Adults.	Non-adults.	Adults.	Non-adults.	Adults.	Non-adults.	Adults.	Non-adults.	

Its suitability to local conditions.

7. Tribal life in Balūchistān lends itself admirably to a census on these lines. The conditions are primitive and patriarchal. The unit of society is not the individual but the joint family. In a typical household father, mother, sons and daughters live under the same roof and work together for the support of the whole family. One and all follow the lead of the head of the household. His religion is their religion; his tribe is their tribe. For even though a man marry a woman of another sect or alien race, she leaves her old faith and tribe behind her when she enters his household. Even as regards occupation

there is little scope for individualism. One of the sons perhaps is employed in the levies, but his earnings go into the common pot; indeed the billet he has secured is regarded as a billet secured for the family as a whole, to be passed on to another member of the family as convenience may suggest. In short, once we know the particulars regarding the head of a family, we can make a shrewd guess at the corresponding particulars for the various members of his whole household.

Record of other particulars.

8. In spite, therefore, of the absence of a column in the tribal schedule corresponding to the column headed 'means of subsistence of dependants on actual workers' in the standard schedule, there was little difficulty in collating the required information when the stage for tabulation was reached. Nor was any column provided for the recording of birthplace. Curious though it may seem, questions on this score are apt to be suspect in a land where tribal responsibility is a tangled yarn of birth in the tribe and residence in the tribe, and tribal responsibility is law: even as it was, several Kākaṛ families staying within Lūṇī limits beat back to their own country as soon as the census was a-foot, for fear that the records might condemn them to a life sentence of double tribal responsibility, first in their own Kākaṛ tribe and again among the Lūṇī. But it was not the possibility of arousing unrest that suggested the omission. In Balūchistān statistics of birthplace have too little value to be worth the trouble of grappling with the obvious difficulty of differentiating between the various members of a household. As a test of migration, for instance, they are as unnecessary as they are uncertain: aliens can be sifted from tribesmen without extraneous assistance; the two constituents of the population live to all intents and purposes in separate communities, and even where they mingle, there is scant danger of confusion between them. But the birthplace of all obvious aliens and also of Hindus and others who, as far as race went, might or might not be natives of Balūchistān was duly recorded, to enable us to trace the main streams of immigration to their sources. As for education, so little headway has it made among the tribesmen that it seemed safer to ascertain particulars of literacy and knowledge of English village by village. Had the household been taken as the unit, there would have been a lively danger that the enumerators, finding the columns blank for household after household, might leave them blank as a matter of course throughout. Statistics of infirmities were collected in the same manner.

No statistics of civil condition or age.

9. Thus the whole range of enquiries which make up the standard Indian schedule was covered in one way or another by the tribal census with two and only two real omissions. But both, though inevitable, are important enough. Statistics regarding civil condition there are none to offer, and the deficiency must be made good, as best it may, from the fairly wide general knowledge we have of the subject of marriage among the tribesmen. And bereft of the flood of light cast on the whole array of statistics in other provinces by the highly complicated—though confessedly not entirely accurate—statistics regarding age, we have to grope our way through our tables with the help of the dim and fitful glimmer that comes from a mere division of the population into minors and adults.

Certain additional statistics.

10. But while the Balūchistān schedule fell short to this extent of the standard schedule used elsewhere in India, in other respects it went beyond it. Most important of all was the provision made for an elaborate classification of the races into tribes, clans, sections and subsections. Though these details do not figure largely either in the following report or the Imperial tables, they are of much administrative value and ethnological interest, and will be fully analysed in a separate volume hereafter to be published under the authority of the Local Government. Our schedule again provided for statistics not only of religion but also of sect, chiefly with a view to discovering how far the curious Zikrī sect had been making headway. Of greater interest is the classification of the tribesmen according to the nature of their dwellings into nomad, semi-nomad and settled, a subject which will be treated at length in the third chapter. And finally by recording any second language spoken freely by all members of a household over and above the language ordinarily regarded as their mother-tongue, we have endeavoured to portray a remarkable feature of Balūchistān, and have collected statistics of no small linguistic interest.

Remarkably little double-counting.

11. So much for the tribal schedule; let me now turn to the tribal census itself. The most obvious drawback to any non-synchronous census lies in the danger of double-counting to which it is exposed. From this danger we issued with far greater success than the nomadic habits of so many of the tribesmen allowed us to count on. The various precautions that were taken it would be tedious to detail. Nor is it necessary; the conditions as a whole were after all very largely in our favour. Though the tribal census was anything but synchronous in the technical sense of the word, it was in so far synchronous that it was begun, conducted, and wound up more or less simultaneously in nearly all parts of the country. Better still, it was found possible so to arrange our programme that most of the enumeration fell within the summer, the one season of the year when the shifting elements of the population are comparatively settled. By taking the family and not the individual as the census unit, the risk of double-counting was largely discounted. The enumerators moreover set out on their work equipped with an intimate local knowledge, which enabled them both to detect omissions not only of families but of individuals, and also to exclude from the count casual visitors to the locality, whose proper place of enumeration was with their family elsewhere. The unavoidably large extent of an enumerator's beat in the native states, though in some ways unfortunate, was obviously in itself a very valuable safeguard against double-counting. And when the schedules eventually reached the central office, the small number of the people enumerated (or rather, the much smaller number of the families to which they belonged), coupled with the minute tribal details accompanying the name of the head of each family, rendered it possible to subject the results to a very real scrutiny. It may safely be said that there was little, if any, double-counting within the tribal census itself. A certain amount of double-counting of individuals, first under the tribal census and later under the regular census, was doubtless inevitable. But such cases were certainly not numerous; individual tribesmen do not over-lap into the regular areas except incidentally as sepoys or police and the like. And by excluding from the tribal census any members of a household who were expected to be resident in regular areas on the census night, and by clearing those areas as far as possible on that night of all tribesmen not ordinarily resident in them, we were able to reduce double-counting to a negligible quantity. In a word, I do not consider that this source of error has had an appreciably disturbing influence on the census.

Double-counting owing to migration from the province.

12. One potential form of double-counting lay unfortunately beyond our control. While we were at pains to exclude from the tribal census individual tribesmen who had left their homes for trade or in search of work down-country and were not expected back from their travels within the year, we were obviously unable to make similar allowances in the case of whole families of Jhalawān Brāhūīs who might or might not have made their way back from their winter quarters in Sind by the time of the Indian census. There is unhappily no very certain means of dividing up the total returns of Brāhūīs actually enumerated in Sind into those who were mere birds of passage already included in the tribal census of Balūchistān, and those who have taken up a more or less permanent abode in Sind and were consequently left out of account in our census. The number of the latter is known to be considerable. A large proportion of them are settlers who were fortunate enough to secure land in the canal colonies some fifteen or twenty years back in those strange days when the value of canal lands was still unrealised and enterprising colonists were scarce. Of late years they have been reinforced by hundreds of their kith and kin, attracted by the demand for labour to the prosperous plains of Sind, which offered them a pleasant refuge both from the long drought in their own hills and from the payment of tribal dues to their chiefs. But when all allowance is made for those who have thrown in their lot with Sind, it is reasonably certain that several migratory Brāhūīs were counted in Sind who had already been included in the tribal census of Balūchistān. Not that their numbers are so great as might have been expected; for the rains in the Brāhūī country were timely and fairly abundant, and many families were already on their homeward tramp by the time of the Indian census. Indeed had the date of the census been fixed a bare month later, the plains would have been wellnigh cleared of the last of them. Whatever may be the number covered by the double-counting of these amphibians of the hills of Balūchistān and the plains of Sind, it

does not of course affect the accuracy of the census of either province. Duplication only occurs when the returns of both flow together into the census of India, engulfed in whose mighty totals it is too insignificant to raise even a ripple of disturbance.

13. But if we succeeded, within the limits of our own province at any rate, in avoiding the great pitfall of double-counting that besets a non-synchronous census, we could hardly hope for the same measure of success in escaping the danger of omissions with which every census, even a thorough-going synchronous census, has necessarily to contend. To any one who has travelled amid the jumble of mountains that darken the map of Balūchistān, or along the bare wastes that leave so much of it blank, and has seen the seemingly inaccessible crannies, the seemingly waterless desolations in which the nomad finds a resting-place on his wanderings, the impossibility of avoiding omissions can come as no surprise. To all who have taken an active part in the census the surprise has been that the omissions were so few. In organising the scheme of operations I resigned myself to a low standard of accuracy as inevitable. I was oppressed by the obvious difficulty of rounding up within the census the backward and largely nomadic peoples scattered so sparsely over the vast area covered by this rugged frontier province. But as soon as I was able to watch the organisation in progress, I found my gloomy anticipations falsified all along the line. The standard of efficiency with which we wound up was very different from the standard with which we set out; the organisation was in fact a great deal more effective than its author dared to hope for. The enlistment of the interest of the tribal chiefs in the census, the modification of the standard schedule in deference to tribal susceptibilities, the entrusting of the actual enumeration to men who knew the tribesmen, their manners and their country—herein lay the main secrets of our success. In the regular districts, where the existence of a trained revenue staff was more or less a guarantee of efficient enumeration, few omissions were anticipated, and still fewer appear to have occurred. And if conclusions derived from a careful personal check up and down the country and from repeated general enquiries can be trusted, the percentage of omissions was hardly higher throughout the native states and tribal tracts, which are only indirectly under our administration. In all probability it reached its highest in Jhalawān and more especially in the Mēngal country, where political trouble called for a military demonstration as recently as 1908 and has not wholly subsided. **Inevitable omissions.**

14. But though we must plead guilty to sins of omission, it is obviously impossible to make amends by nice calculations of the actual percentage of loss. I believe it to have been remarkably small. So much is certain. The census has been a very real enumeration of the population, unvitiated by estimates or guess-work. It has suffered inevitably from the inherent defects of a non-synchronous census. But a non-synchronous census has, after all, compensating advantages of its own, not the least of which is the greater time that can be devoted to the actual enumeration, to the accurate ascertaining and recording of the requisite particulars, and to the local checking of the results. That the census has been far more trustworthy than any synchronous census of Balūchistān on the standard Indian schedule could possibly have been—even if political, to say nothing of financial, considerations had permitted the flooding of the country with the gigantic swarm of enumerators required to undertake it—of this I have no doubt whatever. **General conclusions.**

15. To our frontier tribesmen everything connected with the census pointed to war and the preparation for war. So far from this having any disturbing influence, it found a sympathetic echo in their warlike hearts, and left them with the comfortable feeling of having discovered what the extraordinary trouble was about. All our pretty parables of the good farmer who takes stock of his farm or the careful housewife who counts her chickens before and after they are hatched, they brushed aside as child's talk. War they understood, and war or the preparation for war was of course the object of the census; the one thing they were unable to square with this rooted idea was the fantastic counting of the womenfolk. Now it so happened that the opportunity of the census was taken to collect certain additional information for administrative purposes, and our enquiries embraced the numbers of their donkeys and camels **Rumours of war.**

and plough oxen, water-mills and hand-mills and musical instruments, harmless unnecessary information, designed to cover up the real object of our inquisition—a rough idea of the arms in the possession of our various tribes. But trust a tribesman to see through so thin a disguise. Even as the tribes were being numbered to gauge the supply of men-at-arms, so the camels and the oxen and the asses were being numbered for future service as transport. The mills were to grind corn for the combatants. And the whole force was to march forth to battle to the stirring strains of the sackbut, the psaltery and all kinds of music.

Other gossip.

16. Sometimes, however, their thoughts took a more peaceful turn. Though nothing could shake the general conviction that the primary object of enumerating the blind, the deaf, the leper and the insane, was to weed wastrels from the fighting strength of the tribe, it was gravely argued by some that the benign government was contemplating a form of Old Age Pension for these unfortunates in honour of the King Emperor's accession. The tribesmen were at first exercised by the encyclopædic nature of our enquiries. But they soon fell into the spirit of the thing. "I should like you to put down my poor old sheep dog," said one waggish Paṭhān. "It's a great pity," quoth a hoary-headed Brāhūī lady, "that you're leaving out our cooking-pots, you would otherwise have numbered everything there is to number among us." The fisherfolk of Sōnmiānī went one further, and gravely presented me at the close of the check of their village with a list based on their catches for the season, in which not only the numbers but the names of the fishy tribes on the Bēla coast were faithfully recorded. In another village we were asked if we would mind waiting a few days, as several of the womenfolk were hourly expected to add to the census. Over the counting of the women many heads were wagged. Some folks thought that government's sole object was to give its servants something to do; but they had to admit that there was probably something behind it after all, when some wiseacre pointed out that the graves were being left uncounted. In the wilds of Makrān it was whispered that one woman in every forty was to be shipped to England, and sent to the marriage-market, or else to the shambles for the production of *mōmiyāī*, that precious juice which exudes from dead bodies and is a panacea for all ills; happily the sinister rumour died down almost as soon as it was born. But I must not forget the most laughable idea of all. In the course of some ethnological research I had asked one of my staff to make some discreet enquiries regarding female circumcision as it exists among certain of our races. As good luck would have it, he soon fell in with a garrulous Makrānī midwife who regaled him with several bits of first-hand gossip. By the next day she must have got to know that he was connected with the census, for she came bustling up with eyes starting out of her head, and dropping her voice to a hoarse whisper exclaimed: "There now! And I never guessed why you're counting the women, dullard that I was! And it's as plain as a pikestaff that government is going to circumcise the lot of us!" The old lady must have been sadly disappointed to find that the expected boom in her trade never came off at all.

Frontier incidents.

17. The good humour with which the tribesmen entered into the census was not the least pleasing feature in our work. There were a few little rifts in the general harmony, it is true; but these one learns to expect on the frontier. For months it looked as if K͟hārān would have to be left out altogether; for the chief had declined roundly to have anything to do with government in any shape or form, and adopted an attitude so obstructive as to fire his uncle with the fatuous idea that we would look on unmoved while he put an end to him and usurped the chiefship. From this fool's dream he was rudely awakened by the appearance of troops on the scene, which speedily paved the way for the peaceful census of K͟hārān at the eleventh hour. One of the enumerators in the Shīrānī country was kidnapped and left to kick his heels for a few days on the other side of the border. The enumerator in the heart of the Mēngal country was beaten and his precious schedules were torn to shreds and thrown to the winds. But none of these incidents were consciously directed against the census; they were merely the effervescence of that spirit of independence which frontier tribesmen still think it necessary to display from time to time. Nor do they darken the general impression of goodwill and

kindly welcome on the part of chiefs and tribesmen alike, with which my two assistants and I came back from our tours.

18. And our touring took one or other of us into wellnigh every part of the country. For success clearly hung on the amount of personal inspection we could devote to the operations. It may help to conjure up something of the physical conditions of the country if I give a few bare facts about our tours. Apart from journeys by rail and by sea, we covered in all 6,041 miles by road between the three of us. By road? It was often a sorry apology for a camel-track. But to myself crude figures convey little—a pathetic confession, I suppose, for a census officer to make—and I have amused myself by calculating that one would have to tramp three times from John o'Groats to Land's End and back and once again to Land's End, to top the mileage of our wanderings. As for the enumerators, they must have put a girdle round about the earth among the lot of them. **Heavy touring involved.**

19. Here then is one very obvious reason for the unavoidably high cost of the operations, for it goes without saying that one cannot travel in the wilds of the frontier without tents or escorts. The costliness of the Balūchistān census was so very different from the admirable economy with which a census is conducted elsewhere in India, that I am tempted to hide the figures (from all but the unnaturally curious) in the obscurity of a subsidiary table. But the bare details must out. In confessing to a cost of Rs. 57-1-10 or Rs. 110-7-6—there are two complicated systems of accounts to choose from—for every thousand souls we enumerated, I can probably claim the melancholy distinction of having conducted the most expensive enumeration in India during the present operations. But I cannot accept this conventional measurement of the cost in terms of numbers as in any way appropriate to the peculiar circumstances of Balūchistān. On the contrary, it would not be difficult to make out a case to prove that the very smallness of our scattered population tends unavoidably to heighten the cost of a census, and that an increase in the population would tend to cut the expenses down. To any one who knows the country or takes the trouble to turn to it on the map, a much more appropriate method of reckoning the cost of the census is to look not to the numbers enumerated but to the area over which they are scattered. Judged in this light 0-5-8 (or if the other account system is preferred, 0-10-11) for every square mile is no inglorious record. I doubt whether any other province, however much more favourable its general conditions, could hope to enter the lists against it. **Cost of the operations.**

20. But it would be churlish to turn from this unconventional census to the unconventional report without a word of thanks to those who enabled me to carry out the one and to write the other. In this one feature of the census I have suffered from the embarrassment of numbers. Indeed the people I had to count were so few and my fellow-workers so many, that I find it a little hard to realise that any of the work fell to me at all. In the assistants who were given me at various stages I was fortunate indeed. During the greater part of the active operations I had at my back the ripe experience and sound judgment of R. B. Dīwān Jamiat Rāi, C.I.E., and even when he was recalled to other duties, he continued to give me his invaluable help at every turn. In K. S. Mirzā Shēr Muhammad I had an ideal assistant to undertake the first real census of the Brāhūi country: a Brāhūi himself, he knows it from corner to corner, and a good deal of his knowledge of his race is reflected in these pages. Upon the shoulders of M. Gul Muhammad fell the burden of the tabulation of the statistics, and the zest he put into it enabled me to turn from this dreary drudgery to more enlivening parts of the census. How much work my head clerk, L. Chōith Rām, has saved me, he alone knows. And as I pen the last words of this report, I become conscious of the debt I owe to Colonel Archer not only for the many suggestions he has made from the fulness of his knowledge of Balūchistān but also for the stimulating interest he has throughout taken in the operations, and to Mr. William Archer for laboriously reading the proofs from cover to cover. But I suppose the people to whom I owe most are the tribesmen themselves, and the chiefs above all. It was thanks very largely to their great if somewhat amused kindliness that, with the help of my staff, I was able not only to count heads but to get some sort of peep at the thoughts inside them. And thus what would otherwise have been arid labour proved a pleasant and very interesting duty. **Acknowledgments.**

CHAPTER I.

POPULATION.

Statistical data.

Subject.	Tables		
	Imperial.	Provincial.	Subsidiary.
Area, houses and population	I	......	......
Density	......	I	I
House-population	......	......	IV
Political Agencies and *tahsils*	......	I, II	......
Race	XIII	......	II
Towns and villages	III	......	III

Descriptive and Historical.

21. Balūchistān—it would be pedantry, I suppose, to insist on Balōchistān—is the extreme north-west buttress of the Indian Empire. Its 134,638 square miles sprawl out into an irregularly shaped block of country, generally described in defiance of all geometrical definitions as oblong. It is bounded on the south by the Arabian Sea, with a small inlet of Muscat territory round Gwādar; on the east it is bounded by Sind, the Panjāb and the North-West Frontier Province; on the north by independent territory and Afghānistān; on the west by Persia. At the tip of the horn that juts out on the north-west stands Kōh-i-Malik Siāh, an otherwise unenviable desolation which enjoys the double distinction of being the most westerly point of all India and the meeting-place of three great countries, Afghānistān, Persia, and the Indian Empire. Not without justice does Balūchistān claim high rank among the frontier provinces of India. For 520 miles it marches with Persia, for 723 miles with Afghānistān, for 38 miles with independent territory. There are 471 miles of coast-line along the Arabian Sea; the precise length of the inconsiderable Muscat frontier is a matter in hot dispute. **Geographical.**

22. It is a land of contradictions and contrasts. From a bird's-eye view the general impression would probably be a chaotic jumble of mud-coloured mountains, for all the world like a bewildered herd of titanic camels. Yet it contains many a rich valley and upland plateau, and at least one broad plain as flat and low-lying as any in India. For a brief and fitful season its rivers are rushing torrents; for the greater part of the year there is hardly a trickle in their giant beds. On the maps there are three large lakes of limpid blue—very different from the gloomy swamps of reality. But the maps are crammed full of unconscious irony; and if you come to the country after poring over these elaborate patchworks of well-defined rivers, refreshing oases of green, and named localities innumerable, small wonder if you condemn it on sight as a land of rivers without water, of forests without trees, of villages without inhabitants. The whole outlook seems bleak and bare. Yet you have only to scratch the soil and add a little water, and you can grow what you please. But often enough nature is so perverse that where **Descriptive.**

there is land, there is no water, and where there is water, there is no land. Probably no province in India can show so vast a range of climate. The winter cold of the uplands baffles description. Even in Quetta (and Quetta, high-lying though it is, is surrounded by mountains five thousand feet higher) it is bitter enough. It is a mildish winter when eggs are not frozen solid; a few years back coveys of chikor were driven into the heart of the market-place benumbed and starving. Yet the readings of the thermometer give but a poor idea of the rigours of the winter, as everybody knows to his cost who has faced the happily infrequent blast of iciness that is driven over the snow-capped Khwāja Amrān. As for the mid-summer heat of the Kachhī plain, I can only fall back on the hackneyed local proverb of the superfluity of Hell to depict that burning fiery furnace. The sun beats fiercely even above the passes: I have met tribesmen loud in their praises of the telegraph service along the Nushkī trade-route; it was not the speedy despatch of messages that appealed to them—that they have found at times an unmitigated nuisance; it was the grateful shade shed by the telegraph poles all along the road. On first acquaintance a newcomer is tempted to sum up Balūchistān as 'a vast country, mostly barren,' unconsciously echoing the unflattering verdict passed on Makrān more than a thousand years ago by the Arab traveller and historian, Al Istakhrī. Yet among those who have sojourned long enough in Balūchistān for their first impressions to fade away, there are few who have not fallen under the mysterious spell cast by this wild country and its wild inhabitants.

Population.

23. The contrast between Balūchistān's imposing area and its modest population is almost grotesque. A scanty rain-fall and lack of perennial water are enough in themselves to make a sparse population a foregone conclusion. Yet the extraordinary sparseness of the population will probably come as a surprise to most people who have any conception of the vastness of the country. 834,703 souls, all told, were actually enumerated during the census. True, if we are seeking to gauge the normal strength of Balūchistān, we should in fairness add somewhat to this humble total. For the country, largely inhabited as it is by nomadic peoples, is extravagantly affected by the nature of the seasons: given a good season it will attract thousands from across its borders; given a bad season, it will send them back, with many thousands of its own besides. Now when the census was being taken, conditions were more or less normal in the Paṭhān part of the country; but in Chāgai and Makrān and still more markedly in Jhalawān, conditions were not a little unfavourable. Yet, when all allowances have been made, it probably takes a pretty good season to raise the numbers above a million. Let me try to bring the contrast between area and population into bolder relief. Balūchistān contributes $\frac{1}{13}$th to the area of the Indian Empire, yet it has contributed little more than a paltry $\frac{1}{377}$th to the teeming millions enumerated at the current census. Though there is not much to choose between Balūchistān and the Panjāb in the matter of area, the Panjāb lost considerably more people from plague alone in the last four years than can be found to-day in the whole of Balūchistān. Or put it another way. So vast is Balūchistān that if the British Isles, Channel Islands and all, were lifted up and dumped down on it, there would still be room for over thirteen thousand square miles of surrounding sea. So insignificant is its population, that it falls far short of the births in the British Isles in a single year.

Retrospect and forecast.

24. It may be that the population was much greater in the dark backward of time. This at any rate is the thought that forces itself upon most people who have seen the extensive *gabr-bands* studded up and down the country to the west, especially in parts that now are all but desert. Most of these 'dams of the fire-worshippers' were palpably designed to hold up mountain torrents for agricultural purposes. A few seem to be remains of terraced fields. Here and there they look more like watering-places for men or beasts. But be they what they may, it is clear that they were the handiwork of a race of thrifty husbandmen, people very different from our devil-me-care tribesmen of to-day. Whether Balūchistān under present conditions could support a much larger population than it actually does, is open to question. Geologists indulge in

gloomy prophecies of its gradual desiccation and ultimate depopulation. But large schemes for damming up its mighty floods are now being evolved, and should they come into being, the census reports of the future may have a very different tale to tell. Yet though scientific irrigation on a large scale might easily spell a tremendous increase in population, one need not necessarily be a pessimist to have an uneasy feeling that without wise guidance it might also spell a deterioration in the breed. It is not merely that material prosperity has an awkward habit of bringing compensating disadvantages in its train. In Balūchistān, society rests on an ancient tribal system, which, admirably suited though it is under existing primitive conditions to people and country alike, is peculiarly sensitive to changes of all kinds, and sensitive above all to any change in the communal or quasi-communal tenures of land on which it is partially grounded. It is a sturdy breed of up-standing men that Balūchistān has produced under the tribal system. And an increase in mere numbers would be poor consolation, if an improvement in environment brought with it not simply a break-down of the tribal system, but a deterioration in the breed, such as sets in with pathetic rapidity among Brāhūīs who settle down in the enervating prosperity of Sind.

The tribal system.

25. Though the term 'tribal system' is constantly on our lips, it is curiously difficult to define. The truth is that the tribal system is not one and immutable throughout the country. It is to be found in all stages of evolution—from infancy to maturity, from maturity to senile decay. And different races and even different tribes within the same race have evolved characteristic varieties of it, suited to their peculiar needs. But however numerous the varieties, there are certain broad features of similarity running through them all. If I were asked to describe rather than to define the typical tribal system, I should be inclined to say that it is the negation of individualism; individualism is certainly its most insidious enemy. Ask a wayfarer in Balūchistān who he is, and he will simply reply that he is a Brāhūī or whatever his particular race may be. Press him further, and he will say he is a Bangulzai; then, if that does not satisfy you, he will add that he is a Badūzai, and clinch matters by saying that he is a Ṭēngizai. Further cross-examination may perhaps elicit the more intimate detail that he is an Āghālizai. The information is now complete: he is a member of the Āghālizai group of the Ṭēngizai section of the Badūzai clan of the Bangulzai tribe of Brāhūī. A glimpse of tribal society peeps out from these answers, I think. Society under the tribal system is no random collection of individuals: it is a living organic whole, made up of organisms within organisms. And the most rudimentary organism of all is the family. Nowadays a typical tribal family consists of the father and his unmarried sons; from a purely formal point of view the wives and the daughters are rather part of the family's wealth, than actual members of it. In olden days the family probably included the eldest living male and all his descendants, and the smallness of the modern family is perhaps a symptom that the system is beginning to decay from within. Now in the family the most obvious bond is the common blood that runs through all its members. But common blood is not sufficient in itself, for a division of the family property results at once in the fissure of the family into several smaller organisms of the same kind. Common blood, common property, common weal and woe, these are the bonds that bind the family together. And the same bonds operate with varying force all up the line, till the tribe itself is reached. True, the bond of common blood in the tribe is often enough imaginary or fictitious; it is none the less real for all that. Even the bond of common property still holds good in some form or other, though it may be somewhat hidden out of sight if tribal tenure of land has passed into severalty. The bond of common weal and woe now looms largest, simply because it is the most material and practical bond of the three, and forms the basis of that communal or tribal responsibility which is the immediate connecting-link between the tribal system and our administration. Corresponding to the patriarch at the head of every well-ordered tribal family, there are leaders at the head of the groups and sections and clans of every well-ordered tribe, all taking their proper place in the tribal hierarchy, with the tribal chief at the pinnacle of them all. And just as strangers may be found as guests within the family circle, alien groups may be found sheltering within the tribe; but whereas the tribe is constantly absorbing such *hamsāya*, 'sharers of the same shade' as they

are called, into the tribal organism, there is no customary method of adopting strangers—other than females on marriage—into the family. And finally, just as there are dependants attached to the family, yet not members of the family, so in the tribe, yet not of the tribe, there are alien elements—Sayyid, Hindu, Lōṛī and the rest—all more or less parasitic, who serve the spiritual and temporal needs of the tribesmen. The family is in fact the tribe in germ.

Racial ties.

26. When we mount from the tribes to the larger whole to which these belong in fact or theory, we find that the bonds that bind race together are fragile indeed. Common blood now runs in a very thin trickle: little though we know of the ancestry of any of our three principal races, Brāhūī, Balōch or Paṭhān, we know that they are of a very mongrel composition. The bond of common land has worn down to a mere matter of hazy territorial boundaries. As for the bond of common weal and woe, it all but snapped on the arrival of British rule and the removal of necessity for union against a common foe. But racial bonds are present none the less, and the most potent of all is the inheritance of a common *rivāj* or body of customary law, which remains in principle pretty much the same throughout the race, though the evolution of details may have been very diverse among the many tribes. So much for the present state of affairs. But time was when national if not ethnical unity was a real thing in Balūchistān. For out of seemingly hopeless heterogeneity the old Ahmadzai K͟hāns succeeded with consummate statecraft in welding together a powerful Confederacy embracing wellnigh all the tribes of Balūchistān south of Quetta. And uniting Sarāwān and Jhalawān, as the Confederacy was called, were much the same bonds as unite the family and the clan and the tribe. Common blood, to be sure, there was little enough in the strict sense of the word, for the members of the Confederacy were drawn from multitudinous sources; nevertheless membership gave to one and all what amounts to much the same thing, and what fiction often converts into the same thing—common status. That the K͟hāns knew the strength of the bond of common land, they have left evidence behind them in the tribal lands of the Kachhī. But the vital bond of unity was the bond of common weal and woe; and the common weal of Kalāt in the golden age of Nasīr K͟hān the Great made Balūchistān one commonweal in the modern sense of the word. It is worth while to take a fleeting glance at the Kalāt of those by-gone days, the better to understand the Balūchistān of to-day. For Balūchistān under British rule is the lineal descendant of the old Brāhūī Confederacy, with the important Paṭhān country north of Quetta thrown in. Balūchistān after all is really a misnomer. To be of geographical significance, it should include Persian Balūchistān. Politically, the best title would be Brāhūīstān, the land of the old Brāhūī nation. It is only in the not uncommon use—or rather misuse—of Balōch as a synonym for Brāhūī, that the present title can find justification at all.

Ancient history.

27. We need not linger over the ancient history of the country. Nor would our curiosity be rewarded if we did. Of ancient Balūchistān strangely little is known, yet it lies on one of the great highways trodden by the many conquerors of India. Achaemenian, Macedonian, Arab, G͟haznivid, Mog͟hal, Afshārid, Durrānī, have sojourned in it, and after a brief sojourn passed on, leaving scarce a trace behind. A few mounds, a few coins, a few bits of pottery, a few legends, possibly a few names, are almost all that remain in the country as a memorial of their sojourn, unless perchance some of their blood still runs attenuated in the veins of the people. And though the mists that brood over ancient Balūchistān are fitfully broken by Persian poet and Greek and Arab historian, nothing stands out clear from the written records except a vivid picture of Alexander's amazing march through the wastes of Makrān. Of the ancient inhabitants of the country they tell us tantalisingly little. From the Greeks we hear of the Gadrosi, the Oreitai, the Arabiti, who vainly sought to oppose Alexander on his march — strange names in which the eye of faith has variously read (among others) the present-day Gadra or Gadōr of Las Bēla, the Hōt of Makrān or the Hōṛū of Jhalawān, and the Arabs or the people about the Hab river. In the Arab chronicles we read of the Mēd and the Jat. And while there seems little danger in recognising here the modern Mēd of the coast and the Jaṭṭ of the plains, we may well pause before we follow others in tracing their ancestry back to the Medes and the Gethae of the classics. It is a wise instinct to be mistrustful of the lure of imagined similarity of sounds.

At this stage of ethnological knowledge it is well to accept the tribes as we find them, without attempting what seems at present the unprofitable task of probing into their origins. That the Balōch slowly made their way hither from a westerly direction some time between the 7th and the 15th centuries; that the Paṭhāns have been lodged here round the Takht-i-Sulemān from time immemorial—so much seems tolerably certain. But whence and when these Brāhūīs, who speak a Dravidian tongue and point to sacred Aleppo as their ancient home, really came to Balūchistān, is as much of a puzzle as who they really are.

The rise of the Brāhūī Confederacy.

28. Nor can we trace the process by which the Ahmadzai or rather the Mīrwāṛī, once apparently an insignificant section of the Kambrāṛī Brāhūī, rose to be rulers of the country. Perhaps the Mīrwāṛī had some accidental advantage over their fellows—a little more valour, a little more shrewdness, a little more wealth, and therefore a little more means of displaying that hospitality which is an irresistible loadstone to Brāhūī and Balōch to this day. Perhaps a mysterious halo of sanctity surrounded some family among them: what was spiritual influence in the beginning may have developed into temporal power in the end; the tribesmen perchance went forth to seek a holy peace-maker, and found a ruler. Whatever the history of the rise of the Mīrwāṛī may be, the Khānate certainly sprang from mean beginnings. Tradition has it that when the petty chieftains in the neighbourhood of Kalāt, tired of their dissensions, called upon the Mīrwāṛī to place one of their number at their head, none of the elder members would deign to accept the offer, and it was passed on to Mīr Hassan who stood far down the line. From the time of Mīr Hassan is supposed to date the division of the tribes into Sarāwān and Jhalawān, those above and below Kalāt, and it was as Sarāwān and Jhalawān that the Confederacy came to be known. From him too is supposed to date the furnishing of men-at-arms by the various tribes in set proportions, and also the allotment of certain lands and miscellaneous service for the upkeep of the ruler's position. But all this is vaguest tradition. Not till 1660, the year of the succession of Mīr Ahmad, from whom the dynasty takes its name, do we reach anything like history. And even here it is threadbare history at best, and the annals of the dynasty are little more than a string of names down to Mīr Abdulla, to whose political sagacity and martial enterprise during his rule from 1715 to 1730 the consolidation of the Confederacy appears to have been due.

Its constitution under Nasīr Khān the Great.

29. But famous ruler though he was, he is overshadowed by his son, Nasīr Khān the Great. There is no need to follow Nasīr Khān through his long career, either in his hard apprenticeship at the Kandahār court, his military training with Nādir Shāh's army of conquest, or his long rule of forty-four years. It is the Kalāt constitution, on which he placed the coping-stone, with which alone we are concerned. Even here we have to peer through a haze of tradition, before we can make out its main outlines; its details are hopelessly blurred. Brāhūīs themselves look back on everything connected with their national hero through rosy-coloured spectacles. But even though their enthusiasm may partially succeed in distorting our vision, it would perhaps matter little after all. The Kalāt constitution as the Brāhūīs think it ought to have been is a matter of hardly less lively interest to us than the constitution of Kalāt as it really was. For practical purposes at any rate the Brāhūī's Utopia is of greater moment than the reality: it is far more important that our own policy should reflect the fond dreams of the people, than that it should be susceptible of being traced back by learned research to historical precedent.

The Khān and the Chiefs.

30. The old analogy—half metaphor, half reality—will help us again. The Confederacy was a family writ large, a fraternity of tribes, a mutual co-operation society, all the members of which contributed to the welfare of the whole, and derived their welfare from it. The Khān—or *Bēglar Bēgī*, the Chief of the Chiefs, to employ the title conferred by Nādir Shāh—was the father of his people, and it was from the people, through their representatives the chiefs, that he derived his authority. This authority was given him freely by virtue of his birth, for the Brāhūīs have a deep-rooted feeling that a son should sit in the seat of his fathers. And the authority, once given, was loyally acknowledged by virtue of the divinity that hedged his person. And what applies to the Khān himself, applies also to the chiefs. A chief was not, indeed is not, a despot, any more than the Khān. His authority is derived directly

from his tribesmen; in formally recognising his chiefship the Khān (or, for the matter of that, the British government) is simply ratifying the choice of the tribe. And the chief, like the Khān, maintains his position over his people, not merely because they themselves have given it to him as his birthright, nor because he uses it, or is supposed to use it, for their welfare, but very largely because of that semi-religious veneration with which all Brāhūīs and Balōch instinctively regard their rulers. Though this veneration is often severely tried in these self-seeking days, it is marvellous how well it stands the strain.

Decentralisation in internal government.

31. In all internal matters the Khān—I am still speaking of the days when 'Khāns were philosophers and philosophers Khāns'—interfered with the chiefs as little as possible in the control of their tribes. He was in short a staunch upholder of the tribal system, the key-note of which is decentralisation all down the line. The head of the family, the *kamāsha* or section-leader, the *ṭakkarī* or clan-leader, the *sardār* or chief—each was left to the management of his own charge. In the maintenance of his authority in his allotted sphere those above and below him were almost equally concerned. To those below him he was not only the first court of appeal, he was their representative, their mouthpiece and their champion in the larger whole of which their group formed a unit. It must needs have been a serious dispute that would not resolve itself at the interposition of the head of the group, who could bring into play not merely his authority as such, but the pressure of public opinion within the group, the ancient customary modes of conciliation and settlement, the mediation of Sayyids and other holy men, and in the last resort the entreaties of the whole body of womenfolk. And on the measure of success with which he carried his group with him, hung the measure of his influence with the powers above him. A chief was naturally inclined to lean on a *ṭakkarī* who showed that he had the corporate goodwill of the clan behind him by never allowing disputes to pass beyond him to the chief. Similarly the influence of a chief with the Khān depended on his authority over his tribe, and this in turn depended very largely on his making every officer in the tribal hierarchy control his own particular group. And when disputes did come before the Khān, either because a chief could not or would not bring about a settlement between his own tribesmen, or because two chiefs were at loggerheads among themselves, they were heard by the Khān in his Darbār, and justice was swift, simply because, though delay—like justice itself—cost the litigants nothing, it cost the Khān a good deal, as he charged himself with their maintenance, with their *rōza* and *jīra* as it was called, so long as they remained at his court. And here we stumble up against one of the main secrets to which not only the Khān but the chiefs owed their extraordinary hold over the tribesmen—a lavish display of hospitality. "Hold out a joint," Nasīr Khān used to say, "and the Brāhūīs will flock to you from all sides for a bite."

External policy in the Khān's hands.

32. Unfortunately there is as much truth in the aside with which he concluded. "And when they have torn off the flesh, they will squabble among themselves like dogs for the bone." Not without good cause does he appear to have recognised in a forward policy abroad the best means of securing peace at home. Now while the Khān left the various units a free hand to manage their internal affairs, he kept the foreign policy in his own hands. Here his word was supreme. But it was supreme, simply because he took the precaution to carry his people with him. Just as in the Kandahār representative at his court and in his own representative at Kandahār he had counsellors who could keep his policy from coming into serious conflict with the wishes of the suzerain power, so in his chiefs, and more especially in the Raisānī and Zarakzai, the premier chiefs of Sarāwān and Jhalawān, he had counsellors who could keep it in harmony with public opinion at home. Once he gave the word for war, the conduct of the war rested with the war-council composed of the chiefs and war-tried veterans. The tribesmen ranged themselves under the Sarāwān and Jhalawān banners, and took the field in two wings under the premier chiefs. But though the leadership of the Khān in war-time seems thus to have been somewhat shadowy, it fired the whole army with an ardour born of the pious belief that they were fighting under one who, if not quite divine himself, was under the special favour of the God of Battles.

33. The constitution built up with such admirable statecraft by Nasīr Khān the Great and his forefathers contained one fatal flaw: it provided no safeguard against the consequences of a possible lack of statecraft in the Khāns who were to come after. Before long it began to decay from the top, sapped by a spirit of individualism, which in time spread through the whole organism. The later Khāns gradually—and in the beginning, it may be, unconsciously—attempted to rise from constitutional heads of a Confederacy to autocratic rulers of the country. To this end they began to amass treasure, in striking contrast to Nasīr Khān, who more than once found his privy purse so drained by his lavish hospitality that the trappings of his horses had to be pledged to raise money for his periodical tours through the country. Even when they could bring themselves to spend from their hoards, it was for their own selfish pleasures. There was no shorter cut to the loss of their hold over the tribesmen than this departure from that fine old tradition of hospitality to which their forefathers owed so much of the veneration they inspired. They tampered with the tribal system at every turn. False to the old motto of the Confederacy that "Union is strength," they found the maxim "Divide and rule" more suited to their personal aggrandisement. Whereas their forefathers took pride in being the peacemakers of the Confederacy, they began to undermine the authority of any chief who held his head high, by setting his various *ṭakkarī* against him; chief they played off against chief, seeking to draw the one closer to their side by crushing his rival, with the inevitable result that the chiefs retaliated by sowing dissension within the ruling family itself. Instead of inviting the chiefs to their councils, they leant more and more on the body of alien officials and hangers-on at the court, whose interests clashed all too often with the interests of the tribes. And—perhaps most significant of all—not content with relying on the tribal levies for the prosecution of their foreign policy, they gathered round themselves a mercenary army to enforce their authority at home. The modest ceremonial guard of trusty tribesmen with which Nasīr Khān the Great surrounded himself had developed under Nasīr Khān II into an imposing bodyguard of six officers and six hundred men; by the time of Khudādād Khān it was a standing mercenary army, recruited by adventurers drawn from India and Afghānistān, who were always on the war-path, fighting for the Khān against the members of what it would be irony to call a Confederacy of tribes any longer.

Decay of the constitution.

34. It would of course be folly to suppose that all the faults were on one side, or to ignore the disintegrating influence of accidental causes such as the accession of several of the Khāns while still in their minority. Nor must we overlook the part played by external causes in helping on the decay of the Khānate. Even in the hey-day of its prosperity Kalāt was never a wholly independent power. It appears from the Āīn-i-Akbarī that Mastung alone used to furnish a hundred horse and five times as many foot, besides a tribute in money and grain, to the Delhi kings. Even Nasīr Khān furnished men-at-arms to the rulers of Kandahār, first to Nādir Shāh and then to the Durrānī dynasty that succeeded. The great Khān stood in wholesome awe of the suzerain power. The story goes that he used to keep a pet tiger, which he never failed to visit when one of his rebellious fits was on him. "Its eyes," said he, "are as the eyes of Nādir Shāh; I have only to look into them for my loyalty to return." And though his reign was marred by one outburst of rebellion against Ahmad Shāh, his general loyalty and his gallantry in the field appear to have won for his country a relief from the payment of tribute and some relaxation at any rate in the furnishing of men-at-arms to the suzerain power. The rulers of Kandahār never again made good their hold on Kalāt. What they lacked in authority they seem to have made up in the peremptoriness of their messages, if one may judge by this specimen which still lingers in the memory of the people. "What means this knavery that has come to my ears, Oh Brāhūī, you fox of the hills! Beware, beware! What, have you never heard of the captain of the blood-sucking guard? If I give but the word, he will seize you by the tail and dash your body against the rocks, so that the marrow of your bones will ooze from your nostrils! Beware, beware! And again I say: Beware!" It is possible that a resolute suzerain power would have proved a blessing in disguise to the Brāhūī Confederacy and postponed its break-up

Contributory causes from without.

at any rate for a season. But troubles nearer home left the Durrānī scant leisure to devote their attention to Kalāt.

British administration.

35. Our early interference in Kalāt affairs forms a somewhat characteristic episode in the inglorious history of the first Afghan war. Inspired as it was by a radical misconception of the nature of the Khānate and a curiously perverse misreading of the local politics of the day, it was hardly calculated to arrest the decay of the Kalāt constitution, and by the time Sandeman appeared on the scene, the breach between the Khān and the chiefs was wellnigh complete. But though the old Confederacy was disrupted past repair, Sandeman succeeded in building up a new and wider union on its ruins, and Balūchistān now embraces not merely the old Confederacy of Sarāwān and Jhalawān with its appendages Las Bēla, Kachhī, Khārān, Makrān and Chāgai, but also areas formally ceded by Afghānistān in the second Afghān war, as well as the Paṭhān country to the north, over which Afghān rule had never been wholly effective.

The Sandeman policy.

36. No analysis of his policy could convey an adequate idea of the lasting impress left by Sandeman on Balūchistān. On the frontier personality often counts for more than policy. And the personality of this strong but simple man would live long in the memory of the people, even though the Sandeman policy were infringed, reversed, forgotten. As for the famous policy itself, it is the fashion in some quarters to summarise it airily as 'the bolstering up of the chiefs.' We should do scant justice to Sandeman's political wisdom if we allowed ourselves to be deceived by this plausible catch-word. Had he struck no deeper than this, his vaunted policy would have been little more than a makeshift policy of expediency along the line of least resistance. But Sandeman was no mere opportunist with an instinct for right judgment. He was a statesman gifted with rare imaginative insight and broad sympathies, which enabled him to divine and understand the social institutions, customs, and needs of the people whom he was called upon to rule. He had no belief in short cuts to civilisation, or in the development of the material prosperity of the individual at the expense of the community as a whole. Instead of battering down the walls of tribal society he sought to further its slow but sure evolution towards civilisation by helping the tribesmen to repair them. First and last, his aim was to preserve the ancient tribal system. In so far as the chief is the head and embodiment of the tribal system, he assuredly received Sandeman's whole-hearted support. But Sandeman's support of the other elements in the corporate body of the tribe was none the less whole-hearted because it was exercised in a less ostentatious and less obvious manner. A chief who carried his tribe with him because he never lost sight of the fact that his authority was derived from the tribe, was grounded in the tribe, and was to be exercised for the welfare of the tribe—this was Sandeman's ideal. A chief who flouted his tribal officers, encroached on the ancient liberties of his tribesmen, and sought to change his status from that of a constitutional tribal chief into that of an irresponsible despot, looked for his support in vain. Sandeman never mistook the part for the whole; it was not the chiefs alone, it was the entire fabric of the tribal system that he, like Nasīr Khān before him, laboured to uphold. And the life-blood of the tribal system is tribal law, the essence of which is reconciliation—the satisfaction of the aggrieved, not the punishment of the aggressor. It is on the well-tried lines of ancient custom that the chief and the other tribal officers patch up disputes within the tribe. And it was to provide for the customary settlement of disputes with which the chief failed to cope, or which overlapped into another tribe, to say nothing of disputes between the chiefs and the Khān's personal subjects, that Sandeman set up councils of Elders, or *jirga* as they are called. In other words Sandeman's *jirga* system provided a final court of appeal not altogether dissimilar from the Khān's Darbār in the old days. And finally as a means of enforcing tribal responsibility and at the same time of giving the tribes a stake in the wider government of the country, Sandeman devised a levy system—he employed it by the by less in Kalāt itself than in other parts of the province—under which chiefs and headmen were given allowances in return for the furnishing of tribal levies for tribal work within tribal limits. This again had its counter-

BALŪCHISTĀN

SHEWING ADMINISTRATIVE DIVISIONS.

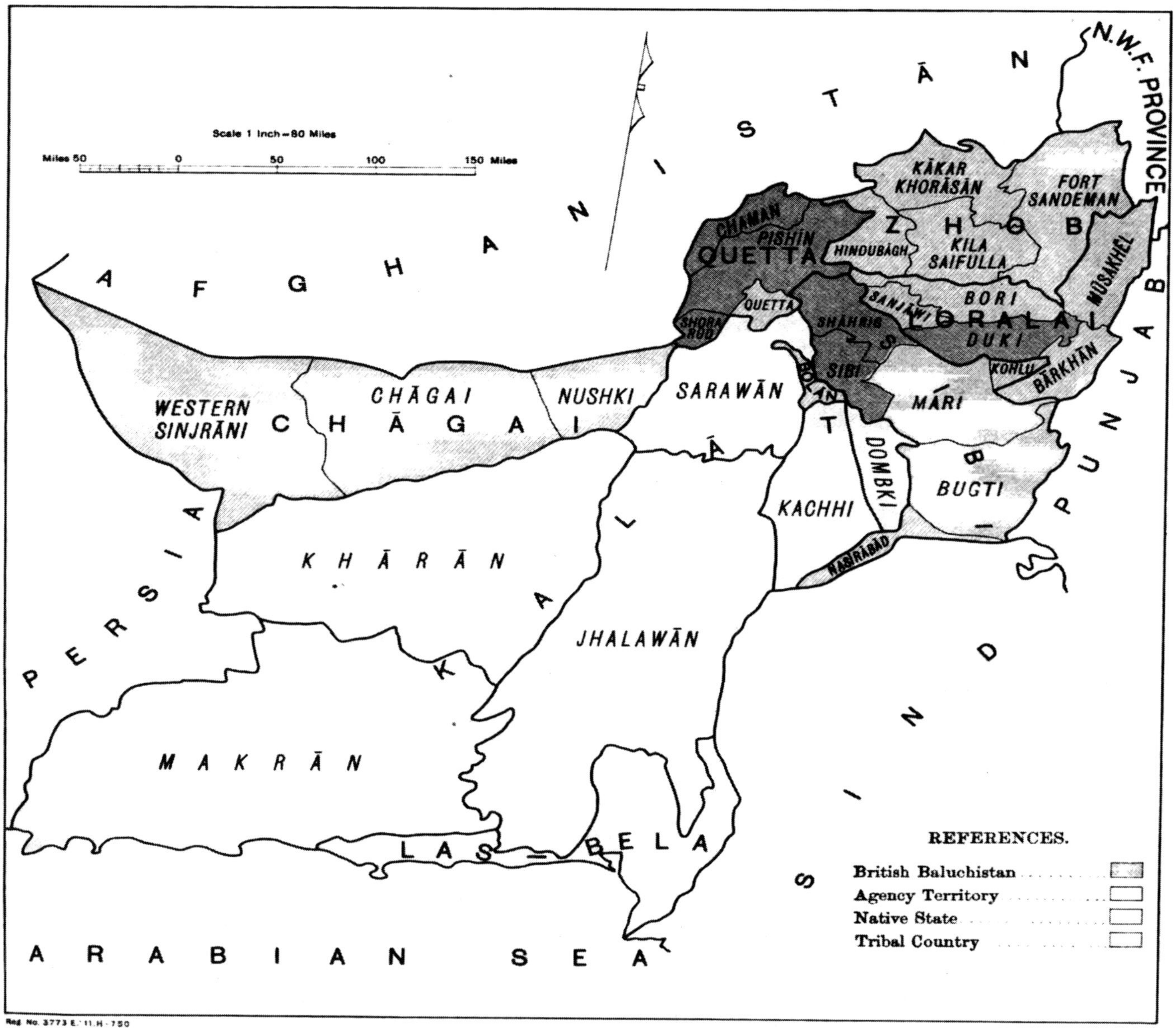

Reg. No. 3773 E.'11.H.-750

part under the old regime in the furnishing of men-at-arms and tribal levies in return for a share in the war-lands. In fact it does not make much demand on the imagination to see in the Sandeman policy a modern revival, half conscious, half unconscious, of the old constitution of Nasīr Khān the Great, remodelled, it is true, to suit the changes in the times.

Modern tendencies.

37. Times have changed again since the days of Sandeman. Here and there tribal bonds have been loosening; chiefs and tribesmen have been drifting apart into individualism; and it almost looks as if the tribal system were slowly sinking into decay. But if there is a spirit of change in the tribal life, there has also been a gradual declension from the Sandeman policy, unwittingly occasioned by the over-emphasis of some particular element in it. From time to time we have fallen into the temptation of bolstering up not the tribal system but the chief, and of regarding him as the creation and creature of government and not of the tribe. On the other hand there has been an unconscious tendency to enlarge the scope of the *jirga* and so to undermine the chiefly authority by placing disputes before a *jirga* without first entrusting them to the chief. And by degrees the levy system has lost much of its purely tribal character and become infected with the fashionable spirit of individualism, and tribesmen may now be found serving in some part of the country with which their tribe has no concern at all. Possibly these and similar departures from the Sandeman policy are for the better after all. It is infinitely more probable that they are for the worse. But even though they are among the causes that make for the loosening of the ancient ties of tribal society, there are other causes of a much more intimate and insidious nature, on which I shall have occasion to touch up and down this work. Nevertheless, if the tribal system should prove to be really in need of a physician, it would probably be hard to prescribe a more invigorating tonic than 'Back to Sandeman'.

Statistical.

Census and administrative divisions.

38. But it is high time to get at closer grips with the census; the fascination which these speculations cast over all disciples of the great Sandeman has already led me too far astray. Now for census purposes we divided Balūchistān into six districts and two native states, a grouping which follows closely on administrative lines, though both the native states, Kalāt and Las Bēla, and one of the districts, Bōlān, are under the charge of one and the same Political Agent. From a legal point of view matters are in a bit of a muddle, as may be judged from the map on the opposite page. The two states stand, of course, apart: in the rest of the province two divisions are recognised, British Balūchistān and Agency Territories. For workaday purposes it is a distinction without a difference, a pallid reflection of past history that vaguely reminds us that the portions which make up British Balūchistān were ceded by Afghānistān at the Treaty of Gandamak in 1879, and that the portions which make up the Agency Territories have been leased from Kalāt, or taken over at the request of the tribesmen, or have fallen on our side of the border as the result of boundary demarcations with Afghānistān. And the legal conception of the country is incomplete. It ignores on the one hand the whole of the Chāgai district, where matters have still to be put on a legal footing, and on the other the Marī and Bugṭī tribal country, once a member though a very unruly member of the Brāhūī Confederacy, now tacked on conveniently if incongruously to the Sibī district. In Chāgai, administration proceeds on the usual lines by executive order, as if it were an ordinary Agency Territory. In the tribal country the reins are slackened, and the tribesmen are given their head as much as possible to follow their own bent, revenue-free.

Quetta-Pishīn.

39. The only portion of the Quetta-Pishīn district which lies outside British Balūchistān is the Quetta *tahsīl*. For while the rest of the district formed part of the Kandahār province up to the Treaty of Gandamak and was then ceded to the British government, Quetta was handed over to Kalāt by Ahmad Shāh in the middle of the 18th century, and is now held by us on perpetual lease. To the Brāhūīs Quetta is known as Shāl, a name much more ancient than their pretty legend that the country was presented by Ahmad Shāh to the mother of the great Nasīr Khān as a *shāl* or shawl. The fact that the town

itself, as distinguished from the surrounding country, is sometimes referred to as Shālkōṭ, is, I suppose, at the bottom of the strange but common idea that the modern name of Quetta is a corruption of *kōṭ*, a fort ; it is simply the Pashtō word *kwaṭa*, a heap. But whether the name contains a sneer at the old Quetta fort— 'that most ancient debris of mud volcano,' as a picturesque but dangerously imaginative authority describes it—or whether there is truth in the local tradition that here was heaped the earth with which some Afghān army of old had burdened itself for fear this daily necessity of Muhammadan life might not be forthcoming in so heathenish a country, I will not stay to enquire.

Quetta-Pishin		**127,648**
Indigenous		87,536
Paṭhān	65,320	
Brāhūī	9,604	
Sayyid	9,716	
Others	2,896	
Semi-indigenous		5,580
Aliens		34,532

The district is essentially Paṭhān, though it merges into the Brāhūī country towards the south and contains a large Sayyid leaven and more aliens than the rest of Balūchistān put together. It consists in the main of upland valleys or plains 4,500 to 5,500 feet above sea-level, squeezed in by ranges of majestic but uninhabitable mountains, which are crowned by a peak overtopping 11,700 feet. The average rainfall varies from 6 inches in Chaman to a humble maximum of 10 inches in Pishīn. But more important than the rain or snow that falls in the valleys, where alone recording-stations are maintained, is the snow on the surrounding heights which feeds the springs and the streams and the *kārēz* or underground channels, chief and most characteristic of indigenous methods of irrigation. Despite the mountainous blocks of uninhabitable desolation which take up so much of the area, many causes combine to make the district not only the most advanced but the most thickly populated in the province : excellent communications by rail and road, fertile soil in the centre of the valleys, sources of irrigation to an extent unusual in Balūchistān, and a large military station in its midst which offers a ready market for its surplus produce. The density of the population—the word has a curious sound in Balūchistān—is of course very unequally distributed. In the Quetta *tahsīl* it stands at an abnormal figure owing to the presence of Quetta itself. But even though the density of the *tahsīl* on the exclusion of Quetta with its 33,922 inhabitants and 20 square miles drops from 100 to 40, its position remains unchallenged. Second on the list—but a very bad second—stands Pishīn, thanks in some measure to two Government irrigation works, the Shēbō canal and the Khushdil Khān reservoir, whose settling influence on the inhabitants is not confined to the fact that they bring some six or seven thousand acres under cultivation every year of favourable rainfall. There is a biggish drop in Chaman. But here conditions are very different : the population is dependent almost wholly on pastoralism, and shifts freely now this now that side of the border ; cultivation there is very little. Shorarūd—valley of the brackish river—comes last ; and last it is likely to remain until its lethargic inhabitants learn to develop the not unpromising agricultural resources of their country.

Density.	
Quetta Pishin	**24**
Quetta	100
Pishīn	17
Chaman	14
Shorarūd	5

Lōralai.

40. The Lōralai district has come into being since the last census, having been formed in 1903 by the severance of Mūsakhēl and Bōrī from Zhōb, and the absorption of Dukī, Sanjāwī and Bārkhān on the break-up of the old Thal-Chōtiālī district. Dukī is the only portion that lies within British Balūchistān. The district consists like Quetta of upland valleys hemmed in by rugged mountains ; but both valleys and mountains lie somewhat lower except towards the west. The mass of the population is Paṭhān ; even the nucleus of the Khetrān, who nowadays claim Balōch status, is probably Paṭhān by origin (§264). The majority of the tribesmen are small cultivating proprietors, but there are not a few who subsist almost entirely on their flocks. The density is less than half the density of Quetta ; at the same time it is much more evenly distributed. Yet the conditions vary not a little. Thus, while Bōrī, Sanjāwī and parts of Dukī are fairly well irrigated, in Mūsakhēl only 35 per cent of the irrigable area has a perennial water-supply ; the rest is dependent on floods. The permanently irrigable area in Bārkhān, the home of the Khetrān, is less than half that in Mūsakhēl ; yet this

Lōralai		**80,769**
Indigenous		65,185
Paṭhān	42,764	
Khetrān	12,926	
Others	9,495	
Semi-indigenous		11,068
Aliens		4,516

Density.	
Lōralai	**11**
Bōrī	10
Dukī	10
Bārkhān	14
Mūsakhēl	9
Sanjāwī	11

is the most thickly populated portion of the district. The truth is that flood irrigation, if less certain, is usually more productive than permanent irrigation; and so long as the rains do not fail, all is well, especially as the district contains excellent grazing-grounds for the herds of cattle and the sheep and goats which form a large portion of the wealth of the tribesmen. But a failure of the rains, which only average about 11 inches, is disastrous in parts that are unprotected by a permanent water-supply.

41. The whole of the Zhōb district lies outside British Balūchistān. Its **Zhōb.**

Zhōb . . .		**70,366**
Indigenous . .		61,104
Paṭhān .	59,541	
Others .	1,563	
Semi-indigenous .		4,954
Aliens[1] . . .		4,308

tribal population is remarkably homogeneous—Paṭhān almost to a man, as befits the ancestral home of the Paṭhān race; many of the odd thousand who now call themselves Sayyid might probably with greater propriety be called Paṭhān like their fathers before them. It is another highland district, broken up in all directions by mountains, which are sometimes well-wooded, more often barren, but, wooded or barren, rarely without a rugged grandeur. Chief among its many valleys is the great alluvial plain fed by the Zhōb river, which gives its name to the district. Except in the large but desolate area known as Kākaṛ Khurasān, conditions are pretty much the same throughout the district. The most populated portion, the Fort Sandeman *tahsīl*, has unfortunately not been surveyed for revenue purposes,

	Density.
Zhōb	7
Fort Sandeman . .	9
Killa Saifulla . .	7
Hindūbāgh . . .	8
Kākaṛ Khurasān . .	2

but seeing that barely four acres in every square mile are cropped annually in Hindūbāgh, where the density is almost as high, it is hardly surprising that there are not seven persons to the square mile in the whole of the district. The rainfall is scanty, varying from 6 inches in Hindūbāgh to about 9 inches in Fort Sandeman, and little rain-crop cultivation is attempted except in the centre of the district. There is a certain amount of irrigation from springs, and still more from streams, though the high banks of the Zhōb river in its upper reaches overtax the by no means despicable engineering ingenuity of the tribesmen. By far the chief source of irrigation is the *kārēz*.

42. The Bōlān Pass and Nushkī Railway district—to give this artificial **Bōlān.**
little district its full official title—is geographically and historically part of Kalāt, and simply owes its creation into a separate entity and its inclusion among the Agency Territories to obvious considerations of administrative convenience. It includes not only the famous pass itself, which starts from Rindlī at the foot of the plains and rises more than 5,000 feet in 54 miles, but also the present alignment of the railway at the lower end along the Mushkāf valley, and so much of the recent railway extension towards Nushkī as lies outside the Chāgai district. It is a mountainous tract cut by numerous hill-torrents, which after heavy rain fling themselves with amazing force and suddenness into

Bōlān . . .		**2,096**
Indigenous . .		852
Brāhūī .	236	
Balōch .	451	
Others .	165	
Semi-indigenous . .		6
Aliens . . .		1,238

the Bōlān river. It has hardly six inhabitants to the square mile. Even so, a large proportion of the population are temporary immigrants at work on the railway; the indigenous inhabitants are chiefly Kūrd and Sātakzai Brāhūīs and Kuchik Balōch; in the spring and autumn it is thronged by swarms of Brāhūīs on their annual migrations. But the importance of this pigmy district lies of course, not in its tiny population, but in the fact that in its historic pass, once trodden by many a proud conqueror of India, now pierced by a railway which ranks among the engineering feats of the world, it possesses one of the main arteries between India and Central Asia.

43. The Chāgai district is called after Chāghai, the head-quarters of the **Chāgai.**
Sanjrānī tribe, which is popularly supposed to have earned its name from the enviable number of *chāh* or wells that it once possessed. But to thousands who have never heard of Chāgai this part of the country is familiar as Nushkī, the terminus of the world-famous trade-route which traverses the district from end to end before it branches off northwards to Seistān. Folk-etymology has been busy with Nushkī also, and refers it back to *nōsh khanē*, 'fall to the food,' a treacherous signal with which the Rakhshānī Balōch are said

[1] In the 4,308 aliens are included as many as 144 Europeans, simply because some troops happened to be marching through the district on the night of the census. The normal European population of Zhōb hardly reaches 30.

to have fallen upon their Moghal tyrants whom they had invited to a feast. Balōch and Brāhūī divide the country between them in almost equal and

Chāgai		16,344
Indigenous		15,175
Balōch	6,688	
Brāhūī	6,485	
Pathān	371	
Others	1,631	
Semi-indigenous		594
Aliens		575

equally small numbers. The district, it is true, was abnormally empty during the census owing to the drought to which it is often exposed. But even at the best of times it is never otherwise than very thinly populated. In many ways it is one of the least inviting parts of the province: hills on the east, hills on the north, hills on the south, hills on the far west, and in the centre vast plains (very occasionally alluvial and fertile, as in the neighbourhood of Nushkī, more often desolate wastes covered with stones or crescent-shaped sand-dunes) 3,000 feet above sea-level on the east, but sloping down westward to the howling wilderness that drains fittingly into the dreary swamp of the Hāmūn-i-Māshkēl. To speak of density and of Chāgai in the same breath is almost laughable:

	Density.
Chāgai	1
Nushkī	3
Chāgai	1
Western Sanjrānī	...

there is barely a man to the square mile in the district as a whole. By far the most populated portion of the country is Nushkī, where there is excellent land and a goodly amount of water but considerable difficulty in wedding the two together. Here the people have taken to agriculture and have become more or less settled. In Chāgai there is little cultivation: in Western Sanjrānī there is hardly any at all. Throughout the district drinking-water is scarce: in many parts it is so impregnated with sulphates and other minerals, that it almost looks as if an extension of the railway onwards from Nushkī were all that is required to turn the district into a resort of future valetudinarians. Backward though the district is, it would be hard to summon a better witness to the benefits of our rule. If it is thinly peopled to-day, it was all but a desert a short generation back; here, at any rate, we can boast that two blades grow where one grew before. And if the development is slow, it is sure and continuous. The trade-route alone is a monument of our enterprise in overcoming the difficulties of nature in this desolate region: its absolute security a monument of our civilising influence on its rugged inhabitants.

44. In Sibī almost all the characteristic features of Balūchistān are to be found in miniature. From a legal point of view the district is as much of a muddle as the province itself. While the Sibī and Shāhrig *tahsīls* are part of British Balūchistān, and Kōhlū and Nasīrābād are Agency Territories, the tribal country occupied by the Marī and Bugṭī is neither the one nor the other; and to add to the confusion, the tribal country occupied by the Ḍōmbkī and Kahērī, which really belongs to Kalāt, is lumped up with the district for most purposes of political control. Matters are cleared a bit if we treat the tribal countries apart. But even in the district proper the physical contrasts are striking enough; whereas Sibī and Nasīrābād are level low-lying plains,

Sibī district proper		82,423
Indigenous		71,290
Balōch	26,342	
Pathān	18,607	
Brāhūī	4,706	
Jatt	12,973	
Others	8,662	
Semi-indigenous		2,056
Aliens		9,077

which in reality belong to the great Kachhī plain, the rest of the district is as mountainous as any portion of Balūchistān. And the jumble of its physical contrasts is borne out by the heterogeneous character of its population, for it is the meeting-ground of all the four chief peoples of Balūchistān. The density of the population is very unevenly distributed. In Nasīrābād it reaches its highest figure—a figure only overtopped in one other portion of Balūchistān. But the conditions here are

	Density.
Sibī district proper	21
Sibī	22
Nasīrābād	41
Shāhrig	12
Kōhlū	13

such as are to be found nowhere else in the province, for one-sixth of its whole area is irrigated yearly from the Sind canals. The density in Sibī is little more than half that in Nasīrābād, yet even so it remains at a figure unusually high for Balūchistān; and here again the irrigated area (irrigated for the most part from the Nāṛi river) is above the normal, averaging about one-fiftieth of the whole. In the mountainous parts of the district the density drops to the ordinary level of Balūchistān districts. There is of course a tremendous range of temperature between the scorching heat of the plains in the summer and the icy cold of the uplands in the winter. The variation in the rainfall is no less marked. In the plains it averages about 7 inches; in the hills it is much greater: in fact Shāhrig with an average of well over 12 inches can usually boast the highest records of the year. Of the various divisions of the district Shāhrig is on the whole the best protected against famine. Even Nasīrābād, for all its canals, is subject to bouts of scarcity, as it is generally the first part of the country under the Sind canal system to feel the pinch when the water runs low. And scarcity comes home with greater force to the people of Nasīrābād, because they have lost much of the nomadic instincts of their forefathers.

Mari-Bugṭī country.

45. The whole of the Marī and Bugṭī tribal country, which is conveniently split up north and south by a mountainous barrier between these two ancient enemies, is much the same in character from end to end: barren, closely packed hills, which gradually break the fall of the great Sulemān range to the plains; hill-torrents and ravines innumerable; here and there good pasturage and a few valley patches of cultivation. Of the two tracts, the Bugṭī country on the south is the bigger by nearly five hundred square miles. It is also the more thickly, or rather the less thinly, populated. Both tribes are nomadic: there are only five collections of huts in the whole country that can be called villages at all. The rainfall is scanty and precarious in both areas, and both are constantly victims to drought, from which the tribesmen escape by extending their migrations to Sind and the Panjāb.

	Density.
Marī country	4
Bugṭī country	5

Kalāt State.

46. The Kalāt state derives its name from its capital Kalāt, often styled Kalāt-i-Sēwa after its possibly mythical Hindu founder, or Kalāt-i-Nasīr after the great Khān, to distinguish it from Kalāt-i-Ghilzai and many another Kalāt. It takes up more than half of the whole area of the province. Yet it falls far short of its area in the palmy days when it not only included Quetta, Nushkī, Nasīrābād, which have been taken over on permanent lease, and the Bōlān, where the Khān's right to levy transit dues has been commuted for an annual subsidy, and the Marī-Bugṭī country over which the Khān's control, it is true, was rarely otherwise than nominal, and Las Bēla, eventually successful in setting itself up as a virtually independent state, but also stretched over to Dājal and Haṛṛand in the Panjāb and down to Karāchī in Sind. And if the Khān's territories have shrunk from their ancient dimensions, so also has his authority. Throughout his state it is wholly effective only over his personal subjects in the crown-lands or *niābat* as they are called; and the independence openly claimed by the chief of Khārān is little more than an extreme case of the independence now enjoyed by the tribal chiefs in all parts of the country. The most numerous race is the Brāhūī, and this is the race to which the ruling family belongs. In some tracts the Balōch are in the majority; in others the Jaṭṭ. There are four or five persons to the square mile in the state as a whole. But the density is so unevenly distributed, varying from 23 in the Kachhī to but 1 in Khārān, that it is well to say a word or two about each of the main divisions.

Kalāt	**359,086**
Brāhūī	138,581
Balōch	83,432
Dēhwār	6,742
Jaṭṭ	60,238
Others	70,093

	Density.
Kalāt	5
Sarāwān	12
Jhalawān	4
Kachhī	23
Ḍōmbkī-Kahērī	17
Makrān	3
Khārān	1

Sarāwān.

47. In olden days all Kalāt or rather the whole Brāhūī Confederacy was divided into two divisions only: the tribesmen of Sarāwān, who lived up-country to the north of Kalāt, and the tribesmen of Jhalawān, who lived down-country to the south; the Kachhī was divided between the two of them. In its 5,230 square miles, accordingly, Sarāwān of to-day retains but a portion of its former magnitude. It is a highland country, in general character not unlike Quetta-Pishīn: its valleys lie between 5,000 and 6,500 feet above the level of the sea; the most majestic peak among its mountain-ranges is Kōh-i-mārān, 'the hill of the snakes,' which reaches up to 10,730 feet. In the centre of the valleys, some of which are spacious and broad, the soil is remarkably fertile; and the wheat, tobacco and orchards of Sarāwān are famous throughout the country; for though the rainfall is scanty as everywhere in Balūchistān and the large dry-crop area accordingly seldom yields a full out-turn, there is a good deal of permanent cultivation by means of *kārēz*, springs and streams. With the exception of the Kachhī plain and the connected Ḍōmkī-Kahērī country, Sarāwān is the most prosperous and thickly populated portion of the state. The Brāhūīs are of course in the great majority: but many of them

Sarāwān	**63,781**
Brāhūī	47,816
Balōch	2,697
Dēhwār	6,537
Others	6,731

still cling to the pastoral pursuits of their fathers, and much of the development of the country has been due to the husbandry of the thrifty Dēhwār.

Jhalawān.

48. In fact, though nature has doubtless treated Jhalawān with a far more niggardly hand, it is quite possible that the real reason for the vast difference between its poverty and backwardness and the development and prosperity of Sarāwān lies in the presence of the thrifty Dēhwār in the one and his absence from the other. No one at any rate can help being impressed by the palpable fact that the Jhalawān, partly from innate laziness, partly from ignorance, fails to make the most of his country. Much of the cultivable area to be found in the valleys between the mountain-ranges and on the *bēnṭ* or flats along the river-courses is either left uncultivated altogether or is merely scratched. It is true the Jhalawān can plead a scanty rainfall and the scarcity of permanent water: the sole means of irrigation at his command are a very few *kārēz*, a few streams, and any channels he can dig at favourable places from the rivers, of which moreover not one has a continuous flow of water throughout its course. A race of husbandmen would doubtless make light of many of the difficulties. But it is perhaps not surprising that a race of nomad pastoralists like the turbulent though hardly warlike tribesmen of Jhalawān should find little inducement in their mountainous country to beat their swords into ploughshares and to turn their shepherds' crooks into spade handles, more especially when they have eked out their pastoral life from time immemorial with a winter migration into the plains. As it is, Jhalawān remains a poor country at best, though it is possible that the census figures, taken in a year which was bad from many points of view, give an unduly unfavourable impression of the sparsity of its population (§ 64).

Jhalawān	**84,398**
Brāhūī	69,553
Balōch	1,443
Others	13,402

Kachhī.

49. An amazing contrast confronts us when we turn to the Kachhī, those much prized war-lands of Sarāwān and Jhalawān both. Here the mountains are left behind for a vast alluvial plain, which except for one small group of hillocks does not rise above 500 feet at its highest point. Hardly anywhere is the rainfall so scanty; but even complete failure is not very disastrous so long as there has been enough rain in the uplands to bring down the Nāṛī and the Bōlān and the Mūla and the Suklēji in full flood, to be dissipated in numberless channels over the country or brought on to the fields by an ingenious system of dams. So fertile is the soil that it is indeed a bad year when three crops are not harvested. The autumn harvest, which consists chiefly of a *jowār* justly renowned for its excellence, is the most important of the three. Given good rains as well as good floods, prosperity smiles on the land: large areas are reclaimed from the seeming desert, and there is an abundance of forage and grazing not only for the live-stock of the country itself—for the far-famed Rind and Magasī breeds of horses and the equally famous Bhāg-Nāṛī and Bālā-Naṛī breeds of bullocks—but also for the camels and sheep and goats which in the winter are brought down in their thousands by the Brāhūīs from the uplands. But if the rain fails both in the uplands and the Kachhī itself, the only refuge from the certainty of scarcity and the probability of famine is a wholesale migration into Sind. Though all the Brāhūī tribes are supposed to own war-lands in the Kachhī, few Brāhūīs actually live here all the year round: the scorching heat of the summer is little to the liking of these mountaineers. The most important elements among the permanent inhabitants are the Magasī and Rind Balōch, of whom the former are still reckoned with Jhalawān and the latter with Sarāwān. More numerous still are the Jaṭṭ, who are to be found everywhere as cultivators.

Kachhī	**92,759**
Brāhūī	4,148
Balōch	28,872
Jaṭṭ	45,102
Others	14,637

Ḍōmbkī-Kahērī country.

50. The Lahṛī *niābat*, commonly known as the Ḍōmbkī-Kahērī country, is an integral part of the Kachhī, and has only been separated from it for census purposes because of the peculiar nature of its administration: for whereas the Kachhī is treated in the same way as the rest of Kalāt, the general control of the Ḍōmbkī-Kahērī country is vested in the district officer of Sibī. It is unnecessary to describe it: it resembles the rest of the Kachhī in its main features. What the Bōlān, the Nāṛī, the Suklēji and the Mūla are to the Kachhī, the Lahṛī and the Chhattar

Ḍōmbkī-Kahērī country	**23,543**
Balōch	4,147
Kahērī Sayyid	800
Jaṭṭ	12,252
Others	6,344

and many smaller hill-torrents are to this portion of it. The chief inhabitants are the Ḍōmbkī and Umrānī Balōch, the Kahērī, who were lately content to be reckoned as Balōch but have now blossomed forth into Sayyids (§ 281), and the Jaṭṭ.

51. As for Makrān (or to be precise Kēch-Makkurān, in distinction to the **Makrān.**
Makrān across the Persian border) I am almost tempted to echo the Lament of Sinān Ibn Selāma: "Thou shewest me the road to Makrān, but oh! the difference between an order and its accomplishment! Never will I set foot in a land whose very name strikes terror within me!" Whatever the origin of the name—and there is a wilderness of guesses to choose from: *maka-araṇya* or the waste of Maka (and of course either the Maka of the Behistūn inscription or the Mekia of Herodotus or the Makara of the Dravidians), the land of Mokrān the great grandson of Noah, *mā-kerān* or the land by the sea, *māhī khurān* or the Ichthyophagoi or fish-eaters, the land of *makr* or deceit—Makrān, has had an evil reputation from time immemorial. To the ancient Greeks, to whom it was known under the name of Gadrosia, it seemed a waterless waste of sun-scorched sand, across which Alexander deliberately chose to pass his army simply to prove, as Arrian puts it, that he could succeed where Cyrus and Semiramis had failed before him. In the Arab chronicles it is commonly described as a vast country, mostly barren. Among natives of other parts of Balūchistān a two-year sojourn in it is regarded as docking ten years off life. Along the grim sea-coast life is barely possible except for a few fisherfolk. Inland the country is gridironed across by three ranges of hills, which enclose valleys of varying width, rising in elevation as the coast is left behind. Though the rainfall is scanty, damp fogs are so frequent and mosquitoes so abundant that every native of the country equips himself with mosquito curtains against both as a matter of course. The rivers are more often dry than not, but they carry heavy floods, and, more important still, leave behind frequent pools of water which are drawn off for irrigation. These pools with a few streams and a hundred odd *kārēz* (or *kahn* as they are called in Makrān) are the only sources of irrigation; outside Kēch and Panjgūr they are rarely to be found at all. Elsewhere most of the cultivation is dry-crop, and more than usually precarious owing to the capricious nature of the rainfall. The real harvest of Makrān, that which provides food for man and beast during the greater part of the year, is the date-harvest. There are date-trees studded up and down most parts of the country; the richest and most famous groves are those of Panjgūr and Kēch. The population is sharply divided into three layers of society: first the *hākim* or dominant landowning families, which consist of the Gichkī and Naushērwānī (§ 269), and the Mīrwāṛī and Bīzānjau Brāhūīs: then the Balōch or middle-class cultivators—for the word Balōch has none of the proud ring in Makrān that it has in eastern Balūchistān (§ 268); and finally the *hizmatgār* or menials.

Makrān	**71,942**
Balōch	35,789
Brāhūī	9,167
Mēd	495
Others	26,491

52. When we pass northwards over into Khārān, there is little change in **Khārān.**
the general conditions, and what there is is hardly for the better. The greater part of the country is one vast plain, which lies about 1,600 feet above sea-level towards the west, and rises some nine hundred feet higher to the east. Into it drain the many streams that run off the surrounding hills. There are some goodly patches of cultivation near the skirts of the hills and along the Māshkēl and Baḍḍō rivers; but an enormous part in the centre, known as the Lut or Rēgistān, is a dreary ocean of shifting sand. There are rich date-groves in Wāshuk and Māshkēl, but wheat is the staple food of the country. The whole country is ruled by the Naushērwānī chief, and the population is divided into the Naushērwānī, the dominant race, and the Balōch (with whom are classed some miscellaneous groups), and the menials.

Khārān	**22,663**
Balōch	10,484
Brāhūī	7,700
Others	4,479

53. If the petty state of Las Bēla can hardly be regarded as typical of **Las Bēla.**
Balūchistān, it contains many of its characteristic features in little. It is mountainous on the east and to the north: in the centre it is flat and low-lying, sloping to the sea: towards the west it stretches out for miles along a narrow strip of coast as barren as that of Makrān. There are several rivers and mountain-torrents, but though their floods are diverted by dams for irrigation, nearly all of

them are dry for the greater part of the year. There is one large lake often as dry as the river-beds. The people are an unusually mixed lot; in fact the tribal system seems hopelessly moribund. The dominant class of Lāsī is divided into five groups known as the *panj-rāj*, which consist of the Jāmōṭ (to which the ruling family of the Jām belongs), Rūnjhā, Angāria, Būrra, and Shēkh (§ 279). There are a fair number of Brāhūīs, chiefly in the north; the fisherfolk along the coast are Mēd (§ 283). The rest of the population is largely composed of servile or menial elements. There are about nine persons to the square mile in the state as a whole. But the density varies considerably in the various parts, and is at its height in the well-cultivated Wēlpaṭ *niābat*. As the rainfall even at its best seldom exceeds seven inches, the country frequently suffers from drought, which drives the poorer classes wholesale over into Sind.

Las Bēla	**61,205**
Lāsī	26,860
Brāhūī	8.017
Mēd	1,993
Others	24,335

Summary.

54. Having hurried through the various districts and states we may now glance back at the country as a whole. Its most striking characteristic is unpeopled vastness—a vastness to which its estimated area fails to do justice. For in its reputed 134,638 square miles no account is taken of the mountainous superstructure reared on their surface. How far it affects the area, there seems no way of ascertaining; at any rate I have been unable to cajole the merest guess out of the survey department. But if these mountainous piles add enormously to the vastness of the province, their barren ruggedness goes far to explain the extraordinary sparsity of the population. And sparse though the population is—so sparse that I can hardly bring myself to talk of density in Balūchistān without an apology—there is a pretty general consensus of opinion that it is about as much as the country under present conditions could support. It is not easy to say how far this opinion is correct. A sceptic might possibly seize upon the not inconsiderable exports of grain from the Kachhī and Mastung (only to be exchanged into luxuries—not necessaries—of life) as an argument against it; and to rebut this argument one might speciously point to the imposing imports of food stuffs without which the alien population, and the Quetta town in particular, could hardly subsist. But these vexed questions of economics may be left to 'sophisters, economists and calculators.' The real assumption at the back of the opinion that the country is severely taxed in supporting its present population is that all the available perennial water is already used up as far as existing methods can use it, and that the only prospect of any expansion in the irrigable area lies in a change of those methods themselves. But though this may be substantially true of the districts, I very much doubt whether it is true of the native states. There has certainly been a considerable extension of the *kārēz* system of irrigation and a consequent expansion of cultivation even in backward Jhalawān during the last few years, and the *kārēz* resources of the country are far from being fully tapped. Not that I have any wish to attempt to prove too much. In one form or another density and rainfall are very closely correlated nearly everywhere in Balūchistān. Where conditions are favourable, as in the Kachhī, density varies with the amount of land that can be brought under cultivation, and this in turn varies very largely with the amount of rain that falls, not necessarily in the particular locality, but in the surrounding uplands. But in less favoured parts, in Khārān for instance or Western Sanjrānī, rainfall is not merely a matter of cultivation, it is a matter of life or death. If the rains fail, there is no water for man or beast, and both must wander on until they find it. The nomadism of a large number of Balūchistān's inhabitants is after all less a habit than a necessity. And though there are signs of change in the air, nomadism to a greater or less degree is still so prevalent that an analysis of the density in the various districts and states and divisions is true only for the particular season of the particular year when the census was taken. Thus if the density of the Kachhī in the scorching summer months[1] is 23, it must be at least half as much again when the bitter cold of the uplands drives the Brāhūīs down-country. A scanty and precarious rainfall, scarcity of culturable land and perennial water, extremes of heat and cold — these are factors which will long make tribesmen cling to their

Density.	
Balūchistān	**6**
Districts	8
States	5

[1] Though the regular areas were censused on the night of the 10th March 1911, most of the non-synchronous areas were censused in the previous summer.

BALŪCHISTĀN

SHEWING DENSITY.

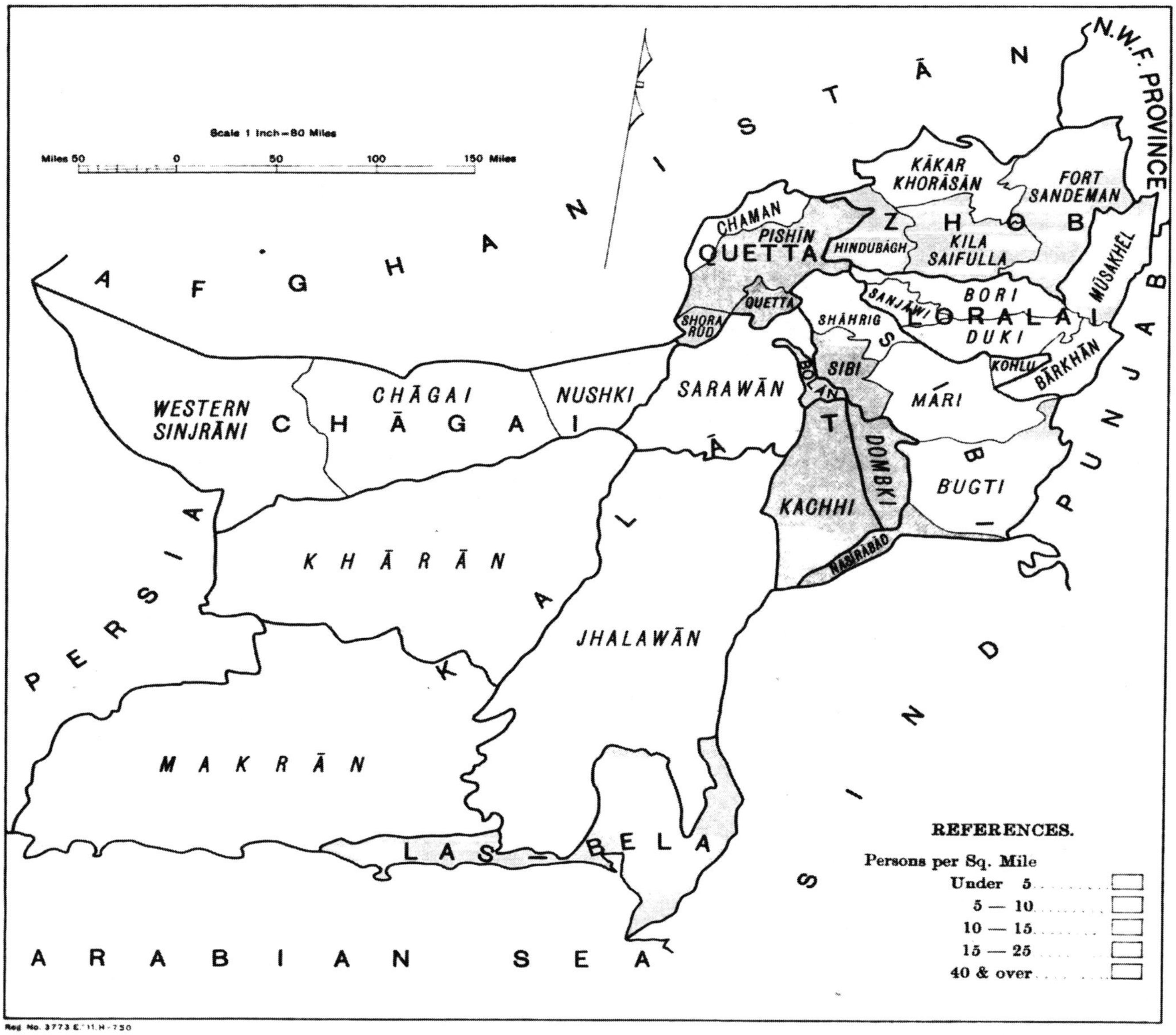

Reg. No. 3773 E.'11.H-750

nomadic habits, and the only thing that is likely to bring about a wholesale change in their mode of life is government irrigation on a large scale.

Towns, Villages, Houses.

55. Though there are nine towns included in our tables, most of them are only towns by courtesy. In fact the only unimpeachable towns among the lot are Quetta and Sibī, and the former at any rate is almost entirely the creation of British rule. And whereas Lōṛalai, Fort Sandeman and Chaman are in some ways characteristically urban, they are after all mere garrison towns that have sprung up during our occupation. Kalāt and Bēla owe their place in the category more to the fact that they are the capitals of the two native states than to anything else. For Bēla is nothing but an overgrown village, the numbers of which are inflated by the inclusion of surrounding hamlets ; Kalāt simply consists of the Kh̲ān's *mīrī* or castle and a largish but half-empty bazaar, whose rows of deserted shops witness pathetically to a bygone prosperity, that has passed over chiefly to Quetta, but partly also to Mastung, now the most thriving township in the state. Were it not for its hoary historical associations, Pishīn, the ancient Fushanj, would not have figured among the towns at all; and it has recently fallen into such decay that it looks as if it would have to drop out of the list at the next census. Such being the nature of our so-called towns, there would be something unreal in any conclusions we might attempt to draw from the proportion of rural and urban elements in the population of the province, and a crude comparison between the reputed urban populations at this census and the last would be hopelessly fallacious, seeing that Kalāt, Bēla and Mastung have been treated as towns for the first time in their history, though they had just as much claims to the title at the last census. But we may safely commit ourselves to this: the proportion of tribal inhabitants our towns contain is in inverse ratio to their urban character. The average tribesman still looks upon a town as a mighty poor place for his family to live in, yet an excellent place in which to secure temporary employment for himself, especially in government service. Towns.

Urban percentage.	
Balūchistān .	**0·4**
Districts . .	0·9
States . . .	0·1

56. How little attraction town-life has for the tribesmen becomes clear on an analysis of the population of Quetta, by far the largest town in the province. To its population of 33,922 the indigenous Paṯhān, Balōch and Brāhūī contribute no more than 1,427. Small though this figure is, its real significance only emerges when we divide it up between the two sexes, for there are but 385 females in the lot. Even though we assume (and we have of course no right to do so) that all the women are permanent residents of the town, this in itself is a pretty clear proof that when the tribesmen shift into the towns, their move is generally a temporary migration of individuals in search of employment. While the whole population of Quetta has increased by 9,338 since the last census, the tribal element in it has merely increased by 88. With the rapid development of the capital of their province into a thriving mart and an imposing cantonment, the military strength of which is second to none in India, the tribesmen have clearly had very little to do. And this development is much more remarkable than the census figures indicate. For the census was taken in the off-season when everybody tries to flit from the winter cold. One has only to glance at the margin, where the results of the census are compared with the results of an enumeration undertaken three summers before, to appreciate how thorough-going this winter exodus is. If we assume (and I see no reason why we should not) that the summer population to-day is at least as great as it was three years back, the winter flitting affects no less than one-fourth of the whole population. And as Quetta is in no sense a summer resort, its normal population must be regarded as much nearer forty-five thousand than the thirty-four thousand actually found in it at the time of the census. Yet Quetta a brief generation ago was a cluster of mud huts sheltering round a ramshackle fort. Quetta.

	Quetta.	Town.	Cantonments.
August '08 .	45,570	24,129	21,441
March '11 .	33,922	17,021	16,901
Winter shortage	11,648	7,108	4,540

Villages.

57. Not only are the tribesmen no lovers of town-life, very many of them are not even villagers. In saying this I may seem to be flying in the face of the statistics, but it is only in rare cases that the statistics are concerned with villages in the ordinary sense of the word. Wherever the country has been parcelled out into revenue villages, we followed the very artificial but orthodox procedure current elsewhere in India and treated the revenue village as our unit; but as often as not a revenue village is not a village at all but a collection of more or less unconnected hamlets. In the native states, where there are no revenue villages, we endeavoured to bring about uniformity by bunching hamlets up together. But even in the districts there was nothing for it but to class as villages a number of localities—possibly altogether innocent of permanent inhabitants—which are regularly occupied by largish groups of people at certain seasons of the year. And the result is necessarily so chaotic that we can hardly hope to glean much enlightenment from the number of the so-called villages in the tables. It is far more to the point to glance at the classification of the villages according to the size of their population. Here it is the smallness of the average village that at once strikes the eye, a smallness all the more remarkable because the average village is not a village in the English sense of the word but a cluster of several hamlets: ninety per cent of the villages into which the whole country has been divided contain less than five hundred inhabitants. For several reasons it is hardly possible to compare these figures with the figures of the last census. But it seems worth while to jot down a few impressions on the subject I have got by gossipping with the people. British rule seems to have affected village-life in curiously different ways. In the Paṭhān country concentration into rudely fortified villages was more or less essential in the old days as a safeguard against attack, and the peace that British rule has brought with it has usually led to a partial break-up of the villages into several smaller hamlets. In the Kachhī, once the happy hunting-ground of the dreaded Marī and Bugṭi marauders, concentration was on a larger scale still, and the first-fruits of the *pax Britannica* was the springing-up of smaller hamlets at the expense of the parent village; but of late years the parent villages have been regaining much of their lost ground, partly as a consequence of healthy natural growth fostered by the increasing prosperity of the country, partly by recruitment from people hitherto nomadic. In the Brāhūī country tribal warfare was more parochial and conducted according to more gentlemanly rules. It was war of tribe against tribe, for tribal honour and glory, not for plunder. Villages were deliberately avoided, even by those who were not pastoral nomads. They were useless as walls of defence: for women and children were inviolate in tribal warfare, and the proper place for these non-combatants when the tribesmen were on the war-path was the fastnesses in the hills. They were sources of weakness and not of strength, for the greatest possible disgrace in a tribal feud was to have one's village burnt by the enemy. In the Brāhūī country, accordingly, British rule has had the effect not merely of enlarging the few existing villages but of causing hamlets to spring up where there were none before. In Makrān, unlike Kalāt proper, an assault on a fort or a siege appears to have been among the regular tactics of tribal warfare. Every petty chiefling had his little fort to which his people flocked for refuge when an attack was threatened. But no chief ever allowed any one else to build a fort or even a mud hut if he could help it, not only because he was jealous of his prerogatives, but also because the mud hut might fall into the hands of his enemy and make it the more difficult to dislodge him. With the advent of our rule times have changed, and there are now mud huts everywhere. Speaking broadly, I fancy that, though the growth of village-life will be slow, it will be sure from now onwards. Different conditions will doubtless give rise to different results. But the most notable trend of evolution, as pastoralism gradually gives way before agriculture, will probably be from tents all the year round to mud huts in the winter, from mud huts to hamlets, from hamlets to villages. Migration into towns will only be general when the tribal system falls hopelessly into decay.

Houses.

58. The mere mention of tents will have made it obvious that the term 'house' is used in our tables in as wide a sense as the term 'village.'

It includes not only houses of sun-dried bricks rarely to be found outside the towns, and the mud huts of the villages, but also *jhuggī* or summer shelters made of branches, and mat tents, known among Paṭhāns as *kiz̲hdʿī* and among the Brāhūīs as *gidān*, and even holes in the hillsides—in short any place where man can lay his head. It is only among the more progressive and well-to-do that sun-dried bricks are used in the construction of a house. Most villagers build their walls of stones and mud; athwart are laid rafters of any wood that is locally procurable; the roof consists of matting generally made of *pīsh* or dwarf-palm leaves; and on top are dumped thick layers of plaster. But certain Umrānī Balōch in the Kachhī deliberately refrain from plastering their roofs, because they assert (and who shall give them the lie?) that one of their forefathers died under a plastered roof. The ordinary village hut is a very primitive affair—four walls and a roof; likely enough there is no door, a hole in the wall covered with a strip of matting doing service instead. As for repairs, even the well-to-do seem to have an inveterate dislike to them: many a chief takes pride in raising imposing edifices for himself; but once raised, they are allowed to fall gradually into ruins. In the colder parts of the country, like Kach Kawās in the Sibī district, the huts are often built into a hollow in the ground, and the roof is made on the slope for the more easy removal of the snow. A *jhuggī* or summer shelter is easily made by driving a few poles into the ground and covering top and sides with strips of matting or with reeds or branches. Though it is a cramped abode, it affords a cool and pleasant refuge from the heat and mosquitoes in the villages, especially if there is water handy to sprinkle over it. But perhaps the most characteristic dwelling in Balūchistān is the *gidān* or *kiz̲hdʿī*, which ordinarily consists of a few bent poles covered over with matting made of goat's hair. But those who live in *pīsh* growing areas generally make their *gidān* of *pīsh*, which if less warm than goat's hair is much less expensive. How chary the people are of changing their ways may be seen by the fact that though the Mardōī Mēngal Brāhūīs near K̲hōzdār in Jhalawān have built several mud huts on their rain-crop lands, they use them almost entirely as barns or cattle-sheds, and only shift out of their *pīsh gidān* if the weather turns unusually cold. The chief has lately built himself a spacious fort; the ladies of his household still prefer to camp out in the courtyard.

House-population.

59. In Balūchistān as a whole there are not quite five persons to each house or tent. But if we exclude the urban areas and thus exclude most of the abnormality arising from the artificial conditions in which aliens live, the house-population goes up to just over five. It makes little or no difference if we split the province into districts and states; the result remains much the same in both. There is even a remarkable uniformity throughout the various minor divisions, with two exceptions. In the Bōlān, the house-population all but drops to two; in the Marī-Bugṭī country, it all but rises to eight. The explanation in the former case is obvious enough; the tiny population of the Bōlān is largely composed of alien railway employés living a life of solitude in gang-huts. In the Marī-Bugṭī country conditions of course are perfectly normal, and the unusual size of the household (which also manifested itself at the last census but not to the same degree) seems clear proof that the joint-family still thrives in these Balōch tribes; for in Balūchistān the term 'house' really covers the household, representing as it does the members of a family that live under the same roof and take their food from the same hearth. But statistics based on localities are a little dangerous after all: even the Marī-Bugṭī country is not inhabited by Marī and Bugṭī alone. So we took the trouble to pick out 8,258 indigenous families at haphazard from all parts of the province and examined them by race and tribe. And our labour was certainly not misspent. Even the bare summary in the margin is not without significance; it is interesting, for instance, to learn that the average Balōch family is 7 persons strong and beats the average Brāhūī household by two. But anybody who has the curiosity to turn to the subsidiary tables for the detailed results, will find more abundant and more serious food for reflection. He will discover, for instance, that there is one disturbing factor that has to be discounted in these statistics: the size of a Balūchistān household is often swollen by servile elements who are

House-population.	
Balōch	7·1
Lāsī	5·8
Jaṭṭ	5·6
Paṭhān	5·2
Brāhūī	5·1
Sayyid	4·5
Mēd	4·3
Sikh	5·1
Hindu	4·6

members of the household but not members of the joint-family in the proper sense of the word. And here what will probably strike him most is the absence of servile dependants among the Paṭhāns. To one who has the preservation of ancient social ties at heart, a much more significant feature in the statistics is the great contrast between the size of the family among the Marī (13·2) and Bugṭī (7·9) and the smallness of the family among their fellow-Balōch (4·2) in the west—in some measure, I cannot doubt, a direct reflection of the robust vigour of the tribal system in the one, and its hopeless decay in the other.

SUBSIDIARY TABLES.

I.—Distribution of the Population Classified by Density.

Districts and States.	Tahsils, etc., with a population per square mile of													
	Under 5.		5—10.		10—15.		15—20.		20—25.		40—45.		100—105.	
	Area.	Population.	Area.	Population.	Area.	Population.	Area.	Population.	Area.	Population.	Area.	Population.	Area.	Population.
BALŪCHISTĀN	**88,219**	**213,672**	**21,695**	**172,901**	**13,709**	**163,953**	**4,411**	**76,838**	**5,229**	**118,340**	**827**	**33,977**	**548**	**55,022**
	65·5	*25·5*	*16·1*	*20·7*	*10·1*	*19·6*	*3·2*	*9·2*	*3·8*	*14·1*	*·06*	*4·07*	*·04*	*6·5*
Districts	**25,590**	**34,669**	**14,563**	**111,696**	**8,479**	**100,172**	**3,052**	**53,295**	**1,169**	**25,581**	**827**	**33,977**	**548**	**55,022**
Quetta-Pishīn	...	...	414	2,079	1,206	17,252	3,052	53,295	...	...	...	...	548	55,022
Lōralai	...	...	2,181	20.714	5,344	60.055	...	...	...	...	...	...	...	...
Zhōb	2,576	4,216	7.739	66,150	...	...	...	...	...	...	...	...	...	...
Bōlān	...	...	353	2,096	...	...	...	...	...	...	...	...	...	...
Chāgai	19,622	16,344	...	...	...	...	...	...	...	...	...	...	...	...
Sibi	3,392	14,109	3,876	20,657	1,929	22,865	...	...	1,169	25,581	827	33,977	...	...
Administered area	...	...	...	...	*1,929*	*22,865*	...	...	*1,169*	*25,581*	*827*	*33,977*	...	...
Mari-Bugṭi country	*3,392*	*14,109*	*3,876*	*20,657*	...	...	...	...	...	...	...	...	...	...
States	**62,629**	**179,003**	**7,132**	**61,205**	**5,230**	**63,781**	**1,359**	**23,543**	**4,060**	**92,759**	...	...	...	...
Kalāt	62,629	179,003	...	...	5,230	63,781	1,359	23,543	4,060	92,759	...	...	...	...
Sārawān	...	...	...	...	*5,230*	*63,781*	...	...	...	...	...	...	...	...
Jhalawān	*20,795*	*84,398*	...	...	...	...	...	...	...	...	...	...	...	...
Kachhi	...	...	...	...	...	...	...	...	*4,060*	*92,759*	...	...	...	...
Dōmbki-Kahēri country	...	...	...	...	...	...	*1,359*	*23,543*	...	...	...	...	...	...
Makrān	*23,269*	*71,942*	...	...	...	...	...	...	...	...	...	...	...	...
Khārān	*18,565*	*22,663*	...	...	...	...	...	...	...	...	...	...	...	...
Las Bēla	...	...	7,132	61,205	...	...	...	...	...	...	...	...	...	...

Note.—The figures in leaded italics denote the proportions per cent which the area and population of each density group bear to the total area and population of the Province.

II.—Racial Distribution in the Regular and Tribal Areas.

District and States.	Indigenous.				Semi-Indigenous.				Aliens.			
	Regular Areas.		Tribal Areas.		Regular Areas.		Tribal Areas.		Regular Areas.		Tribal Areas.	
	Males.	Females.	Males.	Females.	Males.	Females.	Males.	Females.	Males.	Females.	Males.	Females.
BALŪCHISTĀN	***6,505***	***1,942***	***401,258***	***342,689***	***2,133***	***437***	***12,634***	***10,207***	***40,633***	***11,357***	***3,256***	***1,652***
Districts	**6,160**	**1,872**	**176,710**	**151,053**	**2,130**	**437**	**12,032**	**9,687**	**40,308**	**11,287**	**1,841**	**895**
Quetta-Pishīn	2,112	798	45,121	39,505	912	318	2,391	1,959	25,493	8,387	438	214
Lōralai	348	62	34,624	30,151	137	30	6,004	4,897	3,499	569	311	137
Zhōb	946	47	32,545	27,566	537	36	2,478	1,903	3,782	459	58	9
Bōlān	188	42	316	306	4	1	1	...	964	250	19	5
Chāgai	343	93	7,997	6,742	43	9	304	238	294	103	126	52
Sibī	2,223	830	56,107	46,783	497	43	854	690	6,276	1,519	889	478
Administered area	*2,223*	*830*	*36,888*	*31,349*	*497*	*43*	*839*	*677*	*6,276*	*1,519*	*835*	*447*
Marī-Bugṭī country	...	...	*19,219*	*15,434*	...	...	*15*	*13*	...	...	*54*	*31*
States	**345**	**70**	**224,548**	**191,636**	**3**	...	**602**	**520**	**325**	**70**	**1,415**	**757**
Kalāt	345	70	192,239	163,202	3	...	599	518	320	70	1,092	628
Sarāwān	*29*	*2*	*34,684*	*28,494*	*3*	...	*78*	*53*	*69*	*37*	*219*	*118*
Jhalawān	...	...	*46,714*	*37,481*	...	...	*8*	*5*	...	...	*158*	*33*
Kachhī	...	...	*49,738*	*42,963*	...	...	*139*	*119*	*4*	*2*	*310*	*184*
Dōmbkī-Kahērī country	...	...	*12,264*	*10,609*	...	...	*71*	*56*	...	...	*289*	*254*
Makrān	*316*	*68*	*36,813*	*33,902*	...	...	*211*	*201*	*247*	*81*	*111*	*49*
Khārān	...	...	*12,026*	*10,453*	...	...	*92*	*84*	...	...	*5*	*3*
Las Bēla	...	...	32,309	28,434	...	...	3	2	5	...	323	129

III.—Urban and Rural Distribution.

Districts and States.	Average population per		Number per mille residing in		Number per mille of urban population residing in towns with a population of			Number per mille of rural population residing in villages with a population of			
	Town.	Village.	Town.	Village.	20,000 and over.	5,000 to 10,000.	Under 5,000.	2,000 to 5,000.	500 to 2,000.	200 to 500.	Under 200.
BALŪCHISTĀN	***6,618***	***210***	***71***	***929***	***569***	***195***	***236***	***59***	***402***	***281***	***255***
Districts	**8,268**	**233**	**120**	**880**	**684**	**133**	**183**	**60**	**450**	**262**	**223**
Quetta-Pishīn	12,228	220	287	713	925	...	75	35	495	257	209
Lōṛalai	2,936	175	36	964	...	...	1,000	39	370	280	310
Zhōb	3,391	243	48	952	...	...	1,000	48	468	223	254
Bōlān	...	161	...	1,000	...	...	...	...	542	...	260
Chāgai	...	264	...	1,000	...	...	...	...	550	234	214
Sibī	6,597	313	56	944	...	1,000	...	113	441	287	158
Administered area	*6,597*	*295*	*80*	*920*	...	*1,000*	...	*34*	*505*	*300*	*158*
Marī Bugṭī country	...	*362*	...	*1,000*	...	...	...	*285*	*303*	*258*	*154*
States	**3,317**	**194**	**24**	**976**	...	**503**	**497**	**57**	**359**	**299**	**284**
Kalāt	3,472	198	19	981	...	721	279	59	362	287	291
Sarāwān	*3,472*	*177*	*109*	*891*	...	*721*	*279*	...	*355*	*319*	*326*
Jhalawān	...	*201*	...	*1,000*	...	...	...	...	*315*	*400*	*285*
Kachhī	...	*157*	...	*1,000*	...	...	...	*52*	*295*	*291*	*362*
Ḍōmbkī-Kahērī country	...	*1,070*	...	*1,000*	...	...	...	*487*	*480*	...	*33*
Makrān	...	*189*	...	*1,000*	...	...	...	*63*	*432*	*246*	*251*
Khārān	...	*252*	...	*1,000*	...	...	...	...	*480*	*199*	*321*
Las Bēla	3,006	197	49	951	...	...	1,000	47	341	369	243

IV.—House-population among the Indigenous Population (8,258 houses examined).

All indigenous.	House-population.	Family.	Servile dependants.
Balōch	**7·1**	**6·4**	**·7**
Eastern	*8·1*	*7·6*	*·5*
Marī	13·3	13·2	·1
Bugṭī	8·7	7·9	·8
Rind	7·3	5·4	1·9
Magasī	5·7	5·69	·01
Khetrān	5·7	5·7	...
Western	*5·3*	*4·2*	*1·1*
Brāhūī	**5·1**	**5**	**·1**
Sarāwān	*5·1*	*5*	*·1*
Shahwānī	5·7	5·7	...
Raīsānī	5·5	5·2	·3
Jhalawān	*5·1*	*5·0*	*·1*
Māmasanī	5·1	5	·1
Zahrī	4·4	4·3	·1
Paṭhān	**5·2**	**5·2**	...
Kākaṛ	4·6	4·6	...
Paṇī	5·6	5·6	...
Tarīn	5	5	...
Lāsī	**5·8**	**5·4**	**·4**
Jaṭṭ	**5·6**	**5·55**	**·05**
Mēd	**4·3**	**4·2**	**·1**
Sayyid	**4·5**	**4·4**	**·1**
Hindu	**4·6**	**4·6**	**·003**
Sikh	**5·1**	**5·1**	...

CHAPTER II.

VARIATION.

Statistical data.

Subject.	Tables.		
	Imperial.	Provincial.	Subsidiary.
Variation in general	II	......	......
Subdivisional variation	......	I	......
Urban variation	IV	......	......
Variation in density	......	......	V
Racial variation	......	......	VI
Racial variation by districts and states .	......	......	VII
Fecundity of marriage	......	......	VIII

60. Though this is the third census undertaken in Balūchistān, it is anything but easy to measure the rise or fall of the population from one census to another. Before we can indulge in the luxury of drawing comparisons at all, we must be in possession of like to compare with like. But not only are there huge gaps between the areas censused on the three occasions, there is a world of difference in the various methods of enumeration adopted and the degrees of efficiency attained. The census taken twenty years ago was so fragmentary, its methods so primitive, its results so unconvincing that, though I have fought against the temptation to leave it alone altogether, I find it the best policy to succumb. The flimsy and uncertain information that might be won from it would not be worth the elaborate and bewildering calculations I should have to work out and the reader would have to unravel. And great as was the advance that was made ten years later, nearly two-fifths of the country were left untouched. It might be thought that the exercise of a little ingenuity was all that was required to bridge over the hiatus. Unfortunately, the population of considerably more than half the area censused—and still more unfortunately the population of just that portion of the country which ought to serve as a guide for the population left unnumbered—was calculated on very rough and, as it usually proved, very sanguine methods. And if we leave census failings on one side and turn to the real causes which make for an increase or decrease in the population, to wit the ratio of births to deaths, of immigration to emigration, we are almost as much in the dark as we were before. Apart from a very sketchy registration of births and deaths in Quetta itself, registration is unknown in the country, and there is nothing to take its place but what can be gleaned from such vital statistics as we had time to collect from heads of families (§ 67). Nor are we on much firmer ground when we pass on to the ratio between immigration and emigration. Simple though the sum appears to be, it contains one known quantity only. For while the volume of the flow of immigration is easily measured, we can only make a guess at the ebb of emigration (§ 68). **Comparison with past results impossible.**

Area.		Population.		
		Total.	Estimated.	Enumerated.
1891	. 20,568	171,752	142,473	29,279
1901	. 82,950	810,746	459,728	351,018
1911	. 134,638	834,703	...	834,703

61. It will help us in groping our way through the uncertainties that surround us to analyse the population into its main component elements. The **Threefold population.**

chief interest centres throughout round the true indigenous inhabitants of the country—the tribesmen, and their satellites, the Lōṛī, the Dēhwār, the domiciled Hindus and the rest. At the opposite pole stand those who are unmistakably aliens in an alien land—Europeans, Anglo-Indians, and orientals from this or that side of the Indus. And midway between these two classes are people who might fairly be lumped up with the aliens, and yet have some show of claim, grounded in the present or the past, to be treated as indigenous inhabitants. Typical of this class are the Ghilzai Paṭhāns from Afghānistān and the Buzdār Balōch from the Panjāb. For not only have the Ghilzai been wont from time immemorial to pass through Balūchistān on their annual migration into India, a goodish number sojourn here for the winter, and a few have recently come to stay. And though the Buzdār tribe is now settled in the Panjāb, it was of course once indigenous to Balūchistān; several members still keep up a temporary connection with the old country, while a few families seem to have returned for good. These and others like them I have accordingly treated apart, and have divided up the whole population of the country into indigenous, semi-indigenous and alien inhabitants. It is a little difficult at this eleventh hour to apply the same classification to the population of the last census, but I fancy we have got round the obstacles sufficiently well to justify a broad comparison between the results on the two occasions.

Districts.

62. The threefold classification is especially useful when we turn to the districts. Take the districts *en bloc*, or take them piecemeal—in either case there is an increase over the population of ten years back. It is hardly profitable to examine the several districts in any detail. There was a wholesale redistribution of administrative charges shortly after the last census, and though we have done what we could to readjust the population among the newly constituted districts of Zhōb, Lōṛalai and Sibī, there is every reason to fear that we have not met—and could not meet—with full measure of success.[1] But apart from this, much of the district population is of a floating character, moving freely not only across the border and back again, but also from one district to another; and where the population is so fluid, it is idle to linger long over a rise or fall that may be literally ephemeral. Nevertheless some little light is shed on the meaning of the variations in the several districts by an analysis of the three elements in the population. How unevenly these have contributed to the increase of 8·5 per cent in the districts as a whole is seen clearly enough from the margin. In the indigenous population the rate of increase has been modest enough. The semi-indigenous population, on the other hand, appears to have gone up by leaps and bounds, materially affecting the variations in Lōṛalai, Zhōb and Quetta-Pishīn, where it chiefly disperses itself. But this great influx has probably been more apparent than real—a mere consequence, that is, of better enumeration, which could hardly have greater scope than among the wandering Ghilzai, who form the bulk of this element in the population. The increase among the aliens, though less marked, is still considerable, and unquestionably a good deal more genuine. Nearly the whole of it has occurred in Quetta-Pishīn, where the aliens have been responsible for almost half of the goodly increase of nearly 12 per cent in the district population. On paper Lōṛalai shows a substantial increase of over 18 per cent—an increase much too good to be true, and in itself a very pretty proof of our faulty readjustment of the figures for the last census. Much of the increase should clearly be handed over to Zhōb, which otherwise appears to have been almost stationary: spread over the two districts, it would work out to over 9 per cent. But some of it should probably go to the Sibī district: as matters stand, the administered area simply shows an increase of about 5 per cent (representing 4,436 souls), which is more than accounted for by an increase of 2,046 in Sibī town and a remarkable but fictitious jump of 3,632 in the Kōhlū sub-*tahsīl*, the simple explanation of which is that at the last census the Marī colony in Kōhlū was lumped up with the population of the Marī-Bugṭī country—yet another proof of the danger of placing blind reliance on the internal variations in the province. Thrown back at this census on its own resources,

Variation.

	Actual.	Percentage.
Districts . .	+ 32,306	+ 8·5
Indigenous .	+ 17,081	+ 5·4
Semi-indigenous	+ 8,416	+ 53
Aliens . .	+ 6,809	+ 14·3

[1] For one thing, no village statistics were left on record.

the Marī-Bugṭī country not unnaturally finds it hard to show any advance at all. The Bōlān, on the other hand, can boast an increase of over 8 per cent; but its population still remains microscopic. In Chāgai there has been a nominal increase of 4 per cent: that it can show an increase at all is simply due to the fact that Western Sanjrānī, now censused for the first time, is included in its total. Had it not been for the bad season which sent many of its inhabitants out of the district, I should have anticipated a much larger increase, not so much as a result of better enumeration (for though Chāgai was merely subjected to a rough estimate at the last census, rough estimates in Balūchistān have usually overshot the mark) as on account of the strides this district has been making towards development during the past ten years.

63. The threefold classification is of little use when we turn to the states. **States.** Here the population is almost entirely indigenous. Nor do I put much faith in the apparently enormous increase of the inconsiderable semi-indigenous and alien elements, for the excellent reason that the census of 1901 was a mere estimate in which the non-indigenous elements ran the greater risk of being overlooked, because it was based (partially in Las Bēla and wholly in Kalāt) on figures supplied by the tribal chiefs and headmen of sections. And in the nature of that estimate lies the secret of the seemingly serious decline in the state population, a decline all the more marked as half the state area was omitted from the scope of the last census. The explanation of this apparent decline is after all simple enough. Asked to furnish the number of fighting men at their command, chiefs and headmen would have been either more or less than human to have withstood the temptation of putting their numbers at the highest possible pitch. The more out of the way the tribe, the more would the chief be emboldened to pile on the agony. Nothing, for instance, would be more natural than for a chief of Jhalawān to exaggerate unblushingly, where a chief of Sarāwān would have to stick pretty close to actual facts for very shame. Equally natural would it be to find exaggeration much more frequent in the Brāhūī country, where tribal organisation is still strong, than in the Kachhī, which is largely inhabited by Jaṭṭ, who have become so split up that they can hardly be said to have any real tribal organisation at all. In fact where tribal bonds are loose or lacking altogether, it is not exaggeration of numbers that an estimate based on the assumption of the existence of such bonds is likely to produce, but wholesale omission. This or something like this was clearly the chequered history of the census of 1901 in the various parts of the country to which those methods were applied.

Variation.

	Actual.	Percentage.
States	– **8,349**	– **1·9**
Indigenous	– 10,531	– 2·5
Semi-indigenous	+ 973	+ 640·1
Aliens	+ 1,209	+ 89

64. The estimates for Jhalawān were suspect from the beginning. They **Kalāt.** were regarded as inflated not only by the district officer, but by the officials primarily responsible for them. My predecessor, however, while recognising the possibility of exaggeration in individual cases, came finally to the conclusion that the figures had not been vitiated in any serious degree, and saw confirmation of his conclusion in the discovery that the density in Jhalawān worked out to very nearly the same figure as the density in Sarāwān. And here he unwittingly put his finger on a very telling proof that his conclusion could not hold water. For that Jhalawān is incomparably more thinly populated than prosperous Sarāwān, there is no possible question. How gradually and grudgingly we have come to realise the extraordinary dearth of inhabitants in many parts of this vast province may be traced in the successive attempts that were made to gauge the population of the three tracts omitted from the operations of the last census. Working on the analogy of Chāgai, my predecessor assessed the population of Western Sanjrānī at over nine thousand souls; a couple of years later he found cause to cut down his estimates to six thousand; the writer of the district gazetteer would not commit himself to as many hundreds. More interesting still is the case of K͟hārān and Makrān. On the basis of the density in the Marī-Bugṭī country my predecessor assessed their population at 229,655; as soon as he was able to have a rough estimate made on the spot, the figures went down with a bang to 97,800; and big though the drop, the total is still some three thousand in excess of the figures for the

present census. Now if we could assume that in 1901 the same degree of error crept into the rough estimates of Jhalawān as into the rough assessments of Khārān and Makrān, and could assume further that the forces that make fro progress and decay had operated evenly during the past ten years in all three parts of the country, the present-day population of Jhalawān would pan out to 92,306 souls, as against the 84,398 actually enumerated at this census. And though it is hardly more than a coincidence, I am inclined to think that this figure would not be very wide of the mark. The district officials, it is true, seem fairly confident that our census netted in pretty nearly all there were to be found in Jhalawān. But parts of this somewhat backward tract were in so troublous a condition as to make it probable on the face of it that a fair number of the inhabitants escaped enumeration. It is at the same time almost certain that there had recently been a considerable exodus from the country to avoid not only the political trouble but the prevailing scarcity. Thus we should not be far wrong, I fancy, in reckoning the actual population of Jhalawān in 1911 at about 90,000, and its potential population in a good and peaceful year at about 100,000. But if I am not mistaken, Jhalawān is nowadays slowly draining into Sind (§ 78), and unless conditions take a turn for the better, it may be long before Jhalawān sees 100,000 inhabitants again. Even in Sarāwān, which is much too well-known from end to end for the chiefs to have launched out into wild over-statements of their tribal strength like the chiefs of Jhalawān, there appears on paper to have been a slight drop since the last census. On the other hand there appears on paper to have been a gigantic increase of over 40 per cent in the low-lying plain composed of the Kachhī and the Ḍōmbkī-Kahērī country. Such an increase can hardly be genuine, even though this plain is acutely sensitive to the nature of the seasons and was certainly in much better case during the present census than it was ten years before. I have no doubt that a very large proportion of the apparent increase is simply due to the facts that many of its tribal inhabitants were lumped up at the last census with their tribes in Jhalawān and Sarāwān, and that hundreds of Jaṭṭ and others of similar character were overlooked, simply because enumeration on a tribal basis breaks down hopelessly when it is applied to people who have lost their tribal organisation.

Las Bēla.

65. We need waste little time over the petty state of Las Bēla. Most of its inhabitants are less unruly and less unsettled than the tribesmen of Kalāt, and it was found possible in a largish portion of its area to conduct the former census on more orthodox and trustworthy lines. Not that the whole of the apparent increase of nine per cent in its population from the one census to the other can be placed to its credit. Something at any rate must clearly be put down to a more effective enumeration. Nevertheless, though there is nothing in the economic history of the past ten years taken by themselves to explain a rate of increase which, even after due allowance is made on the score of better enumeration, remains at a figure abnormal for Balūchistān, it becomes explicable enough when it is remembered that at the date of the last census the state was only just beginning to recover from a bout of scarcity long drawn-out, and had not had sufficient time to attract back the many hundreds of its inhabitants who had taken refuge in India.

Summary.

66. The more clearly the nature of the problem is realised, the more hopeless it appears to attempt to measure the increase or decrease that has occurred in the population of Balūchistān during the last ten years. Where —as in a large portion of the district area—there was a reasonable amount of uniformity in the methods adopted at the one census and the other, some allowance at any rate ought to be made for the palpable improvement that has come over those methods. Where the methods were widely different—and even the districts had their roughly estimated areas in 1901—much greater allowance ought to be made for errors of exaggeration and the lesser errors of omission. In dealing with areas that have never been censused before, we are of course thrown back on sheerest conjecture. It is idle to enter upon a disquisition on the economic conditions that prevailed before the last census and in the ten years that followed. For large numbers of the people never stay in the country to see the lean years out. On the first symptoms of scarcity they decamp wholesale, and abroad they remain till they get news of better times

in their own country. In other words, adverse conditions have little permanent effect on the population; they simply lower it for the time being. It is only when dire calamities come suddenly and act swiftly that the people are baffled in their attempts to escape; and from such—save for a fierce outbreak of cholera in Makrān and a terrible earthquake in the Kachhī—Balūchistān of recent years has happily been spared. It is more to the point to take a broad view of the conditions that prevailed during the census operations of 1901 and 1911. In the Paṭhān country conditions were much the same in 1911 as they were in 1901; in the Jhalawān part of the Brāhūī country they were a good deal worse; in the Lāsī and the Jaṭṭ and the typically Balōch countries—that is to say, in Las Bēla, in the whole area occupied by the Kachhī plain, and in the Marī-Bugṭī country—they were distinctly more favourable; in Chāgai they were distinctly worse. As Makrān, Khārān and Western Sanjrānī were not censused in 1901, comparisons are a little irrelevant, but it may be said that Makrān was certainly not at its best, that Khārān was unusually well populated, and that Western Sanjrānī seems to have been as full—or as little empty—as it ever is. This hasty review is in itself enough to show how dangerous an artless comparison of the two sets of statistics would be, even if there had been no gaps in the last census and its methods of enumeration had been above reproach. Amid so much that is doubtful, guess-work is really vain. But if guess I must, the convenient guess that is nearest to hand will do as well as any other. It is quite possible that if the total for 1901 is held to cover not only the portions that the last census professed to cover but also the portions that it left untouched, it is about as near as we are likely to get to the true facts for 1901. That the alien population has increased with great rapidity is a demonstrable fact; it must not be assumed that it will be able to keep up the same pace much longer. In all probability the explanation of the great increase in the semi-indigenous population lies largely in the fact that we were more successful than our predecessors in enumerating the elusive Powindahs. As for the tribesmen and other indigenous peoples, the very general impression is that they are barely holding their own: if one year finds more in the country than another, this is simply because large numbers of them are nomadic—or to use their more expressive term, *khāna-ba-dōsh*, 'house-a-back'—people ready to shift in or out of the country at a moment's notice, as conditions change for the better or the worse.

Variation.

	Actual.	Percentage.
Balūchistān	**+ 23,957**	**+ 2·9**
Indigenous .	+ 6,550	+ ·9
Semi-indigenous	+ 9,389	+ 58·6
Aliens . .	+ 8,018	+ 16·4

67. It will be many a long day before we can put this general impression to the test of vital statistics. In the absence of any registration of births and deaths outside Quetta town, we utilised the census machinery to ascertain from 6,641 fathers in all parts of the country the number of children that had been actually born to them and the number still alive. The results of our enquiry are summarised in a table at the end of this chapter; the gist of them is given in the margin. But the statistics must be read with some reservation. Our enumerators unfortunately ignored sterile unions as irrelevant to the object of the enquiry. Nor were they able to make any nice distinction between the issue of an only wife and the issue of a plurality of wives, contemporaneous or successive. Not that sterile unions appear to be common in this country; when they do occur, they are usually short-lived: if the husband is palpably the one to blame for the childlessness of the union, the wife appeals to the elders for a dissolution of the marriage; if the wife is the one at fault, the husband takes to himself another wife—to beat the first withal, as the proverb says. And though the average tribesman usually marries again if his first wife dies, probably not one in a dozen takes a second wife if his first is alive and has borne him children. The fathers of course were of all ages: some no doubt were in the vigour of manhood; others must have had a foot in the grave. Vital Statistics.

Average family per father.

	Births.	Survivals.
All .	*5·9*	*3·6*
Balōch .	6·5	4·1
Brāhūī .	4·8	3·0
Paṭhān .	6·0	3·4
Lāsī .	5·6	4·2
Jaṭṭ .	5·8	3·9
Sayyid .	5·4	3·3
Miscellaneous .	6·0	3·9
Hindus .	5·2	2·8

There is in consequence considerable disparity in the ages of the surviving children. In a word, the general purport of the statistics is nothing more than this: 6,641 fathers, taken at haphazard from among the indigenous population in all parts of the country, were found to have had 38,912 children, of whom 23,837 were still alive; and in considering these statistics we have to make allowances for the omission of sterile unions on the one hand, and on the other for the fact that several unions had not reached the maximum of their fecundity. It ought to be possible to weave many a pretty theory out of the various figures that go to the making of this result. But I have been unable to stumble across any statistics exactly comparable, and am thus in the ignominious position of having to leave to others the task of gauging the precise value of my contribution to the problem. I hardly like to commit myself to more than the general conclusion that the fecundity of the average marriage in Balūchistān seems respectably but hardly surprisingly high. Of the various races the Balōch are the most prolific with 6·5, the Brāhūis are the least prolific with 4·8. If we analyse the birth-rate by localities, Makrān comes out an easy first with 7·8, and this has had its effect in raising the Balōch figures; Sarāwān and Jhalawān, the heart of the Brāhūi country, is a bad last with 4. As for infant mortality in Balūchistān, it is very commonly believed to be appalling: but whether this is borne out by our statistics, which show that 387 out of every 1,000 children have predeceased their fathers, I hesitate to say, for several European countries a few decades ago could cap our dismal figure with a somewhat analogous and an even more dismal death-rate under the age of five. In Jhalawān, however, the children seem to die off like flies, for not one in two was found to have survived its father; and as the birth-rate itself is painfully low, the outlook would be hopeless indeed, were it not for the consolation that it would take a much larger set of statistics than those before us to drive home the mournful suspicion that the peoples of Jhalawān are rapidly dying out. This then is the conclusion of the whole matter: though a man of Balūchistān can reasonably hope to beget a goodly family of 5 or 6 children, he cannot look to see more than 3 or 4 survive him. And this is surely a very meagre surplus margin to carry on to the next generation, seeing that it has to replace the man and his wife or wives, sterile unions and deaths before maturity. So meagre is it, that to say that the tribal population is standing still, is possibly to overstep the mark.

SUBSIDIARY TABLES.

V.—Variation in Relation to Density.

NOTE.—The 1901 census was largely based on estimates, which were for the most part unduly sanguine; on the other hand vast areas were omitted. As these two factors possibly balance one another (§ 66), no adjustments have been attempted in this or the following tables.

District or State.	Mean density per square mile. 1911.	1901.	Percentage of variation, 1901-11. Increase + Decrease —
BALŪCHISTĀN	*6·19*	*6·02*	+ *2·95*
Districts	**7·64**	**7·05**	+ **8·45**
Quetta-Pishīn	24·45	21·86	+ 11·88
Lōṛalai	10·73	9·08	+ 18·20
Zhōb	6·82	6·76	+ 0·92
Bōlān	5·93	5·48	+ 8·26
Chāgai	0·83	0·79	+ 4·17
Sibī	10·46	10·03	+ 4·31
Administered area	*21*	*19·86*	+ *5·69*
Marī-Bugṭī country	*4·78*	*4·72*	+ *1·19*
States	**5·23**	**5·33**	— **1·94**
Kalāt	4·90	5·08	— 3·60
Las Bēla	8·58	7·86	+ 9·03

VI.—Racial Variation.

RACE.	1911. Regular Census. Persons.	Males.	Females.	Tribal Census. Persons.	Males.	Females.	Variation, 1901-11. Increase + Decrease —
BALŪCHISTĀN	*63,007*	*49,271*	*13,736*	*771,696*	*417,148*	*354,548*	+ *23,957*
Indigenous	**8,447**	**6,505**	**1,942**	**743,947**	**401,258**	**342,689**	+ **6,550**
Balōch	1,158	889	269	168,032	91,070	76,962	+ 68,960
Brāhūī	1,473	1,146	327	166,314	91,949	74,365	— 124,432
Paṭhān	3,499	2,938	561	184,594	99,210	85,384	+ 5,019
Lāsī	...	...	...	27,779	14,857	12,922	+ 1,162
Jaṭṭ	432	324	108	77,965	42,346	35,619	+ 19,005
Sayyid	238	202	36	21,058	10,806	10,252	+ 6,696
Other Musalmān	906	518	388	81,162	41,949	39,213	+ 30,579
Hindu	733	481	252	14,252	7,641	6,611	} — 439
Sikh	8	7	1	2,791	1,430	1,361	
Semi-indigenous	**2,570**	**2,133**	**437**	**22,841**	**12,634**	**10,207**	+ **9,389**
Balōch	18	11	7	3,076	1,709	1,367	+ 1,405
Paṭhān	2,552	2,122	430	19,765	10,925	8,840	+ 7,984
Aliens	**51,990**	**40,633**	**11,357**	**4,908**	**3,256**	**1,652**	+ **8,018**
European	4,210	3,382	828	...	...	...	+ 731
Anglo-Indian	123	64	59	...	...	...	+ 1
Oriental	47,657	37,187	10,470	4,908	3,256	1,652	+ 7,286
Trans-Indus	*6,379*	*5,332*	*1,047*	*761*	*464*	*297*	...
Cis-Indus	*41,278*	*31,855*	*9,423*	*4,147*	*2,792*	*1,355*	...

VII.—Racial Variation by Districts and States.

Districts and States.	TOTAL.	Indigenous.	Semi-indigenous.	Alien.
BALŪCHISTĀN	***+ 23,957***	***+ 6,550***	***+ 9,389***	***+ 8,018***
Districts	**+ 32,306**	**+ 17,081**	**+ 8,416**	**+ 6,809**
Quetta-Pishīn	+ 13,561	+ 4,174	+ 2,984	+ 6,403
Bōlān	+ 160	+ 142	— 56	+ 74
Chāgai	+ 655	— 48	+ 583	+ 120
Lōralai, Zhōb, Sibī	+ 17,930	+ 12,813	+ 4,905	+ 212
States	**— 8,349**	**— 10,531**	**+ 973**	**+ 1,209**
Kalāt	— 13,445	— 16,611	+ 1,081	+ 2,085
Las Bēla	+ 5,096	+ 6,060	— 108	— 876

VIII.—Fecundity of Marriage.

(Among the indigenous people.)

PARTICULARS.	Number of fathers.	Number of births.	NUMBER OF SURVIVALS. Total.	Non-adult.	Adult.	Average births per father.	Average survivals per father.	Deaths per mille births.
			(i) By locality.					
BALŪCHISTĀN	***6,641***	***38,912***	***23,837***	***13,883***	***9,954***	***5·9***	***3·6***	***387***
Districts	**4,226**	**24,948**	**15,064**	**9,323**	**5,741**	**5·9**	**3·6**	**396**
Quetta-Pishīn	696	4,273	2,323	1,548	775	6·1	3·3	456
Lōralai	1,121	6,927	3,936	2,413	1,523	6·2	3·5	432
Zhōb	780	4,543	2,746	1,876	870	5·8	3·5	396
Bōlān	126	654	330	207	123	5·2	2·6	495
Chāgai	263	1,393	882	541	341	5·3	3·4	367
Sibī	864	4,900	3,092	1,839	1,253	5·7	3·3	369
Mari-Bugṭī country	376	2,258	1,755	899	856	6	4·7	223
States	**2,415**	**13,964**	**8,773**	**4,560**	**4,213**	**5·8**	**3·6**	**372**
Kalāt	2,244	12,819	7,920	4,093	3,827	5·7	3·5	382
Sarāwān	*377*	*1,561*	*1,008*	*615*	*393*	*4·1*	*2·7*	*354*
Jhalawān	*223*	*842*	*394*	*211*	*183*	*3·8*	*1·8*	*532*
Kachhī	*693*	*4,153*	*2,572*	*1,114*	*1,458*	*6*	*3·7*	*391*
Ḍōmbkī-Kahērī country	*317*	*1,606*	*1,026*	*570*	*456*	*5·1*	*3·2*	*361*
Makrān	*526*	*4,110*	*2,503*	*1,325*	*1,178*	*7·8*	*4·8*	*391*
Khārān	*109*	*547*	*417*	*258*	*159*	*5·1*	*3·9*	*238*
Las Bēla	171	1,145	853	467	386	6·7	5	255
			(ii) By race.					
Musalmān	**6,321**	**37,232**	**22,951**	**13,430**	**9,521**	**5·9**	**3·6**	**384**
Balōch	1,628	10,536	6,747	3,740	3,007	6·5	4·1	360
Brāhūī	891	4,270	2,677	1,595	1,082	4·8	3·	373
Paṭhān	2,254	13,549	7,736	4,985	2,751	6	3·4	429
Lāsī	87	486	369	216	153	5·6	4·2	241
Jaṭṭ	730	4,246	2,839	1,354	1,485	5·8	3·9	331
Sayyid	429	2,330	1,414	901	513	5·4	3·3	393
Miscellaneous	302	1,815	1,169	639	530	6	3·9	356
Hindu	**320**	**1,680**	**886**	**453**	**433**	**5·2**	**2·8**	**473**

CHAPTER III.

MIGRATION.

Statistical data.

SUBJECT.	TABLES.		
	Imperial.	Provincial.	Subsidiary.
Birthplace	XI	......	......
Race	XIII	......	......
Nomadism	......	I	IX
Brâhûis in Sind	......	......	X
Loss and gain over "migration"	......	......	XI

Birthplace no criterion of migration.

68. In departing from the orthodox method of gauging the ebb and flow of migration by the statistics of birthplace, I have been largely influenced by the uneasy feeling that birthplace is a singularly treacherous guide to rely upon after all. Stated in the rough, the theory seems to be simply this: that persons enumerated in one province but born in another are emigrants from the latter to the former. On this theory all migration difficulties at once resolve themselves into a delightfully easy sum of addition and subtraction. Take the population actually enumerated in the province; subtract the population born elsewhere; add the population born in the province but absent at the time of enumeration (but how you are to get the figures from Afghānistān or Persia, for instance, I cannot tell you), and you arrive at once at the so-called natural population—the population of the province purged of its alien immigrants and with its absent emigrants restored to it once more. A very pretty theory this, but one that will never reflect the real facts of life so long as immigration and emigration exist. For until migration ceases, there will always be people born where, according to the theory, they should not be born—outside their mother country. I freely admit that errors will tend to adjust themselves where emigration and immigration are fairly equal in volume; I admit also that birthplace statistics may be put to other and more legitimate uses. But I cannot help thinking that, if we frankly laid ourselves out to collect statistics not of birthplace but of mother country, we should get much more useful results. And the results, I fancy, would be much more trustworthy at the same time. As it is, I have a shrewd suspicion that birthplace statistics in India are plentifully adulterated with statistics of mother country: in the primitive society of Balūchistān, at any rate, mother country is so uppermost in the minds of the people that it naturally prompts their ready answer to a question about birthplace. Better still would it be to collect statistics of birthplace and mother country both[1]; the people would then know what we were driving at, and we ourselves could tackle the statistics without the uncomfortable feeling that we were racking them beyond their legitimate uses. As a guide to emigration, birthplace statistics are a makeshift at best, only to be pressed into service in the absence of something better. In Balūchistān we have no need to rely on such a broken reed. Here there is a great gulf fixed between aliens and the true natives of the country,

Census population	834,703
Subtract "immigrants"	58,500
Add traceable "emigrants"	76,273
"Natural" population	852,476

[1] An alternative suggestion that involves no change in the standard schedule is put forward in the footnote at page 46.

and it will probably be many generations before it is bridged. Race, and race alone, suffices (except in a few very special cases) to weed out the immigrants and to sift the whole population into three heaps—indigenous, semi-indigenous and aliens (§ 61).

Only partly recorded.

69. And, truth to tell, I have discarded birthplace for another and a very different reason. While in the regular areas we fell into line with the rest of India and recorded birthplace as a matter of course, we were faced in the tribal areas with the obvious difficulty of recording the birthplace of individuals on a schedule which applied to the family as a whole. Had the matter been of vital importance, we could, I dare say, have found a way round the difficulty. But if birthplace is of little value in tracing the movement of aliens into the province, it is of still less value in tracing the movement of the indigenous population from one part of the province to another. So shifting are many sections of the indigenous population, that what is true of it in the spring is almost certainly wide of the mark in the summer or autumn or winter. Where movement is so common, local knowledge—backed, as we took care to back it, by general statistics of nomadism (§ 71)—is a much safer guide to the many channels in which it flows than any bookish comparison between birthplace and the place of enumeration at some particular date. And this constant movement is itself a factor which in some ways would tend to invalidate birthplace statistics in direct proportion to their accuracy. For the winter exodus of the Brāhūīs to the plains, for instance, would be marked by births all along the march, and Quetta and Bōlān and Sibī and Las Bēla would be accredited with more Brāhūīs than is their proper due. Not that scrupulous accuracy could be expected. Strange though it may seem to us, many a tribesman would be at a loss to give the birthplace of all the members of his family. It would not seem strange to the tribesman himself, whose life is often spent in one long weary tramp—here to-day, gone to-morrow. And even if his poor memory found room for such worthless lumber as the precise sites of the various and, very possibly, nameless localities where his offspring first happened to see the light of day, what should he know of their position in the several districts, whose boundaries belong for the most part to the artificial geography of British administration? Thus all that seemed really necessary in the tribal areas was to record the birthplace, first, of those whose race stamped them as aliens, then of Hindus and others who (as far as race went) might or might not be natives of Balūchistān, and finally, in a few special cases, of tribesmen who were enumerated in some part of the country with which they had no recognised concern. In other words, not only did we assume that all members of races and tribes indigenous to Balūchistān were actually born in Balūchistān, and ignore the existence of inevitable exceptions to the general rule, like births on the other side of the Afghān frontier or births in Sind during the winter migrations of the Jhalawān Brāhūīs down-country; we also assumed that all members of races and tribes indigenous, in some sense, to the district in which they were enumerated, were actually born in that district, and ignored the existence of inevitable exceptions to the general rule, like births in the course of wanderings outside it. In either case the exceptions, though common enough, are mere accidents; had they been recorded, we should have had to exercise a deal of caution in groping our way through the treacherous fog of statistics.

Shifting character of the population.

70. Probably no feature of Balūchistān life impresses a new-comer more forcibly than the apparent fact that the population, such as it is, is always on the move. If he travels through Zhōb and Lōṛalai at the fall of the year, he will come across swarms of Afghān Powindahs on their yearly journey into India, shedding some of their numbers here and there to seek pasturage during the winter within Balūchistān itself. If he travels up the Bōlān, he will have to thread his way through a moving mass of Sarāwān Brāhūīs, leaving their native highlands with their wives and their children, their flocks and their herds, for the warmth of the Kachhī. And if he travels up the Mūla or any of the other passes to the south, he will be met by hosts of their Jhalawān brethren, wending their way into Sind. These are extreme cases, where whole masses of the population move down-country like a slowly advancing glacier. But wherever he travels, he will—if only he travel long enough—come across families camped in blanket-tents, or living in temporary huts made of bark or dwarf-palm leaves or similar material, or even sheltering in holes in the hillside.

And if he chance to revisit the spot a short while later, he will find the tents gone, or their places taken by others, and the huts maybe abandoned, and the holes tenantless. As for the permanent villages which jostle one another on the maps, he will look for most of them in vain. Even in the more settled parts of the country many of the permanent villages he descries from afar are permanent only in the sense that the same structures on the same sites serve as dwelling-places year after year: to-night there may be no room for the traveller to sleep in; to-morrow, before he awakes, half the inhabitants may have flitted, to summer abroad in the open. Now and then he may be drawn to a village of fairish size, only to regard it as a village of the dead, until he stumbles up against a few unfortunates who have been left behind to look after the crops.

71. If the picture appears to be overdrawn, it is well worth while to glance at the bald figures in the margin. They are the gist of not the least important of the special statistics we collected in the tribal census. Of the total population netted in by that census, only 54 per cent spend their days, year in, year out, in a permanent dwelling. Thirteen per cent divide their time between life in a village and life in the open. As many as 33 per cent have no roof worth the name to bless themselves with at all. Significant though these figures are, they lose nothing in significance when it is remembered that they relate not to individuals but to whole families of men, women, and children; and that they include neither temporary migrants who were censused in the regular areas within Balūchistān or in India, nor the swarms of nomad families who had wandered into Afghānistān and Persia owing to the drought. Even more significant do they become with a little sifting. A large proportion of the settled population is taken up by the Jaṭṭ, Dēhwār, Hindu, Sayyid, and other satellites or parasites of tribal life. If we wish to examine the mode of life of the true tribesmen of the country, we must leave these out of the count, and turn to the Brāhūī and the indigenous Balōch and Paṭhān. Among these, nomadism still claims no less than 40 in every hundred as its own; 18 are now wavering in their allegiance; only 42 have freed themselves wholly from its thrall.[1] Nomadism.

Tribal Census.	
Nomad	255,338
Semi-nomad	96,995
Settled	419,363

72. The migrations of the three peoples have much in common. All three are largely seasonal migrations. All three are migrations not of casual individuals but of whole families. At bottom all three are induced in a greater or lesser degree by three interrelated causes—extremes of heat and cold, pastoralism, lack of perennial water and culturable land. Put in a very general way—there will be enough evidence brought forward presently to check the generalisation—it may be said that the Brāhūī is affected in the main by the first of these causes; the Balōch by the second; and the Paṭhān by the third. Though the world itself has scarce bounds for the adventurous spirit of the individual Paṭhān, the Paṭhān family of this country (in striking contrast to the Powindah) rarely wanders far from home. The Balōch, if we take the Marī or Bugṭī as typical, circles round and round his own country, only occasionally leaving its limits for Sind or the Panjāb, except of course under the pressure of drought. Home-keeping though the Brāhūīs are, it is they who are perforce driven furthest afield in their wanderings. Its causes.

73. Among Paṭhāns nomadism flourishes in many forms. There are nomads pure and simple, living wholly on their flocks, constantly moving their *kiẕhdʻī* or blanket-tents from place to place in search of pasture and more congenial climates, but usually keeping pretty close to the same old beaten tracks. More characteristic of Paṭhān nomadism are the semi-nomads. Of these, large numbers live partly on their flocks and partly on agriculture—some relying more on the former, some more on the latter—and usually quit their blanket-tents for huts on their fields in favourable seasons of the year. There are others, dependent almost wholly on agriculture, who possess lands in different parts of the country, and shift their quarters with the different sowing and harvest seasons. Then there are villagers who leave their villages in the Paṭhān nomadism.

Paṭhāns.	
Nomad	24
Semi-nomad	33
Settled	43
	100

[1] The percentages in this and the following paragraphs necessarily relate to those censused in the tribal areas only. There is nothing to show the mode of life of the few thousand tribesmen censused in the regular areas: it would certainly be rash to assume (though it was found convenient to do so in Provincial Table I) that all or even the majority of them are settled.

warmer months and squat on their fields close by, where some live in *kizhdᵃi*, others in summer shelters; most of these last have doubtless been returned as settled. Over and above all these, there are of course temporary migrants, drawn chiefly from the settled classes, who wander off to India or Afghānistān in search of labour and trade. That the Kāsī is the only tribe of any importance in which all the tribesmen are settled, is a suggestive commentary on the nomadic character of the Paṭhāns of this country. The varying degrees of nomadism in the larger tribes are given in a table at the end of this chapter. An analysis of the figures in any fulness would be a very laborious undertaking. Happily there is no need to attempt it. The details are of hardly more than local interest; their main features are fairly familiar to local officers; and to map out the itineraries of the several tribes would be to cover ground that has already been worked elsewhere. One or two facts, however, should be borne in mind. On their seasonal movements, tribes cross and recross from one district to another, the general trend being from the uplands to the lowlands in winter, from the lowlands to the uplands in summer. Moreover, these movements sometimes extend beyond the confines of Balūchistān either into independent territory, as in the case of the Shīranī, or into Afghānistān, as in the case of the Achakzai and the Baṛēch. And lastly, although one type of nomadism may seem more characteristic than others in some particular tribe, other types exist almost always side by side with it.

The Powindahs.

74. Of the Paṭhāns known as Powindah, *pᵃvᵃnda* or "nomads" *par excellence*, I need say little. Though Balūchistān has been one of the regular stages on their annual migrations from time immemorial; though several of them treat it as their journey's end, some never going further south, a few never going further north; and though a small colony of refugees has taken up its abode in Balūchistān apparently for good, the Powindahs as a body hail from Afghānistān and are hardly to be classed among our indigenous inhabitants. Chief among the clans that visit us year by year are the Sulemānkhēl, the Nāsar, the Kharōṭ, the Tarak and the Andaṛ—Ghilzai all, it would seem, though in a recent authority[1] the term appears to be more especially confined to the Sulemānkhēl. They first begin to swarm into Balūchistān in October, and gradually spread over the northern districts. Thence the main body moves slowly on into India. Here they pass the winter, grazing their flocks in the plains, bartering furs and dried fruits and other goods brought from the highlands, plying their camels for hire, or engaging in manual labour. Towards the beginning of March the first stragglers re-enter Balūchistān on their homeward journey. But with the Powindahs who extend their migration into India, our statistics have little to do; for we took pains only to enumerate those who actually wintered in Balūchistān and the few early stragglers who had already passed up from India by the date of the census. Thus, nearly all our nomad and semi-nomad Powindahs (to use a tautology) are at least semi-indigenous to Balūchistān; the "settled" Powindahs (to use a contradiction in terms) are members of the tiny Ghilzai settlement.

Powindahs.	
Nomad	81
Semi-nomad	5
Settled	14
	100

Balōch nomadism

75. There is a smaller degree of nomadism among the Balōch than among either the Paṭhāns or Brāhūis. This is chiefly due on the one hand to the settled character of the Rind and the Magasī and the other tribesmen who have colonised the plain which stretches over the Kachhī and Nasīrābād and the Ḍōmbkī-Kahērī country, and on the other to the more unstable yet settled character of many Balōch in Makrān, where there are a fairish number of permanent villages and a still larger number of temporary hamlets, which are regularly shifted at periodical intervals. But these Balōch of the east and west are no longer true to the ancient Balōch spirit, that spirit of unfettered pastoralism that inspires many a famous ballad:—

Balōch.	Eastern.	Western.
Nomad	39	36
Semi-nomad	4	6
Settled	57	58
	100	100

For a fort the Balōch has his hills!
What wind-catching mansion is grander?
White sandals he has for a steed,
In his brother a sword and defender.

[1] *The Encyclopædia of Islām*, page 153.

For the old-fashioned Balōch we must turn to the Marī and Bugṭī, the great majority of whom never sleep under a roof, but move up and down their country with their flocks, rarely resting a week in the same encampment. Most of their movements are confined to their own tribal limits; but there is a seasonal overflow into Sibī and into neighbouring districts in the Panjāb and Sind, while several Marī pay regular visits to the Kōhlū valley, where some families have even settled for good. Or we must go to Khārān, where the ancient nomad spirit is still strong—so strong, indeed, that I fancy that many of the tribesmen who have been returned as settled are really semi-nomads who only live in permanent villages for a few months in the year. Even Makrān, with its large proportion of settled Balōch, is the scene of constant movement. Some of the tribesmen spend their life circling round and round within a limited beat; others wander all over the country. The very fisherfolk on the coast are infected with the wander-spirit when the date-harvest of Kēch and Panjgūr is in full swing. During the whole four months of that rich harvest both these favoured spots are centres of attraction to men, women and children, from far and near. And apart from nomadism altogether, the individual Makrānī shares with the Paṭhān the distinction of being the most adventurous traveller beyond the borders of Balūchistān.

Brāhūī nomadism.

76. More interesting and in some ways much more important than the nomadism of the Paṭhān and Balōch is the winter migration of the Brāhūīs into the Kachhī and Sind. This seasonal migration must be as old as the Balūchistān hills themselves; life would hardly be possible for man or beast without a refuge from them in the rigours of the winter. Yet it is probable enough that the tide sets to-day in a very different direction. The streams must once have run northwards into Afghānistān—there are still plenty of Brāhūīs in Shōrāwak—and westwards into Persia; for the easy channels that now lead into Sind and the Kachhī (which of course was once a part of Sind) were long blocked at the mouth by a hostile power. But a vigorous body of nomad tribesmen could not be debarred indefinitely from the promised land that lay within such easy reach. It was no mere motives of ambition or aggrandisement or territorial greed that made the Khāns lead their tribal hosts time after time against Sind. The Brāhūī swarms were borne down into the plains by the irresistible force of gravity. Nor, I think, shall we read traditional history aright, unless we regard the earlier at any rate of the much-fabled expeditions against Sind, not as organised expeditions at all, but as furtive attempts, often frustrated and as often renewed, on the part of small nomadic groups to win pasturage for their flocks in the genial plains that lay at their borders. Not that it was by their own prowess that the Brāhūīs at length wrested the long-coveted Kachhī from Sind. It fell to them almost by accident, when things looked blackest. Their warrior hero Mīr Abdulla, who of all men seemed destined to lead them into the promised land, had fallen in battle with the Kalhōra of Sind, and the remnants of his shattered army had fled to the hills. But a greater power now appeared on the scene, greater than either Kalāt or Sind. And as soon as Nādir Shāh set foot in Sind with his all-conquering army, Nūr Muhammad the Kalhōra threw himself on his mercy. The story goes how Nādir Shāh sent Nūr Muhammad laden with chains to Nasīr Khān's[1] tent, and bade the Khān slay the Kalhōra and so avenge his father's death. But the Khān, to his deathless renown and, as it turned out, to the lasting gain of his countrymen, sent the Kalhōra away with a robe of honour. "I'm a mere Brāhūī," he explained to Nādir Shāh, "too faint-hearted to butcher my enemy in chains." "And by the by—" he added, "a poor Brāhūī can ill afford a *shalvār*, or pair of breeches." So Nādir Shāh took the hint, and gave him the Kachhī as his *shalvār*. And to this day, a Brāhūī talks of the Kachhī as Abdulla Khān's blood-money or as Nasīr Khān's *shalvār*; and whenever he is asked why he is off to the Kachhī, he will say it's to get him a new *shalvār*.

Brāhūīs.	
Nomad	60
Semi-nomad	13
Settled	27
	100

Sarāwāns migrate to the Kachhī, Jhalawāns to Sind.

77. The Khān reserved a goodly portion of the Kachhī for the ruling house, and divided the rest between the Sarāwān and Jhalawān tribes, allotting

[1] As a matter of fact, it was not Nasīr Khān but his brother Muhabbat Khān who was actually ruling at the time; but the former's presence in the camp is enough to make the Brāhūī regard him and not his worthless brother as the hero of the episode.

to the former the lands towards the Bōlān, and to the latter the lands towards the Jhalawān hills. The initial division of the spoil may have been fair enough, but the fact remains that the Sarāwāns are to-day in happy possession of the lion's share. More enlightened, then as now, than their brethren of Jhalawān —thanks very largely to closer touch with the wider world—they apparently lost no time in getting their Jaṭṭ villeins to improve the lands they had acquired, and seized every possible opportunity to filch still more from the lands reserved to the Khān, with the result that they now possess not merely rich culturable lands but—what is almost of greater importance to the tribesmen at large—ample tracts of pasture. So firm a footing have the Sarāwāns gained in the Kachhī that it takes an exceptionally bad season to force them to extend their winter migration in any numbers beyond its limits. It is otherwise with the Jhalawāns, next-door neighbours to the Kachhī though many of them are. And the difference in the past history and the present stage of development of these two great branches of the Brāhūī Confederacy is mirrored in the interesting figures in the margin. It would seem that the Jhalawāns never learnt to appreciate their share of the spoils at its full value until it was too late. They failed to make good the possession of much of their land, and allowed themselves to be jockeyed out by the Jaṭṭ. And so it has come about that, though most of the chiefs have Kachhī domains to which they themselves resort, the Jhalawān tribes at large have been gradually elbowed out of the Kachhī, and are driven by the inhospitable nature of their Jhalawān hills to seek a winter home in Sind.

	Sarāwāns.	Jhalawāns.
Nomad	34	75
Semi-nomad	29	5
Settled	37	20
	100	*100*

Jhalawān migration to Sind becoming permanent.

78. Nothing in the emigration statistics can vie in interest with this Jhalawān emigration into Sind. As the Bombay figures of race and birthplace give us a very vague idea of it, I had the less scruple in bothering my courteous colleague in Bombay for duplicate slips of the 60,389 Brāhūīs enumerated in Sind.[1] It is a pity that the various tribes to which these Brāhūīs belong were not recorded; among the lot there must be a sprinkling of Sarāwāns, possibly even of people who in Balūchistān would not be reckoned as Brāhūīs at all; on the other hand, I have little doubt that many Jhalawāns (and indeed other Brāhūīs) might have been found masquerading as Balōch (§ 277). But with all their shortcomings, the statistics doubtless give us in the rough a fairly faithful picture of the Jhalawān migration. Look at the picture from whatever standpoint I will, it seems to have the same tale to tell—that the once purely seasonal migration is tending to become permanent, that Jhalawān is slowly but surely draining into Sind. Take, first and foremost, the way that the numbers of Brāhūīs in Sind have been going up by leaps and bounds in the last twenty years. To-day there are more than twice as many as there were in 1891; in the last ten years alone they have increased by over 12,000. A flood of light would pour on to the statistics, if we could compare the relative numbers of those who returned Sind and those who returned Balūchistān as their birthplace at each succeeding census; unfortunately, the figures for the present census are the only ones on record. Birthplace divides the sixty thousand odd Brāhūīs now enumerated in Sind almost half and half between the two countries. This might be thought a very natural reflection of the way that the Jhalawāns divide their time between this country and that. But apart from the fact that they actually spend much more of the year in Balūchistān, patriotic Brāhūīs (as I know by experience) are far more likely to give Balūchistān than Sind as the birthplace of their Sind-born children, simply because birthplace conveys to their mind not so much place of birth as mother country (§68). In short, I am inclined at the outset to read a good deal of permanent settlement into the figures of those Brāhūīs who are supposed to have been born in Sind; to regard them in the main as a catalogue not merely of Brāhūīs actually born in Sind but of Brāhūīs who, wherever born, have now settled in Sind for good and all. This may seem a daring generalisation, but that there is something in it may be seen from the highly significant way in which birthplace

[1] My experiment might be worth a more extended trial. One would simply have to copy the entries of persons born in India but not in the province of enumeration on double slips, tear off the duplicates and send them to the province of birth. Should this be too much of a good thing, the procedure might at least be adopted for any particular castes or tribes in which the various provinces are specially interested.

divides these Sind Brāhūīs all down the line in matters of sex-proportion, civil condition, language, literacy and occupation. Take sex-proportion, for instance. Among Sind Brāhūīs as a body, there are 809 females to every 1,000 males. Divide them up according to birthplace, and the proportion among the Sind-born jumps to 865; among those born in Balūchistān it drops to 758. There must be some very potent influences at work to produce so wide a discrepancy, influences much more far-reaching than mere accident of birthplace. Take language. For every Brāhūī in Sind who talks Sindhī, there are roughly four who speak Brāhūī. Divide them up by birthplace: for every Sind-born Brāhūī who speaks Sindhī, there are but two who speak Brāhūī; yet for every Balūchistān-born Brāhūī who speaks Sindhī, there are nine or ten who still speak their mother tongue. Clearly no accident of birthplace can explain away discrepancies such as these, or the similar discrepancies that might be traced in other branches of the statistics. We are here face to face with no mere seasonal migration, but with a migration that in a large part has already developed into permanent settlement. The crude figures of language and race are enough to show that this must be so. Just look at this amazing paradox: in the last twenty years the Brāhūīs in Sind have more than doubled their numbers, yet the Brāhūī language has not even held its ground; in the last ten years alone the Brāhūīs have gone up by well over 26 per cent, yet the Brāhūī language has gone down by 40. To me these figures came as a revelation. Conscious though I was that Brāhūī must almost inevitably succumb if brought into real and lively conflict with Aryan languages, I little thought it would succumb so swiftly and seemingly without a struggle. Conscious though I was that Sind was luring Brāhūis away from their own country, I little thought that Jhalawān was veritably draining into Sind.

Sind Census.

	Brāhūīs.	Brāhūī speakers.
1881	...[1]	24,510
1891	29,907	28,984
1901	47,758	47,898
1911	60,389	28,930

79. And the explanation? Well, a searching analysis of the many causes that are leading to the self-expatriation of the Jhalawāns would probably carry us far afield. Yet it is not difficult to picture the gradual stages by which a typical Jhalawān settles down in Sind. Visiting Sind winter after winter, he may well come to look upon it as a land of ease and drowsihead after his own inhospitable mountain country. Things that he learns to treat as necessaries in Sind, at home are luxuries; things that are pleasant luxuries in Sind, at home he has to go without altogether; and a change comes over his whole standard of living accordingly. To-day it irks him to be clothed as his chief was clothed a couple of generations ago; to-day he has no stomach for the handful of parched wheat which was once his only provision on a journey; he must needs have his ball of leavened dough, his slice of mutton and his pat of butter. Small wonder that, once having tasted of the flesh-pots of Sind, he is loth to quit that pleasant land. After all there are few temptations for him to shift. Labour is abundant; judged by his humble standards, it is highly paid; and—better still—though many kinds of labour are beneath his dignity at home, in Sind his dignity is no man's business but his own. At first, perhaps, he simply intends to drag out his stay in Sind a few months longer than usual; but the more he puts off the evil hour, the more difficult he finds it to tear himself away. And if in the end he can resist the call of his hills no longer, the dreariness and the hardships of the old home-life come back to him with doubled force on his return. It is not only the slothful ease and the fine food and fair clothes that he misses; crushed by the demands of his tribal chief (for unlike his brother of Sarāwān he usually has to pay revenue to his chief—no one seems to know why) he yearns for his untroubled life in Sind, where he was free to go his own way so long as he kept on the windy side of the law. If this is indeed a faithful picture of the typical Jhalawān's progress, it is a foregone conclusion that the last scene of all will see him settled in Sind—lock, stock and barrel. And every Brāhūī family settled in Sind is a loadstone for others. This, to be sure, is one of the most characteristic features in the past and present history of the Brāhūī settlement in Sind. It began ages ago when a few Brāhūī families acquired plots of land on the canals, and speedily found themselves the centres of attraction for their kith and kin. To-day this process of attraction often takes a more peculiar form. Many a Jhalawān on his winter wandering finds it hard to resist the temptation of marrying off his

Influences at

[1] The race figures for 1881 are unfortunately not on record.

women at a high bride-price to some Sindhī husband. But bride-price is not the only thing that he has in his eye. If the Sindhī husband fancies that, once having married the lady and paid up like a man, he is quit of her family for good and all, he is mightily mistaken. Her kinsmen and kinswomen unto the third and fourth degree will hang like a millstone round his neck. For what says the Brāhūī proverb ? Never spread out your rug, save where you intend to lie upon it.

Emigration to India.

80. Of the volume of emigration to other parts of India we can get some sort of inkling from the statistics of people born in Balūchistān but enumerated in other provinces. Precise enough in themselves, the statistics are of course far less illuminating than they seem. They professedly relate only to persons enumerated elsewhere whom birthplace—not necessarily birth—marked out as natives of Balūchistān. Birthplace was the sole determining factor: race and mother country went by the board. At one time the net must have been cast too wide, at another drawn too close: we have doubtless had thrown back on us several whose one accidental concern with Balūchistān was that they happened to be born in it; we must have been deprived of others, true sons of Balūchistān though they were, because they happened to be born outside it. Of other disturbing potentialities in the statistics, I will mention but one. That an Afghān must be a native of Afghānistān may well have seemed to an enumerator in some distant corner of the Indian Empire as self-evident as that a Balōch must be a native of Balūchistān. In either case he would be sorely tempted to take the answer regarding birthplace for granted; and who shall blame the overworked man for falling into the temptation, when question and answer had to be bandied to and fro in mutually unintelligible languages ? And the very large majority of cases where Balūchistān pure and simple, and not some particular district in Balūchistān, was put down as the place of birth, makes me suspect that the temptation proved irresistible often enough. But it would be ungenerous to look a gift-horse too closely in the mouth. We must take the statistics for other provinces as we find them, merely tempering our faith in the happy knack of largish numbers to round themselves with the mental reservation that these and other sources of error must be at the bottom of any returns in which local knowledge seems to scent out something wrong.

Its chief directions.

81. A case in point is the Hyderabad State, notoriously a happy hunting-ground for huckstering Sayyids and Paṭhāns of Pishīn, which has returned a paltry total of 181 persons born in Balūchistān; a goodish number of those shown as born in Afghānistān have probably never set foot in Afghānistān at all. Possibly an example of the reverse is to be found in Baroda: for what 41 natives of Balūchistān were doing there, I cannot imagine; there were none ten years ago. I am told that there were 11 solitary females from Khārān enumerated in Bengal; I should be sorry to believe it. To the 39 males in the Andamans we must regretfully plead guilty. But these, like the 20 in Kashmir, and the 30 in Burma, and the 126 in Madras, even the 1,064 in the Central Provinces, are mere driblets after all. It is more interesting to follow up the broader streams of emigration that flow into the provinces on our borders. The volume of emigration into the Panjāb and the North-West Frontier Province has risen in ten years from 3,445 to 8,973. It is made up of migrations of all kinds—casual, temporary, seasonal and permanent, but it seems almost hopeless to attempt to differentiate between them. It is recruited chiefly from Paṭhāns and Balōch. Intermarriage, especially among the Balōch, trading and transport, especially among the Paṭhāns, and pastoralism, are among the chief causes that give rise to it. But the main flood of emigration, 69,373 in volume, finds its way into the Bombay Presidency, where, however, it rarely advances further than Sind. The stream of Brāhūīs which flows down in a broad and ancient bed into Sind is joined by many rivulets. To Sind come the Makrānī in quest of day-labour in the Karāchī docks or on the canal-works, the Lāsi from Bēla, and the Balōch from Nasīrābād and the Marī and Bugṭī hills, seeking to tide over bad times at home by field labour.

Its nature analysed by sex-proportion.

82. It requires no local knowledge to realise that the Brāhūī migration to Sind is not the only element in the emigration to the Bombay Presidency that is of a family character. One can see this at once from

the comparatively large proportion of females in the figures. And though there are palpable but inevitable gaps in the argument, I fancy that we shall not be far wrong if we use sex-proportion as a basis for a wider generalisation. Let us shut our eyes for the moment to the ambiguities attaching to birthplace, and accept the figures of the Balūchistān-born enumerated in other provinces as a sufficiently accurate indication of the numbers of the emigrants from Balūchistān to India. Now we know that most of the emigration from Balūchistān is either of a family character or else confined to individual males; with the exception of an occasional woman who leaves the province to get married, there is no emigration of individual females. We know, further, that there are 845 females to 1,000 males in the indigenous population of Balūchistān (§ 138). As males are much more subject to the drain of emigration than females, the female proportion should obviously be pitched lower. But we will let it stand; any adjustment would only accentuate the point I am driving at. And my point is this. According to our very rough-and-ready line of argument, every 845 females in the so-called emigrants can be fairly paired off with at least 1,000 males. And as there are 31,765 female emigrants in all, 37,592 males out of the grand total of 44,266 are at once disposed of. In other words, if we ignore the emigration of a few females on marriage, gloss over other difficulties, and accept the argument in principle, we seem to be well on the safe side in concluding that over ninety per cent of the emigration to India is of a family character, and that 6,674 male emigrants or thereabouts make up the balance. We can even go one step further, I think, and assume that this surplus emigration is made up of able-bodied men, for the boys of Balūchistān are not given to running away from their parents and seeking their fortunes abroad.

Emigration out of India.

83. But what of emigration out of India? Though the main channels that lead into India are fairly easy to follow, we are thrown back almost entirely on our own resources in tracking up the streams that flow beyond its limits. Except into Persia and Afg̲h̲ānistān they flow, it is true, in very languid trickles: constantly on the move though the tribesmen are, they rarely venture out of the beaten tracks, and we may ignore the few but gallant adventurers like the Makrānī, who takes an occasional trip across the sea to Muscat and the neighbourhood, or like the Paṭhān, who is ready to seek his fortunes in Australia or China or Turkistān or Somaliland or Uganda. But it is a very different matter with emigration into Afg̲h̲ānistān and Persia. Many Paṭhāns on the Afg̲h̲ān frontier would be hard put to it to say whether they were domiciled in Afg̲h̲ānistān or Balūchistān: hundreds of families are equally at home on this and that side of the border, shifting their quarters as often as pasture, or friction with their neighbours, or trouble with the different powers that be, may make it desirable. Much the same applies to Shīrānī Paṭhāns, who divide their time between Balūchistān and independent territory, to many Brāhūīs and Baṛēch Paṭhāns who hover between Nushkī and the Afg̲h̲ān district of Shōrāwak, and to the frontier Balōch who hover between Makrān, K̲h̲ārān or Çhāgai on the one side and Persia on the other. On the north-east frontier conditions were fairly normal at the time of the census. But conditions on the west and the north-west were so generally unfavourable that not only has there been a serious wastage of Brāhūīs and Balōch who waver on the borderland, but numbers of Brāhūīs ordinarily domiciled in Chāgai and numbers of Balōch ordinarily domiciled in Makrān had passed over into Afg̲h̲ānistān and Persia, seeking a refuge from the drought. Within a month of the closing of the census the tide had begun to turn, and the population of Chāgai alone went up by 10 per cent.

Immigration.

84. The wastage in the indigenous population owing to the drought was not the only cause that made for an unduly low census of Balūchistān. So long as the census of India is fixed at an early date in the year, so long will the numbers of aliens returned in Balūchistān and more especially in its capital town (§ 56) be an inadequate representation of the wave of immigration; for during the winter months there is always a temporary flow back into India, chiefly affecting the women and children. The main inducements that bring aliens to the country are Government service, labour and trade. The majority of the Europeans are absorbed in the army: the

Aliens	56,898
Europeans	4,210
Anglo-Indians	123
Natives	52,565

European commercial community, though vigorous and growing, is still in its infancy. The aliens from India not only man most of the billets in the army, the police, and the administration, they monopolise most of the trade in the towns, and a good deal of the labour market. They come from far and near, but the chief recruiting-grounds are the Panjāb and the North-West Frontier, the United Provinces, and Bombay. From the Panjāb Balūchistān draws most of its sepoys, policemen, and clerks; from the United Provinces most of its gardeners, washermen and other domestic servants; from Bombay, or rather from Sind, many of its traders. The extent to which the alien population follows in the wake of Government, and thrives under its protection, very largely by supplying its multifarious needs, may be gathered from the fact that it packs itself almost entirely into civil and military stations. If the British Government ever quitted Balūchistān, the great mass of the immigrants would quit it at the same time. All that would remain would be a stream of Powindahs sojourning as of old for a brief season on their wanderings, and here and there a few petty but adventurous traders.

SUBSIDIARY TABLES.

IX.—Nomadism among Selected Tribes.

Tribe.	Tribal Census. Nomad. Males.	Nomad. Females.	Semi-Nomad. Males.	Semi-Nomad. Females.	Settled. Males.	Settled. Females.	Regular Census. Males.	Regular Census. Females.
Balōch (indigenous only)	**34,941**	**28,572**	**4,311**	**3,615**	**51,818**	**44,775**	**889**	**269**
(*i*) *Eastern*	*24,192*	*19,050*	*2,336*	*1,863*	*34,392*	*29,499*	*431*	*156*
Bugtī	10,541	8,160	25	23	313	292	14	2
Ḍōmbkī	364	284	38	36	2,678	2,276	29	8
Jakhrānī	52	40	...	...	59	49	...	...
Khetrān	639	604	443	401	6,278	5,774	12	2
Magasī	631	467	...	...	9,119	7,525	22	13
Marī	10,094	7,981	1,396	1,020	954	720	64	4
Rind	1,864	1,514	428	378	14,454	12,378	192	59
Umrānī	...	...	6	5	500	460	14	4
Others	7	...	...	...	37	25	84	64
(*ii*) *Western*	*10,749*	*9,522*	*1,975*	*1,752*	*17,426*	*15,276*	*458*	*113*
Brāhūī	**55,588**	**44,335**	**12,228**	**9,968**	**24,133**	**20,062**	**1,146**	**327**
(*i*) *Original nucleus*	*5,514*	*4,448*	*437*	*370*	*2,279*	*1,914*	*72*	*18*
Ahmadzai	...	...	...	...	7	9	8	1
Iltāzai	63	40	...	...	22	31	...	...
Gurgnāṛī	958	785	13	13	147	117	6	2
Kalandrāṛī	759	567	97	91	279	216	3	...
Kambrāṛī	810	657	133	110	727	642	9	7
Mīrwāṛī	990	798	16	11	444	395	...	...
Rōdēnī	237	203	34	32	446	366	7	...
Sumalaṛī	1,697	1,398	144	113	207	138	39	8
(*ii*) *Sarāwān*	*10,277*	*8,246*	*8,680*	*7,077*	*11,035*	*9,259*	*623*	*173*
Bangulzai	2,229	1,838	1,461	1,226	2,560	2,118	127	36
Kūrd	491	388	894	725	510	432	33	3
Lahṛī	1,641	1,260	616	436	1,011	828	46	6
Lāngav	1,077	852	3,675	3,087	1,175	997	80	36
Māmashahī	869	742	197	134	1,013	829	64	18
Raisānī	104	77	71	58	894	743	24	6
Rustumzai	...	...	1	...	332	299	8	16
Sarparra	118	111	302	261	726	623	67	4
Sātakzai	654	514	5	5	48	37	13	7
Shahwānī	1.918	1,470	1,029	779	1,840	1,602	107	25
Zagr Mēngal	1,176	994	429	366	931	756	54	16
(*iii*) *Jhalawān*	*39,391*	*31,276*	*2,610*	*2,126*	*10,320*	*8,479*	*376*	*130*
Bizanjav	5,099	4,260	30	19	777	673	...	...
Hārūnī	369	310	104	93	197	170	4	2
Māmasanī	5,864	4,754	181	152	1,375	1,088	54	21
Mēngal	12,096	9,242	790	637	2,125	1,664	188	63
Nichārī	1,327	1,075	50	30	617	461	66	15

IX.—Nomadism among Selected Tribes—*continued.*

Tribe.	Tribal Census. Nomad. Males.	Nomad. Females.	Semi-nomad. Males.	Semi-nomad. Females.	Settled. Males.	Settled. Females.	Regular Census. Males.	Regular Census. Females.
Pandrānī	320	238	191	144	599	514	5	1
Sājdī	1,769	1,421	16	14	453	336	1	1
Zahrī	12,547	9,981	1,248	1,038	4,177	3,573	58	27
(*iv*) *Miscellaneous*	*406*	*365*	*501*	*395*	*499*	*410*	*75*	*11*
Nighāṛī	141	131	400	313	177	149	...	...
Pirri-Kāṛī	259	228	9	6	10	5	...	...
Rēkīzai	2	2	89	75	245	198	...	...
Others	4	4	3	1	67	58	75	11
Paṭhān (indigenous only)	**24,000**	**19,884**	**32,994**	**28,440**	**42,216**	**37,060**	**2,938**	**561**
Bābī	2	1	1	3	159	140	11	6
Baṛēch	104	102	18	15	274	210	84	47
Jafar	91	72	165	132	429	391	5	1
Kākaṛ	10,091	8,238	20,935	17,705	25,037	21,118	1,689	260
Dāwī	*16*	*12*	...	...	*130*	*116*	*10*	...
Dumaṛ	*715*	*560*	*1,412*	*1,134*	*2,081*	*1,781*	*59*	*13*
Lamaṛ	*46*	*43*	...	...	*228*	*175*	...	...
Sanzarkhēl	*6,233*	*5,029*	*15,663*	*13,327*	*8,055*	*6,941*	*693*	*91*
Sargaṛa	*27*	*14*	*476*	*448*	*736*	*612*	*26*	*4*
Snaṭia	*2,348*	*1,993*	*2,796*	*2,298*	*7,244*	*6,039*	*557*	*74*
Targhaṛa	*597*	*485*	*552*	*465*	*6,418*	*5,335*	*208*	*34*
Others	*109*	*102*	*36*	*33*	*145*	*119*	*141*	*44*
Kāsī	...	...	1	1	657	615	47	16
Lūṇī	296	266	7	4	1,185	1,049	8	1
Paṇī	1,984	1,649	8,484	7,538	4,481	4,191	296	52
Main branch	*584*	*480*	*482*	*433*	*2,343*	*2,262*	*87*	*43*
Isōṭ	*394*	*316*	*942*	*879*	*124*	*103*	*55*	...
Mandōkhēl	*164*	*137*	*2,278*	*2,031*	*142*	*123*	*79*	...
Mūsakhēl	*809*	*666*	*4,774*	*4,192*	*877*	*802*	*73*	*9*
Zarkūn	*43*	*51*	*8*	*3*	*995*	*901*	*2*	...
Shirānī	128	122	2,012	1,845	2,307	2,017	91	30
Tarīn	11,264	9,397	1,305	1,156	6,851	6,664	657	117
Abdāl Achakzai	*8,453*	*6,926*	*426*	*329*	*1,903*	*1,765*	*417*	*53*
Spīn Tarīn	*718*	*624*	*821*	*777*	*1,149*	*1,015*	*25*	*5*
Tōr Tarīn	*2,093*	*1,847*	*34*	*30*	*3,795*	*3,882*	*164*	*45*
Others	...	...	*24*	*20*	*4*	*2*	*51*	*14*
Zmarai	14	13	63	39	610	482	7	...
Others	26	24	3	2	226	183	43	31
Ghilzai	**7,560**	**6,139**	**450**	**371**	**1,341**	**982**	**1,538**	**205**
Kharōṭ	1,599	1,262	12	13	40	26	99	6
Nāsar	1,187	1,033	47	50	214	154	69	15
Suiemankhēl	1,946	1,503	91	59	277	199	510	58
Tarak	1,014	779	7	8	176	147	152	33
Others	1,814	1,562	293	241	634	456	708	93

X.—Brāhūīs Censused in Sind.

District or State of enumeration.	Total.			Born in								
				Balūchistān.			Sind.			Other Provinces.		
	Persons.	Males.	Females.	Persons.	Males.	Females.	Persons.	Males.	Females.	Persons.	Males.	Females.
Total	***60,389***	***33,383***	***27,006***	***29,901***	***17,012***	***12,889***	***29,749***	***15,952***	***13,797***	***739***	***419***	***320***
Hyderabad	3,445	1,852	1,593	879	532	347	2,513	1,283	1,230	53	37	16
Karachi	10,147	5,612	4,535	2,264	1,334	930	7,860	4,267	3,593	23	11	12
Larkana	21,698	11,878	9,820	14,030	8,042	5,997	7,579	3,811	3,768	80	25	55
Sukkur	4,624	2,611	2,013	1,644	986	658	2,811	1,527	1,284	169	98	71
Thar and Parkar	1,089	598	491	96	50	46	984	542	442	9	6	3
Upper Sind Frontier	19,110	10,684	8,426	10,955	6,054	4,901	7,750	4,388	3,362	405	242	163
Khairpur	276	148	128	24	14	10	252	134	118	...	...	.

XI.—Loss and Gain between Balūchistān and India by Birthplace.

Province or State.	Born in other Provinces but enumerated in Balūchistān. "Immigrants." 1911. Males.	1911. Females.	1901. Males.	1901. Females.	Variation 1901-11. Males.	Variation 1901-11. Females.	Born in Balūchistān but enumerated in other Provinces. "Emigrants." 1911. Males.	1911. Females.	1901. Males.	1901. Females.	Variation, 1901-11. Males.	Variation, 1901-11. Females.	Gain + / Loss − to Balūchistān 1911. Males.	1911. Females.	1901. Males.	1901. Females.
Total	*33,302*	*9,007*	*28,411*	*6,411*	*+4,891*	*+2,596*	*41,266*	*31,765*	*41,364*	*28,903*	*+2,902*	*+ 2,862*	*−10,964*	*−22,758*	*−12,953*	*− 22,492*
Ajmere-Merwara	193	14	162	6	+ 31	+ 8	13	10	11	2	+ 2	+ 8	+ 180	+ 4	+ 151	+ 4
Andaman Nicobar	..	..	..	..	..	..	39	..	..	..	+ 39	..	− 39	..	..	..
Baroda	5	2	..	..	+ 5	+ 2	31	10	..	..	+ 31	+ 10	− 26	− 8	..	..
Behar and Orissa	53	10					18	1								
Bengal	80	45	99 (Behar and Orissa, Bengal, Assam)	47	+ 40	+ 12	75	38	25	11	− 396 (Behar and Orissa, Bengal, Assam)	+ 47	− 134	− 10	− 570	+ 25
Assam	6	4					180	30	644	11						
Bombay	3,660	1,298	3,373	962	+ 287	+ 336	39,385	29,988	38,141	27,528	+ 1,244	+ 2,460	− 35,725	− 28,690	− 34,768	− 26,566
Burma	19	20	8	15	+ 11	+ 5	27	3	6	2	+ 21	+ 1	− 8	+ 17	+ 2	+ 13
Central India	99	34	231	25	− 132	+ 9	25	5	..	..	+ 25	+ 5	+ 74	+ 29	+ 231	+ 25
Central Provinces and Berar	66	58	77	13	− 11	+ 45	971	93	173	4	+ 798	+ 89	− 905	− 35	− 96	+ 9
French and Portuguese Settlements	163	20	113	10	+ 51	+ 10	..	..	..	..	..	..	+ 163	+ 20	+ 112	+ 10
Hyderabad	61	15	41	8	+ 20	+ 7	171	10	13	..	+ 158	+ 10	− 110	+ 5	+ 28	+ 8
Kashmir	794	105	382	67	+ 412	+ 38	17	3	15	1	+ 2	+ 2	+ 777	+ 102	+ 367	+ 66
Madras	82	58*	106	40	− 24	+ 18	116	10	16	7	+ 100	+ 3	− 34	+ 48	+ 90	+ 33
Mysore	30	27	18	14	+ 12	+ 13	8	3	2	5	+ 6	− 2	+ 22	+ 24	+ 16	+ 9
N.-W. F. Province	3,391	709	89†	4,198 (N.-W. F. Province and Panjab)	+ 4,297 (N.-W. F. Province and Panjab)	+ 1,809 (N.-W. F. Province and Panjab)	226	43	2,137 (N.-W. F. Province and Panjab)	1,308 (N.-W. F. Province and Panjab)	+ 484	+ 44	+ 19,648	+ 4,655	+ 15,835	+ 2,890
Panjab	18,878	5,298	17,883				2,395	1,309								
Rajputana	741	109	1,087	47	− 346	+ 62	140	70	48	9	+ 92	+ 61	+ 601	+ 39	+ 1,039	+ 38
Sikkim	..	..	..	..	..	..	..	1	..	..	..	+ 1	..	− 1	..	..
United Provinces	4,900	1,135	4,474	898	+ 426	+ 237	429	138	133	15	+ 296	+ 123	+ 4,471	+ 997	+ 4,341	+ 883
	81	46	269	61	− 188	− 15	..	..	..	..	..	..	+ 81	+ 46	+ 269	+ 61

* Includes Travancore. Males. 3 Females. 2

† Yāghistān and Wazīristān only.

CHAPTER IV.

RELIGION.

Statistical data.

SUBJECT.	Tables.		
	Imperial.	Provincial.	Subsidiary.
General	VI	......	......
Local distribution	......	II	XII
Urban religions	V	......	... .
Christian sects	XVII	......	......
Variation in Christianity	......	......	XIII

Statistical.

85. Islām easily tops the list of religions in the province, claiming as its own nearly 94 per cent. of the total population. The summary in the margin puts the matter in a nutshell. Of the indigenous population, Islām claims over 97 per cent.; the residue are Hindu or Sikh. By profession indeed, all tribesmen are Musalmān—for I suppose the Zikrīs must be reckoned as Musalmāns, though they are certainly not Muhammadans. The semi-indigenous population is Musalmān to a man. But though Balūchistān is essentially a Musalmān country, most of the main religions found in India can nowadays count on their local devotees, thanks to the steady influx of strangers from far and near. Animism, which seems to be the only absentee of any importance, is no exception at all, for animism is the mainspring of the religious beliefs of many tribesmen who profess and call themselves Musalmāns. For the present, however, we will assume that the various religious labels have their usual connotations, and take the statistics as we find them. A discussion of the tribesmen's actual beliefs and usages may be reserved to the end. **General review.**

	Indigenous.	Semi-indigenous.	Aliens.
Musalmān	734,610	25,411	22,627
Hindu	14,985	...	22,617
Sikh	2,799	...	5,591
Neo-Hindu	...	...	724
Christian	...		5,085
Parsee	...	...	170
Jew	...	...	57
Jain	...		10
Budhist	...	...	16
No religion	...	...	1

86. The fact that, except for the few old Hindu families dotted here and there, all indigenous peoples of Balūchistān—Paṭhāns, Balōch, Brāhūī, Jaṭṭ, Mēd, Lōṛī and the rest—are professedly Musalmān, greatly simplifies the task of analysing the statistics, for it enables us to treat the whole country in its religious aspect as a whole. No difficulty was experienced in ascertaining the various sects under which the Musalmāns range themselves. But the simplicity of the results as they are depicted in the margin is a little misleading. The Islām of the average tribesmen is so crude that it would be a trifle unreasonable to expect them to have any very clear idea of the sect to which they are supposed to belong. All but a very humble minority are Sunnī. Perhaps it would be nearer the mark to say that the haughty majority are obsessed by a fanatical abhorrence of the very name of Shīah. This abhorrence is strong simply because it is absolutely unreasoning. It is shared to the full by many **Islām.**

Musalmān	**782,648**
Sunnī	749,909
Shiah	4,823
Zikrī	27,588
Ahmadī	47
Ahl-i-Hadis	17
Sūfī	1
Chūhṛa	263

who have never heard of the word Sunnī at all. Great was the wrath of a Jāmōṭ when the enumerator, taking his cue from his loud execrations of the Shīahs, remarked that he was putting him down as a Sunnī. "Sunnī yourself!" was his indignant retort. "How dare you dub me Sunnī?"—the simple explanation of his ebullition lying in the fact that *sunnī* or something very like it means ill-fated in Lāsī. The truth is that Shīah to most tribesmen is not so much the antithesis of Sunnī, as something unspeakably abominable in itself. And it will be a rude awakening if the day comes when they discover that to the Sunnī of India their own religious practices appear tainted with Shīah heterodoxy. The only tribesmen who have proclaimed themselves to be Shīah are certain sections of the Ḍōmbkī Balōch, with the Chief at their head; and even these have bowed to the prevailing prejudice by styling themselves not Shīah but Jafarī. To all appearance, the only distinctive features of these local Shīahs are that they leave the hair on the upper lip untrimmed, don dusky turbans during the Muharram, mourn round a bier lamenting "Yā Hussain! Yā Hussain!" on the eve of the tenth day, and preface all new undertakings with the invocation "By the help of Ghaus Bahāwal Haq!" Most of the other Shīahs enumerated in Balūchistān are Hazāra from across the border.

The Zikrī sect.

87. The curious Zikrī sect has its head-quarters in Makrān, but it also spreads into south-western Jhalawān and Las Bēla, while a fair number of its sectarians were doubtless censused in Sind. It is strongest among the Makrānī, the Sājdī, Māmasanī and Bīzanjav Brāhūīs, and the Sangur in Las Bēla. It appeals more especially to the nomadic and lower classes. But though it is looked upon with contempt, and has been subject to a certain amount of persecution from the days of Nasīr Khān the Great onwards, it has always attracted a few men of higher status, and it may be questioned whether there are any real signs of its decay. Persecution, as usual, seems to give it new strength. For its gradual disappearance, one must probably look to the slowly increasing association of its followers with the wider world. In its origin it is apparently a backwash of the Mahdawī movement, started in India by Sayyid Muhammad Jaunpūrī towards the close of the 15th century. How the movement flowed into the country—whether directly from India or by a circuitous route through Persia—it is difficult to say. There is a good deal of obscurity and confusion in all that pertains to the sect. The very identity of the Mahdī who is claimed to have supplanted Muhammad as God's latest Prophet is curiously shadowy. Whoever the Mahdī may have been in the beginning, he is certainly Muhammad Jaunpūrī no longer, except to a few mullas who have begun to pick up a smattering of book-learning. To the mass of the people he is known variously as Mulla Murād (perhaps the Gichkī chief of that name who broke the Bulēdai power in Makrān) or more commonly, if more vaguely, as Ḍāī, who is believed to have miraculously extracted a new holy writ of revelation from the heart of a living tree. The sect is known more or less indifferently both among themselves and others as Zikrī or Ḍāī: Zikrī, because they hold that the age for *numāz* or prayer has given way to the age for *ẕikr* or the mention of God (for is it not written in the Koran "Make *ẕikr* of Me, that I make *ẕikr* of you," and again "Verily We have sent down the *ẕikr*, and verily We will guard it"); Ḍāī or Ḍāhī, because they are followers of Ḍāī, so styled because he was the bringer of the *ḍāh* or "alarm." But there is confusion everywhere. The Koran itself is known to them as *ḍāī*, though the "alarm" that Ḍāī brought them was presumably the new revelation he found growing in the tree. The word *ḍāī*, by the by, bears a superficial resemblance to the Arabic *dā'i*, "propagandist," so common in Persian revivalist history; but the sounds are really distinct, and though a phonetic relationship is perhaps not altogether impossible, the partial coincidence of meaning is probably a pure accident.

Zikrī	**27,588**
Makrān	16,433
Jhalawān	4,970
Las Bēla	6,068
Khārān	116
Quetta	1

Its tenets.

88. The Zikrī faith is a curious jumble of Islām. In form it is the negation of Muhammadanism. "There is no God but God, and the Mahdī is His Prophet" is the cardinal article of the faith. In reality it is not so much a negation of Muhammadanism as a hazy imitation of it. Zikrīs accept the Koran but repudiate its orthodox interpretation, ignoring everything that

tells against them, exaggerating everything that can be twisted to their side. All down the line they are sturdily protestant. Instead of the pilgrimage to Mecca, they trudge on the ninth day of the Zī-ul-hajj to Kōh Murād, a hill in Kēch a few miles from Tūrbat, close by the sacred tree of the new revelation, which still survives the ruthless hewing of bigoted Sunnīs. Instead of *zakāt* or alms at one-fortieth, they preach the bestowal of a tithe of their worldly goods. But their most distinctive dogma is the iniquity of *numāz*, and their most distinctive practice is the performance of *zikr*. By rights it should be performed six times a day according to an elaborate ritual, but as a rule three times appear to suffice: at dawn, at noon and at night. Regular services or *kishtī* are held on set occasions in circular places of worship called *zikrāna*. In villages there is some special spot, surrounded by a wall or dwarf-palm enclosure, set apart as the *zikrāna;* but nomads merely mark out a circle with small white stones, wherever they happen to be encamped. Though women worship apart from the men in the villages, both sexes worship together among the nomads. The congregation group themselves round in a ring, while the priest stands in the centre and conducts the service. He intones the praises of the Mahdī, and the congregation chime in after him. At first all is reverential quiet and orderliness, but the service soon degenerates into fanatical ecstasy, and ends in an uproar. The harrowing tales of promiscuity at the end of the service and of the deflowering of brides by the priests seem to be fabrications of bigoted orthodoxy. Though their form of worship is grotesque and their faith founded on the grossest superstition, the Zikrīs seem simple and harmless folk enough.

Apparent extinction of the Tāib sect.

89. It is a little surprising that the Tāib or "Penitents" have fallen out of the returns. This quaint puritanical sect was started some twenty or thirty years ago by Hājī Muhammad Fāzil, a Raīsānī Brāhūī of good birth, and at one time attracted a fair congregation in the Kachhī. The universal brotherhood of all Musalmāns—a reaction by the by against exclusively tribal bonds of good and ill—the seclusion of women, and the repudiation of the saints and their worship, appear to have been chief among the founder's doctrines. How far the many eccentricities attributed to the sect were really part of his teaching, how far they were later extravagances of his followers, or simply the invention of their scoffing neighbours, it is not easy to determine. He clearly made a stand against undue show and expenditure at domestic ceremonies: at weddings the customary drummings were forbidden; mournings for the dead were abandoned altogether. His followers appear to have carried his puritanical ideas a good deal further. The sound of a drum became their idea of the embodiment of all that was sinful; every good Tāib stuffed his ears against such naughty music. In the founder's preaching much stress was laid on the sanctity of the marriage-tie. Bride-price was forbidden. The marriage-service was celebrated afresh weekly, or at any rate fortnightly, throughout life. An erring wife had to wear bells on her fingers and bells on her toes as a public penance, when first she returned to the bed of her forgiving husband. So much seems fact. But these practices gave rise to a sheaf of absurd and unrepeatable yarns regarding conjugal relations among the Tāib, which lost nothing in the telling because a Tāib is taught to answer abuse with meekness. The ridicule heaped on the sect may possibly account for its bashful absence from our returns. But it is by no means impossible that the sect has been killed by ridicule altogether.

Hinduism.

Hindu . .	37,602
Indigenous . .	14,985
Aliens . . .	22,617

90. Proverbially elastic though the term is, Hinduism is stretched almost to breaking-point in Balūchistān. It is not merely that the Hinduism of the domiciled Hindu families (§287 *seq.*) is widely different from the Hinduism they see practised among the alien immigrants; there is precious little in their religion that would pass for Hinduism in more enlightened parts of India. It almost looks as if the singular freedom from persecution which the old Hindu families have always enjoyed at the hands of their Musalmān over-lords had given Islām greater scope to impart its subtle influence to their inward beliefs and outward practices. Knowing no sacred books but the Sikh scriptures, and with priests (Brahmans though they may be) as ignorant of the Shāstras as themselves, these benighted Hindus have allowed nearly all their rites and ceremonies to become coloured with an Islāmic tinge. They reverently resort to Muhammadan shrines; they invoke Muhammadan saints; in times of trouble they are glad of the help of charm-mongering mullas. It is not uncommon to find them observing Muhammadan

fasts, or participating in the Muharram and other Muhammadan festivals. They have little scruple in performing the investiture with the sacred thread at Muhammadan places of sanctity. Still less scruple have they in keeping Muhammadan men-servants and maid-servants to sweep their dining-floor, to fetch their water, to cleanse their eating-vessels and their cooking-pots. Not only they themselves but their Sārsut Brahmans drink freely from water-skins; they even use these waters of defilement—*horresco referens*—in their offerings to the family deity. How those who indulge in such practices as these, who know nothing of caste but the difference between Hindu and Brahman and Musalmān, who know nothing whatever of caste-rules, who have allowed members of their community in the past to take Musalmān women to wife, who still resort not infrequently to the unspeakably heretical practice of divorce—how men who unblushingly perpetrate these and similar outrages on what Hinduism professes to deem most sacred, can claim admittance to the Hindu brotherhood and find a welcome, I am at a loss to understand. But these are happily matters on which one who is himself outside the pale can hardly be called upon to sit in judgment.

No returns of Bām Mārgī.

91. As for sect, the old Hindu families care less than nothing. At a pinch, they may be able to remember that they are supposed to belong to the orthodox *Sanātan-dharma;* but this shred of knowledge is beyond the reach of most of them. There is accordingly little of interest in the statistics of Hindu sects that we collected. In fact the only matter of any real interest lies in one curious omission. But though it is notorious that Sāktaism, the worship of the female energy, thrives not only in Quetta under the name of Bām Mārgī, but also in Bārkhān and Mēkhtar under the name of Dēv or Andar or Sundarī Mārgī, I was hardly surprised that it found no place in our returns. Even in India the worshippers draw a veil over their unsavoury worship; not a word is willingly allowed to leak out regarding their rites. And the rites, it would seem, are unholy indeed. They are based on the observance of the so-called "five M's"—each of the five a reckless outrage on something that Hinduism esteems holy. And the greatest of these is *Maithun* or Lechery—the more unspeakable the lechery, the more meritorious the worship. How far the local sects indulge in the worse abominations of the ritual, it is impossible to say: not only do the worshippers in Balūchistān disavow their sect, a novice is only admitted under awful vows of secrecy after his good-faith has been shrewdly put to the test. Of an initiation I can, however, give some slight account on unimpeachable authority. The congregation meets at dead of night within closed doors and the novice is brought into the assembly blindfolded, with ear-rings of dough dangling from his ears. First he is made to swear a solemn oath never to divulge a word of aught that hereafter shall be revealed to him; then he is conducted through a weird ritual which centres round the adoration of Durga; and the initiation is crowned by a feast at his expense. The chief items in the fare are flesh and wine and *bhang*, but the all-important feature of this part of the ceremonial is that four or five worshippers—and the more diverse their castes, the better—should eat out of the same platter, drink out of the same cup, wash their hands and mouth in the same basin, and wind up the orgy by swilling down the filthy water. If this wanton flouting of common decency at initiation is a fair sample of the worship itself, it would be only in keeping for the local worshippers to luxuriate in the unmentionable abominations attributed to the sect elsewhere. "A perverted but reasonably innocent form of eccentricity" is the verdict passed on the local ritual by apparently well-informed opinion. And if it were true, as is sometimes asserted, that all women are excluded from the revels, this verdict might stand. But Sāktaism with woman barred seems such a strange contradiction in terms, that one doubts whether the apparently well-informed opinion is particularly well-informed after all.

Sikhism and Neo-Hinduism.

92. Of the later developments from Hinduism, I need say but a word. Nearly all the old Sikh families of the country belong to the great Sahjdhārī branch of the Sikh faith: few if any are Kēsdhārī—the only branch that is Sikh in the sense in which a recruiting officer would use the term. And here, by the by, we seem to be in the presence of an unmistakable change in the age.

Sikhism . .	**8,390**
Kēsdhhāri . .	4,613
Sahjdhārī . .	3,777

Time was, and not so very long ago, when the Sahjdhārī Sikhs still clung to Hinduism as the ancient mother of them all. At this census but 13 Sahjdhāris were found in the whole of Balūchistān who did not, apparently deliberately, omit all mention of Hinduism from their returns. As for Neo-Hinduism, neither Ārya nor Brahmō can claim any congregation among the domiciled community. These reform movements are so far confined entirely to the alien Hindus from down-country and it will be long before they are able to strike root in the old Hindu families of Balūchistān.

Ārya	674
Brahmō	50

Christianity.

93. Among religions which have no adherents in the indigenous population is Christianity, for conversion of the tribesman plays no direct part in the work of the good Samaritan undertaken by missionary effort in Balūchistān. The increase of a thousand odd souls in the Christian fold since the last census is merely another phase of immigration; Quetta alone accounts for nearly the whole of it. As for the various denominations, the tables may almost be left to tell their own tale. The Christian population shifts from year to year, and the chief factor in the ups and downs of the sects is the territorial composition of the British regiments who happen to be stationed in Quetta. It is perhaps worth mentioning that the five Europeans for whom no denomination has been recorded, expressly stated that they belonged to no denomination at all; and that of the couple whose beliefs are recorded as "indefinite," the European is a disciple of Theosophy and the native a Unitarian. Of the 752 Indian Christians, the Anglican Communion claims 418, and Roman Catholicism 278, leaving 56 to be divided among other denominations. Goanese servants form the bulk of the native Roman Catholics. The ranks of the Anglican Communion are largely swelled by converted Chūhṛa or sweepers, who have been locally given the jocular nickname of Chūhaṛkhēl, a tribal appellation they may possibly affect in all seriousness before long.

Christianity	5,085
Europeans, etc.	4,210
Anglo-Indians	123
Indian Christians	752

Miscellaneous.

94. There remain 254 followers of religions locally so microscopic in strength that they have had to be swept together into one incongruous heap. All but 15 were censused in the towns; all but 51 in Quetta. Chief among the lot are the Parsees, whose numbers remain almost stationary—the males have gone up by six, while the females have gone down by two—though one might not unnaturally have anticipated a substantial increase in this sturdy trading community, in sympathy with the remarkable expansion of Quetta. The Jews have gone up by nine; the Jains by two. The Budhists appear in our statistics for the first time. One solitary individual (a French cook by the by), who stoutly declared that he was of no religion at all, has the field to himself; indeed he is the only man in the length and breadth of India to sum up his beliefs in such blank negation.

Zoroastrianism	170
Judaism	57
Budhism	16
Jainism	10
No religion	1

Descriptive.

Local Islām skin-deep.

95. So much for the statistics. In so far as they relate to the alien population, we need not trouble to go behind them. But the living beliefs of the tribesmen of Balūchistān have little to do with the religions which they profess, or the various sects under which they range themselves. There is as much difference between the Islām of the average tribesman and the highly developed Islām of the Indian *maulvi*, as between the Hinduism of the domiciled Hindu families and the Hinduism of orthodox Brahmanism. As regards outward observances the Paṭhān stands no doubt on a fairly high level; for all his ignorance of the inner meaning of his Faith and his weakness for ancestor-worship he is usually as punctilious over his prayers and his fasts (if not over the pilgrimage and alms-giving) as his more enlightened co-religionists; what he lacks in doctrine he is quite capable of making up in fanatical zeal. The Balōch lags far behind. Though there are signs of a religious revival, ancient custom still holds sway in the vital affairs of his life; to him religious precepts are little more than counsels of perfection; religious practices little more than the outward and awe-inspiring marks of exceptional respectability. Among the Brāhūīs a truly devout Musalmān, learned in doctrine and strict in practice, is rarer still; with the vulgar mass Islām is merely an external badge that goes awkwardly with the quaint bundle of superstitions which have them in thrall.

Ignorance of the very name.

96. To judge by the answers made to the enumerators on the score of religion among the wilder sections of the community in all parts of the country

it would almost seem as if many people had never heard of Islām and Musalmān at all. "Put me down the same religion as the chief" was perhaps the commonest answer of the lot; its absurdity becomes apparent when it takes the form "I used to follow the Mēngal chief, but I've shifted quarters and adopted the religion of the Bangulzai." "I'm a Kākaṛ by birth, so of course I'm Kākaṛ by religion;" "I'm a Mīr Zangī" (the name of some dead worthy in the tribe); "my religion is Mulla Ishāq" (the name of the village priest)—these are typical of many others. More amusing but hardly less common was the non-committal request "Just wait till sun-down, and I'll enquire of the mulla." I do not mean to imply that Islām is a sealed book to the more advanced in the community. But when such answers among the ruck of the people raise scarce a smile and certainly occasion no surprise, it is sheer waste of time to attempt to discuss how far the spirit of Islām permeates the life of our tribesmen.

Ignorance of fundamental doctrines.

97. Even as regards the external practices of religion there is extraordinary ignorance everywhere. Many are the tales told of the utter darkness that broods over the wilder parts of Jhalawān. And though, thanks to the security of British administration, some light is flickering in from Sind, it will be long before it penetrates into the furthermost corners of the country. A wayfaring mulla may still run some risk of being driven from a Jhalawān encampment for scaring the flocks with his cry to prayers—a strange and unlucky sound to the unaccustomed ears of the nomads. Nor would I be surprised if history repeated itself any day, and some peddling Hindu were hauled off his nag to read the marriage service—surely an everyday task for so learned a bookworm—and were made to join in the feast and stay overnight, in case the bridegroom stood in need of an amulet to help him through his ordeal. Even among the Balōch in the Bōlān, I have come across a case of a disputed marriage where the mulla naively admitted to the court that he for one could not swear to the marriage, for the simple reason that he was still in the dark as to how a *nikāḥ* should be performed; but if the reciting of the *kalima* could do the trick, man and wife they undoubtedly were, for he had recited the *kalima* with the best of them. Such crass ignorance would hardly be found among Paṭhāns, who are usually great sticklers for religious practices. Yet in any Yāsīnzai Kākaṛ hut you may see a string hanging from the roof during the winter months, in which the goodman of the house ties a knot whenever the cause for an ablution arises, to serve as a reminder of the number of ablutions he must get through, when summer comes and washing is less of a nuisance.

Universal observance of circumcision.

98. There is, however, one religious ordinance rigorously observed by everybody, and that is the one which finds no mention in the Koran. I do not doubt that the reason for the universality of circumcision is that it is older than religion itself. The only uncircumcised followers of the Prophet I have ever heard of in Balūchistān were among Mahsūd recruits, and these of course do not belong to the indigenous population at all. Now while the well-to-do get their sons circumcised at an early age, the poor may find it necessary to postpone the ceremony for some years; like all ceremonies it is largely a matter of money. But it must be performed before puberty at all cost; and the sooner the better, for a male is no full Musalmān until he has been circumcised. As a rule the operation is entrusted to a barber, who generally seizes the opportunity to use his razor when the lad's attention is distracted by the supposed appearance of some strange bird in the sky. In most tribes it is a point of honour for the lad to retaliate by giving the barber a blow or a tug of his beard, and the force he puts into the blow or tug is regarded as the measure of his pluck. In some tribes this belabouring of the operator is almost a recognised portion of the ceremony, and if the boy is too small or too upset to play his part, one of the bystanders acts for him. As a rule the foreskin is carefully threaded and tied round the boy's ankle. The colour of the thread is a matter of no small moment: thus the colour among Brāhūīs must be red, among the Marī Balōch it must be green. The Snaṭia Kākaṛ Paṭhān vary the custom by tying the foreskin round the boy's neck. And on the boy it remains, a sure talisman against evil spirits, until his wound is healed; it is then buried under a green tree. This at any rate is the common practice; but some Brāhūīs prefer to bury the foreskin forthwith in damp earth, as the simplest means of healing the burning of the wound. Though womenfolk are ordinarily debarred from the ceremony proper, they generally perform some ceremonials while it is going on. The Brāhūī mother, for instance, puts a hand-

mill on her head, the kinswomen put a Koran on theirs, and they stand facing the west and pray for the lad's welfare, until the circumcision is over. Among the Marī the mother stands in the centre of singing women, bearing in her hands an upper mill-stone, which is sprinkled with red earth and covered with rue, an iron ring, a green bead and a red cloth, tied together by a red thread—all symbolical, I imagine, of procreative virility. Among the Brāhūīs, the Gichkī, the people of Khārān and possibly others, a father is expected to make over some piece of property to his son on the occasion of his circumcision. This custom, by the by, has landed one of the biggest Gichkī chiefs in an awkward fix. For years he had remained sonless. To his delight a son was unexpectedly born to him late in life, and in the exuberance of his pride he endowed him on his circumcision with the bulk of the family property. Unfortunately the old gentleman married again in his dotage, and as his young wife has recently presented him with sturdy twins, he is now at his wits' end trying to get his first-born to cancel the deed of gift.

Female circumcision.

99. Among the Gharshīn Sayyids of Mūsakhēl, the Khetrān, and the Jat—and the list should probably be longer—circumcision is looked upon as almost as essential for the other sex. Precise details of female circumcision are naturally not easy to secure in Balūchistān. Indeed the wonder is not that we know so little about it, but that we know anything at all. Many tribesmen themselves would be hard put to it to say much on the subject, even if they cared to do so; for the operation is generally conducted apart among the women with no small amount of secrecy. Unfortunately, our information is not only meagre but confused. But it seems pretty clear that there are two distinct methods of female circumcision: among some peoples the tip of the clitoris is clipped off, among others the *labia* are scarified; in both cases the operation is performed by some discreet old dame with a razor. Now while the operation is usually described as being performed at about the same age as circumcision proper in the case of the boys, there is yet another operation of a similar kind performed among these Gharshīn Sayyids and the Jat (but not among the Khetrān) on the bridal night. It is sometimes described as if it were an alternative operation; in all probability it is not alternative but additional. Among the Jaṭṭ (and also apparently among the Jafar Paṭhān and the Marī Balōch, but here our information is very vague) the bridal operation appears to be the only one practised at all. But of female circumcision and artificial defloration (for this is clearly what the bridal operation really amounts to) I shall have something to say in another place (§177).

Mullas and mosques.

100. Perhaps the most obvious among the outward signs of the Paṭhān's superior orthodoxy, as compared, let me say, with the Brāhūī, is his attitude towards the priesthood. Though the Paṭhān of Balūchistān is far from being as priest-ridden as his brethren in Tīrāh, he treats his mullas with marked respect and often bows himself deferentially to their influence, even in matters that might be thought purely secular. With such a feeling abroad, it is only in the nature of things that the priestly profession should be popular among Paṭhāns and that the priesthood outside the Paṭhān country should be largely recruited from within it. In nearly every Paṭhān mosque there are a number of *tālib-i-'ilm* or "searchers after knowledge," youths preparing themselves for the priesthood under the mulla's guidance. The mosques are humble enough structures in themselves, but they are imposing edifices compared with the so-called mosques in the Brāhūī country. Brāhūī mosques are as plenty as blackberries. It is just as well that nothing is more easy to make, for a mosque is frequently required on the spur of the moment in all sorts of out-of-the-way places; a corpse, for instance, which has been disinterred from its temporary resting-place for burial in the family graveyard, must lie in a mosque at every halting-stage on the weary march home. Range a few stones in a ring; leave a small opening on the east; raise a small arch on the west—and the Brāhūī's mosque is complete. My own impression is that these so-called mosques are much older than Islam itself, probably developments of something of the nature of magic circles. Mosques in the ordinary sense of the word are conspicuously rare in the Brāhūī country. As for a mulla, he is no doubt useful for marriages and burials and the like; but he is looked upon as a somewhat despicable creature at the best, and in any case "the power of a mulla should reach as far as the mosque," say the Brāhūīs,—and no further. In fact what a Brāhūī

wants from his mulla is not so much spiritual guidance, as amulets and charms and an inexhaustible supply of all kinds of magic. Small wonder that his country swarms with a disreputable band of wandering impostors.

Shrines and saints.

101. But even among Paṭhāns the respect paid to a mulla is as nothing compared to the reverence paid to Sayyids and other holy men; among Brāhūīs this reverence is carried to a higher pitch still. And great as is the reverence paid to the living, it is altogether dwarfed by the worship paid to the dead. Throughout the country, among the Paṭhāns, the Brāhūīs, the Balōch and the rest, the number of *pīr* or saints, of their *ziārat* or shrines, is veritably legion. "There is no God but God" is the grand confession of the Faith. But it is often little more than lip-worship after all. Ask a Brāhūī to swear by God, and he'll swear briskly enough, without bothering himself overmuch about the truth. But ask him to swear by his patron saint, and he'll boggle a mighty long time before you can get the oath out of him, and his knees will knock together when at last he brings the holy name to his lips.[1]

Paṭhān shrines and ancestor-worship.

102. The most striking feature about Paṭhān shrines is the fact that the majority and certainly the holiest are shrines of sainted ancestors, *nika* or "grandfathers" as they are called; such, among countless others, is the well known shrine of Sanzar Nika, the progenitor of the great Sanzarkhēl branch of the Kākaṛ tribe. It would be difficult to find any spot of importance in the country, whether a village graveyard, or a boundary between two tribes, or a spring of water, or an imposing mountain top that is not hallowed by the presence of a shrine. And to Paṭhān ideas there could be no site for a holy shrine more fitting than the crest of the majestic Takht-i-Sulemān, the mountain home of their far-away ancestor Qais Abdur Rashīd, with its many fabled associations of Solomon, who is revered not merely as a prophet of old but as a near contemporary of Saul, from whom Abdur Rashīd was thirty-seventh in descent. Its very inaccessibility gives the shrine an added sanctity and grandeur.

Brāhūī shrines.

103. Nowhere are shrines held in greater worship than in the Brāhūī country. A place without a shrine is a place to be avoided; a shrineless road is wearisome, unlucky, unsafe. Happily there are very few of either. For the typical shrines of the Brāhūī country are not the domed shrines one sees in Las Bēla and the Kachhī and occasionally in Jhalawān, but rough piles of stones, strewn about almost at random, often surrounded by a rude wall. They can be descried from afar by the rags and tatters that flutter from the collection of poles stuck up over them. Though a shrine is often the actual grave of some saint, almost anything seems to serve as an excuse. One shrine may mark the spot where the saint disappeared below the earth; another the spot where he performed some miracle; another, more humble in origin but none the less worshipful for that, the spot where he said his prayers. Hither come all who are in need, sickness, or any other adversity, to entreat the saint for the fulfilment of their desires, vowing to sacrifice this or that in return—the barren woman to pray for children, the sick to pray for health, the traveller for a safe return from his travels, the hunter for luck in the chase. Hard by most shrines of high reverence there are sacrificial altars, where the attendants preside at the sacrifice and receive a set portion of the flesh as their wage before it is distributed in alms.

Family shrines.

104. So well provided are Brāhūīs with saints and shrines, that every household in the land has its patron saint who watches over its destinies, and its own peculiar shrine to which it resorts to pay him homage or to supplicate him for some boon. There is hardly a domestic ceremony of any importance that does not culminate in worship at the family shrine. And if the two parents worship different saints, the saint of the goodman of the house has the pre-eminence in the family worship. It is to him, for instance, that the first shavings of the heads of the children are dedicated. But the mother will see to it that her own saint is not slighted, and will propitiate him in due course with a portion at any rate of subsequent shavings. And if in times of stress the father's saint proves of no avail, she will turn to her saint for succour, and it will be a fine feather in

[1] Judging by an incomplete collection of my own, I fancy that a collection of solemn oaths among various peoples would be both interesting and suggestive. And in Balūchistān at any rate it would have practical value. It is, for instance, a useful tip to know that the best way to make a Zikrī speak the truth is to make him swear that he'll break Mula Rahmat's griddle if he speaks false.

her cap if he succeeds where her husband's saint has failed. Now at all well-ordered shrines of holiness there are mangers containing *khwarda* or loose earth, which the members of the family rub on their faces and hands when they visit the shrine, and carry home with them against the day of sickness. And though all sorts and conditions of men are welcome to worship at a shrine, divine wrath will surely fall on man or woman who takes of the *khwarda* at a shrine that is not the shrine of his family saint.

Apparent survivals of the *lingam*.

105. Countless offerings are littered about a shrine: tiny bags stuffed with hair, the first-fruits of childhood's locks; baby dolls and cradles, pathetic mementoes of many a childless woman; leading-strings of camels, that speak of hazardous journeyings and rich merchandise; horns of wild animals and other spoils of the chase; on the coast maybe, the grisly jaw-bone of a shark. All these tell their varied tale of anxious yearnings or pious gratitude. But there are multitudinous odds and ends less easy to classify in this homely museum. For the wild Brāhūī is a snapper-up of unconsidered trifles, and pounces on any little thing that strikes his fancy as he trudges along the road, only to deposit it with childlike faith in the first shrine he comes across. But though his idle wonderment at freaks of nature accounts for much in the weird collection of sticks and stones to be seen in most shrines, this explanation seems occasionally to fail. Some shrines there are in which largish stones, polished and, to all seeming, chiselled with devoted care, occupy the place of honour in the niche towards which the worshippers direct their prayers. In a certain Chāgai shrine there stands a stone, some two feet high, with a flat base and a rounded, bullet-shaped head, too lifelike, it would seem, to be other than the conscious work of men's hands. It is hard to avoid the conclusion that in this far-off shrine the pious Musalmān is bowing his head all unwittingly before a *lingam*, an ancient relic of pre-Islāmic times. Similar in character appear to be a couple of conical stones at the shrine of Pīr-Sultān-ul-Āfirīn in Zahrī, reverentially kissed by all who come to worship. Their shape and their polished surface seem unmistakable evidence of their long-forgotten origin. The tops of the stones by the by are pierced through from side to side, and the keepers of the shrine never tire of telling how the saint used to run ropes through the holes and spend the livelong night with the stones hung round his neck, lest errant thoughts should disturb his holy meditations. So runs the pious tradition. It seems almost sacrilege to add the materialistic detail that each stone must be a good five and twenty pounds in weight.

Shrines of special interest.

106. There are of course far-famed shrines like Shāh Bilāwal which attract their votaries from all parts of the country. But these are so well known that we may pass them by, and glance at one or two shrines remarkable for some quaint characteristic or other. Such are the shrine of Pīr Chattan Shāh in Chashma, half a mile from Kalāt, in the neighbourhood of which no hemp or tobacco may be grown; the shrine of Bībī Nēkzan at Ziārat hard by, a shrine of such sanctity that no one may sleep on a bedstead in the village, though it lies a mile or so away; the shrine of Māi Barēchānī or Gōndrānī in Las Bēla, where no one may stay more than two nights or he will be overwhelmed with a shower of stones from heaven; the shrine of Pīr Chatta at a sacred spring near the mouth of the Mūla pass, the fish in whose holy waters no man may eat on pain of grievous loss or death; the shrine of Shāh on the track between Zahrī and Kōṭra, that massy sheet-rock cleft in three places by a blow wherewith the fourth friend of the Prophet once felled a runagate fire-worshipper, who cowered behind it.

Dog shrine in Jhalawān.

107. A shrine dedicated to a dog would be a bit of an oddity anywhere, and something more than an oddity in a Musalmān country. Yet such a shrine is to be found in the Kīrthar hills. And this is the pious legend that clings to it. Once upon a time there was a dog that changed masters as a pledge for a loan. Now he had not spent many days with his new master before thieves came at dead of night and took off ever so much treasure. But he slunk after the rogues and never let them out of his sight till he had marked down the spot where they buried the spoil. And on the morrow, he barked and he barked and made such a to-do, there was nothing for it but for the master of the house to follow him till he came to the spot where the treasure was buried. Well, the owner was pleased enough to get his goods back, as you may guess. And round the dog's neck he tied a label whereon was writ in plain large letters that the debt

was discharged; and with that he sent him packing to his old master. So the dog bounded off home, as pleased as pleased could be. But his master was mighty angry to see him; for he was an honest fellow, and much as he loved his dog, he set more store on being a man of his word. And as a warning to all breakers of pledges he hacked him limb from limb. But when in the end he saw the label round his neck, and heard of all that he had done, he was exceedingly sorry. So he gathered up the limbs and buried them in a grave. Had the limbs been the limbs of a true believer and not the limbs of an unclean beast, he could not have made more pother over the burial. And to the grave of this faithful dog Jhalawān folk resort to this day. And there they sacrifice sheep, and distribute the flesh in alms, in the certain belief that whatsoever they seek, that they will surely find.

Another in the Pathān country.

108. If it is a trifle curious for a dog, and a dead dog at that, to be an object of worship in backward Jhalawān, it is doubly curious to find a parallel among Paṭhāns, who profess to be such sturdy Musalmāns that one would naturally expect them to be imbued with a wholesome abhorrence of this unclean animal. Hard by the shrine of the sainted Husain Nika stands the shrine of his dog. Never was there so wonderful a dog, we are told. A world of trouble it used to save its holy master. For, whenever visitors came along, it would bark—for every visitor a bark, no more, no less. Now one fine day, up came four men to see the saint. But the dog barked thrice, and then lay down. And when the saint arose, lo! there were not three men but four. And he was so incensed that, without staying to ask the why or the wherefore, he slew the dog then and there. Well, there was an end to the dog, there was no doubt about that. But imagine the remorse of the saint, I ask you, when the fourth man stood revealed as an unbelieving Hindu, who in his naughtiness had dressed himself up for all the world like a true believer. All that a saint could do to make amends, Husain Nika did. For he gave the dog a decent burial, and ordered that he himself should be laid to rest close to the grave of his dog. Nay, he ordained this moreover—that whosoever should come to worship at his shrine should first worship at the shrine of his dog. And so it was, and so it is to this day.

Stones of reproach.

109. So rude are many of the shrines and mosques that a stranger might well be excused for lumping up into the same category the countless artificial collections of stones strewn all over the country. But a little local knowledge soon enables one to read the meaning of some at any rate of these on their face. Such, for instance, are the stones of reproach in the Bugṭī country, called *phiṭ-ḍhērī*, which tell of some tribesman's black deed, incest maybe or flight from the field or foul murder. Of these cairns there is no mistaking the meaning, for they are generally topped by a stone as black as the black deed itself. And their size alone is enough to suggest that the larger cairns dotted about Balūchistān are memorials of some famous battle-field. But I have never been able to differentiate between the various kinds of cairns in the Brāhūī country, where they are often enough the most conspicuous features on the landscape. If a man is a miser, his neighbours vent their spleen by piling up a cairn against him; if a man flies from battle, a cairn will commemorate his cowardice; if a man brings down a fine head, there will be a cairn where he stood and another where the beast fell; if a man dies heirless, a cairn will be raised to his pitiful memory. Every little thing seems to prompt the Brāhūī to pile one stone upon another. A whole mile along the path from Pandrān to Zahrī is dotted out by cairns half a dozen yards apart—they cover the hoof-marks of the horse on which some saint of old gambolled on his way. Fifty years ago a man was done to death by his rutting camel, and to this day cairns mark the course of his desperate flight and the scene of his cruel death. Yet one cairn looks very much like another, and all suffer the same fate. If they lie on the beaten track, they grow in height week by week; each passer-by will add his stone to the pile, but whether with a muttered prayer for the heirless wretch or a curse for the coward or the miser, heaven alone knows; much depends, I suppose, on his frame of mind. And to add to the confusion there are everywhere circles of stones, called *chāp-jahī* or dancing plots, which mark the sites of the frequent dances of some wedding-procession from the village of a Brāhūī bridegroom to the village of his bride.

110. We seem to get interesting glimpses of the religious development of the tribesmen in their attitude towards the forces of nature. Here, I fancy, we are in the presence of great, if seemingly gradual, changes. Old and cherished superstitions are slowly breaking up with the advancing tide of civilisation. In a short time many of them will lose all vitality, only lingering on in weird and unintelligible survivals or here and there perhaps in harmless games, their original meaning entirely lost to tribal memory. Typical instances in my mind are ancient customs relating to rain-making—how priceless a gift in Balūchistān, only those who have lived in this arid country can appreciate—casually mentioned to me as relics of a bygone age, too obsolete or obsolescent and too puerile for my notice. But it is well worth while to catch at the old ideas before they fade away. For the old ideas are not only valuable for their own sake; they are valuable as throwing light on the newer ideas that are displacing them. And though I shall have little to say about rain-making or pest-driving or fruit-producing in Balūchistān that is not familiar to everybody who has dabbled in anthropology, it is after all the common kinship of the human mind, evidenced all the world over in the very universality of such ideas, that lends them half their interest and more than half their value. **Attitude towards nature.**

111. In the old days a halo of divinity surrounded the leaders of the Brāhūī Confederacy. Accredited with authority over the forces of nature, they were held directly accountable for seasons good and bad. When famine was sore in the land, the Brāhūī would look to the Khān to exercise his divine powers and bring down the rain for which the earth cried out. Then would the Khān doff his fine clothes for the woollen overcoat of the peasant, and drive a yoke of oxen across a rain-crop field. Twice has my informant himself seen the ruler of the country put hand to the plough to compel rain to fall; and so efficacious was the second ploughing that the people began to fear another Deluge. But my informant is now an old, old gentleman, and the ruler he saw ploughing was Nasīr Khān II, who has been dead these sixty years and more. The last attempt at rain-making by a Khān was apparently in the early days of Mīr Khudādād. The Jām of Las Bēla and the various chiefs were doubtless credited with similar powers in the old days; but when the Zarakzai chief recently tried his hand, he ploughed from dawn to night-fall with never a drop of rain to reward him—"and small's the wonder, when he had no right to the chiefship at all," muttered a malcontent who was watching him. **Brāhūī rain making.**

112. But happily for them, the Brāhūīs are not wholly dependent on their chiefs. When the flocks are dying for want of rain, a sham-fight is arranged between the womenfolk of two nomad encampments. The opposing forces come together in the afternoon at some lonely place, armed with thorn-bushes, their head-dress thrown back and girt round their waist. Here, unseen by the men, they belabour one another till blood begins to fall. And with that they call a truce, for the falling of blood will surely induce the falling of rain. In some tribes the men take matters into their own hands. The men of one encampment march off to another in the neighbourhood, and there make a great noise, and are soused with water for their pains. Then they are given alms and sent about their business. Both customs appear to be on the wane; but it is safe to prophesy that the women will be the last to abandon theirs. **Sham-fights among adults.**

113. Less obvious is the idea underlying another old rain-making custom, now fast degenerating into a game occasionally played by boys in Kalāt and other settled villages in times of drought. One of the boys acts as the *pīrakā*, dressed up like a little old man (for this is what the word means) with a hoary beard of cotton-wool on his chin, a felt cap on his head, a *zōṛ* or felt coat on his back, and a string of *gungaṛā* or bells jingling about his waist. Round his neck his comrades put a rope and drag him through the village. And when they come to a door, they stand and shout this Dēhwārī doggerel:— **The boys' game of *pīrakā*.**

The buffoon! The old manikin!
Down fell the grain-bin
On top of poor granny!

This is the signal for the goodman of the house to come out with an offering of money or grain. And the *pīrakā* shakes himself and makes his bells jingle and bellows like a camel, while the boys shout in chorus :—

Good luck to the house of the giver!
And a hole in the bin of the miser!

And so they move on from house to house. In the end their collections are clubbed together, a pottage is prepared and distributed among the people, and the game is closed with prayers for rain. I suppose the *pīrakā's* bellowing and the jingling of the bells are imitative of thunder and the swish of rain, but I can volunteer no explanation for his general get-up, unless his snow-white beard is imitative of snow; the game at any rate is generally played in the uplands in the late autumn.

The girls' game of *tiktālo*.

114. There is a somewhat similar rain-making game among the girls. Each girl makes herself a small wooden frame called *ṭikṭālo*, something like the framework of a kite, by tying two sticks crosswise, joining the ends at top and bottom with two more sticks, and tying another stick right down the centre as a handle. Then they go in a body through the village, attended by a female minstrel, and sing at each door :—

Ṭikṭālo! Māṭālo!
Kāsim's dwelling, I'll plait you your tresses!
House of Raīs, mulberries and raisins!
Arbāb's house, white bread and roast meat!
Rush, rain, rush!

Raīs and Arbāb are the titles of headmen among the cultivators, but I can throw no light on the identity of Kāsim; the bread and the meat and the fruits are symbolical, no doubt, of the produce that the earth will yield if only the rain will fall. Having collected doles from house to house in the village, they give them away in alms and pray for rain. Not until the time comes for the distribution of the dainties do the males or the older women take part in the fun.

Rain-stopping.

115. One or other of these rain-making devices is occasionally so successful that folks have found themselves before now in danger of being swamped in the inundation conjured up by their own magic, like Goethe's *Zauberlehrling*. So it's just as well, even in Balūchistān, to be armed with antidotes to banish the rain when it becomes a nuisance. Some people stop rain by hanging a wooden ladle out in the air; others believe in putting antimony in a cock's eye; women light a small fire in the open and damp it down with green leaves, to make it send up a column of smoke into the sky. Any one who can put two and two together will surely admit that the rain is bound to die away if it falls on a dead body; so the Jamālī Balōch of Las Bēla are doubtless wise in their generation in never taking their dead out to burial if it's raining, unless of course there has been enough rain and to spare. But corpses are not always procurable, and I am assured on all hands that the best all-round device to stop rain is to run a thread through a frog's mouth and then let it go with the thread tied round it. Unfortunately the hated miser, who hoards up grain in his bins and spends his days praying for drought, has learnt to turn the frog to his own base uses. When the rains are withheld, folks soon begin to suspect that he has hidden some frogs away in his house in a jar of water, and so stopped the rain. And sure enough, driven to desperation, they have more than once ransacked some miser's house and exposed his shameful trick. At least so they tell me. The survey department may possibly have wondered why their constructions are occasionally demolished in the wilder parts of the Brāhūī country. It may be of interest to them to know that they are joint-accused with the hoarders of grain, and stand charged with locking up the rain by means of their survey pillars.

Rain-making among Paṭhāns.

116. To most Paṭhāns any attempt at rain-making by human agency would savour of blasphemy. The common idea is that above the heavens there are vast oceans of water—so vast that if God gave the word for them to fall, the earth would become a mere bubble floating on a mighty sea. And when clouds are scudding overhead, a Paṭhān will say that they are thirsty and hurrying off to their drinking-grounds. So if there is drought in the land, it is to God that he turns, and calling his comrades together he goes in a procession to some open

field, and there slaughters a sheep and offers up prayers for rain. But that which a Paṭhān thinks rank blasphemy to-day, he may have regarded in a very different light yesterday. For an interesting rain-making custom still survives in what is now a mere boys' game. In times of drought boys make a round bag out of white cloth and stuff it with rags. And they paint the eyes and nose and mouth of a woman on one side of the bag, and bedaub the face with flour, and stick a pole through the bag, and go in a body from house to house, one of their number carrying the doll, or Lāḍō Laḍanga as it is called. At each door they sing this chorus :—

" Lāḍō Laḍanga ! What do you want ? "
The sky's muddy rain is what I want ;
The earth's green grass is what I want ;
One measure of flour is what I want ;
Flavoured with salt—that's what I want !
Argōṛe ! bargōṛe !
God grant you a son to redound to your glory !
Amen.

And the mistress of the house may be relied upon to give them a dole in return for their flattering prayer.

Rain-stopping among Paṭhāns.

117. To a Paṭhān the stopping of rain must seem simple enough. For he has a sheaf of devices to choose from. Throw a handful of salt on the fire ; nail a horse-shoe on to the wall, well out the reach of the rain ; plaster a *patīra* or wheaten bannock on a rubbish-heap ; put a Koran into an oven when the fire is out, and bring it back to your room and distribute alms—it doesn't seem to matter much which of these methods you adopt, all are pronounced to be immediately effective. But after all the only ones to dabble in rain-stopping are the grain-hoarders who always hanker after drought, and the women who get bored with a few days' rain. Two other Paṭhān ideas about rain are perhaps worth adding. Paṭhān lasses are fond of scraping up the last titbits on the dish with their fingers and licking them off, much to the disgust of the old ladies, who know well what the consequences will be. " For the hundredth time of asking," they will say, " don't lick the pot, or there'll be a downpour on your wedding-day." And any Paṭhān can tell you that if you want to change your sex, all you have to do is to go and roll underneath a rainbow.

Rain-making by holy men.

118. But in these days even Brāhūīs are beginning to lose faith alike in the efficacy of their own magic over the powers of nature and in the divine right, or, at any rate, the divine power of their chiefs, and are tending more and more to rest their trust in the advocacy of their holy men with the Almighty. In almost every locality throughout the land there is some holy man who receives a share of the produce known as *ṭuk* as a retaining-fee to produce rain, ward off locusts and mildew, and otherwise control nature for the good of the community. In the more civilised parts the *ṭuk-khōr* or fee-receiver is a Sayyid, but in the wilder parts any holy magic-monger may be found playing the part with apparently equal success. They go to work in various ways. In Bāghbāna a Shēkh reads some charm and lures distant clouds to the valley by waving his turban in its direction. But if there has been some hitch over his *ṭuk*, he is quite capable of driving the clouds over the hills and far away. Not that a *ṭuk-khōr* has always the best of the matter. If rain holds off, the people seek to spur his flagging efforts by stopping his payments. If this fails, and their distress is great, they bind him hand and foot with a rope and leave him to swelter in the blazing sun the livelong day, holy Sayyid though he may be, in the pious hope that he will repent him of his slackness, and call in his frenzy upon God and his sainted forefathers to save his honour by sending rain. There is nothing like this, so I am told, for bringing a lazy *ṭuk-khōr* to his senses ; instance could be piled on instance to prove that rain has fallen within a few hours of his punishment.

Locust driving.

119. Some holy men specialise in one particular department of nature. Such is the *Makṛī* or Locust Sayyid of Ḍhāḍar, who holds his title by virtue of having the locusts under his charm. Father passes on the charm to son, brother to brother, by simply spitting into his mouth. For a day or two the only result is that the man initiated into the mystery goes stark staring

mad. But the madness soon passes off, leaving a wonderful power in its place. For when a swarm of locusts infests the country, all the Sayyid has to do is to catch a locust, spit in its mouth, and let it go. Off it flies spreading the news among its fellows, and in alarm they take to flight towards pastures new, where Sayyids cease from troubling. Not so long ago the people presented a petition to a native official, complaining that the *Makṛī* Sayyid was so slack that the locusts had become a burden. The Sayyid was summoned, and at once explained that it was the people's own fault for falling into arrears with the payment of his dues. The official assured him that, if that was all, he would be personally responsible that there were no grounds for complaint on that score in future. "I knew it," rejoined the Sayyid, "and took the precaution to spit on a locust before I came along." And lo and behold, the people presently rushed up with the news that the locusts had just taken to flight.

Ridding wheat of rust.

120. At least once every five years a disease, variously known as *surkhī* or *rattī*, 'red rust,' attacks the wheat in Kalāt, and the more thickly growing and well-watered the crop, the severer the attack. It comes with the *nambī*, the moist south-wind, which carries it rapidly from field to field; but it soon disappears if the wind veers round to the north. If the *gōrīch* or north-wind doesn't blow, they get Sayyids to read charms over some earth and fling it on the fields. But if this fails, the Brāhūīs are not yet at their wits' end. They get hold of a boy seven years old, bathe him, and deck him out in red clothes, and make him drive a red kid through the fields attacked by the red rust. The kid is then slaughtered and the meat distributed in the name of God. A most effective remedy this, they tell me.

Fruit-producing.

121. They have a pretty way in Makrān of dealing with a mango tree or date-palm that fails to give fruit. The owner gets a couple of friends to bear him company and strides up to it in a threatening manner. "What's all this?" he bawls. "No fruit? D'you think you can make a fool of me? I'll soon show you're mightily mistaken." And with that he gives it a stroke with his axe. Thereupon his comrades fling themselves upon him and seize his hands: only let him spare the poor thing this once and it'll be on its best behaviour in future, they'll be bound. But he wrenches himself loose, and gives it another blow before they can stop him. In time of course they wheedle him into a more forgiving frame of mind, and turn to the tree and say, "Harkee, brother Mango! We've begged you off this time, or by the Almighty he would have had you down. And now that we've given our word for your good behaviour, you'd best bear fruit next year and plenty of it, or you'll catch it with a vengeance." It's marvellous, I'm told, what a bit of bluster will do to make a mango tree or date-palm mend its ways.[1] Yet sometimes they resort to more artistic methods still. The owner comes and reasons quietly with the tree. "What's up with you," says he, "that you won't bear fruit?" "Oh!" say his comrades, "he's simply sick to death of a bachelor's life. A wife is all he wants." Off goes the owner, and back he comes with fine new clothes, all red and green, and spreads them over the tree. And a sheep is killed, and rice is boiled, and the kinsmen are called together, and they sit them down to a wedding-feast to the beating of drums and the singing of songs. But before they break up, they take pains to make it clear to the tree that all the jollity is in his honour, and in return he will kindly behave himself prettily ever after.

Miscellaneous superstitions.

122. These, of course, are very obvious instances of that anthropomorphic humanizing of Nature, that fusion or confusion of natural objects and human beings, which seems so ingrained in the primitive mind. The same fundamental feeling of kinship and sympathy between themselves and Nature is still alive in the peoples of Balūchistān, though magic-mongering has often transmuted it so ingeniously for its own uses, that many survivals of it run the risk of being unrecognized. In a sense far less metaphorical than Shakespeare's can one say that life in Balūchistān still finds tongues in trees, books in the running brooks, sermons in stones, and good—or harm—in everything. When the stone that is strung across a Paṭhān's grave is rocked to and fro in the wind, it is sending up prayers for the peace of the soul; the pebbles that are

[1] Remarkably close parallels (even down to the dialogue), hailing from such different parts of the world as Malay, Japan, Bulgaria, Sicily and Armenia, are given by Dr. Frazer in *The Golden Bough*, Pt. I, vol. ii, pp. 20 seq. And the same notion, I suppose, is embedded in our old saying: *A woman, a spaniel, and a walnut tree—The more you beat'em the better they be*. This is a delightful instance of the universality of the working of the human mind (§ 110).

strewn over the grave of some wild Brāhūī are themselves a coverlet of prayers, still and motionless though they lie. And anthropomorphism had probably been at work before magic added its touch to many objects of nature, and transformed them into warning signs or harbingers of luck. Human fate is writ large on the shoulder-blade of a fresh-killed kid for those that can read it; if a partridge runs across your path from the left, it is as though it said 'Turn again, Whittington.' But notions of this kind are almost without number. Anthropomorphism may even have had a hand in the framing of the first and last rule of Brāhūī life (a rule followed also by many Balōch, though the enlightened of both races are rapidly freeing themselves from its shackles) never to go in the direction of the Star. For the Star is very commonly muddled up with the *chiltan*, the forty *mardān-i-ghaib* or invisible beings, who seem to be always luring unwary mortals to their own invisible realms. In its zigzagging but appointed course, the mysterious Star is now south or east or north or west in the heavens, now sunk beneath the earth; and woe betide the man that ventures to follow in its track. But happily every Brāhūī knows the date of its appointed course. On the 3rd the Star is in the south; so if there's a corpse in the house and the door faces the south, the only way to get the corpse out-of-doors is to batter down a wall that has a more favourable aspect. This is bad enough in all conscience; but the battering down of all four walls is of no avail on the 9th or the 19th or the 29th, for these are the three days when the Star is in its underground quarters, and the burial will have to be postponed to the morrow. And after anthropomorphism has done its work, one touch of magic is all that is needed to make many an inanimate object spring to life, an obvious potentiality for good. Of such the Brāhūī rules of life are full. Tie the knuckle-bone off the hind-leg of a wolf round your leg, and you'll travel all day long and never tire. Pop a wolf's eye into your turban, if ever you want to sleep with one eye open. Hang a wolf's tooth round your child's neck, and there'll be no chance of the evil spirits troubling it. Give it a morsel of dried wolf's guts to eat, if it is threatened with consumption. Put the skin of a hyena's forehead into your grain measure, and your heap of wheat will increase. And if you're crazy with love, the skin will prove a very potent love-charm into the bargain. But the Dēhwār of Kalāt knows a love-charm worth two of that; and if ever you come across a much-wooed Dēhwār lassie, you may lay ten to one that she has got hold of a *kus-i-kaftār*—the dried genitals of a hyena bitch. Then there's the other side to the question. There are a whole host of taboos, things that are possibly all very well for other folk, but unspeakably evil for oneself. A Lāshārī Balōch will never touch *ālṛō*, a succulent plant of which women especially are very fond, partly because of its taste, partly because of the pleasant sound it makes when they munch it; a Marī Balōch will never touch tripe; a Rind Balōch will never touch camel's flesh; a Chīstī Sayyid of Kalāt will not eat sheep's head after dark; a Bikak Chhuṭṭa will never eat *bik* or kidneys at all; nor will a Dē-laṛau Chhuṭṭa eat *laṛau* or guts. Somewhat different are the fads of the Umrānī Balōch, who hate the very sight of a long-necked drinking-vessel called *ghuggī*, and of the Jamālī Balōch, who can't stand burning cow-dung. These seem more akin to the various abominations of the menials and artisans of the Kachhī, where the tool called *pēnr* is an abomination to the weavers, *wakhā* or bits of rotten hide are an abomination to the cobblers, uncrushed pulse to the minstrels, a lemon to the grain-parchers, brinjal to the carpenters, and honey to the barbers. A chief in the Kachhī used to have fine sport in the old days in trying to make the menials bring the names of their pet abominations to their lips; the very mention of them on the lips of others was enough to make them weep and wail and rend their clothes.

123. But if I once embark on a voyage among superstitions and magic of Jinns. this nature, it would be many a weary page before I could reach the haven where I would be. As it is, it may be thought that I have already drifted far enough from my subject; yet the uncharted seas of religion abound too much in magic and superstitions for me to steer wholly clear of them. But on one other topic I must touch before I bring these fragmentary impressions of religious life in Balūchistān to a close. For a sketch of Balūchistān religion with the spirits of darkness left out would be as bald as Paradise Lost without the Arch-fiend. Here at any rate I return to the thick of my subject. Not even

in the Occident have they yet succeeded in pitchforking the devil out of religion; and in Islām the Iblīs and the Jānn and the Jinn and the Shaitān and the Ifrīt and the Mārid have all their appointed spheres. In Balūchistān everything untoward seems to be put down to the Jinns—sickness among the children, murrain among the cattle, sudden death among the men. But worse perhaps than all, is the way the Jinns plague the poor women. I have before me the records of a case that occurred only a few months ago, where a council of Paṭhān Elders held an inquest over a woman who had evidently come by a violent death, and gravely pronounced that she had been strangled by a Jinn; and the official in charge of the case, himself a Balōch, as gravely endorsed their verdict. In the length and breadth of the land it would probably be hard to find a household where a woman has not been possessed of a devil at some time or another. But if the Jinns are abroad, ever on the watch to do mischief, there are happily talismans and amulets and charms to keep them at their distance. And even though a Jinn makes good his foothold in a woman, there are Sayyids and other holy men to eject him with their holiness and their prayers. Even if these fail, there are Shēkh or devil-dancers to lure him out with their dancing. But this is ground where it will be better for me to stand aside and allow a man of the country to take up the parable.

Shēkh or devil-dancers.

124. Now as soon as a Jinn has entered into a woman (says a Brāhūī friend of mine[1]), she falls to the ground, poor thing, in a dead faint, shivering and trembling, with eyes fast shut, with teeth clenched, and arms and legs flung this side and that. And for the space of an hour or more she can utter never a word, and is deaf to the cries of her sorrowing kin. By these signs we know full well that a Jinn has got her in his grip, and our first thought is to summon some holy man who shall drive the evil spirit forth with prayers and incantations and charms. Well, it's not for me to decry the skill of mulla or Sayyid in the casting out of devils; in truth the efficacy of their amulets and charms is the measure of their power among the people. But old-fashioned folks set more store by the Shēkh and his dancing. Now a Shēkh is not a member of any one tribe or race. You may come across one here and there all up and down the country. By his long, long hair you will know him, and his skill on instruments of music, and his power over the Jinns. Some Jinns he has forever under his spell, and with these to do his bidding he can win the mastery over others. So if mulla and Sayyid have failed to free the hapless woman from the spell, her kinsfolk call in a Shēkh at dead of night. But first they gather together men that are cunning on instruments of music. And when the Shēkh enters the assembly where the woman is laid, the minstrels strike up a measure, and play right lustily. And as he listens to the strains, the Shēkh's limbs tremble beneath him; and he rocks to and fro, and his face is as the face of a man in agony. For the wild music breeds a madness within him, so that he becomes like one possessed. And lo! he starts to his feet and dances madly, whirling round and round and ever round. And his long, long hair now floats in the air, and anon it sweeps the ground. On he dances, and the music grows yet more wild and the dance yet more crazy. And when he is so spent with his whirlings that the sweat drips from him in great drops, he cries aloud on Ali Bēzāt and Lākā and his other saints, to help him in this his hour of bitter stress. Now when the frenzy is upon him, men and women gather round him eagerly—the old ladies foremost in the press—and question him touching this or that, bidding him prophesy: is it a boy or a girl that neighbour's wife will bear him? is there rain in the air? will father return this month or the next from his travels? and how will his business speed, for good or for ill? And to all their questions he will make answer, if so be the Jinns are in the humour to prophesy. And haply some old crone will totter forward with a blue thread in her hand, mumbling up many a prayer that a son may be vouchsafed her daughter, and will piteously entreat the Shēkh to tie a knot in the thread that it may safeguard the child against the Jinns. And the Shēkh will tie the knot, sure enough, but a deal he will mutter of the sacrifices she must offer, and the rich presents she should give him. Then one in the company will cry out for

[1] Here and elsewhere I have drawn freely from an essay on Brāhūī autobiography, which I hope shortly to publish in separate form.

sweetmeats, and all the assembly take up the chorus. So with a wild toss of the head, the Shēkh calls upon the Jinns, and lo! at a whisk of his hand sweetmeats come tumbling from the air. Or he takes an empty bowl and waves it aloft, and then shows it to the people all brimming with blood. And oftentimes he goes apart and talks aloud, as though he were holding communion with the spirits of darkness. And the hairs bristle on the heads of all that hear him. For 'tis in truth a gruesome thing to hear strange talk and weird sounds in the dead of night.

125. By and by the Shēkh returns to the assembly, and speaking like one who speaks in his sleep, he tells how he has wrestled long and manfully with the spirits of darkness. Maybe he will say that the Jinn must be appeased with the sacrifice of a he-goat or a ram of this colour or that. Or he will say there is nothing for it but *alēj*. Now *alēj* is a sacrifice that is made after this fashion. The beast must be slaughtered before the very eyes of her that is seized of the devil. And a little wool is soaked in its blood, and smeared on her hands and feet and forehead. But the flesh is cooked and served among the assembly. And so, please God, the devil is cast out for good and all. But often enough it all begins over again before long. For some women seem never free from the Jinns. They are always flying into a rage and beating their faces and plucking out their hair; Heaven alone knows why. Nothing provokes them more than the smell of roasting meat. So no one is surprised if a neighbour pops in when a joint is on the roast, and begs for a bit to soothe some Jinn-ridden woman next-door. But truth to tell, there are women so lost to shame as to put on the airs of one that is possessed of a devil, and all to compass some private end. One, I daresay, has a grudge to pay off against her husband. Another may fancy that folk will eye her with reverence when they know that she is in league with the Jinns. But of such idle women, and their tantrums, and the airs they put on, and the nuisance they are, I will say naught. The Jinns are of a surety a dread and awesome company. Trouble enough do they give us, and small's the need to add thereto trouble that is mockery and vanity.

The casting out of the devil.

SUBSIDIARY TABLES.

XII.—Distribution of the Population by Religion.

District or state.	Number per 1,000 of the population who are				
	Musalmān.	Hindu.	Sikh.	Christian.	Others.
BALŪCHISTĀN	***938***	***45***	***10***	***6***	***1***
Districts	**911**	**62**	**13**	**12**	**2**
Quetta-Pishīn	836	104	19	36	5
Lōralai	950	37	11	1	1
Zhōb	968	18	10	2	1
Bōlān	678	250	51	12	9
Chāgai	974	23	2	1	...
Sibī	926	62	9	2	1
Administered area	*899*	*84*	*13*	*2*	*2*
Marī Bugṭī country	*989*	*11*	...	...	...
States	**965**	**28**	**7**	...	...
Kalāt	963	28	9	...	...
Sarāwān	*982*	*16*	*2*	...	...
Jhalawān	*994*	*6*	...	...	...
Kachhī	*910*	*77*	*13*	...	...
Ḍōmbkī-Kahērī country	*874*	*54*	*72*	...	...
Makrān	*997*	*2*	...	1	...
Khārān	*998*	*2*	...	...	...
Las-Bēla	970	29	1	...	...

XIII.—Variation in Christianity.

Sect.	1911						Total.		Variation + or —.
	European.		Anglo-Indian.		Indian.				
	Males.	Females.	Males.	Females.	Males.	Females.	1911	1912	
All denominations	3,382	828	64	59	495	257	5,085	4,026	+ 1,059
Anglican Communion	2,270	600	28	30	239	179	3,346	2,857	+ 489
Baptist	7	3	...	...	...	...	10	17	— 7
Congregationalist	2	...	...	...	...	...	2	...	+ 2
Lutheran	1	...	...	...	1	...	2	...	+ 2
Methodist	118	40	...	4	19	10	191	165	+ 26
Minor Protestant denominations	1	...	...	...	4	2	7	5	+ 2
Presbyterian	111	28	2	...	8	11	160	90	+ 70
Roman Catholic	868	155	34	25	223	55	1,360	736	+ 624
Sect not returned	3	2	...	...	...	...	5	154	— 149
Indefinite beliefs	1	...	...	...	1	...	2	2	...

CHAPTER V.

AGE.

Statistical data

SUBJECT.	Tables.	
	Imperial.	Subsidiary.
General	VII	..
Puberal distribution by race . . .	...	XIV
Puberal distribution by locality . . .	...	XV

Age statistics in the regular areas.

126. The only members of the community whose specific age was recorded were those censused in municipalities, military stations, and the few other scattered areas where the census was taken on regular lines. But the conditions here are so abnormal and accidental that it seems sheer waste of time to dwell on the statistics. The ages of the aliens, who of course form the bulk of this part of the population, simply reflect the artificial character of their temporary sojourn in Balūchistān; the ages of the few indigenous inhabitants simply reflect the artificial character of their temporary sojourn outside their tribal country. In both cases there is an abnormally low proportion of the very young and the very old, and an abnormal deficiency of females except among the children. The urban population in Balūchistān (for this is what the regular areas give us in effect, though on the one hand they do not include all of our so-called towns and on the other include several petty localities which cannot be called towns, to say nothing of a few travellers by rail, road and sea) is made up for the most part of men in the prime of life actively engaged in earning their livelihood. As the census was taken before the coming of spring, it gives a somewhat exaggerated idea of the scarcity of females among the aliens, for many of the alien women move down-country during the rigours of winter. Most aliens send away their children at an early age. Few tribesmen bring either wives or children from their homes at all.

Specific age not recorded elsewhere.

127. Out in the districts, conditions are of course so normal and at the same time so primitive that accurate age statistics would have thrown a welcome flood of light on the darkness caused by the utter lack of registration of births and deaths in the country. Unfortunately they were not to be had. For one thing, age is a matter beyond the grasp of the ordinary tribesman. Ask a well-grown youth his age, and he will very possibly say ten or twelve. The answer, by the by, may not be quite so absurd as it sounds; in all probability it is roughly so many years since he was breeched. Ask another, and he will perhaps say twenty or thirty; if you look dubious, he may raise it to forty or fifty—even to sixty or seventy, if only you look dubious long enough. A third will say frankly that he has no idea, but supposes that you are lettered enough to know better. But similar difficulties crop up in every part of India, and had these been all, we would have got over them, I dare say, in much the same way and with much the same degree of plausible success as other provinces. In Balūchistān, however, we are faced with a far more formidable difficulty, and though the ages of the males might have been registered after a fashion, in the case of the female sex all reference to age had to be left discreetly alone.

Owing to sexual jealousy among the tribesmen.

128. Specific questions of any kind regarding individual women are questions best avoided in Balūchistān. Questions that touch on the marriage state

however remotely—and questions of age touch it much more nearly in the minds of the tribesmen than in the mind of the most fastidious spinster at home—are questions that are rarely safe outside the frigid atmosphere of the courts. It is a little difficult for any one who has not actually lived on this frontier to appreciate the extreme delicacy of the subject. Let me try to give some faint idea of it with the help of a few illustrations. Take the case of the stranger who came to a Brāhūī camp, asked politely after the health of his hospitable host and his brothers and his sons, and incautiously wound up with the hope that his wife was in the best of health. The courteous bearing of the Brāhūī turned to a blaze of wrath. "And what concern is it of yours," he roared, "whether my wife is sick or whole?" And brandishing his sword he sped the flying guest. Or take the case of the guard placed over a cholera camp some ten years ago, who was accused and found guilty of "blackening" a Brāhūī woman, all because he laid a hand on her to keep her from quitting the camp—the evidence hardly amounted to more. Or take an extraordinary case which occurred among the Marī Balōch while the census was in progress, where a maiden was claimed in betrothal by two men of different sections of the tribe, and was done to death by her father because (so he said) he felt that she was "blackened" by a claim he was unable to countenance. Among Paṭhāns, sexual jealousy seldom touches so absurd a pitch; but matters are bad enough. Where the Paṭhān lives cheek by jowl with Brāhūī or Balōch, he affects much the same measure of reticence. Removed from their influence, he is, it is true, amenable within reason, but he remains at all times keenly sensitive to the opinions of the outside world. On the part of the Dumaṛ, for instance, there seemed no reason to anticipate any real objections to the standard schedule, for so little addicted are they to jealousy where their unmarried women-folk are concerned, that they still regard the provision of a maiden for the night as one of the first duties of hospitality (§175). But as soon as they got wind of objections raised by a neighbouring tribe, they at once mounted the high horse, and gave me the flat answer, as they called it, that nothing would induce a Dumaṛ to submit to a catechism about his women which was held to be too searching for his neighbours.

Age statistics would have been untrustworthy.

129. To have bade our enumerators go forth and record the women of such tribes individual by individual on the inquisitive lines of the ordinary census, would have been like asking them to take lighted torches into cellars full of gunpowder. After all, as one philosopher among the tribesmen consolingly remarked, even if the standard schedule with its prying questions regarding age and marriage state could have been adopted, we should not have got at the truth. "Put the case" said he, "that I had (which Heaven forbid!) an unmarried daughter of thirty-two in my house; do you suppose for a minute that I would own up to her? Never a bit! I would plead guilty either to an unmarried daughter of twelve or a married daughter of thirty-two; or rather, now that I come to think of it, it's much more likely that I would hold my tongue, and not mention her at all. And even granted that honour and decency allowed us to give the ages of our women, do you think we know them ourselves? I guess your zealous enumerators would always be wanting to have a peep at the wenches to see if they were really of the age we said they were. Or do you imagine," he added with a grin, "that our pious and wealthy friend Mr. Sayyid So-and-so, who, as all the world knows, has married five wives, though the holy law allows him but four at a time, would publicly acknowledge the presence of the fifth?"

Methods justified by the full record of females.

130. Thus by denying ourselves the luxury of statistics regarding both age and marriage, we thereby denied the tribesmen even the shadow of an excuse for the wilful concealment of their women. Under a more inquisitorial system such concealment must have been inevitable in many tribes. As it was, the most minute check and countercheck in all parts of the country and among all races revealed not the slightest evidence of it. The trouble we took to temper our enquiries to the susceptibilities of the tribesmen was more than repaid by the candour of their answers: judged by what has come to be regarded as the touchstone of census work in India, our methods stood justified to the full. The only member of the household who ever ran any risk of being omitted was the useless old granny, not because there was the vaguest wish to conceal her

existence, but simply because she was apt to be forgotten or ignored, as an unnecessary encumbrance who had outlived her utility. And whenever record and check refused to tally, it was the regular thing to seek the explanation in the person of the old lady, and roars of laughter never failed to greet the goodman of the house when he stood convicted of having overlooked the poor old body at the time of record or check. But the enumerators themselves soon learnt to eye her as a potential source of error, and the cases in which she finally escaped being recorded must have been few indeed.

Division into adults and non-adults.

131. And so, though we were losers in one direction, we were for that very reason gainers in another. And the balance was unmistakably in our favour. It is much more important to have the bare numbers of females complete than to have fanciful ages and very possibly fanciful marriage particulars of such females as the tribesmen might condescend to acknowledge. Not that age data are altogether lacking : unsatisfying though the information may be, it is something at all events to have the population divided up into those above and those below the age of puberty. A wholly inoffensive division this, one would think. Yet even here we were treading on dangerous ground, and we found it advisable to temper our enquiries to the whimsies of the particular races we were enumerating. True, there is little false modesty about the Paṭhān on the score of *balūghat* or puberty ; indeed one hoary-headed old dodderer waxed quite querulous at finding himself recorded as *bāligh*, and kept harping on the embarrassingly intimate detail that it was many a weary year since his last *iḥtilām*. Not even with regard to his women does the Paṭhān resent the point-blank question, though he appreciates the pious circumlocution "Has she started prayers yet?" which puts matters in just as clear and much more polite a manner. But the Balōch professed himself scandalised at the very mention of puberty; happily he saw no indecorum in dividing up his household into those over and under thirteen—or whatever the age that might catch our fancy. And the Brāhūī went one further. To his fastidious mind a definite age smacked as much of impropriety as the word puberty itself, and it was no small relief to find that our object could be attained just as well and without loss of decency by a mere division into big and small.

Puberty, unlike age, fact not fiction.

132. In abandoning years of age and confining ourselves to puberty, we score at any rate in the elimination of nearly all element of fiction. Puberty is not simply a matter of certainty in the family, it is a matter of common knowledge in the village. It is accordingly a little curious to stumble on so few ceremonial customs connected with it. There is of course the breeching of the budding youth. Among the Marī Balōch and the Sanzarkhēl Kākaṛ of Lōṛalai and probably other Paṭhāns, a lad's first breeches (which by the by have distinctive red strips tacked on to the legs) are ignominiously pulled off by his comrades before he is suffered to wear them in peace. But breeches often forestall puberty nowadays, and Brāhūīs usually don them at quite an early age. A Brāhūī mother sometimes passes sweetmeats round among the women of the house with a meaning smile when her son first takes razor to shave himself about the middle. For a Paṭhān girl to begin to say her prayers—or, as they put it, to stand up for *numāz*—is the signal that she has passed the threshold to womanhood. The Brāhūī custom is much more picturesque. The mother takes three small stones at sun-down, and placing them thus ° o °, bids her daughter jump over them thrice. "For"—and here I will quote my informant's own words—"if this be done duly and in order, three days and no more will be the span of her monthly issue. Now and then, to be sure, she may be troubled longer : but that it never lasts beyond four or at the most five days, I have the warrant of an old dame who knows all about it. And surely to a man who ponders over such things, 'tis strange to find three stones on the threshold of womanhood. For it's three stones a husband throws when he banishes a wife from bed and board." As a matter of fact, there can hardly be any closer connection between the three stones on the two occasions than that they serve in each case to emphasise the number three—at puberty for the purpose of magical telepathy ; at divorce as a mnemonic.

Local ideas.

133. Whether scientists would rest content with the local definition of puberty, I do not know. The only sign of adolescence a tribesman looks for in

his daughter is the appearance of her first period of uncleanliness; the only signs he looks for in his son are the cracking of the voice, the sprouting of hair, and the intrusion of sex in his dreams. Old folks will have it that puberty is reached much sooner in these degenerate days than in the good old days of their fathers. This, they say, is but one sign out of many that the end of the world—a never-flagging topic among Brāhūī greybeards—is surely nigh. But as they also say that puberty comes earlier to the rich than to the poor, a sceptic might take them at their word, and, putting two and two together, read therein a sign that the times were on the mend. It is just possible that increased exposure to the temptations of town-life may breed thoughts in some of the rising generation calculated to encourage the early arrival of puberty; but a general speeding-up of puberty is, I suppose, an old wife's tale. It is easy to see how the idea may have arisen. The breeching of lads, which is the outward sign of puberty, was put off in olden times as long as possible because unbreeched lads were as inviolate in tribal warfare as a woman or a Hindu or a Lōṛī (§ 288). But the need has gone for any such precaution, and lads are nowadays breeched betimes, though truth to tell, one may still see in outlying parts youths in garb scant enough to bring a blush to the cheek of averted propriety.

The age of puberty.

134. But whether or no there has been any speeding-up of the age of puberty, the fact unfortunately stares us in the face that we are unable to assign any particular age to puberty, varying as it does with the individual, with the race, with sex and with environment. Hence, much as I appreciate the accuracy of our statistics, it is a trifle embarrassing to know what to do with them now that I have got them. Comparison with other statistics seems scarcely feasible, for it would be hard to lay one's hands on any statistics that are really comparable. Here, on the one hand, is the division of the Balūchistān peoples on the basis of puberty; there, on the other, are the complex classifications of the populations of India and Europe on the basis of age. The gulf between them can only be bridged by a common denominator. I can hardly drive a line through the statistics for India at some critical age like twelve or thirteen, and expect any very satisfying results from a comparison with the puberal cleavage in Balūchistān. Nor can I reverse the process and reduce our own statistics to terms of age. For what critical age could I select with any confidence? To fix upon the age of fifteen is merely to cut the Gordian knot in the first likely place that catches my eye. Not but what it might be difficult to find a better. Fifteen may err on the safe side; yet the margin is not so great as those accustomed to life in the warmth of India may imagine. It seems to fit the males fairly well when we take them in the mass, though it probably oversteps the mark among the Jaṭṭ and other dwellers of the plains, where development seems to set in much more rapidly than in the uplands. But if it fits the males, it must necessarily fail to do justice to the superior precocity of the other sex; for a lass, as the Brāhūīs say, is like barley that shoots up apace, whereas a lad is like the more precious wheat that is slow of growth.

Rapid female development.

135. This female precocity seems to be writ large over our statistics, even when—in an endeavour to discount the local dearth of females—we take a thousand of either sex and use puberty to divide each thousand into two heaps. Only among the erratic Hindus do the girls appear to have any difficulty in outstripping the boys in the race towards maturity. In the heats run off among the Brāhūīs and the Balōch and the Paṭhāns the girls make good their lead with curious regularity. Among the Jaṭṭ, and still more among the Lāsī, it looks as if the girls were beginning to flag; but this is probably an optical illusion, the truth being that Jaṭṭ and Lāsī girls have little time to increase their lead in the warmth of the plains, where the first lap in the race of life is shortened by the early arrival of puberty. Sayyid girls, on the other hand, show their brothers a remarkably clean pair of heels. Here the gap between the two sexes is so wide that, were the precocity of females the only factor in the case, our statistics might well be suspect. But though I certainly believe in this female precocity, I am of

Non-adults in 1,000 of each sex.

	Males.	Females.	Male excess.
Indigenous	*391*	*366*	*+25*
Sayyid	420	367	+53
Miscellaneous	376	342	+34
Brāhūī	386	360	+26
Balōch	397	372	+25
Paṭhān	412	390	+22
Jaṭṭ	366	347	+19
Lāsī	372	361	+11
Sikh	325	308	+17
Hindu	315	316	−1

course conscious that there are many other factors at work—far too many, I confess, for the comfort of one who has no statistical bent. One obvious factor that plays havoc with this Sayyid proportion is matrimony. For while Sayyids cheerily recruit the number of their women by taking wives from outside their hallowed circle, they suffer no corresponding loss in the number of their girls for the simple reason that they disdain to give their daughters to outsiders in exchange. Among the Sayyids—to put it bluntly—there is many a woman that was never a Sayyid at birth. The full force of this matrimonial disturbance is probably concentrated on the Sayyid statistics, though the reverse of it, of course, dissipates itself over several of our other races. On the statistics of the province as a whole, it is hardly felt at all. If Sayyids take a woman or two from outside the province, others (like the Brāhūīs) make up for it by sending a few of their daughters abroad; but the totals on either side are small, and the balance within the province remains, I fancy, pretty constant. It is very different with emigration, which disturbs the proportions throughout, and probably to a much greater degree. Unlike nomadism, which removes whole families from the province and thus fails to affect the balance, emigration upsets the balance not only among the several races but in the province as a whole by carrying off full-grown men and consequently exaggerating the relative number of boys in the population that is left behind. If only we knew to what races the emigrants belonged, a simple readjustment of the racial proportions would allow us to tackle them with renewed confidence. Unfortunately, all that emigration statistics tell us is that apart from the emigration of whole families (which does not concern us) there was a surplus emigration of males — full-grown males, we may safely assume — nearly 7,000 strong (§82); all that local knowledge can tell us is that most of them were probably drawn from the Sayyids and Paṭhāns and from the Makrānī Balōch and others of Makrān. Their absence from the province of course throws an unnatural damper on the proportion of men in it, and gives an unnatural fillip to the proportion of lads. The best we can do to put things straight is to lump the whole lot up with the total number of men in the indigenous population. This done, the number of lads in every 1,000 males drops from 391 to 384, and the true excess of lads over girls drops from 25 to 18. And, if this were the full measure of female precocity in Balūchistān, it would amount to nothing very serious after all. But there is at least one other disturbing influence to be taken into account — the fact (for it seems a well-established fact, though it runs in the teeth of all European experience) that there is much more infant mortality among the daughters than among the sons of Balūchistān (§162).

136. When we turn to the fluctuations in the relative number of children among our various peoples, we pass on to what should prove a much more fascinating topic, for, other things being equal, the greater the proportion of children in a race, the more hopeful the prospect of its healthy development in the coming generations. Take our three chief races, for instance. On the face of it, things look rosy enough for the Paṭhāns, not nearly so rosy for the Balōch, far from rosy for the Brāhūīs. And this may be a reasonably true account of the relative prospects of the Brāhūīs and Paṭhāns. But a glance at the margin, where the childhood proportions are contrasted with extracts from our birth statistics (§67), makes one feel at once that there must be something wrong with the place of the Balōch on the list. And, sure enough, up crop the same old difficulties to spoil our simple calculations. Thus, if birth or rather survival statistics are any criterion at all, the Lāsī and the Jaṭṭ should be at the top of the list or near it, instead of sinking, as they do, towards the bottom. The obvious explanation for their humble position on the list is not that they breed little or rear few, but that their children ripen early to maturity in the warmth of the plains they inhabit. The influence of locality is perhaps best seen in the local statistics themselves. In Las Bēla, which is hot enough, the average number of children in every 1,000 of the population is 369; in the Ḍombkī-Kahērī country, which is hotter still, it is 359; in the Kachhī, which is hottest of all — show me the tract in India that can vie with this burning fiery furnace!—

Proportion of children.

Non-adults in 1,000 persons.

	Non-adults.	Survivals per father.
Indigenous	*379*	*3·6*
Paṭhān . .	402	3·4
Sayyid . .	395	3·3
Balōch . .	385	4·1
Brāhūī . .	375	3
Lāsī . .	367	4·2
Miscellaneous .	360	3·9
Jaṭṭ . .	357	3·9
Sikh . .	317	—
Hindu . .	315	2·8

it is 348, the lowest childhood proportion in the whole of Balūchistān with the sole exception of the hopelessly exceptional case of Bōlān. And in illustration of other disturbing factors, let us turn to the sacred people that all but heads the list. That the Sayyids are really entitled to a highish place, I do not question: they marry early, they marry often, they live in comfort, and their children ought to thrive. But -- and here is the rub — the presence of two mutually repellent but very possibly unequal factors leaves us in doubt whether we can take Sayyid childhood proportion at its face value. On the one hand, the relative number of Sayyid children is artificially lowered by matrimonial customs, which bring alien women into the Sayyid fold; on the other, it is artificially heightened by emigration, which drives many Sayyid men out of the country. And looking at the not particularly high survival rate among the Sayyids, I am inclined to think that the proportion of children among them is artificially exaggerated. So here, once more, we sorely feel the absence of any information regarding race in our so-called emigration statistics. And all we can do is to repeat the old process and add the emigration surplus to the adult figures for the whole province, with the result that the provincial proportion of children drops from 379 to 376. But I am far from satisfied with the lame and impotent conclusions that I have been able to draw from this puberal division of the Balūchistān peoples. With proper handling it ought to be made to yield some very pretty results, I think. But my own confession of bungling will surely provoke some learned statistician to prove how dismally I have failed. And with this sincere but unflattering hope I gladly retire.

SUBSIDIARY TABLES.

XIV—Puberal Distribution by Race.

(*Indigenous only.*)

RACE OR TRIBE.	Non-adults per mille persons.	PUBERAL DISTRIBUTION OF 1,000 OF EACH SEX.			
		NON-ADULTS.		ADULTS.	
		Males.	Females.	Males.	Females.
INDIGENOUS	*379*	*391*	*366*	*609*	*634*
Balōch	**385**	**397**	**372**	**603**	**628**
Eastern	384	393	372	607	628
Western	389	403	372	597	628
Brāhūi	**375**	**386**	**360**	**614**	**640**
Original nucleus	371	384	356	616	644
Sarāwān	368	376	359	624	641
Jhalawān	378	393	360	607	640
Miscellaneous	398	400	396	600	604
Paṭhān	**402**	**412**	**390**	**588**	**610**
Kākaṛ	397	405	388	595	612
Paṇī	400	415	382	585	618
Tarīn	419	430	407	570	593
Lāsi	**367**	**372**	**361**	**628**	**639**
Jaṭṭ	**357**	**366**	**347**	**634**	**653**
Sayyid	**395**	**420**	**367**	**580**	**633**
Miscellaneous	**360**	**376**	**342**	**624**	**658**
Hindu	**315**	**315**	**316**	**685**	**684**
Sikh	**317**	**325**	**308**	**675**	**692**

XV—Puberal Distribution by Locality.

(Indigenous only.)

DISTRICT OR STATE.	Non-adults per mille persons.	PUBERAL DISTRIBUTION OF 1,000 OF EACH SEX.			
		Non-Adults.		Adults.	
		Males.	Females.	Males.	Females.
BALŪCHISTĀN.	***379***	***391***	***366***	***609***	***634***
Districts	**395**	**404**	**386**	**596**	**614**
Quetta-Pishīn	417	431	400	569	600
Lōṛalai	395	399	391	601	609
Zhōb	390	401	377	599	623
Bōlān	298	244	376	756	624
Chāgai	385	382	389	618	611
Sibī	383	390	375	610	625
Administered area	*373*	*381*	*363*	*619*	*637*
Marī Bugṭī country	*405*	*408*	*401*	*592*	*599*
States	**366**	**380**	**350**	**620**	**650**
Kalāt	366	381	348	619	652
Sarāwān	*362*	*371*	*351*	*629*	*649*
Jhalawān	*371*	*391*	*346*	*609*	*654*
Kachhī	*348*	*364*	*330*	*636*	*670*
Ḍōmbkī-Kahērī country	*359*	*364*	*354*	*636*	*646*
Makrān	*373*	*394*	*351*	*606*	*649*
Khārān	*411*	*424*	*396*	*576*	*604*
Las Bēla	369	373	364	627	636

CHAPTER VI.

SEX.

Statistical data.

SUBJECT.	TABLES.	
	Imperial.	Subsidiary.
Actual population—		
Variation by age	VII	......
Natural population—		
Variation by 'migration'	......	XI
Indigenous population—		
Variation by locality	......	XVI
Variation by race	......	XVII
Variation by nomadism	......	XVIII

Sex-proportion in the actual and natural populations.

137. Unless a country is entirely cut off from all intercourse with the outside world, there is of course no reason to expect the sex-proportion of its population to coincide with the sex-proportion of the population born in it. Emigration and immigration upset the balance at once. In so far as an undue number of males is usually carried to and fro on their flood, they often tend to counteract each other; but it is only when they are equal in volume and alike in character, that it is safe to ignore their disturbing influence. The population actually enumerated in Balūchistān is a very artificial medley, made up of indigenous inhabitants of the country, large numbers of alien immigrants, and a sprinkling of people who are hardly the one or the other (§ 61).

	Males.	Females.
Actual population .	1,000	790
Natural population	1,000	833

It is accordingly not surprising that the sex-proportion is also artificial, for there is as usual a great deficiency of females among the immigrants, a deficiency exaggerated in the statistics by the by owing to the particular season of the year when the census was taken. If we endeavour to adjust matters by weeding out of the population those born outside Balūchistān and by bringing in those born within it but enumerated elsewhere in India (for all who had ventured outside the limits of India are of course beyond our control[1]), the sex-proportion is materially altered. But the natural population, as the resultant of these simple sums in addition and subtraction is called, is a very unnatural population after all (§68). It simply reflects the accident of birthplace, and even that it fails to reflect faithfully. For all it amounts to is the total number of persons, whatever their creed, their race or mother country, who happen, first, to have been born in Balūchistān, and, further, to have been enumerated within the Indian Empire at the time of the census. There is a place in it allotted to my child, simply because she happens to have been born in Quetta: my Brāhūī orderly is sent packing, simply because he happens to have been born in Karāchi. Much that is of interest could, I suppose, be gleaned from a comparison of sex in the actual and natural

[1] This is not strictly accurate. I have since received the returns of 242 persons (including 15 females) who were born in Balūchistān but censused in Ceylon, Uganda and Malaya.

populations of Balūchistān. But a glance at the two sets of statistics fails, I confess, to whet my curiosity. For neither the one nor the other can profess to represent the sex-proportion among the true natives of the country—among those, that is, whose home, like the home of their fathers before them and the future home of their sons and their sons' sons after them, is Balūchistān.

Paucity of females in the indigenous population.

138. And so, rather than look on this picture or on that, I prefer to turn to the sex-proportion among those who are natives of Balūchistān in the living sense of the word. Here we leave the shifting sands of accidental birthplace for the firm ground of birth-right or race. All aliens are bundled out of the statistics neck and crop, and the semi-indigenous may go with them. Of the emigrants from this country there are so few whom there is any point in hailing back, that I propose for the present to leave one and all where they are. For on the great tidal wave of emigration into Sind are borne not so much casual individuals as whole families—men, women, children and all; and for aught we care, with our present object in view, whole families may go and welcome, for in the mass they obviously leave sex-proportion as it was before. Once the stream of family emigration is cut off, the drainage into Sind and Bombay dwindles away to little. To other parts of India emigration runs in mere driblets: and even in the Panjāb, where the stream is a little stronger, it is swollen by the emigration of family groups. Emigration beyond India need not concern us at all. Even if we could come by the statistics, they would hardly tell one way or the other; here again emigration is almost wholly of a family character, except to countries outside the regular beat, like Ceylon or Malaya, where it is so small as to be negligible. The net result is that there appear to be six or seven thousand males who should, properly speaking, be added to our figures (§ 82)—to be distributed for the most part among the Paṭhān, the Sayyid, and the Makrānī. If a dearth of males in Balūchistān were in question, or if males in Balūchistān were for some strange reason more likely to evade enumeration than females, I should certainly be loth to let these male deserters escape my clutches. As it is, I prefer for the present to leave them where they are. For to me it falls to discuss an abnormal dearth of females, and I shall clearly run less risk of being suspected of overstating a case, remarkable enough as it stands, if I refrain as long as possible from calling these male absentees back to the province, and deliberately forgo a tempting opportunity of laying the colours on thicker at the outset.

Indigenous population.

Males.	Females.
1,000	845

Intense desire for male issue.

139. Now there is a curious conflict of opinion among the people themselves as to the modern drift of the proportion between the two sexes. Brāhūī gaffers are always harping on the lamentable increase of females as the world grows older, gloating over it with melancholy pride as not the least of the many signs that the next world, which is to be heralded in by a grievous famine of males, is surely nigh. Yet the tribesmen at large, unconsciously glorifying their old tribal struggles, which in reality seem usually to have been very bloodless affairs, are fond of airing the view that the relative number of females has recently gone down by leaps and bounds, simply because the males are no longer subject to the drain of war. Unfortunately we are not in a position to check either notion further, for ancient statistics there are none. But of the dearth of females in Balūchistān at the present day, even judged by the low standards of India, there is no possible question. The people themselves complacently attribute it in no small measure to their overwhelming desire for male issue, a desire which is as intense among the mothers of Balūchistān as it was among the mothers of the Jewish world, where by the by it had roots much more ancient and much more deep down in human nature than that divine hope of bearing the promised Messiah in which we were taught to believe. And without in any way posing as being of the tribesman's artless faith in the direct power of the wish to become father to the fact in this simple manner, I cannot but feel that the intensity of the desire for male issue and the universality of the belief in the inherent inferiority of the female sex are factors not to be overlooked in any discussion of sex-proportion in Balūchistān.

Fertilising customs.

140. To leave a son behind is the lifelong prayer of every man in the country. To have no children at all is of all calamities the most calamitous.

But hardly less pitiable is the plight of the man who has nothing but daughters; for a daughter (as the shrewd proverb puts it) is little better than a gift to your neighbour after all. Nevertheless the first concern of a newly wedded couple is to get a child at all cost, no matter what the sex; for, as far as I can make out, there is a very general scepticism regarding the possibility of regulating the sex of the first-born. If the various fertilising customs connected with the marriage ceremonies fail to achieve their object, folks soon look around for the cause. Should the wife peak and pine, the Brāhūīs put all the blame on the husband, and it is for him to try what drugs and charms and the like can do to set him right; and in passing I may add that actual impotency is almost everywhere regarded as ample grounds for the wife to appeal to the Elders for a dissolution of the marriage. But if the wife grows fat and well-liking, the blame for the sterility of the union rests obviously with her. Throughout the length and breadth of the land a barren wife is a very fruitful source of gain to holy men and beggars and quacks and magic-mongers of all kinds. Possibly they may content themselves with palming off some charm or amulet on her. But highly prized though these are, they do not exhaust the resources at their command. One very favourite device is to hold a staff against a wall and make the barren woman pass under it thrice; other faith-curers with more dramatic instinct vary the cure (or are they perhaps simply retaining a more archaic form of it?) by crooking one leg against the wall to make the archway. Shrines, needless to say, are a very popular resort of the barren woman. Some shrines have a greater fertilising reputation than others, and the most famous of all is perhaps Shāh Wasāwa's *kandī*,[1] a tree that grows in the Nasīrābād *tahsīl*. The legend connecting the saint with this tree is a little too broad to be repeated here, but we have the saint's own word for it that any woman who comes to the tree and embraces it in true faith, shall be the joyful mother of children. Unfortunately the tree was hacked down some little time ago by a priest out of jealousy or bigotry. The people at first threatened to wreak their vengeance on the priest for this act of sacrilege, but quieting down wrapped the trunk in a shroud and gave it decent burial. True, the roots have begun to sprout afresh; but I understand that the enthusiasm of the women has been somewhat damped. If all else fails, the last resource known to the Brāhūīs and Marī Balōch in cases of barrenness is to snip off the tip of the woman's clitoris (§178). The cure is possibly much more common than my reports seem to imply—I have also heard of a case by the by in Makrān—for this is a matter that the women keep dark from their menfolk as much as possible.

Sex diagnosed from the expectant mother's condition.

141. So intense is the universal yearning for a son that once conception becomes certain, the sex of the unborn babe arouses very lively speculation. Nature is ransacked for portents. The condition of the goodwife herself is of course full of them. The various signs are not always read in quite the same way; but the general idea that a son taxes the mother much more severely than a daughter is rarely challenged. You can read the sex in her whole demeanour: if she is weak and ailing and listless and querulous, it's surely because there's a male child in her womb slowly sapping her strength. You can read it in her face: for she can only hope to keep her plump cheeks and bonny looks during this trying time if she has nothing but a daughter to nourish. You can read it in her gait: for small's the wonder if shoulders droop and feet drag behind her when a son is bearing down upon her; (but a Jaṭṭ thinks it's a much better symptom if she unconsciously starts off with her right foot). You can read it in her figure: for a daughter humbly nestles low down and towards the left; but a son sits higher up, as befits his lordly sex, and of course on the right. You can read it in her appetite: for though a son requires more nourishment, she is so weakened by his demands and so nauseated by his lusty kicks, that she is left with small inclination for food. You can read it in her nipples: for they flush red at the joyous prospect of a son, but grow black (as a sign of mourning I suppose) if a daughter is coming to suck them.

The milk test.

142. But the milk in her breasts is perhaps more tell-tale than anything else. Among the Brāhūīs, the Jaṭṭ and the people of Makrān at any rate, there is a wide-spread belief that it varies in consistency with the sex of the babe in

[1] Prosopis Spicigera.

her womb. If the milk is thick, such strong food is obviously being stored up for a son; if it is thin, they must just resign themselves to fate. But as it is not easy to say whether milk is thick or thin by merely looking at it, a simple plan is to draw off a little from her breasts and test it in water: all is doubtless well if it sinks to the bottom; but there's sure to be a girl coming if it spreads out and dissolves. Another of their tests is to sprinkle a few drops on a stone and lay it out in the sun: and it's a sad business if the milk runs off, instead of caking on the stone. A still more favourite test is to pick a louse from her hair and plunge it into some of her milk: then if the milk is thick and strong enough to drown it, there can be no mistake about the coming of a boy. All this seems more or less rational on their premises—whether the premises themselves are founded on fact, let the man of science up and speak for himself, as a Brāhūī friend of mine is fond of saying whenever I look sceptical over any of his Brāhūī notions. But in some parts of Makrān they go about the test in a bewilderingly topsy-turvy manner. Instead of testing the anxious mother's milk, they simply take a louse off her head and pop it into some milk drawn from another woman. This time they are anything but pleased if it dies, for it is only if it struggles back to life that they can be confident of a boy. In Zāmrān they are not satisfied with the test of a single louse, but prefer to make matters trebly sure by picking three from her head.

Other forms of divination.

143. According to the Brāhūīs the Black Snake is blinded when its path is crossed by a woman great with a male child, though heaven only knows what mischief it might do were she not protected by the male life within her. I am sorry, by the by, to have to leave the identity of the Black Snake a mystery. In Turbat they use any snake killed in the house to solve the problem of the unborn's sex: they simply make the woman step over its dead body, and then they fling it aloft in the hope that it will fall on its back; for it means a daughter for certain if it falls on its belly. But there are other forms of divination by throwing things in the air in this part of Makrān; in fact it seems to be as popular here as divination by throwing orange-peel is in our nurseries. The future mother, for instance, pats some ashes from the hearth into a cake, and on its face she sets a mark which she fondly imagines resembles a skeleton, and shutting her eyes she flings it in the air with the cry "Everybody feeds on the food you cook, so speak the truth." If it falls face upwards, she is a happy woman that day. Or she takes a flat stone, marks the face of it with a circle, and throws it aloft, conjuring it by the true Faith to speak the truth, with an inward prayer that it may fall with the circle upwards. Nowhere does the expectant mother appear to be so inquisitive as in Makrān: nowhere else at any rate do there seem to be so many devices at her command. Thus she marks one of the beads on a rosary, and beginning with the marked bead she tells them over in pairs, muttering the names of all the prophets she can think of, and is highly disgusted if there is a bead left over at the end, for this is a sure sign of the coming of a girl. Or she shuts her eyes tight, and does all she can to make the tips of her middle fingers on either hand meet together across her breast.

Abortion not practised.

144. I cannot help thinking that the women must persist in their experiments, like their magpie-counting sisters in England, until the result comes out to their liking. At any rate, great though their disappointment must be when divination fails to tell in their favour, I have never heard the slightest whisper of attempts at abortion except among the Chhuṭṭa Mēngal of Samōṭri,—and among wild and hopelessly uncivilised Makrānīs of Pasnī and Kulānch. Among the former, the practice is reported to be dead: and it is not impossible that my informant has confused abortion with female-infanticide, of which the Chhuṭṭa were once accused. Among the latter, folks who have already a surfeit of daughters are supposed to attempt abortion by stuffing Akh[1] leaf fibre or else *kinnī kāṭhī*[2] wrapped in wool up the vagina, or by dosing the unfortunate woman with powdered asafœtida. Whether either treatment is really successful, I cannot say. They certainly sound more efficacious, if less ingenious, than the reputed devices of the guilty Brāhūī woman, who is supposed to cover up the possible consequences of her amours by swallowing a roasted locust of

[1] *Asclepias Gigantea.*

[2] Rhizome of the Sweet Flag or *Acorus Calamus.*

the kind found in the Akh plant, or raw pigeon dung, or the roast anus of a wolf. But except in cases of illicit intercourse, which obviously stand on a different footing, the Brāhūīs, like the people of Balūchistān generally, allow nature to run its course without let or hindrance at all stages of life. Abortion is universally looked upon as something sinful, unholy, abominable; it could hardly be otherwise among people whose earnest prayer is to have as many children, or at any rate as many sons, as possible.

145. And, unskilful though local midwifery methods may sound to a doctor's ears, the tribesmen according to their lights devote much care to the safety of mother and child during pregnancy and confinement; nor, as far as I have been able to ascertain, do they make any appreciable difference if divination has pronounced the unborn babe to be a girl. The kindliness shown by Brāhūīs, for instance, to the future mother is pleasant reading enough. After the first three months are out, she is relieved, as far as may be, of the heavy drudgery about the house. Not that she is suffered to sit idle the livelong day—this would only make it more difficult for her when her time comes ; on the contrary, she is encouraged to keep on the move, especially towards the end. In matters of diet she almost runs the risk of being killed by kindness : of every edible thing that is brought into the house she must be given a bite, for if she should catch sight of anything and her craving for it should be left unsatisfied, it would be almost certain to bring on a miscarriage ; so if, as happens often enough, she gets a craze for clay or fullers' earth, they never dare to lift a finger to stop her, in spite of a shrewd suspicion that she is injuring not only herself but the babe in her womb. After the seventh month she lives apart from her husband. Against the spirits of darkness she is shielded at every turn ; threads of blue cotton are tied round her big toes; she is not allowed to go into a dark room by herself; above all things she must not look upon a corpse. But among all our races elaborate precautions are taken to prevent miscarriage. Amulets and charms and the like are of course in great demand. In many parts of Makrān the pet talisman is a *band*—a knotted goat's hair thread to be got from any holy man—which must be hammered with a stone and thrown into running water as soon as the delivery is safely over. In Pasnī and Kulānch any amulet that is used is washed after the delivery, and the water in which it is washed is poured on to the roots of some tree. But throughout Makrān they are so afraid of the spells of some spiteful enemy that, though amulets and charms are all very well in their way, the pregnancy is kept dark as long as possible ; which leads one to wonder whether the shamefaced attempts at concealment of their honourable condition on the part of our own women have not deeper roots than false modesty or false vanity. With the same object the people of Makrān carefully gather up the combings of the woman's hair and the parings of her nails and eventually bury them in a shroud. But do what one will, accidents will of course happen, and should miscarriage occur by some unhappy chance about the third month, a Brāhūī woman will often wrap the noisome thing in antimony and swallow it whole, in the certain faith that it will quicken once more in her womb and be born in due course.

Precautions against miscarriage.

146. The birth itself seems usually a simple affair, especially among nomads ; and it is no uncommon experience for the goodman to leave his dwelling in the morning with never a suspicion of coming events, only to be greeted by an infant's cry on his return. It may, to be sure, be a very different matter, as Brāhūīs and Balōch know to their cost, if the voice of a virgin or a woman with child is allowed to strike the ear of the poor wife. So it is no small comfort that there are a sheaf of devices to help her in her distress. If you have a leaning towards charms, this Persian couplet is recommended by Brāhūīs as the very best of all :—

The birth.

I have no place to dwell in and my ass hath none.
Spouse of a farmer ! give birth, give birth to a son !

It should be written down (and the mulla is of course the proper man to do it for you) on two bits of paper ; the one should be tied to the woman's thigh, and the other placed where she can gaze upon it. Another very favourite device, especially among the Ḍombkī Balōch and the Brāhūīs, is to make her drink off some water in which any old gentleman has kindly dipped his beard. In parts of Las Bēla the husband (who by the by is very generally suspected of unkindness to his wife if her labour is troublesome) passes himself over her body, or else he washes her hands and feet in water, and makes her drink it off ; in the Kōlwah tract in Makrān he rubs her belly with his feet. If it is past her full time and there are still no signs of labour, the Brāhūīs fear she must be in for the long weary period of a mare. This would be indeed a serious business, were there not easy means of passing on the curse to the proper quarters. All that need be done is to give the woman any water that is left in the pail after a mare has swilled her fill, or to make her crawl under the belly of a mare that is in foal.

A son.

147. Even at birth the two sexes appear to affect the mother in different ways. At any rate the Paṭhāns will have it that females are so full of original sin that they are up to their mischievous pranks from the very beginning and give their poor mother far more pangs than their brothers, who of course comport themselves throughout life much more closely in accord with divine law. On all sides the birth of a son is hailed with delight. Among Brāhūīs the young mother is left for a while in the saddening belief that she has been delivered of a daughter, lest her exceeding great joy should be too much for the poor thing in her prostration. Much ado is made over the breaking of the news to the father, who generally retires to a neighbour's house during the crisis. Not only the father but the other kinsmen and close friends of the family are expected to tip those who manage to be first with the glad news. Almost everywhere shots are fired to celebrate the event. But among the Ḍōmbkī Balōch shots are only fired if the birth takes place by night ; in the day-time the glad tidings are announced by the weird cry "Mistress So-and-So has been delivered of an ass's colt !" There are one or two other quaint touches in Ḍōmbkī birth-customs : whether a son or a daughter is born to him, no Ḍōmbkī would allow embers to be removed from his hearth for full seven days ; if he is blessed with a son, a drain is dug through the wall by the side of the house-door, and it is left to run for a week. But the Makrānīs seem stranger folk still. Just as they endeavour to conceal pregnancy for as long as possible, so they make a show (and doubtless for the same reason) of keeping the birth dark for at least six days, and when at the last they announce it, they announce it (and again for the same reason) all wrong, giving out that it's a boy if it's a girl, and that it's a girl if it's a boy. Here, as elsewhere, the father is usually supposed to absent himself. In Panjgūr he betakes himself into the jungle, and though he returns briskly enough at the glad news of a boy, he is not allowed to set foot in the house itself till the fourth day. In other parts of Makrān he has to keep himself in readiness to assist in troublesome labour, and in Pasnī and Kulānch he may even be called upon to lend the midwife a helping hand at the delivery itself.

A daughter.

148. At the birth of a daughter no guns are fired. In truth this is no time for joyous sounds. A gloom falls over the household. Even the midwife has to be content with half fees ; there are no tips at all for the officious bearers of the bad tidings. Among the Brāhūīs at large the unfortunate man whose first-born is a daughter is thought to be a weaker vessel than his wife ; among the Zahrī he is beaten seven times with a shoe, though he can compound for his beating (possibly a modern refinement) by standing a feast to his neighbours. But though no rejoicings herald the arrival of a daughter into the world, there is consolation for the family in the thought that it is at any rate better off than it was before. A son, no doubt, means honour and strength to the family, and another worker to increase its wealth. But a daughter is wealth itself. For the time being, to be sure, the capital is locked up, and there is one more mouth to feed. But a girl takes a hand in the household labour at an early age, and when after a few years she is turned into money in the shape of a bride-price, they will be either woefully unbusinesslike or woefully unlucky, if they cannot show a goodly balance to their credit in the end.

Scarcely a trace of female-infanticide.

149. This by the by is the gist of the answers received on all sides, whenever we sounded the tribesmen on the existence of the practice of female-infanticide. It may possibly be thought that female-infanticide is hardly a subject on which we are likely to elicit any very trustworthy information, though there is perhaps something in these pages (which contain after all mere gleanings from our researches) to suggest that in Balūchistān we have at times a knack of getting fairly close to the intimate life of the people of the country. But our questionings

were neither direct nor clumsy : regarding the seamy side of their own customs tribesmen may well be tongue-tied ; their tongues wag freely when they are invited to dilate on the shortcomings of their neighbours, who are generally their rivals and as often as not their hereditary and exceeding bitter enemies. As it is, the only people I have any grounds for suspecting are the chiefly families in the Marī and Bugṭī Baloch, and the Chhuṭṭa, a numerically insignificant branch of the Mēngal Brāhūīs, apparently Jaṭṭ in origin. Yet even their enemies agree that female-infanticide is now dead among both Marī and Bugṭī, where it owed its existence to the custom of strict endogamy of females within the chief's family. Even among the Chhuṭṭa (who, significantly enough, do not go in for bride-price) it is said to be dead, except possibly in the case of twin daughters, who still appear to be regarded as too much of a good thing altogether. With these exceptions—female-infanticide in the past but possibly not very distant past among the Marī and Bugṭī chiefly families, female-infanticide dying if not already dead in the small Chhuṭṭa community,—and with the further possible exception of casual female-infanticide in isolated families already overburdened with female children, I have been unable to trace its existence in Balūchistān ; and all whom I have consulted, tribesmen and experienced officials alike, agree with me in believing it to be practically non-existent in the country.

Unlucky children possibly survivals of ancient infanticide.

150. It is possible that in the unlucky children of to-day—children in whom some physical abnormality is eyed as the harbinger of grievous ill-luck to the household—there are preserved traces of bye-gone infanticide in the dark ages of some far distant past, when the ill-luck seemed so imminent and so deadly that the only remedy was death. Of such ill-starred children Balūchistān has plenty and to spare. First—at any rate most common of the bunch—is the girl that grinds her teeth in her sleep, who is so universally regarded as a danger to the house that the list of the various local cures seems interminable : hanging a blue bead or a sheep's vein to her ear, tying a jay's feather or a broken harp-string round her neck, slapping her in her sleep, striking her on the teeth with a coin (but it must have the creed of the true Faith written on it), pouring powdered charcoal or sand or ashes into her mouth, branding her on her big toe—and many another crafty device. Others in the throng are the Brāhūī girl with the whorl of her hair at all forward on her head, and the Brāhūī child or the Makrānī child of Pasnī and Kulānch born with two front teeth, and the Brāhūī child that cuts its upper teeth before the lower. A truly dread calamity is this last, one that fills the mother with an overwhelming terror that she cannot explain. And it is only putting the difficulty further back if we hazard the guess (and no one would be more horrified at the idea than a modern Brāhūī) that it is a faint echo of the agonising terror of the Brāhūī mother in the long-forgotten past, when her child was torn from her arms and done to death to save the family from the awful consequences of those upper teeth, which to this day are the signal for infanticide in many East African tribes. I have not come across any suggested explanation of this cruel but wide-spread superstition. Even the ingenious author of *The Golden Bough* dismisses the subject for once without further comment, only mentioning it in connection with certain customs which seem rooted too deep down in the blackness of the savage mind for the modern mind to probe[1]. But the answer to the riddle lies perhaps on the surface after all. Is it not simply but another instance of the portentous character of the abnormal ? Though the authorities are at sixes and sevens regarding the details of dentition, one and all seem agreed that the lower teeth in the normal child come first throughout. And as most of the authorities hedge their limited statistics with the confession of ignorance that dentition seems to vary with race and climate and environment, it would not be surprising if more comprehensive enquiries revealed the fact that the premature cutting of the upper teeth is least common, in other words most abnormal, among those peoples and in those countries where it is regarded as most unlucky. But though the abnormal is nearly always portentous, it seems sometimes almost a toss-up whether it will be read to prophesy fair things or foul. Take twins, for instance. Nearly all our races regard them as lucky, no matter what their sex, though no amount of good luck that a couple of girls at a birth may bring can be expected to reconcile folks wholly to their disappointment at missing a boy. Most Paṭhāns look upon twins

[1] J. G. Frazer's *Totemism and Exogamy*, Vol. IV, p. 194.

as emblems of God's good-will, and the Zarkūn playfully cast lots to decide which breast each should have for its very own. But among the Chhuṭṭa a couple of girls at a birth is regarded as so unlucky that they are still suspected of putting them out of the way (§149). And though in Pasnī and Kulānch it is the best of good omens if one of the twins is born head-foremost with a caul over its face and the other is born sucking its right thumb, for both to be born otherwise than head-foremost is the worst of bad omens, even apparently though both are males and a caul cover the faces of both. Which of the two presentations is the normal and which the abnormal, I must leave to the doctors to decide. One curious thing about such symptoms of ill-luck is that the males sometimes know little or nothing about them. I remember cases when they have dismissed the matter as a thing of the past or else as something of which they have dimly heard in some other tribe, only to return with scared faces a few days later to tell me of the terror they had spread among the female members of their household by mooting the idea casually regarding their own offspring. So true is it that the women have longer memories than the men, that they are not only the mothers of our children but the custodians of ancient custom from one generation to another.

Turning the womb.

151. Now though the people at large feel themselves helpless to regulate the sex of the first-born, they have several devices to avoid the birth of a second daughter. Thus among the Brāhūīs the midwife loses no time in making the young mother of a new-born daughter gulp down a hot broth prepared from a fresh-killed chicken, heavily spiced with cinnamon, pepper and the like; for this will turn the womb, as the expression is, and prepare it for the conception of a son. To quote my Brāhūī informant: "If nothing be done, she will bear daughter after daughter; and if there be no change at the third, seven daughters will be the lot of the unhappy father. This is what the midwives say, and surely they should know; but how far a man of science may believe them, let the man of science up and say for himself." The corresponding remedy among Paṭhāns is for the young mother to swallow something sour (pickles, for instance, or curdled milk) immediately after the delivery of a daughter: this should have the desired effect, though to be on the safe side she should really swallow the testicles of a cock. Not but what some folks think it enough to call their girl Bula-Nista, No More—of the Feminine Gender. The Makrānīs of Pasnī and Kulānch go one further, and pride themselves on being able to regulate the sex absolutely after the first delivery, by simply dieting the young mother forthwith with either a cock or a hen according as a son or a daughter is required, and stuffing a pellet of opium three days later as far up the vagina as possible.

The statistics.

152. Now and then, to be sure, all devices are in vain, and many a father pulls a rueful face over the superfluity of girls that has fallen to his lot. I have even heard of a plague of daughters in a whole community. A few years ago a famous band of Shīrānī outlaws made overtures to be allowed to leave their sanctuary in Afghānistān and return in a body to their old country. Theirs was a piteous plight, they said: from the day they had left their native soil, the birth-rate among them had gone from bad to worse, and, more alarming still, their womenfolk had lost all power of bearing them sons. Whether they had any theory to account for the calamity, I never heard; that they had the decency to read in it divine displeasure at their acts of outlawry, I very much doubt:—the Shīrānī remains a Shīrānī still. But this, to be sure, is a case that it would be hard to parallel. The indigenous peoples of Balūchistān as a body are quite content with what they doubtless regard as the direct results of their admirable efforts at the regulation of sex. And well they may be. For in the mass there are only 845 female encumbrances to every 1,000 males among them. To those who are accustomed to the Western European standard of 1,038 females, even to those who have become hardened to the humbler Indian standard of 953 or thereabouts, the Balūchistān figure may seem an impossible one. And yet, so far from being an understatement of the female element in the indigenous population, it undoubtedly errs on the other side, for the surplus of males among the emigrants from the country (§82) is incomparably greater than any leakage of females that could possibly have occurred in the enumeration.

Females to 1,000 males.

(Indigenous only.)

Balūchistān	**845**
Districts	836
States	852

153. The disturbing influence of emigration on sex-proportion, however, is a factor in the problem which for the present it is convenient to ignore. As for an appreciable leakage of females in our returns, I myself feel not the slightest uneasiness. When the scheme of operations was hatching out, my uneasiness, I confess, was great. But the various safeguards we finally decided to adopt were thorough-going enough to allow me to embark on the census with a comforting amount of assurance. While the active operations were in progress, we had plenty of opportunities of testing our safeguards, and every apparent reason to be well satisfied with the result. And looking dispassionately at the coldblooded statistics, I can detect nothing in them to shake my confidence. There were two possible dangers that stared us in the face throughout our operations: the intense and almost universal strain of sexual jealousy among the tribesmen to be enumerated, and a casual strain of inefficiency among those who were to enumerate them. Hence my first instinct in scrutinising the statistics was to play the sceptic and use one or other of these dangers to put them to the test. Had there been any leakage of females, it would clearly reveal itself, I thought, where sexual jealousy is known to be strong or the calibre of the enumerators was suspected of being weak. Thus, with an eye on the character of the tribesmen, a sceptic would confidently anticipate a much lower female proportion among Paṭhāns at large than in the Dumaṛ section, whose sexual laxity is a crying scandal (§175). Yet what are the facts? The Dumaṛ proportion does not exceed 817, and falls short of the proportion among their fellow Paṭhāns by 24. Or the sceptic might turn to the scum of the land, and look for consolatory proof of the unreality of the low proportion among the tribesmen in an extravagantly high proportion among the Jat, that degenerate race that stoops to the very prostitution of its women (§179). And he would find to his disappointment that, so far from the proportion of females among the Jat being unusually high, it is actually as low as 803. Again, with an eye on the possibility of treachery in the ranks of the enumerators, our sceptic might pardonably expect to see tell-tale signs that there had been far less leakage in the districts, where the existence of a trained administrative staff would probably inspire even him with a fair degree of confidence in the efficacy of our methods, than in the states, where at the outset (though not in the end) there was some little misgiving on this score among ourselves. And again he would be disappointed. He would find the highest proportion just where he hoped to find the lowest: in the states the proportion is 852; it is 16 lower in the districts. And in despair the hardened sceptic would perhaps turn to the figures for the last census, seeking here at any rate the wherewithal to feed his cynical forebodings. Unfortunately for him, and unfortunately for me, those figures were necessarily marred by guess-work in too many parts of the country to serve any very useful purpose. Yet, as I scan the comparative statistics where comparison is at all justifiable, one or two notable points of agreement catch my eye. In the indigenous population of what is now the three districts of Sibī, Zhōb and Lōṛalai, the female proportion was 839 in 1901; it is 837 to-day. A curious rise from 782 to 803 in the Marī-Bugṭī country came to me at first as a bit of a shock, for here also there was little to choose between the standards of enumeration adopted at this census and the last. But this is one of those comforting exceptions that in reality help to prove the rule. The statistics in 1901 were artificially adjusted by swamping the tribal country with hosts of tribesmen who had been counted elsewhere, with the result that the female proportion in the tribal country was lowered to very nearly the same level as the female proportion among the tribesmen. At this late stage the only thing to do is to ignore the local figures altogether and to content ourselves with comparing the figures of the tribes. At the present census the female proportion works out to 778 among the Marī and Bugṭī both. This is a low figure with a vengeance—much too low to be true, one might almost think. Yet though the proportion in 1901 worked out to 790 among the Bugṭī, it was actually as low as 773 among the Marī, and as low as 780 in both put together. Here, at any rate, the census of 1901 has proved a friend in need: it has come to our rescue at the very point where scepticism threatened to deliver its shrewdest attack.

Their reliability.

154. The very small quota of females among the Marī and Bugṭī prepared me for a fairly wide range of sex-proportion in the country at large. But on

Local variation.

marshalling the several divisions of Balūchistān in the order of their sex-proportions — the Bōlān population is too pigmy to take into account — I was somewhat surprised at the extent of the range. The order itself is bewildering enough. Glancing first at the top, I was tempted to conclude that the more backward and deserted a locality, the higher the proportion of females in it. Glancing at the bottom, I was tempted to conclude the exact opposite. And in the end, as I glance at the list as a whole, I am almost tempted to conclude that all conclusions are vain. There are incongruities everywhere. The Kachhī, I suppose, is less characteristic of Balūchistān than any other division in it; yet its female proportion is nearest the average. It is a flat, low-lying plain; yet in sex-proportion it takes its stand by the side of the mountainous district of Quetta and comes almost midway between the two adjacent and mountainous districts of Zhōb and Lōṛalai. Physically and racially Zhōb and Lōṛalai — or, better example still, Chāgai and Khārān — are about as much alike as any two parts of the province; yet they are widely severed in the order of sex-proportion. The list has an embarrassing air of impartiality about it: it seems to baffle our every attempt to trace in it any certain correlation between altitude or rainfall or density or environment and a high or a low rate of females. There is hardly a single generalisation to which it proffers support, that it is not equally ready to assail. And the only safe but withal unsatisfying conclusion appears to be this — that in Balūchistān, whatever the reason, conditions are generally more unfavourable to female birth or female life in the north-east than in the south-west; and that amid the multitudinous factors that enter into the mysterious struggle for the mastery between the two sexes, locality has its appointed part to play.

Makrān	915
Las Bēla	880
Khārān	869
Dōmbkī-Kahērī	865
Lōṛalai	864
Quetta Pishīn	853
Kachhī	850
Zhōb	824
Sibi administered	823
Sarāwān	821
Chāgai	820
Marī Bugṭī	803
Jhalawān	802

Racial variation.

155. So on we pass to glean what enlightenment we can from the racial characteristics of the people. Again I give the main statistics in the margin; and again I marshal them in the order of the relative number of females. And again there is an amazing range of variation in the sex-proportion. But this time there is no disputing the validity of the title to the first place, at any rate among the Musalmāns. For while the Sayyids condescend to take the daughters of other races to wife, they are much too high and mighty to give their own in exchange. Nowhere else, I fancy, do matrimonial customs upset the balance to such a degree; but they are obviously weights in the scale that must be taken into account throughout. The high female proportion among the peoples lumped up as Miscellaneous is largely due to a plethora of females among the Ghulām, who form a fourth of their number. As the proportion among the Ghulāmazād (who are simply Ghulām that have risen to the status of freedmen) is only 828, race has clearly precious little to do with the Ghulām proportion of 1,121; it is merely a reminder that a female Ghulām has much less opportunity, and indeed much less temptation, to alter her status than her brother. The Lāsī proportion is well above the average, yet it falls short of the proportion in the Lāsī country by 10. The last four places on the list are occupied, significantly enough, by the four races of tribesmen who interest us most. The Paṭhāns with 841 and the Balōch with 840 stand almost neck to neck. The Jaṭṭ with 837 follow hard on their heels, leaving the Brāhūīs a long way behind with 802. But I must not forget the domiciled Hindus and Sikhs, whom I have put in a class by themselves. Among the Hindus the female proportion is 845, identically the same as the general proportion among the indigenous Musalmāns. Among the Sikhs it stands at the extraordinarily high figure of 948, a figure that puts even the Sayyids to shame. But the domiciled Sikhs are less than 3,000 strong, and the abnormality of their female proportion is a danger-signal that should bring us to a dead-stop: we are no longer within the region of large numbers where we can safely trust ourselves to averages.

Sayyid	935
Miscellaneous	933
Lāsī	870
Paṭhān	841
Balōch	840
Jaṭṭ	837
Brāhūī	802
Sikh	948
Hindu	845

Internal variation among the Brāhūīs.

156. And though I am alive to the perils of embarking on any conclusions once outside the deep waters of large numbers, I will venture a little closer to

the shoals in the case of our three most important races. And first let me turn to the race that has the smallest share of females. Despite much variation in the Brāhūī tribes, there is curiously little variation in the main divisions of the Brāhūī race. Somewhat to my surprise, the Brāhūī nucleus tops the list with 812; then come the Sarāwān tribesmen with 809; the Jhalawān tribesmen and the small miscellaneous group are bracketted last with 797.

Brāhūīs	[illegible]
Nucleus	812
Sarāwān	809
Jhalawān	797
Miscellaneous	797

In the Jhalawān country itself the proportion among the Jhalawān tribesmen dwindles to 792 — a figure low enough to arouse the worst suspicions in the mind of the sceptic. But his suspicions will be lulled, I fancy, on finding that there is not a whit of difference in the proportion among the 10,000 odd Jhalawāns enumerated in Sarāwān. Quaintly enough, though the general Brāhūī proportion in Jhalawān is only 795, the proportion among the Sarāwān tribesmen in Jhalawān is 36 higher than in their own Sarāwān country; but there are so few Sarāwāns in Jhalawān that this is probably a mere freak begotten of inadequate numbers. And a notable gallery of freaks awaits anybody who has the curiosity to turn to the sex-proportions in the several tribes. These freaks have a morbid fascination of their own, but it is hardly less interesting and it is certainly much more edifying to revert to the Brāhūī race as a whole, and observe the significant way in which its proportion of females tends to go up in sympathy with the general female proportion in localities where Brāhūīs are found in any numbers. In Quetta and Chāgai, it is true, the proportion among the Brāhūī inhabitants is actually a trifle lower than the Brāhūī average. It is very different in the three tracts where females are most abundant. In Makrān the Brāhūī proportion rises to 817; in Las Bēla to 840; in Khārān to 843; in none of the three, I need hardly say, does it touch the local average. This, then, is the general conclusion: the proportion of females among Brāhūīs is extremely low, but tends to rise above the racial average in tracts outside the Brāhūī country proper where the local proportion is high.

And among the Balōch.

157. The influence of locality seems to stare us in the face when we turn to the Balōch. For measured in terms of sex, there is a wide gulf fixed between the essentially territorial divisions of the race that we have adopted. The female proportion among the Eastern Balōch is 824: were we to eliminate the Khetrān with their superabundance of women—as we apparently ought, for it is extremely doubtful whether they are Balōch at all (§264)—it would drop as low as 811.

Balōch	[illegible]
Eastern	824
Western	871

Among the Western Balōch it stands at the very respectable figure of 871. And as we mark the ups and downs of the Balōch proportion in the various parts of Balūchistān, we seem justified in enunciating this general rule: sex-proportion among the Balōch is a trifle lower than the average for Balūchistān, and tends to rise or fall above or below its own normal in sympathy with the proportion in the general population of the particular locality in which they live. The rule obviously holds good in seven out of the eleven tracts where the Balōch are to be found in reasonably large numbers—in Makrān, Las Bēla, Khārān, Sarāwān, Kachhī, and the Ḍōmbkī-Kahērī and Marī-Bugṭī countries. In all these tracts, whether the Balōch proportion is higher than the Balōch normal or not, it falls short of the proportion of the locality. And the only exceptions to the rule are Lōṛalai, which is no exception at all, for the so-called Balōch of Lōṛalai are the Khetrān; Chāgai, where the Balōch divide nearly the whole of the population with the Brāhūīs, who of course bring the proportion down; and Sibī, where, for some obscure reason, the Balōch proportion overtops the local proportion by 7.

And among the Paṭhāns.

158. We are much less likely to be able to trace the influence of locality in the case of the Paṭhāns, for unlike the Brāhūīs and Balōch who are dissipated abroad in many and various parts of the province, the Paṭhāns are massed in a more or less homogeneous block of country covered by the four districts of Zhōb, Lōṛalai, Quetta-Pishīn and Sibī; and to make matters worse, they bulk so large in the indigenous population of three of these districts as to exercise a dominant force on the local proportion of females. Yet the influence of locality

	All Paṭhāns.	Kākaṛ.	Tarīn.	Panī.
Balūchistān	841	819	863	881
Lōṛalai	860	836	904	880
Quetta-Pishīn	841	823	859	...
Zhōb	827	816	...	836
Sibī	851	789	859	956

seems to peep out from the figures in the margin, notably from the curiously constant superiority of Lōṛalai over Quetta, and of Quetta over Zhōb; the Sibi figures, I confess, seem hopelessly capricious. Of all the statistics, those for Lōṛalai and Zhōb interest me most. Where Lōṛalai can boast a female proportion of 860 among Paṭhāns at large, with 836 among the Kākaṛ and 880 among the Paṇī, Zhōb comes limping behind with 827, 816 and 836. Notwithstanding the strong family likeness that runs through the physical conditions of the two districts, it certainly seems as if these variations were in some degree the results of an influence, subtle though potent, exercised directly or indirectly by locality. And when we turn the table sideways and focus our eyes on the three main branches of the race, the Kākaṛ and the Paṇī and the Tarīn, and watch them maintaining their relative order in sex-proportion amid the ups and downs of the figures for Lōṛalai and Quetta and Zhōb, it is hard not to feel that we are at the same time in the presence of some sort of tribal or racial influence. The Sibī figures are frankly beyond me, unless an explanation for their vagaries is to be found in the alacrity with which the enterprising Paṇī male wanders abroad, or in his readiness to indent on the Kākaṛ for his wives—and anybody can get a Kākaṛ girl for the asking (§ 169)—while disdaining to give the Kākaṛ any daughters of his own in return.

Effect of nomadism. 159. But to say that there seems something in the locality, something in the tribe or race, that works for a rise or fall in the female population, is a very different thing from saying that there is something in the air of a country, something in the blood which runs through the tribe or race, that makes it easier for a man of Balūchistān to breed more sons if he lives in one part of the province, or happens to belong to this tribe or that. Even if we had any warrant to indulge in such wide conclusions, we should have hardly reached the first stage on our journey. Sex-proportion is a tangled yarn which cannot be undone by the breaking of a couple of strands in this simple fashion. Even granted that a man of such and such a tribe, living in such and such a locality, actually begets more sons than falls to the lot of ordinary mortals in Balūchistān, there may still be something in the life of his tribe or in the life of his locality that will soon readjust the balance and humble his pride. And infinitely complex though the problem is, I can confidently point to one unmistakable factor of this character. In scanning our statistics of nomadism (§71), nothing struck me more forcibly than the way in which the proportion of females gradually rises as the people themselves rise from wholesale nomadism to a life that is wholly settled through a life that is half-way between. And no one, I think, who takes the trouble to glance aside at the margin, will feel disposed to dispute my statement.

	Nomad.	Semi-nomad.	Settled.
Paṭhān .	828	862	878
Balōch .	818	839	864
Brāhūī .	798	815	831

The upward movement is refreshingly constant in the three main races; and in the light of what I have already written of the influence of race, it is not uninteresting to note how the Paṭhān maintains his superiority in female numbers over the Balōch, and the Balōch his superiority over the Brāhūī, in all the changing walks of life. To the general rule that females are more abundant among those that are settled and more scarce among those that are nomad, than among those who are now the one and now the other, exceptions are of course to be found in the several tribes, especially where the tribal strength is inconsiderable, or unevenly dissipated under the three heads. But the tendency is at once too marked and too regular, alike in the country at large and throughout its dominant races, to be brushed aside as an idle curiosity in coincidences. And one reason for it lies, I suppose, in the somewhat paradoxical antagonism that exists between nomadism and emigration in the modern sense of the word. As far as sex-proportion goes, the antagonism is complete. Whereas nomadism lures whole families from the province and leaves sex-proportion where it was, emigration lures the males from the settled families and alters sex-proportion very considerably. Not that this can be the sole explanation, or the female proportion would remain fairly constant among the Brāhūīs, who, even when they reach the stage of settled life, are little affected by the emigration of individual males. There is, I fancy, a still more potent factor at work. It is possible (if scarcely probable) that nomadism in Balūchistān showers its favours or curses on boys and girls with an impartial hand. But no one who has seen the woman of Balūchistān trudge heavily burdened along the road with her lord and master stepping briskly ahead, or has watched her wearily pitch the tent while he looks on with a critical eye, can doubt that nomadism tells far more hardly on the women than it does on the men.

160. Thus in the simple fact that nomadism, from which many a family in Balūchistān has still to emerge (§ 71), is careless of the female life, we have some sort of explanation ready to hand for our notable shortage of females. But whether one of the penalties of quitting life in the open for life under a roof is a growing incapacity to breed a proper quota of boys, is an interesting question on which discretion bids me keep my insubstantial opinion to myself: I unfortunately did not think of putting myself the question until it was too late. To the wider question whether the paucity of females in Balūchistān is in any way due to a paucity of females at birth, our birth statistics (§ 67) supply me with an answer as remarkable as it is decided. If I may generalise from the number of births we recorded (and 38,912 seems a fair round sum), and if I am right in believing the statistics to be untainted by inaccuracy (and even tribesmen have no excuse and little scope for romancing on such a theme with their neighbours for an audience) — then, if so much be granted, there are but 799 daughters born to the indigenous peoples of Balūchistān for every 1,000 sons. Pitted against the Western European birth-proportion of 948, this can hardly be called a paucity of females: it is a veritable famine. So remarkable is the figure that it might well be left to stand by itself in glorious isolation. But pointed questions as to the possible influence of race and locality on sex-proportion at birth press themselves so insistently upon me, that I have placed a few other statistics beside it in the margin, statistics primarily racial, yet in the subdivision of the Balōch into Eastern and Western automatically illustrative of the influence of locality at the same time. If the Western Balōch are left out of account, no very great deviation from the normal is displayed by the races, among whom the Brāhūīs, curiously enough, come out top. And the general conclusion, I take it, is that blood or race has comparatively little to do with the sex-proportion at birth among the peoples of Balūchistān—a conclusion the reverse of unwelcome to one who has some inkling of the heterogeneous character of our so-called races, and who knows how the Brāhūīs, for instance, have gone recruiting among the Paṭhāns and the Balōch and the Jaṭṭ and the Persians and into other less reputable quarters. A much more potent influence seems to be exercised by locality. Not only does it proclaim itself in the enormous difference in sex-proportion between the Eastern and the Western Balōch, we seem to trace it in the variations among the districts, notably in the wide range between the two Paṭhān districts of Zhōb and Lōralai, where Lōralai beats Zhōb by almost a hundred. As Makrān can boast the triple distinction of having the highest birth-rate generally, the highest female birth-rate (for we may ignore Bōlān), and the highest proportion of females in the living population, one is tempted to seek a causal correlation in Balūchistān between the blessing of large families, the curse of daughters, and a plague of females in the living population. But there are statistics in plenty to warn us off any hasty generalisations in the matter. Thus, though Paṭhāns are much more prolific than Brāhūīs, they seem much more lucky in begetting sons for all that; and though fecundity is above the average in the Marī-Bugṭī country, it is here that the female proportion in the living population almost reaches its lowest ebb.

Sex-proportion at birth.

Sex-proportion at birth.

Balūchistān	799
Western Balōch	902
Brāhūī	815
Paṭhān	797
Eastern Balōch	787

Emigration.

161. The task before me has undergone a wondrous change indeed. I set out to justify our census results in the face of a paucity of females in the living population. I have now to justify the number of females enumerated at the census in the face of a famine of females at birth. Well might we wonder how a birth-proportion of 799 could convert itself into a proportion of 845 in the living population, had not Western European statistics already made us familiar with the marvellous rapidity with which females recover from the disadvantage in numbers which handicaps them at birth. Indeed, if we could argue blindly from Western European females with their proportions of 948 at birth and 1,038 in the living population, it would follow that the Balūchistān proportion of 799 at birth should eventually convert itself into a proportion of

875 in the living population. There is, however, too lively a difference in the factors that come to the assistance of the female sex in the two cases, for us to allow ourselves to be cajoled by the sweet simplicity of the Rule of Three. In both cases, I do not doubt, emigration is the factor that plays the most important part. But the very nomadism of our peoples is a sign that they have still to reach that stage in evolution where emigration in the European sense of the word becomes really active. Nomadism, or the emigration of families, leaves sex-proportion untouched : it is the more highly developed emigration of individuals that disturbs the balance. The volume of this emigration of individuals from Balūchistān has already been gauged, very roughly I admit, at 6,674 males (§82). Were we to restore these 6,674 truants to the bosom of their families, the sex-proportion among the indigenous peoples would drop from 845 to 832. Our calculation, no doubt, wants a little rounding off, but it would apparently call for more mathematics than I have forgotten to avoid arguing in a circle, and I will let it stand at that—832 seems about as near as we are likely to get to the adjustment of sex-proportion in the province. It is a pity that we cannot adjust the figures for the races and the districts in a similar manner ; but in furnishing the numbers of the so-called emigrants from Balūchistān, other provinces left us without a clue to their race and, far more often than not, without a clue to their district (§80). Only in the case of the Brāhūīs are we at all on certain ground ; and in the discovery that the Brāhūī sex-proportion was 809 among those censused in Sind against 802 in Balūchistān, we stumble upon a pretty proof that a Brāhūī, wanderer though he is, is not overfond of emigrating by himself. But so much our local knowledge could tell us before. Elsewhere local knowledge is too uncertain to be of much help. The utmost we can safely say is this—that if we were in a position to make the necessary adjustments, it is chiefly among the Sayyids and the Paṭhāns and the Balōch of Makrān that we should have to make them, and that the result would be an appreciable lowering of their sex-proportions.

Variation by age. 162. In the steady rise of the proportion of Western European females from birth upwards, emigration is clearly not the only factor—though in the prime of life it is certainly the most potent factor—that comes into play. Yet another is unmistakably the European female's superior tenacity on life, both at the outset and towards the decline. When we return to the birth statistics of Balūchistān and compare sex-proportion among the young generation whose fathers are still alive, the result is an extraordinary reversal of what European statistics would lead us to expect. So far from rapidly overhauling the males, the females, both in Balūchistān at large and among the Brāhūīs and the Paṭhāns and the two branches of the Balōch, fall further back in the race. To those who are convinced that rules which hold good in Europe must necessarily hold good the wide world over, the only explanation would lie in some violent and artificial disturbance of nature, such as female infanticide or the deliberate neglect of female children. Of female infanticide I have been unable to find any real trace (§ 149). As for neglect of female children, the only sign of it seems to lie in the extra care and devotion which the doting mother lavishes on her sons, and that her favouritism is marked enough to exercise any great influence on the sex-proportion, I very much doubt. A far more disturbing factor, I fancy, is to be found in nomadism, which probably bears harder on the females even in childhood, and never more so than at the critical period of puberty, which may well be doubly critical amid the discomforts of a gypsy life. The influence of this factor is very possibly accountable for the marked drop among the non-adult Brāhūīs. But it is hardly profitable to waste much time over variation in sex-proportion on this or that side of puberty, not merely because the dividing-line is uncertain and variable and is usually crossed by the girls at a much earlier age than by the boys (§ 135), but because it is almost entirely among the adults that the drain of emigration comes into play. The exceptions to the general rule that individual emigrants are drawn from males who have already reached manhood, are so few that we

Birth statistics.

	At birth.	Among survivals.
Balūchistān	799	778
Western Balōch	902	830
Brāhūī	815	775
Paṭhān	797	795
Eastern Balōch	787	771

Census statistics.

	Non-adult.	Adult.
Balūchistān	792	879
Western Balōch	804	916
Brāhūī	748	837
Paṭhān	796	873
Eastern Balōch	780	853

may safely add the entire bulk of the surplus emigration to swell the figures of the male adults. This done, the female proportion in Balūchistān would run from 799 at birth, and 792 among the non-adults, to 856 among the adults. Even so, the females still gain perceptibly on the males in the latter half of life. And yet I am doubtful whether much of the apparent sprint towards the end is not largely an optical illusion arising from the fact that there are relatively more females to enter upon the second lap in the race, so unevenly does the dividing-line operate in the case of the two sexes. At any rate, it is certainly my impression and the impression of all whom I have consulted, that so far from the women of Balūchistān gaining lost ground as the years roll on, they usually age more rapidly and die off earlier in life than the males.

Sex-proportion possibly dependent on ease of parturition.

163. This impression, it is true, runs counter to the well-established experience of the female's superior tenacity on life in Western Europe. But as European experience is already stultified in Balūchistān both by the amazingly low proportion of females at birth, and also by the drop in the proportion of girls among the surviving children, it seems high time to disabuse ourselves of the idea that European rules of life necessarily hold good from pole to pole. What the causes are that bring about the extraordinary disparity between the sexes at birth, I hardly venture to suggest. Of the influence of race, it is impossible to speak with confidence in view of the motley elements that go to the making of our races; yet I am certainly not prepared to deny its existence. Much more clearly do our statistics seem to point to the presence of locality among the multitudinous influences that work — sometimes maybe directly sometimes indirectly, often at cross-purposes, and always in an infinitely complex manner — for the mysterious determination of sex. In any attempt to analyse the inner nature of those influences we seem to be mocked by our statistics: no sooner do they prompt us to set up one theory, than they supply us with the handiest weapon to overthrow it. They certainly bid us beware of pressing them too far; for though our birth statistics are all very well in the mass, they become dangerous playthings as soon as we split them up among the several races. Of the making of theories regarding the determination of sex, there is no end. Theorising is veritably in the air. Who indeed may escape the infection? Yet though I myself would fain unburden myself of a theory, I should have to thumb over many a weary tome before I could safely claim it as my own. Nothing in the voluminous literature that has been written round the subject of sex has impressed me more than the great disparity in sex-proportion between still-births and births that are safely brought to a happy issue. Thus, while the female proportion among living births in Belgium is as high as 955, the proportion among still-births is (or was when the statistics were collected) as low as 735. The explanation, of course, lies chiefly in the larger body or rather the larger head of the male that makes him much more chary of adventuring into the world than his smaller-headed sisters who have a far less perilous journey before them—a fact that helped to inspire Galton with his famous saying that the physical proportions of a race are largely dependent on the size of the female pelvis. Whether the female pelvis is unusually large or the infant's head unusually small in Balūchistān, I cannot say. But that parturition is much more easy and expeditious in Balūchistān than it is in Europe, there can hardly be any question. If this be true, it must needs follow that still-births are far more rare. And if this in turn be true, it is surely folly to expect the peoples of Balūchistān to rest content with the same relative number of males as are born to the peoples of Europe. It is upon the vaunted civilisation of the West that the full force of the primeval curse appears to have fallen: and to that curse is added, it would seem, this further curse, that a lower number of males are safely brought to the birth. In these simple facts, I suggest, lurks part, at any rate, of the explanation for the much-debated disparity in sex between Europe and the races of the East. And adapting Galton's dictum to my own purposes, I would sum up my theory in a nutshell: the sex-proportion of a race is largely dependent on the ease of parturition

Conclusion.

164. I do not claim that rarity of still-births is the only factor in the problem, but it seems a factor that in Balūchistān is much more certainly operative than any of the thousand and one theories that have been advanced on the determination of sex elsewhere—theories that seem to multiply in pairs

year by year, for hardly is a theory started to fit one set of facts than its contrary is started to prove another. And one and all they seem to remain mere theories still. With all our science we have not pierced much deeper into the mystery of sex than the Paṭhān who calls the last of a succession of daughters Bula-Nista, No More—of the Feminine Gender; or the Brāhūī midwife who stuffs the unfortunate mother of a new-born daughter with hotly spiced chicken-broth, to ensure that when next she is brought to bed, it shall be for a son; or the Brāhūī shepherds who never wash their heads during the lambing season for fear the ewes should suffer over much in their birth-pangs and bring forth nothing but male young. Perhaps the true philosophy after all is that of the Balōchī lullaby, in which the young mother for all her pride in her infant daughter cannot bide her exceeding great longings for a son:—

Sons and colts are in God's hand—
God's to keep and God's to send.
Were they goods on a market-stall,
Princes would buy one and all,
Beggars would get none at all.
Lulla, lulla, lullaby,
Lulla, Moonface, lullaby.

At any rate, if this has less rhyme, it has certainly more reason than Herrick's whimsy:—

Who to the North, or South, doth set
His bed, male children shall beget.

SUBSIDIARY TABLES.

XVI.—Sex Variation by Locality.

(*Indigenous population only.*)

Locality.	VITAL STATISTICS.			CENSUS STATISTICS.		
	Number of births recorded.	FEMALES TO 1,000 MALES AMONG.		FEMALES TO 1,000 MALES.		
		Births.	Survivals.	Non-adult.	Adult.	All.
BALŪCHISTĀN	***38,912***	***799***	***778***	***792***	***879***	***845***
Districts	**24,948**	**796**	**798**	**799**	**861**	**836**
Quetta-Pishīn	4,273	792	764	792	900	853
Lōṛalai	6,927	839	824	847	875	864
Zhōb	4,543	740	764	774	858	824
Bōlān	654	1,083	1,115	1,065	570	690
Chāgai	1,393	816	807	836	809	820
Sibī	4,900	796	844	784	847	823
Marī-Bugṭī	2,258	711	711	789	813	803
States	**13,964**	**805**	**746**	**785**	**894**	**852**
Kalāt	12,819	816	756	773	894	848
Sarāwān	*1,561*	*839*	*810*	*776*	*847*	*821*
Jhalawān	*842*	*799*	*759*	*711*	*861*	*802*
Kachhī	*4,158*	*718*	*677*	*772*	*894*	*850*
Ḍōmbkī-Kahērī	*1,606*	*817*	*791*	*842*	*878*	*865*
Makrān	*4,110*	*929*	*816*	*817*	*979*	*915*
Khārān	*547*	*765*	*709*	*812*	*912*	*869*
Las Bēla	1,145	696	656	858	893	880

XVII.—Sex Variation by Race.

(Indigenous population only.)

Race.	Vital Statistics.			Census Statistics.		
	Number of births recorded.	Females to 1,000 males among		Females to 1,000 males.		
		Births.	Survival.	Non-adult.	Adult.	All.
MUSALMAN	***37,232***	***797***	***772***	***791***	***880***	***845***
Balōch	**10,536**	**827**	**790**	**789**	**874**	**840**
Eastern	6,815	787	771	780	853	824
Western	3,721	902	830	804	916	871
Brāhūi	**4,270**	**815**	**775**	**748**	**837**	**802**
Original nucleus	369	757	692	752	850	812
Sarāwān	2,070	821	803	774	830	809
Jhalawān	1,684	840	775	732	840	797
Miscellaneous	147	633	600	791	802	797
Paṭhān	**13,549**	**797**	**795**	**796**	**873**	**841**
Kākaṛ	7,904	807	816	785	843	819
Paṇi	2,699	754	756	810	931	881
Tarīn	1,399	803	697	818	898	863
Others	1,547	818	877	796	915	866
Lāsi	**486**	**687**	**604**	**843**	**886**	**870**
Jaṭṭ	**4,246**	**716**	**669**	**792**	**863**	**837**
Sayyid	**2,330**	**792**	**806**	**816**	**1021**	**935**
Miscellaneous	**1,815**	**819**	**810**	**850**	**982**	**933**
HINDU	***1,680***	***858***	***947***	***855***	***863***	***860***
Hindu	**1,680**	**858**	**947**	**847**	**844**	**845**
Sikh	...	...	...	**899**	**971**	**948**

XVIII.—Sex Variation by Nomadism.

(Tribal Census only.)

Race and tribe	Percentage of population that is			Females to 1,000 males.		
	Nomad.	Semi-nomad.	Settled.	Nomad.	Semi-nomad.	Settled.
Balōch	**38**	**5**	**57**	**818**	**839**	**864**
Eastern	39	4	57	787	798	853
Western	36	6	58	886	887	877
Brahūi	**60**	**13**	**27**	**798**	**815**	**831**
Original nucleus	67	5	28	807	847	840
Sarāwān	34	29	37	802	815	839
Jhalawān	75	5	20	794	815	822
Miscellaneous	30	35	35	899	788	822
Paṭhān	**24**	**33**	**43**	**828**	**862**	**878**
Kākaṛ	18	37	45	816	846	843
Paṇi	13	56	31	831	883	935
Tarīn	56	7	37	834	886	973
Others	8	26	66	908	899	870

CHAPTER VII.

MARRIAGE.

Statistical data.

SUBJECT.	TABLES.	
	Imperial.	Subsidiary.
Marriage in general	VII	......
Marriage by religion	XIV	......
Marriage in the indigenous population	......	XIX
Marriage among Brāhūīs in Sind	......	XX

Fragmentary statistics.

165. There is some irony in prefacing this chapter with an imposing list of statistical data, for if statistics were the only data for a discussion of marriage in Balūchistān, the chapter would never have been written at all. Not only are there no statistics for the tribal areas, the bulk of the statistics for the regular areas are concerned with aliens and can be of little interest to anybody. And the only statistics that an enquirer into the matrimonial life of Balūchistān has to guide him are statistics for 8,447 indigenous inhabitants who happened to be censused in the regular areas. Small though the number is, it might give us a not unlifelike picture of matrimony in miniature, if only these 8,447 persons were typical representatives of the province. Unfortunately, with more able-bodied men among them than women and children put together, they are so unrepresentative a crowd that the picture is grotesque in its distortion. There are of course one or two obvious but rough-and-ready devices for bringing it into some sort of focus. We can, for instance, easily raise the number of females to their proper proportion of 845 to 1,000 males (§152) ; nor is there anything—save a not unjustifiable scrupulosity in selecting the age of (say) fifteen as the universal dividing-line of puberty—to prevent us from similarly raising the number of children to their proper proportions of 391 among 1,000 males and 309 among 845 females (§135). And artificially touched up though it is, the picture in the margin gives, I do not doubt, a much less distorted reflection of actual facts than the crude statistics themselves. But in a picture where so much faking is needed there is little chance of catching an entirely faithful likeness. One feature of it, the enormous disparity of the married in the two sexes, strikes me as being ludicrously distorted. And this seems a defect at once unavoidable and ineradicable. To none has life in the regular areas such attractions to offer as to bachelors, and it is accordingly probable on the face of it that the picture should exaggerate the proportion of the unmarried and consequently exaggerate the polygamous tendencies of their married brethren. A pretty clear confirmation of this is to be found on extracting the Brāhūī statistics and comparing them with the statistics for their fellow tribesmen censused in Sind. On the female side there is a very close agreement in the two sets of statistics : thus to every 1,000 Brāhūī males, there are 300 Brāhūī spinsters in Balūchistān, and 317 in Sind. So far, so good : one could hardly have hoped for so gratifying a vindication of such rude adjustments of our flimsy statistics. But when we find that 1,000 Brāhūī males in Balūchistān are supposed to

Indigenous population.

	Unmarried.	Married.	Widowed.
1,000 males	**670**	**296**	**34**
Non-adult	385	6	...
Adult	285	290	34
845 females	**319**	**422**	**104**
Non-adult	289	20	...
Adult	30	402	104

contain no less than 686 bachelors among them or 114 more than their proper quota in Sind, it becomes fairly obvious that in this apparent plethora of bachelors our adjusted statistics give us a picture that is sadly out of drawing.

Of Balūchistān marriage in general.

166. Juggle with the statistics as we may, they are meagre and unsatisfying at the best. But when in default of marriage statistics we turn to marriage customs, it is a very different matter. The country bristles with them. Here the trouble is to pick and choose, and to pack into a small compass. Many customs of interest must needs be shorn of their interest and swept together into a dull heap of generalisation; and all that can be spared to enliven the prevailing dullness are a few customs a little more quaint or a little more characteristic than the rest. Now take a broad view of the country as a whole, and you will find that an ordinary marriage proceeds very much in this wise: first and foremost—and very possibly while girl and boy are both immature—come negotiations (ostensibly set afoot by the boy's party) for the transfer of ownership in the girl from one family to another in consideration of a bride-price; hard on the heels of successful negotiations follows a public ceremony of betrothal, in which the contract is announced in open assembly; and finally—after lass and lad have both passed from childhood to youth—comes the wedding ceremony, hallowed by what is nowadays regarded as the high religious ritual of the *nikāḥ*, when that contract is ratified and fulfilled. Polygyny up to the Islāmic limit of four wives is open to all. But it is an expensive luxury that not one man in ten is likely to be able to afford. And though the very high and mighty have occasionally overstepped the limits of orthodoxy in the past without raising a scandal, those tolerant days are probably over. Divorce lies in the hands of every husband: he has only to throw three stones and bid his wife be gone, and the deed is done; but tribal opinion is a wholesome safeguard against a wanton abuse of the husband's unfettered powers. Widow-remarriage (except maybe in the proudest families) is the very general rule, continued widowhood the very rare exception. It would be unthrift indeed for tribesmen to suffer such easily convertible capital to lie idle. Nevertheless it is much more correct to keep a widow in the family than to dispose of her elsewhere. In most tribes she is the recognised perquisite of her deceased husband's brother; if he is unmarried or childless, the chances are that he'll avail himself of it briskly enough, especially as he usually gets her without paying a penny even though there are sons to inherit their father's estate. The freedom of choice that British rule has granted to widows has done little to shake his rights; indeed tribal opinion on the propriety of the match is sometimes so strong as to convert an apparent privilege into an irksome duty. And though no one has a prior claim to her hand in tribes (chiefly Balōch) where it is customary for a widow to revert to her parent's dominion (§190), it is hardly too much to say that second marriage with the brother's widow is at the bottom of most of the polygamy from one end of the country to the other.

Bride-price.

167. But a man's prescriptive right to the hand of his brother's widow is of course a thing apart. The workaday man has usually to purchase his wife with a price. And the principle of it seems reasonable enough. Bride-price is simply back-payment for the girl's upbringing in her father's house. Most Brāhūī tribes carry out this idea with businesslike pedantry: for the bridegroom has to pay not only *lab* or bride-price proper, which goes to the father, but also a *shīr-pailī* or milk-share, which goes to the mother; he has, in fine, to compensate the mother for the suckling, and the father for the subsequent maintenance of his bride. This intimate relationship between bride-price and maintenance is brought out very clearly in the case of widows. As a general rule a widow continues to receive board and lodging during her widowhood from the husband's estate; so it's only fair that her husband's heirs should appropriate the bride-price when she marries again. But where a widow returns to her parents' roof and dominion, as she does among most Balōch, it is equally fair that her bride-price should go to them and not to her husband's heirs. As for the bride-price itself, not only does it vary in different tribes, it has its ups and downs within the same tribe: looks, social position and youth—these have their market value even among tribesmen. Individual

variations in fact are too great for it to be easy to strike the average in any particular tribe. And even if we could be certain of the averages, it would be unsafe to assume a necessary correlation between a high bride-price and a low proportion of females, in the teeth of the multitudinous factors that enter into the determination of the bride-price in the several tribes. In one respect most tribes have the same tale to tell: the rates have gone up enormously all round in quite recent times. Yet I see in this no reason to suppose that the tribesmen themselves are becoming any more conscious of the shrewd pinch of the scarcity of women among them than they were before; in all probability it is simply the natural and direct outcome of the increase of wealth in the country. Facts that stare us in the face with census statistics before us do not necessarily make themselves felt in everyday life. The most intelligent Bugṭī Balōch I know was dumbfounded when it was put to him that in his tribe there were not enough women to go round. Yet here, if anywhere, the pinch should be felt, for there are only 778 females to 1,000 males in the tribe. And here, if anywhere, we ought to find bride-price pitched inordinately high. But what are the facts? Among the Bugṭī bride-price has never been otherwise than modest, and, with the avowed intention of encouraging cousin-marriage, they have recently decided to do away with it altogether.

Marriage by exchange probably older.

168. But if bride-price holds the field to-day as the most characteristic basis of marriage, it is not the only system in Balūchistān, and the probability is that its spread among many of the peoples is comparatively modern. Thus, though I have cited the Brāhūī custom of *shīr-pailī* to illustrate the principle underlying it, it is beyond cavil that, whereas the Brāhūīs have practised *shīr-pailī* from time immemorial, they have copied the bride-price itself almost within living memory from the Paṭhāns. A much older form of marriage in Balūchistān, I fancy, is marriage by exchange, which under many names—*sar*^{a}*ī*, *vaṭāndra*, *kanōvaṭī*, *adal badal*, to mention but a few—flourishes in one form or another among all races to this day. Such a marriage system is in keeping with the whole spirit of a country where most affairs are conducted on a brotherly basis of mutual co-operation—where one tribesman, for instance, subscribes something as a matter of course in *bijjār* or *baspan* towards the marriage expenses of a fellow-tribesman, in the certainty that he will be re-paid with a like subscription when his own turn comes round in the course of time. Even nowadays the family that has the least bother in finding brides for its sons is the family with an equal number of daughters to give in exchange. But the principle of bride-price is present in the germ even in marriage by exchange, which after all is little more than marriage by barter in disguise. Where the two parties have like to exchange with like, there is of course no scope for anything but exchange pure and simple. But if one of the two girls is of tender age or a widow, and the other a ripe maiden, it is (and was) the regular thing to give something in addition as a make-weight—some cash perhaps, or preferably the promise of a girl yet unborn, very possibly the issue of the projected union. But the exchange was never a promiscuous exchange: it was confined to a certain limited circle. Thus widen the circle as you will, a Paṭhān girl should properly marry a Paṭhān, a Balōch girl a Balōch, a Brāhūī girl a Brāhūī.

Bride-price sometimes a change for the better.

169. But according to strict old custom the circle should be drawn much closer. A Paṭhān girl is still supposed to marry within her parental tribe, and it has become a standing sneer against the Kākaṛ among other Paṭhāns that anybody can get a Kākaṛ girl for the asking—or rather for the paying. Far narrower was the circle among certain sections of the Balōch. To this day a daughter of the Bugṭī chiefly family is never suffered to marry outside it; she is doomed either to become one among the several wives of some near kinsman or to pass her days in spinsterhood. But the lure of bride-price has opened up an avenue of escape to the daughters of some of the neighbouring chiefly families among the Balōch, which were once under the thrall of the same strict marriage law. And regarding this particular instance of hypergamy (or should we not rather call it hypergamous endogamy?) let me quote the son of Bugṭī chief. "Just because we decline to give our daughters to the Khetrān chief, for instance, and yet freely take his daughters to wife ourselves, you must not rush

to the conclusion that we think ourselves a cut above him, any more than you are to imagine that the Bugṭī looks down on the Mazārī or the Mazārī on the Bugṭī, because each chiefly family declines to offer matrimonial alliances to the other. The truth of the matter is simply this:—we are bound hand and foot to an ancient but somewhat awkward custom; the custom itself implies no superiority one way or another." Now though all this need not shake our conviction that the custom is anciently founded on superiority of some sort, it may well make us chary of launching out into wholesale generalisations from hypergamy to status, as I myself was tempted to do in the case of the Bugṭī and Khetrān. Custom is a hardy plant that often preserves its characteristics even when it is transplanted to a different soil and a different environment. Thus this particular custom probably grew up generations ago out of the obvious superiority of the chief's family over the rest of the tribe: once the custom had struck firm root, it could easily survive later contact with families of equal or even higher status in other tribes. It would of course be dangerous to prophesy on such a matter: but when the future chief of the great Bugṭī tribe recognises, however imperfectly, something of the awkwardness and anomaly of an existing custom, no one would be surprised if his family followed the suit of other Balōch chiefly families before long and consigned the custom to limbo.

Sometimes a change for the worse.

170. So far bride-price can fairly claim to have had some hand in the breakup of cramping customs. But many hard things are said about bride-price, and it must be confessed that as a solvent of ancient customs its influence is sometimes too powerful altogether. The worst thing about it is that it constitutes an obvious temptation to offer one's daughter to the highest bidder—though it is only fair to remember that this temptation is not wholly unknown in countries where the unveiled mention of bride-price would now be received with protestations of horror. Take, for instance, its influence among the Brāhūīs. In the old days neither the tribal circle nor the immediate family circle appears to have been regarded as the true marriage-circle. Cousin-marriage, no doubt, is to-day as common among Brāhūīs as it is elsewhere in Balūchistān—perhaps even more so, for the Brāhūī, putting great faith in his proverb that though it takes a good sire to breed a good colt, it takes a good mother to breed a good son, favours cousin-marriage as the simplest means of keeping the stock pure. But in olden time cousin-marriage seems to have been accidental rather than deliberate, the exception not the rule. Among Jhalawāns in particular it used to be the correct thing for one group of families to interchange marriages generation after generation with another group which belonged very possibly to quite a different tribe altogether. Such a group called the other its *shalvār* or breeches—for breeches are as essential to a Brāhūī bride as a bridal veil to a bride in Europe. And the only decent excuse for not sticking to one's ancestral *shalvār* was the chance of worming oneself into a better. But the introduction of bride-price has altered all this. The *shalvār*, once so fair, so honoured, so cherished — (for I prefer to let a Brāhūī of the old school tell the tale of the degeneration of his race himself) — is now a sorry patchwork of rents and tatters: of a truth it barely holds together at all. In these latter days the Jhalawān has grown ashamed of his threadbare *shalvār*, and doffing his old rags he hunts and grasps for a fat bride-price with the best of 'em. The higher a man's rank and the greater his substance, the more he claims. As for the poorer folk, ill-content with what they may look to get from one of themselves, they bundle their women off to Sind — for all the world as if they were taking them to market. Gone past recall is the day when there was truth in the proud boast that a Jaṭṭ was about as good as a Brāhūī's shoe.

Betrothal age.

171. But be the past what it may, bride-price is nowadays the great crux in the negotiations which are bandied to and fro between two households as a prelude to the normal betrothal. In the family councils neither the future groom nor the future bride is expected to take part. In fact the girl is rarely old enough to lift up her voice at all. To put off her betrothal till she has reached puberty is certainly unusual. For it to be put off once puberty is passed would be looked upon in most tribes as a flouting of the decencies on the part of her family, only to be excused by some physical or mental defect in the

girl herself. It is much more common for her to be contracted away before ever she is born, either by a loving compact between expectant mothers, or as part-payment of a bride-price or bloodmoney. But though there can be no question of the antiquity of these customs, I am inclined to think that an ordinary betrothal is contracted nowadays at a much earlier age than it used to be. That this is true of Paṭhāns seems clear from the survival of certain antiquated customs which still crop up from time to time and cause not a little embarrassment among the people, who are not sure whether there is enough life in them to be respected or not. Such for instance is the *ar* custom, where a youth claims a girl by flinging a sheep's head into her father's house, or the custom of blazing away with his gun just inside the door, or of snatching off her head-dress with the shout that the girl is his, or the analogous custom of the rape of the lock. For these customs presuppose not only virility on the youth's part, but also sufficient age on hers to make her an object of his desire. Even more obvious is this in the recognised custom of *maṭīzgai*, where the young couple take matters into their own hands and elope. In a country which is still enslaved to the bloodfeud and where women are chief among the causes that lead to it, it is only natural that the tribesmen should have learnt the wisdom of fixing up a betrothal before the girl is old enough to put a spoke in their wheel. The Paṭhāns go one further. At once more priest-ridden and less conservative of their ancient customs than Balōch or Brāhūī, they are endeavouring to merge betrothal and marriage into one, not merely in order to come into line with *sharīat* (in which the *nikāḥ* of course takes the place of both), but also in order to draw the betrothal-tie taut once and for all by hallowing it with the *nikāḥ*.

Marriage age.

172. But even Paṭhāns still recognise the existence of two stages, betrothal and marriage, on the ordinary road to wedlock. Though they insist on the finality and all-sufficiency of a betrothal whenever it suits their purpose, nobody ever takes part in a betrothal without looking forward to a marriage ceremony in due course as a natural and proper climax. Nor does it make much difference whether the *nikāḥ* has been read at the betrothal or no; the reading of the *nikāḥ* is usually regarded as an absolute essential at the marriage. And even though Paṭhāns frequently betroth away a girl while she is yet of tender age, and muddle up betrothal and marriage to such an extent that it is often puzzling to know whether she is veritable wife or trysted maid, there is no attempt to forestall puberty: not until she is actually ripe for wedlock does her family pass her on to the family of her husband. And the same is true of the tribesmen generally; as they themselves point out, a child-wife has absolutely no attraction for a man who wants his wife to be a sturdy helpmate about the house. Now, if we ignore exceptional cases on either side of the line—the very big folk who seem to be drifting into child-marriage as the correct thing for the gentility, and the very poor who may take years scraping together the wherewithal for the bride-price—the popular idea of the proper age to marry is a year or so after puberty for a girl, and half a dozen years later for a youth. And on the whole the popular idea seems to be borne out pretty closely in practice.

Polygyny not incompatible with scarcity of women.

173. For the groom to be a few years elder than his bride is not only natural in itself and fairly common in most parts of the world, it is doubly natural and doubly common in countries where girls are in a minority and have to be bought with a price. Indeed, if I were asked to explain how polygyny and scarcity of women can exist side by side in Balūchistān, I should begin by saying that polygyny, though open in pleasant theory to all, is in cruel fact a privilege of which only the well-to-do can ordinarily hope to avail themselves. And I should go on to point out that, while there are no spinsters above a certain early age (except some lady with the fatal gift of high birth, or here and there some wretch hopelessly deformed or insane), a few full-bodied men, though doubtless very few, pass their lives in bachelorhood to the day of their death. Both facts are significant, as far as they go. But I should lay the stress elsewhere. The average girl passes into the married estate almost as soon as she passes over the threshold into womanhood, and in the married state she remains either with her first husband or — after a short spell of divorce or widowhood — with a second or a third; the average man is not married till

some years after the age of puberty is passed, and often fails to replace or supplement a first wife by a second, provided children or rather sons have been born to him. The enormous influence of disparity in marriage age between the two sexes in a country where widow re-marriage is the general rule, seems sometimes imperfectly realised. In casual conversation I once heard it so stoutly denied that I was provoked into working out the ludicrous calculation which (not without a blush) I here reproduce. The whole thing of course is farcical—gaps, hypotheses, and figures and all; yet it serves its purpose. Though polygyny is law in Balūchistān and polyandry is unknown, I fancy that if we stretched the two words so as to cover plurality of marriage of all sorts—the re-marriage of the widowed and divorced, to say nothing of what the Paṭhāns at any rate would call the re-marriage of the betrothed—we should find that polyandry in this wide and untechnical sense is far more common than polygyny.

Suppose (among other wild suppositions)
(*a*) there are 1,000 men to 850 women,
(*b*) 48 is the life of one and all,
(*c*) men marry at 24, women at 16,
(*d*) all widows re-marry immediately.

Then
$1{,}000 \times 24 =$ total male married years,
$850 \times 32 =$ total female married years,
Excess $= 3{,}200$ female married years,
∴ there's (i) a wife for each man from his wedding day to death; and (ii) 3,200 female married years over for the polygynists.

Now suppose
(*a*) 12 per cent are polygynists, *i.e.*, 120 in all,
(*b*) 90 with one extra wife, 20 with two, 10 with three,
(*c*) each lives in monogamy for the first four years, and then becomes polygynist up to his limit.

Then
Total number of female married years required for 20 years of polygyny

$$= \left\{ (90 \times 1) + (20 \times 2) + (10 \times 3) \right\} \times 20 = 3{,}200$$

But these are forthcoming.
Q.E.D.

Free-love among Sanzarkhēl Paṭhāns.

174. Now in throwing a modern religious glamour over the ancient custom of betrothal and thus pulling the betrothal-knot as tight as it will go, the Paṭhāns not only obviate future complications—and of all complications a refractory maiden is possibly the worst—their conscience is more or less salved in countenancing cohabitation by a betrothed couple before marriage as being sanctioned by the *nikāḥ*. The *nikāḥ* thus serves as a decent cloak to cover up a flagrant scandal which, if no longer so confirmed a custom as it used to be, is still common enough in many tribes, loth though they may be to admit it. Yet bastardy is nowhere tolerated: pre-nuptial pregnancy simply hurries the marriage on, and the only punishment that awaits the impatient youth is the inconvenience of having to pay up any arrears of bride-price on the nail. But in certain Paṭhān tribes a youth, even at the present day, need not wait till betrothal for permission to traffic with the other sex. Among the Sanzarkhēl Kākaṛ of Zhōb and Lōṛalai there still survives—under the innocent name of *majlis*, or as Pashtō pronounces it *m*^{a}*jl*^{a}*s*, 'meeting' or 'assembly'—a curious species of licensed free-love between the unmarried lads and lasses of the village. A lad who wants to join the lists of love has only to appoint a tryst with some maiden that has caught his fancy as she stood at the well or loitered along the road. Or if he cannot get a message through to her, he creeps to her bedside at dead of night. Likely enough the coast is clear, for unmarried maidens sleep apart from the rest of the household. A soft pressure of her hand or a gentle squeeze of her nose is the customary invitation to join the game. If the lad isn't to her liking, she tries to put him off with some excuse; if he persists in his unwelcome wooing, she raises her voice until her father or mother calls out to the intruder to be gone and not make himself a nuisance. But if she shows herself ready for the sport, he tip-toes out of the house and she follows hard at his heels. At the first *majlis* the couple should content themselves with breaking the ice, by merely talking of love till the peep of dawn. Any familiarity on the lad's part, even though she may have lured him on to it, should be instantly repulsed, and the meeting broken off, never to be renewed. For this is only the first stage in the game, and goes by the name of *d*^{a} *kh*^{a}*le m*^{a}*jl*^{a}*s*, *majlis* by word of mouth. But if the course of love runs smooth, the meetings soon ripen into *w*^{a}*oh m*^{a}*jl*^{a}*s*, the dry *majlis*. Yet though they kiss and toy to their heart's content, actual intercourse is still against the rules of the game; and if the youth does not play fair, the lass will tell on him among the other lasses of the village, and he will find himself barred from future revels. But once her wedding-day is in sight, the time is now ripe for *lund m*^{a}*jl*^{a}*s*, the third and last stage of all. This, I am assured, is almost a thing of the past. But in olden days it was

apparently the regular thing for a girl to enter upon it freely, heedless of consequences which marriage would presently gloss over, though the precaution was usually taken to resort to some crude preventive, most commonly the one that is as old as the days of Onan. And on the very night of her wedding she would slip away for one last hour with her lover, for marriage put a final stop to the game. Prevalent though this curious custom still is in one form or another, at any rate among more unsophisticated tribesmen, there is doubtless a good deal of hyperbole in the statement made by one of my many informants that the odds are on every single lad, certainly on every lad of mettle, having played the game at one time or another with every single lass in the village. Yet this is very possibly a true presentation of Sanzarkhēl society a couple of generations ago.

Girl-hospitality.

175. Analogous is the custom, once common and still current in the same tribes, of providing an unmarried but marriageable girl for the better entertainment of any guest who stays in the house overnight. If the host has an unmarried daughter or sister in his household, well and good; otherwise he sends over to borrow one from his neighbour, not without a word of apology to his guest. Now whereas the explanation usually offered for *majlis* is the encouragement of manliness in the youth of the tribe—partly because the favours of the lasses are an incentive to feats of manliness, partly because *majlis* itself is believed to develop manliness—the explanation always[1] offered for this particular form of the custom is simply old-fashioned hospitality on the grand scale. And this of course is the explanation generally accepted for similar customs elsewhere. Yet girl-hospitality, curiously enough, seems to be extended among the Sanzarkhēl Kākaṛ when ordinary hospitality is withheld: a short time back, at any rate, a stranger who came to a village known to no one, the guest of no one, had only to ask the first youth he met for the whereabouts of the likeliest lasses in the village, if he wanted to join in. But the custom has been abused by strangers who were not Paṭhāns at all, and girl-hospitality like *majlis* is rapidly on the wane, even among the more uncivilised elements of society, though the Sanzarkhēl are probably a little too previous when they affect to put a very innocent interpretation on both, or try to make out that they are only really current among the Dumaṛ, whose claims to kinship with the Kākaṛ are usually scouted (§257). Paradoxical though it may seem, these three customs of prenuptial licence—cohabitation between betrothed, *majlis*, and girl-hospitality—go hand in hand with the most stringent insistence on the sanctity of the marriage-tie. According to strict old custom the wages of adultery is death to wife and paramour alike: if they escape the clutches of the outraged husband and his kinsmen, there arises a bloodfeud that only a blood-settlement can wipe out.

The tokens of virginity among Brāhūis.

176. Prenuptial licence of any kind is entirely foreign to the Brāhūī, who demands vivid proofs of the chastity of his bride, and is absolved by public opinion from all guilt if he slaughters her on the bridal bed when there are none forthcoming. But for a description of the scene at the Brāhūī nuptials I had better go to a Brāhūī himself. "Now when bride and groom are left alone at last, the two mothers sit without, attended by a few old ladies of the kindred, keeping watch and ward to the end that they may be as witnesses hereafter. They are all on the alert for the call that shall summon them within. And they wait and wait, and still maybe there is no call. And the bride's mother twits the groom's mother touching the sluggishness of her son. But the other is not at a loss for the reason: there must be magic abroad, it could not be else. And sure enough, the groom may presently call out in distress, bidding his mother hurry away for some holy water to undo the spell that has been cast upon him. Off bustles the old dame post-haste, and the priest, taking some water, breathes a potent charm over it, and she's back with it as fast as her old legs can carry her. And let's hope the charm will work this selfsame night; for the longer the delay, the greater the disgrace to the groom. And the moment it's all over, he calls the old ladies in. They don't stand on the order of their going, I'll be bound, but hasten in and eagerly

[1] I am wrong. Some local theorists, I now find, explain it as the crystallisation into a voluntary custom of what was once the enforced prerogative of the early Moghal tyrants.

scan the bridal apparel for the tokens of virginity. And if the stains are all she could wish, great is the exaltation of the mother of the bride. Aloft she holds the cloth in triumph, and displays it with pride to each lady in turn; and one and all they rejoice in her rejoicing. But the cloth is treasured up by the mother, for it is her glory. And when the young men come to greet the groom on the morrow, they greet him with the eager cry: 'Are you a lion or a jackal?' Not a word does he answer in his pride, but carelessly spreads out his skirt that they may see the tokens of virginity wherewith he took pains to stain it." The scene conjures up that well-known passage in Deuteronomy, from which indeed I have borrowed the translation for the central feature of the custom: "If any man take a wife, and go in unto her and hate her. And say,—I took this woman, and when I came to her, I found her not a maid: Then shall the father of the damsel, and her mother, take and bring forth the tokens of the damsel's virginity unto the elders of the city in the gate: And the damsel's father shall say unto the elders, I gave my daughter unto this man to wife, and he hateth her;—saying, I found not thy daughter a maid; and yet these are the tokens of my daughter's virginity. And they shall spread the cloth before the elders of the city. And the elders of that city shall take that man and chastise him....But if this thing be true, and the tokens of virginity be not found for the damsel: Then shall they bring out the damsel to the door of her father's house, and the men of her city shall stone her that she die." (XXII.,13-21.)

Artificial defloration among the Jaṭṭ and others.

177. But in publicly exhibiting the stains on the bridal raiment the Brāhūis do not stand alone. The custom is found also among the Balōch and Jaṭṭ of the Kachhī. But among the Jaṭṭ and probably among some if not all the Balōch tribes, the stains are the outcome of artificial deflowering a few hours previous to consummation. The Jaṭṭ make no secret about it, though they themselves are somewhat in the dark, as the operation is done by an old woman in private. The instrument she uses is a razor; the operation consists, one would presume, in the rupture of the hymen or the scarifying of the place where the hymen ought to be; yet some of my accounts seem rather to imply the circumcision of the clitoris or *labia*. To staunch the bleeding they burn an old shoe and sprinkle a rag with the ashes and hold it to the wound for a few minutes. But the one and only permanent cure for the wound is consummation. And at consummation the wound breaks out anew, thus ensuring the desired flow of blood on the bridal couch, which otherwise might not be forthcoming owing to the common disappearance of the hymen from natural causes when marriage is comparatively late. How far this custom is to be regarded as common to the Balōch, it is difficult to say. My own impression is that it is fairly wide-spread among the Balōch of the east. In the first place, it undoubtedly prevails among the Marī families who have taken up their residence with the G͟harshīn Sayyids of Mūsak͟hēl. It is therefore probable enough that it prevails in the Marī *tuman* at large; and this seems amply confirmed from other indirect sources. And if, as I see no reason to doubt, it prevails among the Marī, it is at least not improbable that it prevails among their neighbours the Bugṭī, with whose customs the Marī have much in common. Whether it prevails among other true Balōch of Balūchistān there is little or no direct evidence to show. Yet it can hardly be a mere coincidence that the only people other than Jaṭṭ and Balōch among whom I have been able to trace the custom, should happen to be people who are known to have come under Balōch influence, though the prevalence of the custom among them may of course be evidence not so much of Balōch influence as of Jaṭṭ influence on and through Balōch. The custom prevails, for instance, among the Jafar Paṭhān, who like most remnants of the Miāna stock left in Balūchistān (§255) have been considerably infected by Balōch ideas. The G͟harshīn Sayyids, who, half Sayyid though they may be, are also off-shoots from the Miāna, make no bones about the prevalence of the custom among themselves. At the same time, they state definitely that it is not a regular practice among the Buzdār Balōch who live with them as *hamsāya* on the same terms as the Marī; but these Buzdār hail from the Panjāb and do not belong to Balūchistān. That the custom does not appear to exist among

the Khetrān is much more remarkable; for of all offshoots from the Miāna stock this is the one that has been most affected by Balōch influence, and, curiously enough, the Khetrān, like the Gharshīn Sayyid, make no distinction of sex in the circumcision of their children (§ 99). On the other hand, among the Jat, that quaintly debased people who, though their claims to Balōch descent are probably unfounded, have been closely associated with the Balōch time out of mind (§ 285), the custom seems to be as prevalent as female circumcision in childhood.

178. These curious operations in girlhood and on the bridal night are usually lumped together in Balūchistān as mere varieties of one and the same practice, female circumcision. Like its counterpart among the males, female circumcision is vaguely regarded as a religious ordinance, an initiation into the Islāmic fold, a necessary preliminary all women must go through before their acts of charity can become acceptable to God. It is supposed to have a scriptural origin: for Hagar was circumcised to appease Sarah's jealousy, according to a legend too familiar, I imagine, to bear repeating here. Apart from its religious aspect, the bridal operation at any rate is supposed to ensure the woman's fecundity, to deaden her passions, and at the same time to quicken the passions of her spouse. And, finally, unkind outsiders look upon it as an ingenious and deep-laid plot to prove that the bride is what all too often she is not—a spotless virgin. There may be a grain of truth in all these local suggestions: though none of them may hit on the ultimate origin of the customs, each may have played its part in the later stages in helping them to survive. In Balūchistān it certainly seems awkward to apply the orthodox explanation that artificial defloration is grounded in some primitive dread of menstrual blood, for the blood in this country appears to be always carefully left on the bridal couch and on the groom's garment, and to be an object of solicitous interest to the community, as proving not only the virginity of the bride but the virility of the groom. We could no doubt account for the anomaly by assuming that the exhibition of the blood-stains is a much later development, possibly a mere aping (as local theorists suggest) of a totally different custom among a neighbouring people. But there is perhaps a little too much readiness to reduce similar customs the wide world over to one and the selfsame origin. On the whole I am inclined to trace both the girlhood and bridal operations of Balūchistān to a desire to facilitate the physical union of the male and female by the removal of all possible obstructions. At any rate, if this is not the mainspring of the customs—and crude and primitive though the motive seems, it may not be quite primitive enough to account for what are apparently ancient customs of widely different peoples—this idea has almost certainly played its part in their preservation. And the idea is undoubtedly still alive. Among the Marī, who apparently perform the bridal operation as a matter of course, and again among the Brāhūis, who otherwise have nothing to do with female circumcision in any shape or form, the snipping off of the tip of the clitoris is a not unusual device to overcome either complete barrenness or a stubborn perversity in bearing nothing but females; and the removal of a stoppage seems the only possible rationale of this strange piece of native surgery.

Its origin.

179. If local theorists are right in thinking that the bridal operation has anything to do with proofs of virginity, it is a little humorous to find it common among the Jat (§285). For whatever store a Jat may set by the chastity of his bride—and though he certainly takes pride in displaying the bridal stains, this may be less to show off her virginity than his own virility—he sets absolutely none on the chastity of his wife. It's a common saying that a tribesman who puts a camel out to graze with a Jat becomes thereby the *bhōtār* or master of the Jat's wife. He strolls up every now and then to have a look at his camel and more than a look at the lady of the house. As he comes in, the Jat goes out. The *bhōtār* leaves his shoes or his stick outside the tent as he enters. If the Jat on his return still finds shoes or stick outside, he shuffles with his feet or gives a discreet cough; if this is insufficient, he shouts out "Master! the horse has got loose!" or "Master! a dog has made off with your shoes!"—hints too broad to be ignored much longer. The presence of a

Post-nuptial licence among the Jat.

visitor who comes along while the Jat is away will be advertised by his shoes outside the tent; or some obliging old lady will keep a look-out for the husband and tip him the wink with the stock euphemism "There's a stallion after the mare." Though this is regarded as an ancient and honourable custom, and the husband, we are assured, takes no small pride in his wife's conquests, it has of course a mercenary side to it. The *bhōtār* makes presents in one form or another; if he is a big man in his tribe, there are a number of ways in which he can help the family.

Wedding buffoonery.

180. It goes perhaps without saying that divorce is unknown among the Jat. It would be a little out of place considering the keen and kindly interest the husband takes in his wife's amours; but it is hardly necessary to go as far as one of my informants, who finds the explanation for the absence of divorce in the charitable conclusion that the happiness of his wife is the first and last ambition of a Jat. But if there is no divorce among the Jat, there is plenty of widow-remarriage, though the lady can please herself whether to live as widow, mistress or wife. If she makes up her mind to remarry, her late husband's brother has no claim to her hand, and the bride-price goes to her parents. Her second wedding seems to be regarded as a huge joke. The women make the unfortunate mulla the butt for the broadest of jests; they stitch up his clothes and play him every trick they can think of, and he's a lucky man if he escapes with his breeches on. To add to his misery, he only gets half the usual wedding-fee. Not that a mulla is indispensable even at the marriage of a Jat maiden. Any old greybeard can conduct the service just as well, though all he may be able to recite is some Jaṭkī or Balōchī song he happens to remember. Among some Zikrī sectarians (§87) it is a more or less regular thing for a water-skin to be inflated with the mulla's holy breath, and a marriage to be solemnised (possibly miles off) by deflating it into the bride's face. But though this sounds sheer buffoonery to us—we can almost fancy we have read of it in Gulliver's Travels—it is not buffoonery to the people themselves, but dire earnest. Even among the dominant races a wedding service is not the solemn ceremony one might expect. Young Brāhūī bloods are always on the watch to catch the mulla tripping over the service and do their best to disconcert him with jocular interruptions. There is of course much more scope for buffoonery in the ceremonies that lead up to the *nikāḥ*; thus the lads and lasses in the two assemblies would not consider the ceremonial anointing of the bridal couple with henna complete, if they did not manage to bedaub the groom's father and mother all over into the bargain. But for wedding buffoonery at its height we must turn elsewhere.

Puch-kūn among Makrān menials.

181. Among the Nakīb and other low classes on the Makrān coast a marriage is regularly made the excuse for a gross piece of horse-play, which goes by the appropriately gross name of *puch-kūn*. It would have made Rabelais shake his sides, but decency forbids any attempt on my part to depict it in detail; it is only in the chaste disguise of a dead language that I could venture to do so. There are several variants of the custom, but the central figures in the mummery are usually a man and a boy, dressed up as bridegroom and bride, who are ushered into the assembly by a party of youths amid much clapping of hands and bawling of wedding songs. And when the pair are seated, up comes a man and calls upon the bride roundly to choose between the paltry groom and one whose manhood is famed from the coast of Makrān to the furthermost corner of Balūchistān. The groom's best man tries to push him aside, but is flung head over heels for his pains. Then despite all the groom can say or do, the intruder seizes the bride round the head, and tousles her about, until—"Hullo! what's this?" he bellows in amazement—But here the curtain must drop with a rush, and I can say no more than that the discomfiture of bridegroom and rival alike is the final tableau in the scuffle. Though this buffoonery, which is often gone through at a circumcision as well, is believed to serve as a wholesome reminder that matrimony isn't such a bed of roses as the happy couple may imagine, it looks very much like a fertilisation custom.

Hājī Murda among Pathans.

182. Of much the same character is a farce called *Hājī Murda* or the Dead Pilgrim, which is acted before a Paṭhān bridegroom and his male friends on the

wedding eve. Most of the dialogue is in Persian, with a strong flavour of Pashtō to make it all the more ludicrous. The scene opens with Hājī lying stark on the ground, covered by a sheet. On one side stands a barber, saying again and again that Hājī's dead; on the other stands Hājī's father, yelling that he's alive. To make sure the barber lifts up Hājī's limbs one by one, but they drop back lifeless; in one part only is there any sign of life. "Humph! there's life enough here," says the barber, "but the rest of him's as dead as a door nail." And again the father yells back that Hājī's alive. So the barber ties a shoe about his middle and with meaning but indescribable gestures tries to spur Hājī back to life. When all proves in vain, he bursts out into song, punctuating each line with a yell that Hājī's dead, which the father drowns with a yell that Hājī's alive :

Hājī gorged on carrots, carrots full of dust ;
Hājī's paunch is swollen, swollen full of must.
Hājī, dearest husband, my slim cypress tree !
Hājī's grave is just the place to make a jakes for me !

Then the father bids Hājī's eyes to open, and legs and arms to move, and the moment he touches his heart, Hājī leaps to life. This is the cue for a shepherd to enter, driving imaginary flocks before him with his crook, and bawling as he comes along :

A shepherd's life's not a life at all !
I am sick of rising before the morn,
I'm sick of these goats with the crumpled horn,
I'm sick of these fat-tailed sheep unshorn.
Oh why was I ever a shepherd at all ?
I graze the flock in shady dells,
I drive the flock upon the hills,
The flock I water at the rills,
Plague take the goats and sheep and all !

A lamb is promptly bought of him, and slain in honour of Hājī's wedding. Then up speaks his father :

Limping craftsman, ply your craft !
Shear him trim both fore and aft !

"Touch that nasty mangy poll ?" says the barber, "not I !" And he sticks to his word, though two men step forward and solemnly pronounce the head to be free from mange. So the father tries to wheedle him with promises :—

I'll give you a cloak and a turban so bonny,
I'll fill you your skirts to the brim full o' money.
Limping craftsman, ply your craft !
Shear him trim both fore and aft !

("Not I !" says the barber. "Then take *that* !" says the father, giving him a clout on the ear.)

I'll give you a cloak and a turban so bonny,
I'll fill you your skirts to the brim full o'money,
I'll give you a damsel to be your sweet honey.
Limping craftsman, ply your—

But at the word "*damsel*" the barber flourishes his tackle, and shears away right lustily. Yet his only reward when his task is done is to have his face blackened and to be kicked out of the village.

Pantomime before Pathān brides.

183. Though I cannot pretend to understand all the points in the farce, it looks like a fertilisation custom at bottom. That this is the character of the

mummery that goes on among the women is clear enough. Here there are two leading ladies in the cast, the one young and the other old. The girl waddles on with a pillow strapped round her middle.

Dearie, dearie, dearie me!
How many months may the little one be?

says the old crone in deeply sympathetic tones.

Dear aunt of mine, may I die for thee.
A month and a day must the little one be!

replies the girl. And again the old crone mumbles

Dearie, dearie, dearie me!
How many months may the little one be?

and the answer comes pat—

Dear aunt of mine, may I die for thee.
Two months and two days must the little one be!

So it goes on till it gets to *Nine months and nine days must the little one be.* And the words are hardly out of the girl's mouth before she begins to groan and moan, and to writhe about in such agony that it takes two or three women to hold her down. And between her moans she curses herself for a fool ever to have thought of marriage at all, and cries out to her friends

Oh maidens all, be warned of me,
How bitter the fruit on the wedlock-tree!

And she points her warning to such purpose that the maidens run off and hide their faces. But when matters are at their worst, the pillow begins to descend, and with one last mighty strain she is delivered of her burden. Shrieks of laughter greet the climax. The only one in the room to keep her countenance is the real bride herself. At any rate if she cannot contain her feelings, she can at least conceal them, for she sits with her face covered by a wrapper. But not a scream or a giggle may escape her, for a Paṭhān bride must sit like a statue, and a whispered word to her bridesmaids is all that may pass her lips.

Self-effacement of the bride.

184. Now I have gone out of my way to describe wedding buffoonery, not merely because it is mildly interesting in itself, nor because in one form or another it is regarded everywhere as only fit and proper at a wedding, but chiefly because it is the one explanation local theorists have to offer for a curious shrinking from the wedding and the wedding ceremonies that is often displayed by the bride, her groom, her brother, and her father. It will probably be found hard to believe that this shrinking or self-effacement, which is essentially a customary thing, is not more deeply grounded in the case of the men. But maidenly modesty—real or assumed—is very possibly sufficient to account for most of the bride's coy bashfulness. There is after all nothing strange in a bride comporting herself during the ceremonies as though she were an unwilling participant in them; and it is apt to become a bit of a nuisance to be pestered with ingenious traces of bride-capture at every turn, where a simple explanation lies ready to hand in the natural modesty with which many peoples, belonging to very different stages of development, expect a bride to clothe herself. A Brāhūī maiden, for instance, is supposed to sit with eyes tight shut and a handkerchief to her face, from the moment she is decked out for the bridal until she is handed over to her groom. Nor should she utter a word, save of course for a frightened whisper when she is called upon by the witnesses to nominate her proxy father at the wedding. And not only ought a bride to hedge herself round with an air of maidenly reluctance, she is supported by kinswomen and a bodyguard of bridesmaids, whose chief object seems to be to protect her from her groom. Thus when the witnesses to a Brāhūī wedding come to the women's apartment to ascertain the name of the bride's proxy father, they must be prepared for a deal of trouble before the door is unbarred to admit them. And much the same trouble awaits the groom himself after the wedding is over, for the bride's mother and married sisters

slam the door in his face when he seeks to enter the bridal chamber. Among some sections of the Jaṭṭ one of the bridesmaids takes her stand at the door and bangs him over the head with a thorn-bush as he comes along. A Khetrān wedding-service is preceded by the unloosening of the bride's plait—one of many Hindu touches in Khetrān domestic customs, by the by—which is only carried out after a sham-fight in which the company range themselves in two parties, the one striving in vain to defend the bride against the onslaughts of the other. Those who would read bride-capture into this custom will be disappointed over the composition of the contending armies : it is the bachelors and the spinsters, and not the bride's kin, who champion her cause ; the ranks of the enemy are filled by the married. Yet they may possibly find consolation in the thought that the fight must have lost its ancient character ; for the issue is greeted with weeping and wailing by the mother and the other kinswomen of the bride. Now when the fight is over and the plait is unloosed the bride runs out in the open to swing with her playmates. And this at any rate seems an example of an outworn custom. For there can be little doubt that a much older form of the custom (though possibly not the oldest) is being enacted when she occasionally runs off with her playmates to the jungle, and there remains in high dudgeon until she is coaxed back by her father at night-fall. Not even when the bride is left alone with her groom is her air of reluctance always laid aside. A Brāhūī bride is often tutored to resist his advances, and a scuffle may ensue between them, only to be ended by his buying her over with presents.

Self-effacement of the groom.

185. Now if we are to see traces of bride-capture in much of the bride's reluctance, as some theorists would probably have us do, are we to see traces of bridegroom-capture in the reluctance that is sometimes displayed by the groom? There seem far fewer instances of it—I have found none at all among the Brāhūīs—yet such as occur are very marked. Among the Sanzarkhēl Kākaṛ Paṭhāns the one person who is conspicuous by his absence from the procession that wends its way from the groom's house to the house of the maiden to bear her off on the morrow for the wedding, is the groom himself. And in the customary delay of three days after the wedding during which he must refrain from coming near his bride, and the subsequent period during which he is often supposed to defer consummation, may perhaps be seen indications that at least as much bashfulness is expected from him as from his bride. However this may be—and I will return to the subject presently (§ 189)—much more significant for present purposes is the fact that among the Mūsakhēl Paṇī and some if not all Sanzarkhēl the groom hides himself on the return of the bridal procession from the maiden's house, and remains in hiding for full three days.

Self-effacement of the bride's brother.

186. As for the bride's brother, there is a wide-spread idea that he at any rate should efface himself from the wedding festivities. Thus as soon as the procession arrives to bear his sister away on the morrow for the wedding, a Sanzarkhēl youth leaves the house for the night—for very shame, they say, that anyone should dare to carry off his sister while he is there to prevent it. This custom seems to reach its height in Makrān, where the bridegroom has generally to buy off the bride's brother (or, in default of a brother, her first cousin) with what is known as *kamān-bahā* or bow-price. This bow-price used by rights to consist of a horse and a sword and a gun ; but nowadays cash is often given instead. The gift of a horse and a sword and a gun seems clearly symbolical of the self-disarming of the bridegroom, just as the customary award of a sword and a gun as part of the bloodmoney throughout Balūchistān is symbolical of the disarming of the murderer and his kin, and is a survival of a custom, still current among Brāhūīs, whereby the disarming of the aggressor in public assembly constitutes a substantial compensation to the aggrieved. And a similar idea seems to be at the back of the very name of the custom. For *kamān-bahā* can hardly mean anything else but the price that must be paid to the bride's brother, before he will consent to lay down his bow and arrows that otherwise would be lifted in her defence. Chary though I am of seeing traces of marriage by capture at every turn, it certainly looks as if we had something very much like it here.

And yet I am not sure whether the deep-rooted feeling that there is something humiliating in one's own flesh and blood being handed over in wedlock outside the family, no matter how high the station of the groom, might not account for it after all. It is a little strange that the bow-price should go to the brother or first cousin and not to the father or head of the family. This may be simply another sign that betrothal and marriage used to be instituted much later in life in the days of old, when the father might often have one foot in the grave before the marriage was complete and would naturally look to the son to champion the honour of the family. Possibly the explanation lies deeper. (§188.)

Self-effacement of the father.

187. Among Brāhūīs there is a very strong feeling that a daughter's wedding is no place for a father. In olden days it would have been a scandal for him to put in an appearance at all; he was expected to quit the house, leaving his wife's brother in possession to act as the head of the family. Folks, to be sure, are not quite so strait-laced nowadays, but it is still considered the correct thing for the father to keep himself in the background during the festivities; in any case he should be spared the buffoonery with which the groom's father has to put up (§180). And not only should the bride's father make himself scarce at the wedding, his very name is never mentioned during the ritual: whenever the bride's name occurs in the *nikāh*, it is coupled with the name of her mother and her mother alone. Learned Brāhūīs have a vague idea that their practice has Islāmic sanction: in the Day of Judgment one and all will be summoned by the names of their mothers; for God, to Whom all secrets are opened, will put no one to shame by revealing his sinful parentage. Nor is a daughter's wedding the only occasion when a father's name is avoided: in speaking of the dead, whether male or female, old-fashioned folk would always refer to So-and-so, *shīr-mich* or milk—sucker of such and such a woman. Now in glossing over the father's name at the *nikāḥ* the Balōch of Khārān and Makrān follow the Brāhūīs. Yet the Balōch of the Kachhī and also the Jaṭṭ specify both parents. And so do the Paṭhāns. Nevertheless even among Paṭhāns the mention of the father's name looks at times like an innovation; for among the Sanzarkhēl of Bōrī (and I daresay elsewhere) the father's name comes as an after-thought at the end of the formula: "Do you accept as your wife Musammāt So-and-so, the daughter of Mistress So-and-so, the grand-daughter of Mistress So-and-so (the mother's mother), and daughter of Mr. So-and-so?"

Apparent survivals of mother-kin.

188. It certainly seems as if glimpses of bygone mother-kin—glimpses of days when the family centred round the mother, and her brother and not her husband was its natural head—peep out from some of these customs; notably from the payment of bow-price not to the bride's father but to her brother[1]; from the omission or the slurring over of her father's name in the marriage service; and from his self-effacement at the wedding, more especially as this used to be coupled with the prominence of her maternal uncle. And these and other instances of the kind are all the more significant because they are found in a country where the father is now a patriarch of the patriarchs. But space and time forbid a plunge into the eddies of the controversy which rages round this subject of mother-kin. I can only pause on the brink and fling over a few other local customs to those engaged in the wordy struggle. It is quite clear, for instance, that a Brāhūī mother's rights in her child received formal and tangible recognition ages before the Brāhūī father had learnt to assert his. For nothing can be more certain than that she claimed a milk-price on the marriage of her daughter (§167) ages before her husband dreamt of claiming a bride-price for himself. Nor is marriage the only occasion when the milk-price crops up; until a Brāhūī mother has expressly renounced all mother-rights in her dead child, no one would dream of removing the body to the grave.

[1] There is, however, a hitch in the argument. The first cousin to whom the bow-price goes in default of a brother (§186) is the son of the paternal and not, as of course should be the case if the argument is to hold good, of the maternal uncle. So we would apparently have to assume that the paternal cousin has managed under modern conditions to acquire for himself rights which under strict old custom either did not exist at all or else were enjoyed by the maternal cousin. Though there is a little awkwardness in both assumptions, neither can be said to be impossible. If I had to choose between them, I should plump for the former.

189. But mother-kin is not merely the antithesis of father-kin, it is of course opposed also to the rights of the husband. And generations after the merging of mother-kin into father-kin was complete, this opposition might well continue to be felt in the clashing of the rights of the parents on the one hand and the rights of the husband on the other. Take, for instance, the simple question whether a girl is married in her father's house or in the house of her groom. With luck the answer ought to throw a glimmer of light on the subject; for a bridegroom can only hope to be allowed to remove his bride from her parental roof in a society where the father or rather the husband has firmly established himself as the head of the family. Now it is in the bride's house that a Brāhūī wedding is performed, and—much more significant—the young couple must abide in it for at least three days after the wedding; indeed in high Jhalawān families it is a point of honour for her parents to keep them much longer. So great store do Brāhūī parents set by this ancient custom that many a young husband wrings a goodly portion of the bride-price and the milk-price out of them by simply threatening to pack up at once and be gone with his bride. A Balōch wedding, on the other hand, is solemnised in the bridegroom's house, the *nikāḥ* being read the very evening of the bride's arrival; if she has not reached puberty, custom must nevertheless be fulfilled and the girl must be brought to the bridegroom's house, though consummation is of course deferred till she has left girlhood behind. There is some diversity of practice among the Paṭhāns, but as a very general rule the wedding is celebrated in the house of the groom. The *nikāḥ* is sometimes read the moment she arrives. Sometimes she has to wait; and wait she obviously must, if the bridegroom has hidden himself away. During this period of delay, which ordinarily lasts for three days, she is treated like a guest, and it is essential that some kinswoman should sleep by her side. Even after the marriage is solemnised, she often continues to share her bed with a kinswoman for three nights more; and when her husband eventually joins her, he is expected in some tribes to defer consummation for a considerable period. I suppose that those who are hot on the tracks of mother-kin will say that the Brāhūī custom is a very obvious survival of it; that mother-kin has given way entirely to father-kin in the Balōch custom; that the curious Paṭhān custom lies midway on the road to final evolution. That ancient mother-kin is the explanation of the Brāhūī custom seems not unlikely. Taken by itself the Balōch custom hardly proves anything one way or another. As for the Paṭhān custom, I confess I find the implied argument as far-fetched and unsatisfying as the local theory that the bridegroom's sole object in delay is to bring his bride's pre-nuptial peccadilloes to light. As the custom prevails more particularly in those tribes that still go in wholesale for pre-nuptial amours, it may sound ironical to suggest that this ostentatious but in many cases doubtless fictitious delay is simply an ostentatious but equally fictitious display of bashfulness on the part of the young couple—topsy-turvily analogous to the ostentatious and yet in reality bashful departure of the English bridal couple, who hasten away from home and the curious eyes of their kith and kin. But I forgot. Even the honeymoon has been glorified into a splendid survival of the flight of the groom after the capture of his bride.

In the restriction of the husband's rights.

190. But we must pass on to other and possibly more convincing evidence of ancient mother-kin. Once the bride-price has been paid over and the possession of the girl has been transferred from her parents to her husband, the authority of the husband over his wife appears at first sight to be so absolutely unrestricted in Balūchistān that one is apt to conclude that the parents' rights in her are dead. Nevertheless, whereas a Paṭhān or Brāhūī woman is transferred permanently out of her parental family on marriage and does not return to it on widowhood, the ordinary rule among the Balōch is for her to remain a member of her husband's family only so long as he is alive; on his death she reverts to her parents.[1] The custom is still unfixed

In the retention of parental rights.

[1] The rule may be stated categorically of all the great *tuman* in the east, with the special exception of the Khetrān. Among western Balōch the rule is often the reverse: *e.g.*, a good deal of the recent trouble in Khārān was due to the refusal of Sir Naurōz's son to hand over his father's widow to his uncle. But even among eastern Balōch the rule is only absolute in cases of ordinary marriage. Thus among the Ḍombkī and Umrānī, a woman given in marriage as compensation for murder remains with her husband's family on widowhood; given as compensation for adultery she reverts to her parents. Among the Jamālī the rule seems the other way round. Among the Bulēdī she remains with the deceased husband's family in either case.

among the Khetrān, who for practical purposes are usually regarded as Balōch (§264): whether Khetrān parents are to retain or renounce their hold over their daughter on her widowhood is a matter which is regularly defined in the marriage settlement. But the rights of husband and parents overlap in a still more interesting manner. Among all three races—Paṭhān, Brāhūī, Balōch—tribal law looks to the husband to avenge adultery with the blood of the guilty couple; and if the paramour manages to escape his clutches, he should slay his wife none the less. Now according to tribal theory the husband in so doing simply acts as executioner: it is the paramour who has signed her death-warrant; her blood is on his head, and it is with bloodmoney alone that he can wipe out the bloodfeud. Among Paṭhāns the husband receives every penny of it. And this is exactly what one would expect on tribal premises. As Balōch parents merely make a temporary transfer of their daughter and recover their rights in her on her husband's death, it would seem only fair that they should receive some small compensation for their potential loss. In point of fact they receive not a penny. Yet among Brāhūīs two-thirds of the bloodmoney go to the wife's parents. That Brāhūī parents should receive any of the bloodmoney at all—still more that they should receive the lion's share—seems altogether irrational, seeing that they relinquished their other rights in their daughter for good and all when they handed her over in marriage. I can only assume that their title to two-thirds of her bloodmoney is a relic of the days when the parents' rights over their married daughter were very considerable indeed. And I fancy that research would reveal the fact that the killing of an adulterous wife was once a right or a duty that fell primarily on the parents and not on the husband, and that (except when he caught her red-handed in adultery) he was only justified in acting as executioner if the parents were absent, or had delegated the execution to him. This idea, I fancy, is still alive. Here, for instance, is a curious case that occurred the other day, which also illustrates the stringency of 'the unwritten law' in Balūchistān. An adulterous wife was killed by her Brāhūī husband on the spot: the paramour escaped and took sanctuary for a while: then thought better of it, and returned home: dug himself a grave, and sent word to the woman's kinsmen that he was awaiting their coming. He hadn't to wait long.

In the prominence of the maternal uncle.

191. And finally let us return to the maternal uncle who has already appeared on the scene (§ 187) and frequently plays a prominent part in the family life, which seems hardly intelligible except on the theory that he once played the most prominent part of all—as the brother, and therefore the owner or natural defender, of the mother. It is for him (to take a few striking instances) to put some rupees—eventually the barber's perquisite—under his nephew's feet at a Marī circumcision; at a Brāhūī circumcision it is he who leads the lad up to the wooden pot for the operation; it is he who furnishes him with his first breeches among the Khetrān. Both these occasions, circumcision and breeching, are significant enough, for both are connected directly or indirectly with the boy's entrance to manhood. But the maternal uncle, unlike the paternal uncle, is always bobbing up in domestic customs. Indeed throughout Balūchistān he is regarded as a much nearer and a much dearer and more loving kin than the uncle on the father's side. The country is full of wise saws to prove it, just as it is full of saws (and Brāhūī saws in particular) to prove that the faults and virtues of a son are derived not so much from his father as from his mother—in short, that it is the mother and not the father who is the boy's nearest kin.

Inheritance confined to male agnates.

192. But if such ideas and such customs really hark back to the days of mother-kin, those days are long since dead. To-day the position of husband and father is supreme, and in nearly all parts of Balūchistān inheritance is strictly confined not merely to males, but to those who can trace their descent through males. So far from females being reckoned among the heirs, they are not the least valuable assets in the estate. There is, it is true, a faint-hearted tendency springing up to give women the shares to which Islām entitles them. At present the tendency is little more than pious fiction. If it ever develops into reality, the consequences will be far-reaching indeed. At the stage when property still consists of flocks and herds and a few sticks of furniture, the

division of a dead man's estate among the various members of his family into the fractional shares laid down by religion is as easy in practice as it is certainly equitable in principle. But times change: pastoral life begins to give way before agriculture, and the possession of land comes to be vital to the tribe even though life is still largely nomadic. Yet so long as the land remains the joint property of the tribe, the partition of the property of a deceased tribesman into the requisite fractions gives rise to little tribal inconvenience. On the inevitable evolution from tribal ownership to severalty the difficulties begin in real earnest. With the death of each relative the whole family is plunged into a pretty mathematical problem, often difficult enough to work out on paper, a thousandfold more difficult to work out on the land itself. Complexity succeeds complexity, until confusion reigns supreme. But confusion would become chaos, if our tribesmen suddenly changed their own simple if selfish methods. And it is not merely on the score of complexity that *sharīat* or Muhammadan Law is ill-suited to our tribes in their present stage of development. It strikes at the very root of the tribal system itself. Once women are admitted to full rights of inheritance and put in actual possession of land, land will constantly be passing out of the family. Even if our tribes were strictly endogamous, this would have serious consequences impossible wholly to foretell. But as women are married freely outside the tribe, the land would pass not only from the family but from the tribe itself, and the tribal system would be threatened with its death-blow. This was perceived by the chief fathers of the families of the children of Gilead in the days of Moses, and the one remedy for the tribes of Balūchistān would be the remedy Moses propounded for the tribes of Israel, 'Only to the family of the tribe of their father shall they marry, so shall not the inheritance...remove from tribe to tribe' (Numbers XXXVI 6, 7). In a word, unless and until our tribes go in for a radical readjustment of their marriage customs, the exclusion of women from the inheritance is dictated by the primary instinct of tribal self-preservation. It is no accidental coincidence that Makrān and Las Bela, where the women have in great measure made good their claims to inheritance, are just those parts of Balūchistān where the tribal system seems hopelessly in decay.

193. Thus in Balūchistān at large a woman might seem to be a mere chattel, an object of barter from birth to death; marriage simply a transfer of property by the parents to the husband's family in consideration of a bride-price. And heavy though his outlay may be, the husband should soon be able to make money out of his investment. There is at any rate a good deal of force in the retort made by a tribesman, taxed with improvidence in marrying while head over ears in debt: a wife does more work than a couple of bullocks, and with luck will breed enough in a few years to pay for her bride-price thrice over. Even if it prove a barren marriage, she need not represent so much money thrown away or remain so much capital locked up. The husband can divorce her, merely stipulating for the proceeds if—one may almost say when—she re-marries, and thus recover a fair proportion of what he had to pay for her. Out of her infidelity, sad to relate, he can make yet more. Even on widowhood she constitutes a valuable and, as a rule, an easily realisable asset of his estate; or else (as among some Balōch) she reverts to her parental family, only to be disposed of afresh. Death and death alone removes her finally off the market. It's a sorry existence that these gleanings of custom conjure up, sordid and drab from the cradle to the grave. Yet the truth of the picture seems borne out only too well by the casual glimpses we get of a tribeswoman in actual life—a drudge about the house, a beast of burden on the march, in the courts a chattel in dispute, and too often a thing of dishonour. In strange and pleasant contrast are the little maidens at play, as happy as the day is long. It is not simply that the tiny tots are 'regardless of their doom': they are as well nourished and as well looked-after as their urchin brothers. And the sight of their happiness and the love that has evidently been lavished upon them at this one period of female existence when the curtain is lifted from the inner life, should give us pause. That life cannot always be one long sunless tragedy. Though customs and customary law reveal the narrow dreary limits within which it must be ordered, they tell us little or nothing of what the ordinary humdrum woman can make of her unpromising

Status of women.

environment. For life seen in the courts is life seen at its worst, here as elsewhere. Of the love of parents, of affection in the husband's house, we necessarily know little, and arguing rigidly and unimaginatively from customs to the inner life, we are at times inclined to regard their existence as an impossibility. It would be vain to attempt to prove too much. Yet amid much in the women-customs of the tribes that is repugnant to our more advanced ideas and a direct offence against their own religion, there is a good deal not unsuited to their stage of development. And though we are tempted to think that some of the customs are more than flesh and blood could bear, I fancy that if we could peep behind the scenes and watch the customs being enacted in flesh and blood in an everyday household, we should find the average woman adapting herself to her environment with a matter-of-fact resignation not at all incompatible with happiness.

Apologia for bride-price.

194. Thus, objectionable though we may think the payment of bride-price in the abstract, it has much to recommend it in practice. To its credit must be placed first and foremost the absence of female infanticide in the tribes. Indeed should any recrudescence of female-infanticide (§ 149) ever come to light, the most effective remedy would be not legislation, but the introduction of bride-price where bride-price does not exist, or the doubling of it where it does. It ensures the careful nurture of the child from infancy to maidenhood, and tends to invest the young wife on entry into her husband's home with a respect in some degree proportionate to its size. It acts as a very valuable check against wholesale and unbridled polygyny. The system of bride-price lends itself readily no doubt to abuses, some of which, by a curious tragic irony, indirectly owe their birth or growth to the peace and security of our administration. But it is the abuses rather than the system itself that call for check. To abolish the system at this stage of tribal development would be to reap a rich crop of greater evils, the nature and offshoots of which it would be impossible to foresee.

And for the contracting of unborn babes.

195. Or take a custom which outrages our ideas still more violently. Among Paṭhāns one of the commonest ways of patching up a bloodfeud is to give a couple of girls born and a couple of girls unborn, as part of the settlement. That is to say, the aggressor makes his peace with the aggrieved party by handing over a couple of girls in marriage and by covenanting to give two more, yet unborn, in the course of time. To us it might seem difficult to conceive anything more monstrous than thus to dispose of infants before they see the light of day. Yet look at the idea for a moment from another point of view. The contracting of unborn babes is not confined to settlement of bloodfeuds. Among Brāhūīs in particular it is often a love-match arranged between two expectant mothers in token of the affection they bear one another, much in the same way as among ourselves two friends are fond of interweaving schemes for carrying on their love to the next generation in a marriage between their prospective offspring. With us it is an ideal, a fond dream that usually goes the way of all dreams. With the Brāhūīs it eventuates into fact. And if we are able to accept without many qualms the fundamental principle of the tribesmen that it is for the parent to make matrimonial alliances for their children, it seems hypercritical to cavil at their desire to take time by the forelock by arranging a love-match at the very beginning of things. That love is the deity that presides over the arrangement of marriages of girls and unborn babes in the settlement of a bloodfeud, it would be ridiculous to pretend. Yet the fact remains that no other means of preventing the further shedding of blood can rival this apparently iniquitous system. And the reason is obvious. Not only is peace secured for the time being by the more or less immediate operation of marriage-ties between the parties, it is strengthened progressively as the years go on by the prospect of fresh alliances, until it is cemented anew by marriages in the next generation when the girls are grown to maturity.

The influence of women.

196. Now if women were mere chattels, as lasting a peace would be secured by the immediate payment of half their value in money or kind and a promise to pay the other half after a lapse of sixteen years or so. The truth is that women cannot be reduced to terms of money, whatever tribesmen and professed misogynists like them may imagine or pretend to imagine. To treat them

as soulless abstractions is to ignore the fundamental laws of human nature which govern the relations of man and wife, or mother and child. It argues in fact a singular shortsightedness to look upon tribeswomen as chattels and nothing more. They are human beings with rights as well as duties, though the latter may bulk so large in our eyes as to crowd the former out of sight. So far from being mere chattels, the average wife and the average mother exercise a very real influence over their menfolk, none the less potent because it is exercised in the background. To say that the hand that rocks the cradle rules the tribe, would be hyperbole. Yet cases are on record of the paramount influence of women in the tribe. Witness the widowed lady who a couple of generations ago ruled the Zahrī and hence all Jhalawān with a strong hand not only during the minority of her son but also after his death. Or witness the skill and statecraft with which Musammāt Gulsana managed the Jōgizai tribe when it was thrown into confusion on the murder of her father, the great Bangal Khān. Nor is it simply in the political world that tribeswomen have been known to play a significant part. In the spiritual world there is no personage of greater reverence and influence than Bībī Mariam, Chishtī Sayyid of Kalāt. And if the women can thus make their influence felt in the larger spheres of tribal life, it is certainly not inoperative in the home-life of individual families.

XIX.—Civil Condition among the Indigenous Population.

(*Regular areas only.*)

RACE	0—15.						15 AND OVER					
	MALES			FEMALES			MALES			FEMALES		
	Unmarried	Married	Widowed	Unmarried	Married	Widowed	Unmarried	Married	Widowed	Unmarried	Married	Widowed
All Indigenous	**961**	**15**	...	**634**	**44**	...	**2,586**	**2,630**	**313**	**72**	**947**	**245**
Balōch	106	2	...	77	8	...	200	547	34	9	152	23
Brāhūī	128	...	...	98	5	...	497	477	44	11	183	30
Pathān	311	2	...	187	13	...	1,552	944	129	17	265	79
Others	416	11	...	272	18	...	337	662	106	35	347	113

XX.—Civil Condition among Brāhūīs censused in Sind.

BIRTHPLACE	0—15						15 AND OVER					
	MALES			FEMALES			MALES			FEMALES		
	Unmarried	Married	Widowed	Unmarried	Married	Widowed	Unmarried	Married	Widowed	Unmarried	Married	Widowed
All	**12,957**	**215**	**16**	**9,908**	**502**	**18**	**6,132**	**12,714**	**1,349**	**701**	**13,023**	**2,854**
Sind	8,042	128	8	6,649	258	8	2,524	4,769	481	393	5,319	1,170
Balūchistān	4,780	84	7	3,195	234	10	3,512	7,780	849	294	7,505	1,651
Other provinces	135	3	1	64	10	...	97	165	19	14	199	33

CHAPTER VIII.

EDUCATION.

Statistical data.

SUBJECT.	TABLES.		
	Imperial.	Provincial.	Subsidiary.
Education by religion and age .	VIII	......	......
Education by race . .	IX	......	XXII
Education among Musalmāns .	......	......	XXI, XXII
Education by locality .	......	II	XXI

197. Without laying the slightest pretension to scrupulous accuracy, I fancy that our literacy statistics only need a little judicious weeding to yield a fairly true account of the general progress of education in the country. Education, to be sure, is a high-sounding title to give to what often falls short of the three R's, and the word progress has a somewhat strong flavour of irony about it. Our educational standard amounted to nothing more than the ability to decipher a letter and pen a reply; and, even so, I am not prepared to vouch that every one of our self-styled literates could really reach this humble standard. We had to take the statements, especially in the case of the women, more or less on trust. Among ourselves reading and writing are so correlated that it requires a mental effort for us to conceive of a man that can read and yet is unable to write. But in Balūchistān, where the goal of indigenous education is the reading of the Koran, scores who can read Arabic glibly cannot write a word. And as our enumerators could not be allowed to set themselves up as an examining board, the chances are that a fairish number who would be floored at having to write a letter, have found their way among the literates. On the other hand, there must have been a few genuine literates who escaped our notice; for reading and writing, though rare accomplishments among the tribesmen, hardly impress the tribal mind as being of any importance or even particularly reputable. And this is the upshot of the statistics. In every thousand persons we can produce no more than 33 who profess to be able to con a letter and scrawl a reply. Of the lot 31 are males. But if general literacy is at a low ebb, literacy in English is extraordinarily high by comparison. Of the 31 males who are literate, no less than 7 are prepared to back themselves as literate in English. Among female literates English, it would seem, has greater attractions still. Nearly every couple that can read and write at all contains one who claims to be able to read and write English. **General.**

Literates per mille.

	Males.	Females.
Literate . .	31	2
English-literate	7	1

198. There could be no happier proof of the futility of wasting one's ingenuity over the literacy statistics of the province as a whole. The study of English has no lot or part in the tribesman's life; still less is it the concern of the tribeswoman. The bulk of these apparently advanced students of English are either English themselves or natives of India from down-country. Their presence in the statistics obscures the only thing of real interest that the statistics have to tell. To get at it, we must sweep the boards of all aliens, and **Literacy among the indigenous inhabitants.**

look at the state of literacy in the country when the country is left to its true indigenous inhabitants. And it will clear matters still further if we weed out the domiciled Hindus at the same time. They are an unusually literate lot, these old Hindu families. Among them book-learning is passed on from father to son, to be used of course in the way of business. And in Hindu business it is a matter of workaday precaution to indulge in a script of one's own; accordingly, though every domiciled Hindu who returned himself as literate may actually be able to write to his father and read his reply, I doubt whether it follows that a Hindu, let us say, in K͟hārān could necessarily carry on a free correspondence with a Hindu, let us say, in the Kachhī. Purged of the aliens, the semi-indigenous and these domiciled Hindus, the statistics go down with a bang. Literacy must now be reckoned, not as so much in a thousand, but as so much—or rather so little—in ten thousand.

Literacy by race.

199. In every 10,000 indigenous Musalmāns there are but 47 who were found to reach our modest requirements. Yet, painfully low though this figure is, it gives an extravagant idea of the amount of literacy among those whom we have come to regard as the real tribesmen of the country. For, if we muster the races in the order of their scholastic attainments, we find the Sayyid, the Lāsī, and the Jaṭṭ at the top of the list, and the Paṭhān, the Balōch and the Brāhūī at the bottom. To those who know something of the country, there is little in the list to awaken surprise. It is after all only in the fitness of things that the Sayyid should head the list in virtue of his sacred calling; it is only in accord with his general attitude of contempt towards book-learning that the Brāhūī should be relegated to the bottom. It will doubtless be the first instinct of the enthusiastic educationist, flushed with the prospect of finding a rich harvest of literacy where his schoolmasters are abroad in the land, to trace the reason for the ups and downs of the several races in the varying educational facilities offered by the localities they inhabit. But his enthusiasm will receive a cold shock when he discovers that the districts, the very centre of his scholastic activities, can only reckon 46 literates in 10,000 of the population, while the backward states, to which he has still to devote his attentions, can boast their 48. To these figures our educationist may perhaps demur, for even he will confess that his schooling leaves the womenfolk unaffected. But if we narrow the statistics down to the males, his record becomes worse still: in the states there are 89 literates in 10,000 males; in the districts there are but 84. For my own part, though I would not deny the direct influence of our schools or question the likelihood of their giving an increasingly better account of themselves as time goes on, I confess to resting much greater faith in the indirect but vivifying influence of our administration, in the gradual pacification and settlement of the country, and in the growing contact of our peoples, thanks to our roads and our railways, with other and more enlightened communities. After all, what hampers the march of education among the Balōch and the Paṭhāns and the Brāhūīs, is not merely the bigotry or the suspicions or the prejudices of the tribesmen, but also—and perhaps even more—the self-sufficiency of their tribal society, which secludes them from the wider movements in the world outside them, and the nomad life that has so many of them in its grip.

Literates per 10,000.	
Sayyid	170
Lāsī	68
Jaṭṭ	57
Paṭhān	50
Miscellaneous	44
Balōch	38
Brāhūī	32

Literacy by language.

200. But this is only one side of the picture. A settled life of husbandry and contact with a wider civilisation may explain why the Lāsī and the Jaṭṭ should stand higher in the educational scale than the Brāhūīs and Balōch, or why literacy should have struck root in Las Bēla or Quetta, and wilted away in Zhōb. They are no reasons why the states as a whole should be more advanced than the districts. To understand this paradox we must turn to the languages in which literacy is claimed. As the language of present-day official education is Urdū, we might naturally expect to see Urdū drive all other languages out of the educational field. And if only we persevere long enough, this may possibly be the dismal issue. But the day is not yet. Persian, the ancient literary language of the province, still maintains its supremacy. For every indigenous Musalmān that can read and write Urdū, there are more than two that can read and write Persian. Of the 2,121 literates who have been returned among the Balōch, Brāhūīs and Paṭhāns, 1,544 have returned themselves as literate in

Persian; 553 only have returned themselves as literate in Urdū. And this to my thinking is the most striking moral that the statistics have to tell. It is surely a useful straw that shows which way the educational wind is blowing. In fact, I am sorely tempted to ascribe much more destruction than construction to our present educational efforts, and to seek the explanation for the backwardness of literacy in the districts in the greater scope that has here been offered for what I cannot but regard as our misdirected zeal.

Indigenous education. 201. This is a hard saying. Yet it has not been petulantly provoked by some illusion in the statistics. It has been forced upon me gradually by what little knowledge I have of the tribesmen themselves. But an end to this dreary prologue. The statistics have held the stage long enough. It is time to ring up the curtain on actual life. There is quite a pretty little scene among the tribesmen when a lad first enters the mosque for his schooling. His father presents the mulla with a plate of sweetmeats topped by a couple of rupees. And the mulla makes the lad repeat *Bismilla* after him, and puts him through the alphabet before the proud friends of the family who have assembled for the occasion. Learning proceeds very slowly: first comes the study of a simple Arabic primer, with a little general instruction in Persian; then a few simple verses of the Koran. The day when the lad has read the Koran from cover to cover is kept as a high day and holiday. Sweetmeats are distributed among the kith and kin; the lad is dressed up in gay clothes and tipped by his relatives; the mulla is given sweetmeats and cash and a new turban. The rejoicings of this day are never repeated, however much further the lad may prosecute his studies; and as for the mulla, he simply receives a fee called ‘Īdī on every ‘Īd festival. But further than this a lad is hardly likely to go, unless he is to become a *tālib-i-‘ilm*, training for the priesthood. Then he will study various books on religious topics, though at the end it may be doubted whether he is really much wiser than he was before. If he wants to become really learned, he will go from mulla to mulla, for a mulla is rarely versed in more books than one, and in all probability cannot write at all. Reading is no doubt a religious accomplishment, and in pious theory at any rate a useful and desirable accomplishment, even for a tribesman. Writing is on a completely different footing: it is purely secular, worldly, and more or less dangerous. It must not be supposed that a lad is taught simply to rattle the Koran off by heart. What he reads he of course rarely understands; in the narrowest sense of the word the reading itself is genuine enough. The pity is that education usually stops at reading; the short and to us inevitable step onwards to writing, which might be calculated to put a little life into the mechanical reading, is taken by very few.

Pathān attitude towards education. 202. As the mullas are the only people (with the obvious exception of the Hindu traders) who go in for education as a matter of course, and as they are the sole teachers outside the Government schools, the amount of literacy in the different parts of the country tends to vary directly with their position and influence. There is thus more book-learning among Paṭhāns than among Brāhūīs or Balōch; more in the Quetta-Pishīn district, where a strong mulla influence dates back to the old days of Kandahār rule, than in Zhōb and Lōṛalai. But education is at a low ebb even among Paṭhāns. In one sense the Paṭhāns have laid to heart the Prophet's injunction "Seek thou knowledge though it be in China," for they are world-wide travellers. But though a learned man commands respect among them, they are themselves no very ardent seekers after knowledge in the ordinary sense of the word. They regard book-learning as a matter that ill repays them for the time and labour that must be spent on it. Not but what the pious and the well-to-do will make shift to send their boys to the mosque between the ages of six and twelve to get a grounding in the Koran: the pious, because they would encourage their sons to become mullas; the well-to-do, because they seem to be beginning to look upon a smattering of religious learning as the right thing for people in their station.

Brāhūī and Balōch attitude. 203. Among Brāhūīs and Balōch there is usually a very different feeling on the subject. Book-learning may be all very well for the mulla, and a learned mulla is useful enough when it comes to the prescribing of charms and amulets. But for the rest—"who wants his son to become a mulla?" as one of the chiefs indignantly exclaimed, scandalised at the suggestion that he should give his son a decent education. For a bookworm and a mulla are regarded as one and the same thing by the countryside. To call a Brāhūī a mulla is to use a very ugly term of reproach. If you want to taunt him with cowardice, there will be an added sting if you call him a mulla—a cowardly mulla, who sits in the mosque where the leopard can't get at him, as the Brāhūī proverb puts it. In many chiefly families, no doubt, it is becoming fashionable for the sons to receive an education of sorts. And so long as this is confined to the education of the old school, all goes well. But the results of a more up-to-date education have been far from encouraging. A little modern book-learning is a dangerous thing for a budding chief. It makes him discontented with the ancient ways of his fathers, and his discontent is usually advertised to the tribesmen and the outer world by a change in dress and manners. It is often said that the Balōch and Brāhūī are more naturally aristocratic in their political leanings than the Paṭhān. But Balōch and Brāhūī alike remain amenable to their chief only so long as their chief remains one of themselves. His manners, dress and customs may be a little more fine, a little more grandiose than theirs; they must be the same in kind. As soon as a chief turns up his nose at ancient customs and apes the manners and dress of aliens, it is a sure sign that he is already beginning to lose his hold over his tribesmen. Not until the mass of the tribesmen turn their thoughts to education, will it be altogether safe for any but the strongest minds among the chiefs to go in for it themselves. And that day lies far ahead. For education is instinctively regarded as a mysteriously insidious enemy of ancient custom: and ancient custom is dearer to the tribesmen than anything else; it is more revered than religion itself.

Urdū education uncongenial and apparently unsuitable.

204. Education has thus an uphill journey before it in Balūchistān. But need the road be quite so uphill as the one we are taking? There is, I think, a much easier if more winding road that leads to the same goal. We blame the reluctance of the tribesmen to avail themselves of the great boon of education we hold out to them. But I fancy we are putting the blame on the wrong shoulders, like the teacher in the Balōchī proverb who could not teach and whacked the boys instead. We profess to hold out to them a vernacular education, but the education we offer is not racy or vernacular at all: it is simply the vernacular education of Hindustān, with which the Central Asiatic civilisation of Balūchistān has no natural concern. And what the more intelligent tribesmen object to is not so much education itself, as a foreign system of education. It is not simply that Urdū is a foreign tongue, which must be laboriously mastered before education can begin at all, or that the teacher is usually as ignorant of the language of his pupils as they are of his. These are defects in the system burdensome enough to the boys; they are not the defects that worry the parents. To the tribesmen at large Urdū is the language of alien India, of its alien courts of justice and its alien modes of administration; it breathes strange ideas, ideas which menace their ancient manners and institutions. This is what is at the back of the minds of the shrewder tribesmen when they decline to send their lads to our schools. Call it sentiment, if you will: were it nothing more, it would be enough to give us pause. To one who is not bold enough to scoff at sentiment, and who feels, though none can measure, the great but subtle influence of alien language on thought and manners and customs, there is much in the prejudice against Urdū education to awaken his sympathy. The tribesmen after all are not condemning the system altogether unheard: they have given it some sort of trial, half-hearted though it has been. And they ought to know what they are talking about when they describe the local product of our Urdū education as an unnatural hybrid, a cross between a tribesman and a Panjābī that combines the poorer qualities of both, always fidgeting under the good old customs of his fathers, always aping new-fangled ways which sit ill upon him. To use their own parable, he is like the crow of the Persian fable that never succeeded in learning to run like a partridge, but only managed to forget how to hop like a crow.

A plea for the indigenous agency.

205. The quack remedy is of course a more heroic dose of Urdū education still. But when the old prescription so palpably disagrees with the patient, is it not wiser to alter the prescription? The key-note of administration in Balūchistān is home-rule—the self-government of the frontier, as far as may be, by the tribesmen themselves along the ancient lines of tribal custom. And it would be only in harmony with the whole tenor of our administration if our educational system were directed to helping the tribesmen to educate themselves after their own methods. To be consistent with our general policy, our object

should be to turn the young generation into better tribesmen, not into artificial individualists—to make them not different from their fathers, but better, more fully developed. And as in administration, so in education, we are only likely to achieve success by quickening the existing system. The success that has marked the employment of ancient machinery in administration, should at any rate make us hesitate before we scrap the ancient machinery in education. However difficult it may be to work through or with the mullas, the sole indigenous scholastic agency in the country, the experiment would deserve a patient trial even on grounds of mere policy: as long as their monopoly is threatened by our entrance into the educational field, so long will the dead-weight of their powerful influence be thrown into the scale against our educational efforts.

And for Persian education.

206. As regards the vehicle of ed machinery may seem at a disadvantage. None of the three tribal vernaculars will ser seemr purpose. Brāhūī is never reduced to writing; Balōchī hardly ever, notwithstanding the rich and interesting collection of ballads it can boast; and though a few Pashtō works, chiefly of a religious character, figure among the books conned by the budding mulla, Pashtō in Balūchistān is not a written language like the Pashtō of the North West Frontier. And if we must turn to other languages, Arabic, on which existing education seems to be grounded, is as dead a language to the tribesmen as Latin is to the average schoolboy at home; and though it would be a mighty educational force if the grandeur of the Holy Book of Islām and not merely the grandeur of its sounds could reach the tribesmen, it must be confessed, that, as matters now stand, an Arabic education would be as artificial to the tribesmen as Urdū education itself. There remains Persian. Now, though Arabic may seem to be the basis of indigenous education, this is only because it leads on to the reading of the Koran. But it is in Persian that the Koran is usually expounded, and the teaching of Persian and the reading of Persian classics are almost invariably parts of the mulla's curriculum. Persian was and still is the official language of the K͟hān's Darbār; all correspondence between the K͟hān and the chiefs and between one chief and another is conducted in it; it is the common language of the polite world; it is understood by thousands; it is admired by all. In the form of Dēhwārī it is actually one of the vernaculars of Balūchistān; Balōchī is its first cousin; Pashtō is a near kin. Better still, the whole spirit of Persian is in a very real if indescribable manner attuned to the spirit of the country. Speaking, not of course as an educationist, but as a census officer who not only counts heads but tries to read what is inside them, I cannot but feel that the returns of literacy among the tribesmen, and among Brāhūīs and Balōch more especially, would be much less dismal reading at the next census, if we ceased to kick against the pricks, and contented ourselves with fostering a sound but simple education through the indigenous agency on the foundation of this magnificent language and its magnificent literature. Such an educational system would not come up against a deadwall of passive resistance such as now confronts us, and on this foundation it ought not to be difficult—though one may doubt whether it would be worth the while—to build up an education in Urdū for the more robust spirits among the tribesmen who want to go further than their fellows.

Strong feeling against English education.

207. Strong though the prejudice is against Urdū education, it is doubly strong against English. But of English education they hardly know except by hearsay: an English-knowing tribesman is very rare indeed. One of the Balōch chiefs, an admirable blending of the natural wit of the old school and the acquired wisdom of the new, tried the experiment of giving his eldest son a smattering of English. As the youth went to the dogs, all the blame was of course piled on to the English education, and English is accordingly a subject that is ruthlessly banned from the studies of his brother. Even among the more enterprising Paṭhāns the prejudice is strong. The common idea is that the man that learns English will be sure to mumble English on his death-bed instead of reciting the *Kalima*; and to die with English on the lips is to take a passport to Hell. Small wonder that the death-bed scene of the wretch that knows English is a favourite theme of the sensational story-teller and an awful warning to others.

And against female education.

208. And all that has been said about education generally applies with a sevenfold force to the education of women. A tribesman looks upon female

education as something highly unbecoming. Among Paṭhāns, no doubt, it is considered in theory only right and in practice harmless enough for a girl to be put through her paces in the Koran and a few devotional books, and there is all the less harm in this as in ninety-nine cases out of a hundred the modicum of learning is forgotten as soon as it is acquired. Further than this, the Paṭhān considers it would be mischievous to go: and even this is more than Brāhūī or Balōch would approve of. Education casts a blight on the sex, they think. Teach a woman to read, and she will read love-stories. And what conceivable use could she put writing to but the penning of love-letters ?

SUBSIDIARY TABLES.

XXI.—Literacy among Musalmāns by Locality.

District or state.	LITERATES									LITERATES IN 10,000 INDIGENOUS MUSALMĀNS OF EITHER SEX	
	TOTAL			ALIEN		SEMI-INDIGENOUS		INDIGENOUS			
	Persons	Males	Females	Males	Females	Males	Females	Males	Females	Males	Females
BALŪCHISTĀN	***7,306***	***7,093***	***213***	***3,507***	***177***	***140***	***1***	***3,446***	***35***	***86***	***1***
Districts	**5,182**	**4,989**	**193**	**3,349**	**173**	**129**	**1**	**1,511**	**19**	**84**	**1**
Quetta-Pishīn	2,843	2,712	131	1,961	126	49	1	702	4	149	·9
Lōṛalai	581	572	9	371	8	49	...	152	1	44	·3
Zhōb	563	561	2	414	1	...	...	147	1	44	·3
Bōlān	80	76	4	67	3	...	...	9	1	179	29
Chāgai	200	189	11	76	10	2	...	111	1	135	1
Sibi	915	879	36	460	25	29	...	390	11	69	2
Administered area	*891*	*855*	*36*	*458*	*25*	*29*	...	*368*	*11*	*97*	*3*
Mari Bugṭi country	*24*	*24*	...	*2*	...	...	...	*22*	...	*11*	...
States	**2,124**	**2,104**	**20**	**158**	**4**	**11**	...	**1,935**	**16**	**89**	**·8**
Kalāt	1,683	1,672	11	136	4	11	...	1,525	7	82	·4
Sarāwān	*438*	*437*	*1*	*29*	...	*5*	...	*403*	*1*	*118*	·3
Jhalawān	*131*	*131*	...	*3*	...	...	...	*128*	...	*27*	...
Kachhi	*515*	*510*	*5*	*17*	*1*	...	...	*493*	*4*	*108*	*1*
Dōmbki-Kahēri country	*89*	*89*	...	*4*	...	...	...	*85*	...	*77*	...
Makrān	*412*	*407*	*5*	*82*	*3*	...	...	*325*	*2*	*87*	·5
Khārān	*98*	*98*	...	*1*	...	*6*	...	*91*	...	*76*	...
Las Bēla	441	432	9	22	...	...	...	410	9	130	3

XXII.—Literacy among Indigenous Musalmāns by Race.

(NOTE.—Several literates returned themselves as literate in more than one language; hence the apparent discrepancies in the language percentage)

RACE	Literates per 10,000	Female literates to 1,000 male literates	NUMBER PER CENT OF TOTAL LITERATES WHO ARE LITERATE IN						
			Persian	Urdu	Arabic	Sindhi	Lande	English	Other languages
Indigenous Musalmāns	*47*	*10*	*67*	*25*	*9*	*9*	*3*	*1*	*1*
Balōch	**38**	**19**	**77**	**22**	**4**	**9**	**1**	**1**	**1**
(i) *Eastern*	*21*	*39*	*57*	*40*	*8*	*13*	*1*	*2*	*3*
Bugṭī	4	...	...	100	...	...	...	...	...
Khetrān	25	...	29	66	20	...	6	3	...
Magasī	20	129	91	11	3	9	...	...	...
Marī	11	...	25	71	4	...	...	...	...
Rind	26	12	76	27	9	23	...	1	...
(ii) *Western*	*70*	*8*	*89*	*10*	*2*	*6*	*1*	...	...
Rakhshānī	61	...	87	17	...	3	...	1	...
Brāhūī	**32**	**7**	**82**	**16**	**7**	**1**	**1**	**1**	**2**
(i) *Original nucleus*	*43*	*16*	*84*	*16*	*8*	...	...	*2*	...
(ii) *Sarāwān*	*51*	*7*	*84*	*16*	*7*	...	*1*	*1*	...
Bangulzai	30	...	89	9	6	3	...	...	...
Lāngav	67	...	89	12	1	...	...	1	...
(iii) *Jhalawān*	*17*	*6*	*77*	*14*	*9*	*4*	*1*	*1*	*4*
Bizanjav	13	...	93	7	7	...	7	...	...
Māmasanī	24	...	94	3	6	...	...	...	3
Mēngal	21	...	55	20	20	11	...	...	2
Zahrī	10	...	91	25	...	...	...	3	...
(iv) *Miscellaneous*	*131*	...	*74*	*29*	*3*	...	*8*	...	*6*
Paṭhān	**50**	**2**	**65**	**35**	**17**	...	...	**2**	...
Kākaṛ	41	2	65	31	20	...	...	3	...
Sanzarkhēl	*21*	*8*	*57*	*26*	*31*	...	...	*2*	*2*
Snaṭia	*78*	...	*65*	*36*	*12*	...	...	*4*	...
Targhaṛa	*45*	...	*86*	*6*	*14*	...	...	...	...
Paṇī	52	...	57	32	19	...	...	1	1
Musakhēl	*14*	...	*76*	*18*	*12*	...	...	*6*	...
Tarīn	50	5	78	41	11	...	...	1	...
Abdāl Achakzai	*30*	...	*79*	*69*	*16*	...	...	*2*	...
Tōr Tarīn	*75*	...	*90*	*15*	*9*	...	...	...	...
Lāsi	**68**	**22**	**7**	**49**	**2**	**54**	**11**	...	...
Jaṭṭ	**57**	**9**	**69**	**18**	**14**	**14**	...	**1**	...
Sayyid	**170**	**11**	**76**	**21**	**8**	**8**	...	**1**	...
Other Musalmāns	**44**	**14**	**55**	**20**	**2**	**10**	**22**	...	**3**
Darzāda	35	...	92	3	11	...	...	...	3
Ghulām	2	...	...	60	20	20	...	...	...
Lōṛī	5	...	40	60	...	40	...	...	...

CHAPTER IX

LANGUAGE.

Statistical data.

SUBJECT.	TABLES.	
	Imperial.	Subsidiary.
General	X	......
Bilinguity by locality	......	XXIII
Bilinguity and race	......	XXIV
Race and bilinguity	......	XXV
Loss of racial language	......	XXVI

Statistical.

209. Though we did our best to make up for other deficiencies in the tribal areas by conducting a highly elaborate linguistic census, my treatment of the statistics themselves will be very slight. And this for two reasons. The many languages spoken by the strangers within our gates, however interesting in themselves, have little or no interest to Balūchistān : they simply reflect the main features of immigration already reflected by the statistics of birthplace—only in a slightly different and perhaps less distorted manner. And elaborate though our statistics of the languages native to Balūchistān, their full statistical value must necessarily remain buried until we have others to compare with them. No gap in the last census was so regrettable—certainly none was so utterly unnecessary—as the omission to record the languages of the indigenous peoples. If language were perfectly stable—if we could assume, for instance, that every Brāhūī speaks Brāhūī, and every Balōch Balōchī—we might readily reconcile ourselves to the absence of linguistic statistics and get along quite comfortably with the statistics of race. But such assumptions, as we know, would be wide of the mark. Even at the present moment some language, unless I am mistaken, is elbowing out another here and being elbowed out by yet another there. One has only to look at the gradual disappearance of Brāhūī among the Brāhūīs of Sind (§78) to realise how rapid the shifting of language may be, and to regret the more that statistics of the last census are not forthcoming to compare with the linguistic statistics of this. **No linguistic census in 1901.**

210. It was partly in the hope of being able to fathom the changes that are going on that I subjected the indigenous inhabitants to a bilingual census, and recorded not merely their mother-tongue but also any other language that is spoken freely and naturally outside the family circle by all members of the household. For at a humble stage of development nobody will burden himself with a second language if his mother-tongue will carry him everywhere in his ordinary walk of life ; and where the mother-tongue is associated as a matter of course with another, there is evidently a struggle for existence in progress which can only end, be it soon or be it late, by the weaker going to the wall. Moreover, this bilingual census of ours is a useful reminder that there is a good deal of intercourse between the various layers of Balūchistān society, a fact which is patent to the man on the spot, but a fact which might easily be lost sight of by outside readers—if any there be—of Balūchistān census reports. Not **Bilingual census in 1911.**

that our bilingual statistics give a full idea of this intercourse. It must be remembered that the statistics are essentially family statistics, not the statistics of individuals. Had they been collected individual by individual, the statistics of mother-tongue would doubtless have been almost identically the same. But there would have been a goodly rise in the statistics of the secondary language. For we ignored the many precocious individuals who single themselves out from the ruck of the family by mastering some language unknown to the rest : the only secondary language in which we were interested was the one spoken freely in addition to their own by the family as a whole. And though this distinction rendered it almost impossible to extend the bilingual census to the regular areas—and we made no attempt to do so—it served incidentally as a simple but not ineffective test that the secondary language was in reality a living thing and no chance accomplishment.

Chief local languages.

211. Balūchistān is the scene of a three-cornered duel between Iranian, Indian and Dravidian. Not that there is any great harmony within the ranks of the competitors themselves. Balōchī and Pashtō, the two great champions of Iranian, are old and inveterate rivals, among whom the honours rest for the time being with Balōchī. The local champions of Indian are a ragged and ill-assorted regiment commonly known as Jaṭkī or Jadgālī, the members of which, though banded against their common enemies, are fighting among themselves for the supremacy of Sindhī or Western Panjābī (§ 228). Brāhūī alone, the sole champion of Dravidian, shows a united front to the foe. And well it may. For unlike Iranian, whose forces are strengthened by a constant influx of allies more especially from Persia and Afghānistan, and unlike Indian, which is steadily reinforced from India, Brāhūī has friends nowhere. So great is the preponderance of Iranian that, ignoring the presence of the 7,579 speakers of Dēhwārī (§ 221), I will divide the Iranian army into its two main divisions, and follow the fortunes of the four chief languages of Balūchistān—Balōchī, Pashtō, Brāhūī and Jaṭkī. And as the forces of Pashtō in particular are unduly swollen not merely by the semi-indigenous but also by aliens, I will clear the field of all outsiders and allow fair play for the indigenous Musalmāns to fight out their battles among themselves. And the present state of their wordy warfare may be gathered from the margin. Balōchī still holds the mastery. But Pashtō presses it hard, and if it were allowed assistance from outside, it would press it harder still. Yet the battle is not always to the strong, and the final issue will almost certainly not rest with Balōchī. It may not even rest with Pashtō, stubborn language though it is. In despised Jaṭkī there is a yet more dangerous rival in the field. For though Jaṭkī has a lot of ground to make up, many of the conditions are in its favour, and no one would be particularly surprised at its ultimate triumph. Brāhūī, I fear, is no longer in the running.

Balūchistān vernaculars.

Iranian		468,119
Balōchī	*232,987*	
Pashtō	*227.553*	
Dēhwārī	*7,579*	
Indian		155,351
Dravidian		145,299
Unclassified		253

Languages of indigenous Musalmāns.

Balōchī	229,935
Pashtō	201,775
Brāhūī	145,167
Jaṭkī	141,464
Other languages	16,269

Racial distribution.

212. As a rule, of course, language follows race. But we stand in no need of the assistance proffered in the margin to realise that not all our races are able to maintain proper discipline in their ranks. Between the almost unswerving loyalty of the Paṭhāns to their mother-tongue and the infidelity of the Brāhūīs to theirs, there is all the difference in the world. Among Paṭhāns the only outside language that seems to be able to make any serious headway is Jaṭkī, and the only tribes that show any real tendency to succumb to its wiles are the Jafar and the Paṇī—or rather the main branch of the Paṇī long settled in the Jaṭkī atmosphere of Sibī. It is Jaṭkī again that is by far the most successful in weaning the Balōch away from the language of their race. Even though its conquests would be notably diminished if we excluded the Khetrān.

Linguistic distribution per mille of each race.

	Balōchī.	Pashtō.	Brāhūī.	Jaṭkī.	Others.
Indigenous Musalmāns	313	275	198	192	22
Balōch	870	4	17	108	1
Paṭhāns	1	974	2	21	2
Brāhūīs	210	8	773	8	1
Jaṭṭ	48	2	3	878	69
Lāsī	52	...	30	918	...
Sayyids	43	707	52	151	47
Miscellaneous	502	16	123	248	111

BALŪCHISTĀN
SHEWING
LINGUISTIC DISTRIBUTION.

(N.B.—The linguistic boundaries are very approximate only.)

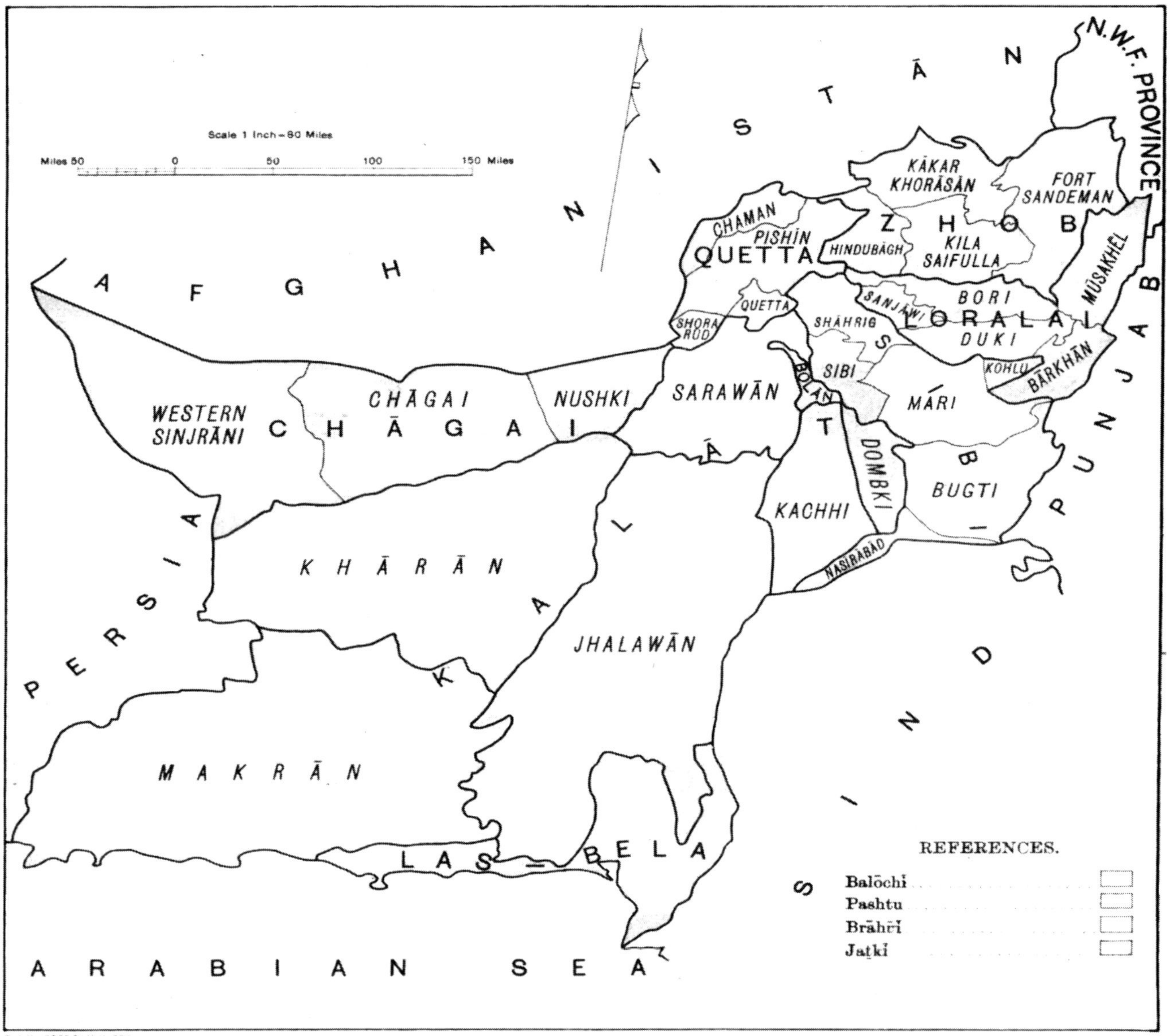

from the Balōch ranks (§264), the fact remains that it has already effected a footing in the very citadel of the Balōch, for it has won over deserters from among the Bugṭī and Magasī, and deserters, at once more numerous and more notable, from among the Rind. But Jaṭkī is worming itself everywhere. Its hold over the Jaṭṭ and the Lāsī is of course only in the nature of things. Nor is there much significance in the number of its adherents among those I have classed as miscellaneous, for in many cases there is no rival in the field to challenge its claim to being their mother-tongue. But there is a good deal of significance, I think, in its signal success among the Sayyids, seeing that most of the Sayyids of Balūchistān live in a Paṭhān environment and that many of them are in all probability Paṭhān or half-Paṭhān by origin (§259). Only the Brāhūīs seem to be able to resist its advances. And here one is almost tempted to mistrust the accuracy of our statistics in face of the remarkable statistics we received from Sind, where half the total number of Brāhūīs enumerated were returned as speakers of what we should call Jaṭkī (§78). But I am not disposed to explain away the apparent paradox by the easy assumption that the enumerators in either province were seriously at fault. There is, in the first place, an obvious difference in the nature of the two statistics: in Balūchistān the Brāhūīs were given the opportunity of entering two languages in their returns; in Sind of course, they had to plump for one; and we shall see in the sequel that the Brāhūīs of Balūchistān affect Jaṭkī very considerably as their secondary language. And in the second place—and this perhaps is even more to the point—of the Brāhūīs enumerated in Sind it is only among those who declared Sind (and not Balūchistān) as their birthplace that there is any serious abnormality in the Jaṭkī returns. In short, I have no hesitation in finding in the analysis of the linguistic statistics of the two provinces yet another confirmation of my conviction that most of the Brāhūīs who were censused in Sind and nominally born in Sind have taken up their abode in Sind for good and all, and belong to Balūchistān no longer.

213. Linguistic territories have no impassable frontiers to set casual trespassers at defiance or to resist insidious but wholesale encroachments. Yet with all its great but inevitable imperfections, the map on the opposite page, which purports to show the general dispositions of the contending forces, merits more than a fleeting glance. Pashtō is massed on the north-east. Balōchī is entrenched in a great block of country on the west and in a more confined but much more thickly populated block on the east, with a small outpost to the south. The Jaṭkī forces are split up. But its disposition is not so unfavourable as one might think; for in reality it consists in strategical positions from which it can sally forth and wear down its enemies at leisure. It has already driven a wedge through Balōchī in the east and between Balōchī and Pashtō further north, and is beginning to drive a wedge between Balōchī and Brāhūī on the south. Brāhūī stands at bay in the centre of the country, surrounded by foes on all sides, with advanced guards of Dēhwārī and Balōchī planted in its very middle. On the map Brāhūī shows a brave enough front. But in looking at the map, one must of course bear in mind the varying density of the several parts of Balūchistān: even Balōchī, strongest of the local vernaculars though it is, looms disproportionately large on the map, because its stronghold in the west is the most thinly populated tract in the country. The map loses nothing in interest on comparison with the equally rough map that serves as frontispiece, on which I have endeavoured to show the distribution of the various races. The first thing that strikes the eye is the ousting of Brāhūī by Balōchī among the Brāhūīs of Makrān; yet the Balōchī inroads into the very heart of the Brāhūī country—into Sarāwān and the southern portions of Jhalawān—are perhaps more remarkable still. The Brāhūī tribes chiefly affected by these Balōchī encroachments are, first and foremost, the Mīrwāṛī, reputed to be Brāhūīs of the oldest and purest Brāhūī stock of all; the Sājdī and the Bīzanjav and the Lāngav; and in lesser degree the Kambrāṛī (another branch of the ancient stock) and the Māmasanī and the Bangulzai. It is to these conquests among the Brāhūīs and to its even more extensive conquests among the miscellaneous peoples that Balōchī owes its superiority in numbers over the Balōch race. And so far it has had to put up with comparatively few desertions from its ranks, though the full significance of the losses it has suffered at the hands of Jaṭkī, notably in the Kachhī among the Rind and the Magasī, is not to be

Geographical distribution.

measured by their actual numbers or the small show they make on the map. On the map, indeed, Balōchī seems to have sustained a much more serious loss in the apparent surrender of Bārkhān to Jaṭkī ; but a possibly truer way of interpreting the facts would be to regard the Khetrān as only imperfectly won by the Balōch race from the Paṭhāns (§ 264). Viewed in this light the Jaṭkī assimilation of Bārkhān would constitute a very signal loss sustained by Pashtō. But with this exception—if indeed it is any exception at all—Pashtō has yielded little ground, though it has had to admit defeats at the hands of Jaṭkī in Mūsakhēl among the Jafar and in Sibī among the Paṇī.

Bilingual struggle.

214. We may now turn aside and watch a different and perhaps more interesting phase in the linguistic warfare—the stealthy encroachments of the enemy in the innocent guise of a subsidiary language. In these indirect tactics Jaṭkī, Balōchī and Brāhūī prove themselves much greater adepts than Pashtō, which shows as little inclination to foist itself on outsiders as a subsidiary language as it does to press home a frontal attack. But if Paṭhāns make no effort to impress their language on outsiders, they are equally deaf to the overtures of others, whether what they offer is a principal or a subsidiary language. In fact, only 3 per cent of the Paṭhāns profess to be bilingual at all. A telling contrast to this policy of linguistic aloofness is afforded by the ingenuousness of the Balōch and Brāhūīs in admitting subsidiary languages into their midst. Here the insidious enemy "comes not single spies, but in battalions." One Balōch in every three, one Brāhūī in every four, boasts himself to be bilingual, little dreaming that his linguistic tolerance is placing the very preservation of his mother-tongue in jeopardy. And it is these disarming but deadly tactics that render Jaṭkī, as it seems to me, so serious a menace to our other languages. Even the Paṭhāns, who usually—and wisely—disdain the tempting help of a subsidiary language, resort to Jaṭkī almost twice as often as they resort to either Balōchī or Brāhūī. The stealthy inroads that Jaṭkī is making on the Balōch are indeed the most obviously salient feature in the statistics, though I am not sure that, if we could probe a little deeper into the inner meaning of the statistics, its conquests over the Brāhūīs would not prove more notable still. For the statistics clearly call for cautious handling. Thus, take the population in the mass, and it appears that Brāhūī is employed as a subsidiary language more freely even than Jaṭkī. Look to the races who so employ them, and you will stumble up against the extraordinary fact that, while hardly a Jaṭṭ in a hundred is so false to his mother-tongue as to degrade it to his subsidiary language, among Brāhūīs Brāhūī has been relegated to the second place by at least eight in every hundred.

Subsidiary languages per mille of each race.

	All.	Balōchī.	Pashtō.	Brāhūī.	Jaṭkī.	Others.
Indigenous Musalmāns	202	37	6	68	62	29
Balōch	342	18	7	89	194	34
Paṭhāns	30	6	4	7	11	2
Brāhūīs	268	94	10	81	41	42
Jaṭṭ	132	32	1	21	14	64
Lāsī	143	32	...	79	17	15
Sayyids	167	27	23	97	8	12
Miscellaneous	272	42	4	175	23	28

Forecast.

215. But the statistics are much too complex for an academic analysis to enable us to follow the fickle fortunes of the combatants in the linguistic warfare that is now being waged in Balūchistān. Even in the case of one and the same language, statistics, to all appearances identical, may in reality denote very different things : here perhaps they are the spoils of victory ; there the admission of defeat. That a language figures prominently as a subsidiary language, may well be a proof of its powers of attack ; it may equally well be the first symptom of rout. In itself, therefore, it helps us little to combine the two aspects of a language—principal and subsidiary—into one whole, and measure the result against the similar totals of its rivals. The full meaning of the bewilderingly multitudinous factors that go to the making of these deceptively simple totals can only be gauged by local knowledge at its highest power. But one or two of the main processes seem unmistakable. Thus, if an outside language is associated freely with the language of the race, the chances are that the day is not far distant when the racial language will have to struggle to hold its own ; if the racial language is being constantly relegated to the second place, the chances are that decay has already set in. Accordingly, though it is

Principal and subsidiary combined.

Balōchī	257,281
Pashtō	206,209
Brāhūī	195,516
Jaṭkī	186,723
Others	37,479

obviously a sorry case of the blind leading the blind, the thought that it will be another ten years before statistics can be collected to contradict me, and many more years before statistics can be collected to prove me wrong, emboldens me to venture on a word of prophecy. The large reinforcements received by Brāhūī from its subsidiary figures seem to me but one among many lamentable signs that Brāhūī has entered on its decline ; that it will be able to resist the inroads of Balōchī on the one side and of Jaṭkī on the other for many generations more, I very much doubt. Yet in the nearly equal reinforcements that Jaṭkī receives from its subsidiary figures I seem no less clearly to see a foreshadowing of the ultimate success of Jaṭkī, now numerically the weakest of our vernaculars, all along the line. The full weight of our administration is after all at its back : every advance that is made in our so-called vernacular Urdū education, every advance that is made in the opening up of the country, are in effect advances made by Jaṭkī over the more racy vernaculars of Balūchistān. Balōchī for a time may be able to hold its own ; it may even seem to advance ; for what it loses to Jaṭkī it may possibly more than make up by conquests among the Brāhūīs and the miscellaneous peoples. But any success, I fancy, will be momentary, and only serve to hasten on the day of Jaṭkī's ultimate triumph. Even Pashtō, which now seems to be marking time, will probably be driven, slowly but surely, further and further back. But the absorption of Pashtō will be many a long day in coming. For the present, Pashtō is secure, thanks not merely to its intrinsic strength and the loyalty it inspires in all Paṭhāns, but also to its resolute refusal to be drawn into the seemingly innocent game of give and take. Not alone to race or country does a policy of glorious isolation offer the best chance of staving off the evil day of absorption.

Descriptive.

216. The neglect that usually falls to the lot of Balōchī seems to be fostered by two curious fallacies. There is first the very common notion that it is of little practical value in Balūchistān. It is difficult to trace the origin of this extraordinary delusion. It certainly runs absolutely counter to our statistics. Balōchī is spread over more than half the area of the whole province ; it is the principal language of nearly a third of the indigenous Musalmāns ; it is spoken freely and naturally by one-twelfth of the remainder as their secondary language. I can only imagine that the delusion is part and parcel of that wider delusion that Balūchistān consists of the Paṭhān districts with the Balōch and Brāhūī country knocked in. And then there is the equally common notion that Balōchī is of no scientific value at all. The truth of the matter is that Balōchī has suffered from its very simplicity. I can think of no language a smattering of which is easier to acquire, especially for a man with a nodding acquaintance with Persian. The grammatical structure is refreshingly simple and straightforward ; the pronunciation comes trippingly to the tongue ; the vocabulary is by no means extensive. But it's a case of lightly come, lightly go. The facility with which a smattering is acquired is only equalled by the facility with which it is forgotten. And so arises the extraordinary delusion that Balōchī is not worth mastering at all—a delusion crystallised in ninety-nine cases out of a hundred in the verdict that Balōchī is a bastard Persian at best. **Iranian family : Balōchī.**

217. The verdict is curiously wide of the mark. In contrast let me quote the conclusion of Professor Geiger,[1] who has done so much to further the study of Iranian philology : "Of all the dialects"—he is speaking of Iranian dialects in general—"Balōchī is raised to a pre-eminence of its own by virtue of the marked antiquity of its phonetics. It has preserved the old tenues in all positions, even after vowels and liquids. In this respect accordingly it stands on a level with the older Pahlavi. In Persian the transition of the tenues after vowels and liquids to voiced spirants took place between the third and sixth century after Christ. In a word, Balōchī represents in the all-important matter of consonantal system a stage of language left behind by Persian some fifteen hundred years ago." So with equal justice we might almost invert the common verdict and speak of Persian as a bastard Balōchī. This at any rate would bring out the fact that Balōchī preserves a much more archaic form of **Its important place in Iranian.**

[1] *Grundriss der iranischen Philologie, I, 2, p. 417.*

the parent language than Persian. But old beliefs die hard, and it will be many a long day before the idea that Balōchī is a mongrel patois of Persian is finally consigned to limbo. In the meantime the popular delusion must be rudely assailed, for it is without question chief among the stumbling-blocks in the way of a more genuine study of the language. And though this is hardly the place for a philological discussion, I am tempted to follow Professor Geiger's lead, and to go a little deeper into the question of the antiquity of Balōchī.

Eastern and Western Balōchī.

218. A wedge of Brāhūī splits Balōchī into two main divisions, Eastern and Western Balōchī. Though it must not be imagined that the two are mutually unintelligible, the differences between them are real enough, and a Balōch from the east finds it at first not a little difficult to make himself fully understood by a Balōch from the west. In point of fact the two divisions of the language hardly come into any very real contact. As might perhaps have been expected from its geographical isolation, it is in Western Balōchī, and more especially in that branch of it known as Makrānī, that the purer form of the language has been preserved. Not only is its phonetic system older, its vocabulary is less overloaded with loan-words; its verbal and other terminations are on the whole less subject to curtailment. But within each of the two main divisions there are several dialects, clearly distinguishable by difference in phonetics alone, to say nothing of the degree in which the terminations are clipped and modified, and other characteristics of the kind. Certain of the Eastern Balōchī dialects are fairly generally, if somewhat vaguely, recognised; for each of the main tribes—Marī, Bugṭī, Rind, Magasī, Ḍōmbkī—is eager to claim its own particular dialect as the standard language. In Western Balōchī, where the boundaries are geographical rather than tribal, there is more diversity still; the ramifications strike much deeper than the large and obvious territorial divisions of Makrān, Khārān and Chāgai.

Uneven phonetic development in the dialects.

219. Now when we come to study individual dialects, we find that the case is not quite so simple as Professor Geiger, perhaps unconsciously, would lead us to imagine. What he says regarding the antiquity of Balōchī phonetics is hardly correct in its entirety of any single dialect taken by itself. For the Balōchī consonantal system has developed itself among the many dialects in a curiously uneven manner. One dialect, for instance, has faithfully maintained the original sounds in one portion of its consonantal system, and has evolved variations of its own in another; in a second dialect we are faced with the exact converse. In other words, there is no one dialect which has preserved the whole consonantal system of the parent stock in its archaic purity, and we are left to piece it together by a process of selection. To illustrate my meaning I will turn to Western in preference to Eastern Balōchī, not only because it is more archaic, but also because the existence of the many sharply defined dialects within it has hardly been recognised at all. Take for instance these typical variations in the two Makrānī dialects spoken in Kēch and Panjgūr:—

OLD PERSIAN.	MODERN PERSIAN.	MAKRĀNI KĒCHĪ.	 PANJGŪRĪ.
pitare, father	*pidar*	*pit*	*pis.*
mātare, mother	*mādar*	*māt*	*mās.*
brātar, brother	*birādar*	*brāt*	*brās.*
zāmātar, son-in-law	*dāmād*	*zāmāt*	*zāmās.*
mahrka, death	*marg*	*marg*	*mark.*
makhshi, fly	*magas*	*magisk*	*makisk.*

This comparative statement almost tells its own tale. For the preservation of the original consonants *t*, *z*, *k*, we look to Persian in vain, and have to turn to Makrānī Balōchī. But even Makrānī preserves the archaic sound in both the dialects I have selected in the case of *z* only. And while Kēchī has retained the final *t*, it has, like Persian, forsaken final and medial *k* in favour of *g*. On the other hand Panjgūrī has struck out a line of its own in the radical change of final *t* to *s*, yet at the same time has clung conservatively to the ancient hard guttural. How uneven the consonantal development has been in the various dialects, may further be seen in the fact that Kēchī, while preserving an original final *t*, shows a distinct tendency to oust an initial *d* by the corresponding cerebral : *ḍumb*, tail, *ḍumbag*, sheep, *ḍuwāl*, wall. Panjgūrī on the other hand preserves the original forms : *dumb, dumbag, duwāl.* Instances in which both these dialects (and indeed Balōchī generally) preserve, while modern Persian discards, an original final *d*, are fairly common : Pahlavi *mūd*, hair, modern Persian *mū*, Kēchī *mud*, Panjgūrī *mūd*, is a case in point. This particular instance, by the by, is doubly interesting as illustrating a curious vowel variation in the two dialects, Kēchī, unlike Panjgūrī, having a tendency to shorten an original long *ū* : Panjgūrī *mūd*, hair, Kēchī *mud* ; Panjgūrī *sūt*, profit, Kēchī *sut* ; Panjgūrī *būta*, was, Kēchī *buta*. In the dialects spoken in Mand and along the coast, *ū* is regularly changed to *ī* : *mīd, sīt, bīta*—one illustration out of many of the interestingly close connection of these particular Makrānī dialects with Eastern Balōchī.

220. But the subject of dialectical variations is at once too wide and too technical to be pursued further. Nor are the data available, for the study of Balōchī dialects has hitherto been neglected. The neglect is curiously ill-deserved. A careful analysis of the phonetic system of any one dialect would be labour well spent. It is the first step towards a comparative survey of the many phonetic systems now surviving in the Balōchī language, the results of which would be not only valuable in themselves, but of wide philological interest. The need for research into the related subjects of dialectical characteristics in vocabulary and grammatical system, I must leave to plead its own cause. So much however seems obvious. The longer the research is put off, the greater the difficulties that will attend it, and the less rich the results. Changes are in the air. Boundaries, both tribal and geographical, are gradually shifting and becoming absorbed. To a large extent this process is an inevitable outcome of our administration, and it is the more incumbent on us to record existing dialectical variations before they become merged into uniformity. **Importance of the dialects.**

221. As the local study of Balōchī has been so perfunctory, it is hardly surprising that no one has taken the trouble to analyse Dēhwārī at all. But though Dēhwārī really seems a genuine case of a debased dialect of modern Persian, the mere fact that the lonely Dēhwār settlement in the Brāhūī country is several centuries old, is enough to lend the language an interest and importance which intrinsically it may hardly possess. To judge by the Dēhwārī of Mastung—for even Dēhwārī can boast its dialects—the vocabulary is for the most part ordinary Persian, but there are a few old forms and not a few corruptions. Among isolated peculiarities I may note *giftan*, Persian *giriftan*, to seize ; *shishtan*, P. *nishastan*, to sit ; *var khēstan*, P. *bar-khāstan*, to stand up ; *indākhtan*, P. *andākhtan*, to throw ; *shū*, P. *shauhar*, husband ; *umsāl*, P. *imsāl*, this year ; *umrōz*, P. *imrōz*, to-day ; *īsā*, P. *īn sāat*, this moment ; *īzmā*, P. *īn zamān*, this time. Here are some of the more general features : a preference for the *majhūl* sounds (*bēnī*, P. *bīnī*, nose ; *-ē*, P. *-ī*, the indefinite article ; *mē-*, P. *mī-*, the verbal affix ; *ārōs*, P. *'arūs*, bride ; *to*, P. *tu*, thou) ; a tendency to change an *a*-sound to *u* (*-um*, P. *-am*, I am ; *-um*, P. *-am*, my ; *hum*, P. *ham*, also) ; the avoidance of an ancient or modern *b*—especially medially or finally—in favour of *v* or a diphthong (*āv*, P. *āb*, water ; *shav*, P. *shab*, evening ; *taustān*, P. *tābistān*, summer ; *va*, P. *ba*, on) ; the clipping of final consonants (*ma*, P. *man*, I ; *ī*, P. *īn*, this ; *kho*, P. *khud*, self ; *kudā*, P. *kudām*, which ? *da*, P. *dar*, in ; *es*, P. *ast*, is ; *-an*, P. *-and*, are ; *āya*, P. *āyad*, comes ; *ko*, P. *kun*, do ; *zū*, P. *zūd*, quickly) ; a tendency to vowel-shortening (*kah*, P. *kāh*, grass ; *-ra*, P. *-rā*, the dative-accusative suffix, often, by the by, cut down to *-a* : *e.g.*, *gurga*, to the wolf). There is of course a fair sprinkling of loan-words, chiefly Brāhūī. In the choice of the words it borrows, Dēhwārī is anything but fastidious ; even sounds foreign to Persian find a ready welcome : *e.g.*, *ḍaggī*, cow ; *ṭāng*, leg ; *jōṛ*, well. **Dēhwārī.**

222. These illustrations have been taken from the Dēhwārī spoken in and round Mastung. At least two other dialects are ordinarily recognised, the Dēhwārī spoken by the Dēhwār of Kalāt, and that spoken by the Sayyids of Kirānī near Quetta. But there are a few local varieties besides. Thus there is a sufficient difference between the Dēhwārī of Mastung and the Dēhwārī of Prīngābād, which is only six miles off, to supply the people of **Dialects.**

Mastung with a stock of anecdotes at the expense of their neighbours. If they want to give you an idea of the Prīngābād jargon in a nut-shell, they will mimic it in the story: *sag haba kard, gau ḍaba kard, tāte-um talangāv shud, pā-ēsh var-dāshtum, tah-i-khurchū kardum,* "the dog barked, the bullock shied, my aunt took a toss, so I hauled up her legs and put them in the saddle-bag," the chief point of the jest lying in the use of the weird words *ḍaba, talangāv, khurchū.* But their favourite jibe is at Prīngābād hospitality. The story goes that a Brāhūī once put up in a Dēhwār's house in Prīngābād. "Get half a dozen *gaṭōr* ready," cried the host, "and let's give him a feast!" Now as *gaṭōr* means a lamb in Brāhūī, the Brāhūī remarked deprecatingly that *one* would be quite enough for him. But *gaṭōr* means something very different in the Prīngābād jargon, as he learnt to his disgust when he found that he was expected to make a feast off a single onion. And *Prīngāvātnā gaṭōr* has passed into a proverb.

Pashtō.

223. That Pashtō belongs to the Indo-European family of language, there is of course no possible doubt. But doubt seems to creep in, as soon as the circle is drawn closer. Its Indian affinities are so obvious that it has been classed as Indian; its Iranian affinities so obvious that it has been classed—and this is the orthodoxy of to-day—as Iranian. And whereas Trumpp, making a manful endeavour to combine both aspects of the language into a higher unity, pronounced it an Iranian language transitional into Indian, a learned Paṭhān has given me a suggestive essay to prove that it is an independent offshoot from the great mother stock[1]. I am scared by my very slender knowledge off any attempt to follow the lead of my ingenious friend. Nevertheless I cannot help thinking that we have settled down to the Iranian theory pure and simple a little too complacently, and that, though Trumpp overstated his case and stated it wrong, science would be advanced if some philologist took up Trumpp's position anew, and attempted a saner restatement of his case.

Phonetics.

224. With rashness born of ignorance I will point out what look to my untrained eye a few gaps in the harness of the champion of Iranian origin. Is Professor Geiger absolutely unassailable, for instance, in asserting that the cerebrals *ṭ* and *ḍ* exist for Pashtō in Indian loan-words only? What of *ṭapuṭs*, the kite, *ṭ^{a}ghan*, coward, *ghaṭ*, stout, *ṭs^{a}ṭ*, the nape of the neck, *p^{a}ṭ*, hidden? What of *ḍak*, full, *ḍaḍa*, side, *ṭs^{a}nḍa*, edge, *gēḍa*, belly? Are all these and many others which to a Paṭhān's ears ring as pure and as ancient and as racy as any word in his language—are they all loan-words? If they are loan-words indeed, some at any rate are loan-words of such hoary antiquity as to make one wonder where on earth loan-words end and Pashtō undefiled can be said to begin. And again, is Geiger absolutely unassailable in asserting that *ṛ* and *ṇ* and *sh* (and also presumably *zh*, though he does not say so) are later developments sprung from sound-groups which originally had nothing cerebral about them? What remote period, one may ask, first witnessed the development of the *ṛ* in *ṛund*, blind, in *ṛang*, razed, in *mōṛ*, sated, in *g^{u}ṛ^{a}ng*[2], snot, in *laṛam*, scorpion? of the *ṇ* in *rūṇ*, radiant, in *kīṇ*, left, in *sp^{a}ṇsai*, thread, in *kāṇai*, stone, in *maṇa*, apple, in *ghaṇa*, a kind of spider, in *zāṇa*, the demoiselle crane, and in *z^{a}ṇai*, lad? of the highly characteristic *sh* in *sh^{a}h*, good, in *sh^{a}dza*, woman, in *sh^{a}nd^{a}l*, to bestow, and in *k^{u}sh^{a}l^{o}w^{a}l*, to kiss? That his explanation of *ṇ* as the coalescence of $r+n$ and of *ṛ* as the coalescence of r + a dental may possibly hold good in isolated words like *pāṇa*, Avesta *parena-*, and *m^{a}ṛ*, dead, Avesta *mereta-*, or even in groups of words of like formation, is surely not enough. Every language has its pet peculiar sounds which, in season or out of season, it is always lugging in. And nothing would be more natural for such to be the common fate of the cerebrals *ṭ* and *ḍ* and *ṛ* and *ṇ* and the semi-cerebrals *sh* and *zh* (I hardly know what else to call them); for to a Paṭhān they seem as much at home as any other sounds in his armoury—to ordinary strangers they seem his very sword and buckler. And if Pashtō is really so unmistakably and so undilutedly

---

[1] This essay by K. S. Muhammad Gul Khān, Ganḍapur, who has as pretty a knowledge of his mother-tongue as any Paṭhān I have ever met, has furnished me in one form or another with most of the material used in my note.

[2] Though the distinction between the ^{a}-sound and the ^{e}-sound has become a commonplace in Pashtō transliteration, the analogous and equally marked though not equally common distinction between the ^{u}-sound and the ^{o}-sound has never, I fancy, been noticed before.

Iranian in its phonetics, where has the *f*- sound gone, and how is it that, like ancient Indian, it can get no nearer to *f* than *p*, so that even common loan-words like *faqīr*, beggar, and *fāida*, profit, have to become *pakīr* and *pāida* before they can issue from the lips of a Paṭhān[1] ?

225. When we pass from the region of sounds and words to grammatical structure, almost all traces of Iranian character seem to vanish into thin air. Where is the sweet simplicity of Persian and other modern Iranian languages — that delightful absence of inflection in noun and pronoun and adjective, that harmonious conjugation of the verb, that easy and natural flow of the sentence? In Pashtō we look for them in vain. Here we are treading on very un-Iranian soil. In the past and throughout that maze of tenses allied to the past—the imperfect, the perfect, the pluperfect, the dubious past, the past conditional, the correlative conditional, and the past optative—a transitive verb agrees not only in number but in gender with its logical object; its logical subject is in the inflected instrumental. And piled on the complexity in the verb is the complexity in the pronoun: *z*^{a}*h dē waham* or *tā z*^{a}*h waham*, I beat you; *mā t*^{a}*h wahalē* or *t*^{a}*h mē wahalē*, I was beating you; *tā z*^{a}*h wahal*^{a}*m* or *z*^{a}*h dē wahal*^{a}*m*, you were beating me. And when, on top of all, we find similar bewildering constructions applied to nouns like *s*^{a}*ṛai*, man, and adjectives like *st*^{a}*ṛai*, tired, and interrogatives like *tsōk*, who? and relatives like *tsōk chi*, whoever, we feel that if Pashtō is really an Iranian language transitional into Indian, as Trumpp would have us believe, it has overleapt its goal with a vengeance: it has out-Heroded Herod. And Pashtō has several pretty little idioms all to itself. The infinitive noun, for instance, is plural: *halta tl*^{a}*l grān dī* (not *dai*), going there is a difficult matter. And plural again are certain words like *sh*^{a}*h*, good, *bad*, ill, *ts*^{a}*h*, what? *hits na*, nothing: *tā ts*^{a}*h k*^{a}*ṛī dī* (not *k*^{a}*ṛai dai*) what have you done? I will notice one more idiom only, and then pass on. Certain verbs like *kh*^{a}*nd*^{a}*l*, to laugh, *zh*^{a}*ṛ*^{a}*l*, to weep, *l*^{a}*mb*^{a}*l*, to bathe, *d*^{a}*ng*^{a}*l*, to jump, which one would naturally look upon as intransitive, are in the past used in the third person masculine plural only, regardless of the number or gender of the logical subject, which is of course in the instrumental: *mā ukh*^{a}*nd*^{a}*l*, I laughed; *sh*^{a}*dzē ukh*^{a}*nd*^{a}*l*, the woman laughed.

226. Whenever I try to conjure up the influences of race and environment on language, Pashtō at once springs to my mind. The overbearing virility of the turbulent Paṭhān and the austerity of his rocky, rugged mountains seem to have entered into the very soul of his language, with its ruthless docking of syllables (as in *vrōr* and *lūr*, the Persian *birādar* and *dukhtar*, and the English brother and daughter), with its crabbed concatenation of consonants (as in *skhw*^{a}*ndar*, a steer, *ngw*^{a}*shēd*^{a}*l*, to limp, *ngh*^{a}*rd*^{a}*l*, to swallow, *nghwat*^{a}*l*, to hear), with its resolute raucous gutturals, and—I add it with an apology to Professor Geiger—with its stubborn stubby cerebrals. And yet, for all its harshness, it is a language of much rude grandeur, capable of expressing every shade of thought with wit and point and force—a worthy organ of speech for a shrewd and masterful race. I have often wondered whether the solution to the curious problem connected with its bifurcation into two great divisions does not perhaps lie as much in the different physical surroundings of the northern and eastern Paṭhāns as in their different social surroundings. The dialect spoken north and east is called by the Pukhtān^{a}h who speak it Pukhtō[2]; the dialect spoken south and west is called by the P^{a}shtān^{a}h who speak it P^{a}shtō. The difference in the included vowel is worth noting; but the difference in the included consonant is more important still. For this is one of the main distinctive features in the two branches. P^{a}shtō possesses four characteristic sounds *ts*, *dz*, *sh* and *zh*, whereas Pukhtō is content to get along with the much more ordinary *s*, *z*, *kh* and *g*, which P^{a}shtō of course also possesses into the bargain. Thus while a P^{a}shtun will say *tsōk*, who? *dzān*, body, *sh*^{a}*h*, good, *zhal*^{a}*ī*, hailstone, the Pukhtun will say *sōk*, *zān*, *kh*^{a}*h*, *gal*^{a}*ī*. There are of course other variations: Pukhtō tends, for instance, to displace *z* or *zh* by *j*, as in *jaba*, P^{a}shtō *z*^{a}*ba* or *zh*^{a}*ba*, tongue, *jāma*, P^{a}shtō, *zāma*, or *zhāma*, jaw; to displace *s* by *sh*, as in *shta*,

Grammatical structure.

P^{a}shtō and Pukhtō

---

[1] Here we must take care not to judge the spoken sound by the written symbol: a Paṭhān will often, perhaps usually, write فقير and فائده; but he will pronounce them *pakīr* and *pāida* none the less. This by the by is also a very common stumbling-block in dealing with Balōchi manuscripts.

[2] Such at any rate is the pronunciation in Peshāwar, the headquarters of Pukhto; but P^{a}khto and P^{a}khtān^{a}h are also heard.

P^{a}shtō *sta*, is or are, *dersh*, P^{a}shtō *dērs*, 30; it has also a growing tendency to drop an initial *v* before *r* as in *rōr*, P^{a}shto *vrōr*, brother, *rō rō*, P^{a}shtō *vrō vrō*, slowly, *ruk*, P^{a}shtō *vr^{a}k*, lost. But the four sounds *ts*, *dz*, *sh*, *zh* form the real barrier; and in speculating which of the two branches represents the elder and purer form of the language, it seems hard to avoid giving the seniority to P^{a}shtō, which remains in possession of these shibboleths. And this is after all only as it should be; for the Takht-i-Sulēmān, to which every Paṭhān looks reverently as the ancestral home of his race, lies in the P^{a}shtō and not in the Pukhtō country.

Local dialects. 227. Be this as it may, it is with the P^{a}shtō branch alone that we are concerned in Balūchistān; Pukhtō is of course to be heard, but not on the lips of indigenous tribesmen. Chief among the many local dialects is Kākaṛī, one of whose pet peculiarities is the change of *ē* in standard P^{a}shtō to *a*: *r^{a}sazh^{a}m* for *r^{a}sēzh^{a}m*, I arrive; *r^{a}pazh^{a}m* for *r^{a}pēzh^{a}m*, I tremble; *dars* for *dērs*, 30; *ts^{a}lwasht* for *ts^{a}lwēsht*, 40. But the two idiosyncrasies that seem to strike non-Kākaṛ Paṭhāns more than anything else are, first, the employment of the masculine vocative termination for the feminine gender also: *vrōr-a*, oh brother! *mōr-a*, oh mother! *khōr-a*, oh sister!—and second, the childish regularisation of irregular plurals: *zōeān*, *saṛīān*, for *zām^{a}n*, sons, and *s^{a}ṛī*, men. Perhaps the chief characteristic of the Lūṇī dialect, which in general is very similar to Kākaṛī, is the softening of *ts* to *ch*, as in *chōk* for *tsōk*, who? The Shīrānī changes *ē* sometimes to *a*, like the Kākaṛ, and sometimes to ^{a}*ī* as in *dr^{a}ī* for *drē*, 3; another peculiarity of his is an occasional changing of *w* preceded by a consonant to *b* as in *dba* for *dwa*, 2. The Mandōkhēl is fond of lengthening short *a*, and of assimilating *sh* and *zh* to the harsher *sh* and *gh*: *shpāzh* for *shpazh*, 6; he is also fond of changing a medial *w* to *m*: *nimī* for *niwī*, 90. But more important still is his conversion of the ancient *z*-sound in many words to *d*: *de mā*, my, instead of *zmā*; *de mūzh*, our, for *zmūzh*. These are of course but a few local dialects gathered from the bunch—just enough to show that grubbing into the P^{a}shtō dialects of Balūchistān would not be labour lost. But before I leave the subject, I cannot refrain from citing a bit of the Prodigal Son translated into a dialect that has earned a spurious local notoriety merely because it rejoices in the special names of Tarīnō or Chalgarī:—*yā saṛi gha dwa zōyē wī; pa haghō chī waṛake wata wo wai, chi ē piyāra dagha tā māl chī mā barkha wina, agha māta wala au hagha khpala duniā wawēshia; . . . hagha zṛah dā ghwasht sarkuze chī khwaṛah agha chōḍī wiya nas ḍak kaṛe; chā watah na lōwṛah; biyā hōsh chī rāgha wēwai; mā piyār gha dughumre mazdurān gha tsatta nōri wiya au zah warzha ya miṛēzhī.* But enough and more than enough of this jarring gibberish; it is less a P^{a}shtō dialect than a hotchpotch of execrable pronunciation and still more execrable grammar. It is spoken by the Vaṇēchī and Makhiānī of Shāhrig and Dukī, and it looks mighty like proof positive that these so-called Spīn and Tōr Tarīn are not Tarīn at all (and their Paṭhān origin is otherwise suspect) but Indians and possibly Jaṭṭ (as Chalgarī, the name of their jargon, suggests) who have become affiliated to the Paṭhāns, but have still to assimilate the language of their adoption.

Indian family. 228. Of that bewildering bundle of local Indian languages, commonly bunched together in Balūchistān under the delusively convenient title of Jaṭkī, I know far too little to have much to say. They clearly fall into two main groups according as they slide into Sindhī on the one side, and into Western Panjābī on the other. In parting them into the two groups we get disappointingly little help from the statistics. Where the local term for a dialect has been faithfully recorded by the enumerators, the blame of faulty classification rests of course with us, provided always that the local term itself is distinctive and unambiguous. But there's the rub. The commonest local term of all is Jaṭkī (or, as the Balōch call it, Jadgālī or Jagdālī). But not only is Jaṭkī the first and last refuge of ignorant enumerators, it is used indiscriminately up and down the country for both the Sindhī and the Western Panjābī varieties of the language. Nor is it possible to sift Jaṭkī into two heaps according to the racial or sectional divisions of the people that speak it. Thus though the majority of the Abṛā Jaṭṭ, with the Waḍēra at their head, speak the Sindhī form, large numbers of them speak the other. Nor does locality come to our rescue: the two branches occasionally overlap even in the same village, and must often slide insensibly into one another.

Sindhī branch	**94,115**
Jaṭkī unspecified	38,570
Jaṭkī Sindhī	14,940
Lāsī	40,605
Western Panjābī branch	**66,216**
Jaṭkī unspecified	16,766
Siraikī	31,254
Jaṭkī	1,519
Khetrānī	16,071
Jafarkī	606

Dialects.

229. The consequent chaos is much too great to be satisfactorily reduced to order, and the division of Jaṭkī I have attempted in the margin is little more than guesswork. It is merely based on the one apparently certain fact that at least two-thirds of those that dub their language Jaṭkī speak that form of the dialect which is closely allied to Sindhī. Regarding the more specific terms that have been recorded, one can generalise with a tolerable degree of confidence. That Lāsī belongs to the Sindhī branch, as the contact of Las Bēla with Sind would lead one to suppose, there is no question; indeed the Lāsī boasts (I know not with what justice) that his speech is one of the purest forms of Lāṛ Sindhī to be found anywhere. No less unmistakably does Siraikī, 'the language of the upper country', range itself on the opposite side; it seems in fact to be not the least important representative of Western Panjābī. And it is on this side that Khetrānī, the language of the Khetrān Balōch (§264), after having been bandied to and fro between Sindhī and Balōchī, must finally be allotted a place. But though Western Panjābī is writ large over its grammatical structure, it is impregnated with Sindhī influence even in such intimate parts of it as *ā̃*, I, *chhā*? what? *bā*, two; and Balōchī, if it has done nothing else, has undoubtedly furnished some useful contributions to its vocabulary. I have presumed, and probably correctly, that Hasankī, which has been returned by one or two Silāchī Khetrān living in Tallī, is the same dialect under a different name, though the one slight specimen of it that I have seen contains a few peculiarities in the vocabulary. Jafarkī, which has been returned by a few Jafar Paṭhāns, is manifestly near akin to Khetrānī, though fairly marked differences of vocabulary are only to be expected. Whether Jaṭkī, the language of the Jaṭṭ (§280) has really any claims to a name of its own is doubtful, to say the least; personally I have never been able to discover in it any characteristic divergences from the Western Panjābī branch of Jaṭkī; at the same time I would not be surprised to meet a Jaṭṭ who spoke the Sindhī form of Jaṭkī and yet insisted that his speech was Jaṭkī none the less. But this Indian branch of languages is clearly the most unsatisfying part of our linguistic census, chiefly because my own ignorance of it did not fully forewarn me of the difficulties that lay ahead. So here again is an inviting opening for local research, and at the same time a useful reminder that care will be needed at the next census to ensure that the various local terms are scrupulously recorded, and, in all cases of ambiguity, eked out with distinguishing symbols.

Dravidian Family: Brāhūī.

230. And surrounded on all sides by the Indian and Iranian languages there is one language that bears no affinity to either. The time has now come for Brāhūī to take its place unchallenged as a member of the Dravidian language-group. Not without a struggle has its birthright been won. In the early days it was claimed on evidence so meagre and frail, that the claim inevitably aroused a healthy scepticism, which gathered strength—a very counterfeit strength after all—from the awkwardness of the ethnological conundrum which a recognition of the linguistic kinship seemed to involve. The evidence now available is clear, ample, decisive; and Brāhūī can be debarred from entering into its birthright no longer: its Dravidian descent has become a mere commonplace of philology. But here philology stops short. Who the Brāhūīs themselves are, and how it has come about that a people living in the wilds of Balūchistān speaks a language akin to the languages of Southern India, are questions that must be left to ethnology. Though philology has presented ethnology with a very pretty riddle, it is not bound to present it with the answer. Yet I for one would not be surprised if a hint were gathered in the course of time from deeper researches into comparative phonology, grammar and vocabulary.

Dravidian affinities in grammatical structure.

231. It is of course in its grammatical system that Brāhūī blabs out the secret of its parentage. There is no need to bother ourselves here with the dry details of the evidence; it has been my lot to deal with them elsewhere.[1] The

[1] The Brahui Language, Part I, Introduction and Grammar, by Denys Bray, Calcutta, 1909.

main heads of the argument are all we want, and I have no scruples in plagiarising the following summary of them from my own writings. The language is agglutinative, and in this aspect it belongs, speaking in the broadest sense, to the same stage of development as the Dravidian language-group. This, indeed, proves little or nothing; but the argument of kinship rests on a surer foundation than a casual analogy of structure. The grammatical relations of the noun in Brāhūī are shown, as in Dravidian, by means of suffixes, and most, if not all, of the suffixes, whether expressive of case-relations or of plural number, are traceable to the same source as Dravidian. Even more direct is the evidence of the pronoun, that faithful repository of the secret of a language's origin. Of the personal pronouns, the pronoun of the second person in both numbers is in essentials the same as in Dravidian, and a Dravidian relationship is discernible in the pronoun of the first person, despite the ravages wrought by phonetic decay. The reflexive in Brāhūī and Dravidian has preserved one uniform type with singular consistency. The Brāhūī demonstratives are only explicable in the light of their Dravidian counterparts. The family likeness is but thinly disguised in the interrogatives, and several of the indefinite pronouns are stamped with the same birthmark. The Dravidian relationship of the first three numerals, often, though perhaps erroneously, regarded as only less significant witnesses to the origin of a language than the personal pronouns, is hardly open to question, and it is interesting to find that Brāhūī and Dravidian, in the absence of an ordinal proper formed from the first cardinal, employ the same device and even, it would appear, the same root to express it. The case of the verb is naturally more complex, but the evidence cannot be gainsaid. The most palpable analogies are to be found in the pronominal terminations of the plural, in the formation of the causal, and above all in the organic negative conjugation. These are, however, far from exhausting all the relevant points in the evidence; indeed, though the Brāhūī verb is not devoid of characteristic peculiarities of its own, it may safely be said—and the remark applies with equal force to the language as a whole—that a full understanding of it would be impossible without the help of the Dravidian languages. There can be but one verdict on this evidence. This verdict is not that of Caldwell, who summed up his final position in the words "The Brāhūī language, considered as a whole, seems to be derived from the same source as the Panjābī and Sindhī, but it evidently contains a Dravidian element," but the converse, first suggested by Lassen in the early days of the study of the language and reasserted by Trumpp more than a quarter of a century ago. The Brāhūī language is sprung from the same source as the Dravidian language-group; it has freely absorbed the alien vocabulary of Persian, Balōchī, Sindhī and other neighbouring languages; but in spite of their inroads its grammatical system has preserved a sturdy existence.

Dravidian affinities in vocabulary.

232. So much for the outline of the argument from Dravidian affinities in grammatical structure, a somewhat sketchy development of which takes up the greater part of the Introduction to my work on the Brāhūī language. There seems, however, a tendency on the part of some scholars to regard evidence from affinity of vocabulary as of equal if not of greater importance. The line of argument is a little difficult to follow. If by some freak Brāhūī divested itself of those suffixes which it has inherited from the Dravidian mother-stock and adopted Iranian or Aryan devices for the declension of its nouns and pronouns and for the conjugation of its verbs, if it substituted for its organic negative conjugation, so characteristically Dravidian, the ordinary mechanical device of adding a negative adverb to the affirmative conjugation, and finally purged its grammatical structure of such last remnants of its Dravidian origin as its personal, reflexive, interrogative and demonstrative pronouns, it is hard to see how it could be said to remain a member of the Dravidian language-group any longer, even though its vocabulary were as heavily interlarded with Dravidian words as it now is with words borrowed from Indian and Iranian languages. That it once belonged to the Dravidian language-group might possibly be demonstrated. To attempt to prove that it still belonged to it, would be like attempting to prove that the late President of the United States was a subject of the Queen of Holland. But once affinities in structure have been proved, we may confidently turn for corroboration and enlightenment to the secondary evidence afforded by affinities in the vocabulary.

What proportion of the Brāhūī vocabulary is taken up by words inherited from the original Dravidian stock, it is, of course, very difficult to estimate. They are clearly in a great minority. But it is a minority of stalwarts. It is composed almost entirely of words to express the most fundamental and elementary concepts of life[1] :—substantives like mouth, ear, eye, brain, sleep; adjectives like big, small, new, old, sweet, bitter; the numerals one, two, three; pronouns like I, thou, he, we, you, they, self, who? what? how many? other; verbs like to be, become, do, stand, come, give, eat, speak, hear, see, understand, take, strike, fear; and adverbs like formerly, yet, to-day.

Possible sidelights on ethnology.

233. The positive evidence that can be gleaned from a comparative vocabulary is, I'm afraid, too flimsy to allow us to draw any very definite conclusions as to the state of society in the days when the Brāhūī language (not necessarily, it should be observed, the Brāhūī people) was still in contact with other Dravidian languages. But everything seems to point to the conclusion that the Brāhūī-speakers of those days were pastoralists, breeding (*hīn-*, to kid, to lamb, Tamil, Malayāḷam, Kanarese, Telugu *īn-*) sheep and goats (*hēṭ*, she-goat, Tam., Mal., Kan., *āḍu*, Tuḷu *ēḍu*, Tel. *ēṭa*, he-goat, goat) for the sake of their milk (*pālh*, Tam., Mal. *pāl*, Kan., Tel., Kui *pālu*) and other produce. Without attempting to weave pretty theories out of the fact that the Brāhūī word for house (*urā*) is the equivalent of the Dravidian word for village (*ūr*), one may safely assume that like many a Brāhūī of the present day, these pastoralists did not herd together in villages, but moved freely from place to place in search of water (*dīr*, Drav. *nīr*) and fresh pastures for their flocks. They were undoubtedly armed with the bow (*bil*, Tam., Mal., Tel. *vil*, Kan. *bil*, Tuḷ. *biru*). They were probably not men of the plains but men of the hills (*mash*, Drav. *mal-*). But further clues as to their locality seem to fail us. For though it evidently swarmed with stones (*khal*, Tam., Mal. *kal*, Kan., Tuḷ., Tel. *kallu*) and worms (*pū*, Tam., Mal., Kan. *puḻu*, Tel. *puruvu*, Tuḷ. *puru*, *Kurukh put'ū*) and scorpions (*tēlh*, Tam., Mal. *tēḷ*, Kan., Tuḷ. *čēḷ*, Tel. *tēlu*) and hares (*murū*, Tam., Mal. *muyal*, Kan. *mola*, Tuḷ. *muyera*, Tel. *nosalu*, Kui *mrāḍu*) and rats or mice (*hal*, Tam., Mal. Tuḷ. *eli*, Tel. *eluka*, Kan. *ili*, Gōṇḍī *alli*)—these are unfortunately incident to most, if not all, parts of India and many other countries into the bargain.

Danger of negative evidence.

234. Much further than this we can hardly rely on a comparative vocabulary to guide us. It would even be rash to conclude that they were unable to count beyond three or were ignorant of the use of metals, simply because the Brāhūī language now draws on foreign languages for names for metals and numerals from four upwards. One might as well argue that they could not tell man from woman, because they now express the idea woman by *arvat*, the Persian *aurat*, or by *zaīfa*, a corruption of the Arabic word for 'weak.' Negative evidence of this description has the awkward habit of stultifying itself by proving too much. It is always dangerous, and never more so than in a case like this, where it seems plausible and attractive, just because positive evidence is tantalizingly defective. From comparative philology we may fairly look to receive more help, though we shall probably have to wait a longish time for it.

Unclassified: Lōṛichīnī or Mōkkī.

235. There is a certain appropriateness in winding up a survey of the languages of this province with Lōṛi-chīnī or Mōkkī, the cant of the Lōṛīs, for it's a hotchpotch of the lot. A language in the ordinary sense of the word it is not. It is an artificial jargon, which the Lōṛīs have mechanically invented on the basis of the language of the people among whom they live, and which they more especially employ when they want to keep their meaning to themselves. Thus if they go to officiate at a wedding, and only come in for unappetising scraps of food after the tribesmen have feasted on the dainties, they will vent their spleen to their heart's content in their Mōkkī gibberish. And yet so successfully and universally is the jargon used, that it seems doubtful whether its artificiality suffices to debar it from being classed as a language. However artificial its origin and character, it is at any rate acquired naturally and as a matter

[1] My selection is confined to words whose Dravidian cousins can hardly fail to be readily recognised: *bā*, *khaf*, *khan*, *milī*, *tugh* (cf. also *tungān*, asleep); *hal-*, *chun-*, *pūr-*, *mut-*, *han-*, *khar-*; *as-*, *er-*, *mus-*; *ī*, *nī*, *ō*, *nan*, *num*, *ōfk*, *tēn*, *dē(r)*? *ant*? *aff*? *pēn*; *ar-*, *ma(r)-*, *ka(r)-*, *sal-*, *ba(r)-*, *īt* and *ti(r)-*, *kun-*, *pā(r)-*, *bin-*, *khan-*. *chā-(ta—*, *tiā-*) and *tir—*, *hal-*, *khal-*, *khul-*; *must*, *annā*, *ainō*.

of course by Lōṛī children; it is no longer, it would seem, simply a secret patter; it is becoming a language for the home-circle. Not that the Lōṛīs admit that its origin is artificial at all. On the contrary, they plume themselves on the fact that it is one of Nature's secrets that has been vouchsafed to them and to them alone. The story goes that Mōkō, as the Brāhūīs call the spider, revealed the spider-language to 'Alī, the Prophet's cousin, on the occasion when he took refuge in a cave. And 'Alī passed on the secret of the spider-language to Sarmast, the father of all Lōṛīs (§284).

Main characteristics. 236. As one might expect, there are several varieties of the patter though a strong family resemblance runs through them all. I will confine myself to three, the Mōkkī spoken by the Lōṛīs of Sarāwān, Jhalawān and Makrān. The same key opens the main secret of all three. It is all very simple. Take any word from any language, and turn it inside out: *ṭēp*, belly, Jaṭkī *pēṭ*; *dohā*, God, Balōchī *hudā*; *chukak*, dog, Brāhūī *kuchak*; *randum*, man, Persian *mardum*. But though this is their chief device for obscuring the meaning of everyday words, there are several others. Sometimes they add a suffix:—*ōsk*, for instance, which is particularly common in Sarāwān Mōkkī, *e.g.*, *hāth-ōsk*, hand; -*kāī* is no less commonly used by the Lōṛīs of Jhalawān, *lumk-kāī*, for *mulk-kāī*, land. Prefixes are affected still more, notably by the Lōṛīs of Sarāwān, who have a large stock to choose from: *e.g.*, *ni-lab*, bride-price, Brāhūī *lab*; *na-tauk*, necklace, Persian *ṭauq*; *la-pūlī*, nose-ring, Brāhūī *pūlī*. Sometimes they go to the other extreme and clip the word short: *āndī*, silver, for *chāndī*; *sōm*, nose, apparently for *sōmāb*, Brāhūī *bāmus*. Or they resort to sound-changes, and this is the chief characteristic of the Mōkkī of Makrān. Some of these seem natural, like *wapt*, seven, for *hapt*; *washt*, eight, for *hasht*, *wash*, six, for *shash*, *wad*, hundred, for *sad*. Others like *kashkar*, army, *lashkar*, are clearly arbitrary. A few words, like *mak*, man, *nodō*, woman, wife, *gōm*, rupee, *rautag*, to beat, seem peculiar to Mōkkī, but even these may be changelings, stolen from some language or other.

Illustrations. 237. So simple are the general rules for the making of this artificial language, that it might seem lamentably deficient as a secret vehicle of communication. But the thin disguise of isolated words and the obscurity of connected sentences, blurred in the rapidity of speech, are two very different things, and both Brāhūī and Balōch admit freely that Mōkkī is beyond them. As Mōkkī has not before, I fancy, attained to the dignity of print, it seems worth while to reproduce a sentence or two taken down from the mouth of a Lōṛī of Jhalawān: *hēk makkiē hud chabak atant; sikānēn chabak udkī tiberā kāmārīt: tibar mānkīā biban sāmānkāī rahbā hamōrī ki mānkī rahb hubīt; harchī tibara lām hubīta, hamōrīān rahb jōhāinta banīta; zāb rōch na gwasta ki sikānēn chabak udkī lām chum jōhainta o rūdēn lumkīā lāgīta ō gō chingirīān udkī lāmā rēbān jōhāinta; har vakhtkāī udkī rudustēn lāmā rēbān jōhāintaī, hamā lumkā bir zabanēn ḍukālkāīe parāvalīt ō hamē randum hairān hubīt; hamōrī guḍā lāgīt ō gō hamā lumkāī rahsh randumīā vatārā ōkāēnt.* Even to a man initiated into some of the mysteries of the patter, this is a little baffling, unless he has happened to take an interest in the Linguistic Survey of India, and to have waded through multitudinous versions of the parable of the Prodigal Son.

General survey. 238. Here ends our review of the languages of Balūchistān. But the list is certainly not complete. If none of the more important languages of the country have been left out, there are dialects of which we are but awkwardly conscious, and without doubt others of whose very existence we are complacently ignorant. The country is a veritable Babel, an ideal hunting-ground for the philologist. Unfortunately philology is not likely to flourish very happily among officers whose work and anxieties leave scant time and less appetite for scientific research. Nor—from a narrowly official point of view—is it perhaps to be encouraged. On the frontier at any rate it is better with Sandeman to be able to speak one language and that to the point, though the language, like his, be of one's own devising, than with Bekker to be silent in seven, though the silence cover a knowledge of their every phonetic and linguistic law.

A word to the linguist. 239. But a practical knowledge of at least one of the frontier languages is a very different matter. None but a Sandeman or a Nicholson can win success without it. And with so many officers now on the frontier with an admirable grip of this dialect of Pashtō or that dialect of Balōchī, it seems a pity that it has gone out of fashion to impart such knowledge to the world. It is, I fancy, a feeling of diffidence that is largely to blame. Men are shy of putting their knowledge on paper for fear of placing on record at the same time their palpable lack of trained scholarship. Such diffidence is intelligible enough, but it is none the less mischievous. For as things now are on most parts of the frontier, it is impossible for the professional philologist to be abroad in the land, and advance in the scientific knowledge of the frontier vernaculars can only be won, first by the spade-work of the man on the spot, and then by the microscopic analysis of the scholar in the study. The material after all lies everywhere to hand ; the ground is vast ; it has only been scratched here and there ; it hardly matters where the claim is pegged out. Hear accurately, describe what you hear accurately, and it is of comparatively little account if the results—grammar, vocabulary, folk-lore or the like—are strung together in a hopelessly unscholarly form. You will have given some scholar the food he has been craving for, and it will not be your fault if you fail to add a humble contribution to the advancement of knowledge between the two of you.

A word to the philologist.

240. I have been lured into this digression by reading some pathetic appeals, written in Germany more than a quarter of a century back and reiterated with plaintive persistency at various intervals, for fresh material on Balōchī from Balūchistān. The pathos lies in the sad fact that the appeals never reached the ears to which they were addressed. If instead of being buried in the obscurity of a German philological Journal, they had been directed in a letter to the Local Government or the Government of India, they would long ago have been answered by a goodly sheaf of material. Strange though it may possibly seem, officers on the frontier, stationed maybe a hundred miles and more from nowhere and a thousand miles from a reference library of any pretensions, have rarely an opportunity and rarely, it must be confessed, a desire to turn over the pages of philological Journals.

A word to the man who is a bit of both.

241. And having drifted into this digression, I may as well go one step further before this chapter on language is brought to a close. Though the Balōchī handbooks of Hitū Rām, Dames and Mockler, have done yeoman service in giving past generations something of a grip of Balōchī, they have outlived their day, and the time has come for a fuller and more accurate treatment of the language. The work on the Pashtō spoken in this province has still to be written. What is now wanted, over and above an analysis of our many subsidiary dialects, are practical handbooks and vocabularies of the two main languages. To overlay them with philology would be seriously to impair their practical utility. But even from a severely practical point of view their utility would be enhanced, not impaired, by a short preface giving a few sidelights on the scientific interest of the subject. One need not be a budding Bopp to derive stimulus from broad philological facts. The interest of even the most humdrum student who takes up a language from a material and unimaginative motive will be awakened on finding that the despised Balōchī, for instance, occupies the pride of place as the most archaic of living Iranian languages, or that the relationship of such common but unfamiliar-looking Pashtō words as *las* and *lūr* to *das*, *decem*, *zehn*, ten, and to *dukhtar*, *Tochter*, daughter, is only obscured by the normal change of the dental to *l* in Pashtō, or that the language of the Brāhūīs of Balūchistān can claim the languages of the Tamils and others of Southern India as its next-of-kin.

Conclusion.

242. As I glance over this chapter, I am oppressed with the feeling that it is less a record of our knowledge than a confession of the measure of our ignorance. Yet a recognition of ignorance is after all the first step towards knowledge, and it is in the hope that this trite maxim will stand justified at the stock-taking ten years hence, that I have emphasised the gaps in our knowledge of the many languages of Balūchistān. But even this cursory review of our local vernaculars raises thoughts of a wider reach. How little, when all is said and done, do we know of language as a whole and the subtle influence on it of race or environment. For the last half hour I have sat at my open window some twenty yards from a Quetta thoroughfare, listening idly to the voices of the passers-by. Hardly a word, hardly an articulate sound has reached my

ears, and yet there has been little doubt as to the identity of the various languages as they floated towards me on the air. Pashtō, Brāhūī, Balōchī, Jaṭkī, Persian, Panjābī, Urdū, English—each has gone by with its indescribable but tell-tale accent or timbre or intonation, that living but intangible something which no transliteration can convey in dead print. I cannot but feel that we are standing on the threshold of a far-reaching revolution in our linguistic methods—a belated revolt against the fashionable tendency of philology to degenerate into an arid study of written symbols. And I for one look forward to the day when the second edition of the monumental Linguistic Survey of India will include, as a matter of course, not an appendix of comparative lists of written words, but a supplement of phonographic records, which will enable us to compare the living sounds themselves.

XXIII.—Local Distribution of the Four Chief Languages.

(Indigenous Musalmāns only.)

DISTRICT OR STATE	BALŌCHI			PASHTŌ			BRĀHŪI			JAṬKI		
	Total	As principal language	As subsidiary language	Total	As principal language	As subsidiary language	Total	As principal language	As subsidiary language	Total	As principal language	As subsidiary language
BALŪCHISTĀN	*257,281*	*229,935*	*27,346*	*206,209*	*201,775*	*4,434*	*195,516*	*145,167*	*50,349*	*186,723*	*141,464*	*45,259*
Districts	**77,278**	**69,624**	**7,654**	**203,865**	**199,858**	**4,007**	**27,892**	**21,118**	**6,774**	**59,934**	**38,576**	**21,358**
Quetta-Pishin	1,194	1,019	175	77,009	75,046	1,963	12,895	10,571	2,324	47	46	1
Lōṛalai	3,203	1,935	1,268	46,894	45,612	1,282	99	99	...	16,871	16,163	708
Zhōb	5	5	...	60,972	60,970	2	97	97	...	...	...	...
Bōlān	690	649	41	29	23	6	737	171	566	...	...	...
Chāgai	11,277	8,860	2,417	303	262	41	9,206	5,790	3,416	4	3	1
Sibi	60,909	57,156	3,753	18,658	17,945	713	4,858	4,390	468	43,012	22,364	20,648
Administered area	*26,579*	*24,401*	*2,178*	*18,658*	*17,945*	*713*	*4,830*	*4,381*	*449*	*41,487*	*20,954*	*20,533*
Marī Bugṭī country	*34,330*	*32,755*	*1,575*	...	...	...	*28*	*9*	*19*	*1,525*	*1,410*	*115*
States	**180,003**	**160,311**	**19,692**	**2,344**	**1,917**	**427**	**167,624**	**124,049**	**43,575**	**126,789**	**102,888**	**23,901**
Kalāt	165,916	147,795	18,121	2,286	1,913	373	158,779	118,282	40,497	84,376	63,701	20,675
Sarāwān	*19,661*	*13,746*	*5,915*	*2,094*	*1,776*	*318*	*57,406*	*39,311*	*18,095*	*491*	*39*	*452*
Jhalawān	*17,451*	*14,615*	*2,836*	*75*	*75*	...	*77,428*	*67,048*	*10,380*	*2,215*	*1,890*	*325*
Kachhi	*33,637*	*29,720*	*3,917*	*83*	*44*	*39*	*15,189*	*3,663*	*11,526*	*64,610*	*47,672*	*16,938*
Ḍōmbki Kahēri country	*5,049*	*4,460*	*589*	*19*	*3*	*16*	*267*	*205*	*62*	*16,966*	*14,014*	*2,952*
Makrān	*70,984*	*69,889*	*1,095*	*12*	*12*	...	*1,006*	*989*	*17*	*86*	*86*	...
Khārān	*19,134*	*15,365*	*3,769*	*3*	*3*	..	*7,483*	*7,066*	*417*	*8*	...	*8*
Las Bēla	14,087	12,516	1,571	58	4	54	8,845	5,767	3,078	42,413	39,187	3,226

XXIV.—Bilinguity and Race.

(*Indigenous Musalmāns only.*)

Language and race	Both as principal and subsidiary language	As principal language: Total	Without subsidiary language	With subsidiary language	Principal to: Balōchī	Pashtō	Brāhūī	Jatkī	Others	As subsidiary language
Balōchī	**257,281**	**229,935**	**154,464**	**75,471**	...	**750**	**32,636**	**35,561**	**6,524**	**27,346**
Balōch	150,211	147,151	93,884	53,267	...	584	14,810	32,364	5,509	3,060
Paṭhāns	1,451	271	161	110	...	...	87	5	18	1,180
Brāhūīs	50,861	35,168	21,522	13,646	...	40	11,797	1,517	292	15,693
Others	54,758	47,345	38,897	8,148	...	126	5,942	1,675	705	7,413
Pashtō	**206,209**	**201,775**	**194,099**	**7,676**	**1,238**	...	**3,550**	**2,183**	**705**	**4,434**
Paṭhāns	183,758	183,132	178,816	4,316	866	...	1,075	2,030	345	626
Balōch	1,959	737	686	51	48	...	3	...	...	1,222
Brāhūīs	3,101	1,407	33	1,374	201	...	1,160	8	5	1,694
Others	17,391	16,499	14,564	1,935	123	...	1,312	145	355	892
Brāhūī	**195,516**	**145,167**	**110,803**	**34,364**	**17,593**	**2,189**	...	**6,760**	**7,822**	**50,349**
Brāhūī	143,310	129,666	100,593	29,073	15,356	1,654	...	5,273	6,790	13,644
Balōch	17,913	2,861	1,372	1,489	998	14	...	367	110	15,052
Paṭhāns	1,696	339	262	77	27	35	...	...	15	1,357
Others	32,597	12,301	8,576	3,725	1,212	486	...	1,120	907	20,296
Jaṭkī	**186,723**	**141,464**	**120,427**	**21,037**	**7,481**	**1,416**	**5,981**	...	**6,159**	**45,259**
Others	121,555	117,933	101,368	16,565	5,140	219	5,149	...	6,057	3,622
Balōch	50,993	18,212	15,291	2,921	1,972	619	236	...	94	32,781
Paṭhāns	6,025	3,967	3,075	892	278	578	36	...	...	2,058
Brāhūīs	8,150	1,352	693	659	91	...	560	...	8	6,798
Other Languages.	**37,479**	**16,269**	**6,219**	**10,050**	**1,034**	**79**	**8,182**	**755**	...	**21,210**
Balōch	5,912	229	129	100	42	5	3	50	...	5,713
Paṭhāns	762	384	180	204	9	13	159	23	...	378
Brāhūīs	7,289	194	22	172	45	...	127	...	..	7,095
Others	23,486	15,462	5,888	9,574	938	61	7,893	682	...	8,024

XXV.—Race and Bilinguity.

(Indigenous Musalmāns only.)

Race and language	Principal language			Subsidiary language to					
	Total	Without subsidiary language	With subsidiary language	All	Balōchī	Pashtō	Brāhūī	Jaṭkī	Others
Baloch	**169,190**	**111,362**	**57,828**	**57,828**	**53,267**	**51**	**1,489**	**2,921**	**100**
Balōchī	147,151	93,884	53,267	3,060	...	48	998	1,972	42
Pashtō	737	686	51	1,222	584	...	14	619	5
Brāhūī	2,861	1,372	1,489	15,052	14,810	3	...	236	3
Jaṭkī	18,212	15,291	2,921	32,781	32,364	...	367	...	50
Other languages	229	129	100	5,713	5,509	...	110	94	...
Pathāns	**188,093**	**182,494**	**5,599**	**5,599**	**110**	**4,316**	**77**	**892**	**204**
Pashtō	183,132	178,816	4,316	626	...	...	35	578	13
Balōchī	271	161	110	1,180	...	866	27	278	9
Brāhūī	339	262	77	1,357	87	1,075	..	36	159
Jaṭkī	3,967	3,075	892	2,058	5	2,030	...	...	23
Other languages	384	180	204	378	18	345	15	...	...
Brāhūīs	**167,787**	**122,863**	**44,924**	**44,924**	**13,646**	**1,374**	**29,073**	**659**	**172**
Brāhūī	129,666	100,593	29,073	13,644	11,797	1,160	...	560	127
Balōchī	35,168	21,522	13,646	15,693	...	201	15,356	91	45
Pashtō	1,407	33	1,374	1,694	40	...	1,654	...	...
Jaṭkī	1,352	693	659	6,798	1,517	8	5,273	...	...
Other languages	194	22	172	7,095	292	5	6,790	8	...
Other Musalmāns	**209,540**	**169,293**	**40,247**	**40,247**	**8,448**	**1,935**	**3,725**	**16,565**	**9,574**
Jaṭkī	117,933	101,368	16,565	3,622	1,675	145	1,120	...	682
Balōchī	47,345	38,897	8,448	7,413	...	123	1,212	5,140	938
Pashtō	16,499	14,564	1,935	892	126	...	486	219	61
Brāhūī	12,301	8,576	3,725	20,296	5,942	1,312	...	5,149	7,893
Other languages	15,462	5,888	9,574	8,024	705	355	907	6,057	...

XXVI.—Loss of the Racial Language.

(*Indigenous Musalmāns only.*)

Race and Tribe	Non-racial Language			
	Balōchī	Pashtō	Brāhūī	Jaṭkī
Balōch	...	**737**	**2,861**	**18,212**
(*i*) *Eastern*	...	*673*	*629*	*18,051*
Bugṭī	...	40	4	615
Ḍōmbkī	...	13	43	271
Khetrān	...	459	...	13,667
Magasī	...	1	36	829
Marī	...	45	45	3
Rind	...	68	458	2,639
(*ii*) *Western*	...	*64*	*2,232*	*161*
Rakhshānī	...	34	1,945	3
Rind	...	...	6	...
Sangur	...	...	...	14
Brāhūī	**35,168**	**1,407**	...	**1,352**
(*i*) *Original nucleus*	*4,332*	*26*	...	*76*
Kambrāṛī	1,200	...	...	36
Mīrwāṛī	2,155	...	...	29
(*ii*) *Sarāwān*	*12,496*	*1,346*	...	*209*
Bangulzai	2,358	11	...	61
Lahṛī	32	13	..	20
Lāngav	8,556	54	...	30
Shahwānī	702	...	...	11
(*iii*) *Jhalawān*	*18,300*	*26*	...	*1,032*
Bīzanjav	7,692	...	...	50
Māmasanī	3,588	4	...	140
Mēngal	642	22	...	376
Sājdī	3,992	...	...	...
Zahrī	2,221	...	...	445
(*iv*) *Miscellaneous*	*40*	*9*	...	*35*
Paṭhān	**271**	...	**339**	**3,967**
Jafar	...	...	...	1,127
Kākaṛ	29	...	7	73
Dumaṛ	...	...	...	*2*
Sanzarkhēl	*11*	...	*1*	*20*
Snatia	*8*	...	*4*	...
Targhaṛa	...	...	...	*1*
Paṇī	32	...	164	2,402
Main branch	*26*		*164*	*2,196*
Mūsakhēl	*6*	...	...	*11*
Shīrānī	...	...	5	62
Tarīn	...	...	34	38
Abdāl Achakzai	...	...	*15*	*5*
Spīn Tarīn	...	...	*19*	*1*
Tōr Tarīn	...	...	...	*31*
Lāsī	**1,447**	...	**830**	...
Burra	9	...	...	...
Jāmōṭ	1,108	...	660	...
Rūnjhā	...	...	45	...
Jaṭṭ	**3,789**	**144**	**263**	...

CHAPTER X.

INFIRMITIES.

Statistical data.

SUBJECT.	TABLES.	
	Imperial	Subsidiary
Infirmities by age	XII (i)	......
Infirmities by locality	XII (ii)	......
Infirmities by race	XII A	......
Incidence by locality and race	......	XXVII
Female incidence by locality and race	......	XXVIII

243. Until all enumerators are doctors who know every man, woman and child in the locality, it is vain to look for an accurate census of infirmities, though all that be attempted is the apparently simple enumeration of the insane, the deaf-mute from birth, the blind of both eyes, and the leper. Technical knowledge is the only safeguard against errors of diagnosis ; local knowledge the only safeguard against wilful concealment. In some degree, no doubt, our local enumerators were able to secure us from the latter. Yet we can hardly hope in all cases to have got behind the decent veil with which folks endeavour to screen the infirmities of their women from curious outsiders, or to have been unaffected by the excusable optimism that leads parents to shut their eyes to the infirmities of their children long after they stare others in the face. And if our statistics suffer from a vein of optimism, they suffer still more from a less admirable but hardly less human vein of pessimism—pessimism that dubs the village simpleton a lunatic ; that glorifies the dim vision of the aged into total blindness, and the tongue-tied or stone-deaf into congenital deaf-mutes ; that reads leprosy into any skin-disease if only it is loathly enough. **Statistics inevitably imperfect.**

244. In fact the utmost we can expect to glean from a census of infirmities is a very rough idea of their general prevalence in the country. And the denser the population, the greater the chance of lighting somewhere near the truth ; for statistical truth is hardly to be found except in the deep well of large numbers. In a population so scanty as ours the information we can pick up from the statistics is scarcely likely to be worth very much, and my remarks will be correspondingly brief. In Balūchistān as a whole every 10,000 persons have in their midst 38 who are reputedly suffering from one or other of the four infirmities with which we are concerned. If we divide the population almost half and half between the districts and states, the incidence of the infirmities in bulk and of every infirmity taken by itself is much higher in the states than in the districts. In the districts there are 27 afflicted persons in every 10,000 ; there are 48 in the states. The difference is much too marked and too uniformly distributed throughout the infirmities to be accidental. Nor can it be entirely due to the idiosyncrasies of the enumerators. Some of the difference clearly arises from the very much larger element of aliens in the districts ; for the **General results.**

Infirm per 10,000.	
Balūchistān	*38*
Districts	27
States	48

aliens are mostly full-bodied men, who usually take care to leave the lame ducks of their families behind in the home-country. And something at any rate may fairly be put to the credit of the medical department, which so far has had little scope for carrying its ministrations into the states; unfortunately infirmities were recorded in too confined an area at the last census for us to attempt to take stock of the progress towards health during the last ten years.

Relative prevalence of infirmities.

245. By far the most common of the infirmities is blindness, which easily overtops the rest put together. It works havoc in the Kachhī plain and the connected Ḍōmbkī-Kahērī country, and is distressingly prevalent in Makrān and Chāgai. And this bears out the ordinary idea that blindness flourishes in excessive heat and glare, which certainly seem—rightly or wrongly—to be predisposing factors of glaucoma and cataract. Of these two great causes of blindness, cataract is much the more common in Balūchistān, though glaucoma is a regular scourge all over the Kachhī. And herein lies a gleam of hope for the gradual diminution of blindness in the country. The numbers who come in for operation are already on the increase; and each successful operation may be relied upon to play its part in thinning the ranks of those who would otherwise be content to be couched—very likely into total blindness—by the local quacks. Another very fruitful local source of blindness is smallpox. Others are granular lids, especially in association with ingrowing eye-lashes, and ophthalmia, especially at or shortly after birth. The amount of blindness among young children which might have been avoided by a little antiseptic washing must be appalling. In comparison with blindness the other infirmities seem almost dwarfed into insignificance. Deaf-mutism is the commonest; yet for every victim it claims, blindness claims three. For some unknown reason it is relatively more prevalent in Las Bēla than elsewhere, with Chāgai a close second. There are rather more than half as many insane as there are deaf-mutes; and Las Bēla has again the melancholy distinction of heading the list with the largest number in proportion to its population. Leprosy, real or imaginary, claims 83 victims in all, or 1 in every 10,000. Makrān is accredited with a third of the lot, but I cannot pretend to be confident of the accuracy of the diagnosis anywhere. Indeed, medical opinion declines to regard leprosy as a local disease at all, though I am told that several genuine cases have been observed among immigrants from Afghānistān, especially among the Hazāra.

Incidence of infirmities.

Blindness	64
Deaf-mutism	21
Insanity	12
Leprosy	3
	100

Racial variation.

246. Turning to race, I am not surprised to find that of all our peoples the Sayyids are the most immune from the four infirmities. It would be pleasant to think that this is but the natural privilege of a sainted race or the natural reward for a holy life. But I fear we must seek a more mundane explanation in the health of the localities where they live and the better surroundings in which their lot is ordinarily cast. And locality and decent surroundings have probably a good deal to say to the comparatively clean health-bill of the Paṭhāns, who are usually next-door neighbours to the Sayyids and very nearly as immune. Among the Brāhūīs the standard of living is markedly lower, and the proportion of infirmities, apparently in consequence, appreciably higher. Why the Balōch should be much less healthy than the Brāhūī is a little less obvious; but we have only to go down lower to the infirmities among the various tribes to find the explanation lurking in locality once more. That all three, Paṭhān and Brāhūī and Balōch, should escape far more lightly than the Jaṭṭ and the Lāsī, who dwell in the hottest parts of the country, is intelligible on the face of it. It is, of course, through blindness that locality is able to exercise a determining influence on the figures throughout: it is blindness, for instance, that makes the Balōch appear much more subject to infirmities than the Brāhūīs, and gives the Jaṭṭ, who live in the burning heat of the Kachhī plain, their unenviable position at the top of the sick-list. Deaf-mutism and insanity levy their heaviest toll among the Lāsī of Las Bēla. Leprosy appears to be most active among the miscellaneous peoples—which is only as it should be, for many of them stand low in the social scale; the Sayyids alone are reputed to be altogether free from the scourge.

Infirm per 10,000.

Jaṭṭ	62
Lāsī	57
Balōch	47
Miscellaneous	45
Brāhūī	32
Paṭhān	28
Sayyid	26

Infirmities among the females.

247. Classed according to the number of their victims among the women, the various infirmities range themselves in the same order as before; blindness stands unchallenged at the top; leprosy stands unchallenged at the bottom. The Balōch woman heads the list of the insane, the Brāhūī of the lepers, the Sayyid (curiously enough) of the deaf-mute; the women of the miscellaneous peoples head the list not only of the blind but of all the afflicted put together. On paper the women as a whole appear to escape far more lightly than the men; in reality they suffer a good deal more than the crude statistics would imply. The proportion of afflicted among them looks unduly small simply because their total number is much smaller than the total number of males: glancing at the statistics we must throughout bear in mind this abnormal scarcity of females in Balūchistān. If we readjust the statistics and compare the proportion of the afflicted among equal numbers of either sex, we find that instead of there being 66 afflicted females to 100 afflicted males, there are as many as 83. As for blindness, it actually affects the females most; in an equal number of either sex there are 110 blind females to 100 blind males. And this of course is the one infirmity where we have come to expect the females to be at least as great sufferers as the males. In the other infirmities the males, here as elsewhere, reassert their unenviable but apparently well-established superiority of variability.

Afflicted females to 100 afflicted males.	
All infirmities	66
Blindness	87
Deaf-mutism	39
Insanity	38
Leprosy	26

Local ideas.

248. But it is hardly worth while to pursue the statistics further; the smallness of our numbers threatens to vitiate any conclusions we might attempt to draw from them. So much do I feel this difficulty that I for one take more interest in the local ideas about the infirmities than in the statistics themselves. The country folk are firmly convinced that smallpox is responsible for most of the blindness among them; but old age comes in of course for a good deal of the blame, and so does fever at all periods of life. Local theories, however, usually vary with local characteristics; and it is only natural that blindness should be attributed along the desolate Nushkī trade-route to the whirling dust, on the Makrān coast to powdered shells driven with the sand, and in the Kachhī to the intolerable heat and glare of the summer months. Not only are the heat and the glare believed to be directly injurious to the sight, they make the salt perspiration drip into the eyes, or else set up a peculiar kind of headache known as *lōtī*, the natural issue of which is blindness or insanity or both. The unfortunate inhabitants of the Kachhī, perhaps the most scorching tract in all India, are very subject to *shab-kōrī* or night-blindness during the months of June, July and August; all treatment appears to be vain: there is nothing for it but to wait patiently for the break in the heat, when the nuisance passes off of itself. Insanity is variously regarded as the outcome of an excessive and heating diet, the result of a sudden shock, the punishment for perjury, or the malicious contrivance of the Jinns. But Kachhī folk put it down to the burning heat like most of their ills, and regard it as one of the ordinary endings of that racking headache they call *lōtī*. Deaf-mutism is ordinarily looked upon as an infliction sent by the Almighty over which man has no control. But the Brāhūīs are convinced that it is the inevitable result of loquacity on the part of the parents at the very first beginning of things; in fact such strong believers are they in pre-natal or rather preconceptional influences that it is one of their first principles to turn out all animals from the vicinity of the conjugal chamber, lest the child of the union be born marred with the characteristic of some brute beast. Though I believe the country to be almost free from leprosy, there is a vague wide-spread dread of it. Most people attribute the scourge to the eating of fish, which may account for the reason why fish is regularly tabooed in several parts of the country. But the more learned in such matters tell me that there is scant danger in fish if you adopt the simple precaution of not taking milk or mutton or fowls or onions along with it. Then there are hundreds who think that leprosy comes from union with a woman in her impurity. More curious is the notion that it arises from ablutions with water that has been left standing in the sun in a copper vessel. But none of these theories appeal to the wise men among the Brāhūīs, who tell me that it simply comes from eating the flesh of a peacock which has just devoured a snake. Local cures are interesting enough. But the subject would lead too far afield even for a report as rambling as this. And in any case I could hardly hope to

provide such entertaining reading as the following paragraph, which I first came across in the *Paignton Observer*, and which appears to be going the round of the provincial press, as I came across it a month later in the *Herts and Essex Observer*: "In Baluchistan, when a physician gives a dose, he is expected to partake of a similar one himself as a guarantee of his good faith. Should the patient die under his hands, the relatives, though they rarely exercise it, have the right of putting him to death, unless a special agreement has been made for freeing him from all responsibility as to consequences; while, if they should decide upon immolating him, he is fully expected to yield to his fate like a man." One almost wishes—for the sake of local colour—that there were a grain of truth in it.

SUBSIDIARY TABLES.

XXVII.—Incidence of Infirmities.

NOTE—The fact that one deaf-mute male in Chāgai and one blind male in Sibī were also returned as insane accounts for the apparent discrepancy in the total.

PARTICULARS	NUMBER AFFLICTED PER 100,000.										
	ALL INFIRMITIES.			INSANE.		DEAF-MUTE.		BLIND.		LEPER.	
	Persons.	Males.	Females.	Males.	Females.	Males.	Females.	Males.	Females.	Males.	Females.
					(i) By locality						
BALŪCHISTĀN	*380*	*409*	*343*	*57*	*28*	*103*	*50*	*235*	*260*	*14*	*5*
Districts	**274**	**309**	**227**	**44**	**14**	**93**	**43**	**165**	**167**	**7**	**3**
Quetta-Pishin	139	172	90	33	2	52	23	86	63	1	2
Lōṛalai	297	342	240	51	19	80	31	191	184	20	6
Zhōb	293	322	253	64	23	92	57	161	170	5	3
Bōlān	477	201	1,159	67	...	67	...	67	1,159	...	...
Chāgai	563	571	553	88	55	220	83	274	401	...	14
Sibī	350	399	284	34	9	133	60	226	213	7	2
Administered area	*404*	*431*	*367*	*38*	*9*	*141*	*54*	*248*	*301*	*6*	*3*
Marī-Bugṭī country	*221*	*321*	*97*	*26*	*18*	*114*	*71*	*171*	*13*	*10*	...
States	**484**	**515**	**447**	**71**	**40**	**114**	**57**	**308**	**344**	**22**	**6**
Kalāt	471	501	437	66	32	95	49	318	349	22	7
Sarāwān	*450*	*544*	*334*	*117*	*31*	*114*	*52*	*296*	*247*	*17*	*4*
Jhalawān	*207*	*222*	*189*	*30*	*14*	*66*	*29*	*107*	*125*	*19*	*21*
Kachhī	*612*	*650*	*568*	*62*	*21*	*118*	*66*	*466*	*479*	*4*	*2*
Ḍōmbkī-Kahērī	*748*	*768*	*724*	*79*	*28*	*87*	*9*	*602*	*687*	...	...
Makrān	*556*	*554*	*557*	*55*	*61*	*93*	*58*	*337*	*435*	*69*	*8*
Khārān	*379*	*388*	*370*	*91*	*47*	*74*	*48*	*223*	*275*	...	...
Las Bēla	560	603	511	104	91	227	105	254	315	18	...
					(ii) By race						
Indigenous Musalmāns	**399**	**445**	**344**	**60**	**29**	**117**	**53**	**253**	**257**	**15**	**5**
Balōch	468	519	407	55	35	126	60	322	308	16	4
Brāhūī	322	341	297	62	35	85	64	174	189	20	9
Paṭhān	280	339	209	57	16	108	34	166	157	8	2
Lāsī	572	707	418	148	77	310	70	236	271	13	...
Jaṭṭ	625	653	590	37	22	150	81	464	487	3	...
Sayyid	258	345	165	54	10	73	48	218	107	...	...
Miscellaneous	450	490	406	71	30	97	33	287	333	35	10

XXVIII.—Incidence of Infirmities among Females.

PARTICULARS	Females afflicted per 1,000 afflicted males				
	All infirmities	Insane	Deaf-mute	Blind	Leper
	(i) By locality				
BALŪCHISTĀN	*661*	*381*	*386*	*874*	*258*
Districts	**539**	**226**	**341**	**741**	**353**
Quetta-Pishīn	348	40	300	485	1,000
Lōṛalai	538	304	306	767	222
Zhōb	585	269	459	785	500
Bōlān	2,333	...	...	7,000	...
Chāgai	769	500	300	1,160	...
Sibī	536	217	337	709	200
Administered area	*624*	*167*	*284*	*890*	*833*
Marī-Bugṭī country	*242*	*400*	*500*	*61*	...
States	**738**	**481**	**425**	**949**	**224**
Kalāt	737	406	432	930	256
Sarāwān	*503*	*220*	*375*	*683*	*167*
Jhalawān	*683*	*357*	*355*	*940*	*889*
Kachhī	*742*	*290*	*475*	*872*	*500*
Ḍōmbkī-Kahērī	*814*	*300*	*91*	*987*	...
Makrān	*914*	*1,000*	*571*	*1,173*	*38*
Khārān	*830*	*455*	*556*	*1,074*	...
Las Bēla	741	765	405	1,084	...
	(ii) By race				
Indigenous Musalmāns	**654**	**407**	**386**	**860**	**267**
Balōch	657	529	397	804	200
Brāhūī	698	448	608	870	368
Paṭhān	520	241	264	794	250
Lāsī	514	455	193	1,000	...
Jaṭṭ	756	500	453	879	...
Sayyid	447	167	625	458	...
Miscellaneous	774	400	317	1,082	267

CHAPTER XI.

CASTE, TRIBE AND RACE.

STATISTICAL DATA:—TABLE XIII.

The chief races of Balūchistān.

249. The heading of this chapter is none of our devising. Appropriate enough for India as a whole, it is curiously inappropriate for Balūchistān. Caste, so absorbingly interesting elsewhere, is almost unknown, and though I shall have a little to say on the subject later, that little will be of a purely negative character. In Balūchistān the interest centres round our multitudinous tribal divisions and the parasitical elements grafted on them. We are chiefly concerned with three races, Balōch, Brāhūī and Paṭhān. In using the word race, I am unfortunately laying myself open to the charge of begging a highly debateable question. In justification I can only plead the lack of a better workaday term. It is of course well-established that not one of the groups now designated as Balōch, Brāhūī and Paṭhān is entirely homogeneous in its composition. There is, for instance, no doubt of the presence of Jaṭṭ elements in all three, or of the Paṭhān origin of several of the Brāhūī tribes. But even if the Balōch and the Brāhūī and the Paṭhān are originally offshoots from one and the same stock, they have certainly differentiated with such persistence that they may well be treated nowadays as different species. In describing them as three distinct races, I am at any rate describing things as they now are or at least as they appear to be to the peoples concerned, who are content to accept the broad dividing-lines of looks, dress, language, manners, customs, without probing too deeply into questions of origin. And after all is said and done, is it so very certain that the nucleus of all three is derived from the same stock? Far from regarding a common origin as certain,—except of course a primeval all-embracing origin of the chief branches of mankind—I regard it, I confess, as altogether unproved and not a little improbable. But here again I have set foot on dangerous ground and am running in the teeth of the latest conclusions of anthropometry, which lump all three together, in company with the Jaṭṭ and the Dēhwār and the Lōṛī and the Mēd and the Ghulām—strange bed-fellows with a vengeance—as constituents of the one Turko-Iranian race.

No theory as to origins.

250. But though I incline to back unscientific but first-hand experience of the peoples themselves against this amazing result of scientific methods, I have no theories to offer regarding the origins of the races. It almost seems as if the whole question were insoluble at the present stage of ethnology. Whether we look upon the races as mere variations from one and the same stock or whether we look upon them as distinct species, we are equally groping in the dark; in either case the opinion we affect is little more than an opinion after all. Philology, anthropometry and the other keys that were to unlock the door and reveal the secrets of race—they all seem to have failed us dismally. But if the time has apparently come for a serious reconsideration of ethnological methods, the time is certainly not past for a careful description of the races as we find them. And this we may look to the Ethnographical Survey of Balūchistān to give us in due course. Here I can hope to do little more than pass the chief peoples of the country in review.

The Paṭhāns.

251. And I will begin with the Paṭhān, not merely because his is the most numerous race in Balūchistān, but because he is so conveniently positive about his origin and his genealogies, and therefore comparatively easy to deal with. Of his supposed identity with the Πάκτυες of Herodotus or the Παρσυῆται of Ptolemy, he knows nothing. The lineage he traces is more ancient still, for he claims to be sprung from Malik Ṭālūt, known to us as King Saul, the son of Kish. Seven and thirty generations separate King Saul from his descendant Qais Abdur Rashīd. And Abdur Rashīd, as befits the ancestor of such sturdy Musalmāns as the Paṭhāns, was among the earliest of the converts to Islām, though his home was far away towards the Takht-i-Sulemān. Nay, he was even counted among the honoured friends of the Prophet himself, and his deeds of valour in the cause of the true faith were rewarded by this glorious prophecy from the Prophet's own lips: "God will raise up a mighty seed from this man, and he will be firm in the faith, and the strength of his tribe will be as the strength of the keel of a ship." And in token thereof he hailed him Patan or Batiyan: for the interpretation of the name (heaven knows in what language) is keel. And Abdur Rashīd married Sarah, the daughter of Khālid the victorious, and by her he had three sons, Saraban, Ghurghusht and Baitan, from one or other of whom all true Paṭhāns are sprung. So, at least, runs the tradition recorded by Niamat Ullah some three hundred years ago; and he has screeds of genealogies to back his statements.

Paṭhāns	**214,517**
Indigenous	188,093
Semi-indigenous	22,317
Aliens	4,107

Genealogies.

252. It seems high time that these musty genealogies were subjected to the search-light of modern criticism. Until this is done, there is nothing for it but to follow them as blindly, though hardly with the same implicit faith, as the Paṭhān himself. Not that I propose to thread my way through their labyrinthine mazes; he who will can find them in any book on the Paṭhāns. A bare skeleton of the chief ramifications in the pedigree is all that we require—just enough to show the groupings of the representatives of the race still to be found in Balūchistān.

Abdur Rashīd	Saraban	Sharkhbūn	Tarīn		37,411
			Shīrānī		8,562
			Barēch		854
			Miāna	Lūṇī	2,816
				Jafar	1,286
				Zmarai	1,228
		Kharshbūn	Kāsī		1,337
	Ghurghusht	Bābī			323
		Dānī	Kākar		105,073
			Paṇī		28,675
	Baitan	Bībī Mato	Ghilzai		18,586

Now Saraban had two sons, Sharkhbūn and Kharshbūn. The descendants of the former are of much greater importance for us than the descendants of the latter, whose only local representatives worthy the name of tribe are the Kāsī. For from Sharkhbūn are sprung the Tarīn, the Shīrānī and the Barēch, together with the Miāna offshoots—the Lūṇī, the Jafar and the Zmarai, to say nothing of the Khetrān, now ranked as Balōch (§ 264) and the Gharshīn, now ranked as Sayyid (§ 259). But important as is this Saraban branch of the Paṭhān race, it is overshadowed in Balūchistān by the Ghurghusht. Of the three sons of Ghurghusht, two, Bābī and Mandō, concern us little, though there are a few scattered Bābī in Quetta-Pishīn and Kalāt, and it is just possible that the Mandōkhēl may be the descendants of Mandō (§ 258). But from Dānī are descended not only the Kākar, the largest of all the Paṭhān tribes in the country, but also the Paṇī with its numerous offshoots. With the third great branch of the Paṭhān race we need hardly bother ourselves at all; for though in the Ghilzai we have enumerated a goodly number of the descendants of Baitan, the Ghilzai are not truly indigenous to Balūchistān (§ 74).

Tarīn.

253. With this skeleton pedigree as a guide, we may now follow up the main Paṭhān tribes in the country. Tarīn, the son of Sharkhbūn, the son of Saraban, had three sons, Spīn, Tōr and Bōr—White, Black and Brown; according to somewhat apocryphal accounts, there was a fourth son Zhaṛ, Yellow, descendants from whom are supposed to be traceable among the Zhaṛkhēl Dēhwār and the Raisānī Brāhūī. The Spīn Tarīn, who are chiefly located in Shāhrig and Sanjāwī, are the least numerous of the three; their strongest clan, the Vaṇēchī—indeed they set up as a tribe with a *sardār*

Tarīn	**37,411**
Spīn	5,134
Tōr	11,890
Achakzai	20,272
Others	115

of its own—are a quiet, peaceful community, whose unmixed Paṭhān origin (partly perhaps for that very reason) is not altogether above suspicion. The Tōr Tarīn, who are scattered over Sibī, Quetta-Pishīn and Lōṛalai, are more than twice as numerous; and here again there seem to be many alien elements in the largest clan, the Makhīānī. But much the most important both in numbers and everything else are the Bōr Tarīn, better known as the Abdāl. Not only is this the stock from which the present ruling family of Afghānistān is sprung, it includes the Achakzai, one of the most prominent Paṭhān tribes in the province. The Achakzai have had a pretty bad reputation from time immemorial, which probably explains why Ahmad Shāh, Durrānī, himself a Sadōzai Abdāl and therefore a kinsman of theirs, took the precaution of removing them to a convenient distance from the parent-stock. They nowadays occupy the whole of the Khwāja Amrān range on the Chaman border, and swarm over southern Afghānistān as far as Herāt.

Shīrānī.

254. The precise classification of the Shīrānī, however obvious on paper, is in reality a very pretty little problem, which ultimately resolves itself, as may be gathered from Niamat Ullah, into a struggle of father-kin *versus* mother-kin. For Sharkhbūn, the son of Saraban, first married a Kākaṛ wife and by her had one son, Shīrānī. Marrying again, he begat several other sons, and in course of time made up his mind to single out Tarīn, the eldest of them, to be *malik* or leader after him, an act of injustice which so incensed Shīrānī that he threw in his lot with his maternal grandfather Kākaṛ, swearing that he had done with the Sarabanī, and that he and his sons' sons after him would remain Ghurghushtī for ever. But whether a tribe is Sarabanī or Ghurghushtī is in these days of course a purely academic question. The Shīrānī, or Marānī as they like to be called, are settled round the Takht-i-Sulemān. Those on the east of the range (who do not properly belong to this province) are known as Largha, those on the west are known as Bargha; but there is a good deal of chopping and changing between the two. One of the chief clans, the Harīpāl, claims Sayyid descent from Harīf, a Sayyid who married a Shīrānī wife and took up his quarters with the Shīrānī tribe; but Niamat Ullah knows nothing of this: on the contrary, he specifically states that Harīpāl was the son of Char, the son of Shīrānī. Of all the tribes within our borders the Shīrānī are possibly the most uncivilised; they are certainly the most turbulent at the moment. "A dog that knows you won't bite you," says the proverb, "but the better a Marānī knows you the greater his relish in devouring you."

Shīrānī . . .	3,552

Miāna branch.

255. We may pass over Baṛēch, another son of Sharkhbūn (for the number of his descendants in Balūchistān is too small to give them any special significance), and turn to his brother Miāna. It has been the curious fate of such descendants of Miāna as are left in Balūchistān to have come under Balōch influence. Thus among the Lūnī, who reside in Dukī and who prefer to be called Durrānī (on no better grounds, as far as I know, than that their ancestor Miāna was a brother of Tarīn, the ancestor of the Durrānī Abdāl), the chief's title is not *sardār* but *tumandār*. More marked is the Balōch influence on the Jafar, who live in the neighbouring *tahsīl* of Mūsakhēl, and speak a Jaṭkī language called Jafarkī among themselves (§ 229) and Pashtō or Balōchī among their neighbours. The general impression that there is a good deal of Balōch blood in the tribe is perhaps confirmed by the practice of the artificial defloration of their brides (§ 177). The same custom exists again among the Gharshīn, who though related to the Miāna stock, have now been classed as Sayyid (§ 259). Curiously enough it does not exist—though female circumcision does (§ 99)—among the Khetrān, who though apparently descended from Miāna can be classed as Paṭhān no longer, for they have definitely taken on Balōch status (§ 264). In fact the only local descendants of Miāna who have kept clear of Balōch influence seem to be the Zmarai. But the name Zmarai (which by the by means lion) does not figure in the genealogies; and it is possible that this numerically insignificant tribe is not Miāna after all.

Lūnī	2,816
Jafar	1,286
Zmarai	1,228

Kāsī.

256. But while the descendants of Sharkhbūn have flourished, the Kharshbūn branch of the Sarabanī is almost extinct in Baluchistān. With the

exception of a few isolated families of the Zamand its sole representatives are the Kāsī, (or Kā̃sī as they are sometimes called), a tribe which has acquired an importance out of all proportion to its numbers owing to the richness of its lands in the neighbourhood of Quetta. But despite their wealth, or perhaps on account of it, the tribesmen have a bad name among their neighbours for cowardice, untrustworthiness, and self-righteousness. If there's any mischief a-foot, the Kāsī is supposed to be at the bottom of it. "'Twas the will of God, but the deed of the Kāsī" is a common proverb. A curious physical defect has earned them the nickname of *zhaṛ-ghāshe*, yellow-tooth. And thereby hangs a tale that their neighbours love to tell at their expense. A harmless wayfarer once passed through their village with a greyhound on leash. Thinking to get a rise out of him, they cried out: "Hallo there! D'you want to sell that mongrel of yours?" And the man replied that he was willing enough, if they could give him his price. "All very well," said his baiters, "but let's have a look at its teeth; you can't palm off a toothless old mongrel on the likes of us." "Look at its teeth if you will," said the man, "but you may take my word for it that the hound is no Yellow-tooth like some I wot of." And with a grin he was quit of his tormentors.

Kāsī	1,337

Kākaṛ.

257. So much for the Sarabanī. Of the sons of Ghurghusht, we may pass over Bābī, because his descendants are few and scattered, and Mandō, because he either left no descendants in Balūchistān (and Niamat Ullah seems to imply that he left none at all) or they have forgotten their origin and trace back to the Paṇī (§ 258). But from Dāni, the son of Ghurghusht, is sprung first and foremost the Kākaṛ, which is not only the largest Paṭhān tribe in the province, but accounts for one-eighth of the whole population. But to call the Kākaṛ a tribe would perhaps be a misnomer. For the connection between the great clans of which it is composed has become so slight, that each may fairly claim to be treated as a tribe by itself; indeed the same may be said of some of the sections in the several clans which have increased and multiplied and come into separate political prominence. By far the largest of these clans, or tribes as I prefer to call them, is the Sanzarkhēl, which is chiefly located in Zhōb and Lōṛalai. The most influential group in the tribe is the Jōgīzai (a subsection of the Jalālzai), who provided the "King of Zhōb" in the days of Ahmad Shāh, and are still regarded with religious veneration by the tribesmen. One of the largest of the Sanzarkhēl groups is the Dumaṛ, but there seems to be some doubt whether these are true Kākaṛ at all. According to the Kākaṛ, they are descended from a *ḍum* or minstrel in Sanzar's service. According to the Dumaṛ themselves, they are descended from one of Sanzar's sons by a Shīrānī widow—a pedigree which obviously indicates uneasiness as to the purity of the breed. But according to Niamat Ullah's genealogies, Dum was the son of Dāwī, the son of Dānī, and on this showing the Dumaṛ and the Kākaṛ and the Paṇī all belong to different branches of Ghurghusht. The Snaṭia, who are next in strength to the Sanzarkhēl among the Kākaṛ, are mainly located in Quetta-Pishīn; but there are also a good number in Sibī, and a few in Zhōb. The Targhaṛa are less widely dispersed than the Snaṭia, keeping almost entirely to Quetta-Pishīn. Though a well-recognised tribe or clan of the Kākaṛ, it is generally believed that they are not true Kākaṛ, and it is certain that there is a large alien infusion among them. Of the Sargaṛa, the smallest of the four main Kākaṛ divisions, the majority now live in Quetta-Pishīn, but their real home is supposed to be Zhōb. How little tribal cohesion there is in this division may be seen from the fact that, when the Māndazai of Quetta-Pishīn recently endeavoured to renew their ties of kinship with the Sargaṛa of Hindūbāgh, their overtures were met with silence. As for the Dāwī and the Lamaṛ, their numbers are too small for them to be of any political interest, though as remnants of once famous branches of the great Kākaṛ tribe, they are interesting enough.

Kākar	105,073
Sanzarkhēl	56,032
Snaṭia	23,349
Targhaṛa	14,089
Sargaṛa	2,843
Lamaṛ	492
Dāwī	284

Paṇī.

258. Paṇī, like Kākaṛ, was a son of Dānī, the son of Ghurghusht. But the connection between the Kākaṛ and the Paṇī tribes has long since faded away;

indeed so little cohesion is there among the various clans of the Paṇī themselves that it is only by a stretch of the imagination that we can call some of them Paṇī any longer. They are a very scattered lot. Not only are they to be found in Sibī, Zhōb and Lōṛalai, and in lesser numbers in Quetta-Pishīn, they are dispersed into Afghānistān, the North-West Frontier Province, and far into southern India. In Balūchistān the only group that still clings to the actual name of Paṇī are the Sibī Paṇī, whose history dates back to Bāra Khān who lived about the middle of the fifteenth century and was the founder of the great Bārōzai section which supplied the rulers of Sibī and the surrounding country under Afghān rule. It is round these Bārōzāi that the Sibī Paṇī range themselves, though the Ismailkhānzai have separated themselves off from the main stock, and have set up in opposition in Sāngān. The Paṇī of Zhōb and Lōṛalai have severed their connection altogether. Dropping the very name of Paṇī, they have taken on separate names, and constituted themselves into separate tribes, though still acknowledging a shadowy Paṇī lineage. The most powerful of these are the Mūsakhēl, who are chiefly to be found in the *tahsīl* of that name in Lōṛalai, and are divided into two main divisions, the Bēlkhēl, the senior branch, and the Lahrzai, each under a chief of its own. Then there are the Mandōkhēl, who also claim Paṇī descent but repudiate anything more than a sentimental connection with the Paṇī of Sibī. As Mandō is the name of one of the three sons of Ghurghusht, it has sometimes been assumed that these Mandōkhēl must be his direct descendants. They themselves lay no pretensions to this pedigree, but trace back to Mandō, the son of Paṇī, the nephew of Mandō, the son of Ghurghusht. And whatever may be the real worth of these misty genealogies, it seems quite clear that, when a tribe deliberately forgoes a proud but plausible pedigree, the chances are that there is more truth in the more modest ancestry it claims. According to their own account (and Paṇī accounts back them up) they broke off from the main Paṇī tribe some twenty generations ago for good and all. They are now a fairly united tribe under one *sardār*, priding themselves on the purity of their many sections. Another offshoot from the Paṇī stock is the small nomad tribe of the Isōṭ. Yet another apparently is the Zarkūn, who chiefly live in Dukī and Kōhlū. But the origin of the Zarkūn is a little obscure, and if they are Paṇī in reality, the probabilities are that they are not a direct offshoot from the main tribe but an offshoot from its offshoot the Mūsakhēl. And finally there is one small Sāfī offshoot which has been classed as semi-indigenous, and another which has affiliated itself to the Sibī Paṇī.

Paṇī	**28,675**
Sibī Paṇī	6.714
Mūsakhēl	12.202
Mandōkhēl	4,944
Isōṭ	2,812
Zarkūn	2,003

Pathān Sayyids.

259. The brief account of the Ghilzai given elsewhere (§74) will suffice for these sons of Baitan; for the Ghilzai are not true indigenous inhabitants of Balūchistān. There remain three groups, half Paṭhān, half Sayyid, to which I must refer. Bowing to public feelings of commendable piety, I have classified the Ustrāna and the Gharshīn and the Mashwānī as Sayyid, and not as Paṭhān. And on this point it is interesting to note what Niamat Ullah has to say. "Several clans among the Afghān nations are Sayyids; such are the Ishturānī among the Shīrānī, the Mashwānī among the Kākaṛ, the Gharshīn among the Miāna. Nevertheless they are now numbered among the Paṭhāns. For they never style themselves Sayyids, saying with one voice: 'Ill-seeming were it and against reason, were we to style ourselves Sayyids, seeing that we have left their order, and have joined the nation of the Afghāns to have our kith and our kin and our commerce among them. Our fathers, moreover, have declared that whosoever of their sons shall take upon himself the title of Sayyid, the same is no son of theirs.' This thing was spoken of in the reigns of Sikandar and Shēr Shāh, and the high personages among them did not gainsay this saying." But the tide has turned, for there is plenty of gainsaying in these days, and it seems wisest to withhold the proud title of Sayyid from them no longer (§ 281).

Tribal and racial composition.

260. These old genealogies of Niamat Ullah would decidedly repay study. Even at the lowest estimate they reflect the general ideas current about the Paṭhāns some three centuries ago. It is interesting enough to compare his antiquated statements with present facts, and not a little curious to find so

many of the names he mentions still surviving among the tribes as we know them now, despite the ease with which new names spring up and old names die out in the mysterious ebb and flow of human generation. Take, for instance, the insignificant Jafar tribe, one of our puny remnants of the Miāna stock. Among its tiny sections—and they are all tiny—are the Rawānī, the Sōmat and the Surānī. Not only is Jafar himself reckoned by Niamat Ullah among the sons of Miāna, so are Sōmat and Rawānī; and Sur figures among Miāna's grandsons. Yet the Jafar might seem a singularly unpromising field for comparative research, for not only is it a very small tribe, it is a tribe that has departed from pure Paṭhān standards: it has adopted a Jaṭkī language; its customs, apparently, have been tinged with Balōch influence. And this reference to Balōch influence suggests another point. It has been assumed time and again that there is no surer indication not merely of Balōch influence but of Balōch infusion than the tribal ending *-ānī*, which figures, for example, in Rawānī, Surānī. Yet when we find that the names of these two petty sections were living names among the Miāna three hundred years ago, and that one of them bore the damningly tell-tale termination even then without raising the slightest suspicion in the not uncritical mind of Niamat Ullah, this sort of argument seems clearly a trifle dangerous. Not that the racial or tribal purity of the Paṭhāns was perfect in Niamat Ullah's days or even in Niamat Ullah's opinion. He has constantly to eke out his genealogies with "adopted sons," and the concluding words of his treatise are a *caveat* against the vain pretensions of outsiders to Paṭhān descent. Still less is the Paṭhān's theory as to the purity of his tribe—the theory that it consists of a body of kinsmen, all descended on the male side from one common ancestor—borne out in fact to-day. Out of his own mouth can we condemn him. For there is hardly a Paṭhān tribe which does not make shift to explain the presence of this or that section in its midst as the descendants of some adopted son, or of some fugitive from another tribe, or—most pathetic of all his confessions of ignorance—of some foundling. And the absorption of strangers must have been easy enough in the old days when the land was the common property of the tribe, to be distributed and redistributed among the tribesmen from time to time. But though traces of periodical allottings of land still linger here and there, there is none of that thorough-going tribal commonalty of land such as still exists among the Marī Balōch (§ 266). The days of wholesale affiliation are apparently over. Even the affiliation of individual refugees from other tribes is fast going out of fashion; refugees are often a good deal more bother than they are worth. Taken in bulk as a race or individually as tribes, the Paṭhāns are much less of a medley than either Brāhūī or Balōch. The only real tendency towards fissure is within the tribe itself; clans, I fancy, will still break off from the parent tribe to form other tribes of their own, as the Mandōkhēl and the Mūsakhēl have done before them. And though the presence of the Khetrān among the ranks of the Balōch (§ 264), and the existence of a clan composed largely of Shīrānī elements among the Marī (§ 263), and the plentiful admixture of Paṭhāns of various kinds among the Brāhūīs generally (§ 272), are living witnesses of a fairly extensive race-change in the past, there is none—at any rate among the Paṭhāns within the country itself—at the present day.

Tribal constitution.

261. Those who have had dealings with the aggressively democratic Paṭhān of Tīrāh are sometimes inclined to imagine that the more aristocratic spirit that animates the Paṭhāns of Balūchistān must be due to the genius of Sandeman. But here, at any rate, the influence of Sandeman has clearly been overrated; indeed there is evidence that our Paṭhāns are somewhat more democratic now than they were before his time. Nor will it suffice to put everything down to contact with the undemocratic Brāhūī and Balōch; except in very narrowly confined areas the contact has never been effective enough to have produced such far-reaching results. The true explanation, I fancy, is that the democratic spirit, which is at once the glory of the Paṭhāns who live outside their ancient mother country and the despair of those who have to deal with them, is a comparatively modern development after all. To my mind, this is almost suggested in the genealogies themselves, in the tracing back of the tribe to an eponymous hero. In any case, one has no need to peer between the lines of Niamat Ullah's work in order to find evidences of an early subordination of the tribe to a chief-

ship. Take, for instance, the story that Shīrānī left the tribe of his father because his younger half-brother Tarīn was to be made *malik* over his head (§ 254). Or take the lengthy story leading up to the Sayyid origin of the Ustrāna and Mashwānī, which tells how the wife of a certain Shīrānī appealed to "Hamīm, Shīrānī, the chief of that nation," when her husband proposed to set up their son as master of the family to the exclusion of the son she had had by her former Sayyid husband; and which concludes with an agreement made by "the heads of the three tribes, the Kerranians, the Kākaṛ and the Shīrānī." Coming to historical times, we find that nearly all the great Paṭhān divisions had their chiefs or rulers or even so-called kings: there were the chiefs of the Achakzai; the Bārōzai governors of Sibī, the chiefs of the Paṇī; the Jōgīzai "Kings of Zhōb," the chiefs of the Sanzarkhēl. Wherever we know that a tribe has had a serious struggle for existence in historical times, we find a chief figuring prominently in its history. And there are plenty of chiefs to-day: there are chiefs of the Jōgīzai, the Mūsakhēl, the Mandōkhēl, the Isōṭ, the Lūṇī, the Jafar, the Zmarai, the Abdullazai, the Mēhtarzai, the two divisions of the Dumaṛ, the Pānēzai and the Sārangzai of Sibī, and others besides. Nevertheless, it would be a bold man who would prophesy that the Paṭhāns of Balūchistān will always remain true to their older tribal organisation. Among Paṭhāns there is little of that blind faith in heredity, that has been so marked a characteristic of the Balōch and the Brāhūī; and probably there never has been. The survival of the "tenth transmitter of a foolish face" at all costs is no part of the Paṭhān's political creed. The present tendency is apparently two-fold: on the one hand the power of the older chiefs seems to be decaying and their influence becoming more and more confined to the clansmen living in their immediate neighbourhood; on the other, new men are constantly rising into prominence and, having gathered a following around them, setting themselves up in authority as leaders of smaller sections. None the less, these leanings towards democracy are leavened by a strong clannish feeling and a robust racial pride, and the Paṭhān seems much better fitted in character than either Balōch or Brāhūī to march with the changes in the times.

The Balōch.

262. A mass of curious legends and a noble cycle of epic ballads have gathered round the early history of the Balōch. In one group of legends the scene opens in Arabia, and after an interlude in Aleppo shifts to Persia, where it wavers between Kirmān and Seistān. In another group it is in Persia that the scene opens; it does not shift to Arabia till long after, in the days of the Prophet; on his death it shifts to Aleppo, and back again to Persia. Yet even this latter group of legends seeks, incongruously enough, to associate the ancestry of the Balōch with the Prophet, by tracing the descent of Jalāl Khān—the father of Rind, Lāshār, Kōrāī, Hōt and their sister Jatō, who are generally accepted as the five progenitors of the race—either to the Prophet's uncle Mīr Hamza and a fairy wife, or else (less directly but still honourably) to a slave of his son-in-law 'Alī. And over all hangs the magic of Arabia. Much has been done to sift the grains of history from these interesting ballad and legend cycles; and no one has laboured more industriously in the field than Dames, whose enthusiasm alone should fire others to carry on the work, partly by collecting the many ballads that still remain on the lips of men, partly by analysing them in the light of the few scattered references to the race that are to be found in more historical records. But at our present stage of knowledge the only facts that seem to emerge clearly from the tangled yarn of tradition are that the nucleus of the Balōch made its way into Balūchistān from Kirmān and Seistān through Makrān, and that internal dissensions soon dissipated large swarms of them further afield. One can almost trace the last stages on their journeying to Balūchistān in many of the tribal names: Bug, Lāshār, Magas, Dasht, Gishkaur, Bulēda, Dōmbak, Kahnat. And of their later dispersal eastwards there is eloquent witness in the fact that Balūchistān, notwithstanding its title as "the land of the Balōch," contains to-day but a fraction of the Balōch scattered broadcast over the Panjāb and Sind.

Balōch.	
Balūchistān . . .	172,473
Sind	601,908
Panjāb	532,499

The Eastern Balōch *tumans*.

263. In the oldest ballads the Balōch are grouped in four and forty *bōlak* or clans, four of which, however, were not true Balōch at all but composed of servile elements. Nowhere, unfortunately, is a complete list of these

bōlak given. Piecing the older references together, we get a string of twenty-six names, but it is of course hardly likely that all or even the majority of the twenty-six figured among the original forty-four. Many of these twenty-six names still survive, but survive for the most part merely as names of minor sections; the word *bōlak* itself survives no longer for the Balōch save in the name of the Ghulām Bōlak, a section of the Rind. It is only a few of the great

Eastern Balōch	111,919
Rind	31,267
Magasī	17,777
Marī	22.233
Bugṭī	19,370
Ḍōmbkī	5.713
Khetrān	14.153
Others	1,406

tuman—the characteristic tribal organisation of the Eastern Balōch of the present day—that bear the same name as one of the *bōlak* of old. Prominent among these is the Rind, now a *tuman* in the Kachhī. But powerful though the Rind *tuman* is and proud though its name, it must not be supposed that the pedigree of all its tribesmen or even of most of its tribesmen would bear close scrutiny. In its neighbour and hereditary rival, the Magasī, we have a typical example of the absorption of an ancient *bōlak* by a modern *tuman*; for the Lāshārī *bōlak*, whose feuds with the Rind are the theme of many a stirring ballad, has been swallowed up by the Magasī with a host of less distinguished elements besides. Both these strong and well-organised *tumans* were once doughty members of the old Brāhūī Confederacy, and the Rind still ranks with Sarāwān and Magasī with Jhalawān. It is a little amusing, by the by, that the amateur philologist, in delving into the old geographers for ancient analogies to modern names, never hit upon the brilliant derivation of Magasī by metathesis from the Massagetæ of Herodotus and Strabo. But the name is probably of no great antiquity, and is presumably derived from Magas in Persian Balūchistān. Here at any rate the Rind can boast an advantage over his ancient foe; his is the proudest of all Balōch names, the name not only of one of the ancient *bōlak*, but of the eldest among Jalāl Khān's sons. But though the word Rind is often used as if it were synonymous with Balōch, and though there are Rind wherever the Balōch are to be found—in Makrān, in Sind and in the Panjāb—this does not mean that even those who call themselves Rind or profess a Rind descent (and their name is legion) look upon the Rind *tumandār* as their nominal leader or on the Rind *tuman* of to-day as the purest representatives of their race. The idea would be contemptuously scouted, for instance, by the great Bugṭī tribe, who are full of protestations of their Rind descent. But they protest, methinks, too much. In reality they are probably as heterogeneous as their ancient rivals the Marī, whose mixed composition may be gathered from the facts that each of its three clans traces a different descent, and that one of the three, the Lōharānī-Shīrānī, openly proclaims the Paṭhān origin of half of its members in the latter part of its name. Neither Bugṭī nor Marī figures among the ancient *bōlak*, and the names are probably fairly modern. As there are several localities in Persia that go by the name of Bug, it seems likely enough that Bugṭī is another geographical formation, though where the ending *-ṭī* can have come from seems a bit of a poser. Some there are who say that they are not Bugṭī but *bagg-a-ṭīh*, "camel-slaves," just as there are others who say that the Marī are *marēṭa* or "slaves" pure and simple.[1] The Marī once on a time were content to retort that they were *marī* or "braves" (I am not clear what language came to their rescue); but they have recently got to hear of some place called Dasht-i-Marī in Persia, and falling a victim to the prevailing fashion of geographical derivations, have given this out as their ancestral home; before long they will doubtless weave a pretty legend around their exodus from Dasht-i-Marī under the leadership of some hero of old. The Ḍōmbkī, like the Rind, are a remnant of one of the ancient *bōlak*. In the ballads they are styled "the greatest house among the Balōch." As they are the hereditary recorders or custodians of Balōch genealogies and legendary chronicles, this may perhaps savour of self-praise. But of their high rank there is no question. Not that blue blood runs through all sections in the *tuman*. Some like the Sangiānī are Jaṭṭ, others

[1] The opprobrious meaning (real or imaginary) that attaches to several Balōch tribal names is probably responsible for many of the honorific nicknames, like Zarkhānī, the Golden Bugṭī; Phullēn, the Flowery Marī; Bādshāh, the Royal Rind; the literal meaning of Rind itself seems to be Scoundrel. The Magasī are similarly Jang-dōst or War-lovers. Of a different character are Mīrālī and Khatbūriā, the second names of the Bulēdī and Chānḍia.

like the Ghaziānī are freed slaves; the Gabōl are the descendants of the ancient slave *bōlak* of that name. And even those who claim Balōch descent, claim it in different ways. Lāshārī, Laghārī, Bulēdī, Khetrān are among the multifarious elements in the *tuman*. But the nucleus is, or is supposed to be, purest Rind. Yet this is but one example taken at haphazard out of the bunch to show how miscellaneous is the composition of even the proudest Balōch *tumans* of to-day (§ 298).

Khetrān.

264. But not only have many isolated sections acquired Balōch status by the once easy process of becoming assimilated into one or other of the great *tumans*, it is hardly too much to say that Balōch status has been acquired by a whole tribe. For take the curious case of the Khetrān. Here we have the quaint spectacle of a tribe with a Jaṭkī language (§ 229), with a weird Hindu vein running through its domestic customs (§ 184), and a Paṭhān vein running through its tribal law, with vague traditions of Paṭhān origin and still vaguer traditions of Hindu connection, none the less making good its claims to Balōch status, not on the grounds of Balōch blood (to which very few sections can lay pretensions) but on the grounds of Balōch dress, manners and tribal constitution. Nor is the acknowledgment which the great Balōch tribes extend to these claims academic only; it takes the eminently practical shape of matrimonial alliances. As for traditions—the Mazārānī, the chiefly section of the *tuman*, trace descent from Mazār, a Tarīn, who fled to Bārkhān from his home in Vihōa (in Dēra Ghāzī Khān) to escape the clutches of some Moghal emperor, whose wrath he had roused by harbouring a goldsmith who had embezzled money and jewels from the State treasury. But there are other and stronger traditions of descent not from Tarīn but from his brother Miāna, the son of Sharkhbūn, the son of Saraban, the son of Qais Abdur Rashīd—a tradition which appears to have solid foundation in the presence of the Silāch and Maṭṭ sections: for the latter are Laṭ Paṭhān, and Laṭ and Silāj were both sons of Miāna. And lastly there are persistent but muffled traditions of descent from Khetrān, the son of Rām, a Khatrī chieftain who lived in the Gomal and set the Moghal at defiance, until he had to retire to Vihōa. There seems a germ of truth in all three traditions, though one can hardly hope to piece the real story together at this late date. It is quite possible that various Miāna and Tarīn sections broke off from the main stocks, and, ousted from their ancient home, migrated eastwards, and became so mixed up with Jaṭṭ elements and especially with Jaṭṭ women, and so infected by their Balōch environment, that on their return westwards they returned not only with their numbers reinforced by Jaṭṭ and Balōch recruits, but with a Jaṭkī language, a Hindu tincture in their domestic customs, and what is more important still, with a Balōch constitution, and Balōch dress and manners. That the name of the *tuman* has any direct connection with Khetrān, the son of Rām the Khatrī, or with *khēt*, a field—both common suppositions even among scholars—I very much doubt. Nobody, I imagine, but the Paṭhān himself treats his ancient genealogies as gospel, but when they are ordinarily accepted for practical purposes in other cases, I fail to understand the conspiracy of silence regarding Niamat Ullah's explicit statement that Khatran (possibly connected with *kihtar*, 'minor') was the second son of Ashkun, the son of Miāna, especially when the modern version of the eponymous hero's name is so easily explained as being the form imposed by folk-etymology during the stay of the tribe in a Jaṭkī-speaking country. Two of the clans, the Ispānī (to which the chiefly section, the Mazārānī, belongs) and the Phallēt, are known collectively as Ganjūra, possibly after some eponymous hero—at any rate no one seems to have a better suggestion to offer. The name is used of these two clans in contradistinction to the Dhiṛa, whose name is supposed to be derived from *dhiṛa*, a heap. As a matter of fact there seems little to choose between all three in the matter of homogeneity, and though the Dhiṛa or "heap" certainly contains Jaṭṭ elements, it also seems to contain more true Balōch than the rest of the *tuman* put together.

The rise of the tuman.

265. This of course is an extreme case. But a somewhat similar process, though on a much less wholesale scale, has possibly been at work in the formation of all the *tumans* as we now know them. For the Balōch tribal system of to-day is clearly a comparatively late development in Balōch history. To

my mind at any rate the scene conjured up by the ancient traditions of the Balōch wanderings in Persia is that of a vast nomadic horde, loosely knit together by some consciousness of common blood, and herding in clans in which that consciousness of common blood was more vivid, yet even in those early days strengthening its numbers by giving harbourage to aliens, who were made to dwell servilely in clans by themselves. And as the horde passed slowly onwards, groups recruited from different *bōlak* seem to have gathered round leaders of valour and enterprise, and to have broken off from the parent horde—at first maybe temporarily or experimentally—to essay expeditions of conquest. Many of these unions would doubtless revert to the horde. Others, more successful or inspired by greater faith in their new-found leaders, would endure; and endure they certainly would if their raids were crowned with the acquisition of land. Many of those that endured would naturally enough take their names from the places where they were consolidated or had won themselves a footing. The names of the old *bōlak* would often be absorbed or even forgotten amid the crowd of clashing elements that had gone to the making of the new groups. And just as the horde itself had opened its ranks to aliens, so the hybrid groups—and with much more urgent cause—would open their ranks to aliens of well-tried prowess, prowess tried very likely by themselves in battling against them. In short, the modern *tuman* seems to have risen on the ruins of the Balōch horde and its ancient clans. As its very name—*tuman*, the Turkish *tūmān*, "the ten thousand"—almost seems to imply, the *tuman* is not an ethnical clan like the ancient *bōlak*, but a tribe on the war-path, warring first with the alien peoples that stood in its way, and warring later with any rival *tuman* that disputed its spoils—and the echoes of that warfare are to be heard not only in the famous fights between the Rind and the Lāshāri but in the hereditary feuds that now keep the Balōch from any real union. This or something like this would at any rate explain much that seems otherwise inexplicable in the fragmentary history of the Balōch that has come down to us. It would explain the bewildering medley which now forms the *tuman*; it would explain the obviously modern and geographical ring of many of the tribal names; it would explain how the names of the ancient *bōlak* have been lost altogether or submerged or dispersed among many different *tumans*; and it would explain how the *tumans* contain one and all not only elements that are to be found in other *tumans*, but even elements whose origin is frankly acknowledged to be alien and not Balōch at all.

Modern recruitment.

266. And the same processes of disintegration and assimilation would continue long after the *tumans* had come into being. In the old days of tribal warfare numbers must have meant not only strength but existence itself in the constant struggle a *tuman* had to wage with its neighbours. Small wonder that it offered a safe refuge and a warm welcome not only to malcontents from some rival *tuman* but even to aliens, who would be attracted to it by the success of its forays and by the prospect of sharing in its fat spoils. Once settled in the tribal country, it was only a matter of time for the alien *hamsāya*—these "sharers of the shade," as they are called—to take on Balōch status by the easy process of becoming members of the *tuman* of their adoption. In the common bloodfeud they shared from the outset; for the term *hamsāya* implies that the refugee will receive protection on the one hand, and on the other will place his powers at the disposal of his protector. Once they had made it clear that their settlement in the tribal country was no mere sojourn, and that they had finally thrown in their lot with the *tuman*, they were admitted to blood-kinship and given wives from among the tribeswomen. And finally they were accorded rights in the tribal land, and so took their place as fully fledged members of the *tuman*, ranking as tribesmen with those who had belonged to the *tuman* from time immemorial. It will be observed that the grand climax in the process of affiliation is not admittance to the blood-kin but participation in the tribal lands. It is land and not blood that is nowadays the corner-stone of the tribal system; once an alien has made good his right to tribal land, he and his sons after him will find the fiction of common blood just as good as common blood itself. And from the particular tenure of land prevailing in any particular *tuman* we can probably glean some idea of its future recruitment. At first no doubt all land was the common property—or rather the common grazing-grounds or common hunting-grounds—of the *tuman*. At a later stage it

became subjected to a periodical and temporary distribution among the members. At a later stage still the distribution became crystallised once and for all. The difficulties which beset the affiliation of a *hamsāya* clearly increase as land-tenure in the tribe thus drifts from commonage to severalty. Thorough-going commonage is a thing of the past; the days when it once existed must have been halcyon days for waifs and strays who sought admittance into a *tuman*. But out of the intermediate stage the *tumans* have not wholly passed. Periodical divisions of land are still the order of the day in the Marī *tuman* at large, in two clans and one isolated section of the Bugṭī, and among the Kuchik Rind. The shares are determined by the drawing of lots with pellets of sheep or goat droppings. The distribution is usually a distribution by males—or *kēr-mēz* to use the forcible vernacular expression, unfortunately untranslateable in unbiblical language; very occasionally it goes by families. The Marī *tuman* with its wholesale allotting and re-allotting of land should suffer from no lack of candidates for affiliation. But there is a feeling of uneasiness in the *tuman* that augurs ill for its future; and so long as this feeling lasts, it is unlikely that aliens will be attracted in the same numbers as in the palmy days of the *tuman*. Nor is it likely that they will find so warm a welcome: mere numbers are no longer the source of strength that they once were; and it will not be surprising if the idea soon springs up among the tribesmen that the fewer the numbers, the greater the share that will fall to themselves at the next division. In the Bugṭī *tuman*, where most of the lands have been already parcelled out, affiliation ought to present more difficulties; but it probably presents more attractions. All lands held by the Ḍōmbkī have been permanently divided, and of the few *hamsāya* who may seek shelter in this *tuman*, fewer still can expect to become regularly absorbed. In the Magasī country, and to a modified extent in the Rind country, the *tumandārs* have managed by hook or by crook to get the proprietary rights into their own hands, and the future of these *tumans* thus rests in a peculiar degree on the character and policy of their *tumandārs*.

267. In saying that strangers take on Balōch status by first becoming members of a *tuman*, I have slurred over one important step in the process. In the ordinary course affiliation is primarily affiliation into some section or at any rate into some clan, and not into the *tuman* as a whole. For a *tuman* is no mere concourse of tribesmen, but an organism of organisms. It is made up of clans or *ṭakar*; each clan is made up of sections or *phallī*; each *phallī* of smaller subsections or *pāṛa*; each *pāṛa* of groups of *lōg͟h* or households. Though this is the most common terminology, there are several variants: in the Khetrān *tuman*, for instance, the clan is called *ḍhak* (*ḍak*, *ḍag* or *ḍhiṛ*), the section is called *lōh*, the subsection *phallī*, and the family group *kahōl* or *ṭabar*. There are variants again in the tribal officers. But it will probably repay us best to glance at the Marī organization, not simply because it is fairly typical, but because it seems to be unusually archaic. At the head of the *tuman* is the *tumandār*, now hereditary and hedged round with divinity. At the head of each *ṭakar* or clan there is a clan-leader or *waḍēra*, also hereditary. At his side there is an executive officer called the *mukaddam*, the working man of the clan, who owes his office to selection, though he is usually selected from some particular section. But the *waḍēra* and the *mukaddam* do not deal direct with individual tribesmen, but work through the many *mōtabar*, the chosen heads of the various *phallī* and *pāṛa*. Now though the *tumandārī* is to-day strictly hereditary, passing from father to son, it has had a suggestively chequered career. We are told how the first *tumandār* of all was one Bijār, a Rind; how on his death his grandson sold the *tumandārī* to an Aliāṇī Rind called Wazīr; how Wazīr on his death-bed passed over his sons in favour of a Bulēdī; how even as late as the close of the eighteenth century the *tumandārī* was sold yet again to one Mubārak K͟hān, who handed it over to his father Bahāwalān, the most famous of the long line of Marī *tumandārs* and the founder of the chiefly dynasty of to-day. Reading between the lines of this fragmentary history, we seem to find our general theory of the Balōch *tuman* confirmed: for it is hard to avoid the conclusions that the first leader of the Marī 'ten thousand' was a successful warrior who induced adventurous spirits to break off from their *bōlaks* and leave the horde to try their fortunes

Tuman organization.

under his leadership; that his earlier successors won and held their chiefship by personal prowess; and that the *tumandārī* became an hereditary office after a long process of time. To borrow a pregnant distinction from Tacitus, the *tumandār* was a *dux* ages before he blossomed into a *princeps*—he was first a war-leader and only later did he manage to transform himself into an hereditary chief. And we get a curious sidelight on these suggestions from the survival in the *tuman* of yet another officer in the Marī tribal hierarchy, the *rāh-zan*. In these latter days the *rāh-zan* or "highway robber" is little more than a man with an honorary but honoured title, ranking in virtue of his high but leisured office next to the *tumandār* himself. In the old days of tribal warfare he was (like the Teutonic *Heretoch*, the Welsh *Dialwr*, and the Scotch *Toisech*) the war-chief who led the tribe forth to battle. Originally devised no doubt to counteract an almost inevitable failure of the hereditary principle in the *tumandārī* when tried in the fire of warfare, the office is itself succumbing in these days of peace to the hereditary principle. Though still in the gift of the *tumandār* to bestow on some warrior of proved valour, it has become in practice more or less confined to one particular family, and on the death of the last *rāh-zan* the title was conferred almost as a matter of course on his son. But this inglorious ending to the *rāh-zan's* warrior career is clearly a direct consequence of the enforced peace under British rule. Had tribe been left free to war with tribe, the *rāh-zan's* office could hardly have thus degenerated into an hereditary sinecure. It is much more likely that at some crisis of great stress in the *tuman* he would have brushed the *tumandār* aside. And history, we may well imagine, would repeat itself. The *dux*, having overturned the *princeps*, would seek to secure his new-won position to his son and son's sons after him, and a new *princeps* would arise, only to fall in his turn before another *dux* who had to be appointed to lead the tribal hosts in the field. This after all is no mere empty conjecture; it is a fairly true picture of the rise of kingship in Europe. Nor is the Marī *rāh-zan* a solitary figure in Balōch politics. There is a *rāh-zan* among the Bugṭī; but in this *tuman* the *tumandārs* seem to have been strong enough or themselves warriors enough to keep him from rising to any eminence.

The Western Balōch.

268. I have dwelt at some length on the *tuman* and its organisation, not simply because the great *tumans* dwarf other Balōch in political importance, but because the *tuman* is the most characteristic form of Balōch society to be found in Balūchistān. I must pass by the smaller communities among the eastern Balōch like the Umrānī, of whom Balūchistān retains a mere remnant, and the Kahērī, but lately a section of the Rind now beginning to blossom forth into Sayyids (§ 281), and scattered offshoots from great *tumans* domiciled in Balūchistān no longer, like the Buzdār, Lag͟hārī, Gurchānī, Kasrānī. Far more interesting to us than these are the Balōch in the west. Here Balōch society runs on very different lines. The only community at all akin to a *tuman* is the Rak͟hshānī, one of the ancient *bōlak*, but now a somewhat disrupted and amorphous tribe of Brāhūī rather than Balōch pattern, with its chief head-quarters in the Chāgai district and with offshoots in K͟hārān and Makrān and Persia. To see the western Balōch in his most typical surroundings we must go to Makrān, where the Balōch won his first footing in Balūchistān. Says the old ballad: "Those that followed Chākar (into India) became Jaṭṭ; those that stayed behind remained Balōch." But a somewhat similar fate was reserved for those that never followed Chākar further into Balūchistān than Makrān. They did not indeed become Jaṭṭ like so many of the Balōch who wandered off into Sind and the Panjāb, or like them forget their language. Balōch they remained, but Balōch in a land where the word Balōch came in time to be almost a term of reproach, like the word Balōch in the eastern Panjāb. Crushed under the heel of dominant classes, they are Balōch in humble distinction to their proud masters —whether these are the alien Gichkī or the Brāhūī Mīrwāṛī or the Naushērwānī, who likely enough are Balōch themselves. And yet, if we are searching for the ancient *bōlaks* of the Balōch race, it is in Makrān that we seem to have most chance of finding them: Rind, Lāshārī and Hōt, proudest *bōlaks* of all; Gōrgēj and Pu͟zh, two *bōlaks* akin to the Rind and both of ancient renown; Bulēdī (known in Sind as Burdī) who preserve the name of an old-world *bōlak* in their nickname Mīrālī; Rak͟hshānī, the *bōlak* which has transmitted its name

Western Balōch	87,271

to the tribe in the north; Khōsa, from which have sprung two great *tumans* in the Panjāb and Sind; Dōdāī and Kalmatī, ancient names now otherwise lost; Dashtī and Gabōl, two out of the four servile *bōlak*. Yet with the one exception of the Rind, who are not only numerous but still hold their heads high, these are at best but feeble and scattered remnants for all their high ancestry, proud names and little more—living proofs, it almost seems, of the inability of the effete *bōlak* to struggle against the more youthful and vigorous *tuman*.

Balōch status.

269. In the west of Balūchistān, more even than in the east, does the word Balōch convey status rather than race. For it is applied not only to this flotsam and jetsam from the old *bōlak* and also to others who can plausibly make out a case for Balōch descent, but to people like the Kishānī, who claim to be Shāhwānī Brāhūīs, and the Barr, who are popularly supposed to be Bedouins, and the Kēnagizai, who are seemingly Jaṭṭ, and even to people of much lower origin. On the other hand, it is hard to find any other classification for the Naushērwānī and the Gichkī, who in their own country are the *hākim* or dominant classes as opposed to the Balōch. And perhaps it is idle to hunt about for any other. For though the Naushērwānī claim descent from Kaianian Maliks, there is some significance in the historical fact that both Nādir Shāh and Ahmad Shāh styled the Khārān *hākim* of their day as "Naushērwānī, Rakhshānī Balōch," and it is not improbable that they may be Balōch after all. The Gichkī, it is true, are in very different case. Whether or no they are Rājpūt who came from Karanga, now part of Barōda, as an old Kāṭhiawāṛ chronicle relates, it is quite certain that they were originally Hindus from India, who made their way to Makrān somewhere about the sixteenth or seventeenth century and rapidly conquered the Balōch inhabitants. But the conquerors were themselves conquered by the conquered. Their religion became Musalmān, their language Balōchī. Indeed so powerful is the Balōch genius in assimilating aliens, that in the language spoken by the Gichkī of to-day is preserved, it would seem, not merely the purest but the most archaic form of Balōchī to be found anywhere.

Naushērwānī	333
Gichkī	554

The Brāhūīs.

270. No people in Balūchistān has of late years provoked so much speculation outside it as the Brāhūīs, chiefly owing to the fact that they speak a Dravidian language in about the last place in India where a Dravidian language would be expected. The Brāhūīs themselves have taken a very languid interest in their past—possibly because there are among them so few who are true Brāhūīs at all. They know little about the history of their remarkable and not inglorious rise into something like a nation three or four centuries ago. Of their remoter past, which, if less glorious, must have been more remarkable still, they have hardly an inkling. They are a people singularly incurious and unimaginative, devoid of all touch of that poetic instinct which prompts others to chronicle the history of their origin and the deeds of their fathers, or to invent both where both are forgotten. Though largely recruited from the Balōch and the Paṭhān, they have no ballads like the one and no genealogies like the other. A few traditions are all they can produce to illumine the mystery that broods over their origin. If only their traditions were conflicting enough and definite enough their illumination might serve. It is after all easier to piece together the truth from conflicting traditions than to extract it out of a tradition that has become crystallised into set genealogies or the conventional theme of an epic. But the bald Brāhūī traditions are hardly such stuff as history is made of. They are little more than far-away echoes of tradition among the Balōch.

Brāhūīs	167,787
Brāhūī nucleus	15,047
Sarāwān	55,370
Jhalawān	94,708
Miscellaneous	2,662

The Brāhūī nucleus.

271. Like the Balōch, the Brāhūīs are sprung from the loins of Mīr Hamza, the Prophet's uncle; like them, they have wandered in from Aleppo. But while so much is treated as gospel, there are too many rival versions of the intermediate gaps for any one to be regarded as less apocryphal than the others. Not that there is any great difference between them. According to one fairly typical account, the Brāhūīs trace their lineage from the seven sons of Gwahrām, the son of Brāho or Ibrāhīm, who was descended more or less

immediately from the Prophet's uncle. But the links are often left out in order to claim the descent of the seven brothers direct from Mīr Hamza. Thus the Prophet's uncle, who according to Islāmic tradition died without issue, is accredited with one batch of four sons and a daughter, the forefathers of the Balōch (§ 262), and with another batch of seven sons, the forefathers of the Brāhūīs. I hardly like to mention yet another son, Sarmast, the forefather of the Lōṛī (§284), for both Brāhūī and Balōch are of course scandalised at the impertinence of the Lōṛī in fabricating so preposterous and impious a fable. But though seven brothers usually figure in Brāhūī traditions, there is some disagreement as to the number, and even more as to their identity. One tradition opens with the statement that Gwahrām had three sons, Gurgīn, Sumāl and Kalandar. But as the story develops, it appears that there were more than three sons after all; indeed Hassan, the youngest of the lot, turns out to be the real hero of the story, for as the future father of Ahmad (to say nothing of Iltāz and Kambar) he is the ancestor of the Ahmadzai, the ruling family of Kalāt. It is not till we get to the fag-end of the story that we learn that there were yet two other brothers, Mīrō and Rōdēn, who suddenly walk upon the scene as if we knew all about them already. In the same story casual mention is made of a brother of Gwahrām called Zagr, and this is the first and the last occasion that he is mentioned in the narrative, though he crops up in another tradition, but this time not as Gwahrām's brother but as Brāhō's father. Zagr's place among the ancestors of the Brāhūīs is, I am told, a matter known only to very old folk; it certainly forms no part of the ordinary body of tradition. Other accounts give the name of Gwahrām's sons as Kambar, Gurgīn, Kalandar, Sumāl and Rōdēn—the last by a slave mother, a common and significant touch in Balūchistān genealogies. And from Kambar sprang Mīrō, from Mīrō sprang Ahmad, and from Ahmad sprang Iltāz. But there are several other ways of ringing the changes on these four: Mīrō is sometimes regarded as the forbear of the other three; the ex-Khān used to say that Kambar was the father of Ahmad and Iltāz and related in some shadowy way to Mīrō. The one and only deduction that we can safely draw from all this is that Brāhūīs of modern times regard the following, and the following only, among the many Brāhūī tribes as belonging to the true Brāhūī stock: first the ruling family, the Ahmadzai, and its collaterals, the Iltāzai; then the Mīrwāṛī and the Kambrāṛī (both closely connected with the ruling house, though the Kambrāṛī, unlike the Mīrwāṛī, no longer bask in reflected glory), together with the Gurgnāṛī, the Sumālāṛī, the Kalandrāṛī, and—despite the servile strain in their blood—the Rōdēnī. It would be hardly safe to add the Zagr Mēngal, for the isolated but reputedly ancient traditions regarding Zagr's ancestry receive little countenance from the public opinion of to-day, which usually lumps up the Zagr Mēngal into the same category as the Mēngal.

Brāhūī nucleus	**15,047**
Ahmadzai	25
Iltāzai	156
Mīrwāṛī	2,654
Kambrāṛī	3,095
Gurgnāṛī	2,041
Sumālāṛī	3,739
Kalandrāṛī	2,012
Rōdēnī	1,325

Sarāwān and Jhalawān.

272. These then are the Brāhūīs of the Brāhūīs—the Brāhūī nucleus, to use an ugly term in default of a better. The rest of the Brāhūī tribes are supposed to be the descendants of strangers who in the early days threw in their lot with this Brāhūī nucleus, and in so doing took on Brāhūī status. The curious thing is that in course of time these strangers dwarfed the original stock in importance, and became, as it were, more Brāhūī than the Brāhūīs themselves. For if we except the ruling family, the true Brāhūī tribes have fallen into the background. The political importance has passed from them to the tribes of Sarāwān and Jhalawān. And it is as somewhat insignificant members of the latter group that the true Brāhūī tribes are nowadays reckoned, chiefly, I suppose, because of territorial reasons; but in the Darbār of the old Confederacy they seem to have sat in the centre, dividing the great lines of Sarāwān and Jhalawān. Now there are at least five races which are popularly supposed to have been the recruiting-grounds of these Sarāwān and Jhalawān tribes, and of the small miscellaneous group which, though generally included loosely among the latter, seems properly to fall under neither: Paṭhān, Balōch, Jaṭṭ, Persian and aboriginal. And this is how popular opinion usually attempts to class them :—

Reputed origin.	Sarāwān.	Jhalawān.	Miscellaneous.
Paṭhān . . .	Bangulzai . . Raisānī Ruṣtumzai (Raisānī) Shahwānī Sarparra Sātakzai (Kūrd)	Zarrakzai (Zahrī) Khidrānī (Zahrī) Jattak (Zahrī) Nīchārī (?)	
Balōch . . .	Lāngav . . . Lahṛī Kūrd	Bīzanjav Pandrānī Mūsiānī (Zahrī) Ḍānya (Zahrī) Bājōī (Zahrī) Sājdī	Rēkīzai
Persian . . .	......	Māmasanī[1] Hārūnī (Māmasanī) Sannāṛī (Zahrī)	
Jaṭṭ	Māmashahī (?)[1] .	Mēngal Zagr Mēngal. Sāsōlī (Zahrī) Lōṭiānī (Zahrī) Natwānī	
Aboriginal	Māmashahī (?) . .	Nīchārī (?)	Nighāṛī
War-captives from India .	......		Pirrikāṛī

Heterogeneous character of the tribe.

273. But this racial classification of the several tribes is at best true only in the rough. It merely reflects public opinion, and public opinion goes largely by the origin, or reputed origin, of the chiefly family and its immediate clansmen; and, even so, public opinion is by no means unanimous. If it went by the reputed origin of the majority in a tribe, the classification would be very different. Take, for instance, the Bangulzai. The tribe has been classified as Paṭhān, simply because the Saidzai, the chiefly clan, are supposed to be Sārangzai Snaṭia Kākaṛ; but most of the clans profess to be Rind Balōch, while the Badūzai claim to be Arab. And it is well to bear in mind that the true Brāhūī tribes are just as much of a mixture as the rest. Take, for instance, the Sumālāṛī. The Saiadzai, the largest clan in the tribe, are said to be Paṭhān Sayyids; the Sheikh Hussainī are said to be Hārūnī Māmasanī, and therefore Persians; the Balōkhānzai, the Mūsāzai, Dādūzai, Rāzānzai, Nidāmzai, Aidōzai, and Gwahrāmzai are supposed to be Kūrd, and therefore Balōch; the Lōkī Ṭappurī, to judge by the tradition that their ancestors were purchased for a *lōk* or camel and a *ṭappur* or felt, are apparently descended from slaves; as for the Būrakzai and the Sīkhī, nobody seems to know who they are or where they came from. In a word, if we accept the popular accounts of the origin of the various elements in this true Brāhūī tribe, the true Brāhūī strain in it amounts to but one-eleventh of the whole. Indeed, whatever the mother-stock of a tribe, whether true Brāhūī or alien, it is the rule and not the exception for the nucleus—the chiefly family and those related to it, the *rāj-o-kabīla* as they are called—to be in a large minority to the *barōk* or new-comers, who have tacked themselves on to the tribe from time to time.

Brāhūī origin untraceable.

274. In the multifarious elements that have gone to the making of the tribes and the race one ought, I suppose, to find clues to the past history of the Brāhūī. But it is very difficult to get beyond insubstantial generalities. Traditional history is painfully meagre. We hear that Kalāt, which has been

[1] This is the way the names are locally pronounced; but in finer language they are brought back to their presumably original forms, Muhammad Hasnī and Muhammad Shahī.

knit up with the destinies of the Brāhūīs ever since they emerged from obscurity, was at various times called Kalāt-i-Sēwa, Kalāt-i-Nichārī, and Kalāt-i-Balōch—to the Afghāns of to-day by the by it is known as Kalāt-i-Nasīr; that the shadowy Sēwa dynasty according to one account voluntarily abdicated in favour of the Mīrwāṛī, according to another was forcibly expelled; that the Mīrwāṛī in turn had to make way before the Moghal; that the Brāhūīs at the invitation of the Dēhwār and with the active help of Raisānī Paṭhāns made good their occupation once again. And then there are vague but persistent accounts of fights with Balōch and fights with Jaṭṭ. Though these traditions are sometimes given piecemeal, they are sometimes arranged consecutively, as if one event followed closely on the heels of another; but the order is often reversed, and in any case there must have been a good deal of telescoping. The vague impression left on my mind is that the Brāhūī nucleus, the Kambrāṛī and the Sumālāṛī and the rest, first came to the front about the time of the Balōch migrations, and that their prowess under the leadership of the Mīrwāṛī may have had something to do with the wave of Balōch emigration beyond the confines of Balūchistān. But who these Brāhūīs were, and whether in those days also they spoke a Dravidian tongue; whether they came from the east or the west or the north or the south, or whether they were housed in Balūchistān from time immemorial, I cannot pretend to guess. If we assume that they came from the east, they may perhaps have brought their Dravidian language with them—but even if these baseless assumptions were granted for the sake of argument, they would not entitle us to assume that they brought any Dravidian blood with them at the same time. If we assume that they came from the west, it is tempting to identify them with the Kōch, so often coupled with the Balōch in Persian and Arab chronicles—but these equally baseless assumptions would carry us little further than we were before. If they spoke another language when they arrived in the country, they presumably picked up their present language from some people who were there before them; but if we assume—and this would simply be an assumption as baseless as the others—that they picked it up (let us say) from the Nīchārī, the only result would be to shift the linguistic problem one step further back.

Rise of a military Confederacy.

275. But while it seems safest in our present state of ignorance to be shy of any rash assumption as to the origin of the Brāhūīs, there is little harm in letting imagination attempt to follow the stages by which they rose from obscurity. According to my vague view, the Brāhūī nucleus in the early days was a fairly compact body, in which the Mīrwāṛī, an offshoot from the Kambrāṛī, gradually took the lead. Issuing successfully under Mīrwāṛī leadership from the conflicts with the aborigines (whoever they may have been) and the Balōch and the Jaṭṭ and any others that stood in their way, they must have found little difficulty in attracting recruits from all quarters, even from the ranks of their late enemies. Not the least striking proof of the fullness of their success is the very large Paṭhān element among them; for Paṭhāns are ever chary of sinking their own race except to join a vigorous and rising power. Once settled in Kalāt and the neighbourhood, the Brāhūīs seem to have spread themselves over the country, and in consequence to have undergone a certain amount of disintegration, the Brāhūī nucleus drifting apart into their clans, and their new-found allies into communities of their own. And from these clans and communities were in course of time developed what we now call tribes. Though it is improbable enough that the tribes at their birth were either as numerous or as heterogeneous as the tribes of to-day, it is hardly likely that they were truly homogeneous even then; in any case the original tribal stock must soon have become crossed by malcontents from other tribes and by fugitives or adventurous spirits from outside. But coincident with this partial disintegration there was a gradual organisation of the several tribes into a Confederacy under the leadership of the Ahmadzai, who though apparently a junior branch of the Mīrwāṛī, soon forced their way to the front. The successful welding of the Confederacy seems to have been due in no small measure to the statecraft of the Ahmadzai leader—the Raīs as he was first called, the Mīr as he was called later, the Khān as he is called to-day. Nevertheless it was of course self-interest—or, to use the local phrase, common weal and woe—that ultimately kept the Confederacy together. And it is not

difficult to guess in what that common weal and woe consisted. Though the rise of the Brāhūīs appears to have been as successful as it was rapid, it can hardly be supposed that they had the field entirely to themselves. The Confederacy was in origin a combination for offence and defence, an organisation on a war-footing. It was split up first and foremost into the two great territorial divisions of Sarāwān and Jhalawān, with the true Brāhūī tribes either loosely associated with the Jhalawāns or treated loosely as a thing apart. At the head of the territorial divisions were leading tribes who carried the divisional banners, which after many a hard-fought struggle between the Mēngal and the Zarakzai and between the Shāhwānī and the Raisānī now rest with the Zarakzai on behalf of Jhalawān and with the Raisānī on behalf of Sarāwān. And in the *dasta* or wings into which Sarāwān and Jhalawān still range themselves (nowadays chiefly in the prosecution of ancient feuds), we seem to see survivals of a further subdivision of Sarāwān and Jhalawān for the purposes of war. And mobilisation for war was always in the air. Not only had the tribes to find fighting-men to carry on the little wars of the Confederacy, they soon had to supply their *sān* or quota of men-at-arms to the army of the suzerain power; for the Brāhūīs were not left long undisturbed in the independent position they had won for themselves. Yet even though they had to acknowledge the suzerainty of an outside power, the Confederacy in the glorious days of Nasīr Khān the Great became not only a powerful military organisation but a political common-weal from which it is hard to withhold the title of nation.

Its decline and fall.

276. But the forces that kept the Confederacy together—the need of showing a united front to a common enemy, the prospect of sharing in the common spoils, the wisdom and personality of their leader—gradually weakened one by one. The Brāhūīs were left more and more undisturbed in the possession of their unalluring hills; the prospects of further territorial expansion faded away; the Khān's authority was undermined because he tried to pervert it from its proper function. Animated no longer either by a common fear or a common greed, and headed by a leader whose ambition was to establish a despotism, the Confederacy became racked in civil war. The anarchy that prevailed during the long rule of Mīr Khudādād was really the death-knell of the Confederacy; it was only our appearance on the scene that patched up the breach between the Khān and the chiefs, and kept the shadow of a Confederacy alive. And the break-up of the Confederacy was the prelude to the disintegration of the tribe, and is likely, as it seems to me, to prove the prelude to the decay of the race. On a superficial view, it might be thought that, though the long rule of Mīr Khudādād Khān, which was little more than one long struggle between the tribes and his mercenary army, shook the Confederacy from its foundations, it must also have encouraged the consolidation of the individual tribes. And such was perhaps the case for the time being. But the snapping of the ancient ties that kept the larger union together seems to have put too great a strain on the ties that bound the tribe. The snapping of ancient social ties became, as it were, the fashion; and the most characteristic feature of modern Brāhūī history is constant fissure. In Sarāwān the Rustumzai, once merely a clan of the Raisānī, has broken off from the mother-stock and set up as a tribe on its own; the Sātakzai has broken off still more recently from the Kūrd. In Jhalawān the Hārūnī has broken off from the Māmasanī; as for the Zahrī, it can hardly be called a tribe any longer: it is a mere reminder that the Zarakzai and the Mūsiānī and the Bājōī and the Khidrānī and the Jattak and the rest, were once clans of the most powerful tribe in all Jhalawān. Matters have got to such a pitch that it is often exceedingly hard to say what constitutes a tribe. To say what sections and subsections belong exclusively to the tribe, and what tribesmen to the subsections, is harder still. Before long it may become hard to say what constitutes a Brāhūī at all.

Modern disintegration.

277. For disintegration has set in, all down the line. Not only have clans broken off from the mother-stock and constituted themselves into tribes, sections and groups and individual tribesmen are constantly breaking off from the tribe. Sometimes they affiliate themselves definitely to another tribe; sometimes they simply shift their quarters and change their old beats, quietly biding the day when they will have to throw in their lot with some tribe or another, not without the hope that that day may never come at all. In Makrān and elsewhere

outside the Brāhūī country proper it was quite a common experience at this census for members of some well-known section of some well-known Brāhūī tribe to return themselves, not as Brāhūīs, but as Balōch. And I shrewdly suspect that so far from the sixty thousand odd Brāhūīs enumerated in Sind (§ 78) being the only Brāhūīs in Sind at the time of the census, there are many Brāhūīs in Sind who prefer to masquerade as Balōch; and the numbers who will take up this disguise will certainly increase as time goes on; for the Balōch are a very strong community in Sind, and their name ranks high because of the Balōch descent of the former Tālpūr rulers. In Balūchistān we took it upon ourselves to adjust these apparent anomalies to the accepted notions of Brāhūī and Balōch. But I am not sure that we were right. Certainly if the present tendency gathers force in the next ten years, it will be a very pretty problem at the next census to decide who are to be recorded as Brāhūī, and the best course will possibly be to abide by the strict letter of what the tribesmen tell us. The precise extent to which these tendencies towards tribal disintegration and racial change have been operative since the last census, we are unfortunately not in a position to measure. The apparent decrease in the number of the Brāhūīs is colossal; the apparent multiplication of the tribal sections and subsections is perhaps more striking still. But we must of course discount a very great deal of both. In the first place the last figures were mere estimates. In the second place they emanated from the chiefs, and the ideas of a chief as to what clans and sections and subsections and groups belong to his tribe are by no means the same as the ideas of the tribesmen themselves. But great as have been our difficulties in drawing up a reasonably correct classification of the Brāhūī tribes, it seems safe to prophesy that the difficulties of our successors are likely to be still greater. If, however, my prognostications prove false, as I hope against hope that they may, it will be an extremely interesting study to trace the causes that have led to the unexpected arrest of what seems now to be a very unmistakable tendency towards dissolution.

The future of the race.

278. To me the only chance for the Brāhūī appears to lie in a resuscitation of some wider union on the lines of the old Confederacy; but this at present seems Utopian enough, unless in the Jirga system wisely reformed and jealously administered a new lease of life is given to the tribal hierarchy and hence to tribal unity, and the wider racial unity takes fresh roots in the consciousness of the possession of a common body of customary law (§26). It almost looks as if a loosely knit Confederacy were the one form of social community really suited to the Brāhūī genius. The old Confederacy had at least this in its favour: it possessed a territorial unity and a geographical isolation, all the more effective because of the uninviting character of the country. But not only have the individual tribes no territorial cohesion worth the name, the lack of it is accentuated by the nomadic character of the tribesmen, which disperses them abroad among other tribes and into other countries. Every tribe, it is true, can boast its tribal head-quarters; but this is often little more than the head-quarters of the chief and his immediate clansmen; the majority of the tribesmen are scattered over the face of the country. And here I find it interesting to contrast the Brāhūī with the Balōch. With a tribal constitution very similar to that of the Brāhūī (on this score one has only to compare what has been said generally of the one in §31 with what has been said equally generally of the other in §267), and with the same baleful heritage of nomadism to contend with, the great Balōch *tumans* of the east can boast a solidarity with which no Brāhūī tribes can vie. The Rind and the Magasī Balōch must once have been as nomad as any Balōch have ever been, or as any Brāhūīs are to-day. They were once active members of the Brāhūī Confederacy, and like other members of the Confederacy received their share of the Kachhī war-lands; but, unlike the Jhalawāns who allowed themselves to be ousted out of large slices that fell to their share (§77), and unlike the Sarāwāns who left the Jaṭṭ tenants in possession and simply use the Kachhī as a farm of which they enjoy the produce and to which they resort for the winter, the Magasī and the Rind quietly set themselves to colonise their lands, with the result that they are now compact, self-sufficient *tumans*, occupying a tribal territory of their own.[1] Confronted

[1] I am of course taking the Magnsī and Rind *tumans* as I now find them in Balūchistān; the offshoots from the ancient stock of both are of course legion.

with this example of what might have been, the Brāhūīs would probably say that the comparison is unfair, for hillmen like themselves can never take to a life in the plains; in face of the growing expatriation of the Jhalawāns to Sind (§ 78), they can hardly solace themselves with this excuse much longer. But to drive my point home, let me turn to other Balōch who are still as nomad as the Brāhūīs and almost as thorough-going hillmen. I cannot doubt that the Marī and Bugṭī *tumans* owe a tremendous amount of their admirable tribal cohesion to the cunning way in which nature has provided each with its own territory, cut off not only from the outside world, but also from each other (§ 45). It is this lack of isolated, well-defined tribal territory that has helped on the dispersal of the Balōch in the west, where disintegration has reached a pitch that leaves Brāhūī disintegration far behind. And added to the absence of natural checks to Brāhūī disintegration there are a multitude of positive disintegrating forces, such as the growth of a selfish individualism among the tribesmen at large and most significant of all among the chiefs, the inevitably disintegrating influence of peace under a foreign administration, the increasing tendency to migrate beyond the limits of the country, and the consequent tendency to settle outside it. Taking one thing with another, I am forced to the regretful conclusion that unless the many disintegrating influences are arrested and some counter-influence, such as the purging and strengthening of the Jirga system, speedily arises to put new life into tribal and racial unity, the Brāhūī tribes have seen their best days, and that the Brāhūī race is doomed in the future, let us hope in the very distant future, to absorption into some more virile community.

279. Etymologically the word Lāsī means simply inhabitant of Las Bēla. **Lāsī.** In older writings the word Lumri is often used in this sense, but Lūmṛiya or Nūmṛiya is properly confined to such Lāsī as live south of Bēla town. But though the term Lāsī is thus frankly of territorial and not racial connotation, it indicates status nevertheless; for not all inhabitants of Las Bēla come within the category. It applies primarily to the *panj-rāj* or five dominant communities, Jāmōṭ, Angāria, Shē<u>kh</u>, Burrā and Rūnjhā, and is extended by courtesy to the many various groups more or less loosely affiliated to them. In theory all five are equal; if the superior claims of the Jāmōṭ are often tacitly admitted, this is simply because it is to the Jāmōṭ that the ruling family, self-styled the Jamshēdī, belongs. In theory each is supposed to be endogamous; but breaches of the rule are common enough. In theory again no full member of the *panj-rāj* would give his daughter in marriage to a member of one of the affiliated groups; he does so in practice for all that. One and all, it need hardly be said, take wives from all and sundry. Even if the motley crew that have managed to get themselves tacked on to the *panj-rāj* are left out of count, the Lāsī seem to be a somewhat heterogeneous collection, though this is very different from saying that it is necessary to accept as gospel the pedigrees that the *panj-rāj* have concocted for themselves: that the nucleus of the Jāmōṭ is Qurēshī Arab; that Angāria was a hero who hailed from Arabia; and Burrā a hero of the great Samma tribe of Sind; that the Rūnjhā are Rājpūt, and the Shē<u>kh</u>, if not actually Sayyid, something mighty like it.

Panj Rāj	**27,779**
Jāmōṭ	9,724
Angāria	3,146
Shē<u>kh</u>	4,432
Burrā	5,374
Rūnjhā	5,103

280. I fancy that these Arab and Rājpūt legends are largely Lāsī inventions, **Jaṭṭ.** possibly unconscious enough, to cover up a Jaṭṭ origin. The truth is that the term Jaṭṭ or Jadgāl has a contemptuous ring in Balūchistān, and all who can are at pains to rake up some other ancestry for themselves. I have often been tempted to regret that the famous though reckless derivation of Jaṭṭ from the classical Gethae has not filtered down from the studies of ingenious theorists and come home to the business and bosoms of the men of the country. We should then perhaps have heard less of the Arabs and more of the Jaṭṭ, and been in a far better position to judge of the real racial divisions of Balūchistān. As it is, I have every now and then had to pick my way warily, for fear of treading on some one's corns. Yet many of those who are Jaṭṭ self-professed, like the Abṛā and others of the Kachhī, are fine up-standing men and excellent husbandmen. Though perforce occupying an inferior position to their tribal overlords, they hold

Jaṭṭ	**78,400**

themselves proudly aloof. The Brāhūī, for instance, may mouth out his haughty saying that a Jaṭṭ is about as good as his shoe, yet many a Jaṭṭ home is presided over by a Brāhūī mother; the Jaṭṭ wives of Brāhūī husbands could almost be counted on one's fingers; and it is only in the best Brāhūī families that they are found. Unfortunately for the Jaṭṭ, he has little or no tribal cohesion, and his one hope for a rise in the social world is the coming of that day when tribal bonds shall be broken, and he can enter free and unhandicapped upon the race of life, an individual pitting himself against individuals. And in that race the proud tribesman of to-day will be hard put to it to hold his own.

Sayyids.

281. How many of the twenty-two thousand odd Sayyids enumerated in Balūchistān would find a place in the Sayyid peerage that used to be kept up by the Naqīb-us-Sādāt under the Khalifa's orders, it would be interesting to know. Not a single one, was the unexpected verdict of a Musalmān critic, whose lifelong experience of Balūchistān and Afghānistān and curious reading in the by-paths of Islāmic history made me think that his opinion on such a subject would be worth inviting. But I fancy his opinion was expressed in an unusually sceptical and splenetic mood. He certainly shuffled out of it when called upon to give chapter and verse for his dogmatic assertion. As a matter of fact, I can conceive no more unprofitable and invidious task than to probe too shrewdly into this complex and delicate question. While I am conscious that a goodly number of those whose claims to the revered title of Sayyid have been acknowledged in our tables, are really trespassers and usurpers, I thought it best to exclude none from the hallowed circle whose title is generally recognised by the people at large. Room has thus been found, for instance, for the Mashwānī, the Ustrāna and the Gharshīn, who for a long time were content to rank as Paṭhāns (§ 259) and for the Kahērī, who for a long time were content to rank as Balōch (§ 268).

Sayyids . .	22,183
Indigenous . .	21,296

Dēhwār.

282. The Dēhwār are a peaceful, law-abiding people, simple and unaffected in manners, homely thrifty husbandmen. The bulk of them are settled in Sarāwān, where they are divided between Kalāt and the Mastung valley into two main communities, each under an *arbāb* or leader of its own; of recent years a small colony has gone over into the Quetta district. How they first came to settle down in Sarāwān, nobody knows. They have evidently been there for many generations. The vague but very persistent tradition that they had a large hand in the setting up of Brāhūī rule seems to be borne out both by the nature of the services they still render to the ruling house (the repairing of the Kalāt battlements, for instance) and the privileges they still enjoy. The honour of having played the chief part in the overthrow of the earlier tyrants is supposed to rest with the Ḍōḍakī, one of the chief sections in the Kalāt group. And the story that attaches to their name is this. They had sworn an oath never to take up arms against the tyrant—whoever he may have been, for the story is told indifferently of a Moghal and of Sēwa, the Hindu. Crushed by his oppressions, they at last hit upon a method of putting him out of the way and at the same time of keeping to their oath. They baked a number of *ḍōḍī* or loaves, with a thin layer of dough round largish stones, and with these they pelted him to death. The name Dēhwār itself seems clearly a descriptive appellation,—a mere variation of Dēhkān, common enough in Central Asia—people who live in *dēh* or villages, in distinction to nomad tribesmen. So it is not surprising to find that these Dēhwār are a very heterogeneous community. All the main peoples of Balūchistān seem to have been laid under tribute to swell their numbers. There are some, like the Zhaṛkhēl (§ 253) and the Yūsufzai, who claim to be Paṭhāns; others, like the Hōtizai, who claim to be Balōch; and others, again, like the Saulāi, who claim to be Brāhūī. And in addition there are many who claim to have come from Persia, Arabia or Afghānistān. But the nucleus is supposed to be Tājik, chiefly, I fancy, because of their name and their Persian language (§ 221). Unfortunately the word Tājik is often brought in when origin is uncertain, or when a humble origin has to be covered up. But the important thing for us is that, however heterogeneous their origin, the Dēhwār are to-day a very homogeneous community, homogeneous in every way—looks, manners, language, occupation and all.

Dēhwār . .	7,326

283. Over the pedigree of the Mēd, ingenuity has surely run riot. They *may* be the Mēd of the Arab chroniclers. If so, they must have changed a good deal since the days, described in the earliest chronicles of all, when they were a pastoral people living on the banks of the Indus and, unlike their neighbours, were

Mēd 2,494

unaccustomed to boats. They *may* be the Ichthyophagoi of Alexander's time—at any rate they occupy the same locality and follow the same calling. If so, they must have changed a good deal since the days when they had long claw-like nails and shaggy hair, and cut the growth of neither; when they lived in huts made of shells and the off-scourings of the sea; when their clothing was the skins of wild beasts; when they fed not only on sun-dried fish but on the flesh of sea-monsters cast ashore in stormy weather. And if they are the Ichthyophagoi of 325 B. C. and also the Mēd known to the Arabs centuries later, it is a pretty little piece of unexpected atavism that the fisherfolk of the Makrān coast should have reverted to their old haunts and their old calling after a spell of pastoral life inland. When, however, I am asked to go back much earlier still and to regard them as a colony of the ancient Medes, I can only repeat what Herodotus gravely remarked in like case of the Sigynnae on the Danube: "How they can be a colony of the Medes, I am at a loss to imagine. Not but what anything can happen—given plenty of time." But the Mēd is sufficiently interesting in himself, without our interest having to be tickled by guesses at his origin. He is an excellent fisherman and, though the K͟hōja has managed to get a good deal of the fish-trade into his own hands, a very fair man of business. And there is money enough to be made, what with the export of dried fish to India and Africa, of air-bladders to England for the making of isinglass, of shark fins to China, to become one of the ingredients, I suppose, of some Chinese dainty. He can manage his tiny crafts, his dug-outs and his luggers, with the best of them—and well he may, for though he rarely ventures far from the shore in the one, or further than Muscat and the Malabār coast in the other, storms rise in these parts with alarming rapidity. For all his humble fisher-life he can hardly be classed as a menial; in Las Bēla at any rate he is looked upon as *k͟hānwāda*, a man of respectable family enough. He is remarkably prolific—I have never seen so many chattering children in any Balūchistān village as along the coast of Las Bēla and Makrān. Like all true sons of the sea, he is intensely superstitious: if he toils all night and catches nothing, somebody must have bewitched the fish, so off he goes to the mulla for a charm; if he spends the night ashore, it's as much as his life is worth to poke his nose outside the door, and even indoors a night-light has to be kept burning to scare the Jinns off; if he is ill, the *gwāt* or Spirit of the Wind must have laid him low, and the Mother of the *gwāt*—some man or woman who poses as the invoker of the *gwāt*—must be called in to sing and dance him into a healing trance. And withal he is a cheery, breezy fellow, with the salt of the sea about him, though the unspeakable stench of the drying-yards in his villages is to most of us an effective barrier to a closer acquaintance.

284. Of more than local interest, I fancy, are the Lōṛī, who ought to have little difficulty in worming themselves into any congregation of the catholic brotherhood of gypsies all the world over. They are dispersed throughout the whole Lōṛī.

Lōṛī . . . 10,996

country, and reach far away into Persia and beyond. Asked about their origin, they usually spin some yarn connecting them with the particular race among whom they live: they hail from Aleppo; they are descended from Sarmast, youngest of the sons of Mīr Hamza, the Prophet's uncle; it was under Chākar the Rind that they came first to Makrān and on into Balūchistān; and much more in the same strain. Asked about the meaning of their name, they usually explain that old father Sarmast was luckless enough to get overlooked when Mīr Hamza's patrimony was being divided up, and there was nothing left him but a *lōṛ* or share in the lot of his more fortunate brothers. As a matter of fact, they are not over-fond of the name of Lōṛī, and many of them much prefer to be called Sarmastāṛī after their legendary ancestor, or Lōpī, for which they have no explanation to offer at all, or else to be dubbed *usta*, short for *ustād*, master-craftsman. By craft they are tinkers, first and last; after their own fashion they work well enough in gold and silver; they are not bad hands at carpentry; they are expert beggars; several of them are *ḍōmb* or professional minstrels; the wives of the *ḍōmb* are the midwives of the country. After this long list of their attainments it is not surprising that the tribes to which they are attached—and nearly every section among the Balōch and Brāhūis has its own little Lōṛī group—are fully alive to the value of their services and keep a pretty tight hold over them, taking them along on their wanderings and fiercely resenting any overtures on the part of other tribes to lure them away. In the tribal headmen the Lōṛī have jealous guardians of their petty rights and privileges, and under their protection they lead a charmed if lowly life, for the excellent reason that their blood-money is set at some fancy price, generally twice the blood-money of an ordinary tribesman. Yet the wilder and uncaged life of Makrān is probably much more to the Lōṛī's liking. Here he is not tied to tribal leading-strings, but is free to live his life as he pleases, with no one to say him nay. It is in Makrān, therefore, that we find the Lōṛī in his element. And this is the way this merry, careless, ne'er-do-weel gypsy—this tinker, goldsmith, minstrel, ballad-monger, donkey-coper, juggler, circumciser, quack, this jack-of-all-trades, everything by starts and nothing long—sums up the story of his life: "Wanderers we were born, wanderers we live, and wanderers we shall die. When our bellies are full, we pray. When our bellies are empty, we cheat—for are we not the rightful sharers in the food and the drink of you all? No birthplace nor home nor burying-ground is ours. Our birth is in the jungle and the desert. The desert and the jungle are our home and our grave."

Jat.

285. The Jat usually pose as Balōch, much to the disgust of the Balōch himself. They hark back in approved fashion to Chākar the Rind, and attribute their drop in the social scale either to their refusal to support him in the struggle with the Lāshārī, or to their ancestral profession as camel-drivers, from which they are supposed to derive their name. According to Balōch tradition, so far from having dropped in the social scale, they must have gone up a step or two, degraded though their condition is. For in the old days these Rāvchī or Rauchī, as they are called in the ballads, were little better than savages, living unwashed, unshaven, unclothed, partly on their camels and partly on their women—their two sources of livelihood to this day (§ 179). As for their absurd claims to kinship, the Balōch say that Chākar himself had to warn them of the inevitable consequences of such impertinence, and Heaven proved him in the right by wiping out ten thousand of them in the next battle. But though it seems clear that their claims to blood relationship are really preposterous, it is equally clear that their connexion with the Balōch is of long standing. The bonds between their various sections are of the frailest, and in the individual section it is a case of *kiṛī kiṛī sardārēn*, or "one tent—one chieftain," as the proverb says. Latterly they have begun to awake to the idea that union is not without strength, and some of them are begining to follow, though very gingerly, the lead of their *mōtabar*. But if each man is a chieftain in his own tent, they are a cringing lot to the outside world, submitting with whispering humbleness to any indignity put upon them; sufferance is the badge of all their tribe: even among themselves a flood of abuse or a cuff with the hand or a blow with a shoe is the utmost limit of their valour. Winter and summer they are on the move, in search of grazing for their camels, carrying with them a mat-tent, a hand-mill, some pots and pans, and a few sticks of furniture. They are such notorious evil-livers and expert camel-lifters, that they are not allowed to camp close to a village unless they have taken service with some big man.

Jat 5,680

Ghulām.

286. It is hard to find an equivalent for so antiquated a relic of pre-British days as the Ghulām, but the term "servile dependant" will perhaps do as well as any other. The Ghulām are a very motley crew, the descendants of ancestors imported either by purchase or capture from Africa, Persia, India and Afghānistān. There are *habshī* or negroes; Makrānī half-breeds; Persians or Balōch, whose fathers were captured in border warfare; *marēṭa*, who are popularly supposed to be descended from Mahrattas led into captivity by Ahmad Shāh; Hazāra women from Afghānistān. They are of course an anachronism. But their position in the tribal household is often much too comfortable for them to forfeit it lightly by claiming that full status which is theirs for the asking in any British court.

Ghulām . . . 20,244

The relationship of *ghulām* to master is not so one-sided as it might seem. The *ghulām* have of course to work for their master about the house or farm; but the master has to support them like the rest of the family. When times are hard, the *ghulām* no doubt are the first to feel the pinch. But even though the master himself wants to be quit of them, he may find it no easy matter to shake them off. Not only are they loth to shift for themselves in this world, they have an uncomfortable idea that if their master seeks to earn merit by dismissing them, they will have to take his sins with them into the next. Sometimes the master tries to wash his hands of them as a punishment, only to be pestered by entreaties that he should forget and forgive and take them back into the bosom of the family.

Hindus.

287. The only Hindus I propose to discuss are the old families who have been domiciled in various parts of the country for so long that they have almost as much right to be regarded as indigenous as the tribesmen themselves. In fact, if their own accounts are to be trusted, they date further back than these; for the Hindus of Kalāt town—undoubtedly among the oldest in the community—claim to be offshoots of the mysterious Sēwa dynasty that ruled in Kalāt centuries before the Brāhūī Confederacy took shape. But though the Bhāṭia of Las Bēla punctiliously refer their advent to the year 708 A.D., and the Hindus of Lahṛī tell in all good faith of their journeyings from Aleppo with Chākar the Rind, the early history of these old Hindu families is hopelessly befogged. Everything, however, seems to point to the western Panjāb and Sind as the countries from which most of them came, though isolated families in Nushkī may have immigrated by way of Afghānistān, and a few others may have wandered in from the far corners of India. Originally they may have been as diverse as the villages from which they came and the dates of their coming. To-day the old Hindu families form a more or less homogeneous community. In particular customs no doubt they vary considerably; but common environment has set its common mark on them all. And it is in the effect of an alien environment on Hindus and Hindu caste that the main interest in these old trading families of Balūchistān is centred.

Indigenous Hindus	14,985
Indigenous Sikh	2,799

Their position in the tribal days.

288. In the olden days the Hindu shopkeepers were lumped up with the servile dependants of the tribe. They lived everywhere on sufferance: in the more important villages they enjoyed the direct patronage of the State in return for the payment of a poll-tax; elsewhere they sheltered under the protection of the tribe as a whole or of the chief or some influential headman, whom they had to conciliate with offerings on marriages and other set occasions. They were made to wear red head-gear or red leg-gear as a distinctive dress, and the lowly ass was the best mount they dared to aspire to. They were treated as transferable property, and there were all the makings of a very pretty quarrel whenever a tribesman sought to coin money out of a transfer behind the back of his fellows, or one tribe endeavoured to filch some particularly useful Hindu from another. But this is only one side of the picture. If they ranked in theory a little lower than the lowest because of their idolatrous religion, they were in reality regarded as much more important than many of their betters because of their greater usefulness. And the protection accorded to them was in consequence complete. They were free from persecution and molestation; in any dispute with the tribesmen they could appeal to their protector or the headmen for a fair hearing and a fair settlement; the honour of their women was respected; their religion was tolerated; no one tampered with their customs. In spite of their apparent disabilities, theirs was no unhappy lot. If none were allowed to become very rich, none were poor. Friction between Hindu and Musalmān was unknown, because neither preyed on the other, but each took his proper place in tribal society. Exercising a mutual forbearance—as they still do in outlying parts of the tribal country—both communities lived together in unruffleable harmony, such as is seldom seen where British justice gives every man fair play to play for his own hand. And not only were the Hindus safe from persecution within the tribe, they were—like the Lōṛī, and for similar reasons—as inviolate in tribal warfare as women and unbreeched lads. This protection did not, of course, extend to those among them who took their place in the fighting ranks. And there were many such—though not to many fell the honour of being sung in ballad history like Mārkan, the Hindu hero of a famous battle on the Pab hills

between the Khān and the Burrā of Las Bēla. Nor was it individuals alone who became fired with the martial spirit of a tribesman. The pugnacity of the Rāmzai Hindus of Bārkhān and the so-called Kākaṛī Hindus of Mēkhtar is a byword in the country to this day.

The Panchāyat.

289. In every Hindu settlement of any size is a Panchāyat or governing body of representative men called *panch* or *paryamuns*. At the head of the Panchāyat stands the *mukhī* or president, with his deputy the *chaudhrī*; sometimes the order is inverted. Both offices, which are occasionally vested in one and the same person, are ordinarily held by hereditary right, but hereditary claims have often to give way to the superior claims of an outsider; in a Native State the appointments require the ratification of the ruler. There is a third official, the *ṭahlwa*, who is a paid servant of the Panchāyat. In larger communities, like Kalāt and Bēla and Bhāg, the Panchāyat is composed of a definite number of members especially appointed; in smaller communities everybody of any standing at all takes his place on the governing board as a matter of course. Each Panchāyat is ordinarily a self-contained whole working independently of similar bodies elsewhere, though there is sometimes a shadowy right of appeal to the Panchāyat of a larger community—from Mēkhtar, for instance, to Dukī, and from the petty Hindu community in Afghān Shōrāwak to the more flourishing settlement at Nushkī. But this independence is not inconsistent with a certain amount of reciprocity: thus in cases of grave importance the Lahṛī Panchāyat will invite the Panchāyats of the neighbouring villages of Phulējī and Chhatr and Shāhpur to its counsels and, if necessary, enlist their co-operation in exacting the penalty from a delinquent. The functions of the Panchāyat are to keep the peace in the community, to support its religious institutions, and to preserve its social system. It settles disputes among its members; it maintains the places of worship and feeds religious mendicants; it assists at domestic ceremonies and punishes sins against society. The sanction behind its orders is the force of public opinion; and the extreme penalty it can inflict is *naṛ-khasna*, the withholding of the hookah, that outward emblem of excommunication. But the authority of the Panchāyats is on the wane, as a consequence partly of the institution of courts throughout the country, partly of the fashionable spirit of individualism that has taught men to make light of the severing of old ties and to meet social ostracism by calmly shifting their quarters. But a timely recognition that these useful bodies are losing much of their usefulness will probably result in just that amount of wholesome yet unobtrusive official support that is needed to restore them to their former vigour.

Caste.

290. An important characteristic of these Panchāyats must not be overlooked. Except in Quetta, where the Hindu community has become so overgrown that conditions are abnormal, neither caste nor sub-caste enters into their composition: there is nothing incongruous or unusual in a Panchāyat subscribing impartially to a Sikh Dharmsāla and to the worship of a Dēvī or of Daryā Pīr; or in a Panchāyat (like that of Chūhaṛkōt in Bārkhān) which is composed almost wholly of Arōṛas having a Brahman as its president. In other words, a Panchāyat is a Panchāyat not of caste-members but of the whole body of Hindus in a village community. It is indeed almost always sheer waste of time to question a member of one of these old Hindu families regarding his caste. Brahman he knows and Musalmān he knows; and it is enough for him that he is neither the one nor the other, but a Hindu pure and simple. Most of the families are undoubtedly Arōṛa; some few are very possibly Khatrī; the Bhāṭia of Las Bēla are probably Rājpūt. But these are distinctions too nice for a local Hindu; it is more than possible that he may never have heard the terms before. Nevertheless, though his mind may be a blank as to the name of his caste, he can sometimes give the name of his sub-caste—possibly a hoary name like Ahūja, possibly a newly coined name like Rāmzai or Panjazai, modelled on the name of a tribal section. But it is merely a matter of names after all. The Rāmzai and the Panjazai and the Ahūja may have each some cherished peculiarities of their own. But such peculiarities strike no discord between them. The old Hindu families are a brotherhood of equals; among themselves they know no distinctions valid enough to influence the intercourse of everyday life. And even outside their own select circle few distinctions are recognised. Let a man

but be a Hindu, and they will eat with him and drink with him, and though they will not marry their daughter to him, they will marry a daughter of his with alacrity.

291. They are more broadminded still, for Musalmān influence and Musalmān environment have made themselves felt at every turn. Take for instance the water-question. The Hindus employ the useful *khallī*—goat-skin or sheep-skin—almost as freely as their Musalmān neighbours. Outside Quetta it is even employed for water to be used in places of worship. It seems to defy defilement: that Musalmāns have fetched it from the river or well, matters not a whit. It is somewhat otherwise with the *dilla* or earthen pot. In most parts of the country Musalmān touch renders it unclean; yet in Sibī a Hindu woman is glad enough if her Musalmān sister lends her a helping hand with her *dilla* at the well, and throughout Las Bēla and in many parts of the Kachhī water brought by a Musalmān in a *dilla* is drunk without a qualm. In Nasīrābād, by the by, it is such an everyday matter for a Hindu to prop up his *dilla* against his leather-shod foot when he wants to pour himself out a drink of water, that I can only suppose that no one would be more astonished than he to hear of the horror of orthodoxy at the enormity of his act. As for water in a brass pot, the accepted rule is that water fetched by a Musalmān is clean enough for washing and bathing, but too unclean to drink. In Nushkī and some parts of the Kachhī such niceties are unknown: here they drink the water and wash with the water, and never think twice about it. There is much the same laxity over food. Musalmāns, both male and female, are freely employed as domestic servants, and it is part of their workaday duties to sweep out the kitchen, smear the floor with cowdung, and scour the cooking-pots and eating-vessels. But even local Hindus draw the line somewhere; and they never allow a Musalmān to touch the cooked food, or to enter the kitchen while it is being cooked. Both these restrictions, however, are relaxed in the case of roast meat, of which they are very fond. Here their orthodox scruples are replaced by another of a very different kind: they are as particular as Musalmāns themselves that all flesh they eat should have been *halāl*-ed; if *jhaṭka* is known at all, it is certainly not practised. Away from home the local Hindu throws to the winds the few scruples he may pride himself on at his own hearth. He does not hesitate to borrow a Musalmān's griddle or a Musalmān's oven; nor—unless perhaps another Hindu is looking on—would he turn up his nose at the food some kindly tribesman may have offered to cook for him. Food and drink.

292. Except to a certain extent among the Arōṛas of Nasīrābād, where the Utrādhī consider themselves a cut above the Ḍakhana, there is a free interchange of marriage among all the old Hindu families. There is doubtless a tendency for marriages to be confined within the particular locality; but this is merely a matter of convenience, arising from the accident of distance which separates the various settlements. In Las Bēla again, the Bēlarō who constitute the old-established residents are inclined to keep themselves apart from the Pardēsī, as the later comers are called, notwithstanding the fact that the same sub-castes—the Lohāna and Bhāṭia, for instance—overlap into both; but the artificial barrier between them is constantly broken down. Outside the charmed circle of old families a father would never dream of going for a match for his daughter; not even an alliance into a higher caste would tempt him. Where he himself is concerned, he is much less hide-bound in his tastes. Fifteen or twenty years ago there was a regular epidemic of marriages with Mārwāṛī women, who were imported (especially in the Balōch tribal country) under high-flown but unknown caste-names. In marriages arranged after this fashion, occasional mishaps were only to be expected; but it was too much even for a local Hindu when his new-wed wife settled down to work at the hand-mill with a pious *Bismilla*. The *mésalliance* was hushed up, and the woman was married off to a Musalmān who lived a convenient distance away. Not that marriages—I suppose one must call them marriages—with Musalmān women are altogether unknown. There have been three within recent times which have come to my knowledge: one in Nushkī, another in Jhalawān, and a third on the Makrān coast. In the last case the husband was an orthodox Hindu by religion and a Sirāī Arōṛa by caste. His wife was a Zikrī when he married her, but thanks to his suasions—this is a delightful touch Marriage.

borrowed from my Musalmān informant—she has laid her heresy aside, and is now a devout Sunnī, most punctual in her prayers. The union was happily blessed with numerous offspring, of whom one daughter and three sons survive. The daughter has been married off for a respectable bride-price to a Gichkī, the *nikāḥ* being duly read at the ceremony; the sons are shortly to be circumcised. Though the Musalmān wives in all three cases were of low birth, little difficulty seems to have been experienced in arranging excellent matches for the daughters in Musalmān circles. But such hybrid marriages are probably a thing of the more loose if more harmonious past. I doubt whether they would be tolerated nowadays by either the Musalmān or the Hindu community.

Marriage age.

293. In the old days child-marriage appears to have been unknown. Girls were married off any time between the ages of twelve and eighteen: their husbands were generally three or four years older. But here again old customs are breaking up. There is a growing feeling that the sooner the children are married off, the better. Two influences are at work. Orthodox Hinduism is gradually filtering into the country, bringing with it the conviction that early marriage is a religious duty. And the greater freedom enjoyed by individuals of both sexes under British rule has brought home to the people the apparent advantage of settling their children safely in life, before they reach the dangerous age when they may be tempted to strike out a line for themselves. Needless to say, this idea is doubly operative with regard to the girls: here independence may easily become an alarming scandal. Yet even so, matters are still a long way off infant-marriage in the strict sense of the word, and the lowest age at which boy or girl is known to have been married is seven.

Widow remarriage.

294. Almost more significant from the orthodox point of view is the local attitude towards widow-remarriage. It is prevalent in varying degrees throughout the country. In Kalāt, Mastung and Nushkī it is in somewhat bad odour and relatively infrequent. In the Kachhī the betting is at least three to one that a widow of anything like marriageable age will marry again. In the Marī and Bugṭī country a widow-remarriage entails the payment of twice the usual marriage-fee to the local Panchāyat, which passes on a portion of it to the Brahman and a larger portion to the Lāljī temple in Dera G͟hāzī K͟hān. In Las Bēla the usual fee is cut down by half. In many parts of the country there is none to pay at all. There is considerable disagreement as to the position of the deceased husband's brother in the matter. In Quetta he is ruled out of court entirely; in Dukī he appears to have an absolute right to the widow's hand, and if he prefers to forgo it, he can still claim her bride-price; elsewhere he has usually the prior claim or rather the first refusal, for the lady is supposed to have the last word in the business. And if there are more brothers than one, the lot falls not to the older or the younger, but to the one who is still unprovided with a wife.

Divorce.

295. But a still greater scandal awaits orthodoxy in the existence of divorce. For if divorce is certainly not common, it no less certainly exists. Misconduct is the usual provocative, and divorce is generally accompanied by the payment of compensation. Even in Quetta, where the old families might be expected to have imbibed some of the rigorous ideas of the large orthodox community, or at any rate to comport themselves with a due regard to outward appearances, there have been at least two cases of divorce within recent times. In the first the discarded wife eventually married a Panjābī; in the second, which took place only the other day, she was married off to a local Hindu of Lōṛalai. As a rule it is no doubt felt that it is more decent for the discarded wife to enter upon her new married life in another part of the country, as in these two Quetta cases. But not everybody is so particular. There are two divorcées living with their second husbands in Ḍhādar, with their erstwhile husbands living round the corner.

Future tendencies.

296. It would be a bold man who would venture to dogmatise regarding the directions in which the customs of the old Hindu families will flow on the opening up of the country. There are too many cross-currents. But I cannot help thinking that before long castes will be resuscitated where they have not been wholly forgotten, and usurped where they have. Whether

the old sub-castes like Ahūja will be burnished up, or whether the Rāmzai and the Panjazai and the other fantastic modern creations will be able to hold their own, time alone can show. But it seems pretty clear that the sub-caste is destined to play a larger part in social and more especially in matrimonial life in the near future. Nor would it be surprising if groups like the old Bēlarō and the younger Pardēsī of Las Bēla or the old Taldār and the younger Kachhīwāl of Quetta—artificial distinctions which have grown up around purely residential qualifications—became in course of time rigid endogamous sub-castes. Yet the present tendency, I admit, is in the opposite direction. As the years roll on, the marriage age will probably be pitched lower and lower; and infant marriage may possibly become general in Balūchistān just when enlightenment is banishing it from India. Divorce can hardly hope to survive the influx of orthodoxy for long, though the convenience of it is too apparent among their Musalmān neighbours for the old Hindus to relinquish it without a struggle. Nevertheless, the present tendency seems again in the opposite direction. Widow-remarriage will probably be eschewed by and by among families imbued with a desire to rise in the social scale, but it has taken such firm root in the country at large that it will certainly die hard. A spirit of reform will possibly grow up round the household hearth, but a wholesale reform in matters of food and drink will probably set in last of all; the Hindu population will always be too scattered for the nice observance of the strict rules of diet by a man who goes peddling about the country. It must not be overlooked that while the alien Hindus temporarily settled in Balūchistān are already influencing the old families in some slight degree, they themselves have not remained uninfluenced by the surrounding laxity, at any rate as regards diet. But as I count on having a few orthodox friends among my readers, I prefer to draw a modest veil over their venial and, I doubt not, temporary lapses from the strait path of orthodoxy.

Anthropometry *versus* empirical conclusions.

297. These then are chief among the many peoples of Balūchistān. In a survey like this, it is not easy to bring their peculiarities, characteristics, and points of difference into clear relief. Yet even so it will possibly be a bit of a shock to learn that anthropometry reduces all the peoples so far measured in Balūchistān—and the net has been spread wide enough to catch Balōch, Paṭhān, Brāhūī, Dēhwār, Jaṭṭ, Lōṛī, Mēd and Ghulām—to one and the same race, the so-called Turco-Iranian type. But this is not all. Through the medium of anthropometry the peoples of Balūchistān are now re-united to strange, long-lost kinsmen in the Hunza and the Nagar and the Kāfir and the Hazāra. Well, we will say nothing about the Hunza and Nagar and Kāfir: I doubt whether our Balūchistān peoples have ever clapped eyes on any of them except at the Delhi Darbār. But with the Hazāra they have a pretty intimate acquaintance. And like myself they would probably be hard put to it to imagine a much greater gulf between any two human types than that which exists—to the uninitiated eye—between the Hazāra and, let us say, the Mēd.

Its methods criticised.

298. When the tentative conclusions of science come into such rude conflict with the working pre-conceptions of everyday experience, it is only natural that the layman, even though he may feel obliged to accept unquestioned the premises on which the science is based, should look not a little closely at the actual methods which the science adopts. For here at any rate he may perhaps be a better judge than the scientific man himself. And as far as Balūchistān is concerned, criticisms are ready to hand. There is first and foremost the absurdly small numbers on which the conclusions are framed. And yet one cannot help feeling that even though the numbers had been multiplied a thousandfold, the Nagar and the Kāfir and the Ghulām and the Mēd and the Hazāra and the rest would still have been made to fit the same Procrustean bed. But when we find measurements of Balōch, for instance, among the data, we are entitled and more than entitled to ask who these Balōch were. Judged by their locality, they were Marī and Bugṭī. But what Marī? Shīrānī Marī? But these are commonly supposed to be Paṭhān by origin. Or Baḍḍānī? But these are supposed to be Brāhūī. Or Mohandānī? But these are supposed to be Khetrān. Or Jhing? But these are supposed to be slaves. The questioning in the case of Brāhūīs would be more pointed still. For years I have interested myself in the Brāhūīs, and am still uncertain where to look for a

pure type. The Brāhūis are so mixed, as regards tribes and clans and sections, that I should have thought even the most ardent anthropometrist would have realised it to be a thankless task to measure 198 Brāhūis in the Sarāwān country *en bloc*. In Balūchistān, more perhaps than elsewhere, is it necessary for anthropometry to go to work on cautious and modest lines. The people must be measured tribe by tribe, clan by clan, section by section, and, if it be possible, the measurements should be restricted to families of known pedigree only.

Its premises examined.

299. But the layman seems now in a position to form some opinion on the validity of the premises on which the whole superstructure of anthropometry has been founded. The persistence of the racial head-type—to take the most fundamental premise of all—is an idea entirely at variance with the vivid, if unscientific, impressions of the traveller, who cannot but be struck with the change, for instance, that comes over not only the stature and physique but also, as it seems to him, the head and physiognomy of the product of the European slums in the healthy environment of Australia. And now, if I may put my trust in such of the results of Professor Boas' anthropometrical researches in New York as have come my way, it would seem that anthropometry itself is justifying the conclusions of experience against the premises of anthropometry. These results seem to show clearly enough that even the head cannot escape from the influences of those multitudinous factors that we call environment. For where else can we find the explanation of the fact that the cephalic index of home-born Sicilians is 78 and the cephalic index of Sicilians born in New York is 80, or that the cephalic index of East European Jews is 84 and that of their descendants in New York 81 ?

Cephalic index influenced by environment.

300. But these and other experiments now being conducted by Professor Boas in New York suggest a wider generalisation. They seem to show that the heads of immigrants drawn to New York from all parts of the world are gradually approximating to one and the self-same type. Thus the brachycephalic Jews are losing their brachycephaly, the dolichocephalic Sicilians are losing their dolichocephaly, and both are approaching from opposite directions to a type which for the present we may call the New York type. If these results are confirmed, we have an explanation ready-made for the similarity that runs through the head-measurements so far taken in Balūchistān. We have also an explanation for the surprising coincidence that throughout India the classification of races according to head-measurements falls together in a curiously convenient manner with geographical divisions. In other words, on this showing we must apparently look to anthropometry to give us evidence not so much of common race as of common environment.

And by nursery customs.

301. Now the changes observed in the Jewish and Sicilian population of New York are confined, it appears, to people actually born in the new country, and do not occur among those born, let us say, on the sea-voyage out from home. So far, therefore, we have apparently been concerned with the influence of pre-natal environment only. The nature of this environment is of course not very easy to define; environment after all is a term of the vaguest connotation, one of those Mesopotamian words which conveniently cover a multitude of things unknown. But there appeared a few months ago an article in a German medical journal[1] which attacked the anthropometrical position on the other flank. While anthropometry has long realised the necessity of making allowances for artificial deformations, Walcher, the writer of this short but most interesting article, has demonstrated the ease with which a change from brachycephaly to dolichocephaly or the reverse can be induced—and that in the most natural and unartificial of manners—by simply taking the trouble to lay the babe during the first months of its life either on its side or plumb on the back of its head, according to the particular kind of cephalic index that you desire to produce. Thus, given a ten-day old babe with an index of 79·6, Walcher arranged to have it kept on its side (chiefly by the device of giving it a hard pillow), and made it markedly dolichocephalic with an index of 72·5 in less than eleven months; given a dolichocephalic babe three weeks old, with an index of 78·3, he kept it from lying on its side (chiefly by means of a soft pillow), and so converted dolichocephaly into brachycephaly (with an index

[1] Münchener Medizinische Wochenschrift, 17 Jan. 1911.

of 82·4) in little over ten months. Here are the details of three more of Walcher's experiments in the pre-determination of the head-type :—

Child Erk (b. 14-2-10)		Child Friedrichsen (b. 5-11-09)		Child Butz (b. 2-6-05)	
26-2-10	79·1	11-11-09	78·9	2-6-05	80·6
1-4-10	77·1	1-12-09	84·8	2-8-06	73
3-5-10	76·8	3-1-10	89·08	11-10-10	74·1
2-6-10	73·8	1-3-10	88·6		

The last experiment is the most interesting of the lot for many reasons, not the least of which is the fact that it is spread over a longer period than any of the others. The parents, like their child at birth, are themselves brachycephalic, the father's index being 84, the mother's 83·2 ; so is the three-year old sister with an index of 81·5. The child was under control for 14 months only, and it is expressly stated that it was given a soft pillow (in other words was encouraged to lie on the back of its head) after it left the observer's control, a fact which possibly accounts, in some measure at any rate, for the slight reversion to the original type. Now these experiments are of course tentative, not final. We must await the subsequent life-history of the patients ; we want to know for instance, whether the slight rise in the case of the child Butz and the slight drop in the case of the child Friedrichsen (which occurred apparently while he was still under control) developed still further in later life. But one must needs be a very whole-hearted anthropometrist to anticipate that, great as are the changes arbitrarily or accidentally impressed on the skull in the first months or years of life, they will pass off in due course, and that the original racial types will reassert themselves in the end. This would surely be a miracle indeed—even in the eyes of the anthropometrist himself. So much seems clear. Anthropometry cannot brush aside these established influences of early nursing as mere accidental deviations on this or that side of the normal, which will right themselves when the population is measured up in the mass. True, the manner in which babes are laid to rest in our own nurseries is, for aught I know, a mere toss-up ; it is just possible that, as the child of rich parents is more likely to sleep on a soft pillow than the child of the poor, whose pillow is often hard enough, we ought to anticipate a tendency to brachycephaly in the upper classes and a tendency to dolichocephaly in the lower. But the case is very different among more unsophisticated peoples. Here, if I may judge by our peoples of Balūchistān, custom will be found to reign as supreme in the nursery as in other walks of life, and the anthropometrist will have to recognise that nursery customs are as seriously disturbing factors to be reckoned with as the influence of environment.

Possible practical future for anthropometry.

302. Whether anthropometry will be able to take up the challenge and issue strengthened and triumphant from the difficulties that now beset it, time alone can show. The chances seem against it. Present-day anthropometry at any rate appears to be in somewhat parlous case. That it will not be able to maintain its premises, methods and conclusions in their present form, is tolerably clear. One is reluctant to believe with Walcher that so great a mass of painstaking drudgery can be altogether labour lost. One would rather hope that anthropometry may yet be able so to adapt itself to unforeseen difficulties as to throw some flicker of light on the infinitely complex problem it so lightheartedly set itself to solve. Yet glancing at the photograph of the twin sisters in Walcher's article, I cannot help wondering whether the future of anthropometry does not lie along practical rather than scientific lines. The cephalic indices of these twins at birth are unfortunately not given. At two and a half years the index of the one destined for dolichocephaly was 78·4, the index of the one destined for brachycephaly was 86-2. But not only have their skulls been deliberately moulded at the relentless will of the scientific observer, their faces have undergone changes, apparently *pari passu* with their skulls. And the result is striking indeed. The tragic melancholy of the long-faced dolichocephalic twin is in sad contrast to the jolly visage of her round-faced brachycephalic sister. Not at random surely has folk-anthropometry (if I may coin the barbarous term) ever associated jollity with roundness of face and melancholy with lantern-jaws and lean and hungry looks. And anthropometry would certainly have done the world

good service, though not the service it set itself to do, if it led on to the discovery of an easy, natural, but withal irresistible method of adding to the gaiety of nations.

Head-forming among the Brāhūīs.

303. Though Walcher's article created no little flutter in anthropometrical dove-cots, its main thesis is as old as the hills, at any rate in Balūchistān[1]. "Too many nurses," says the Brāhūī proverb (and the Paṭhāns have a proverb modelled closely after it) "make the babe's head oval," or—as we should put it—"too many nurses spoil the babe's head." The first concern in a Brāhūī nursery on the birth of a child is the moulding of its head and features. There is no time to lose. During the first three days the babe's body is believed to be so plastic that it can be shaped to will, especially if it is not exposed to the air. Whatever is to be done, must be done in the first fortnight, though as a matter of fact most people persevere for full forty days. According to the current idea—and this may be of interest to the anthropometrist—the babe is born with a tapering head. Nothing could be more opposed to Brāhūī standards of beauty and, I may add, to Brāhūī canons of luck. So they bestir themselves at once to set nature right. The methods they adopt are curiously like Walcher's. First and foremost the babe's head must be laid on a soft pillow, millet being the usual stuffing. The object (as in Walcher's experiments) is of course to keep the babe plumb on the back of the head. The forehead again should be neither convex nor concave, but flat; so they keep it wrapped round in a muslin bandage, drawn as smooth and as tight as they can get it. In these matters a girl gives her parents much more anxiety than a boy. A boy, they say, is one of nature's jewels and stands in scant need of embellishment, after all is said and done. But failure in the case of a girl is little short of a disaster; so they bore three or four holes in her ears, with the result that if she chance to turn over to one side on her pillow, the pain soon makes her turn back again to the proper position.

And among the Jatt, Balōch and Paṭhāns.

304. The Jaṭṭ and the Balōch appear to have much the same standards of beauty as the Brāhūīs and much the same methods of conforming to them. So have the Paṭhāns, but as the Brāhūīs have no very high opinion of the results they achieve, and are fond of poking fun at their long "mortar-shaped" heads, I will describe their methods at some length. The first thing the nurse does is to wipe down and dry the babe, body, head and all. Then she carefully rounds the head with her hands. This done, she takes a piece of old muslin and lays it four-folded over the infant's scalp. Then she swathes head and shoulders round with a long strip of cloth, keeping it in place with a band, called *paṭ°ī*, which must be either silk or muslin. In Kandahār they make black silk kerchiefs, called *kalāghi*, especially for this purpose. Thus trussed up, the babe is laid in its cradle on a soft pillow—usually stuffed with millet—with the object of inducing it to lie on the back of its head. Day by day the face is cleaned with a mixture of kneaded flour and ghee, which after use is kept in some safe place for forty days and then thrown into a stream. Every now and then the head is douched with the mother's milk. On the fortieth day the head and the whole body are bathed for the first time. The folded napkin is now discarded, its place being taken by a *rakhchīna*, a female headgear made of silk or some other soft material. But the *paṭ°ī* is considered indispensable for two or three years, to shield the tender head from the air. Not until the child can pronounce *kāṇai* (stone), do they consider that the bones of the head have properly set. But the Paṭhāns in their over-zealous use of the *paṭ°ī* seem frequently to defeat their object, with the result that the head at the end of the treatment is often found to be elongated—"the reverse of natural beauty, as in the case of my own," adds my informant pathetically. Among the womenfolk, I am told, this tendency to elongated heads is exaggerated by the scraping back of the hair into one long plait behind. The Brāhūī, Balōch and Jaṭṭ women, on the other hand, wear their hair in two plaits, which, scented and plastered with gum, stick out like rams' horns on either side. To a Brāhūī's eye it almost seems as if the Panjābī woman were proud of what he calls her "nut-shaped" head, for not only does she scrape back her hair into a

[1]It is not even a novelty in more scientific circles: 'Many facts shew how easily the skull is affected. Ethnologists believe that it is modified by the kind of cradle in which infants sleep." Darwin's *Descent of Man*, Ch. 2.

single plait, she sticks a rounded ornament called *chaunk* on the top of her head, which makes it look more nut-shaped than ever.

The moulding of the features.

305. But as anthropometry does not stop short at the measurements of the head, let us pass on to the deliberate moulding of the features. And here I will confine my remarks to the Brāhūīs, though it must not be supposed that the other peoples of Balūchistān do not have parallel customs. One of the first things they do when a babe is born is to examine the size of its mouth, measuring it against a finger-joint. If it's too large, they compress it within a small ring, rubbing the lips slowly to make them thin. Not less is the care they lavish on the ears and on the nose, which is pinched constantly and pressed upwards. In fact what with pulling and compressing and massaging with kneaded flour and oil, they devote as much trouble to the features of a new-born babe, as a fashionable beauty-doctor in Europe to the wrinkles of his lady patients. They even do their best to train the hair in the way it should grow, for few things are more fraught with ill-luck for a Brāhūī maiden than to have her *baunṛī* or the whorl of her hair at all forward on the head. So unchancy is such a *baunṛī* that a girl had almost better be lame or blind or deaf; she would certainly have just as much prospect of getting a husband. This then is one of the first things a nurse must look to, and it rests with her to coax the *baunṛī* with her deft fingers towards the back of the head. Not even the foot is overlooked, for the Brāhūīs heartily endorse the Persian saying *sar-i-kalān kalān ast, pā-i-kalān ghulām ast*, a large head is the mark of a nobleman, a large foot is the mark of a slave. Not only should the foot be small, it should have a pronouncedly arched instep. To secure this shape, which they call *mōza-pād* or "boot-foot," the nurse massages the foot with oil, pressing the instep up with her thumbs. Bow-legs (a literal translation, by the by, of their own expression *kāmān-pād*) are regarded as a most unlucky formation, and they seek to avoid it by tying the legs together and stuffing wads of rags in between them to keep them straight. To be really effective, the whole course of beauty-treatment should be begun on the day of the birth and be sedulously adhered to for at least forty days. As may be imagined, the womenfolk are kept pretty busy in a Brāhūī nursery.

Similar treatment of domestic animals.

306. So convinced are the Brāhūīs that art should be the handmaid of nature, and so confident are they of the efficacy of their methods that, not even where their domestic animals are concerned, are they content to leave nature alone. The foreheads of their lambs and kids are smoothed and flattened by constant dabbing with the palm of the hand, for a smooth flat forehead is looked upon as a highly desirable feature in sheep and goats. How far the pointed, inward-tapering ears of the Balūchistān breeds of horses are natural, I do not know. The Brāhūī at any rate does not leave such important matters to chance. He takes a rag some eight inches square, cuts two holes in it, and thrusts the ears through, until the rag rests on the forehead. Not only is this treatment designed to pull the ears to the proper shape, it is intended to narrow the forehead. Another point in horseflesh which is much prized is a slender foreleg above the knee, and this they seek to secure by means of bandages, which are left on the legs until they get worn out or fall off of their own accord.

Blue markings on babies among Hazāra.

307. As the results of anthropometry, whatever be their value elsewhere, are stultified by nursery methods in Balūchistān, we must cast round for other means of analysing the racial characteristics of our peoples. Now Baelz[1] has put forward the theory that the appearance of temporary blotches of bluish pigmentation, which he was the first to observe among the Chinese, Japanese, Koreans and Malays, is an universal mark of Mongolian race. That they have been observed also among the Eskimo, he regards as a corroboration of his theory; he seems, by the by, to have overlooked the fact that similar patches have been observed among the Tagals of the Philippines.[2] Here then we are offered something tangible to go upon. And as the Hazāra are popularly supposed to be Mongolian, we have an opportunity of putting Baelz's theory to some sort of test in this country. Now none of the doctors I consulted had ever noticed any such pigmentation among the Hazāra or any

[1] Z. f. E. o. d. B. G., 1901, Heft ii.

[2] Deniker, *The Races of Man*, p. 51.

other peoples of Balūchistān. So I had to fall back on less directly accessible but hardly less authoritative sources of information. But even among the indigenous midwives there was considerable haziness on the subject. Thus the first to whom I applied indirectly for assistance, said that out of the last eight Hazāra babies that she had helped into the world, one had a bluish patch about the size of an eight-anna piece on the arm, and the second had a patch, somewhat smaller, on the lower sacral region. 'Saint-marks' she called them. But a wider enquiry in midwifery circles led to the conclusion that such patches are to be found on all Hazāra at birth, generally on the lower sacral region, the size varying from a four-anna to an eight-anna piece. They tend to disappear early in life, and rarely last after the second year. But I was told of an Hazāra who still has a blue patch on his arm, though he has long left his teens behind him.

And among Brāhūīs.

308. Thus Baelz's theory seemed to find not a little corroboration. So far, so good. But my enquiries at once revealed the presence of similar pigmentation on all Brāhūī babies. Every Brāhūī babe, so my information goes, is born with bluish patches, some two or three inches in diameter, on the buttocks or at the back of the leg above the knee, which fade away in the first month or so after birth. Very occasionally there are also similar patches on the back of the waist and under the shoulder-blades; patches on the front of the body there are none. The colour varies somewhat: generally it is black, but occasionally it is purple, and occasionally reddish. Reddish colouration is the first to disappear; purple the last. The current belief among the midwives is that the discolouration is caused by the impurities in the menstrual blood during the period the babe is stored up in the womb, the nutritious portion furnishing it with its nourishment. Thus on Baelz's theory one ought to be able to make out a good case for the Mongolian origin of the Brāhūīs. An astounding conclusion this. The more's the pity that I cannot adopt it.

And among Balōch, Pathāns, Jaṭṭ and Hindu.

309. I have been careful to reproduce the definite statement of my informants that this pigmentation is to be found on all Brāhūī babies, irrespective of tribe. The assertion is hardly susceptible of absolute proof, but it may be safely accepted as implying that fairly wide enquiries have not discovered the existence of exceptions to the general rule that Brāhūī babies are marked in this manner. Now, as there is every reason to believe that a large number of Brāhūī tribes are not Brāhūī at all, but Paṭhān, Balōch, Persian or Jaṭṭ by origin, one would be led to suspect, if the statement were true, that similar patches would be found among other races of Balūchistān. And this my enquiries show to be the case. Among Paṭhāns the pigmentation seems to be very arbitrary in its occurrence, if my informants' powers of observation can be trusted: among the Tarīn of Pishīn it is frequent in some villages, and appears never to have been heard of in others; among the Achakzai of Chaman, who are also Tarīn, it seems to be common enough; among the Kākaṛ of Lōṛalai it is said to be unknown. Yet it occurs in the neighbouring *tahsīl* of Kila Saifulla, where it is said sometimes to degenerate into obnoxious and even dangerous sores; among the Dumaṛ of Shāhrig blue blotches appear on the buttocks of many infants a couple of days after birth, but though they usually vanish within three months, they are regarded as a disease which is occasionally fatal, and the precaution is often taken of wrapping the infant up in a goat-skin. Among Balōch and Jaṭṭ in various parts of the country the pigmentation seems to be looked for as a matter of course. Even among domiciled Hindus it is, if not universal, at any rate far from uncommon. According to the midwives who practise among the Jaṭṭ, the patches are simply the marks left on the body by the placenta; but then the midwives attribute all sorts of wonderful things to the placenta: should a dog or a cat get at it, the mother's milk runs dry; so the wisest thing is to bury it safely indoors, and if it is covered with rice and molasses, so much the better, as this will insure that the goodwife is shortly brought to bed again. But the learned men pooh-pooh the idea that the placenta has anything to do with the patches; according to them the patches are marks left by the Jinns, and there would be no patches at all, if there were no Jinns to pinch the luckless infant. Unfortunately I have not seen the patches myself, nor presumably would I be competent to express an opinion whether they are essentially the same among the various peoples, and similar

to the pigmentation observed by Baelz and others elsewhere. But now that attention has been drawn to their appearance in Balūchistān, the subject will doubtless be looked into by medical men. My own impression is that similar pigmentation will be found to be common enough among many races of India[1].

310. Where then shall we turn for guidance out of the labyrinthine race-problem of Balūchistān? We should at once issue into the blaze of daylight if only we could put our faith in language and let it lead us wheresoever it will. What could be more easy than to ticket off the Balōch as Iranian, the Jaṭṭ and the Lāsī as Indian, the Paṭhān as Iranian with a strong Indian strain, and the Brāhūī as Dravidian? Unfortunately we have long since learnt to discount the evidence that language has to offer; or rather, while fully recognising that it may contain a clue to the solution of the problem, to regard it as introducing yet another complexity, yet another element that will have to be explained. The history of a language and the history of the people that speak it must obviously dovetail in their later chapters; there is no earthly ground for assuming that their opening chapters and the development of their plots have anything in common at all. Language does not cling immutably and immemorially to race: there is nothing unchangeable about it like the spots of a leopard or the skin of an Ethiopian. And commonplace though all this is, it is just as well to point the moral with a few local illustrations. The Raisānī and the Zarakzai are fairly typical Brāhūīs of to-day; they have been the premier tribes of Sarāwān and Jhalawān far back into the history of the Brāhūī Confederacy. Yet both claim, and claim apparently with justice, to be Paṭhān by origin; and the fact that they speak Pashtō no longer, not even as their secondary language, does not strike them, nor need it strike us, as being in any way irreconcilable with the theory of their Paṭhān origin. Again the home language of the Raisānī chiefly family is not Brāhūī, the language of the tribe as a whole, nor Pashtō, the language of its origin, but Balōchī. Among the Mīrwāṛī, who are Brāhūī if any Brāhūī is, there is hardly a man that can speak Brāhūī at all. The Hazāra speak a Persian of sorts; but whatever else they are, they are certainly not Iranian. This shifting of language is going on almost before our very eyes in Sind, where the Brāhūī is rapidly forgetting the speech of his fathers and taking on the alien language of the alien land of his adoption (§ 78). I will mention but one more case in point, perhaps the most curious of the lot. If we want to hear the purest form of Western Balōchī and at the same time the most archaic form of Balōchī in existence, I have the warrant of the Western Balōch on the one hand and the warrant of Professor Geiger on the other that we must go to the Gichkī. Yet the Gichkī but three or four centuries back were apparently Indian-speaking Rājpūt—at any rate they were neither Balōch nor speakers of Balōchī. Not that language must be ruled out of court where race is in question. Far from it; the evidence it is trying to stammer out may be very much to the point indeed. We cannot, it is clear, class the Brāhūīs as Dravidian; we cannot even assume that they were ever in direct contact with Dravidian races, simply because they now speak a Dravidian language. Nevertheless, if comparative phonology is ever able to work out the road by which the Brāhūī language straggled into Balūchistān, or to prove beyond cavil its exact degree of relationship to the many branches of the Dravidian language-group, that itinerary and that pedigree ought with luck to throw some light on the past history of the Brāhūī-speaking people. But as matters stand, there are too many gaps in the evidence that language has to offer for us to take it at its face value. Of all circumstantial evidence, language is the most dangerous; and I for one do not propose to give a dog a bad name and hang him on the strength of it.

Arguments from language.

311. Still less do I propose to enter into a comparative study of names, ancient and modern, or seek evidences of origin in the similarity of their sounds—or should we not rather say of their looks?—that will-o'-the-wisp that has long flickered its treacherous light over the ethnological obscurity of Balūchistān. Never surely was a country so hapless a victim to loose etymology. Balūchistān itself has been supposed to enshrine the mighty name of Belus or Baal. Then we are asked to step from the sublime to the ridiculous and to read in Makrān

Arguments from similarity of names.

[1] I have, for instance, been told of patches on the babe of a high-caste Brāhman from the Panjāb.

a corruption of *māhi-khurān* or "fish-eaters"—a naïve piece of folk-etymology suggested by the Ichthyophagoi whom Alexander found on the seacoast, on a par with the local idea that Makrān is the land of *makr* or deceit. The Balōch themselves are supposed to be *bad-rōch*, men of "evil day," or *bar-lūch*, "desert-naked" or—and here comes a daring flight of imagination miscalled philology—the ancient Gadrōsi themselves who harassed Alexander on his fateful march through Makrān. This school of etymology is delightfully accommodating. If you feel qualms about fathering the Balōch on to the Gadrōsi (and well you may) you are offered the present-day Gaḍrā or Gadōr in the alternative; you may take your choice: both are found in Las Bēla, but the one is at the bottom of the social scale, the other at the top. Nor is there any lack of representatives for the Oritae, who are coupled in the Greek historians with the Gadrōsi: in modern history they reappear either as the Hōt, an ancient Balōch tribe now fallen on somewhat evil days, or the Hōrū, an insignificant subsection among the Mīr-Hājīzai Mēngal. The Paṭhān or Pakhtūn must of course be the Πάκτυες of Herodotus unless they are the Παρσυῆται of Ptolemy,—though the reason is hardly obvious. The Brāhūī are the *ba-rōh-ī*, "people on the hill" or—as they themselves prefer to put it—*bē-rāh-ī*, "people without roads" or—here again we must nerve ourselves to dizzy flights—men of Biroea, the ancient Aleppo. But imagination runs wilder yet over Brāhūī tribal names. The Mēngal are the Mēn-people, and of course the Min of the Behistūn inscription. The Sājdī with their subsection the Sākazai are the descendants of the great Scythian tribes, the Sagatae and Saki. The Sarparra are similarly the descendants of Strabo's Saraparae, a Thracian tribe whose name was supposed to be derived from their custom of decapitating strangers; and here ancient and modern folk-etymologies meet, for Sarparra—on the basis of the Pashtō *sar prē-kav°l*—is popularly explained in precisely the same way. And not content with identifying the present-day Mēd and Jaṭṭ with the Mēd and the Jat of the Arab historians, they ask us to hark back to the Medes and the Gethae. And so on, and so on; wild guesses all. It is not for me to say that when the bow has been so often drawn at a venture, an arrow has not somewhere hit the mark. But it behoves us now to cry halt, and wait soberly for the slow advance of comparative philology; crimes enough have been committed in its name.

Arguments from customs.

312. No one, I suppose, has grubbed among old and vanishing customs without hoping that he may by accident stumble across some one custom that will give him the clue to the racial origin of the people he is studying. Does any other people, one wonders, toy with stones in quite the same fashion, quite so childishly and yet so seriously as the Brāhūī (§§ 100, 109)? But to be truly racy, the custom must be very primitive; and the more primitive it is, the more likely is it to turn out but another pleasant illustration of the same old grooves in which the human mind works all the world over. Then up crop analogies in occupations and crafts. I am told, for instance, that Brāhūīs and Balōch would be fully qualified to drive sheep and goats and camels in Arabia, because they use the identical calls that the animals already know; that the silver design on Nushkī sword-hilts is characteristically Assyrian; that the stitch or pattern—I forget which—on Brāhūī needle-work is characteristically—I forget what. Unfortunately I neither have the knowledge nor have I had the time to follow up these and similar clues. If the suggestions are really founded on fact, it is possible enough that there may be something behind them. But evidence of this nature is clearly circumstantial evidence at best; and instead of justifying us in rushing to conclusions, it is much more likely to embarrass us with yet another difficulty, by demanding an explanation as to how on earth this Assyrian connection, or whatever it be, can possibly have arisen.

Conclusion.

313. And so we must leave the subject of the origin of our races in Balūchistān with a confession of ignorance. It almost looks as if the whole question of race were insoluble at the present stage of ethnology. First philology and then anthropometry have played us false, and there is nothing in the field to take their place as a ready method of solving the difficulties. A few philologists have kindly warned me that, though they are no readers of census reports, they intend to skim these pages for the solution to the Brāhūī problem. That their flattering curiosity will go unrewarded, no one regrets more than

myself. It is now some years since I closed a short essay on the Brāhūīs and their language with these words: "We can no longer argue with the child-like faith of our forefathers from philology to ethnology, and assume without further ado that this race of Balūchistān, whose speech is akin to the languages of the Dravidian peoples of Southern India, is itself Dravidian; that it is in fact the rearguard or the vanguard—according to the particular theory we may affect—of a Dravidian migration from north to south or from south to north. Such short cuts in ethnology are no longer open to us. The questions with which this essay opened, return to us at its close, but they return with deeper import. Who are these Brāhūīs, whose habitation is in Balūchistān, and whose language has to stretch beyond their utmost ken over so vast a tract of country and over so many alien languages before it can reach its own kin in the languages spoken by the strange peoples in the far-off south?" The question has haunted me ever since. The more I have studied the riddle, the more helpless I feel to unravel it. Now and then I thought the clue was in my hands, only to fling it aside as useless. And the only answer from which I can never get away is the mockery of that fine rhetoric of Sir Thomas Browne: "What song the Syrens sang, or what name Achilles assumed when he hid himself among women, though puzzling questions, are not beyond all conjecture." In sober truth, I feel as much competent to read those classical riddles as the riddle of these Dravidian-speaking Brāhūīs.

CHAPTER XII.

OCCUPATION.

Statistical data.

SUBJECT.	Tables.	
	Imperial.	Subsidiary.
Occupation in general	XV	......
Variation 1901-11	......	XXIX
Occupation by selected tribes	XVI	XXX
Agricultural implements, livestock, etc.	......	XXXI

General.

314. It is a little humiliating to have to confess that the statistics of occupation, which bulk about as large as the rest of the statistics put together, are in some ways the least satisfying of the lot. This is partly due to their very complexity, which invests them with a specious air of minute and scrupulous accuracy they do not really possess. And yet, paradoxical though it may seem, if we must have complexity at all, we should be better off with complexity carried to a higher pitch. All we attempted to record were the principal and subsidiary occupations of actual workers, and the source from which those supported by the labour of others derive their subsistence. This is enough and usually more than enough for a country in the swim of modern civilisation with its highly developed specialisation of labour. But in a primitive country like Balūchistān a man may put his hand to a score of things in the year's work. He himself perhaps may like to say that his chief employment is scratching his little patch of land, though one half of the village may tell you that most of his time is taken up with his flocks, and the other that he would find it hard to make two ends meet were it not for the cultivation of his neighbour's land. And withal it is quite possible that in reality he derived still more from the casual labour he picked up on the railway (which he now prefers to forget), or from the camel-loads of dwarf-palm leaves he bartered in Sind, or from his peddling trip to Makrān in the date-season, or from the asafœtida which he went far afield into Chāgai to collect and down-country to sell, or from any of the other odd jobs he condescended to do during the year. Yet in the end it may be nearer the mark to say that the chief means of livelihood of this apparently active worker is his share in the fruits of the labour of some other member in his family.

Record of occupation in the tribal census.

315. But these are difficulties that attach in varying degrees to a census of occupations throughout India. In Balūchistān we have to face a peculiar difficulty of our own to boot. As the tribal census was a census by families, we were obliged to deduce the occupations of the various members of the family from the occupation recorded for the householder himself, except in special cases where special means were employed to record specialised occupations. As regards the males, there need be little misgiving that in the mass the results are not just about as true to life as they would have been, had the particulars been collected individual by individual in the ordinary way. There remains the

thorny question of the womenfolk. In treating all children, whether girls or boys, as dependants on the main occupation of the head of the family, we can hardly have gone far wrong. In treating all women in the selfsame way, we have at any rate faithfully reflected economic conditions, not indeed as they actually are, but as they present themselves to the minds of the tribesmen at large. Speaking broadly—for in certain parts of the country where the tribal system is breaking up, conditions are a little different—a tribeswoman remains in a state of tutelage her whole life long : as a child she is subject to her father, as a married woman to her husband, as a widow to the heirs of one or the other. In theory she has no occupation at all : she is a mere dependant on the family into which she was born or into which she has married. In actual fact she is one of the hardest workers in the family, though most of her work is household drudgery and other lowly labour that a tribesman considers beneath his dignity. It is, for instance, the man himself who ploughs the land, sows the seed and waters the crops ; the woman helps in the reaping and threshing, and grinds the daily corn. In a nomad family it is the man who sees to the breeding and shearing of his flocks : the woman pitches the tent, does the milking and the churning and the like, and often enough has to take the flocks out to graze. And everywhere she is the hewer of wood and the drawer of water. But to treat her as a farmer in the one case or as a grazier in the other would be to do violence to the deep-rooted prejudices of the tribesmen regarding the position and functions of the sex. Ask any tribesman to enumerate the actual workers in his household, and he will run over the roll of full-bodied men in it ; the women he will lump up with the children as dependants. Put it to him that his women do a vast deal more hard work than any of the men, and he will promptly retort that the same applies to his ox and his ass. Bereft of the labour of his womenfolk, a tribesman's life would be hardly worth living, to judge by the experience of a mulla who recently went on a revivalist mission among the Marī Balōch. Preaching the rigid observance of the fast, the strict performance of the prayers, the punctilious giving of tithes, and the modest veiling of the women, he quickly gathered quite a respectable congregation round him. Even his insistence on the shearing of the luxuriant locks on which a Marī prides himself failed to check the wave of religious enthusiasm. But presently it began to dawn on his congregation that the apparently harmless veil turned their women into drones, and they gradually fell off one by one, until backsliders are now, alas, almost as plenty as converts.

Distribution of occupations.

316. As theory and practice are hopelessly at variance over the proper functions of womankind in Balūchistān, it is obviously safest in reviewing the statistics to look not so much to the number of the actual workers as to the total number supported by the several occupations. To examine each detailed group would be weary work. Nor would it be particularly profitable. The one unimpeachable thing about an occupational census is that the larger the unit, the truer the account it can render of itself. Acting on this cautious principle, I have ranged the occupations under a few general headings which seem to hold out most promise of reflecting the economic life in Balūchistān. And the most striking feature of the figures in the margin is the enormous number of the population that is dependent in some way or other on agricultural pursuits. To most of us Balūchistān probably conjures up a pastoral rather than an agricultural country. But the idea, I fancy, is derived partly from a reminiscence of the state of affairs that existed before our coming, partly from the physical conditions of the country itself, and partly from the fact that the people according to our standards are mighty fine graziers but even to-day precious poor farmers. In the old days of tribal warfare the tribesmen were chary of husbandry, not merely or mainly because they were only just emerging from the pastoral stage, but because husbandry tied them down to one locality and so exposed them to the attacks of their enemy. As the ruined towers dotted over several parts of the country serve to remind us, they only tilled as much land as their towers could command. But peace under British rule has altered all this ; and an observant traveller will come across few patches of really culturable land that have not

Distribution of Occupations.

Agriculture	68
Pasture	11
Industry	4
Administration	4
Trade	4
Transport	3
Domestic service	2
Labour (indefinite)	1
Professions	1
Others	2
	100

been brought under the plough, and will readily admit that if large tracts are left idle here and there, lack of perennial water and a scanty and precarious rainfall are ample excuses. That our statistics do not seriously exaggerate the agricultural tendencies of the population (though taken literally they may exaggerate the position of agriculture as the chief means of livelihood) may be gathered, I think, from the somewhat remarkable census we took of the farm implements and live-stock in the country. In a country where a plough and a couple of oxen go to almost every dozen inhabitants, there is nothing surprising in 68 per cent of the population returning themselves as dependent on agriculture. I am of course not prepared to vouch that all or even the majority are wholly and solely dependent on agriculture or that agriculture really beats pastoralism in the proportion of six to one. Where occupations are combined so freely as they are in Balūchistān, it is inevitable that the more respectable but possibly less lucrative occupation should be singled out, and the less respectable shoved into the background. There are comparatively few people lucky enough to be able to rely entirely on the produce of their land, and several owners of goodly flocks and miserable plots of land have probably returned agriculture as their main source of livelihood. Industry, administration, trade, follow a long way behind. At first I was a little mystified at finding industry the foremost of the three, but the explanation lies of course in the humble nature of our industrial pursuits. Except as basket-makers and well-sinkers, the tribesmen contribute little to the industrial figures; nor do they make any very serious demands on the industry of others: given their carpenters and blacksmiths, they carry on very comfortably by themselves. The backbone of the industrial population is formed by the menial classes that serve the simple needs of the village community and the township: grain-parchers, butchers, bakers, wool-spinners, cotton-weavers, boot-makers, tailors, dyers, barbers, scavengers. True, the needs of the alien population have called one or two of the more highly developed industries into being; but those that follow them are a mere handful, and contain as yet but few of the real natives of the country among their number. In the very modest dimensions of the Industrial table (XV-E) there is eloquent proof how backward industry in the large sense of the word still is in Balūchistān. At first sight it may seem a trifle curious that four per cent of the population should derive their livelihood from administration in a country where the reins of administration are held so lightly as in Balūchistān. But a little sifting would show that the figures are recruited largely from the army, the levy corps, the police and the district levies, and would serve to remind us of two important facts—facts apparently paradoxical and yet in reality closely interrelated—to wit, that Balūchistān is called upon to play a very active and responsible part in the policing of India, and that the keynote of its internal administration under the Sandeman policy is home-rule, the gradual pacification of the frontier by the frontier tribesmen themselves. That there should be almost as many people dependent on transport as there are on trade may sound a little quaint to those who do not know this land of camels; for my own part, I am surprised that the number of those who returned themselves as primarily dependent on pack-animals is only 19,554. It may seem strange that two per cent of the population should be connected with domestic service in the primitive life of Balūchistān; but a large proportion of them are servile dependants, one of the typical features of the country. The only other occupations I have found room for in my list are labour, pure and simple, and the professions. There is little to choose between them in point of numbers; in the majority of cases there is precious little to choose between them in social status either. Indeed in Balūchistān the labourer often looks down upon our so-called professional men, whose ranks include (for statistical purposes only) minstrels [1]

Ploughs and Oxen.

	Ploughs.	Oxen.
Balūchistān	**75,924**	**139,304**
Districts	33,327	60,425
States	42,597	78,879

[1] We even took a census of indigenous musical instruments: not that we seriously wanted the information; our enquiries were merely meant to disarm suspicion when we enquired about rifles. The statistics, too grotesque for the text itself, are sufficiently interesting for a footnote:—

	Dambūra (rebeck)	Sirōz (fiddle)	Rabāb (lute)	Surnā (hornpipe)	Ḍhōl (drum)
Balūchistān	**1,090**	**974**	**313**	**861**	**705**
Districts	376	342	62	719	151
States	714	632	251	142	554

and midwives, the lowest of the low. There remains a miscellaneous group of miners, fishermen, beggars and others, who account in all for about two per cent of the population.

Comparison with the last census impossible.

317. It would be interesting to compare these broad statistics with the similar statistics of a decade back. But comparison is really hopeless. It is not simply that our present scheme of occupations is different, or that wholesale administrative changes have taken place, or that vast areas were left uncensused in 1901. More serious than any of these difficulties is the fact that the bulk of the population censused in 1901 were censused on a tribal basis, and their occupations recorded on the word of the headmen of the tribal sections. The resultant statistics give us inevitably a very distorted picture of the economic conditions that existed ten years ago, and the comparison I have instituted in the margin is full of obvious abnormalities. Nobody believes, for instance, that agriculture has really gone down, or that pastoralism has almost doubled itself in the last ten years. These vagaries are proofs, if any proofs were needed, that the snobbish feeling that agriculture is a cut above pastoralism was already fashionable ten years back, and that our occupational census has been much more searching than that of our predecessors. Grouped together, agriculture and pastoralism show an increase of 5 per cent in the province as a whole, an increase which corresponds closely enough with the nominal increase of 3 per cent in the population. Industry, if we can believe the statistics, has gone up by leaps and bounds. It certainly has not. The apparent increase and the similar increases in the professions and domestic service are chiefly due to the disdain of the tribal leaders to bother themselves overmuch about the parasites of tribal life at the last census. Transport is the only pursuit that appears to have gone down, at any rate in the states. And here, hopelessly inaccurate though I believe the occupational census of 1901 to have been, it seems for once to have hit the mark.

Variation 1901-11 per cent.

	Balūchistān.	Districts.	States.
Agriculture	− 2	+ 5	− 8
Pasture	+ 80	+ 68	+ 90
Industry	+ 125	+ 33	+ 575
Administration	+ 9	+ 2	+ 65
Trade	+ 32	− 20	+ 198
Transport	− 62	+ 38	− 83
Domestic service	+ 110	+ 77	+ 158
Labour (indefinite)	− 24	− 47	+ 70
Professions	+ 163	+ 59	+ 1,400
Others	− 9	− 43	+ 43

Agriculture.

318. But it would be idle to pursue the comparison further. Nor do I propose to go into niceties over the present occupational census. Perhaps the shortest cut to the broad facts concealed in the mass of statistics is to pick out the main occupations of the indigenous peoples, leaving the detailed statistics to leaven the general impressions at which we arrive. And first and foremost comes agriculture. Now, though the ordinary scheme of occupations is almost absurdly elaborate for the very simple life of Balūchistān, we rashly went out of our way to add complexity to complexity by probing a little deeper into the various methods in which the agriculturists pursue their calling. But the results (the gist of which is given in the margin) would hardly tempt me to repeat the experiment. They certainly cannot be taken at their face value. To us a non-cultivating landlord conjures up a picture of the owner of broad acres, living at his ease on the produce of his estate. One has only to cast one's eye down the list of occupations in which the non-cultivating landlord of Balūchistān is prepared to engage (table XV-B), to appreciate how different our conception of the country squire may be from reality. For here in Balūchistān he is not only landlord but stock-breeder, camel-driver, labourer, even beggar. The truth of the matter is that it would be a little difficult to come across a tribesman who cannot call some wretched plot of land his own, just sufficient to enable him to fall in with the prevailing fashion and to glorify it into his main source of livelihood. The typical non-cultivating landlord is not the big chief or the man of wealth who disdains to sully his hands with the plough, but the poor man whose land is too unproductive for it to be worth his while to turn from his flocks or herds to look after it, especially when he can get some one even poorer than himself to do so for him. It is much the same with the statistics of the cultivating landlords and the various classes of tenants. The mere fact that fully a fourth of their number have also returned themselves as dependent on animals, either as breeders or drivers, is enough to make us suspect that agricul-

Non-cultivating landlords	22,531
Cultivating landlords	96,567
Tenants	58,501
Farm and field labourers	4,844

ture is not always their most paying concern. It is only the farm and field labourers whose figures are innocent of all traces of exaggeration. Here indeed the figures err on the other side. They take no account, for instance, of the swarms of people, chiefly pastoralist, who so arrange their gipsy wanderings that they are able to roam from one harvesting to another, both in their own country and in Sind, picking up not only a respectable little livelihood for themselves, but also some excellent grazing for their flocks and herds.

Pastoral pursuits.

319. Yet though the agricultural figures must be taken with a grain of salt, it is after all the spirit of the age that has infected them with their taint of exaggeration. Not only is agriculture rising in the public estimation, peace under our rule is enabling it to encroach on the old pastoral life more and more every day. Were the natural conditions of the country really favourable (and the fact that there are not 500 water mills in the country is a suggestive commentary on this point), the change would be rapid enough. But the supply of perennial water is limited, and a very large amount of the culturable land is dependent on flood or wholly on rain. Land no doubt, as the local proverb says, is a flock that never dies; but rain-crop cultivation, as another proverb puts it, is mighty like hunting the wild ass. If rain-crop land is all the land a family possesses, it is hopeless to rely entirely on so precarious a source of livelihood; and the petty landholder of the country is almost always an owner of flocks or herds. Time was, and not so very long ago either, when the sheep and the goat were the real staff of life in Balūchistān; even to-day they are all that stands between large numbers of the population and starvation or wholesale emigration. "The sheep," Nasīr Khān the Great was fond of saying (and the only reason why he did not mention the goat was that the sheep is the shepherd's pet, while the goat comes in for all his curses), "the sheep is a goodly tree that bears four and twenty fruits: flesh, wool, milk, curds, whey, ghee—" and a multitude of other products, for many of which the English language might be ransacked in vain to supply equivalents. It may perhaps seem a little curious that the prime importance of flocks in Balūchistān should find so faint an echo in the number of shepherds and goatherds: according to our statistics there are merely a couple of thousand actual herdsmen in the whole country. The simple explanation is that most flock-owners look after their flocks themselves; as for grazing, it is the regular thing to entrust it to the children or the poor old father who is getting past work. It is only the larger flock-owners or those who have valuable irrigated lands that engage outside shepherds. And there may be some little difficulty in securing them. For, according to the popular idea, a shepherd's life is not a happy one, and able-bodied youths are loth to take it up except in the last resort.

Pack animals.

320. Although sheep and goats are vital to the existence of so many of its inhabitants, Balūchistān seems to have produced no breeds of any repute outside it. Yet, curiously enough, the local breeds of those luxuries of pastoral life, the ox and the horse, have won a fame far beyond its borders. But it is not the countless sheep and goats, nor the magnificent Bhāg-Nāṛī and Bālā-Nāṛī breeds of cattle, nor even the famous Balōchī mares, that seem to catch the eye of the newcomer, but the apparently ubiquitous camels—especially when he sees them, as he may within half a dozen miles of Quetta, yoked to the plough. And indeed the camel ranks in local importance second to the sheep and the goat alone. With the exception of the patient ass, which is usually looked down upon as the characteristic drudge of the lowly Hindu and other poor creatures, it is the only natural means of transport in the country. In the old days, it is true, pack-animals were in no very great demand. The tribesmen were much more concerned to provide themselves with nags for their raids than with beasts of burden for transport, and merely kept enough camels and donkeys for their own small needs. It was not until the last Afghān war that their eyes were opened to the great profits to be gained from the camel. Rates went up a hundred-fold; everybody who could got hold of a string of camels and rapidly made his fortune. So developed a new and popular occupation, especially among the Sarāwān Brāhūīs, from what was originally a mere matter of personal

Live-stock.

	Camels.	Donkeys.	Horses.
Balūchistān.	**55,087**	**51,614**	**14,044**
Districts . .	23,542	24,902	7,360
States . . .	31,545	26,712	6,684

convenience. But though Government brought the trade into existence and has given it an impetus from time to time, the tribesmen are beginning to have an uneasy feeling that the railway extensions are dealing it its death-blow, and that the game is about played out. With the decline of government needs, the camel transport trade is languishing, and camel-breeding seems somewhat on the wane. But this is probably a merely temporary reaction after an abnormal boom in the trade. The camel still holds the field as the one form of local transport in Balūchistān, and it is difficult to see how it can ever be supplanted off the line of rail.

Barter and trade.

321. But comparatively modern though the regular camel-trade is, the camel itself has been essential to one characteristic means of livelihood in Balūchistān from time immemorial. To a man of Makrān for instance, a couple of camels is a veritable godsend. He loads them up with dwarf-palm leaves ; makes his way down to the coast ; barters his dwarf-palm for dried fish ; packs the fish on his camels ; and carries it off to the nearest date-grove, where he barters it for dates, only to dispose of them elsewhere ; and so he goes the round. This is typical of a very ancient form of trade in the Brāhūī and Balōch countries, and the centre of the trade is Makrān. At the time of the date-harvest, people flock in from far and near, bringing camels laden with fish, dwarf-palm, wheat, tobacco and all kinds of produce, and barter their loads for dates. And the process is repeated in miniature in the dwarf-palm areas. This *gwāchī* trade, as it is called, is almost the only form of trade that the Balōch and Brāhūī tribesmen do not think beneath them. The Paṭhān, curiously enough, is much more of a trader outside his own country than he ever is within it. Perhaps he prefers to trade—if trade he must—outside Balūchistān, on the same principle that the Brāhūī prefers to labour—if labour he must—in an alien country where his dignity as a tribesman will suffer no eclipse ; perhaps he thinks that his own countrymen are too poor to afford him a paying market ; perhaps he has too high an opinion of their business wits. The consequence is that most of the local trade is in the hands of the Hindus, and the only serious challengers of their monopoly are the European and Parsi traders in the towns, the Indian and Persian merchants on the trade-route, the Ghilzai pedlars in the Paṭhān country, and the fishmongering Khōjas on the sea-coast.

Tribal life.

322. We may now take a bird's-eye view of the economic life in the country. Society falls roughly into three main groups. At the top of the economic scale is the town-life, an artificial by-product of our administration, in which the tribesman at present plays but a fleeting part. Then there is the village community, to be seen at its height in the Kachhī, in which again the tribesman hardly plays an active part, only resorting to it every now and then to indulge in some new-found luxury. And lastly there is the tribal life, ranging from the purely nomadic life of the Bizanjav Brāhūī to the settled life of the Magasī Balōch. And this to us is by far the most important of the three. It is difficult to exaggerate its supreme simplicity. Take, for instance, the typical tribal life among Paṭhāns. A Paṭhān tribe with its few parasites is complete in itself. The tribesman is his own house-builder, grazier, husbandman. He may even be his own priest : at any rate there are priests in plenty among his fellow-tribesmen. He has no scavengers : his mode of life is such that one is hardly needed. He has no barbers : it's a case of shave me and I'll shave you—very possibly with a broken bit of glass. He has no midwives : any old crone about the place will perform the kindly office in his family. He has no potters : any vessels his womenfolk cannot make for him, he can get from the peddling Ghilzai, who also supplies him not only with copper-pots and glass bangles but with new-fangled shoes, which have recently driven the home-made rope and hide sandals out of fashion. The Ghilzai indeed is the only outsider on whose services he relies ; and he finds the *kārez*-digging Ghilzai even more indispensable than the Ghilzai pedlar, whose part after all could be easily taken by the tribal Hindu. In the Hindu, from whom he gets his sugar and his oil and his cloth (which his women fashion into garments in his own house) he has a general storekeeper, money-lender, grain-broker, ghee-broker, wool-broker, rolled into one. Almost equally invaluable is the blacksmith-*cum*-carpenter, who for a regular dole at

each harvest, will turn him out sickles and ploughshares, razors and door-chains, knives and daggers. And third and last of the tribal parasites are the itinerant weavers, who make him carpets and tent-coverings from the wool he himself supplies. Among the Brāhūīs and Balōch, though the women may be handier with distaff and needle, there is rather more division of labour in the tribal life, not so much because of their greater needs as because of their great laziness. Among them, for instance, the Lōṛī or blacksmith plays many parts, an indispensable jack of all trades (§ 284) ; the Lōṛī's wife is called upon to perform at least two important functions in domestic life, as go-between in marriage negotiations and as midwife. But life is becoming more complicated everywhere, widening perceptibly as a direct result of our administration. Facilities of communication have taught the tribesmen something of the tempting luxuries to be derived from the village community and the township, though so far neither the one nor the other is itself tempting enough to lure them to dwell in it. The standard of living among the tribesmen has risen out of all knowledge. New needs suggest new means of livelihood to supply them. Occupations which their fathers scorned are gradually being adopted one by one. A labour market has been opened at their doors : even distant markets are beginning to attract them, for labour has become mobile. Hence it is that most of the complex occupational groups that now figure in the census statistics have received recruits even from the tribesmen, though the recruiting is still very languid. But with each succeeding census we may expect that the tribal numbers, now lumped round agriculture and pastoralism, will become increasingly dissipated over the more specialised forms of occupation.

Raiding and thieving as occupations.

323. But primitive as is the economic life of our tribesmen, it was much more primitive before we came to the country. And no picture of present-day Balūchistān would appear in its true light unless it stood out in contrast with the Balūchistān of bygone days. Asked to state their principal occupation, the Marī Balōch mistook our meaning—we incautiously used the ambiguous word *aslī*, which may mean either principal or original—and began to put themselves down wholesale as raiders, and the enumerator (himself a Marī and one of the most intelligent men in the tribe) protested indignantly when the accuracy of his record was called in question. But the forays of the Marī and Bugṭī are things of the past, and in any case they are so well-known that I will turn from these ancient border raiders to those lesser known but notable highwaymen, burglars, cattle-lifters, rifle-thieves—the Achakzai Paṭhān (§253). Though the Achakzai are now on the reform, the old Adam is still alive among them ; indeed it is popularly believed that, when an Achakzai is stricken in years and getting past work, he cannot woo sleep unless he first pilfers something out of his house and hides it away. Not that the Achakzai are all tarred with the same brush. There is of course many an Achakzai, and for the matter of that many an Achakzai section, whose conduct—for Paṭhāns—is irreproachable. Yet in recent times the Usmānzai section are commonly supposed to have been driven by the force of tribal opinion from unsportsmanlike honesty into joining the gentle craft of burglars ; and many of them have accordingly shifted over into Afghānistān in search of a better opening for their new profession, now languishing under the unsympathetic regime of British Government. Some sections specialise in one branch of the profession, some in another. The Ghaibizai Bādīnzai are expert cattle-lifters and confirmed kleptomaniacs on a petty scale, always very chary of risking their hides. The reckless daring of the Hamīdzai Gujanzai stops at nothing. But the real aristocrats of the profession are the Kākōzai Bādīnzai. Their forefather Kākō, I am told, once made an ecstatic flight through the air with a gobbet of flesh between his teeth ; and to a Kākōzai this pious legend is proof positive that burglary is a highly respectable calling for Kākō's descendants. But I dare say I have left out some step in the argument. Anyhow they are such past-masters in the art that their pride in it is almost pardonable ; and if genius is really an infinite capacity for taking pains, they have assuredly good claims to the title.

Burglary as fine art.

324. With a hearty contempt for the botching of amateur cracksmen, they always go over every inch of the ground beforehand, whether they work near home or far afield. It takes a gang of five to bring off a really artistic burglary. They fare forth severally and take service in houses worthy of their

attentions. Each stays with his unsuspecting master long enough to learn all the ins and outs of the house. Then, chock-full of useful knowledge, they throw up service and forgather to compare notes. The honours of the day rest of course with the late servant of the richest house, and off they go to his old haunt to master the topography. On the great night they meet a few miles from the doomed house. If the ground is frozen enough to make tracking difficult, they put on leather shoes called *sug'lê*. But if there's any danger of being tracked, they wrap bits of rug round their feet. They strip themselves almost to the skin, and see to it that what little clothing they keep on is dirty enough to be invisible in the dark. The rest they hand over to the least useful member of the gang, and drop him behind about a mile from the house. Then with pouches crammed with stones, they move forward to within a hundred yards of their quarry, where one is posted as *tsärü* to keep on the look-out. The others make their way stealthily to the house and set to work on the wall, which they breach with a *sīkhcha* or jemmy. As soon as the breach is big enough, the bravest of the gang squeezes through, armed to the teeth. Cautiously he strikes a light and takes a hasty look round. If there's somebody asleep in the room, he calls one of his comrades to stand over the sleeper with a drawn sword, while he himself hands the treasure to the man outside. As soon as he has made a clean sweep, he joins his comrade, and they decamp with the booty. The man on guard gives them a few minutes' grace, and then follows suit, going through the hole backwards, in case the sleeper has been sleeping with one eye open all the time, and should raise the alarm or attack him in the back. Once clear of the house they spread out, each finding his own way to the tryst, where the spoils are to be divided. A lion's share goes to the hero who first entered the breach ; half a share is good enough for the man who looked after the clothes. Not that the fates are always on their side. Many a pretty piece of work has been spoilt by interruption. If there's anything amiss, the man on the look-out attracts his comrades by flinging a pebble towards them. Once the alarm is raised, they take to their heels in different directions. Should one of them run into the crowd, he joins in the hue and cry, bellowing "Stop thief !" with the loudest, but soon lags behind and sneaks off. If the gang is rounded up, they turn and offer a stout resistance pelting their pursuers with stones from their pouches and, if needs must, slashing about them with their swords. If the worst comes to the worst, they abandon their hard-gotten booty, and make off as best they may, but whenever they can, they conceal it in the hopes of recovering it when the coast is clear. In the good old days (and those days are not quite dead) it was a recognised thing for the thieves, if eventually tracked and unable to clear themselves on oath, to disgorge two-thirds of the loot and to retain the rest as *pshep't* or "foot-covering"—a slight sop for all the wear and tear of foot-gear they had been put to. A lad is initiated into the mysteries of the profession as early as possible. He first tries his prentice-hand with the bundle of clothes. Then he acts as scout. Then he is taken along to learn the art of breaching a wall, but all he does at first is to hand the tools and make himself generally useful. If he gets through his probation creditably, he has to enter the house himself and pass out the loot. His apprenticeship is now over: he is fully fledged, a master of the craft, entitled to his full share of the spoil.

Rifle-theft.

325. Of rifle-theft, needless to say, they make a speciality, though in this branch of the business they have nowadays little scope within Balūchistān itself, for long and bitter experience has taught their prey most of the tricks of the trade. Here again their success is due not so much to their skill, admirable though it is, as to their close study of every factor in the problem. The whole surroundings, the petty habits of the sentry, his exact beat, the pros and cons between the moment of greatest drowsiness (when he is nearing the end of his watch) and of greatest stupor (when the relief first comes out from the light into the dark)—everything down to the smallest detail is gone over again and again before they venture upon action. And when such close study of details is combined with consummate skill in stalking behind a screen of leaves or in a goat's skin, small blame to the sentry who to his cost takes the thief on a pitch-black night for a dog or a bush, if indeed his attention is attracted at all before it is too late.

Highway robber.

326. As highwaymen, they are equally artistic in their methods. While the gang lurks in hiding close by, the most raggamuffinly of the lot squats by the roadside, counting his beads with an unctuous piety that allays all suspicion, and keeping up a flow of devout ejaculations as wayfarers pass by. Along comes a caravan too strong to be overpowered. *Allāh y^{a}ū, numūna ya ḍēr dī, chi pa k^{a}m nām^{a} bē-bōl^{a}m* ?—"God is One! but His names are *many!* By which name shall I call him?" bawls the holy man. And the caravan passes slowly and safely on, little dreaming that such innocent and devotional words have saved them from attack. Presently up comes another which ought to fall an easy prey. And at the words *lā ilāha illallāh, allāh y^{a}ū dai, p^{a}r rā g^{a}rz^{a}ī*, "There is no God but Allah! Allah is *One*! So—*down* on 'em!" out rush the gang, pounce on the travellers, strip them of every stitch and their camels of every load, bind them hand and foot, kick them blindfolded into a ditch, and go on their way rejoicing.

XXIX.—Occupational Variation 1901-1911.

Occupation.	TOTAL POPULATION SUPPORTED.								
	In 1901.			In 1911.			Variation Increase (+) Decrease (—).		
	Balūchistān.	Districts.	States.	Balūchistān.	Districts.	States.	Balūchistān.	Districts.	States.
Agriculture	577,557	261,423	316,134	566,400	274,079	292,321	−11,157	+12,656	−23,813
Pasture	51,724	24,471	27,253	93,033	41,194	51.839	+41,309	+16,723	+24,586
Industry	16,523	13.701	2,822	37,233	18,185	19,048	+20,710	+4,484	+16,226
Transport	75,159	13,008	62,151	28,756	17,972	10,784	−46,403	+4,964	−51,367
Trade	22,087	16,776	5,311	29,263	13,452	15,811	+7,176	−3,324	+10,500
Administration	27,762	24,486	3,276	30,393	24,983	5,410	+2,631	+497	+2,134
Arts and professions	4,253	3,923	330	11,169	6,220	4,949	+6,916	+2,297	+4,619
Domestic service	6,807	4,039	2,768	14.294	7,158	7,136	+7,487	+3,119	+4,368
Labour (indefinite)	13,650	10,988	2,662	10,369	5,845	4,514	−3,291	−5,143	+1,852
Others	15,224	9,291	5,933	13,803	5,324	8,479	−1,421	−3,967	+2,546

XXX.—Occupational distribution per 1,000 actual workers among Selected Tribes.

NAME OF TRIBE.	Agriculture.	Pasture.	Industry.	Transport.	Trade.	Administration.	Art and professions.	Domestic service.	Labour unspecified.	Others.
Balōch	**843**	**79**	**11**	**23**	**5**	**11**	**3**	**4**	**5**	**16**
Eastern	*905*	*58*	*8*	*5*	*2*	*6*	*3*	*8*	*4*	*6*
Bugṭī	865	113	4	...	1	1	...	...	11	5
Khetrān	942	23	9	...	1	11	5	3	1	5
Magasī	908	54	11	1	6	2	2	9	4	3
Marī	882	90	12	3	...	7	...	...	1	5
Rind	929	18	5	13	1	11	6	4	4	9
Western	*660*	*143*	*20*	*75*	*15*	*24*	*4*	*4*	*8*	*47*
Rakhshānī and Naushērwānī	618	214	8	88	5	45	5	2	9	6
Brāhūī	**666**	**216**	**7**	**50**	**7**	**26**	**4**	**4**	**13**	**7**
Original nucleus	*640*	*253*	*7*	*80*	*7*	*36*	*2*	*8*	*11*	*11*
Sarāwān	*739*	*83*	*9*	*84*	*7*	*41*	*6*	*7*	*18*	*6*
Bangulzai	770	86	8	70	2	48	6	4	7	4
Lāngav	813	25	17	79	11	13	3	12	26	2
Jhalawān	*627*	*289*	*6*	*32*	*8*	*15*	*8*	*2*	*11*	*7*
Bīzanjav	537	375	5	43	14	4	2	4	4	12
Māmasanī	478	391	5	52	4	22	7	6	20	15
Mengal	557	353	8	37	6	22	3	2	8	4
Zehrī	747	191	4	20	10	11	1	1	12	8
Paṭhān	**802**	**93**	**14**	**20**	**8**	**26**	**10**	**3**	**14**	**10**
Kākaṛ	757	128	10	22	8	29	11	4	19	12
Sanzarkhēl	*743*	*161*	*11*	*15*	*6*	*26*	*9*	*8*	*14*	*12*
Snaṭia	*764*	*81*	*6*	*33*	*9*	*44*	*14*	*8*	*27*	*14*
Targhaṛa	*827*	*31*	*12*	*36*	*19*	*16*	*18*	*4*	*30*	*12*
Paṇī	832	89	25	4	5	30	5	1	1	8
Mūsakhēl	*945*	*16*	*10*	*2*	*1*	*16*	*3*	*1*	*1*	*5*
Tarīn	874	25	12	30	7	17	10	4	11	10
Abdāl Achakzai	*894*	*4*	*8*	*33*	*8*	*20*	*9*	*6*	*12*	*6*
Tōr Tarīn	*875*	*19*	*12*	*34*	*6*	*15*	*12*	*1*	*12*	*14*
Lāsi	**601**	**300**	**28**	**16**	**4**	**18**	**2**	**1**	**11**	**19**
Jaṭṭ	**816**	**45**	**87**	**11**	**4**	**5**	**14**	**4**	**3**	**11**
Sayyid	**749**	**66**	**16**	**16**	**24**	**24**	**90**	**3**	**9**	**3**
Other Musalmāns	**523**	**41**	**192**	**55**	**24**	**22**	**35**	**6**	**21**	**81**
Darzāda	790	7	116	11	13	6	13	9	4	31
Lōṛī	123	8	600	1	5	4	127	6	6	120

XXXI.—Agricultural Implements, Live-stock, etc.

District or State.	Water mills.	Hand mills.	Ploughs.	LIVE-STOCK.				
				Plough bullocks.	Horses.	Donkeys.	CAMELS	
							of settled inhabitants.	of nomads.
BALŪCHISTĀN	***492***	***83,336***	***75,924***	***139,304***	***14,044***	***51,614***	***39,541***	***15,546***
DISTRICTS	**409**	**32,312**	**33,327**	**60,425**	**7,360**	**24,902**	**15,818**	**7,724**
Quetta-Pishīn	197	2,753	5,381	6,350	840	5,261	3,993	551
Lōṛalai	84	8,702	9,645	18,331	2,331	4,018	879	5,315
Zhōb	67	4,267	5,303	9,015	661	4,133	4,261	9
Bōlān	...	93	54	94	18	8	3	3
Chāgai	6	1,225	1,215	830	76	1,355	4,572	372
Sibī	55	15,272	11,729	25,805	3,434	10,127	2,110	1,474
Administered area	*51*	*9,559*	*9,050*	*18,335*	*2,186*	*4,138*	*1,610*	*364*
Marī Bugṭī country	*4*	*5,713*	*2,679*	*7,470*	*1,248*	*5,989*	*500*	*1,110*
STATES	**83**	**51,024**	**42,597**	**78,879**	**6,684**	**26,712**	**23,723**	**7,822**
Kalāt	80	42.838	35,730	67,514	5,725	22,266	19,259	6,564
Sarāwān	*49*	*7,642*	*5,468*	*8,630*	*2,000*	*5,287*	*5,434*	*2,251*
Jhalawān	*15*	*12,162*	*8,478*	*16,608*	*914*	*6,582*	*3,048*	*1,975*
Kachhī	*14*	*14,354*	*13,883*	*27,525*	*2,131*	*3,991*	*5,889*	*896*
Ḍōmbkī-Kahērī country	*1*	*3,510*	*3,634*	*7,274*	*457*	*873*	*761*	*296*
Makrān	*1*	*4,983*	*4,111*	*7,165*	*219*	*5,443*	*3,999*	*1,646*
Khārān[1]	...	*187*	*156*	*312*	*4*	*90*	*128*	...
Las Bēla	3	8,186	6,867	11,365	959	4,446	4,464	1,258

[1] Statistics were unfortunately collected in the Rakhshān circle only.

CENSUS OF INDIA, 1911

VOLUME IV

BALUCHISTAN

Part II—TABLES

PART II.—CONTENTS.

IMPERIAL TABLES.

PROVINCIAL TABLES.

TABLE I.

Area, Houses and Population.

The census of Balūchistān was made up of two parts (*i*) the regular census of towns, bazars and other alien settlements, which was conducted in the ordinary manner on the standard Indian schedule on the night of the 10th March 1911, and (*ii*) the non-synchronous census of the tribesmen and other indigenous inhabitants on a schedule peculiar to Balūchistān, which was carried out during the previous summer, except in K͟hārān, where operations were for political reasons not feasible till the autumn of 1911. The results may be summarized thus:—

	Persons	Males	Females
Regular Census . .	63,007	49,271	13,736
Tribal Census . .	771,696	417,148	354,548
Balūchistān . .	834,703	466,419	368,284

The term 'house' includes not only houses, but also blanket-tents and other movable or temporary dwellings. The term 'village' includes not only villages in the ordinary sense of the word, but also localities which, though possibly containing no permanent dwellings, are regularly occupied at certain seasons of the year. 172,649 souls in all were enumerated in 912 localities of this description in various parts of the country:—

	Periodically inhabited localities	Population		Periodically inhabited localities	Population
Districts .	***253***	***69,956***	***States*** . .	***659***	***102,693***
Quetta-Pishīn .	80	13,893	Kalāt . . .	523	81,979
Lōralai . .	31	12,153	*Sarāwān* . .	*106*	*21,651*
Zhōb . .	15	5,146	*Jhalawān* . .	*260*	*46,416*
Chāgai . .	19	3,724	*Kachhī* . .	*13*	*1,117*
Sibī . .	108	35,040	*Makrān* . .	*111*	*6,045*
Administered area.	*21*	*4,093*	*K͟hārān* . .	*33*	*6,750*
Marī-Bugṭī country	*87*	*30,947*	Las Bēla . .	136	20,714

The various areas have been supplied by the Survey Department and differ—in some cases materially—from those hitherto accepted.

I.—AREA, HOUSES AND POPULATION.

District or State	Area in square miles	Towns	Villages	OCCUPIED HOUSES			POPULATION								
							PERSONS			MALES			FEMALES		
				Total	In Towns	In Villages	Total	Urban	Rural	Total	Urban	Rural	Total	Urban	Rural
1	2	3	4	5	6	7	8	9	10	11	12	13	14	15	16
Balūchistān	***134,638***	***9***	***3,684***	***168,667***	***14,906***	***153,761***	***834,703***	***59,559***	***775,144***	***466,419***	***43,028***	***423,391***	***368,284***	***16,531***	***351,753***
Districts	**54,228**	**6**	**1,564**	**84,689**	**12,671**	**72,018**	**414,412**	**49,609**	**364,803**	**239,181**	**37,660**	**201,521**	**175,231**	**11,949**	**163,282**
Quetta-Pishin	5,220	3	414	27,937	9,731	18,206	127,648	36,685	90,963	76,467	27,391	49,076	51,181	9,294	41,887
Lōṛalai	7,525	1	446	16,512	847	15,665	80,769	2,936	77,833	44,923	2,428	42,495	35,846	508	35,338
Zhōb	10,315	1	276	15,043	581	14,462	70,366	3,391	66,975	40,346	2,941	37,405	30,020	450	29,570
Bōlān	353	..	13	814	..	814	2,096	..	2,096	1,492	..	1,492	604	..	604
Chāgai	19,622	..	62	3,635	..	3,635	16,344	..	16,344	9,107	..	9,107	7,237	..	7,237
Sibī	11,193	1	353	20,748	1,512	19,236	117,189	6,597	110,592	66,846	4,900	61,946	50,343	1,697	48,646
Administered area	*3,925*	*1*	*257*	*16,311*	*1,512*	*14,799*	*82,423*	*6,597*	*75,826*	*47,558*	*4,900*	*42,658*	*34,865*	*1,697*	*33,168*
Marī-Bugṭī country	*7,268*	..	*96*	*4,437*	..	*4,437*	*34,766*	..	*34,766*	*19,288*	..	*19,288*	*15,478*	..	*15,478*
States	**80,410**	**3**	**2,120**	**83,978**	**2,235**	**81,743**	**420,291**	**9,950**	**410,341**	**227,238**	**5,368**	**221,870**	**193,053**	**4,582**	**188,471**
Kalāt	73,278	2	1,824	71,387	1,532	69,855	359,086	6,944	352,142	194,598	3,809	190,789	164,488	3,135	161,353
Sarāwān	*5,230*	*2*	*322*	*12,951*	*1,532*	*11,419*	*63,781*	*6,944*	*56,837*	*35,082*	*3,809*	*31,273*	*28,699*	*3,135*	*25,564*
Jhalawān	*20,795*	..	*419*	*17,095*	..	*17,095*	*84,398*	..	*84,398*	*46,880*	..	*46,880*	*37,518*	..	*37,518*
Kachhī	*4,060*	..	*590*	*16,081*	..	*16,081*	*92,759*	..	*92,759*	*50,191*	..	*50,191*	*42,568*	..	*42,568*
Ḍōmbkī-Kahērī country	*1,359*	..	*22*	*3,791*	..	*3,791*	*23,543*	..	*23,543*	*12,624*	..	*12,624*	*10,919*	..	*10,919*
Makrān	*23,269*	..	*381*	*16,016*	..	*16,016*	*71,942*	..	*71,942*	*37,698*	..	*37,698*	*34,244*	..	*34,244*
Khārān	*18,565*	..	*90*	*5,453*	..	*5,453*	*22,663*	..	*22,663*	*12,123*	..	*12,123*	*10,540*	..	*10,540*
Las Bēla	7,132	1	296	12,591	703	11,888	61,205	3,006	58,199	32,640	1,559	31,081	28,565	1,447	27,118

TABLE II.

Variation in Population since 1901.

Census results in 1891, 1901 and 1911 may be summarised thus :—

Year	Area in square miles dealt with	Population		
		Total	Estimated	Enumerated
1891 . .	20,568	171,752	142,473	29,279
1901 . .	82,950	810,746	459,728	351,018
1911 . .	134,638	834,703	..	834,703

The first census of 1891 was too rough and fragmentary to lend itself for comparison in the following Table.

The figures for 1901 have been adjusted in view of subsequent changes in administrative charges, the chief of which was the splitting up of the Zhōb and Thal-Chōtiāli districts into Lōṛalai, Zhōb and Sibī in 1903. No attempt has been made to adjust the rough estimates in the native states, the sanguine nature of which accounts for the apparent decrease in Kalāt at the present census.

The following areas are included in the census for the first time :—

New census areas	District or State	Method of census	Population
Western Sanjrānī	Chāgai . . .	Enumerated . .	1,620
Makrān . .	Kalāt . . .	Enumerated . .	71,942
Khārān . .	Kalāt . . .	Enumerated .	22,663

II.—VARIATION IN POPULATION SINCE 1901.

District or State	1911			1901			VARIATION 1901-11 INCREASE + DECREASE −		
	Persons	Males	Females	Persons	Males	Females	Persons	Males	Females
1	2	3	4	5	6	7	8	9	10
Balūchistān	***834,703***	***466,419***	***368,284***	***810,746***	***445,520***	***365,226***	***+23,957***	***+20,899***	***+3,058***
Districts	**414,412**	**239,181**	**175,231**	**382,106**	**219,523**	**162,583**	**+32,306**	**+19,658**	**+12,648**
Quetta-Pishīn	127,648	76,467	51.181	114,087	68,945	45.142	+13,561	+7,522	+6,089
Lōṛalai	80,769	44.923	35,846	68,332	38,088	30,244	+12,437	+6,835	+5,602
Zhōb	70,366	40,346	30,020	69,718	39,637	30,081	+648	+709	−61
Bōlān	2,096	1,492	604	1,936	1.483	453	+160	+9	+151
Chāgai	16,344	9,107	7,237	15,689	8,259	7,430	+655	+848	—193
Sibī	117,189	66.846	50,343	112,344	63.111	49,233	+4,845	+3,735	+1,110
Administered area	*82,423*	*47,558*	*34,865*	*77.987*	*43,836*	*34,151*	*+4,436*	*+3,722*	*+714*
Mari-Bugti country	*34,766*	*19,288*	*15,478*	*34,357*	*19,275*	*15,082*	*+409*	*+13*	*+396*
States	**420,291**	**227,238**	**193,053**	**428,640**	**225,997**	**202,643**	**—8,349**	**+1,241**	**—9,590**
Kalāt	359,086	194,598	164,488	372,531	196,279	176,252	—13,445	- 1,681	—11,764
Sarāwān	*63,781*	*35,082*	*28,699*	*65,549*	*36,366*	*29,183*	*—1,768*	*—1,284*	*−484*
Jhalawān	*84,398*	*46,880*	*37,518*	*224,073*	*115,077*	*108,996*	*—139,675*	*—68,197*	*—71,478*
Kachhi	*92,759*	*50,191*	*42,568*	*63,367*	*34,251*	*29,116*	*+29,392*	*+15,940*	*+13,452*
Ḍōmbki-Kahēri country	*23,543*	*12,624*	*10,919*	*19,542*	*10,585*	*8,957*	*+4,001*	*+2,039*	*+1,962*
Makrān	*71,942*	*37,698*	*34,244*	...	...	...	*+71,942*	*+37,698*	*+34,244*
Khārān	*22,663*	*12,123*	*10,540*	...	...	...	*+22,663*	*+12,123*	*+10,540*
Las Bēla	61,205	32,640	28,565	56,109	29,718	26,391	+5,096	+2,922	+2,174

TABLE III.

Towns and Villages Classified by Population.

In this Table column 2 includes 912 periodically inhabited localities (*vide* Table I note). Column 3 includes 2,497 persons counted on road, railway and steamer :—

	Road	Railway	Steamer
Districts	*499*	*1,394*	..
Quetta-Pishīn	..	307	..
Lōṛalai	56	..	..
Zhōb	443	..	..
Bōlān	..	415	..
Chāgai	..	38	..
Sibī	..	634	..
States	..	..	*604*
Makrān	..	..	604

III.—TOWNS AND VILLAGES CLASSIFIED BY POPULATION.

District or State	Total number of inhabited towns and villages	Population	UNDER 500		500—1,000		1,000—2,000		2,000—5,000		5,000—10,000		20,000—50,000	
			Number	Population	Number	Population	Number	Population	Number	Population	Number	Population	Number	Population
1	2	3	4	5	6	7	8	9	10	11	12	13	14	15
Balūchistān	***3,693***	***834,703***	***3,298***	***415,817***	***282***	***189,658***	***90***	***124,368***	***20***	***56,837***	***2***	***11,604***	***1***	***33,922***
Districts	**1,570**	**414,412**	**1,366**	**176,862**	**143**	**96,019**	**49**	**68,841**	**10**	**30,278**	**1**	**6,597**	**1**	**33,922**
Quetta-Pishin	417	127,648	358	42,407	44	28,554	12	17,192	2	5,266	..	..	1	33,922
Lōralai	447	80,769	414	45,955	22	16,263	9	12,501	2	5,994	..	..	..	..
Zhōb	277	70,366	240	31,947	25	15,962	10	15,441	2	6,573	..	..	..	..
Bōlān	13	2,096	11	544	2	1,137	..	..	..	..	..	..	..	..
Chāgai	62	16,344	52	7,315	6	4,583	4	4,408	..	..	..	..	..	..
Sibī	354	117,189	291	48,694	44	29,520	14	19,299	4	12,445	1	6,597	..	..
Administered area	*258*	*82,423*	*211*	*34,372*	*34*	*23,279*	*11*	*14,988*	*1*	*2,553*	*1*	*6,597*	..	..
Marī Bugṭī country	*96*	*34,766*	*80*	*14,322*	*10*	*6,241*	*3*	*4,311*	*3*	*9,892*	..	..	..	..
States	**2,123**	**420,291**	**1,932**	**238,955**	**139**	**93,639**	**41**	**55,527**	**10**	**26,559**	**1**	**5,007**	..	..
Kalāt	1,826	359,086	1,666	203,308	112	76,734	39	52,592	8	20,841	1	5,007	..	..
Sarāwān	*324*	*63,781*	*298*	*36,678*	*17*	*10,527*	*8*	*11,569*	..	..	*1*	*5,007*	..	..
Jhalawān	*419*	*84,398*	*383*	*57,808*	*32*	*21,765*	*4*	*4,825*	..	..	..	..	..	..
Kachhi	*590*	*92,759*	*561*	*60,517*	*16*	*11,170*	*11*	*16,219*	*2*	*4,853*	..	..	..	..
Ḍōmbkī Kahērī country	*22*	*23,543*	*6*	*789*	*8*	*5,817*	*4*	*5,476*	*4*	*11,461*	..	..	..	..
Makrān	*381*	*71,942*	*342*	*35,725*	*27*	*19,086*	*10*	*12,000*	*2*	*4,527*	..	..	..	..
Khārān	*90*	*22,663*	*76*	*11,791*	*12*	*8,369*	*2*	*2,503*	..	..	..	..	..	..
Las Bēla	297	61,205	266	35,647	27	16,905	2	2,935	2	5,718	..	..	..	..

TABLE IV.

Towns Classified by Population with Variation since 1891.

Pishīn, Chaman, Fort Sandeman, Sibī, Kalāt, Mastung and Bēla were not treated as towns in 1891; the three last have now been treated as towns for the first time. Where past figures are available they are printed in italics, but not included in the totals.

IV.—TOWNS CLASSIFIED BY POPULATION WITH VARIATION SINCE 1891.

Town	District or State	Municipality, suburbs, cantonments, etc.	Population			Variation Increase + Decrease —			Males			Females		
			1911	1901	1891	1901-1911	1891-1901	1891-1911	1911	1901	1891	1911	1901	1891
1	2	3	4	5	6	7	8	9	10	11	12	13	14	15
	Baluchistan		***59,559***	***40,033***	***22,476***	***+19,526***	***+17,557***	***+37,083***	***43,028***	***31,757***	***19,329***	***16,531***	***8,276***	***3,147***
	Districts		**49,609**	**40,033**	**22,476**	**+9,576**	**+17,557**	**+27,133**	**37,660**	**31,757**	**19,329**	**11,949**	**8,276**	**3,147**
1. Quetta	Quetta-Pishin		33,922	24,584	18,802	+9,338	+5,782	+15,120	25,269	19,151	15,813	8,653	5,433	2,989
		Cantonments	*16,901*	*11,067*	*7,500*	*+5,834*	*+3,567*	*+9,401*	*13,813*	*9,689*	*6,625*	*3,088*	*1,378*	*875*
		Municipality (and suburbs)	*17,021*	*13,517*	*11,302*	*+3,504*	*+2,215*	*+5,719*	*11,456*	*9,462*	*9,188*	*5,565*	*4,055*	*2,114*
2. Pishīn	Quetta-Pishīn		754	1,552	*532*	—798	+1,552	+754	517	1,316	*415*	237	236	*117*
3. Chaman	Quetta-Pishīn		2,009	2,233	..	—224	+2,233	+2,009	1,605	1,867	..	404	366	..
4. Lōṛalai	Lōṛalai		2,936	3,561	3,674	—625	—113	—738	2,428	3,118	3,516	508	443	158
5. Fort Sandeman	Zhōb		3,391	3,552	..	—161	+3,552	+3,391	2,941	3,139	..	450	413	..
6. Sibī	Sibī		6,597	4,551	*2,914*	+2,046	+4,551	+6,597	4,900	3,166	*2,186*	1,697	1,385	*758*
	States		**9,950**	..	..	**+9,950**	..	**+9,950**	**5,368**	..	..	**4,582**	..	..
7. Kalāt	Kalāt		1,937	*2,000*	..	+1,937	..	+1,937	1,034	*1,068*	..	903	*932*	..
8. Mastung	Kalāt		5,007	..	..	+5,007	..	+5,007	2,775	..	..	2,232	..	..
9. Bēla	Las Bēla		3,006	*4,183*	..	+3,006	..	+3,006	1,559	*2,169*	..	1,447	*2,014*	..

TABLE V

Towns arranged Territorially with Population by Religion.

160 Chūhṛa and 18 Sāhṇsī who returned their religion as such have been classified as Hindu and included in columns 8 and 9 :—

Town	Chūhṛa		Sāhṇsī	
	Males	Females	Males	Females
Quetta Cantonments	2	5	..	..
Quetta Municipality	60	32	8	10
Lōṛalai	3	2	..	..
Fort Sandeman	16	9	..	..
Sibī	10	..	..	..
Kalāt	1	..	..	..
Mastung	4	2	..	..
Bēla	8	6	..	..

Columns 20 and 21 are made up thus :—

Town	Jew		Buddhist		Jain		No religion	
	Males	Females	Males	Females	Males	Females	Males	Females
Quetta Cantonments	5	5	2	..	..	..	..	..
Quetta Municipality	22	15	4	6	8	1	1	..
Fort Sandeman	1	..	1	1	..	..	..	..
Sibī	2	2	..	..	..	..	..	..
Bēla	..	..	1	..	..	..	..	..

V.—TOWNS ARRANGED TERRITORIALLY WITH POPULATION BY RELIGION.

District or State	Town	Population: Persons	Population: Males	Population: Females	Musalmān: Males	Musalmān: Females	Hindu: Males	Hindu: Females	Sikh: Males	Sikh: Females	Ārya: Males	Ārya: Females	Brahmō: Males	Brahmō: Females	Christian: Males	Christian: Females	Zoroastrian: Males	Zoroastrian: Females	Others: Males	Others: Females
1	2	3	4	5	6	7	8	9	10	11	12	13	14	15	16	17	18	19	20	21
Balūchistān .		***59,559***	***43,028***	***16,531***	***22,514***	***9,518***	***13,330***	***4,839***	***2,973***	***748***	***335***	***197***	***19***	***19***	***3,720***	***1,108***	***90***	***72***	***47***	***30***
Districts .		**49,609**	**37,660**	**11,949**	**17,777**	**5,358**	**12,782**	**4,455**	**2,898**	**712**	**335**	**197**	**19**	**19**	**3,713**	**1,106**	**90**	**72**	**46**	**30**
Quetta-Pishīn .	1. Quetta . . .	33,922	25,269	8,653	11,512	3,741	8,439	3,226	1.413	442	260	159	14	9	3,514	990	75	59	42	27
	Cantonment .	*16,901*	*13,813*	*3,088*	*5,568*	*973*	*4,658*	*1,373*	*400*	*68*	*18*	*4*	*2*	...	*3,151*	*657*	*9*	*8*	*7*	*5*
	Municipality (and suburbs).	*17,021*	*11,456*	*5,565*	*5,944*	*2,768*	*3,781*	*1,853*	*1,013*	*374*	*242*	*155*	*12*	*9*	*363*	*333*	*66*	*51*	*35*	*22*
	2. Pishīn . . .	754	517	237	312	144	146	75	55	13	4	5	...	...	...	...	...	...	...	...
	3. Chaman . . .	2,009	1,605	404	694	184	541	175	333	16	7	4	...	...	30	25	...	...	...	...
Lōralai . .	4. Lōralai . . .	2,936	2,428	508	1,075	177	705	226	692	85	13	5	...	2	42	13	1	...	...	...
Zhōb . . .	5. Fort Sandeman .	3,391	2,941	450	1,856	192	859	171	161	63	17	5	2	5	44	13	...	...	2	1
Sibi . . .	6. Sibi	6,597	4,900	1,697	2,328	920	2,092	582	344	93	34	19	3	3	83	65	14	13	2	2
States .		**9,950**	**5,368**	**4,582**	**4,737**	**4,160**	**548**	**384**	**75**	**36**	...	...	...	...	**7**	**2**	...	...	**1**	...
Kalāt . . .	7. Kalāt . . .	1,937	1,034	903	826	734	183	148	25	21	...	...	...	...	...	...	...	...	...	...
	8. Mastung . .	5,007	2,775	2,232	2,591	2,095	181	135	...	...	...	...	...	...	3	2	...	...	...	...
Las Bēla . . .	9. Bēla . . .	3,006	1,559	1,447	1,320	1,331	184	101	50	15	...	...	...	...	4	...	...	...	1	...

TABLE VI.

Religion.

Of the Chūhra community 263 (males 174, females 89) returned themselves as Musalmān, 3,003 (males 1,940, females 1,063) as Hindu, and 33 (males 26, females 7) as Sikh, and have been classified accordingly.

968 Chūhra (males 572, females 396) returned themselves as Chūhra simply, and have been classified as Hindu :—

	Persons	Males	Females
Quetta-Pishīn	123	77	46
Lōralai	35	26	9
Zhōb	44	34	10
Bōlān	15	13	2
Chāgai	1	1	..
Sibī	449	256	193
Kalāt.	285	155	130
Las Bēla	16	10	6

18 Sāhnsi (males 8, females 10) returned as such in Quetta-Pishīn have been similarly classified as Hindu.

The last two columns headed 'Others' are made up as follows :—

	Zoroastrian		Jew		Buddhist		Jain		No religion	
	Males	Females	Males	Females	Males	Females	Males	Females	Males	Females
Quetta-Pishīn .	77	60	27	20	6	6	8	1	1	..
Lōralai . .	1	..	..	..	..	..	..	..	..	..
Zhōb . .	..	..	1	..	1	1	1	..	..	..
Bōlān . .	1	..	..	..	..	..	..	..	..	..
Sibī . .	14	13	4	5	..	..	..	..	..	..
Makrān . .	3	1	..	..	1	..	..	..	..	..
Las Bēla . .	..	..	..	..	1	..	..	..	..	..

VI.—RELIGIONS.

District or State.	Population			Musalmān									
				Total		Sunnī		Shia'		Zikrī		Others	
	Persons	Males	Females	Males	Females	Males	Females	Males	Females	Males	Females	Males	Females
1	2	3	4	5	6	7	8	9	10	11	12	13	14
Balūchistān	***834,703***	***466,419***	***368,284***	***430,850***	***351,798***	***412,460***	***337,449***	***3,410***	***1,413***	***14,765***	***12,823***	***215***	***113***
Districts	**414,412**	**239,181**	**175,231**	**211,828**	**165,528**	**209,038**	**164,729**	**2,581**	**691**	**1**	..	**208**	**108**
Quetta-Pishīn	127,648	76,467	51,181	60,950	45,752	58,862	45,087	1,939	584	1	..	148	81
Lōṛalai	80,769	44,923	35,846	41,955	34,800	41,809	34,762	119	23	..	..	27	15
Zhōb	70,366	40,346	30,020	38,363	29,725	38,247	29,718	106	7	..	..	10	..
Bōlān	2,096	1,492	604	972	450	958	444	7	1	..	..	7	5
Chāgai	16,344	9,107	7,237	8,800	7,116	8,736	7,089	58	24	..	..	6	3
Sibī	117,189	66,846	50,343	60,788	47,685	60,426	47,629	352	52	..	..	10	4
Administered area	*82,423*	*47,558*	*34,865*	*41,701*	*32,374*	*41,342*	*32,318*	*352*	*52*	..	..	*10*	*4*
Marī-Bugṭī country	*34,766*	*19,288*	*15,478*	*19,084*	*15,311*	*19,084*	*15,311*	..	..	..	..	..	..
States	**420,291**	**227,238**	**193,053**	**219,022**	**186,270**	**203,422**	**172,720**	**829**	**722**	**14,764**	**12,823**	**7**	**5**
Kalāt	359,086	194,598	164,488	187,435	158,471	175,132	148,053	656	534	11,640	9,879	7	5
Sarāwān	*63,781*	*35,082*	*28,699*	*34,411*	*28,249*	*34,407*	*28,245*	*3*	*1*	..	..	*1*	*3*
Jhalawān	*84,398*	*46,880*	*37,518*	*46,491*	*37,423*	*43,748*	*35,196*	..	..	*2,743*	*2,227*	..	..
Kachhī	*92,759*	*50,191*	*42,568*	*45,823*	*38,566*	*45,820*	*38,564*	..	..	..	..	*3*	*2*
Ḍōmbkī-Kahērī country	*23,543*	*12,624*	*10,919*	*11,091*	*9,483*	*10,482*	*8,963*	*609*	*520*	..	..	..	..
Makrān	*71,942*	*37,698*	*34,244*	*37,528*	*34,230*	*28,653*	*26,612*	*44*	*13*	*8,828*	*7,605*	*3*	..
Khārān	*22,663*	*12,123*	*10,540*	*12,091*	*10,520*	*12,022*	*10,473*	..	..	*69*	*47*	..	..
Las Bēla	61,205	32,640	28,565	31,587	27,799	28,290	24,667	173	188	3,124	2,944	..	..

VI.—RELIGION—*contd.*

District or State	HINDU		SIKH				NEO-HINDU				CHRISTIAN		OTHERS	
			KĒSDHĀRĪ		SAHJDHĀRĪ		BRAHMŌ		ĀRYA					
	Males	Females	Males	Females	Males	Females	Males	Females	Males	Females	Males	Females	Males	Females
1	15	16	17	18	19	20	21	22	23	24	25	26	27	28
Balūchistān	***25,008***	***12,594***	***3,912***	***701***	***2,105***	***1,672***	***25***	***25***	***431***	***243***	***3,941***	***1,144***	***147***	***107***
Districts	**18,470**	**7,294**	**3,843**	**674**	**550**	**223**	**25**	**25**	**431**	**243**	**3,892**	**1,138**	**142**	**106**
Quetta-Pishin	9,600	3,644	1,731	412	203	84	14	9	301	178	3,540	1,015	119	87
Lōṛalai	2,038	920	788	82	50	16	..	2	33	13	58	13	1	..
Zhōb	1,150	198	553	24	96	42	2	5	25	11	154	14	3	1
Bōlān	416	107	67	21	15	4	3	2	4	8	14	12	1	..
Chāgai	264	112	18	3	11	2	1	..	7	1	6	3	..	..
Sibi	5,002	2,313	686	132	175	75	5	7	61	32	111	81	18	18
Administered area	*4,798*	*2,146*	*686*	*132*	*175*	*75*	*5*	*7*	*61*	*32*	*111*	*81*	*18*	*18*
Mari-Bugṭī country	*204*	*167*	..	..	..	..	..	..	..	..	..	..	..	..
States	**6,538**	**5,300**	**69**	**27**	**1,555**	**1,449**	..	..	..	..	**49**	**6**	**5**	**1**
Kalāt	5,550	4,552	16	9	1,548	1,449	..	..	..	..	45	6	4	1
Sarāwān	*600*	*403*	*16*	*9*	*53*	*36*	..	..	..	..	*3*	*2*	..	..
Jhalawān	*380*	*92*	..	..	*9*	*3*	..	..	..	..	..	..	..	..
Kachhi	*3,748*	*3,428*	..	..	*616*	*572*	..	..	..	..	*4*	*2*	..	..
Ḍōmbki-Kahērī country	*661*	*598*	..	..	*869*	*838*	..	..	..	..	..	..	..	..
Makrān	*126*	*11*	*1*	..	*1*	..	..	..	..	..	*38*	*2*	*4*	*1*
Khārān	*32*	*20*	..	..	..	..	..	..	..	..	..	..	..	..
Las Bēla	988	748	53	18	7	..	..	..	..	..	4	..	1	..

TABLE VII.

Age, Sex and Civil Condition.

As neither specific age nor civil condition was recorded in the areas censused on the special tribal schedule, this Table falls naturally into two parts. In part A the statistics for the regular areas are analysed in full for the province as a whole, and a summary of the statistics for the tribal areas is added to give completeness. Part B contains the puberal and sex statistics for the tribal areas by districts and states.

VII.—AGE, SEX AND CIVIL CONDITION.

PART A—*Balūchistān*.

Age and civil condition	Population			Musalmān			Hindu			Sikh			Christian			Others		
	Persons	Males	Females	Persons	Males	Females	Persons	Males	Females	Persons	Males	Females	Persons	Males	Females	Persons	Males	Females
1	2	3	4	5	6	7	8	9	10	11	12	18	14	15	16	17	18	19
0—1	1,387	703	684	577	292	285	559	287	272	96	47	49	119	57	62	36	20	16
Unmarried	1,387	703	684	577	292	285	559	287	272	96	47	49	119	57	62	36	20	16
Married	..	..	..	..	..	..	..	..	..	..	..	..	..	..	..	..	..	..
Widowed	..	..	..	..	..	..	..	..	..	..	..	..	..	..	..	..	..	..
1—2	490	253	237	218	118	100	160	75	85	26	16	10	67	35	32	19	9	10
Unmarried	489	253	236	217	118	99	160	75	85	26	16	10	67	35	32	19	9	10
Married	1	..	1	1	..	1	..	..	..	..	..	..	..	..	..	..	..	..
Widowed	..	..	..	..	..	..	..	..	..	..	..	..	..	..	..	..	..	..
2—3	953	480	473	408	209	199	371	176	195	60	35	25	81	44	37	33	16	17
Unmarried	953	480	473	408	209	199	371	176	195	60	35	25	81	44	37	33	16	17
Married	..	..	..	..	..	..	..	..	..	..	..	..	..	..	..	..	..	..
Widowed	..	..	..	..	..	..	..	..	..	..	..	..	..	..	..	..	..	..
3—4	921	468	453	417	212	205	355	171	184	47	32	15	75	40	35	27	13	14
Unmarried	921	468	453	417	212	205	355	171	184	47	32	15	75	40	35	27	13	14
Married	..	..	..	..	..	..	..	..	..	..	..	..	..	..	..	..	..	..
Widowed	..	..	..	..	..	..	..	..	..	..	..	..	..	..	..	..	..	..
4—5	857	418	439	394	194	200	302	147	155	49	25	24	82	37	45	30	15	15
Unmarried	857	418	439	394	194	200	302	147	155	49	25	24	82	57	45	30	15	15
Married	..	..	..	..	..	..	..	..	..	..	..	..	..	..	..	..	..	..
Widowed	..	..	..	..	..	..	..	..	..	..	..	..	..	..	..	..	..	..
Total 0—5	4,608	2,322	2,286	2,014	1,025	989	1,747	856	891	278	155	123	424	213	211	145	73	72
Unmarried	4,607	2,322	2,285	2,013	1,025	988	1,747	856	891	278	155	123	424	213	211	145	73	72
Married	1	..	1	1	..	1	..	..	..	..	..	..	..	..	..	..	..	..
Widowed	..	..	..	..	..	..	..	..	..	..	..	..	..	..	..	..	..	..
5—10	3,591	1,905	1,686	1,618	872	746	1,448	764	684	186	94	92	241	120	121	98	55	43
Unmarried	3,567	1,900	1,667	1,611	872	739	1,432	759	673	186	94	92	240	120	120	98	55	43
Married	24	5	19	7	..	7	16	5	11	..	..	..	1	..	1	..	..	..
Widowed	..	..	..	..	..	..	..	..	..	..	..	..	..	..	..	..	..	..
10—15	3,159	2,099	1,060	1,552	1,094	458	1,203	767	436	203	136	67	136	71	65	65	31	34
Unmarried	2,757	1,976	781	1,401	1,053	348	999	702	297	166	122	44	132	68	64	59	31	28
Married	399	121	278	151	41	110	202	64	138	36	13	23	4	3	1	6	..	6
Widowed	3	2	1	..	..	..	2	1	1	1	1	..	..	..	..	..	..	..
15—20	5,665	4,385	1,280	2,922	2,344	578	1,960	1,454	506	524	442	82	189	103	86	70	42	28
Unmarried	3,693	3,516	177	2,090	2,010	80	1,074	1,050	24	330	328	2	158	94	64	41	34	7
Married	1,926	838	1,088	810	319	491	866	391	475	190	111	79	31	9	22	29	8	21
Widowed	46	31	15	22	15	7	20	13	7	4	3	1	..	..	..	..	..	..
20—25	13,255	11,458	1,797	6,270	5,479	791	4,102	3,437	665	1,267	1,117	150	1,459	1,337	122	157	88	69
Unmarried	7,738	7,650	88	3,821	3,789	32	1,890	1,885	5	622	622	..	1,356	1,314	42	49	40	9
Married	5,256	3,584	1,672	2,334	1,599	735	2,118	1,462	651	603	456	147	100	21	79	106	46	60
Widowed	261	224	37	115	91	24	99	90	9	42	39	3	3	2	1	2	2	..
25—30	11,538	9,892	1,646	5,872	5,086	786	3,321	2,778	543	962	850	112	1,234	1,072	162	149	106	43
Unmarried	4 502	4,442	60	2,367	2,335	32	829	826	3	288	287	1	991	971	20	27	23	4
Married	6,565	5,026	1,539	3,293	2,571	722	2,326	1,796	530	595	486	109	236	95	141	115	78	37
Widowed	471	424	47	212	180	32	166	156	10	79	77	2	7	6	1	7	5	2
30—35	7,916	6,522	1,394	4,237	3,553	684	2,322	1,882	440	647	558	89	605	455	150	105	74	31
Unmarried	1,708	1,665	43	1,036	1,013	23	264	260	4	104	104	..	295	280	15	9	8	1
Married	5,685	4,424	1,261	2,923	2,319	604	1,879	1,468	411	490	404	86	307	175	132	86	58	28
Widowed	523	433	90	278	221	57	179	154	25	53	50	3	3	..	3	10	8	2
35—40	4,474	3,776	698	2,243	1,942	301	1,400	1,159	241	419	382	37	350	251	99	62	42	20
Unmarried	559	532	27	316	304	12	97	97	..	36	36	..	108	93	15	2	2	..
Married	3,527	2,924	603	1,748	1,491	257	1,163	949	214	332	299	33	230	149	81	54	36	18
Widowed	388	320	68	179	147	32	140	113	27	51	47	4	12	9	3	6	4	2
40—45	3,854	3,061	793	2,017	1,607	410	1,294	1,024	270	275	238	37	215	156	59	53	36	17
Unmarried	372	356	16	224	214	10	90	89	1	15	15	..	41	36	5	2	2	..
Married	2,960	2,359	601	1,560	1,243	317	967	776	191	225	194	31	163	115	48	45	31	14
Widowed	522	346	176	233	150	83	237	159	78	35	29	6	11	5	6	6	3	3
45—50	1,640	1,334	306	817	672	145	556	449	107	122	105	17	115	83	32	30	25	5
Unmarried	102	96	6	64	63	1	24	23	1	5	5	..	9	5	4	..	..	..
Married	1,242	1,052	190	628	529	99	394	338	56	95	85	10	96	75	21	29	25	4
Widowed	296	186	110	125	80	45	138	88	50	22	15	7	10	3	7	1	..	1
50—55	1,799	1,403	396	1,004	785	219	625	484	141	83	73	10	66	47	19	21	14	7
Unmarried	102	97	5	70	65	5	29	29	..	1	1	..	2	2	..	..	..	..
Married	1,208	1,038	170	676	585	91	405	348	57	62	56	6	48	35	13	17	14	3
Widowed	489	268	221	258	135	123	191	107	84	20	16	4	16	10	6	4	..	4
55—60	401	326	75	210	180	30	127	95	32	28	24	4	24	18	6	12	9	3
Unmarried	20	19	1	13	12	1	5	5	..	1	1	..	..	..	..	1	1	..
Married	263	233	30	142	129	13	74	64	10	20	18	2	20	16	4	7	6	1
Widowed	118	74	44	55	39	16	48	26	22	7	5	2	4	2	2	4	2	2
60—65	709	525	177	415	320	95	231	166	65	29	23	6	20	10	10	7	6	1
Unmarried	44	43	1	28	27	1	18	18	..	1	1	..	2	2	..	..	..	..
Married	378	338	40	226	205	21	125	110	15	11	11	..	12	8	4	4	4	..
Widowed	280	144	136	161	88	73	93	43	50	17	11	6	6	..	6	3	2	1
65—70	103	74	29	58	43	15	35	22	13	6	6	..	3	2	1	1	1	..
Unmarried	5	5	..	5	5	..	..	..	..	..	..	..	..	..	..	..	..	..
Married	46	41	5	29	25	4	12	12	..	3	3	..	2	1	1	..	..	..
Widowed	52	28	24	24	13	11	23	10	13	3	3	..	1	1	..	1	1	..
70 and over	302	189	113	150	92	58	129	78	51	16	15	1	4	3	1	3	1	2
Unmarried	12	12	..	5	5	..	6	6	..	1	1	..	..	..	..	..	..	..
Married	128	108	20	64	53	11	51	43	8	8	8	..	3	3	..	2	1	1
Widowed	162	69	93	81	34	47	72	29	43	7	6	1	1	..	1	1	..	1
Total civil condition specified	**63,007**	**49,271**	**13,736**	**31,399**	**25,094**	**6,305**	**20,500**	**15,415**	**5,085**	**5,045**	**4,218**	**827**	**5,085**	**3,941**	**1,144**	**978**	**603**	**375**
Unmarried	29,788	24,631	5,157	15,064	12,792	2,272	8,499	6,600	1,899	2,034	1,772	262	3,758	3,198	560	433	269	164
Married	29,608	22,091	7,517	14,592	11,109	3,483	10,593	7,826	2,767	2,670	2,144	526	1,253	705	548	500	307	193
Widowed	3,611	2,549	1,062	1,743	1,193	550	1,408	989	419	341	302	39	74	38	36	45	27	18
Total civil condition unspecified	**771,696**	**417,148**	**354,548**	**751,249**	**405,756**	**345,493**	**17,102**	**9,593**	**7,509**	**3,345**	**1,799**	**1,546**	..	..	..	..	..	..
GRAND TOTAL	**834,703**	**466,419**	**368,284**	**782,648**	**430,850**	**351,798**	**37,602**	**25,008**	**12,594**	8,390	6,017	2,373	5,085	3,941	1,144	978	603	375

VII.—AGE AND SEX.

PART B.—*By districts and states (for areas censused on the tribal schedule only).*

District or State	Religion	Persons: Total	Persons: Under puberty	Persons: Over puberty	Males: Total	Males: Under puberty	Males: Over puberty	Females: Total	Females: Under puberty	Females: Over puberty
1	2	3	4	5	6	7	8	9	10	11
Tribal areas	ALL RELIGIONS	[illegible]	*293,974*	*477,729*	*417,148*	*164,249*	*252,899*	*354,548*	*129,725*	*224,823*
	Musalmān	751,249	287,694	463,555	405,756	160,804	244,952	245,493	126,890	218,603
	Hindu	17,102	5,229	11,873	9,593	2,879	6,714	7,509	2,350	5,159
	Sikh	3,345	1,051	2,294	1,799	566	1,233	1,546	485	1,061
DISTRICTS										
QUETTA-PISHIN	ALL RELIGIONS	**89,628**	**37,780**	**51,848**	**47,950**	**21,070**	**26,880**	**41,678**	**16,710**	**24,968**
	Musalmān	89,340	37,715	51,625	47,732	21,031	26,701	41,608	16,684	24,924
	Hindu	235	53	182	179	34	145	56	19	37
	Sikh	53	12	41	39	5	34	14	7	7
LŌRALAI	ALL RELIGIONS	**76,124**	**29,991**	**46,133**	**40,939**	**16,395**	**24,544**	**35,185**	**13,596**	**21,589**
	Musalmān	74,603	29,493	45,110	40,066	16,146	23,920	34,537	13,347	21,190
	Hindu	1,516	496	1,020	869	247	622	647	249	398
	Sikh	5	2	3	4	2	2	1	..	1
ZHŌB	ALL RELIGIONS	**64,559**	**25,456**	**39,103**	**35,081**	14,400	**20,681**	**29,478**	**11,056**	**18,422**
	Musalmān	64,526	25,454	39,072	35,053	14,399	20,654	29,473	11,055	18,418
	Hindu	24	2	22	19	1	18	5	1	4
	Sikh	9	..	9	9	..	9	..	..	..
BŌLĀN	ALL RELIGIONS	**647**	**232**	**415**	**336**	**111**	**225**	**311**	**121**	**190**
	Musalmān	625	229	396	319	108	211	306	121	185
	Hindu	20	3	17	15	3	12	5	..	5
	Sikh	2	..	2	2	..	2	..	..	..
CHĀGAI	ALL RELIGIONS	**15,459**	**6,037**	**9,422**	**8,427**	**3,290**	**5,137**	**7,032**	**2,747**	**4,285**
	Musalmān	15,367	6,014	9,353	8,364	3,281	5,083	7,003	2,733	4,270
	Hindu	79	23	56	52	9	43	27	14	13
	Sikh	13	..	13	11	..	11	2	..	2
SIBI	ALL RELIGIONS	**105,801**	**41,013**	**64,788**	**57,850**	**23,013**	**34,837**	**47,951**	**18,000**	**29,951**
	Musalmān	102,157	39,965	62,192	55,746	22,422	33,324	46,411	17,543	28,868
	Hindu	3,479	988	2,491	1,992	555	1,437	1,487	433	1,054
	Sikh	165	60	105	112	36	76	53	24	29
Administered area	ALL RELIGIONS	**71,035**	**26,948**	**44,087**	**38,562**	**15,162**	**'3,400**	**32,473**	**11,786**	**20,687**
	Musalmān	67,762	26,008	41,754	36,662	14,630	22,032	31,100	11,378	19,722
	Hindu	3,108	880	2,228	1,788	496	1,292	1,320	384	936
	Sikh	165	60	105	112	36	76	53	24	29
Mari-Bugti country	ALL RELIGIONS	**34,766**	**14,065**	**20,701**	**19,288**	**7,851**	**11,437**	**15,478**	**6,214**	**9,264**
	Musalmān	34,395	13,957	20,438	19,084	7,792	11,292	15,311	6,165	9,146
	Hindu	371	108	263	204	59	145	167	49	118
	Sikh	..	..	..	..	..	..	..	..	..
STATES										
KALĀT	ALL RELIGIONS	**358,278**	**130,970**	**227,308**	**193,930**	**73,861**	**120,069**	**164,348**	**57,109**	**107,239**
	Musalmān	345,245	126,873	218,372	186,889	71,619	115,270	158,356	55,254	103,102
	Hindu	10,013	3,137	6,876	5,479	1,731	3,748	4,534	1,406	3,128
	Sikh	3,020	960	2,060	1,562	511	1,051	1,458	449	1,009
Sarāwān	ALL RELIGIONS	**63,641**	**22,986**	**40,655**	**34,981**	**12,950**	**22,031**	**28,660**	**10,036**	**18,694**
	Musalmān	62,571	22,663	39,908	34,342	12,755	21,587	28,229	9,908	18,321
	Hindu	957	285	672	571	171	400	386	114	272
	Sikh	113	38	75	68	24	44	45	14	31
Jhalawān	ALL RELIGIONS	**84,398**	**31,291**	**53,107**	**46,880**	**18,294**	**28,586**	**37,518**	**12,997**	**24,521**
	Musalmān	83,914	31,190	52,724	46,491	18,219	28,272	37,423	12,971	24,452
	Hindu	472	99	373	380	73	307	92	26	66
	Sikh	12	2	10	9	2	7	3	..	3
Kachhi	ALL RELI'IONS	**92,753**	**32,256**	**60,497**	**50,187**	**18,209**	**31,978**	**42,566**	**14,047**	**28,519**
	Musalmān	84,389	29,613	54,776	45,823	16,788	29,035	38,566	12,825	25,741
	Hindu	7,176	2,276	4,900	3,748	1,221	2,527	3,428	1,055	2,373
	Sikh	1,188	367	821	616	200	416	572	167	405
Dōmbki-Kahēri country.	ALL RELIGIONS	**23,543**	**8,437**	**15,106**	**12,624**	**4,585**	**8,039**	**10,919**	**3,852**	**7,067**
	Musalmān	20,574	7,445	13,129	11,091	4,059	7,032	9,483	3,386	6,097
	Hindu	1,262	439	823	664	241	423	598	198	400
	Sikh	1,707	553	1,154	869	285	584	838	268	570
Makrān	ALL RELIGIONS	**71,280**	**26,682**	**44,598**	**37,135**	**14,679**	**22,456**	**34,145**	**12,003**	**22,142**
	Musalmān	71,186	26,665	44,521	37,051	14,665	22,386	34,135	12,000	22,135
	Hindu	94	17	77	84	14	70	10	3	7
	Sikh	..	..	..	..	..	..	..	..	..
Khārān	ALL RELIGIONS	**22,663**	**9,318**	**13,345**	**12,123**	**5,144**	**6,979**	**10,540**	**4,174**	**6,366**
	Musalmān	22,611	9,297	13,314	12,091	5,133	6,958	10,520	4,164	6,356
	Hindu	52	21	31	32	11	21	20	10	10
	Sikh	..	..	..	..	..	..	..	..	.:
LAS BELA	ALL RELIGIONS	**61,200**	**22,495**	**38,705**	**32,635**	**12,109**	**20,526**	**28,565**	**10,386**	**18,179**
	Musalmān	59,386	21,951	37,435	31,587	11,798	19,789	27,799	10,153	17,646
	Hindu	1,736	527	1,209	988	299	689	748	228	520
	Sikh	78	17	61	60	12	48	18	5	13

D

TABLE VIII.

Education by Religion and Age.

In the Christian figures are included 495 male and 257 female Indian Christians :—

Age	Literate			Illiterate			Literate in English		
	Persons	Males	Females	Persons	Males	Females	Persons	Males	Females
0—10	6	2	4	159	77	82	..	..	..
10—15	21	9	12	32	24	8	5	4	1
15—20	36	19	17	27	15	12	19	13	6
20 and over	212	171	41	259	178	81	109	87	22

The more important vernaculars in which literacy was returned are given below. As several individuals returned themselves as literate in more than one vernaculars, the totals do not of course agree with the totals for literacy in the Table.

District and State	Urdu		Hindi		Gurmukhi		Lande		Sindhi		Persian		Arabic	
	Males	Females	Males	Females	Males	Females	Males	Females	Males	Females	Males	Females	Males	Females
BALŪCHISTĀN .	6,514	278	1,439	125	3,694	362	4,801	9	3,097	43	3,383	37	470	35
Quetta-Pishin . .	3,378	191	678	81	1,170	190	265	..	945	25	1,055	19	164	22
Lōralai . .	705	9	158	9	657	51	394	..	92	4	175	1	60	..
Zhōb . . .	600	5	228	9	368	25	95	..	16	..	178	..	49	..
Bōlān . . .	114	3	9	1	77	10	10	..	66	1	22	1	9	1
Chāgai . .	128	10	6	..	31	4	1	1	121	6	169	7	7	1
Sibi . . .	1,099	55	859	25	705	76	1,056	5	286	3	307	2	33	5
Kalāt . . .	300	5	1	..	660	6	2,259	8	1,403	..	1,432	7	89	1
Las Bēla . .	190	..	..	..	26	..	721	..	168	4	45	..	50	5

VIII.—EDUCATION BY RELIGION AND AGE.

District or State.	Religion and Age	Population									Literate in English		
		Total			Literate			Illiterate					
		Persons	Males	Females	Persons	Males	Females	Persons	Males	Females	Persons	Males	Females
1	2	3	4	5	6	7	8	9	10	11	12	13	14
BALŪCHISTĀN	**ALL RELIGIONS**	**834,703**	**466,419**	**368,284**	**27,925**	**26,202**	**1,723**	**806,778**	**440,217**	**366,561**	**6,321**	**5,541**	**780**
	0—10	8,199	4,227	3,972	375	219	156	7,824	4,008	3,816	167	90	77
	10—15	3,159	2,099	1,060	759	568	191	2,400	1,531	860	187	135	52
	15—20	5,665	4,385	1,280	1,469	1,259	210	4,196	3,126	1,070	337	270	67
	20 and over	45,984	38,560	7,424	15,639	14,509	1,130	30,345	24,051	6,294	5,558	4,974	584
	Unspecified	771,696	417,148	354,548	9,683	9,647	36	762,013	407,501	354,512	72	72	..
	MUSALMĀN	**782,648**	**430,850**	**351,798**	**7,306**	**7,093**	**213**	**775,342**	**423,757**	**351,585**	**663**	**659**	**4**
	0—10	3,632	1,897	1,735	56	40	16	3,576	1,857	1,719	..	..	..
	10—15	1,552	1,094	458	194	169	25	1,358	925	433	29	28	1
	15—20	2,922	2,344	578	328	299	29	2,594	2,045	549	55	55	..
	20 and over	23,293	19,759	3,534	3,209	3,090	119	20,084	16,669	3,415	522	519	3
	Unspecified	751,249	405,756	345,493	3,519	3,495	24	747,730	402,261	345,469	57	57	..
	HINDU	**37,602**	**25,008**	**12,594**	**11,877**	**11,500**	**377**	**25,725**	**13,508**	**12,217**	**983**	**976**	**7**
	0—10	3,195	1,620	1,575	94	62	32	3,101	1,558	1,543	4	4	..
	10—15	1,203	767	436	321	260	61	882	507	375	47	46	1
	15—20	1,960	1,454	506	686	618	68	1,274	836	438	82	80	2
	20 and over	14,142	11,574	2,568	5,675	5,468	207	8,467	6,108	2,361	836	832	4
	Unspecified	17,102	9,593	7,509	5,101	5,092	9	12,001	4,501	7,500	14	14	..
	SIKH	**8,390**	**6,017**	**2,373**	**3,896**	**3,707**	**189**	**4,494**	**2,310**	**2,184**	**250**	**248**	**2**
	0—10	464	249	215	30	17	13	434	232	202	1	1	..
	10—15	203	136	67	94	67	27	109	69	40	11	11	..
	15—20	524	442	82	243	219	24	281	223	58	32	32	..
	20 and over	3,854	3,391	463	2,466	2,344	122	1,388	1,047	341	205	203	2
	Unspecified	3,345	1,799	1,546	1,063	1,060	3	2,282	739	1,543	1	1	..
	CHRISTIAN	**5,085**	**3,941**	**1,144**	**4,254**	**3,472**	**782**	**831**	**469**	**362**	**4,109**	**3,372**	**737**
	0—10	665	333	332	163	86	77	502	247	255	157	84	73
	10—15	136	71	65	100	46	54	36	25	11	84	41	43
	15—20	189	103	86	160	87	73	29	16	13	143	81	62
	20 and over	4,095	3,434	661	3,831	3,253	578	264	181	83	3,725	3,166	559
	OTHERS	**978**	**603**	**375**	**592**	**430**	**162**	**386**	**173**	**213**	**316**	**286**	**30**
	0—10	243	128	115	32	14	18	211	114	97	5	1	4
	10—15	65	31	34	50	26	24	15	5	10	16	9	7
	15—20	70	42	28	52	36	16	18	6	12	25	22	3
	20 and over	600	402	198	458	354	104	142	48	94	270	254	16
QUETTA-PISHĪN	**ALL RELIGIONS**	**127,648**	**76,467**	**51,181**	**12,747**	**11,484**	**1,263**	**114,901**	**64,983**	**49,918**	**5,127**	**4,454**	**673**
	0—10	5,726	2,926	2,800	302	172	130	5,424	2,754	2,670	149	78	71
	10—15	2,133	1,402	731	563	429	134	1,570	973	597	162	119	43
	15—20	3,340	2,464	876	980	825	155	2,360	1,639	721	290	234	56
	20 and over	26,821	21,725	5,096	10,118	9,274	844	16,703	12,451	4,252	4,513	4,010	503
	Unspecified	89,628	47,950	41,678	784	784	..	88,844	47,166	41,678	13	13	..
	MUSALMAN	**106,702**	**60,950**	**45,752**	**2,843**	**2,712**	**131**	**103,859**	**58,238**	**45,621**	**385**	**382**	**3**
	0—10	2,414	1,260	1,154	38	28	10	2,376	1,232	1,144	..	..	..
	10—15	1,013	693	320	148	130	18	865	563	302	25	25	..
	15—20	1,590	1,214	376	208	186	22	1,382	1,028	354	45	45	..
	20 and over	12,345	10,051	2,294	1,793	1,712	81	10,552	8,339	2,213	305	302	3
	Unspecified	89,340	47,732	41,608	656	656	..	88,684	47,076	41,608	10	10	..
	HINDU	**13,244**	**9,600**	**3,644**	**4,492**	**4,256**	**236**	**8,752**	**5,344**	**3,408**	**649**	**645**	**4**
	0—10	2,268	1,129	1,139	70	43	27	2,198	1,086	1,112	2	2	..
	10—15	821	531	290	226	189	37	595	342	253	42	41	1
	15—20	1,269	912	357	462	415	47	807	497	310	63	62	1
	20 and over	8,651	6,849	1,802	3,623	3,498	125	5,028	3,351	1,677	540	538	2
	Unspecified	235	179	56	111	111	..	124	68	56	2	2	..
	SIKH	**2,430**	**1,934**	**496**	**1,163**	**1,068**	**95**	**1,267**	**866**	**401**	**145**	**143**	**2**
	0—10	267	143	124	20	13	7	247	130	117	1	1	..
	10—15	124	88	36	61	48	13	63	40	23	11	11	..
	15—20	256	207	49	126	112	14	130	95	35	28	28	..
	20 and over	1,730	1,457	273	939	878	61	791	579	212	104	102	2
	Unspecified	53	39	14	17	17	..	36	22	14	1	1	..
	CHRISTIAN	**4,564**	**3,549**	**1,015**	**3,822**	**3,140**	**682**	**742**	**409**	**333**	**3,718**	**3,075**	**643**
	0—10	600	297	303	148	77	71	452	220	232	142	75	67
	10—15	121	64	57	87	40	47	34	24	10	72	35	37
	15—20	173	98	75	145	83	62	28	15	13	133	80	53
	20 and over	3,670	3,090	580	3,442	2,940	502	228	150	78	3,371	2,885	486
	OTHERS	**708**	**434**	**274**	**427**	**308**	**119**	**281**	**126**	**155**	**230**	**209**	**21**
	0—10	177	97	80	26	11	15	151	86	65	4	..	4
	10—15	54	26	28	41	22	19	13	4	9	12	7	5
	15—20	52	33	19	39	29	10	13	4	9	21	19	2
	20 and over	425	278	147	321	246	75	104	32	72	198	193	10

VIII.—EDUCATION BY RELIGION AND AGE—*contd.*

District or State	Religion and Age	Population: Total: Persons	Total: Males	Total: Females	Literate: Persons	Literate: Males	Literate: Females	Illiterate: Persons	Illiterate: Males	Illiterate: Females	Literate in English: Persons	Literate in English: Males	Literate in English: Females
1	2	3	4	5	6	7	8	9	10	11	12	13	14
LORĀLAI	**ALL RELIGIONS**	**80,769**	**44,923**	**35,846**	**2,166**	**2,083**	**83**	**78,603**	**42,840**	**35,763**	**202**	**190**	**12**
	0—10	412	232	180	7	3	4	405	229	176	..	..	..
	10—15	174	129	45	32	22	10	142	107	35	1	1	..
	15—20	530	480	50	129	122	7	401	358	43	2	1	1
	20 and over	3,529	3,143	386	1,338	1,281	57	2,191	1,862	329	193	182	11
	Unspecified	76,124	40,939	35,185	660	655	5	75,464	40,284	35,180	6	6	..
	MUSALMĀN	**76,755**	**41,955**	**34,800**	**581**	**572**	**9**	**76,174**	**41,383**	**34,791**	**54**	**54**	..
	0—10	154	84	70	1	1	..	153	83	70	..	..	..
	10—15	76	64	12	11	10	1	65	54	11	1	1	..
	15—20	235	223	12	39	38	1	196	185	11	..	..	..
	20 and over	1,687	1,518	169	316	311	5	1,371	1,207	164	50	50	..
	Unspecified	74,603	40,066	34,537	214	212	2	74,389	39,854	34,535	3	3	..
	HINDU	**2,958**	**2,038**	**920**	**895**	**868**	**27**	**2,063**	**1,170**	**893**	**53**	**52**	**1**
	0—10	180	104	76	2	1	1	178	103	75	..	..	..
	10—15	83	57	26	13	9	4	70	48	22	..	..	..
	15—20	161	135	26	44	41	3	117	94	23	1	1	..
	20 and over	1,018	873	145	391	375	16	627	498	129	49	48	1
	Unspecified	1,516	869	647	445	442	3	1,071	427	644	3	3	..
	SIKH	**936**	**838**	**98**	**607**	**575**	**32**	**329**	**263**	**66**	**30**	**30**	..
	0—10	60	34	26	3	1	2	57	33	24	..	..	..
	10—15	15	8	7	8	3	5	7	5	2	..	..	..
	15—20	129	120	9	43	41	2	86	79	7	..	..	..
	20 and over	727	672	55	552	529	23	175	143	32	30	30	..
	Unspecified	5	4	1	1	1	..	4	3	1	..	..	..
	CHRISTIAN	**71**	**58**	**13**	**57**	**46**	**11**	**14**	**12**	**2**	**51**	**49**	**11**
	0—10	6	4	2	..	..	..	6	4	2	..	..	..
	15—20	2	1	1	2	1	1	..	..	..	1	..	1
	20 and over	63	53	10	55	45	10	8	8	..	50	40	10
	OTHERS	**49**	**34**	**15**	**26**	**22**	**4**	**23**	**12**	**11**	**14**	**14**	..
	0—10	12	6	6	1	..	1	11	6	5	..	..	..
	15—20	3	1	2	1	1	..	2	..	2	..	..	..
	20 and over	34	27	7	24	21	3	10	6	4	14	14	..
ZHŌB	**ALL RELIGIONS**	**70,366**	**40,346**	**30,020**	**1,619**	**1,567**	**52**	**68,747**	**38,779**	**29,968**	**271**	**257**	**14**
	0—10	367	201	166	11	8	3	356	193	163	5	3	2
	10—15	164	116	48	27	21	6	137	95	42	1	1	..
	15—20	618	570	48	93	90	3	525	480	45	7	7	..
	20 and over	4,658	4,378	280	1,341	1,302	39	3,317	3,076	241	257	245	12
	Unspecified	64,559	35,081	29,478	147	146	1	64,412	34,935	29,477	1	1	..
	MUSALMĀN	**68,088**	**38,363**	**29,725**	**563**	**561**	**2**	**67,525**	**37,802**	**29,723**	**32**	**32**	..
	0—10	171	89	82	1	1	..	170	88	82	..	..	..
	10—15	88	70	18	6	6	..	82	64	18	..	..	..
	15—20	439	412	27	24	23	1	415	389	26	..	..	..
	20 and over	2,864	2,739	125	391	390	1	2,473	2,349	124	31	31	..
	Unspecified	64,526	35,053	29,473	141	141	..	64,385	34,912	29,473	1	1	..
	HINDU	**1,348**	**1,150**	**198**	**479**	**459**	**20**	**869**	**691**	**178**	**66**	**65**	**1**
	0—10	133	74	59	3	3	..	130	71	59	..	..	..
	10—15	53	31	22	14	10	4	39	21	18	..	..	..
	15—20	99	85	14	34	34	..	65	51	14	6	6	..
	20 and over	1,039	941	98	424	409	15	615	532	83	60	59	1
	Unspecified	24	19	5	4	3	1	20	16	4	..	..	..
	SIKH	**715**	**649**	**66**	**392**	**381**	**11**	**323**	**268**	**55**	**17**	**17**	..
	0—10	44	28	16	2	1	1	42	27	15	..	..	..
	10—15	20	13	7	5	4	1	15	9	6	..	..	..
	15—20	77	71	6	33	32	1	44	39	5	1	1	..
	20 and over	565	528	37	350	342	8	215	186	29	16	16	..
	Unspecified	9	9	..	2	2	..	7	7	..	..	..	..
	CHRISTIAN	**168**	**154**	**14**	**158**	**144**	**14**	**10**	**10**	..	**149**	**136**	**13**
	0—10	8	6	2	5	3	2	3	3	..	5	3	2
	10—15	1	1	..	1	1	..	..	..	..	1	1	..
	20 and over	159	147	12	152	140	12	7	7	..	143	132	11
	OTHERS	**47**	**30**	**17**	**27**	**22**	**5**	**20**	**8**	**12**	**7**	**7**	..
	0—10	11	4	7	..	..	..	11	4	7	..	..	..
	10—15	2	1	1	1	..	1	1	1	..	..	..	..
	15—20	3	2	1	2	1	1	1	1	..	..	..	..
	20 and over	31	23	8	24	21	3	7	2	5	7	7	..

VIII.—EDUCATION BY RELIGION AND AGE—*contd.*

District or State.	Religion and Age	Population									Literate in English		
		Total			Literate			Illiterate					
		Persons	Males	Females	Persons	Males	Females	Persons	Males	Females	Persons	Males	Females
1	2	3	4	5	6	7	8	9	10	11	12	13	14
BŌLĀN	ALL RELIGIONS	2,096	1,492	604	300	274	26	1,796	1,218	578	68	58	10
	0—10	157	82	75	4	3	1	153	79	74	1	1	..
	10—15	59	38	21	8	5	3	51	33	18	4	2	2
	15—20	139	97	42	22	16	6	117	81	36	5	2	3
	20 and over	1,094	939	155	260	245	15	834	694	140	58	53	5
	Unspecified	647	336	311	6	5	1	641	331	310	..	..	..
	MUSALMĀN	1,422	972	450	80	76	4	1,342	896	446	11	11	..
	0—10	70	35	35	1	1	..	69	34	35	..	..	..
	10—15	30	20	10	..	..	..	30	20	10	..	..	..
	15—20	92	66	26	4	4	..	88	62	26	..	..	..
	20 and over	605	532	73	69	66	3	536	466	70	11	11	..
	Unspecified	625	319	306	6	5	1	619	314	305	..	..	..
	HINDU	523	416	107	135	132	3	388	284	104	23	23	..
	0—10	64	37	27	1	1	..	63	36	27	..	..	..
	10—15	23	16	7	3	3	..	20	13	7	..	..	..
	15—20	39	28	11	12	10	2	27	18	9	1	1	..
	20 and over	377	320	57	119	118	1	258	202	56	22	22	..
	Unspecified	20	15	5	..	..	..	20	15	5	..	..	..
	SIKH	107	82	25	53	47	6	54	35	19	7	7	..
	0—10	16	8	8	1	..	1	15	8	7	..	..	..
	10—15	2	..	2	1	..	1	1	..	1	..	..	..
	15—20	4	2	2	2	1	1	2	1	1	..	..	..
	20 and over	83	70	13	49	46	3	34	24	10	7	7	..
	Unspecified	2	2	..	..	..	..	2	2	..	..	..	..
	CHRISTIAN	26	14	12	22	12	10	4	2	2	22	12	10
	0—10	1	1	..	1	1	..	..	..	..	1	1	..
	10—15	3	1	2	3	1	2	..	..	..	3	1	2
	15—20	4	1	3	4	1	3	..	..	..	4	1	3
	20 and over	18	11	7	14	9	5	4	2	2	14	9	5
	OTHERS	18	8	10	10	7	3	8	1	7	5	5	..
	0—10	6	1	5	..	..	..	6	1	5	..	..	..
	10—15	1	1	..	1	1	..	..	..	..	1	1	..
	20 and over	11	6	5	9	6	3	2	..	2	4	4	..
CHĀGAI	ALL RELIGIONS	16,344	9,107	7,237	399	376	23	15,945	8,731	7,214	52	51	1
	0—10	118	65	53	8	7	1	110	58	52	..	..	..
	10—15	56	36	20	19	14	5	37	22	15	..	..	..
	15—20	75	55	20	25	23	2	50	32	18	1	1	..
	20 and over	636	524	112	208	196	12	428	328	100	43	42	1
	Unspecified	15,459	8,427	7,032	139	136	3	15,320	8,291	7,029	8	8	..
	MUSALMĀN	15,916	8,800	7,116	200	189	11	15,716	8,611	7,105	26	26	..
	0—10	68	34	34	4	3	1	64	31	33	..	..	..
	10—15	31	23	8	10	7	3	21	16	5	..	..	..
	15—20	36	26	10	2	2		34	24	10	..	..	..
	20 and over	414	353	61	68	63	5	346	290	56	18	18	..
	Unspecified	15,367	8,364	7,003	116	114	2	15,251	8,250	7,001	8	8	..
	HINDU	376	264	112	169	160	9	207	104	103	15	15	..
	0—10	47	28	19	3	3	..	44	25	19	..	..	..
	10—15	25	13	12	9	7	2	16	6	10	..	..	..
	15—20	35	26	9	20	19	1	15	7	8	1	1	..
	20 and over	190	145	45	121	115	6	69	30	39	14	14	..
	Unspecified	79	52	27	16	16	..	63	36	27	..	..	..
	SIKH	34	29	5	19	17	2	15	12	3	3	3	..
	0—10	2	2	..	1	1	..	1	1	..	..	..	..
	15—20	4	3	1	3	2	1	1	1	..	..	..	..
	20 and over	15	13	2	8	8	..	7	5	2	3	3	..
	Unspecified	13	11	2	7	6	1	6	5	1	..	..	..
	CHRISTIAN	9	6	3	[illegible]	2	1	6	4	2	2	1	1
	0—10	1	1	..	..	..	..	1	1	..	..	..	..
	20 and over	8	5	3	3	2	1	5	3	2	2	1	1
	OTHERS	9	8	1	8	8	..	1	..	1	6	6	..
	20 and over	9	8	1	8	8	..	1	..	1	6	6	..

VIII.—EDUCATION BY RELIGION AND AGE—*contd.*

District or State.	Religion and Age	Population: Total: Persons	Males	Females	Literate: Persons	Males	Females	Illiterate: Persons	Males	Females	Literate in English: Persons	Males	Females
1	2	3	4	5	6	7	8	9	10	11	12	13	14
SIBI	**ALL RELIGIONS**	**117,189**	**66,846**	**50,343**	**3,870**	**3,628**	**242**	**113,319**	**63,218**	**50,101**	**503**	**436**	**67**
	0—10	1,329	682	647	42	26	16	1,287	656	631	12	8	4
	10—15	543	357	186	107	76	31	436	281	155	19	12	7
	15—20	902	681	221	202	166	36	700	515	185	28	21	7
	20 and over	8,614	7,276	1,338	2,240	2,085	155	6,374	5,191	1,183	444	395	49
	Unspecified	105,801	57,850	47,951	1,279	1,275	4	104,522	56,575	47,947	..	..	..
	Administered area	*71,035*	*38,562*	*32,473*	*1,184*	*1,180*	*4*	*69,851*	*37,382*	*32,469*	..	..	..
	Mari-Bugti country	*34,766*	*19,288*	*15,478*	*95*	*95*	..	*34,671*	*19,193*	*15,478*	..	..	..
	MUSALMĀN	**108,473**	**60,788**	**47,685**	**915**	**879**	**36**	**107,558**	**59,909**	**47,649**	**99**	**98**	**1**
	0—10	675	358	317	11	6	5	664	352	312	..	..	..
	10—15	294	209	85	18	15	3	276	194	82	3	2	1
	15—20	478	372	106	37	32	5	441	340	101	6	6	..
	20 and over	4,869	4,103	766	505	484	21	4,364	3,619	745	90	90	..
	Unspecified	102,157	55,746	46,411	344	342	2	101,813	55,404	46,409	..	..	..
	Administered area	*67,762*	*36,662*	*31,100*	*320*	*318*	*2*	*67,442*	*36,341*	*31,098*	..	..	..
	Mari-Bugti country	*34,395*	*19,084*	*15,311*	*24*	*24*	..	*34,371*	*19,060*	*15,311*	..	..	..
	HINDU	**7,315**	**5,002**	**2,313**	**2,088**	**2,013**	**75**	**5,227**	**2,989**	**2,238**	**165**	**164**	**1**
	0—10	496	246	250	15	11	4	481	235	246	2	2	..
	10—15	188	113	75	54	42	12	134	71	63	5	5	..
	15—20	353	265	88	114	99	15	239	166	73	10	9	1
	20 and over	2,799	2,386	413	979	937	42	1,820	1,449	371	148	148	..
	Unspecified	3,479	1,992	1,487	926	924	2	2,553	1,068	1,485	..	..	..
	Administered area	*3,108*	*1,788*	*1,320*	*855*	*853*	*2*	*2,253*	*935*	*1,318*	..	..	..
	Mari-Bugti country	*371*	*204*	*167*	*71*	*71*	..	*300*	*133*	*167*	..	..	..
	SIKH	**1,068**	**861**	**207**	**633**	**592**	**41**	**435**	**269**	**166**	**48**	**48**	..
	0—10	75	34	41	3	1	2	72	33	39	..	..	..
	10—15	42	27	15	19	12	7	23	15	8	..	..	..
	15—20	53	38	15	35	30	5	18	8	10	3	3	..
	20 and over	733	650	83	567	540	27	166	110	56	45	45	..
	Unspecified	165	112	53	9	9	..	156	103	53	..	..	..
	CHRISTIAN	**192**	**111**	**81**	**144**	**84**	**60**	**48**	**27**	**21**	**140**	**84**	**56**
	0—10	47	24	23	9	5	4	38	19	19	9	5	4
	10—15	11	5	6	9	4	5	2	1	1	8	4	4
	15—20	6	..	6	6	..	6	..	..	..	5	..	5
	20 and over	128	82	46	120	75	45	8	7	1	118	75	43
	OTHERS	**141**	**84**	**57**	**90**	**60**	**30**	**51**	**24**	**27**	**51**	**42**	**9**
	0—10	36	20	16	4	3	1	32	17	15	1	1	..
	10—15	8	3	5	7	3	4	1	..	1	3	1	2
	15—20	12	6	6	10	5	5	2	1	1	4	3	1
	20 and over	85	55	30	69	49	20	16	6	10	43	37	6
KALĀT	**ALL RELIGIONS**	**359,086**	**194,598**	**164,488**	**5,745**	**5,720**	**25**	**353,341**	**188,878**	**164,463**	**85**	**82**	**3**
	0—10	90	39	51	1	..	1	89	39	50	..	..	..
	10—15	30	21	9	3	1	2	27	20	7	..	..	..
	15—20	61	38	23	18	17	1	43	21	22	4	4	..
	20 and over	627	570	57	130	122	8	497	448	49	46	43	3
	Unspecified	358,278	193,930	164,348	5,593	5,580	13	352,685	188,350	164,335	35	35	..
	Sarāwān	*63,641*	*34,981*	*28,660*	*971*	*970*	*1*	*62,670*	*34,011*	*28,659*	*10*	*10*	..
	Jhalawān	*84,398*	*46,880*	*37,518*	*274*	*274*	..	*84,124*	*46,606*	*37,518*	*3*	*3*	..
	Kachhi	*92,753*	*50,187*	*42,566*	*2,689*	*2,681*	*8*	*90,064*	*47,506*	*42,558*	*15*	*15*	..
	Dōmbki-Kahīri country.	*23,543*	*12,624*	*10,919*	*1,166*	*1,164*	*2*	*22,377*	*11,460*	*10,917*	*1*	*1*	..
	Makran	*71,280*	*37,135*	*34,145*	*374*	*372*	*2*	*70,906*	*36,763*	*34,143*	*6*	*6*	..
	Khāran	*22,663*	*12,123*	*10,540*	*119*	*119*	..	*22,544*	*12,004*	*10,540*	..	..	..
	MUSALMĀN	**345,906**	**187,435**	**158,471**	**1,683**	**1,672**	**11**	**344,223**	**185,763**	**158,460**	**48**	**48**	..
	0—10	80	37	43	..	..	..	80	37	43	..	..	..
	10—15	20	15	5	1	1	..	19	14	5	..	..	..
	15—20	52	31	21	14	14	..	38	17	21	4	4	..
	20 and over	509	468	46	67	64	3	442	399	43	17	17	..
	Unspecified	345,245	186,889	158,356	1,601	1,593	8	343,644	185,296	158,348	27	27	..
	Sarāwān	*62,571*	*34,342*	*28,229*	*427*	*426*	*1*	*62,144*	*33,916*	*28,228*	*9*	*9*	..
	Jhalawān	*83,914*	*46,491*	*37,423*	*131*	*131*	..	*83,783*	*46,360*	*37,423*	..	..	..
	Kachhi	*84,389*	*45,823*	*38,566*	*515*	*510*	*5*	*83,874*	*45,313*	*38,561*	*14*	*14*	..
	Dōmbki-Kahīri country.	*20,574*	*11,091*	*9,483*	*89*	*89*	..	*20,485*	*11,002*	*9,483*	..	..	..
	Makrān	*71,186*	*37,051*	*34,135*	*341*	*339*	*2*	*70,845*	*36,712*	*34,133*	*4*	*4*	..
	Khāran	*22,611*	*12,091*	*10,520*	*98*	*98*	..	*22,513*	*11,993*	*10,520*	..	..	..
	HINDU	**10,102**	**5,550**	**4,552**	**3,005**	**2,998**	**7**	**7,097**	**2,552**	**4,545**	**11**	**11**	..
	0—10	7	2	5	..	..	..	7	2	5	..	..	..
	10—15	10	6	4	2	..	2	8	6	2	..	..	..
	15—20	4	3	1	..	..	..	4	3	1	..	..	..
	20 and over	68	60	8	18	16	2	50	44	6	3	3	..
	Unspecified	10,013	5,479	4,534	2,985	2,982	3	7,028	2,497	4,531	8	8	..
	Sarāwān	*957*	*571*	*386*	*528*	*528*	..	*429*	*43*	*386*	*1*	*1*	..
	Jhalawān	*472*	*380*	*92*	*143*	*143*	..	*329*	*237*	*92*	*3*	*3*	..
	Kachhi	*7,176*	*3,748*	*3,428*	*1,838*	*1,835*	*3*	*5,338*	*1,913*	*3,425*	*1*	*1*	..
	Dōmbki-Kahīri country.	*1,262*	*664*	*598*	*422*	*422*	..	*840*	*242*	*598*	*1*	*1*	..
	Makran	*94*	*84*	*10*	*33*	*33*	..	*61*	*51*	*10*	*2*	*2*	..
	Khāran	*52*	*32*	*20*	*21*	*21*	..	*31*	*11*	*20*	..	..	..

VIII.—EDUCATION BY RELIGION AND AGE—*concld.*

District or State.	Religion and Age	Population: Total: Persons	Total: Males	Total: Females	Literate: Persons	Literate: Males	Literate: Females	Illiterate: Persons	Illiterate: Males	Illiterate: Females	Literate in English: Persons	Literate in English: Males	Literate in English: Females
1	2	3	4	5	6	7	8	9	10	11	12	13	14
KALĀT—contd.	**SIKH**	**3,022**	**1,564**	**1,458**	**1,009**	**1,007**	**2**	**2,013**	**557**	**1,456**	..	..	..
	15—20	1	1	..	1	1	..	..	..	..	..	..	..
	20 and over	1	1	..	1	1	..	..	..	..	..	..	..
	Unspecified	3,020	1,562	1,458	1,007	1,005	2	2,013	557	1,456	..	..	..
	Sarāwān	*113*	*68*	*45*	*16*	*16*	..	*97*	*52*	*45*	..	..	..
	Jhalawān	*12*	*9*	*3*	..	..	..	*12*	*9*	*3*	..	..	..
	Kachhi	*1,188*	*616*	*572*	*336*	*336*	..	*852*	*280*	*572*	..	..	..
	Dombki-Kaheri country.	*1,707*	*869*	*838*	*655*	*653*	*2*	*1,052*	*216*	*836*	..	..	..
	CHRISTIAN	**51**	**45**	**6**	**44**	**40**	**4**	**7**	**5**	**2**	**23**	**20**	**3**
	0—10	2	..	2	..	..	..	2	..	2	..	..	..
	15—20	4	3	1	3	2	1	1	1	..	..	..	..
	20 and over	45	42	3	41	38	3	4	4	..	23	20	3
	OTHERS	**5**	**4**	**1**	**4**	**3**	**1**	**1**	**1**	..	**3**	**3**	..
	0—10	1	..	1	1	..	1	..	..	..	..	..	..
	20 and over	4	4	..	3	3	..	1	1	..	3	3	..
LAS BELA	**ALL RELIGIONS**	**61,205**	**32,640**	**28,565**	**1,079**	**1,070**	**9**	**60,126**	**31,570**	**28,556**	**13**	**13**	..
	20 and over	5	5	..	4	4	..	1	1	..	4	4	..
	Unspecified	61,200	32,635	28,565	1,075	1,066	9	60,125	31,569	28,566	9	9	..
	MUSALMĀN	**59,386**	**31,587**	**27,799**	**441**	**432**	**9**	**58,945**	**31,155**	**27,790**	**8**	**8**	..
	HINDU	**1,736**	**988**	**748**	**614**	**614**	..	**1,122**	**374**	**748**	**1**	**1**	..
	SIKH	**78**	**60**	**18**	**20**	**20**	..	**58**	**40**	**18**	..	..	..
	CHRISTIAN	**4**	**4**	..	**4**	**4**	..	..	..	..	**4**	**4**	..
	20 and over	4	4	..	4	4	..	..	..	..	4	4	..
	OTHERS	**1**	**1**	..	..	..	..	**1**	**1**	..	..	..	..
	20 and over	1	1	..	..	..	..	1	1	..	..	..	..

TABLE IX.

Education by Selected Tribes and Races.

IX.—EDUCATION BY SELECTED

(Indigenous

Serial No.	Tribe or race	Population			Illiterate			Literate		
		Persons	Males	Females	Persons	Males	Females	Persons	Males	Females
1	2	3	4	5	6	7	8	9	10	11
1	***Indigenous Musalmans***	***734,610***	***398,204***	***336,406***	***731,129***	***394,758***	***336,371***	***3,481***	***3,446***	***35***
2	**Balōch**	**169,190**	**91,959**	**77,231**	**168,551**	**91,332**	**77,219**	**639**	**627**	**12**
3	*(i) Eastern*	*111,919*	*61,351*	*50,568*	*111,680*	*61,121*	*50,559*	*239*	*230*	*9*
4	Bugṭī	19,370	10,893	8.477	19,362	10,885	8,477	8	8	..
5	Ḍōmbkī	5,713	3,109	2,604	5.706	3,102	2,604	7	7	..
6	Jakhrānī	200	111	89	200	111	89	..	..	..
7	Khetrān	14,153	7,372	6,781	14,118	7,337	6,781	35	35	..
8	Magsī	17,777	9.772	8,005	17.742	9,741	8,001	35	31	4
9	Marī	22,233	12,508	9,725	22,209	12,484	9,725	24	24	..
10	Rind	31,267	16,938	14,329	31,185	16,857	14,328	82	81	1
11	Umrānī	989	520	469	985	516	469	4	4	..
12	Others	217	128	89	173	88	85	44	40	4
13	*(ii) Western*	*57,271*	*30,608*	*26,663*	*56.871*	*30,211*	*26,660*	*400*	*397*	*3*
14	Barr	794	447	347	787	440	347	7	7	..
15	Bulēdī	1,340	723	617	1,335	718	617	5	5	..
16	Dashtī	983	553	430	983	553	430	..	..	..
17	Dōdāī	80	44	36	80	44	36	..	..	..
18	Gabōl	86	43	43	85	42	43	1	1	..
19	Gamshādzai	143	89	54	143	89	54	..	..	..
20	Gichkī	554	269	285	535	250	285	19	19	..
21	Gōrgēj	46	24	22	42	20	22	4	4	..
22	Hōt	1,231	641	590	1,227	637	590	4	4	..
23	Kallagī	443	234	209	440	231	209	3	3	..
24	Kalmatī	187	110	77	187	110	77	..	..	..
25	Kaudāī	1,132	607	525	1,124	599	525	8	8	..
26	Kaṭōhar	186	98	88	183	95	88	3	3	..
27	Kēngīzai	460	242	218	460	242	218	..	..	..
28	Khōsa	1,170	607	563	1,114	551	563	56	56	..
29	Kōlwāī	1.054	589	465	1,054	589	465	..	..	..
30	Kulānchī	51	26	25	51	26	25	..	..	..
31	Lāshārī	459	230	229	459	230	229	..	..	..
32	Laṭṭī	209	120	89	209	120	89	..	..	..
33	Lunḍī	116	63	53	116	63	53	..	..	..
34	Mullāzai	512	282	230	486	256	230	26	26	..
35	Naushērwānī	333	149	184	327	144	183	6	5	1
36	Purki	689	352	337	688	351	337	1	1	..
37	Raīs	4,147	2,187	1,960	4,123	2,163	1,960	24	24	..
38	Rakhshānī	16,913	9,087	7,826	16,809	8.983	7,826	104	104	..
39	Rind	9,022	4,736	4,286	8,946	4,662	4.284	76	74	2
40	Sāmī	1,126	627	499	1,121	622	499	5	5	..
41	Sangur	5,798	3,049	2,749	5,798	3,049	2,749	..	..	..
42	Sanjrānī	121	62	59	117	58	59	4	4	..
43	Shahzāda	609	317	292	606	314	292	3	3	..
44	Tankī	2,822	1,574	1,248	2,822	1,574	1,248	..	..	..
45	Wāḍēla	247	130	117	247	130	117	..	..	..
46	Others	4,208	2,297	1,911	4,167	2,256	1,911	41	41	..
47	**Brāhūī**	**167,787**	**93,095**	**74,692**	**167,245**	**92,557**	**74,688**	**542**	**538**	**4**
48	*(i) Original nucleus*	*15,047*	*8,302*	*6,745*	*14,983*	*8,239*	*6,744*	*64*	*63*	*1*
49	Ahmadzai	25	15	10	17	8	9	8	7	1
50	Iltāzai	156	85	71	156	85	71	..	..	..
51	Gurgnāṛī	2,041	1,124	917	2,037	1,120	917	4	4	..
52	Kalandrāṛī	2,012	1,138	874	2,010	1.136	874	2	2	..
53	Kambrāṛī	3,095	1,679	1.416	3,091	1,675	1,416	4	4	..
54	Mīrwāṛī	2,654	1,450	1,204	2,640	1,436	1,204	14	14	..
55	Rōdēnī	1,325	724	601	1,302	701	601	23	23	..
56	Sumālāṛī	3,739	2,087	1,652	3.730	2,078	1,652	9	9	..
57	*(ii) Sarāwān*	*55,370*	*30,615*	*24,755*	*55,090*	*30,337*	*24,753*	*280*	*278*	*2*
58	Bangulzai	11,595	6,377	5,218	11,560	6,342	5,218	35	35	..
59	Kūrd	3,476	1.928	1,548	3,457	1,909	1,548	19	19	..
60	Lahṛī	5,839	3,314	2,525	5,814	3,290	2,524	25	24	1
61	Lāngav	10,979	6,007	4,972	10,905	5,933	4,972	74	74	..
62	Māmashahī	3,866	2,143	1,723	3,855	2,133	1,722	11	10	1
63	Raīsānī	1,977	1,093	884	1,961	1,077	884	16	16	..
64	Rustumzai	656	341	315	645	330	315	11	11	..
65	Sarparra	2,212	1,213	999	2,185	1,186	999	27	27	..
66	Sātakzai	1,278	715	563	1,276	713	563	2	2	..
67	Shahwānī	8,770	4,894	3,876	8,728	4,852	3,876	42	42	..
68	Zagr Mēngal	4,722	2,590	2,132	4,704	2,572	2,132	18	18	..

TRIBES AND RACES.

Musalmāns only.)

LITERATE IN														
Persian		Urdu		Lanḍe		Sindhī		Arabic		English		Other languages		Serial No.
Males	Females	Males	Females	Males	Females	Males	Females	Males	Females	Males	Females	Males	Females	
12	13	14	15	16	17	18	19	20	21	22	23	24	25	26
2,330	10	872	3	117	..	294	4	320	10	40	..	21	9	1
487	7	137	1	8	..	56	..	25	..	6	..	4	4	2
131	5	96	..	8	..	31	..	18	..	5	..	4	4	3
..	..	8	..	..	..	..	..	..	..	..	..	..	..	4
2	..	4	..	..	..	1	..	..	..	2	..	..	..	5
..	..	..	..	..	..	..	..	..	..	..	..	..	..	6
10	..	23	..	2	..	..	..	7	..	1	..	..	..	7
28	4	4	..	..	..	3	..	1	..	..	..	..	..	8
6	..	17	..	..	..	..	..	1	..	..	..	..	..	9
61	1	22	..	..	..	19	..	7	..	1	..	..	..	10
4	..	4	..	..	..	3	..	..	..	..	..	..	..	11
20	..	14	..	1	..	5	..	2	..	1	..	4	4	12
356	2	41	1	5	..	25	..	7	..	1	..	..	..	13
7	..	..	..	..	..	..	..	..	..	..	..	..	..	14
5	..	..	..	..	..	..	..	..	..	..	..	..	..	15
..	..	..	..	..	..	..	..	..	..	..	..	..	..	16
..	..	..	..	..	..	..	..	..	..	..	..	..	..	17
1	..	..	..	..	..	..	..	..	..	..	..	..	..	18
..	..	..	..	..	..	..	..	..	..	..	..	..	..	19
19	..	2	..	..	..	..	..	2	..	..	..	..	..	20
4	..	..	..	..	..	..	..	..	..	..	..	..	..	21
4	..	..	..	..	..	..	..	..	..	..	..	..	..	22
3	..	..	..	..	..	..	..	..	..	..	..	..	..	23
..	..	..	..	..	..	..	..	..	..	..	..	..	..	24
8	..	..	..	..	..	..	..	..	..	..	..	..	..	25
3	..	..	..	..	..	..	..	..	..	..	..	..	..	26
..	..	..	..	..	..	..	..	..	..	..	..	..	..	27
34	..	12	..	5	..	22	..	..	..	..	..	..	..	28
..	..	..	..	..	..	..	..	..	..	..	..	..	..	29
..	..	..	..	..	..	..	..	..	..	..	..	..	..	30
..	..	..	..	..	..	..	..	..	..	..	..	..	..	31
..	..	..	..	..	..	..	..	..	..	..	..	..	..	32
..	..	..	..	..	..	..	..	..	..	..	..	..	..	33
26	..	..	..	..	..	..	..	..	..	..	..	..	..	34
5	..	..	1	..	..	..	..	..	..	..	..	..	..	35
1	..	..	..	..	..	..	..	..	..	..	..	..	..	36
24	..	1	..	..	..	..	..	..	..	..	..	..	..	37
90	..	18	..	..	..	3	..	..	..	1	..	..	..	38
72	2	6	..	..	..	..	..	1	..	..	..	..	..	39
5	..	..	..	..	..	..	..	..	..	..	..	..	..	40
..	..	..	..	..	..	..	..	..	..	..	..	..	..	41
4	..	..	..	..	..	..	..	1	..	..	..	..	..	42
3	..	..	..	..	..	..	..	..	..	..	..	..	..	43
..	..	..	..	..	..	..	..	..	..	..	..	..	..	44
..	..	..	..	..	..	..	..	..	..	..	..	..	..	45
38	..	2	..	..	..	..	..	3	..	..	..	..	..	46
442	..	87	..	4	..	7	..	37	3	4	..	8	1	47
54	..	10	..	..	..	..	..	4	1	1	..	..	..	48
6	..	5	..	..	..	..	..	..	1	1	..	..	..	49
..	..	..	..	..	..	..	..	..	..	..	..	..	..	50
1	..	..	..	..	..	..	..	3	..	..	..	..	..	51
2	..	..	..	..	...	..	..	..	..	..	..	..	..	52
4	..	..	..	..	..	..	..	..	..	..	..	..	..	53
14	..	..	..	..	..	..	..	..	..	..	..	..	..	54
22	..	1	..	..	..	..	..	1	..	..	..	..	..	55
5	..	4	..	..	..	..	..	..	..	..	..	..	..	56
236	..	44	..	2	..	1	..	17	2	2	..	1	..	57
31	..	3	..	..	..	1	..	2	..	..	..	..	..	58
17	..	2	..	..	..	..	..	5	..	..	..	..	..	59
20	..	2	..	..	..	..	..	6	1	..	..	..	..	60
66	..	9	..	..	..	..	..	1	..	1	..	..	..	61
9	..	4	..	..	..	..	..	..	1	..	..	..	..	62
14	..	1	..	..	..	..	..	3	..	..	..	..	..	63
11	..	..	..	..	..	..	..	..	..	..	..	..	..	64
21	..	6	..	..	..	..	..	..	..	..	..	..	..	65
2	..	1	..	..	..	..	..	..	..	1	..	..	..	66
28	..	13	..	2	..	..	..	..	..	..	..	1	..	67
17	...	3	..	..	..	..	..	..	..	..	..	..	..	68

IX.—EDUCATION BY SELECTED

(Indigenous

Serial No.	Tribe or race	Population			Illiterate			Literate		
		Persons	Males	Females	Persons	Males	Females	Persons	Males	Females
1	2	3	4	5	6	7	8	8	10	11
69	*(iii) Jhalawān*	*94,708*	*52,697*	*42,011*	*94.545*	*52,535*	*42,010*	*163*	*162*	*1*
70	Bīzanjav	10,858	5,906	4,952	10,844	5,892	4,952	14	14	..
71	Hārūnī	1,248	674	574	1,245	671	574	3	3	..
72	Māmasanī	13,489	7,474	6,015	13,456	7,441	6,015	33	33	..
73	Mēngal	26,805	15,199	11,606	26,749	15,143	11,606	56	56	..
74	Nichārī	3,641	2.060	1,581	3,641	2,060	1,581	..	..	..
75	Pandrānī	2,007	1,115	892	2,005	1,113	892	2	2	..
76	Sājdī	4,011	2,239	1,772	3,988	2,217	1,771	23	22	1
77	Zahrī	32,649	18.030	14,619	32,617	17,998	14,619	32	32	..
78	*(iv) Miscellaneous*	*2,662*	*1,481*	*1,181*	*2,627*	*1,446*	*1,181*	*35*	*35*	..
79	Nighārī	1,311	718	593	1.311	718	593	..	..	..
80	Pirri-kārī	517	278	239	516	277	239	1	1	..
81	Rēkīzai	611	336	275	607	332	275	4	4	..
82	Others	223	149	74	193	119	74	30	30	..
83	**Paṭhān**	**188,093**	**102,148**	**85,945**	**187,153**	**101,210**	**85,943**	**940**	**938**	**2**
84	Bābī	323	173	150	318	168	150	5	5	..
85	Barēch	854	480	374	849	475	374	5	5	..
86	Jafar	1.286	690	596	1,281	685	596	5	5	..
87	Kākar	105,073	57,752	47.321	104,641	57,321	47,320	432	431	1
88	*Dāwī*	*284*	*156*	*128*	*283*	*155*	*128*	*1*	*1*	..
89	*Dumar*	*7,755*	*4,267*	*3,488*	*7,740*	*4,252*	*3,488*	*15*	*15*	..
90	*Lamar*	*492*	*274*	*218*	*489*	*271*	*218*	*3*	*3*	..
91	*Sanzarkhēl*	*56,032*	*30,644*	*25,388*	*55,914*	*30,527*	*25,387*	*118*	*117*	*1*
92	*Sargara*	*2,343*	*1,265*	*1,078*	*2,308*	*1,230*	*1,078*	*35*	*35*	..
93	*Snatia*	*23,349*	*12,945*	*10.404*	*23,168*	*12,764*	*10,404*	*181*	*181*	..
94	*Targhara*	*14,089*	*7,770*	*6,319*	*14,026*	*7,707*	*6.319*	*63*	*63*	..
95	*Others*	*729*	*431*	*298*	*713*	*415*	*298*	*16*	*16*	..
96	Kāsī	1.337	705	632	1,285	643	632	57	57	..
97	Lūnī	2.816	1,496	1,320	2,807	1,487	1,320	9	9	..
98	Panī	28.675	15,245	13,430	28,525	15,095	13,430	150	150	..
99	*Main branch*	*6,714*	*3,496*	*3,218*	*6,641*	*3,423*	*3,218*	*73*	*73*	..
100	*Isōt*	*2,812*	*1,515*	*1,297*	*2,803*	*1.506*	*1,297*	*9*	*9*	..
101	*Mandōkhēl*	*4,944*	*2,653*	*2,291*	*4,896*	*2,605*	*2,291*	*48*	*48*	..
102	*Mūsakhēl*	*12,202*	*6,533*	*5,669*	*12,185*	*6,516*	*5,669*	*17*	*17*	..
103	*Zarkūn*	*2.003*	*1,048*	*955*	*2,000*	*1,045*	*955*	*3*	*3*	..
104	Shīrānī	8,552	4.538	4,014	8,533	4,519	4,014	19	19	..
105	Tarīn	37,411	20,077	17,334	37,225	19,892	17,333	186	185	1
106	*Abdāl Achakzai*	*20,272*	*11,199*	*9,073*	*20,211*	*11,138*	*9,073*	*61*	*61*	..
107	*Spīn Tarīn*	*5,134*	*2,713*	*2,421*	*5,110*	*2,690*	*2,420*	*24*	*23*	*1*
108	*Tōr Tarīn*	*11,890*	*6,086*	*5,804*	*11,801*	*5,997*	*5,804*	*89*	*89*	..
109	*Others*	*115*	*79*	*36*	*103*	*67*	*36*	*12*	*12*	..
110	Zmarai	1,228	694	534	1,225	691	534	3	3	..
111	Others	538	298	240	469	229	240	69	69	..
112	**Lāsi (Panj Rāj)**	**27,779**	**14,857**	**12,922**	**27,590**	**14,672**	**12,918**	**189**	**185**	**4**
113	Angāria	3,146	1,656	1,490	3,139	1,649	1,490	7	7	..
114	Burrā	5,374	2,933	2,441	5,362	2,922	2,440	12	11	1
115	Jāmōt	9,724	5,203	4,521	9,710	5,191	4,519	14	12	2
116	Rūnjhā	5.103	2,688	2,415	4,964	2,550	2,414	139	138	1
117	Shēkh	4,432	2,377	2,055	4,415	2,360	2,055	17	17	..
118	**Jaṭṭ**	**78,397**	**42,670**	**35,727**	**77,952**	**42,229**	**35,723**	**445**	**441**	**4**
119	**Sayyid**	**21,296**	**11,008**	**10,288**	**20,935**	**10,651**	**10,284**	**361**	**357**	**4**
120	**Other Musalmāns**	**82,068**	**42,467**	**39,601**	**81,703**	**42,107**	**39,596**	**365**	**360**	**5**
121	Darzāda	10,257	5,215	5,042	10,221	5,179	5,042	36	36	..
122	Dēhwār	7,326	4.009	3,317	7.224	3,907	3,317	102	102	..
123	Gadrā	7,201	3,716	3,485	7,133	3,649	3,484	68	67	1
124	Ghulām	20,244	9,545	10,699	20,239	9,540	10,699	5	5	..
125	Ghulāmāzad	7,738	4,233	3,505	7,715	4,213	3,502	23	20	3
126	Gōlā	834	462	372	834	462	372	..	..	..
127	Jat	5,680	3,151	2,529	5,673	3,145	2,528	7	6	1
128	Khōja	367	185	182	317	135	182	50	50	..
129	Kōri	570	308	262	556	294	262	14	14	..
130	Lōrī	10,936	5,912	5,024	10,931	5,907	5,024	5	5	..
131	Mēd	2,494	1,259	1,235	2,489	1,254	1,235	5	5	..
132	Nakib	6,536	3.444	3,092	6,513	3,421	3.092	23	23	..
133	Others	1,885	1,028	857	1,858	1,001	857	27	27	..

TRIBES AND RACES.

Musalmâns only.)

LITERATE IN														
PERSIAN		URDU		LANḌA		SINDHI		ARABIC		ENGLISH		OTHER LANGUAGES		Serial No.
Males	Females	Males	Females	Males	Females	Males	Females	Males	Females	Males	Females	Males	Females	
12	13	14	15	16	17	18	19	20	21	22	23	24	25	26
126	..	*23*	..	*1*	..	*6*	..	*15*	..	*1*	..	*5*	*1*	69
13	..	1	..	1	..	..	..	1	..	..	..	..	..	70
1	..	2	..	..	..	..	..	..	..	..	..	..	..	71
31	..	1	..	..	..	..	..	2	..	..	..	1	..	72
31	..	11	..	..	..	6	..	11	..	..	..	1	..	73
..	..	..	..	..	..	..	..	..	..	..	..	..	..	74
..	..	..	..	..	..	..	..	..	..	..	..	2	..	75
21	..	..	..	..	..	..	..	1	..	..	..	1	1	76
29	..	8	..	..	..	..	..	..	..	1	..	..	..	77
26	..	*10*	..	*1*	..	..	..	*1*	..	..	..	*2*	.	78
..	..	..	..	..	..	..	..	..	..	..	..	..	..	79
1	..	..	..	..	..	..	..	..	..	..	..	..	...	80
4	..	..	..	..	..	..	..	..	..	..	..	..	..	81
21	..	10	..	1	..	..	..	1	..	..	..	2	..	82
606	**2**	**330**	..	..	..	**2**	..	**161**	..	**22**	..	**3**	..	83
5	..	..	..	..	..	..	..	..	..	..	..	..	..	84
4	..	..	..	..	..	..	..	2	..	..	..	..	..	85
3	..	5	..	..	..	..	..	3	..	..	..	..	..	86
278	1	132	..	..	..	..	..	85		11	..	2	..	87
1	..	..	..	..	..	..	..	*1*	..	..	..	..	..	88
15	..	*1*	..	..	..	..	..	*10*	..	..	..	..	..	89
2	..	..	..	..	..	..	..	*1*	..	..	..	..	..	90
66	*1*	*31*	..	..	..	..	..	*36*	..	*2*	..	*2*	..	91
11	..	*25*	..	..	..	..	..	*5*	..	..	..	..	..	92
118	..	*65*	..	..	..	..	..	*21*	..	*8*	..	..	..	93
54	..	*4*	..	..	..	..	..	*9*	..	..	..	..	..	94
11	..	*6*	..	..	..	..	..	*2*	..	*1*	..	..	..	95
15	..	40	..	..	..	..	..	4	..	3	..	..	..	96
3	..	4	..	..	..	..	..	5	..	..	..	..	..	97
85	..	48	..	..	..	..	..	29	..	1	..	1	..	98
38	..	*37*	..	..	..	..	..	*2*	..	..	..	*1*	..	99
6	..	..	..	..	..	..	..	*3*	..	..	..	..	..	100
28	..	*5*	..	..	..	..	..	*22*	..	..	..	..	..	101
18	..	*8*	..	..	..	..	..	*2*	..	*1*	..	..	..	102
..	..	*3*	..	..	..	..	..	..	..	..	..	..	..	103
13	...	12	..	..	..	..	..	3	..	..	..	..	..	104
144	1	76	..	..	..	..	..	20	..	2	..	..	..	105
48	...	*42*	..	..	..			*10*	..	*1*	..	..	..	106
9	*1*	*16*	..	..	..	..	..	..	..	..	..	..	..	107
80	..	*18*	..	..	..	..	..	*8*	..	..	..	..	..	108
7	..	*5*	..	..	..	..	..	*2*	..	*1*	..	..	..	109
3	..	2	..	..	..	..	..	..	..	..	..	..	..	110
53	..	11	..	..	..	2	..	10	..	5	..	..	..	111
13	..	**92**	**1**	**21**	..	**100**	**3**	**2**	**1**	..	..	..	..	112
..	..	4	..	2	..	1	..	..	..	..	..	..	..	113
..	..	7	1	..	..	4	1	..	..	..	..	..	..	114
..	..	..	..	..	..	12	2	..	..	..	..	..	..	115
11	..	78	..	18	..	70	..	2	1	..	..	..	..	116
2	..	8	..	1	..	18	..	..	..	..	..	..	..	117
309	..	**78**	..	**1**	..	**64**	..	**60**	**4**	**3**	..	..	..	118
272	**1**	**76**	**1**	**1**	..	**28**	..	**26**	**2**	**5**	..	..	..	119
201	..	**72**	..	**82**	..	**37**	**1**	**9**	..	..	..	**6**	**4**	120
33	..	1	..	..	..	..	..	4	..	..	..	3	..	121
100	..	20	..	..	..	..	..	2	..	..	..	..	..	122
1	..	25	..	27	..	18	1	..	..	..	..	..	..	123
..	..	3	..	..	..	1	..	1	..	..	..	..	..	124
17	..	1	..	..	..	..	..	..	..	..	..	3	3	125
..	..	..	..	..	..	..	..	..	..	..	..	..	..	126
5	..	..	--	..	..	2	..	..	..	..	..	..	1	127
..	..	1	..	49	..	..	..	..	..	..	..	..		128
1	..	11	..	1	..	9	..	..	..	..	..	..	..	129
2	..	3	..	..	..	2	..	..	..	..	..	..	..	130
4	..	..	..	2	..	1	..	1	..	..	..	..	..	131
28	..	1	..	..	..	..	..	..	..	..	..	..	..	132
15	..	6	..	3	..	4	..	1	..	..	..	..	..	133

TABLE X.

Language.

Linguistic classification has only been attempted in the case of the Local Vernaculars and is accordingly not exhaustive, several alien Iranian, Indian and Dravidian languages given separately in the Table, being excluded from it.

X.—LANGUAGE.

Language	Balūchistān Persons	Balūchistān Males	Balūchistān Females	Quetta-Pishīn Males	Quetta-Pishīn Females	Lōralai Males	Lōralai Females	Zhōb Males	Zhōb Females	Bōlān Males	Bōlān Females	Chāgai Males	Chāgai Females	Sibi: Administered area Males	Sibi: Administered area Females	Sibi: Mari-Bugti country Males	Sibi: Mari-Bugti country Females
1	2	3	4	5	6	7	8	9	10	11	12	13	14	15	16	17	18
TOTAL	**834,703**	**466,419**	**368,284**	**76,467**	**51,181**	**44,923**	**35,846**	**40,346**	**30,020**	**1,492**	**604**	**9,107**	**7,237**	**47,558**	**34,865**	**19,288**	**15,478**
A. Vernaculars of India	*826,410*	*460,047*	*366,363*	*71,105*	*49,517*	*44,801*	*35,810*	*40,104*	*29,998*	*1,470*	*592*	*9,036*	*7,211*	*47,154*	*34,777*	*19,288*	*15,478*
I. Of Balūchistān	**769,022**	**418,752**	**350,270**	**51,454**	**42,622**	**41,329**	**35,182**	**37,106**	**29,589**	**505**	**350**	**8,716**	**7,116**	**40,662**	**32,703**	**19,192**	**15,411**
Iranian	*468,119*	*254,289*	*213,830*	*45,418*	*37,821*	*32,191*	*26,960*	*37,006*	*29,589*	*369*	*314*	*5,360*	*4,426*	*24,810*	*20,069*	*18,206*	*14,568*
Balōchi	232,987	125,192	107,795	595	445	1,998	1,415	19	3	344	307	4,856	4,074	13,531	11,339	18,204	14,568
Dehwāri	7,579	4,111	3,468	37	29	...	...	..	..	...	...	1	1	..	...	..	...
Pashtō	227,553	124,986	102,567	44,786	37,347	30,193	25,545	36,987	29,586	25	7	503	351	11,279	8,730	2	...
Indian	*155,351*	*83,490*	*71,861*	*114*	*114*	*9,068*	*8,193*	*2*	...	*1*	...	*154*	*88*	*13,389*	*10,816*	*868*	*756*
(i) Western Panjābi branch.	*47,931*	*26,653*	*22,278*	*86*	*90*	*8,502*	*7,730*	*2*	...	*1*	...	...	..	*535*	*442*	*14*	*19*
Jafarki	606	327	279	...	...	325	279	2	...	...	...	..	...	...	...	...	..
Khetrāni	16,071	8,412	7,650	..	...	8,177	7,451	...	...		...	...	...	220	196	14	13
Siraiki	31,254	16,914	14,340	86	90	...	...	..	...	1	...	...	...	315	246	...	...
(ii) Sindhi branch	*55,545*	*29,582*	*25,963*	...	..	...	...	..	..	...	...	...		*1,235*	*1,041*	*1*	...
Jatki-Sindhi	14,910	8,025	6,915	...	...	...	...	...	...	...	...	...	...	1,235	1,041	1	...
Lāsi	40,605	21,557	19,048		...	...	...	...	...	...	...	...	...	...	.	...	...
(iii) Unspecified	*51,875*	*28,255*	*23,620*	*28*	*24*	*566*	*463*	...	...	...	...	*154*	*88*	*11,529*	*9,333*	*853*	*744*
Jatki and Jadgāli	50,356	27,415	22,941	28	24	566	463	...	...	...	...	154	88	11,443	9,265	806	709
Jatki	1,519	840	679		...	.	...	...	...	...	...	..	...	86	68	47	35
Dravidian																	
Brāhūi	145,299	80,828	64,471	5,922	4,686	70	29	98	...	135	36	3,203	2,603	2,563	1,818	7	2
Unclassified																	
Lōṛichini	253	145	108	...	1	...	...	...	...	...	...	...	...	...	...	111	85
II. Of other parts of India	**57,388**	**41,295**	**16,093**	**19,651**	**6,895**	**3,472**	**628**	**2,996**	**409**	**965**	**242**	**320**	**95**	**6,498**	**2,074**	**96**	**67**
Bengali	13	11	2	7	2	1	...	...	...	...	...	...	...	1	...	...	...
Bihari	144	120	24	41	5	3	..	2	1	67	17	2	..	5	1	...	...
Gujrati	580	395	185	235	140	8	1	3	...	1	...	2	...	87	24	...	...
Gurung	1	1	...	1		...	...	...	...	...	...	...	..	...	...	...	...
Hindi Western	10,983	8,460	2,523	5,054	1,973	655	114	840	74	106	20	60	8	1,063	303	2	2
Kanarese	2	1	1	...	...	...	...	1	1	...	...	...	...	...	...	...	...
Kashmiri	16	12	4	12	4	...	...	...	...	...	...	...	...	...	...	.	...
Lahnda or Western Panjābi.	168	122	46	112	42	...	...	...	...	...	...	...	...	8	3	1	...
Telugu	20	19	1	19	1	...	...	...	..	...	...	...	...	...	...	...	...
Malayālam	2	2	...	2	...	...	...	...	...	...	...	...	...	...	...	...	...
Marathi	846	753	93	604	83	12	...	50	...	1	1	2	...	34	9	...	...
Oreya	3	3	...	1	...	...	...	...	...	...	...	...	...	2	...	...	...
Pahari, Central	302	290	12	262	12	3	...	...	...	10	...	1	...	10	...	...	...
Pahari, Eastern	1,956	1,591	365	1,472	340	...	...	...	...	...	...	...	...	116	13	3	3
Panjābi	27,542	20,665	6,877	10,534	3,785	2,606	460	1,880	322	695	173	217	67	3,385	1,063	3	1
Rajasthani	324	299	25	3	2	65	6	197	...	1	...	5	2	9	4	6	2
Sindhi	14,429	8,517	5,912	1,267	483	119	47	24	10	82	31	29	13	1,183	651	81	59
Tamil	55	32	23	25	14	...	...	1	1	...	...	2	5	4	3	...	...
Tibetan	2	2	...	...	...	...	..	...	...	...	...	...	...	1	...	...	...
B. Vernaculars of other Asiatic countries	*3,935*	*2,905*	*1,030*	*2,191*	*878*	*81*	*23*	*109*	*10*	*10*	*2*	*70*	*25*	*318*	*23*	...	...
Arabic	78	58	20	8	16	...	...	...	...	...	...	...	...	...	...	...	...
Bukhari	7	7	...	...	...	...	...	...	...	...	...	...	...	...	...	...	...
Chinese	2	2	...	1	...	...	...	...	...	...	...	...	...	...	...	...	...
Hebrew	9	5	4	5	4	..	..	...	...	...	..	...	...	...	...	...	...
Japanese	6	...	6	...	6	.	...	...	...	...	..	...	...	...	...	...	...
Persian	3,833	2,833	1,000	2,177	852	81	23	109	10	10	2	70	25	318	23	...	...
C. European languages	*4,358*	*3,467*	*891*	*3,171*	*786*	*41*	*13*	*133*	*12*	*12*	*10*	*1*	*1*	*86*	*65*	...	..
English	4,349	3,459	890	3,164	785	41	13	133	12	12	10	1	1	86	65	...	...
German	8	7	1	6	1	...	...	...	...	...	.	...	...	...	...	...	...
French	1	1	...	1	...	...	...	...	...	...	...	...	...	...	...	...	...

X.—LANGUAGE.

STATES																		Language
Kalāt																Las Bēla		
Total Kalāt		Sarāwān		Jhalawān		Kachhi		Dōmbki-Kahēri country		Makrān		Khārān				
Males	Females	Males	Females	Males	Females	Males	Females	Males	Females	Males	Females	Males	Females	Males	Females	
19	20	21	22	23	24	25	26	27	28	29	30	31	32	33	34	35
194,598	**164,488**	**35,082**	**28,699**	**46,880**	**37,518**	**50,191**	**42,568**	**12,694**	**10,919**	**37,698**	**34,944**	**12,123**	**10,540**	**32,640**	**28,565**	**TOTAL**
194,462	*164,425*	*35,049*	*28,656*	*46,873*	*37,508*	*50,189*	*42,568*	*12,694*	*10,919*	*37,604*	*34,934*	*12,123*	*10,540*	*32,627*	*28,555*	*A. Vernaculars of India*
188,474	**159,647**	**34,564**	**28,337**	**46,527**	**37,412**	**46,266**	**39,105**	**11,653**	**10,078**	**37,344**	**34,177**	**12,120**	**10,538**	**31,314**	**27,650**	**I. Of Balūchistān**
84,329	*74,134*	*12,538*	*10,608*	*8,120*	*6,824*	*16,325*	*13,567*	*2,427*	*2,049*	*36,629*	*33,817*	*8,300*	*7,269*	*6,600*	*5,949*	*Iranian*
79,048	69,697	7,450	6,336	8,018	6,742	16,297	13,537	2,424	2,043	36,563	33,770	8,296	7,269	6,597	5,947	Balōchi
4,073	3,438	4,021	3,390	49	43	2	...	1	5	...	...	...	...	...	...	Dehwāri
1,208	999	1,067	882	53	39	26	30	2	1	66	47	4	...	3	2	Pashtō
38,418	*32,822*	*236*	*176*	*1,078*	*841*	*27,919*	*23,831*	*9,114*	*7,936*	*53*	*33*	*18*	*5*	*21,576*	*19,072*	*Indian*
16,513	*14,004*	*1*	...	...	...	*16,511*	*14,004*	*1*	...	...	...	...	...	...	...	*(i) Western Panjābi branch*
...	...	...	...	...	...	...	...	...	...	...	...	...	...	...	...	Jafarki
1	...	...	...	...	...	...	...	1	...	...	...	...	...	...	...	Khetrāni
16,512	14,004	1	...	...	...	16,511	14,004	...	...	...	...	...	...	...	...	Siraiki
6,799	*5,874*	*5*	*3*	*50*	*19*	*6,744*	*5,852*	...	...	...	...	...	...	*21,557*	*19,048*	*(ii) Sindhi branch*
6,799	5,874	5	3	50	19	6,744	5,852	...	...	...	...	...	...	...	...	Jatki-Sindhi
...	...	...	...	...	...	...	...	...	...	...	...	...	...	21,557	19,048	Lāsi
15,106	*12,944*	*230*	*173*	*1,028*	*822*	*4,664*	*3,975*	*9,113*	*7,936*	*53*	*33*	*18*	*5*	*19*	*24*	*(iii) Unspecified*
14,399	12,368	215	163	1,028	822	4,388	3,742	8,697	7,603	53	33	18	5	19	24	Jatki and Jadgāli
707	576	15	10	...	...	276	233	416	333	...	...	...	...	...	...	Jatki
																Dravidian
65,693	52,669	21,790	17,845	37,324	29,745	2,003	1,695	112	93	663	327	3,802	3,264	3,138	2,629	Brāhūi
																Unclassified
34	23	10	8	5	3	19	12	...	...	...	...	...	...	...	...	Lōrichini
5,988	**4,778**	**485**	**319**	**346**	**96**	**3,923**	**3,463**	**971**	**841**	**260**	**57**	**3**	**2**	**1,313**	**905**	**II. Of other parts of India**
1	...	...	...	...	...	...	...	...	...	1	...	...	...	1	...	Bengali
...	...	...	...	...	...	...	...	...	...	...	...	...	...	...	...	Bihari
48	9	...	...	...	...	...	...	...	...	48	9	...	...	11	11	Gujrati
...	...	...	...	...	...	...	...	...	...	...	...	...	...	...	...	Gurung
44	22	12	6	4	...	13	10	5	2	10	4	...	...	37	7	Hindi, Western
...	...	...	...	...	...	...	...	...	...	...	...	...	...	...	...	Kanarese
...	...	...	...	...	...	...	...	...	...	...	...	...	...	...	...	Kashmiri
3	...	...	...	...	...	...	...	...	...	3	...	...	...	1	1	Lahnda or Western Panjābi
...	...	...	...	...	...	...	...	...	...	...	...	...	...	...	...	Telugu
...	...	...	...	...	...	...	...	...	...	...	...	...	...	...	...	Malayālam
60	...	2	...	...	...	...	...	...	...	58	...	...	...	...	...	Marathi
...	...	...	...	...	...	...	...	...	...	...	...	...	...	...	...	Oreya
4	...	...	...	4	...	...	...	...	...	...	...	...	...	...	...	Pahari, Central
...	...	...	...	...	...	...	...	...	...	...	...	...	...	...	...	Pahari, Eastern
1,205	958	75	39	18	3	78	46	966	839	65	29	3	2	140	48	Panjābi
5	3	...	...	...	...	5	3	...	...	...	...	...	...	8	6	Rajasthani
4,618	3,786	396	274	320	93	3,827	3,404	...	...	75	15	...	...	1,114	832	Sindhi
...	...	...	...	...	...	...	...	...	...	...	...	...	...	...	...	Tamil
...	...	...	...	...	...	...	...	...	...	...	...	...	...	1	...	Tibetan
117	*59*	*32*	*41*	*7*	*10*	*1*	...	...	...	*77*	*8*	...	...	*9*	*10*	*B. Vernaculars of other Asiatic countries*
50	4	...	...	...	...	...	...	...	...	50	4	...	...	...	...	Arabic
7	...	...	...	...	...	...	...	...	...	7	...	...	...	...	...	Bukhari
1	...	...	...	...	...	...	...	...	...	1	...	...	...	...	...	Chinese
...	...	...	...	...	...	...	...	...	...	...	...	...	...	...	...	Hebrew
...	...	...	...	...	...	...	...	...	...	...	...	...	...	...	...	Japanese
59	55	32	41	7	10	1	...	...	...	19	4	...	...	9	10	Persian
19	*4*	*1*	*2*	...	...	*1*	...	...	...	*17*	*2*	...	...	*4*	...	*C. European languages*
19	4	1	2	...	...	1	...	...	...	17	2	...	...	3	...	English
...	...	...	...	...	...	...	...	...	...	...	...	...	...	1	...	German
...	...	...	...	...	...	...	...	...	...	...	...	...	...	...	...	French

TABLE XI.

Birthplace.

The birthplace of those enumerated on the Tribal Schedule was assumed to be the same as the district or the state in which they were enumerated, except in the case of Hindus and obvious aliens.

The following are chief among the districts from which immigrants are drawn :—

	Persons	Males	Females		Persons	Males	Females
Sind				*Panjab*			
Sukkur . . .	1,275	857	418	Amritsar . .	2,468	1,870	598
Hyderabad . .	706	545	161	Rawalpindi . .	2,442	2,095	347
Upper Sind Frontier .	628	453	175	Jhelum . . .	1,894	1,596	298
Karachi . . .	343	217	126	Sialkot . . .	1,784	1,295	489
North-West Frontier Province				Jullundur . .	1,666	1,320	346
				Dera Ghazi Khan .	1,632	963	669
Peshawar. . .	1,553	1,211	342	Hoshiarpur . .	1,450	1,216	234
Hazara . . .	1,041	901	140	Gujrat . . .	1,214	962	252
				Gujranwala . .	1,194	870	324
				Gurdaspur . .	1,045	773	272

District, State, Province or Country where born.	Balūchistān			DISTRICT OR STATE — Dis — Quetta-Pishīn			Lōralai			Zhōb		
	Persons	Males	Females	Persons	Males	Females	Persons	Males	Females	Persons	Males	Females
1	2	3	4	5	6	7	8	9	10	11	12	13
TOTAL	**834,703**	**466,419**	**368,284**	**127,648**	**76,467**	**51,181**	**80,769**	**44,923**	**35,846**	**70,366**	**40,346**	**30,020**
A. *Born in India*	818,512	453,999	364,513	118,619	68,965	49,655	80,358	44,617	35,741	65,768	37,428	28,340
I. WITHIN BALŪCHISTĀN	776,203	420,697	355,506	95,477	51,391	44,086	75,655	40,719	34,936	61,867	33,906	27,961
Districts	351,439	190,726	160,713	92,199	49,458	42,741	75,541	40,619	34,922	61,800	33,844	27,956
Quetta-Pishīn	93,030	50,059	42,971	91,285	48,887	42,398	720	397	323	228	217	11
Lōralai	74,285	39,929	34,356	70	47	23	74,008	39,710	34,298	125	119	6
Zhōb	62,223	34,021	28,202	368	238	130	390	265	125	61,411	33,473	27,938
Bōlān	732	384	348	12	8	4	..	..	..	..	..	..
Chāgai	14,532	7,918	6,614	92	54	38	2	2	..	2	2	..
Sibī	106,637	58,415	48,222	372	224	148	421	245	176	34	33	1
States	424,764	229,971	194,793	3,278	1,933	1,345	114	100	14	67	62	5
Kalāt	364,021	197,658	166,363	3,277	1,933	1,344	111	98	13	67	62	5
Las Bēla	60,743	32,313	28,430	1	..	1	3	2	1	..	..	..
II. BEYOND BALŪCHISTĀN	42,309	33,302	9,007	23,143	17,574	5,569	4,703	3,898	805	3,901	3,522	379
(a) Adjacent to Balūchistān.	33,234	25,929	7,305	17,544	13,234	4,310	4,040	3,336	704	2,060	2,706	354
(i) *British Territory*	*31,551*	*24,432*	*7,119*	*16,929*	*12,720*	*4,209*	*3,778*	*3,100*	*678*	*2,672*	*2,322*	*350*
Bombay	4,570	3,349	1,221	2,391	1,792	599	117	88	29	89	78	11
N.-W. F. Province	3,575	2,868	707	1,896	1,497	399	366	293	73	569	477	92
Panjāb	23,406	18,215	5,191	12,642	9,431	3,211	3,295	2,719	576	2,014	1,767	247
(ii) *Feudatory States*	*1,683*	*1,497*	*186*	*615*	*514*	*101*	*262*	*236*	*26*	*388*	*384*	*4*
Bombay States	388	311	77	227	178	49	10	9	1	9	9	..
N.-W. F. Agencies, etc.	525	523	2	214	212	2	11	11	..	295	295	..
Panjāb States	770	663	107	174	124	50	241	216	25	84	80	4
(b) Not adjacent to Balūchistān.	8,765	7,129	1,636	5,372	4,167	1,205	650	549	101	835	810	25
(i) *British Territory*	*6,711*	*5,381*	*1,330*	*4,408*	*3,399*	*1,009*	*391*	*311*	*80*	*489*	*472*	*17*
Ajmere-Merwara	207	193	14	20	10	10	3	3	..	177	177	..
Assam	10	6	4	3	2	1	..	..	..	1	..	1
Bengal	125	80	45	111	70		4	3	1	3	3	..
Bihar and Orissa	63	53	10	33	28	5	4	2	2	2	2	..
Burma	39	19	20	36	18	18	..	..	..	..	..	..
Central Provinces and Berar.	124	66	58	53	25	28	53	28	25	3	2	1
Madras	135	79	56	100	58	42	1	1	..	2	1	1
United Provinces	6,008	4,885	1,123	4,052	3,188	864	326	274	52	301	287	14
(ii) *Feudatory States*	*2,054*	*1,748*	*306*	*964*	*768*	*196*	*259*	*238*	*21*	*346*	*338*	*8*
Baroda	7	5	2	2	1	1	1	..	1	3	3	..
Central India	133	99	34	80	50	30	8	7	1	24	24	..
Hyderabad	76	61	15	66	53	13	..	..	..	4	2	2
Kashmir	899	794	105	466	396	70	90	84	6	88	86	2
Mysore	57	30	27	50	26	24	..	..	..	3	1	2
Rajputana	850	741	109	275	229	46	160	147	13	222	222	..
Travancore	5	3	2	..	..	..	..	..	..	2	..	2
U. P. States	27	15	12	25	13	12	..	..	..	..	..	..
(c) French and Portuguese Settlements	183	163	20	133	115	18	12	12	..	5	5	..
(d) India unspecified	127	81	46	94	58	36	1	1	..	1	1	..

PLACE.

WHERE ENUMERATED														
TRICTS									STATES					
Bōlān			*Chāgai*			*Sibī*			*Kalāt*			*Las Bēla*		
Persons	Males	Females	Persons	Males	Females	Persons	Males	Females	Persons	Males	Females	Persons	Males	Females
14	15	16	17	18	19	20	21	22	23	24	25	26	27	28
2,096	**1,402**	**694**	**16,344**	**9,107**	**7,237**	**117,189**	**66,846**	**50,343**	**359,096**	**194,596**	**164,488**	**61,205**	**32,640**	**28,565**
2,075	1,475	600	15,746	8,731	7,015	116,005	65,764	50,241	358,736	194,380	164,356	61,204	32,639	28,565
961	570	391	15,349	8,427	6,922	108,031	59,465	48,566	358,010	193,850	164,160	60,853	32,369	28,484
746	393	353	14,183	7,732	6,451	105,973	58,108	47,865	996	571	425	1	1	..
48	30	18	152	125	27	512	343	169	84	59	25	1	1	..
..	..	..	..	..	..	76	50	26	6	3	3	..	..	..
2	2	..	1	1	..	51	42	9	..	..	..	..	..	..
662	340	322	..	..	..	..	..	..	58	36	22	..	..	..
4	2	2	14,006	7,583	6,423	81	67	14	345	208	137	..	..	..
30	19	11	24	23	1	105,253	57,606	47,647	503	265	238	..	..	..
215	177	38	1,166	695	471	2,058	1,357	701	357,014	193,279	163,735	60,852	32,368	28,484
215	177	38	1,166	695	471	2,054	1,353	701	356,892	193,213	163,679	239	127	112
..	..	..	..	..	..	4	4	..	122	66	56	60,613	32,241	28,372
1,114	905	209	397	304	93	7,974	6,299	1,675	726	530	196	351	270	81
881	711	170	320	241	79	6,449	5,004	1,445	601	438	163	339	259	80
869	*703*	*166*	*299*	*228*	*71*	*6,149*	*4,733*	*1,416*	*581*	*425*	*156*	*274*	*201*	*73*
65	51	14	38	25	13	1,458	997	461	242	197	45	170	121	49
20	15	5	13	12	1	691	558	133	18	15	3	2	1	1
784	637	147	248	191	57	4,000	3,178	822	321	213	108	102	79	23
12	*8*	*4*	*21*	*13*	*8*	*300*	*271*	*29*	*20*	*13*	*7*	*65*	*58*	*7*
..	..	..	1	1	..	61	47	14	15	9	6	65	58	7
..	..	..	..	..	..	5	5	..	..	..	..	..	..	..
12	8	4	20	12	8	234	219	15	5	4	1	..	..	..
225	190	35	73	59	14	1,502	1,278	224	98	66	32	10	10	..
203	*171*	*32*	*56*	*44*	*12*	*1,116*	*947*	*169*	*41*	*30*	*11*	*7*	*7*	..
..	..	..	..	..	..	6	2	4	1	1	..	..	..	..
..	..	..	..	..	..	6	4	2	..	..	..	..	..	..
1	1	..	1	..	1	3	1	2	..	..	..	2	2	..
..	..	..	..	..	..	23	20	3	1	1	..	..	..	..
..	..	..	..	..	..	3	1	2	..	..	..	..	..	..
6	4	2	..	..	..	9	7	2	..	..	..	..	..	..
1	1	..	10	4	6	20	13	7	1	1	..	..	..	..
195	165	30	45	40	5	1,046	899	147	38	27	11	5	5	..
22	*19*	*3*	*17*	*15*	*2*	*386*	*331*	*55*	*57*	*36*	*21*	*3*	*3*	..
..	..	..	..	..	..	1	1	..	..	..	..	..	..	..
..	..	..	..	..	..	20	17	3	1	1	..	..	..	..
..	..	..	..	..	..	4	4	..	1	1	..	1	1	..
20	17	3	12	11	1	207	192	15	14	6	8	2	2	..
..	..	..	..	..	..	3	2	1	1	1	..	..	..	..
1	1	..	5	4	1	148	112	36	39	26	13	..	..	..
1	1	..	..	..	..	2	2	..	..	..	..	..	..	..
..	..	..	..	..	..	1	1	..	1	1	..	..	..	..
2	1	1	2	2	..	6	5	1	23	23	..	..	..	..
6	3	3	2	2	..	17	12	5	4	3	1	2	1	1

XI.—BIRTH-

District, State, Province or Country where born	DISTRICT OR STATE											
	BALŪCHISTĀN			Dis-								
				Quetta-Pishīn			*Lōralai*			*Zhōb*		
	Persons	Males	Females	Persons	Males	Females	Persons	Males	Females	Persons	Males	Females
1	2	3	4	5	6	7	8	9	10	11	12	13
B. *Born elsewhere in Asia*	12,801	9,444	3,357	5,873	4,732	1,141	373	276	97	4,476	2,803	1,673
Afghanistan	10,625	7,694	2,931	4,203	3,333	870	371	274	97	4,476	2,803	1,673
Arabia	230	129	101	..	..	..	..	..	..	..	..	..
Bhotan	1	..	1	1	..	1	..	..	..	..	..	..
Ceylon	1	1	..	1	1	..	..	..	..	..	..	..
China	8	5	3	7	4	3	..	..	..	..	..	..
Japan	7	1	6	7	1	6	..	..	..	..	..	..
Nepal	1,677	1,439	238	1,561	1,334	227	1	1	..	..	..	..
Persia	214	148	66	69	46	23	1	1	..	..	..	..
Russian Turkistan	14	12	2	7	5	2	..	..	..	..	..	..
Straits Settlements & Malaya	6	6	..	..	..	..	..	..	..	..	..	..
Tibet	1	1	..	..	..	..	..	..	..	..	..	..
Turkey in Asia	17	8	9	17	8	9	..	..	..	..	..	..
C. *Born in Europe*	3,323	2,926	397	3,106	2,736	370	34	28	6	120	113	7
United Kingdom	3,287	2,908	379	3,074	2,719	355	34	28	6	120	113	7
England and Wales	*2,275*	*1,989*	*286*	*2,105*	*1,839*	*266*	*23*	*19*	*4*	*95*	*89*	*6*
Scotland	*127*	*104*	*23*	*111*	*89*	*22*	*5*	*5*	..	*7*	*6*	*1*
Ireland	*881*	*812*	*69*	*855*	*789*	*66*	*6*	*4*	*2*	*17*	*17*	..
Channel Islands & I. of Man	*4*	*3*	*1*	*3*	*2*	*1*	..	..	..	*1*	*1*	..
Austria Hungary	2	1	1	..	..	..	..	..	..	..	..	..
Belgium	1	1	..	1	1	..	..	..	..	..	..	..
France	6	3	3	6	3	3	..	..	..	..	..	..
Germany	9	6	3	8	6	2	..	..	..	..	..	..
Gibraltar	6	1	5	6	1	5	..	..	..	..	..	..
Italy	3	2	1	3	2	1	..	..	..	..	..	..
Malta	5	2	3	5	2	3	..	..	..	..	..	..
Portugal	1	1	..	1	1	..	..	..	..	..	..	..
Russia	1	..	1	..	..	..	..	..	..	..	..	..
Sweden	1	..	1	1	..	1	..	..	..	..	..	..
Switzerland	1	1	..	1	1	..	..	..	..	..	..	..
D. *Born in Africa*	8	6	2	4	2	2	1	1	..	2	2	..
Cape Colony	5	4	1	3	2	1	1	1	..	1	1	..
East Africa (British)	1	1	..	..	..	..	..	..	..	..	..	..
Mauritius	2	1	1	1	..	1	..	..	..	1	1	..
E. *Born in America*	37	27	10	31	22	9	2	1	1	..	..	..
Canada	19	15	4	18	14	4	1	1	..	..	..	..
United States	9	6	3	4	2	2	1	..	1	..	..	..
West Indies	3	2	1	3	2	1	..	..	..	..	..	..
America unspecified	6	4	2	6	4	2	..	..	..	..	..	..
F. *Born in Australasia*	19	15	4	14	10	4	..	..	..	..	..	..
Australia	18	15	3	13	10	3	..	..	..	..	..	..
Sumatra	1	..	1	1	..	1	..	..	..	..	..	..
G. *Born at Sea*	3	2	1	..	..	..	1	..	1	1	1	..

PLACE — *concld.*

WHERE ENUMERATED														
TRICTS									STATES					
Bōlān			*Chāgai*			*Sibi*			*Kalāt*			*Las Bēla*		
Persons	Males	Females	Persons	Males	Females	Persons	Males	Females	Persons	Males	Females	Persons	Males	Females
14	15	16	17	18	19	20	21	22	23	24	25	26	27	28
10	9	1	597	375	222	1,138	1,045	93	334	204	130	..	..	..
10	9	1	497	304	193	1,018	937	81	50	34	16	..	..	..
..	..	..	..	..	..	..	..	..	230	129	101	..	..	..
..	..	..	..	..	..	..	..	..	..	..	..	..	..	..
..	..	..	..	..	..	..	..	..	..	..	..	..	..	..
..	..	..	..	..	..	..	..	..	1	1	..	..	..	..
..	..	..	..	..	..	..	..	..	..	..	..	..	..	..
..	..	..	..	..	..	115	104	11	..	..	..	..	..	..
..	..	..	100	71	29	4	3	1	40	27	13	..	..	..
..	..	..	..	..	..	..	..	..	7	7	..	..	..	..
..	..	..	..	..	..	..	..	..	6	6	..	..	..	..
..	..	..	..	..	..	1	1	..	..	..	..	..	..	..
..	..	..	..	..	..	..	..	..	..	..	..	..	..	..
11	8	3	..	..	..	41	32	9	11	9	2	1	1	..
10	8	2	..	..	..	39	32	7	11	9	2	..	..	..
10	*8*	*2*	..	..	..	*34*	*28*	*6*	*9*	*7*	*2*	..	..	..
..	..	..	..	..	..	*2*	*2*	..	*2*	*2*	..	..	..	..
..	..	..	..	..	..	*3*	*2*	*1*	..	..	..	..	..	..
..	..	..	..	..	..	..	..	..	..	..	..	..	..	..
1	..	1	..	..	..	..	..	..	..	..	..	1	1	..
..	..	..	..	..	..	..	..	..	..	..	..	..	..	..
..	..	..	..	..	..	..	..	..	..	..	..	..	..	..
..	..	..	..	..	..	1	..	1	..	..	..	..	..	..
..	..	..	..	..	..	..	..	..	..	..	..	..	..	..
..	..	..	..	..	..	..	..	..	..	..	..	..	..	..
..	..	..	..	..	..	..	..	..	..	..	..	..	..	..
..	..	..	..	..	..	..	..	..	..	..	..	..	..	..
..	..	..	..	..	..	1	..	1	..	..	..	..	..	..
..	..	..	..	..	..	..	..	..	..	..	..	..	..	..
..	..	..	..	..	..	..	..	..	..	..	..	..	..	..
..	..	..	..	..	..	1	1	..	..	..	..	..	..	..
..	..	..	..	..	..	..	..	..	..	..	..	..	..	..
..	..	..	..	..	..	1	1	..	..	..	..	..	..	..
..	..	..	..	..	..	..	..	..	..	..	..	..	..	..
..	..	..	..	..	..	1	1	..	3	3	..	..	..	..
..	..	..	..	..	..	..	..	..	..	..	..	..	..	..
..	..	..	..	..	..	1	1	..	3	3	..	..	..	..
..	..	..	..	..	..	..	..	..	..	..	..	..	..	..
..	..	..	..	..	..	..	..	..	..	..	..	..	..	..
..	..	..	1	1	..	2	2	..	2	2	..	..	..	..
..	..	..	1	1	..	2	2	..	2	2	..	..	..	..
..	..	..	..	..	..	..	..	..	..	..	..	..	..	..
..	..	..	..	..	..	1	1	..	..	..	..	..	..	..

TABLE XII.

Infirmities.

In Part I age is unspecified for 3,111 infirm belonging to the 771,696 souls enumerated on the Tribal schedule.

In both Parts there is a discrepancy in the total number of the infirm, as one deaf-mute male in Chāgai and one blind male in Sibi were also returned as insane.

XII.—INFIRMITIES.

Part A.—*Distribution by Age.*

Age	Population Afflicted			Insane			Deaf-Mute			Blind			Leper		
	Persons	Males	Females	Persons	Males	Females	Persons	Males	Females	Persons	Males	Females	Persons	Males	Females
1	2	3	4	5	6	7	8	9	10	11	12	13	14	15	16
0—1	..	..	..	..	..	..	..	..	..	..	..	..	..	..	..
1—2	..	..	..	..	..	..	..	..	..	..	..	..	..	..	..
2—3	..	..	..	..	..	..	..	..	..	..	..	..	..	..	..
3—4	..	..	..	..	..	..	..	..	..	..	..	..	..	..	..
4—5	..	..	..	..	..	..	..	..	..	..	..	..	..	..	..
Total 0—5	..	..	..	..	..	..	..	..	..	..	..	..	..	..	..
5—10	4	3	1	1	1	..	3	2	1	..	..	..	..	..	..
10—15	3	3	..	1	1	..	1	1	..	1	1	..	..	..	..
15—20	3	2	1	1	1	..	2	1	1	..	..	..	..	..	..
20—25	5	4	1	3	3	..	2	1	1	..	..	..	..	..	..
25—30	5	5	..	5	5	..	..	..	..	..	..	..	..	..	..
30—35	5	4	1	2	2	..	2	2	..	1	..	1	..	..	..
35—40	5	5	..	1	1	..	1	1	..	3	3	..	..	..	..
40—45	5	3	2	2	2	..	..	..	..	3	1	2	..	..	..
45—50	5	4	1	2	2	..	1	1	..	2	1	1	..	..	..
50—55	5	5	..	1	1	..	..	..	..	4	4	..	..	..	..
55—60	3	1	2	..	..	..	..	..	..	3	1	2	..	..	..
60—65	3	3	..	..	..	..	..	..	..	3	3	..	..	..	..
65—70	1	..	1	..	..	..	..	..	..	1	..	1	..	..	..
70 and over	8	2	6	..	..	..	..	..	..	8	2	6	..	..	..
Unspecified	3,111	1,865	1,246	351	249	102	656	473	183	2,023	1,079	944	83	66	17
Total	**3,171**	**1,909**	**1,262**	**370**	**268**	**102**	**668**	**482**	**186**	**2,052**	**1,095**	**957**	**83**	**66**	**17**

XII.—INFIRMITIES.

PART B.—*Distribution by Districts and States.*

District or State	Population afflicted			Insane			Deaf-Mute			Blind			Leper		
	Persons	Males	Females	Persons	Males	Females	Persons	Males	Females	Persons	Males	Females	Persons	Males	Females
1	2	3	4	5	6	7	8	9	10	11	12	13	14	15	16
Baluchistan	***3,171***	***1,909***	***1,262***	***370***	***268***	***102***	***668***	***482***	***186***	***2,052***	***1,095***	***957***	***83***	***66***	***17***
Districts	**1,136**	**738**	**398**	**130**	**106**	**24**	**299**	**223**	**76**	**686**	**394**	**292**	**23**	**17**	**6**
Quetta-Pishīn	178	132	46	26	25	1	52	40	12	98	66	32	2	1	1
Lōṛalai	240	154	86	30	23	7	47	36	11	152	86	66	11	9	2
Zhōb	206	130	76	33	26	7	54	37	17	116	65	51	3	2	1
Bōlān	10	3	7	1	1	..	1	1	..	8	1	7	..	..	..
Chāgai	92	52	40	12	8	4	26	20	6	54	25	29	1	..	1
Sibī	410	267	143	28	23	5	119	89	30	258	151	107	6	5	1
Administered area	*333*	*205*	*128*	*21*	*18*	*3*	*86*	*67*	*19*	*223*	*118*	*105*	*4*	*3*	*1*
Mari-Bugṭī country	*77*	*62*	*15*	*7*	*5*	*2*	*33*	*22*	*11*	*35*	*33*	*2*	*2*	*2*	..
States	**2,035**	**1,171**	**864**	**240**	**162**	**78**	**369**	**259**	**110**	**1,366**	**701**	**665**	**60**	**49**	**11**
Kalāt	1,692	974	718	180	128	52	265	185	80	1,193	618	575	54	43	11
Sarāwān	*237*	*191*	*96*	*50*	*41*	*9*	*55*	*40*	*15*	*175*	*104*	*71*	*7*	*6*	*1*
Jhalawān	*175*	*104*	*71*	*19*	*14*	*5*	*42*	*31*	*11*	*97*	*50*	*47*	*17*	*9*	*8*
Kachhī	*568*	*326*	*242*	*40*	*31*	*9*	*87*	*59*	*28*	*438*	*234*	*204*	*3*	*2*	*1*
Ḍōmbki-Kahērī country	*176*	*97*	*79*	*13*	*10*	*3*	*12*	*11*	*1*	*151*	*76*	*75*	..	..	..
Makrān	*400*	*209*	*191*	*42*	*21*	*21*	*55*	*35*	*20*	*276*	*127*	*149*	*27*	*26*	*1*
Khārān	*86*	*47*	*39*	*16*	*11*	*5*	*14*	*9*	*5*	*56*	*27*	*29*	..	..	..
Las Bēla	343	197	146	60	34	26	104	74	30	173	83	90	6	6	..

TABLE XII A.

Infirmities by Selected Tribes and Races.

XII A.—INFIRMITIES BY SELECTED TRIBES AND RACES.

(*Indigenous Musalmāns only.*)

Tribe or Race	Population			Insane		Deaf-mute		Blind		Leper	
	Persons	Males	Females	Males	Females	Males	Females	Males	Females	Males	Females
1	2	3	4	5	6	7	8	9	10	11	12
Indigenous Musalmāns	***734,610***	***398,204***	***336,406***	***241***	***98***	***464***	***179***	***1,007***	***866***	***60***	***16***
Balōch	**169,190**	**91,959**	**77,231**	**51**	**27**	**116**	**46**	**296**	**238**	**15**	**3**
(i) *Eastern*	*111,919*	*61,351*	*50,568*	*30*	*8*	*73*	*29*	*200*	*142*	*7*	*3*
Bugtī	19,370	10,893	8,477	2	1	16	7	29	2	..	..
Ḍōmbkī	5,713	3,109	2,604	1	1	4	..	20	33	..	..
Jakhrānī	200	111	89	..	..	..	..	..	..	..	..
Khetrān	14,153	7,372	6,781	5	2	5	4	33	21	2	1
Magasī	17,777	9,772	8,005	11	1	7	4	36	30	1	..
Marī	22,233	12,508	9,725	5	1	13	6	16	8	3	1
Rind	31,267	16,938	14,329	6	2	27	8	61	46	1	1
Umrānī	989	520	469	..	..	..	..	..	..	..	..
Others	217	128	89	..	..	1	..	5	2	..	..
(ii) *Western*	*57,271*	*30,608*	*26,663*	*21*	*19*	*43*	*17*	*96*	*96*	*8*	..
Barr	794	447	347	..	..	..	..	..	..	..	..
Bulēdī	1,340	723	617	..	..	..	..	..	..	..	..
Dashtī	983	553	430	1	1	1	2	5	1	..	..
Dōdāī	80	44	36	..	..	..	..	..	..	..	..
Gabōl	86	43	43	..	..	..	..	..	..	..	..
Gamshādzai	143	89	54	..	..	..	..	1	2	..	..
Gichkī	554	269	285	..	..	1	..	3	2	..	..
Gōrgēj	46	24	22	..	..	..	..	..	..	..	..
Hōt	1,231	641	590	..	..	..	..	5	6	..	..
Kallagī	443	234	209	..	..	2	..	1	3	..	..
Kalmatī	187	110	77	..	..	..	..	1	..	..	..
Kaudāī	1,132	607	525	..	..	1	..	..	..	..	..
Kaṭōhar	186	98	88	..	..	..	..	..	..	..	..
Kēngīzai	460	242	218	..	..	..	..	..	..	..	..
Khōsa	1,170	607	563	..	..	..	..	..	..	..	..
Kōlwāī	1,054	589	465	..	..	1	..	3	1	1	..
Kulānchī	51	26	25	..	..	..	..	..	..	..	..
Lāshārī	459	230	229	..	..	..	..	..	..	..	..
Laṭṭī	209	120	89	..	..	..	..	..	..	..	..
Lunḍī	116	63	53	..	..	..	..	..	..	..	..
Mullāzai	512	282	230	..	..	..	..	2	1	..	..
Naushērwānī	333	149	184	..	..	..	..	..	..	..	..
Purki	689	352	337	..	..	..	..	..	..	..	..
Raīs	4,147	2,187	1,960	1	..	..	..	6	7	..	..
Rakhshānī	16,913	9,087	7,826	4	..	11	2	18	20	..	..
Rind	9,022	4,736	4,286	9	9	14	10	28	41	6	..
Sāmī	1,126	627	499	..	1	2	..	1	2	1	..
Sangur	5,798	3,049	2,749	1	4	2	..	4	2	..	..
Sanjrānī	121	62	59	..	..	2	..	..	1	..	..
Shahzāda	609	317	292	..	..	..	..	..	..	..	..
Taukī	2,822	1,574	1,248	3	2	3	1	8	4	..	..
Wāḍēla	247	130	117	..	..	..	..	..	..	..	..
Others	4,208	2,297	1,911	2	2	3	2	10	3	..	..
Brāhūī	**167,787**	**93,095**	**74,692**	**58**	**26**	**79**	**48**	**162**	**141**	**19**	**7**
(i) *Original nucleus*	*15,047*	*8,302*	*6,745*	*3*	*1*	*6*	*5*	*6*	*15*	*3*	..
Ahmadzai	25	15	10	..	..	..	..	..	..	..	..
Iltāzai	156	85	71	..	..	..	..	..	..	..	..
Gurgnāṛī	2,041	1,124	917	..	..	..	1	1	4	1	..
Kalandrāṛī	2,012	1,138	874	..	..	..	..	..	..	..	..
Kambrāṛī	3,095	1,679	1,416	..	..	4	3	..	3	..	..
Mīrwāṛī	2,654	1,450	1,204	..	1	..	1	1	1	1	..
Rodēnī	1,325	724	601	2	..	1	..	2	1	..	..
Sumālāṛī	3,739	2,087	1,652	1	..	1	..	2	6	1	..
(ii) *Sarāwān*	*55,370*	*30,615*	*24,755*	*31*	*10*	*57*	*15*	*80*	*59*	*4*	*2*
Bangulzai	11,595	6,377	5,218	5	2	12	3	27	22	1	..
Kūrd	3,476	1,928	1,548	..	1	..	..	8	3	..	..
Lahṛī	5,839	3,314	2,525	6	2	4	4	11	6	2	..
Lāngav	10,979	6,007	4,972	9	1	10	3	14	8	..	1
Māmashahī	3,866	2,143	1,723	3	..	..	2	3	5	..	..
Raisānī	1,977	1,093	884	..	1	..	1	1	2	..	..
Rustumzai	656	341	315	..	..	1	..	1	..	..	..
Sarparra	2,212	1,213	999	..	..	..	..	5	1	..	..
Sātakzai	1,278	715	563	1	..	..	..	1	4	..	..
Shahwānī	8,770	4,894	3,876	6	2	6	1	7	5	1	..
Zagr Mēngal	4,722	2,590	2,132	1	1	4	1	2	3	..	1

XII A.—INFIRMITIES BY SELECTED TRIBES AND RACES.

(Indigenous Musalmāns only.)

Tribe or Race	Population			Insane		Deaf-mute		Blind		Leper	
	Persons	Males	Females	Males	Females	Males	Females	Males	Females	Males	Females
1	2	3	4	5	6	7	8	9	10	11	12
(iii) *Jhalawān*	*94,708*	*52,697*	*42,011*	*22*	*15*	*33*	*23*	*72*	*63*	*12*	*5*
Bīzanjav	10,858	5,906	4,952	3	1	5	4	8	11	2	..
Hārūnī	1,248	674	574	..	..	..	..	..	1	..	..
Māmasanī	13,489	7,474	6,015	4	4	4	5	17	6	1	..
Mēngal	26,805	15,199	11,606	8	4	13	8	28	18	3	4
Nīchārī	3,641	2,060	1,581	..	1	..	..	3	..	..	..
Pandrānī	2,007	1,115	892	..	..	1	..	..	..	1	..
Sājdī	4,011	2,239	1,772	1	2	2	3	5	12	3	..
Zahrī	32,649	18,030	14,619	6	3	8	3	11	15	2	1
(iv) *Miscellaneous*	*2,662*	*1,481*	*1,181*	*2*	..	*3*	*5*	*4*	*4*	..	..
Nighāṛī	1,311	718	593	..	..	1	..	1	..	..	..
Pirri-Kāṛī	517	278	239	..	..	..	..	..	1	..	..
Rōkīzai	611	336	275	..	..	..	..	..	..	..	..
Others	223	149	74	2	..	2	5	3	3	..	..
Paṭhān	**188,093**	**102,148**	**85,945**	**58**	**14**	**110**	**29**	**170**	**135**	**8**	**2**
Bābī	323	173	150	..	..	..	..	1	1	..	..
Baṛēch	854	480	374	..	..	..	..	3	2	..	..
Jafar	1,286	690	596	..	..	2	1	1	1	..	..
Kākaṛ	105,073	57,752	47,321	36	5	53	18	90	56	3	2
Dāwī	*284*	*156*	*128*	..	..	..	..	..	..	..	..
Dumaṛ	*7,755*	*4,267*	*3,488*	*4*	..	*4*	..	*4*	*4*	..	*1*
Lamaṛ	*492*	*274*	*218*	..	..	..	..	..	..	..	..
Sanzarkhēl	*56,032*	*30,644*	*25,388*	*21*	*4*	*29*	*12*	*58*	*39*	*2*	*1*
Sargaṛa	*2,343*	*1,265*	*1,078*	..	..	*1*	..	*1*	*1*	..	..
Snaṭia	*23,349*	*12,945*	*10,404*	*7*	*1*	*15*	*4*	*14*	*5*	..	..
Targhaṛa	*14,089*	*7,770*	*6,319*	*3*	..	*2*	*2*	*11*	*6*	..	..
Others	*729*	*431*	*298*	*1*	..	*2*	..	*2*	*1*	*1*	..
Kāsī	1,337	705	632	..	..	..	..	..	..	..	..
Lūṇī	2,816	1,496	1,320	..	1	5	..	3	3	1	..
Paṇī	28,675	15,245	13,430	11	4	22	3	34	44	2	..
Main branch	*6,714*	*3,496*	*3,218*	*2*	..	*3*	..	*11*	*20*	..	..
Isōṭ	*2,812*	*1,515*	*1,297*	*2*	..	..	..	*3*	..	*1*	..
Mandōkhēl	*4,944*	*2,653*	*2,291*	*4*	*2*	*11*	*3*	*7*	*8*	..	..
Mūsakhēl	*12,202*	*6,533*	*5,669*	*3*	*2*	*8*	..	*12*	*16*	*1*	..
Zarkūn	*2,003*	*1,048*	*955*	..	..	..	..	*1*	..	..	..
Shīrānī	8,552	4,538	4,014	1	2	1	4	8	6	..	..
Tarīn	37,411	20,077	17,334	8	2	25	3	30	18	1	..
Abdāl Achakzai.	*20,272*	*11,199*	*9,073*	*5*	*1*	*13*	*2*	*19*	*6*	*1*	..
Spīn Tarīn	*5,134*	*2,713*	*2,421*	*3*	*1*	*7*	*1*	*8*	*10*	..	..
Tōr Tarīn	*11,890*	*6,086*	*5,804*	..	..	*5*	..	*3*	*2*	..	..
Others	*115*	*79*	*36*	..	..	..	..	..	..	..	..
Zmarai	1,228	694	534	..	..	..	..	..	1	..	..
Others	538	298	240	2	..	2	..	..	3	1	..
Lāsī (Panj Rāj)	**27,779**	**14,857**	**12,922**	**22**	**10**	**46**	**9**	**35**	**35**	**2**	..
Angāria	3,146	1,656	1,490	4	1	6	1	2	3	..	..
Burrā	5,374	2,933	2,441	9	1	5	1	11	8	..	..
Jāmōṭ	9,724	5,203	4,521	6	6	12	3	11	8	1	..
Rūnjhā	5,103	2,688	2,415	2	1	13	4	4	11	1	..
Shēkh	4,432	2,377	2,055	1	1	10	..	7	5	..	..
Jatt	**78,397**	**42,670**	**35,727**	**16**	**8**	**64**	**29**	**198**	**174**	**1**	..
Sayyid	**21,296**	**11,008**	**10,288**	**6**	**1**	**8**	**5**	**24**	**11**	..	..
Other Musalmāns	**82,068**	**42,467**	**39,601**	**30**	**12**	**41**	**13**	**122**	**132**	**15**	**4**
Darzāda	10,257	5,215	5,042	5	1	2	2	17	22	5	..
Dēhwār	7,323	4,009	3,317	5	..	4	3	18	17	..	..
Gaḍra	7,201	3,716	3,485	6	4	9	5	14	13	1	..
Ghulām	20,244	9,545	10,699	2	3	4	..	15	22	..	..
Ghulāmāzād	7,738	4,233	3,505	4	..	4	..	9	7	..	..
Gōla	834	462	372	..	..	..	..	..	..	..	..
Jat	5,680	3,151	2,529	1	1	5	..	9	10	..	..
Khōja	367	185	182	..	..	..	1	..	..	..	..
Kōrī	570	308	262	..	..	3	..	1	4	..	..
Lōṛī	10,936	5,912	5,024	3	..	6	1	12	9	2	3
Mēd	2,494	1,259	1,235	1	1	1	1	10	11	..	..
Nakīb	6,536	3,444	3,092	3	2	2	..	17	17	7	1
Others	1,885	1,028	857	..	..	..	..	..	..	..	..

TABLE XIII.

Caste, Tribe, Race or Nationality.

XIII.—CASTE, TRIBE,

Caste, Tribe, Race or Nationality	Balōchistān			Districts													
				Quetta-Pishin		Lōralai		Zhōb		Bōlān		Chāgai		Sibi			
														Administered area		Marī-Bugṭī	
	Persons	Males	Females	Males	Females	Males	Females	Males	Females	Males	Fe-males	Males	Females	Males	Females	Males	Females
1	2	3	4	5	6	7	8	9	10	11	12	13	14	15	16	17	18
TOTAL .	**834,703**	**466,419**	**368,284**	**76,467**	**51,181**	**44,923**	**35,846**	**40,346**	**30,020**	**1,492**	**604**	**9,107**	**7,237**	**47,558**	**34,865**	**19,288**	**15,478**
Indigenous . .	***752,394***	***407,763***	***344,631***	***47,233***	***40,303***	***34,979***	***30,213***	***33,491***	***27,613***	***504***	***348***	***8,340***	***6,835***	***39,111***	***32,179***	***19,219***	***15,434***
Semi-indigenous	***25,411***	***14,767***	***10,644***	***3,303***	***2,277***	***6,141***	***4,927***	***3,015***	***1,939***	***5***	***1***	***347***	***247***	***1,336***	***720***	***15***	***13***
Aliens . . .	***56,898***	***43,889***	***13,009***	***25,931***	***8,601***	***3,810***	***706***	***3,840***	***468***	***983***	***255***	***430***	***155***	***7,111***	***1,966***	***54***	***31***
European .	4,210	3,382	828	3,109	740	41	12	132	12	10	7	1	1	73	52	..	..
Anglo-Indian .	123	64	59	44	39	..	1	1	..	2	3	..	..	12	16	..	..
Oriental .	52,565	40,443	12,122	22,778	7,822	3,769	693	3,707	456	971	245	419	154	7,026	1,898	54	31
Trans-Indus.	*7,140*	*5,796*	*1,344*	*3,613*	*1,023*	*317*	*66*	*730*	*46*	*14*	*1*	*79*	*28*	*809*	*67*	*9*	*1*
Cis-Indus .	*45,425*	*34,647*	*10,778*	*19,165*	*6,799*	*3,452*	*627*	*2,977*	*410*	*957*	*244*	*340*	*126*	*6,217*	*1,831*	*45*	*30*
Balōch . . .	**172,473**	**93,819**	**78,654**	**505**	**376**	**8,978**	**7,855**	**27**	**10**	**233**	**221**	**3,637**	**3,052**	**14,666**	**12,156**	**17,916**	**14,045**
Indigenous .	***169,190***	***91,959***	***77,231***	***467***	***361***	***7,903***	***7,058***	***2***	***4***	***231***	***220***	***3,636***	***3,052***	***14,391***	***11,951***	***17,902***	***14,032***
(*i*) *Eastern* .	*111,919*	*61,351*	*50,568*	*346*	*271*	*7,892*	*7,049*	*2*	*3*	*231*	*220*	..	..	*14,289*	*11,897*	*17,890*	*14,025*
Bugṭī .	19,370	10,893	8,477	13	8	67	58	..	..	5	2	..	..	241	198	10,504	8,161
Ḍōmbkī .	5,713	3,109	2,604	9	10	..	..	..	..	..	..	..	..	869	761	..	..
Jakhrānī .	200	111	89	..	..	..	..	..	..	..	..	..	..	111	89	..	..
Khetrān .	14,153	7,372	6,781	2	..	6,710	6,216	..	..	..	..	..	..	646	553	14	12
Magasī .	17,777	9,772	8,005	7	4	6	8	..	..	1	..	..	..	568	466	..	..
Marī . .	22,233	12,508	9,725	15	11	1,054	742	..	..	10	8	..	..	3,644	2,787	7,357	5,345
Rind . .	31,267	16,938	14,329	249	202	52	25	2	3	211	210	..	..	7,631	6,521	8	7
Umrānī .	989	520	469	..	..	..	..	..	..	..	..	..	..	519	469	..	..
Others .	217	128	89	51	36	3	..	..	..	4	..	..	..	60	53	7	..
(*ii*) *Western* .	*57,271*	*30,608*	*26,663*	*121*	*90*	*11*	*9*	..	*1*	..	..	*3,636*	*3,052*	*102*	*54*	*12*	*7*
Barr . .	794	447	347	..	..	..	..	..	..	..	..	..	..	..	..	..	..
Bulēdī .	1,340	723	617	..	..	..	..	..	..	..	..	..	..	..	..	..	..
Dashtī .	983	553	430	..	..	..	..	..	..	..	..	..	..	18	7	..	..
Dōdāī .	80	44	36	..	..	..	..	..	..	..	..	..	..	..	..	..	..
Gabōl .	86	43	43	..	..	..	..	..	..	..	..	..	..	..	..	..	..
Gamshādzai	143	89	54	..	..	..	..	..	..	..	..	89	54	..	..	..	..
Gichkī .	564	269	285	..	..	..	..	..	..	..	..	..	..	1	2	..	..
Gōrgēj .	46	24	22	..	..	..	..	..	..	..	..	..	..	..	..	..	..
Hōt . .	1,231	641	590	..	..	..	..	..	..	..	..	..	..	2	1	..	..
Kallagī .	443	234	209	..	..	..	..	..	..	..	..	..	..	..	..	..	..
Kalmatī .	187	110	77	..	..	..	..	..	..	..	..	..	..	..	..	..	..
Kaṭōhar .	186	98	88	..	..	..	..	..	..	..	..	..	..	..	..	..	..
Kaudāī .	1,132	607	525	..	..	..	..	..	..	..	..	..	..	..	..	..	..
Kēngizai .	460	242	218	..	..	..	..	..	..	..	..	..	..	..	..	..	..
Khōsa .	1,170	607	563	..	..	..	..	..	..	..	..	..	..	..	..	..	..
Kōlwāī .	1,054	589	465	..	..	..	..	..	..	..	..	..	..	..	..	..	..
Kulānchī .	51	26	25	..	..	7	6	..	..	..	..	..	..	..	..	..	..
Lāshārī .	459	230	229	..	..	..	..	..	..	..	..	..	..	..	..	..	..
Laṭṭī .	209	120	89	..	..	..	..	..	..	..	..	..	..	..	..	..	..
Lunḍī .	116	63	53	..	..	..	..	..	..	..	..	..	..	..	..	..	..
Mullāzai .	512	282	230	..	..	..	..	..	..	..	..	..	..	..	..	..	..
Naushērwānī	333	149	184	24	18	2	3	..	1	..	..	..	..	1	2	..	..
Purkī .	689	352	337	..	..	..	..	..	..	..	..	..	..	..	..	..	..
Raīs . .	4,147	2,187	1,960	..	..	..	..	..	..	..	..	..	..	..	..	..	..
Rakhshānī .	16,913	9,087	7,826	82	61	2	..	..	..	..	..	1,870	1,661	80	42	12	7
Rind . .	9,022	4,736	4,286	..	..	..	..	..	..	..	..	34	29	..	..	..	..
Sāmī .	1,126	627	499	..	..	..	..	..	..	..	..	..	..	..	..	..	..
Sangur .	5,798	3,049	2,749	..	..	..	..	..	..	..	..	..	..	..	..	..	..
Sanjrānī .	121	62	59	1	1	..	..	..	..	..	..	61	58	..	..	..	..
Shahzāda .	609	317	292	..	..	..	..	..	..	..	..	..	..	..	..	..	..
Taukī. .	2,822	1,574	1,248	..	..	..	..	..	..	..	..	1,574	1,248	..	..	..	..
Wāḍēla .	247	130	117	..	..	..	..	..	..	..	..	..	..	..	..	..	..
Others .	4,208	2,297	1,911	14	10	..	..	..	..	..	..	8	2	..	..	..	..
Semi-indigenous	***3,094***	***1,720***	***1,374***	***4***	***1***	***1,041***	***786***	***2***	..	..	..	..	..	***251***	***198***	***14***	***13***
Buzdār .	1,224	683	541	4	1	671	529	..	..	..	..	..	..	4	4	4	7
Others .	1,870	1,037	833	..	..	370	257	2	..	..	..	..	..	247	194	10	6
Aliens . .	***189***	***140***	***49***	***34***	***14***	***34***	***11***	***23***	***6***	***2***	***1***	***1***	..	***24***	***7***	..	..
Trans-Indus .	***21***	***21***	..	***1***	..	..	..	..	..	..	..	..	..	***1***	..	..	..
Cis-Indus .	***168***	***119***	***49***	***33***	***14***	***34***	***11***	***23***	***6***	***2***	***1***	***1***	..	***23***	***7***	..	..

RACE OR NATIONALITY.

STATES																
KALĀT														LAS BĒLA		CASTE, TRIBE, RACE OR NATIONALITY
Total Kalāt		Sarāwān		Jhalawān		Kachhī		Dōmbkī-Kahērī country		Makrān		Khārān				
Males	Females	Males	Females	Males	Females	Males	Females	Males	Females	Males	Females	Males	Females	Males	Females	
19	20	21	22	23	24	25	26	27	28	29	30	31	32	33	34	
194,596	**164,488**	**35,082**	**28,699**	**46,880**	**37,518**	**50,191**	**42,568**	**12,624**	**10,919**	**37,696**	**34,244**	**12,123**	**10,540**	**32,640**	**28,565**	**Total**
192,584	*163,972*	*34,713*	*28,496*	*46,714*	*37,481*	*49,738*	*42,263*	*12,264*	*10,609*	*37,129*	*33,970*	*12,026*	*10,453*	*32,309*	*28,434*	*Indigenous*
602	*518*	*81*	*53*	*8*	*5*	*139*	*119*	*71*	*56*	*211*	*201*	*92*	*84*	*3*	*2*	*Semi-Indigenous*
1,412	*698*	*288*	*150*	*158*	*32*	*314*	*186*	*289*	*254*	*358*	*73*	*5*	*3*	*328*	*129*	*Aliens*
15	4	1	2	..	..	1	..	..	..	13	2	..	..	1	..	European
4	..	..	..	..	..	..	..	..	..	4	..	..	..	1	..	Anglo-Indian
1,393	694	287	148	158	32	313	186	289	254	341	71	5	3	326	129	Oriental
215	*108*	*41*	*26*	*9*	*9*	*50*	*47*	*10*	*13*	*104*	*13*	*1*	..	*10*	*4*	*Trans-Indus*
1,178	*586*	*246*	*122*	*149*	*23*	*263*	*139*	*279*	*241*	*237*	*58*	*4*	*3*	*316*	*125*	*Cis-Indus*
44,969	**38,443**	**1,484**	**1,213**	**799**	**644**	**15,774**	**13,098**	**2,276**	**1,871**	**19,026**	**16,763**	**5,630**	**4,854**	**2,868**	**2,496**	**Balōch**
44,560	*38,058*	*1,483*	*1,213*	*799*	*644*	*15,671*	*13,007*	*2,205*	*1,815*	*18,832*	*16,579*	*5,570*	*4,800*	*2,867*	*2,495*	*Indigenous*
19,623	*16,228*	*1,461*	*1,200*	*235*	*173*	*15,670*	*13,007*	*2,205*	*1,815*	*2*	..	*50*	*33*	*1,078*	*875*	(i) *Eastern*
63	50	..	..	..	..	35	27	28	23	..	..	..	..	..	..	Bugṭī
2,190	1,800	..	..	..	..	97	72	2,093	1,728	..	..	..	..	41	33	Ḍōmbkī
..	..	..	..	..	..	..	..	..	..	..	..	..	..	..	..	Jakhrānī
..	..	..	..	..	..	..	..	..	..	..	..	..	..	..	..	Khetrān
9,190	7,527	12	12	151	110	8,977	7,372	..	..	..	..	50	33	..	..	Magasī
226	195	184	156	..	..	14	14	28	25	..	..	..	..	202	137	Marī
7,950	6,656	1,264	1,032	84	63	6,545	5,522	55	39	2	..	..	..	835	705	Rind
1	..	..	..	..	..	..	..	1	..	..	..	..	..	..	..	Umrānī
3	..	1	..	..	..	2	..	..	..	..	..	..	..	..	..	Others
24,937	*21,830*	*22*	*13*	*564*	*471*	*1*	..	..	..	*18,830*	*16,579*	*5,520*	*4,767*	*1,789*	*1,620*	(ii) *Western*
447	347	..	..	..	..	..	..	..	..	447	347	..	..	..	..	Barr
672	574	..	..	3	1	..	..	..	..	669	573	..	..	51	43	Bulēdī
535	423	..	..	..	..	..	..	..	..	534	419	1	4	..	..	Dashtī
44	36	..	..	..	..	..	..	..	..	44	36	..	..	..	..	Dōdāī
37	42	..	..	..	..	..	..	..	..	37	42	..	..	6	1	Gabōl
..	..	..	..	..	..	..	..	..	..	..	..	..	..	..	..	Gamshādzai
268	283	..	..	6	8	..	..	..	..	262	275	..	..	..	..	Gichkī
24	22	..	..	..	..	..	..	..	..	24	22	..	..	..	..	Gōrgēj
627	575	..	..	..	..	..	..	..	..	627	575	..	..	12	14	Hōt
234	209	..	..	..	..	..	..	..	..	234	209	..	..	..	..	Kallagī
51	36	..	..	21	12	..	..	..	..	30	24	..	..	59	41	Kalmatī
98	88	..	..	..	..	..	..	..	..	98	88	..	..	..	..	Kaṭōhar
607	525	..	..	..	..	..	..	..	..	607	525	..	..	..	..	Kaudāī
242	218	..	..	..	..	..	..	..	..	242	218	..	..	..	..	Kēngīzai
607	563	..	..	..	..	..	..	..	..	607	563	..	..	..	..	Khōsā
550	436	..	..	23	24	..	..	..	..	527	412	..	..	39	29	Kolwāī
19	19	..	..	..	..	..	..	..	..	19	19	..	..	..	..	Kulānchī
226	226	..	..	..	..	..	..	..	..	226	226	..	..	4	3	Lāshārī
120	89	..	..	..	..	..	..	..	..	120	89	..	..	..	..	Laṭṭī
63	53	..	..	..	..	..	..	..	..	63	53	..	..	..	..	Lunḍī
282	230	..	..	44	33	..	..	..	..	238	197	..	..	..	..	Mullāzai
120	158	5	2	11	9	..	..	..	..	71	88	33	59	2	2	Naushērwānī
352	337	..	..	..	..	..	..	..	..	352	337	..	..	..	..	Purkī
2,187	1,960	..	..	..	..	..	..	..	..	2,187	1,960	..	..	..	..	Raīs
6,964	5,995	15	10	442	378	1	..	..	..	1,026	909	5,480	4,698	77	60	Rakhshānī
4,702	4,257	..	..	..	..	..	..	..	..	4,696	4,251	6	6	..	..	Rind
627	499	..	..	..	..	..	..	..	..	627	499	..	..	..	..	Sāmī
1,620	1,429	..	..	..	..	..	..	..	..	1,620	1,429	..	..	1,429	1,320	Sangur
..	..	..	..	..	..	..	..	..	..	..	..	..	..	..	..	Sanjrānī
317	292	..	..	..	..	..	..	..	..	317	292	..	..	..	..	Shahzāda
..	..	..	..	..	..	..	..	..	..	..	..	..	..	..	..	Taukī
130	117	..	..	..	..	..	..	..	..	130	117	..	..	..	..	Wāḍēla
2,165	1,792	2	1	14	6	..	..	..	..	2,149	1,785	..	..	110	107	Others
407	***375***	..	..	..	..	***103***	***91***	***71***	***56***	***173***	***174***	***60***	***54***	***1***	***1***	***Semi-indigenous***
..	..	..	..	..	..	..	..	..	..	..	..	..	..	..	..	Buzdār
407	375	..	..	..	..	103	91	71	56	173	174	60	54	1	1	Others
22	***10***	***1***	..	..	..	..	..	..	..	***21***	***10***	..	..	..	..	***Aliens***
19	..	***1***	..	..	..	..	..	..	..	***18***	..	..	..	..	..	***Trans-Indus***
3	***10***	..	..	..	..	..	..	..	..	***3***	***10***	..	..	..	..	***Cis-Indus***

Caste, Tribe, Race or Nationality	Balōchistān			Districts: Quetta-Pishīn		Lōralai		Zhōb		Bōlān		Chāgai		Sibi: Administered area		Sibi: Mari-Bugṭī	
	Persons	Males	Females	Males	Females	Males	Females	Males	Females	Males	Females	Males	Females	Males	Females	Males	Females
1	2	3	4	5	6	7	8	9	10	11	12	13	14	15	16	17	18
Brāhūī	**167,787**	**93,095**	**74,692**	**5,348**	**4,256**	**43**	**6**	**100**	..	**169**	**67**	**3,605**	**2,880**	**2,731**	**1,975**	**7**	**2**
(i) *Original nucleus.*	*15,047*	*8,392*	*6,745*	*740*	*605*	*1*	..	*1*	..	*5*	*1*	*180*	*151*	*102*	*55*	..	..
Ahmadzai	25	15	10	8	1	..	..	..	..	..	..	..	..	..	..	..	..
Iltāzai	156	85	71	..	..	..	..	..	..	..	..	..	..	..	..	..	..
Gurgnāṛī	2,041	1,124	917	34	20	..	..	..	..	2	1	5	2	..	..	..	..
Kalandrāṛī	2,012	1,138	874	59	41	1	..	..	..	..	..	15	10	..	..	..	..
Kambrāṛī	3,095	1,679	1,416	191	146	..	..	..	..	..	..	59	49	17	17	..	..
Mīrwāṛī	2,654	1,450	1,204	..	..	..	..	..	..	..	..	..	..	..	..	..	..
Rōdēnī	1,325	724	601	45	34	..	..	1	..	..	..	9	13	25	13	..	..
Sumālāṛī	3,739	2,087	1,652	403	363	..	..	..	..	3	..	92	77	60	25	..	..
(ii) *Sarāwān*	*55,370*	*30,615*	*24,755*	*3,488*	*2,484*	*33*	*6*	*75*	..	*114*	*62*	*1,926*	*1,531*	*1,290*	*955*	*1*	..
Bangulzai	11,595	6,377	5,218	445	379	7	..	24	..	35	31	7	5	663	485	1	..
Kūrd	3,476	1,928	1,548	254	214	..	..	2	..	41	18	13	7	14	4	..	..
Lahṛī	5,839	3,314	2,525	472	362	..	..	12	..	1	..	7	4	205	176	..	..
Lāngav	10,979	6,007	4,972	723	555	1	..	9	..	3	..	182	143	139	107	..	..
Māmashahī	3,866	2,143	1,723	198	147	..	..	17	..	14	7	14	10	41	26	..	..
Raīsānī	1,977	1,093	884	149	126	3	..	1	..	4	3	22	2	52	40	..	..
Rustumzaī	656	341	315	51	57	..	..	..	..	..	..	..	..	3	3	..	..
Sarparra	2,212	1,213	999	105	89	2	..	8	..	1	..	72	28	25	4	..	..
Satakzai	1,278	715	563	40	31	..	..	..	..	2	..	..	..	17	15	..	..
Shahwānī	8,770	4,894	3,876	1,024	860	6	..	2	..	9	1	9	6	48	24	..	..
Zagr Mēngal	4,722	2,590	2,132	27	24	14	6	..	..	4	2	1,600	1,326	83	71	..	..
(iii) *Jhalawān*	*94,708*	*52,697*	*42,011*	*1,101*	*799*	*1*	..	*23*	..	*48*	*3*	*1,463*	*1,190*	*1,318*	*961*	*6*	*2*
Bīzanjav	10,858	5,906	4,952	3	..	..	..	..	..	..	..	30	26	4	4	..	..
Hārūnī	1,248	674	574	41	28	..	..	1	..	..	..	40	45	3	1	..	..
Māmasanī	13,489	7,474	6,015	117	79	..	..	1	..	2	..	1,222	984	129	95	..	..
Mēngal	26,805	15,199	11,606	492	357	1	..	20	..	42	3	4	5	691	520	6	2
Nīchārī	3,641	2,060	1,581	65	39	..	..	1	..	..	..	5	3	44	5	..	..
Pandrānī	2,007	1,115	392	..	..	..	..	..	..	..	..	..	..	345	273	..	..
Sājdī	4,011	2,239	1,772	..	..	..	..	..	..	..	..	..	..	1	1	..	..
Zahrī	32,649	18,030	14,619	383	296	..	..	..	..	4	..	162	127	101	62	..	..
Bājōī	*2,531*	*1,365*	*1,166*	..	..	..	..	..	..	..	..	..	..	..	..	..	..
Ḍāṇya	*1,441*	*809*	*632*	*25*	*24*	..	..	..	..	..	..	..	..	..	..	..	..
Khidrānī	*2,053*	*1,163*	*890*	*10*	*6*	..	..	..	..	..	..	..	..	..	..	..	..
Jattak	*5,609*	*3,168*	*2,441*	*165*	*115*	..	..	..	..	..	..	*4*	*5*	*70*	*52*	..	..
Lōṭiānī	*1,778*	*974*	*804*	*6*	*9*	..	..	..	..	..	..	..	..	*12*	*7*	..	..
Mūsiānī	*2,140*	*1,138*	*1,002*	..	..	..	..	..	..	*2*	..	*14*	*16*	..	..	..	..
Sāsōlī	*6,618*	*3,679*	*2,939*	*12*	*4*	..	..	..	..	..	..	*86*	*70*	*4*	*3*	..	..
Gar Sāsōlī	*800*	*442*	*358*	..	..	..	..	..	..	..	..	..	..	..	..	..	..
Zarrakzai	*465*	*236*	*229*	*65*	*58*	..	..	..	..	*1*	..	*53*	*32*	..	..	..	..
Others	*9,214*	*5,056*	*4,158*	*110*	*80*	..	..	..	..	*1*	..	*5*	*4*	*15*	..	..	..
(iv) *Miscellaneous.*	*2,662*	*1,481*	*1,181*	*19*	*8*	*8*	..	*1*	..	*2*	*1*	*36*	*8*	*21*	*4*	..	..
Nighāṛī	1,311	718	593	..	..	..	..	..	..	..	..	..	..	..	..	..	..
Pirri-Kāṛī	517	278	239	..	..	..	..	..	..	..	..	..	..	..	..	..	..
Rēkīzai	611	336	275	..	..	..	..	..	..	..	..	5	4	..	..	..	..
Others	223	149	74	19	8	8	..	1	..	2	1	31	4	21	4	..	..

RACE OR NATIONALITY—*contd.*

STATES																
Kalāt														Las Bēla		Caste, Tribe, Race or Nationality
Total Kalāt		Sarāwān		Jhalawān		Kachhī		Dōmbkī-Kahērī country		Makrān		Khārān				
Males	Females	Males	Females	Males	Females	Males	Females	Males	Females	Males	Females	Males	Females	Males	Females	
19	20	21	22	23	24	25	26	27	28	29	30	31	32	33	34	
76,734	**61,947**	**26,396**	**21,417**	**38,748**	**30,805**	**2,255**	**1,893**	**106**	**89**	**5,045**	**4,122**	**4,179**	**3,521**	**4,358**	**3,659**	**Brāhūī.**
6,788	*5,473*	*1,034*	*850*	*4,037*	*3,190*	*35*	*38*	*1*	..	*978*	*771*	*703*	*624*	*485*	*460*	(i) *Original nucleus*
7	9	7	8	..	..	..	1	..	..	..	..	..	..	..	..	Ahmadzai
85	71	..	..	72	49	13	22	..	..	..	..	..	..	..	..	Iltāzai
940	758	90	74	706	565	2	3	1	..	99	79	42	37	143	136	Gurgnāṛī
1,040	809	212	166	725	557	..	..	..	..	99	83	4	3	23	14	Kalandrāṛī
1,219	1,018	221	173	636	519	17	11	..	..	118	107	227	208	193	186	Kambrāṛī
1,352	1,102	..	..	862	685	..	..	..	..	489	415	1	2	98	102	Mīrwāṛī
635	534	295	268	266	221	3	1	..	..	67	41	4	3	9	7	Rōdēnī
1,510	1,172	209	161	770	594	..	..	..	..	106	46	425	371	19	15	Sumālāṛī
23,475	*19,162*	*19,228*	*15,686*	*1,409*	*1,201*	*1,728*	*1,445*	*70*	*65*	*891*	*662*	*149*	*103*	*213*	*195*	(ii) *Sarāwān*
5,192	4,317	3,742	3,122	78	58	968	825	57	50	347	262	..	..	3	1	Bangulzai
1,497	1,203	1,287	1,024	104	98	23	29	..	..	44	28	39	24	107	102	Kūrd
2,528	1,900	2,139	1,620	157	114	208	153	1	..	23	13	..	..	89	83	Lahṛī
4,950	4,167	4,519	3,755	337	333	16	15	..	..	78	64	..	..	..	..	Lāngav
1,859	1,533	1,734	1,440	68	52	37	34	..	..	18	5	2	2	..	..	Māmashahī
862	713	411	340	78	57	319	265	8	15	46	36	..	..	..	..	Raīsānī
287	255	233	212	..	..	54	43	..	..	..	..	..	..	..	..	Rustumzaī
1,000	878	952	850	5	5	27	23	..	..	16	..	..	..	..	..	Sarparra
656	517	649	515	..	..	2	2	..	..	5	..	..	..	..	..	Sātakzaī
3,782	2,976	2,945	2,313	387	312	59	44	4	..	287	242	100	65	14	9	Shahwānī
862	703	617	495	195	172	15	12	..	..	27	12	8	12	..	..	Zagr Mēngal
45,095	*36,063*	*5,859*	*4,641*	*32,258*	*25,554*	*482*	*404*	*32*	*18*	*3,174*	*2,689*	*3,290*	*2,762*	*3,642*	*2,988*	(iii) *Jhalawān*
4,206	3,608	..	..	2,932	2,420	2	1	..	..	1,317	1,134	45	44	1,573	1,314	Bīzanjav
586	490	66	43	314	278	..	..	..	..	14	13	192	165	3	1	Hārūnī
5,862	4,748	549	442	2,594	2,035	13	11	..	..	578	485	2,128	1,775	141	109	Māmasanī
13,089	10,033	3,323	2,569	9,457	7,220	75	76	32	18	199	146	3	4	854	686	Mēngal
1,945	1,534	445	367	1,494	1,165	5	2	..	..	1	..	..	..	..	..	Nīchārī
770	619	139	106	463	374	168	139	..	..	..	..	..	..	..	..	Pandrānī
2,031	1,604	..	..	1,161	857	..	..	..	..	840	729	30	18	207	167	Sājdī
16,516	13,423	1,337	1,114	13,843	11,106	219	175	..	..	225	182	892	756	864	711	Zahrī
1,344	*1,142*	*67*	*49*	*1,274*	*1,092*	*3*	*1*	..	..	..	..	..	..	*21*	*24*	*Bājōī*
784	*608*	*14*	*15*	*764*	*588*	*6*	*5*	..	..	..	..	..	..	..	..	*Ḍāṇya*
962	*702*	*6*	*6*	*907*	*654*	*5*	*4*	..	..	..	..	*44*	*38*	*191*	*182*	*Khidrānī*
2,938	*2,269*	*410*	*345*	*2,377*	*1,803*	*148*	*115*	..	..	*9*	*6*	..	..	*1*	..	*Jattak*
956	*788*	..	..	*921*	*756*	*35*	*32*	..	..	..	..	..	..	..	..	*Lōṭiānī*
1,100	*969*	*93*	*94*	*992*	*870*	*10*	*5*	..	..	..	..	..	..	*22*	*17*	*Mūsiānī*
3,508	*2,816*	*52*	*45*	*2,468*	*1,946*	*1*	*1*	..	..	*200*	*168*	*787*	*656*	*69*	*46*	*Sāsōlī*
442	*358*	*442*	*358*	..	..	..	..	..	..	..	..	..	..	..	..	*Gar Sāsōlī*
117	*139*	*49*	*50*	*68*	*89*	..	..	..	..	..	..	..	..	..	..	*Zarrakzai*
4,365	*3,632*	*199*	*182*	*4,072*	*3,398*	*17*	*12*	..	..	*16*	*8*	*61*	*62*	*560*	*442*	*Others*
1,376	*1,144*	*275*	*240*	*1,044*	*860*	*10*	*6*	*5*	*6*	*2*	..	*37*	*32*	*18*	*16*	(iv) *Miscellaneous*
718	593	5	4	713	589	..	..	..	..	..	..	..	..	..	..	Nighāṛī
278	239	241	207	..	..	..	..	..	..	..	..	37	32	..	..	Pirri-Kāṛī
331	271	..	..	331	271	..	..	..	..	..	..	..	..	..	..	Rēkizai
49	41	32	29	..	..	10	6	5	6	2	..	..	..	18	16	Others

Caste, Tribe, Race or Nationality	Balūchistān			Districts													
				Quetta-Pishin		Lōralai		Zhōb		Bōlān		Chāgai		Sibi			
														Administered area		Mari-Bugṭī	
	Persons	Males	Females	Males	Females	Males	Females	Males	Females	Males	Females	Males	Females	Males	Females	Males	Females
1	2	3	4	5	6	7	8	9	10	11	12	13	14	15	16	17	18
Pathān	**214,517**	**118,582**	**95,935**	**40,486**	**32,603**	**28,389**	**23,976**	**36,348**	**28,952**	**53**	**21**	**591**	**404**	**11,649**	**9,140**	**2**	..
Indigenous	*188,093*	*109,148*	*85,945*	*35,489*	*29,831*	*29,989*	*19,775*	*39,585*	*26,956*	*17*	*7*	*216*	*155*	*10,050*	*8,557*	..	..
Bābī .	323	173	150	80	73	..	..	1	..	..	..	..	..	5	3	..	..
Baṛēch	854	480	374	188	163	..	..	2	..	2	1	173	140	48	19	..	..
Jafar	1,286	690	596	1	..	685	596	4	..	..	..	..	..	..	..	..	..
Kākaṛ	105,073	57,752	47,321	19,813	16,313	9,052	7,565	24,853	20,277	11	4	21	8	3,959	3,124	..	..
Dāwī	*284*	*156*	*128*	*143*	*118*	..	..	*11*	*9*	..	..	..	..	..	..	..	..
Damaṛ	*7,755*	*4,267*	*3,488*	*404*	*336*	*3,205*	*2,716*	*18*	*13*	..	..	..	..	*624*	*413*	..	..
Lamaṛ	*492*	*274*	*218*	*274*	*218*	..	..	..	..	..	..	..	..	..	..	..	..
Sanzarkhēl	*56,032*	*30,644*	*25,388*	*3,117*	*2,752*	*5,676*	*4,709*	*21,576*	*17,746*	*5*	*2*	*4*	..	*258*	*174*	..	..
Sargaṛa	*2,343*	*1,265*	*1,078*	*864*	*705*	*99*	*98*	*300*	*275*	*2*	..	..	..	..	..	..	..
Snaṭia	*23,349*	*12,945*	*10,404*	*7,058*	*5,687*	*23*	*9*	*2,888*	*2,228*	*1*	*2*	*11*	*4*	*2,960*	*2,469*	..	..
Targhaṛa	*14,089*	*7,770*	*6,319*	*7,650*	*6,283*	*37*	*31*	*46*	..	*2*	..	*1*	..	*33*	*5*	..	..
Others	*729*	*431*	*298*	*303*	*214*	*12*	*2*	*14*	*6*	*1*	..	*5*	*4*	*84*	*63*	..	..
Kāsī .	1,337	705	632	657	613	1	..	10	1	..	..	1	..	16	5	..	..
Lūṇī .	2,816	1,496	1,320	1	..	1,483	1,310	1	1	..	..	..	..	5	4	..	..
Paṇī .	28,675	15,245	13,430	84	57	8,946	7,875	3,395	2,838	2	..	6	1	2,433	2,326	..	..
Main branch	*6,714*	*3,496*	*3,218*	*63*	*48*	*457*	*400*	*664*	*547*	*2*	..	*5*	*1*	*1,942*	*1,901*	..	..
Isōṭ	*2,812*	*1,515*	*1,297*	*7*	*7*	*1,429*	*1,256*	*53*	*7*	..	..	..	..	*26*	*27*	..	..
Mandōkhēl	*4,944*	*2,653*	*2,291*	*1*	..	*13*	*7*	*2,635*	*2,281*	..	..	*1*	..	*3*	*3*	..	..
Mūsākhēl	*12,202*	*6,533*	*5,669*	*13*	*2*	*6,380*	*5,612*	*43*	*3*	..	..	..	..	*81*	*40*	..	..
Zarkūn	*2,003*	*1,048*	*955*	..	..	*667*	*600*	..	..	..	..	..	..	*381*	*355*	..	..
Shīrānī	8,552	4,538	4,014	44	50	96	66	4,282	3,817	1	..	1	..	51	30	..	..
Tarīn	37,411	20,077	17,334	14,550	12,501	2,023	1,828	28	21	1	..	5	2	3,446	2,961	..	..
Abdāl Achakzai.	*20,272*	*11,199*	*9,073*	*11,130*	*9,045*	*21*	*13*	*4*	*1*	*1*	..	..	..	*33*	*3*	..	..
Spīn Tarīn	*5,134*	*2,713*	*2,421*	*48*	*54*	*1,714*	*1,555*	..	..	..	..	..	..	*944*	*808*	..	..
Tōr Tarīn	*11,890*	*6,086*	*5,804*	*3,335*	*3,390*	*275*	*260*	..	..	..	..	..	..	*2,469*	*2,148*	..	..
Others	*115*	*79*	*36*	*37*	*12*	*13*	..	*24*	*20*	..	..	*5*	*2*	..	*2*	..	..
Zmarai	1,228	694	534	2	..	686	533	6	1	..	..	..	..	..	..	..	..
Others	538	298	240	69	61	17	2	3	..	..	2	9	4	87	85	..	..
Semi-indigenous	*22,317*	*13,047*	*9,270*	*3,299*	*2,276*	*5,100*	*4,141*	*3,013*	*1,939*	*5*	*1*	*347*	*247*	*1,085*	*522*	*1*	..
Ghilzai	18,586	10,889	7,697	2,072	1,374	5,044	4,111	2,540	1,530	2	..	189	123	947	487	1	..
Kharōṭ	*3,057*	*1,750*	*1,307*	*101*	*49*	*1,350*	*1,084*	*281*	*161*	..	..	*1*	..	*17*	*13*	..	..
Nāsar	*2,769*	*1,517*	*1,252*	*480*	*446*	*927*	*730*	*50*	*24*	..	..	*2*	..	*53*	*48*	..	..
Sulēmānkhēl	*4,643*	*2,824*	*1,819*	*612*	*393*	*377*	*312*	*1,627*	*1,021*	..	..	*109*	*82*	*83*	*7*	..	..
Tarak	*2,316*	*1,349*	*967*	*313*	*214*	*720*	*557*	*210*	*143*	..	..	*51*	*32*	*38*	*8*	..	..
Others	*5,801*	*3,449*	*2,352*	*566*	*272*	*1,670*	*1,428*	*372*	*181*	*2*	..	*26*	*9*	*756*	*411*	*1*	..
Panī Sāfī	804	436	368	10	9	1	1	416	355	1	..	..	..	2	..	..	..
Durrānī	2,927	1,722	1,205	1,217	893	55	29	57	54	2	1	158	124	136	35	..	..
Nūrzai	*1,056*	*579*	*477*	*418*	*347*	*1*	..	..	..	*1*	..	*110*	*92*	*2*	..	..	..
Others	*1,871*	*1,143*	*728*	*799*	*546*	*54*	*29*	*57*	*54*	*1*	*1*	*48*	*32*	*134*	*35*	..	..
Aliens	*4,107*	*3,387*	*720*	*1,698*	*496*	*300*	*54*	*750*	*57*	*31*	*13*	*28*	*9*	*514*	*61*	*2*	..
Trans-Indus	*2,691*	*2,320*	*371*	*1,073*	*235*	*199*	*35*	*577*	*32*	*5*	*1*	*22*	*2*	*382*	*29*	*1*	..
Afrīdī	345	335	10	108	3	4	..	204	7	..	..	..	..	14	..	1	..
Khaṭak	242	204	38	37	12	17	13	51	13	..	..	2	..	97	..	..	..
Mōmand	339	275	64	156	49	46	3	12	4	2	1	..	..	56	6	..	..
Yūsufzai	675	553	122	213	70	71	7	157	5	1	..	7	..	50	4	..	..
Others	1,090	953	137	559	101	61	12	153	3	2	..	13	2	165	19	..	..
Cis-Indus	*1,416*	*1,067*	*349*	*625*	*261*	*101*	*19*	*173*	*25*	*26*	*12*	*6*	..	*132*	*32*	..	..

RACE OR NATIONALITY—*contd.*

STATES																
KALĀT														LAS BĒLA		CASTE, TRIBE, RACE OR NATIONALITY
Total Kalāt		Sarāwān		Jhalawān		Kachhī		Dōmbki-Kahērī country		Makrān		Khārān				
Males	Females	Males	Females	Males	Females	Males	Females	Males	Females	Males	Females	Males	Females	Males	Females	
19	20	21	22	23	24	25	26	27	28	29	30	31	32	33	34	
1,030	**825**	**351**	**262**	**66**	**47**	**341**	**278**	**127**	**122**	**75**	**53**	**70**	**63**	**34**	**20**	**Pathān**
771	***646***	***230***	***186***	***54***	***39***	***304***	***249***	***124***	***120***	***22***	***19***	***37***	***33***	***31***	***18***	***Indigenous***
87	74	38	34	27	18	21	22	..	..	1	..	..	..	..	..	Babī
67	51	24	12	4	5	2	2	..	..	4	5	33	27	..	..	Baṛēch
..	..	..	..	..	..	..	..	..	..	..	..	..	..	..	..	Jafar
43	30	22	16	6	2	4	4	..	..	10	7	1	1	..	..	Kakaṛ
2	*1*	..	..	..	..	*1*	..	..	..	..	..	*1*	*1*	..	..	*Dāwī*
16	*10*	*16*	*10*	..	..	..	..	..	..	..	..	..	..	..	..	*Dumaṛ*
..	..	..	..	..	..	..	..	..	..	..	..	..	..	..	..	*Lamaṛ*
8	*5*	..	..	..	..	*3*	*4*	..	..	*5*	*1*	..	..	..	..	*Sanzarkhēl*
..	..	..	..	..	..	..	..	..	..	..	..	..	..	..	..	*Sargaṛa*
4	*5*	*4*	*5*	..	..	..	..	..	..	..	..	..	..	..	..	*Snaṭia*
1	..	..	..	*1*	..	..	..	..	..	..	..	..	..	..	..	*Targhaṛa*
12	*9*	*2*	*1*	*5*	*2*	..	..	..	..	*5*	*6*	..	..	..	..	*Others*
20	13	20	13	..	..	..	..	..	..	..	..	..	..	..	..	Kāsī
6	5	4	1	..	..	2	4	..	..	..	..	..	..	..	..	Lūṇī
379	333	80	74	13	14	163	125	123	120	..	..	..	..	..	..	Paṇī
363	*321*	*80*	*74*	*13*	*14*	*147*	*113*	*123*	*120*	..	..	..	..	..	..	*Main branch*
..	..	..	..	..	..	..	..	..	..	..	..	..	..	..	..	*Isōṭ*
..	..	..	..	..	..	..	..	..	..	..	..	..	..	..	..	*Mandōkhēl*
16	*12*	..	..	..	..	*16*	*12*	..	..	..	..	..	..	..	..	*Mūsākhēl*
..	..	..	..	..	..	..	..	..	..	..	..	..	..	..	..	*Zarkūn*
63	51	21	26	2	..	40	25	..	..	..	..	..	..	..	..	Shīrānī
24	21	8	4	1	..	14	17	1	..	..	..	..	..	..	..	Tarīn
10	*11*	*1*	..	*1*	..	*8*	*11*	..	..	..	..	..	..	..	..	*Abdāl Achakzai*
7	*4*	*7*	*4*	..	..	..	..	..	..	..	..	..	..	..	..	*Spīn Tarīn*
7	*6*	..	..	..	..	*6*	*6*	*1*	..	..	..	..	..	..	..	*Tōr Tarīn*
..	..	..	..	..	..	..	..	..	..	..	..	..	..	..	..	*Others*
..	..	..	..	..	..	..	..	..	..	..	..	..	..	..	..	Zmarai
82	68	13	6	1	..	58	50	..	..	7	7	8	5	31	18	Others
195	***143***	***81***	***53***	***8***	***5***	***36***	***28***	..	..	***38***	***27***	***39***	***30***	***2***	***1***	***Semi-indigenous***
93	72	20	10	4	1	31	25	..	..	6	6	32	30	1	..	Ghilzai
..	..	..	..	..	..	..	..	..	..	..	..	..	..	..	..	*Kharōṭ*
5	*4*	..	..	..	..	*3*	*3*	..	..	*2*	*1*	..	..	..	..	*Nāsar*
16	*4*	*8*	..	..	..	*8*	*4*	..	..	..	..	..	..	..	..	*Sulēmānkhēl*
17	*13*	*4*	*1*	..	..	*13*	*12*	..	..	..	..	..	..	..	..	*Tarak*
55	*51*	*8*	*9*	*4*	*1*	*7*	*6*	..	..	*4*	*5*	*32*	*30*	*1*	..	*Others*
6	3	1	..	..	..	5	3	..	..	..	..	..	..	..	..	Panī Sāfī
96	68	60	43	4	4	..	..	..	..	32	21	..	..	1	1	Durrānī
47	*38*	*35*	*28*	..	..	..	..	..	..	*12*	*10*	..	..	..	..	*Nūrzai*
49	*30*	*25*	*15*	*4*	*4*	..	..	..	..	*20*	*11*	..	..	*1*	*1*	*Others*
64	***36***	***40***	***23***	***4***	***3***	***1***	***1***	***3***	***2***	***15***	***7***	***1***	..	***1***	***1***	***Aliens***
60	*36*	*39*	*23*	*4*	*3*	*1*	*1*	*3*	*2*	*12*	*7*	*1*	..	*1*	*1*	*Trans-Indus*
4	..	4	..	..	..	..	..	..	..	..	..	..	..	..	..	Afrīdī
..	..	..	..	..	..	..	..	..	..	..	..	..	..	1	1	Khaṭak
2	..	2	..	..	..	..	..	..	..	..	..	..	..	..	..	Mōmand
54	36	33	23	4	3	1	1	3	2	12	7	1	..	..	..	Yūsufzai
..	..	..	..	..	..	..	..	..	..	..	..	..	..	..	..	Others
4	..	*1*	..	..	..	..	..	..	..	*3*	..	..	..	..	..	*Cis-Indus*

Caste, Tribe, Race or Nationality	Balūchistān			Districts: Quetta-Pishīn		Lōralai		Zhōb		Bōlān		Chagai		Sibi: Administered area		Sibi: Mari Bugṭi	
	Persons	Males	Females	Males	Females	Males	Females	Males	Females	Males	Females	Males	Females	Males	Females	Males	Females
1	2	3	4	5	6	7	8	9	10	11	12	13	14	15	16	17	18
Lāsī (Panj Rāj)†	**27,779**	**14,857**	**12,922**	..	..	..	..	..	..	..	..	..	..	..	..	..	..
Angāria	3,146	1,656	1,490	..	..	..	..	..	..	..	..	..	..	..	..	..	..
Burrā	5,374	2,933	2,441	..	..	..	..	..	..	..	..	..	..	..	..	..	..
Jāmōṭ	9,724	5,203	4,521	..	..	..	..	..	..	..	..	..	..	..	..	..	..
Rūnjhā	5,103	2,688	2,415	..	..	..	..	..	..	..	..	..	..	..	..	..	..
Shēkh	4,432	2,377	2,055	..	..	..	..	..	..	..	..	..	..	..	..	..	..
Jaṭṭ	**78,400**	**42,673**	**35,727**	**99**	**71**	**49**	**32**	**3**	..	**5**	..	..	..	**7,217**	**5,756**	**94**	**71**
Indigenous	*78,397*	*42,670*	*35,727*	*99*	*71*	*48*	*32*	*3*	..	*5*	..	..	..	*7,217*	*5,756*	*92*	*71*
Aliens	*3*	*3*	..	..	..	*1*	..	..	..	..	..	..	..	..	..	*2*	..
Sayyid	**22,183**	**11,662**	**10,521**	**5,196**	**5,090**	**2,554**	**2,133**	**643**	**497**	**31**	**14**	**225**	**189**	**1,010**	**799**	**12**	**15**
Indigenous	*21,296*	*11,008*	*10,288*	*4,786*	*4,930*	*2,513*	*2,125*	*608*	*493*	*18*	*9*	*215*	*182*	*866*	*750*	*12*	*15*
Bukhārī	8,726	4,353	4,373	3,015	3,245	555	416	31	33	..	..	83	71	147	146	12	15
Chishtī	670	347	323	..	..	..	..	..	..	..	..	8	6	107	92	..	..
Gharshīn	796	449	347	181	121	212	182	24	15	..	..	..	..	26	25	..	..
Gīlānī	400	202	198	5	4	..	..	..	..	..	..	4	2	2	2	..	..
Husainī	1,287	660	627	11	8	276	286	..	7	..	..	33	31	2	..	..	..
Kahērī	938	494	444	1	2	..	..	..	..	..	..	..	..	69	66	..	..
Karbalā	1,024	458	566	442	548	16	18	..	..	..	..	..	..	..	..	..	..
Khōstī	888	478	410	7	11	10	13	461	386	..	..	..	..	..	..	..	..
Mashwānī	1,008	530	478	472	454	1	..	11	..	1	..	5	..	3	2	..	..
Maudūdī	577	300	277	175	166	..	..	..	..	..	..	..	..	75	62	..	..
Pēchī	830	461	369	6	4	390	311	..	..	..	..	..	..	65	54	..	..
Tāran	1,237	683	554	252	209	165	134	33	21	..	..	..	..	233	190	..	..
Ustrāna	764	416	348	2	3	410	339	..	..	..	..	..	..	1	3	..	..
Others	2,151	1,177	974	217	155	478	426	44	31	17	9	82	72	136	108	..	..
Aliens	*887*	*654*	*233*	*410*	*160*	*41*	*8*	*35*	*4*	*13*	*5*	*10*	*7*	*144*	*49*	..	..
Trans-Indus	*324*	*233*	*91*	*159*	*72*	*13*	*4*	*8*	*4*	..	..	..	..	*53*	*11*	..	..
Cis-Indus	*563*	*421*	*142*	*251*	*88*	*28*	*4*	*27*	..	*13*	*5*	*10*	*7*	*91*	*38*	..	..
Other Musalmāns	**99,509**	**56,162**	**43,347**	**9,316**	**3,356**	**1,942**	**804**	**1,242**	**266**	**481**	**127**	**742**	**591**	**4,431**	**2,548**	**1,053**	**1,178**
Indigenous	*82,068*	*42,467*	*39,601*	*881*	*734*	*736*	*610*	*191*	*158*	*63*	*45*	*531*	*504*	*2,469*	*2,086*	*1,045*	*1,177*
Darzāda	10,257	5,215	5,042	4	5	..	..	..	..	22	19	..	..	41	18	..	..
Dēhwār	7,326	4,009	3,317	278	204	..	..	1	..	8	..	21	13	30	29	..	..
Gadrā	7,201	3,716	3,485	..	..	..	..	..	..	..	..	..	..	..	..	..	..
Ghulām	20,244	9,545	10,699	27	43	27	19	..	..	9	14	132	173	393	418	495	715
Ghulāmāzād	7,738	4,233	3,505	179	178	..	..	..	..	16	7	292	239	71	56	49	47
Gōlā	834	462	372	..	..	..	..	..	..	..	..	..	..	84	67	..	..
Jat	5,680	3,151	2,529	..	..	..	..	..	..	..	..	..	..	1,206	926	320	277
Khōja	367	185	182	..	..	..	..	..	..	..	..	..	..	..	..	..	..
Kōrī	570	308	262	..	..	..	..	..	..	..	..	..	..	..	..	..	..
Lōṛī	10,936	5,912	5,024	375	293	447	373	71	72	8	5	83	78	513	472	175	138
Mēd	2,494	1,259	1,235	..	..	..	..	..	..	..	..	..	..	..	..	..	..
Nakīb	6,536	3,444	3,092	1	..	..	..	..	..	..	..	..	..	35	20	..	..
Others	1,885	1,028	857	17	11	262	218	119	86	..	..	3	1	96	80	..	..
Aliens	*17,441*	*13,695*	*3,746*	*8,435*	*2,622*	*1,206*	*194*	*1,051*	*108*	*418*	*82*	*211*	*87*	*1,962*	*462*	*8*	*1*
Trans-Indus	*4,104*	*3,222*	*882*	*2,380*	*716*	*105*	*27*	*145*	*10*	*9*	..	*57*	*26*	*373*	*27*	*8*	*1*
Hazāra	2,454	2,015	439	1,526	388	61	16	97	7	2	..	50	23	278	5	..	..
Others	1,650	1,207	443	854	328	44	11	48	3	7	..	7	3	95	22	8	1
Cis-Indus	*13,337*	*10,473*	*2,864*	*6,055*	*1,906*	*1,101*	*167*	*906*	*98*	*409*	*82*	*154*	*61*	*1,589*	*435*	..	..
Hindu	**37,602**	**25,008**	**12,594**	**9,600**	**3,644**	**2,038**	**920**	**1,150**	**198**	**416**	**107**	**264**	**112**	**4,798**	**2,146**	**204**	**167**
Indigenous	*14,985*	*8,122*	*6,863*	*163*	*130*	*740*	*607*	*2*	*2*	*1*	...	*137*	*62*	*1,349*	*1,084*	*161*	*137*
Aliens	*22,617*	*16,886*	*5,731*	*9,437*	*3,534*	*1,298*	*313*	*1,148*	*196*	*415*	*107*	*127*	*50*	*3,449*	*1,062*	*43*	*30*
Sikh	**8,390**	**6,017**	**2,373**	**1,934**	**496**	**838**	**98**	**649**	**66**	**82**	**25**	**29**	**5**	**861**	**207**	..	..
Indigenous	*2,799*	*1,437*	*1,369*	..	..	..	..	..	..	..	..	..	..	*38*	*20*	..	..
Aliens	*5,591*	*4,580*	*1,011*	*1,934*	*496*	*838*	*98*	*649*	*66*	*82*	*25*	*29*	*5*	*823*	*187*	..	..
Miscellaneous Aliens	**6,063**	**4,544**	**1,519**	**3,983**	**1,289**	**92**	**28**	**184**	**31**	**22**	**22**	**14**	**4**	**195**	**138**	..	..
European	4,210	3,382	828	3,109	740	41	12	132	12	10	7	1	1	73	52	..	..
Anglo-Indian	123	64	59	44	39	..	1	1	..	2	3	..	..	12	16	..	..
Indian Christian	752	495	257	396	236	17	..	21	2	2	2	5	2	26	13	..	..
Others	978	603	375	434	274	34	15	30	17	8	10	8	1	84	57	..	..

RACE OR NATIONALITY—*concld.*

STATES																
KALAT														LAS BĒLA		CASTE, TRIBE, RACE OR NATIONALITY
Total Kalāt		Sarāwān		Jhalawān		Kachhi		Dōmbki-Kahēri country		Makrān		Khārān				
Males	Females	Males	Females	Males	Females	Males	Females	Males	Females	Males	Females	Males	Females	Males	Females	
19	20	21	22	23	24	25	26	27	28	29	30	31	32	33	34	
498	**421**	..	..	**419**	**375**	..	..	..	..	**79**	**46**	..	..	**14,350**	**12,501**	**Lāsī (Panj Rāj)**
..	..	..	..	..	..	..	..	..	..	..	..	..	..	1,656	1,490	Angāria
..	..	..	..	..	..	..	..	..	..	..	..	..	..	2,933	2,441	Burrā
498	421	..	..	419	375	..	..	..	..	79	46	..	..	4,705	4,100	Jāmōṭ
..	..	..	..	..	..	..	..	..	..	..	..	..	..	2,688	2,415	Rūnjhā
..	..	..	..	..	..	..	..	..	..	..	..	..	..	2,377	2,055	Shēkh
32,578	**27,660**	**66**	**51**	**293**	**208**	**24,412**	**20,690**	**6,593**	**5,659**	**1,214**	**1,052**	..	..	**2,698**	**2,137**	**Jatt**
32,578	*27,660*	*66*	*51*	*293*	*208*	*24,412*	*20,690*	*6,593*	*5,659*	*1,214*	*1,052*	..	..	*2,698*	*2,137*	*Indigenous*
..	..	..	..	..	..	..	..	..	..	..	..	..	..	..	..	*Aliens*
1,812	**1,607**	**447**	**397**	**161**	**135**	**512**	**488**	**509**	**460**	**113**	**68**	**77**	**69**	**179**	**177**	**Sayyid**
1,811	*1,607*	*447*	*397*	*161*	*135*	*512*	*488*	*509*	*460*	*112*	*68*	*77*	*69*	*179*	*177*	*Indigenous*
385	316	50	35	95	69	193	176	42	33	5	3	..	..	125	131	Bukhārī
232	225	134	118	27	26	57	61	12	18	..	..	2	2	..	..	Chishtī
6	4	..	..	6	4	..	..	..	..	..	..	..	..	..	..	Gharshīn
191	190	118	126	6	4	28	25	9	16	30	19	..	..	..	..	Gīlānī
281	250	6	8	..	..	179	158	12	10	44	33	40	41	53	45	Husainī
424	376	..	..	..	..	..	..	424	376	..	..	..	..	..	..	Kahērī
..	..	..	..	..	..	..	..	..	..	..	..	..	..	..	..	Karbalā
..	..	..	..	..	..	..	..	..	..	..	..	..	..	..	..	Khōstī
37	22	20	17	..	..	6	5	..	..	11	..	..	..	..	..	Mashwānī
50	49	36	33	14	16	..	..	..	..	..	..	..	..	..	..	Maudūdī
..	..	..	..	..	..	..	..	..	..	..	..	..	..	..	..	Pēchī
..	..	..	..	..	..	..	..	..	..	..	..	..	..	..	..	Tāran
3	3	..	..	..	..	3	3	..	..	..	..	..	..	..	..	Ustrāna
202	172	83	60	13	6	46	60	3	7	22	13	35	26	1	1	Others
1	..	..	..	..	..	..	..	..	..	*1*	..	..	..	..	..	*Aliens*
..	..	..	..	..	..	..	..	..	..	..	..	..	..	..	..	*Trans-Indus*
1	..	..	..	..	..	..	..	..	..	*1*	..	..	..	..	..	*Cis-Indus*
29,794	**27,668**	**5,664**	**4,909**	**6,005**	**5,219**	**2,529**	**2,119**	**1,485**	**1,282**	**11,976**	**12,126**	**2,135**	**2,013**	**7,161**	**6,809**	**Other Musalmāns**
29,458	*27,508*	*5,609*	*4,879*	*5,989*	*5,207*	*2,445*	*2,055*	*1,477*	*1,271*	*11,803*	*12,083*	*2,135*	*2,013*	*7,093*	*6,779*	*Indigenous*
5,096	4,954	..	..	37	32	..	..	..	..	5,059	4,922	..	..	52	46	Darzāda
3,671	3,071	3,553	2,984	93	65	2	..	1	5	11	6	11	11	..	..	Dēhwār
..	..	..	..	..	..	..	..	..	..	..	..	..	..	3,716	3,485	Gadrā
7,537	8,312	561	620	1,778	1,852	496	498	148	170	3,128	3,772	1,426	1,400	925	1,005	Ghulām
3,626	2,978	647	528	1,489	1,142	434	327	256	203	701	654	149	124	..	..	Ghulāmāzād
378	305	..	..	..	..	..	..	378	305	..	..	..	..	..	..	Gōlā
1,618	1,323	17	12	..	..	922	747	529	426	150	138	..	..	1	3	Jat
..	..	..	..	..	..	..	..	..	..	..	..	..	..	185	182	Khōja
3	2	..	..	3	2	..	..	..	..	..	..	..	..	305	260	Kōrī
3,522	2,959	826	726	1,560	1,209	290	236	100	107	571	526	175	155	718	634	Lōṛī
253	242	..	..	..	..	..	..	..	..	253	242	..	..	1,006	993	Mēd
3,384	3,052	..	..	1,075	901	10	10	..	..	1,925	1,818	374	323	24	20	Nakib
370	310	5	9	4	4	291	237	65	55	5	5	..	..	161	151	Others
336	*160*	*55*	*30*	*16*	*12*	*84*	*64*	*8*	*11*	*173*	*43*	..	..	*68*	*30*	*Aliens*
136	*72*	*1*	*3*	*5*	*6*	*49*	*46*	*7*	*11*	*74*	*6*	..	..	*9*	*3*	*Trans-Indus*
1	..	1	..	..	..	..	..	..	..	..	..	..	..	..	..	Hazāra
135	72	..	3	5	6	49	46	7	11	74	6	..	..	9	3	Others
200	*88*	*54*	*27*	*11*	*6*	*35*	*18*	*1*	..	*99*	*37*	..	..	*59*	*27*	*Cis-Indus*
5,550	**4,552**	**600**	**403**	**380**	**92**	**3,748**	**3,425**	**664**	**598**	**126**	**11**	**32**	**20**	**988**	**748**	**Hindu**
4,783	*4,183*	*439*	*327*	*251*	*78*	*3,564*	*3,334*	*479*	*426*	*22*	*1*	*28*	*17*	*786*	*668*	*Indigenous*
767	*369*	*161*	*76*	*129*	*14*	*184*	*91*	*185*	*172*	*104*	*10*	*4*	*3*	*202*	*80*	*Aliens*
1,564	**1,458**	**68**	**45**	**9**	**3**	**616**	**572**	**869**	**838**	**2**	..	..	..	**60**	**18**	**Sikh**
1,391	*1,342*	*40*	*26*	..	..	*575*	*547*	*776*	*769*	..	..	..	..	*8*	..	*Indigenous*
173	*116*	*28*	*19*	*9*	*3*	*41*	*25*	*93*	*69*	*2*	..	..	..	*52*	*18*	*Aliens*
49	**7**	**3**	**2**	..	..	**4**	**2**	..	..	**42**	**3**	..	..	**5**	..	**Miscellaneous Aliens**
15	4	1	2	..	..	1	..	..	..	13	2	..	..	1	..	European
4	..	..	..	..	..	..	..	..	..	4	..	..	..	1	..	Anglo-Indian
26	2	2	..	..	..	3	2	..	..	21	..	..	..	2	..	Indian Christian
4	1	..	..	..	..	..	..	..	..	4	1	..	..	1	..	Others

TABLE XIV.

Civil Condition by Age for Selected Castes.

The number of indigenous inhabitants censused in the regular areas, where alone statistics regarding age and civil condition were collected, is too small to justify a selection of races and tribes. The Table accordingly consists of a review of civil condition by age among the population censused on the regular schedule, divided into two main groups, indigenous and others, with subdivisions by the main religions.

XIV.—CIVIL CONDITION BY AGE FOR SELECTED CASTES.

Race and Age	Total			Unmarried			Married			Widowed		
	Persons	Males	Females	Persons	Males	Females	Persons	Males	Females	Persons	Males	Females
1	2	3	4	5	6	7	8	9	10	11	12	13
Grand Total	***63,007***	***49,271***	***13,736***	***29,788***	***24,631***	***5,157***	***29,608***	***22,091***	***7,517***	***3,611***	***2,549***	***1,062***
0—5	4,608	2,322	2,286	4,607	2,322	2,285	1	...	1	...	...	...
5—12	4,822	2,688	2,134	4,735	2,657	2,078	87	31	56	...	...	...
12—15	1,928	1,316	612	1,589	1,219	370	336	95	241	3	2	1
15—20	5,665	4,385	1,280	3,693	3,516	177	1,926	838	1,088	46	31	15
20—40	37,183	31,648	5,535	14,507	14,289	218	21,033	15,958	5,075	1,643	1,401	242
40 and over	8,801	6,912	1,889	657	628	29	6,225	5,169	1,056	1,919	1,115	804
A.—Indigenous	**8,447**	**6,505**	**1,942**	**4,253**	**3,547**	**706**	**3,636**	**2,645**	**991**	**558**	**313**	**245**
0—5	556	290	266	556	290	266	...	...	...	...	...	...
5—12	775	460	315	762	454	308	13	6	7	...	...	...
12—15	323	226	97	277	217	60	46	9	37	...	...	...
15—20	801	618	183	572	531	41	223	84	139	6	3	3
20—40	4,635	3,935	700	1,965	1,935	30	2,434	1,818	616	206	152	54
40 and over	1,357	976	381	91	90	1	920	728	192	346	158	188
MUSALMĀN	**7,706**	**6,017**	**1,689**	**3,940**	**3,328**	**612**	**3,298**	**2,412**	**886**	**473**	**276**	**197**
0—5	492	256	236	492	256	236	...	...	...	...	...	...
5—12	666	406	260	655	401	254	11	5	6	...	...	...
12—15	277	197	80	245	190	55	32	7	25	...	...	...
15—20	710	554	156	524	487	37	180	64	116	6	3	3
20—40	4,353	3,718	635	1,936	1,907	29	2,236	1,678	558	181	133	48
40 and over	1,208	886	322	88	87	1	834	659	175	286	140	146
HINDU	**733**	**481**	**252**	**308**	**214**	**94**	**340**	**230**	**110**	**85**	**37**	**48**
0—5	63	33	30	63	33	30	...	...	...	...	...	...
5—12	109	54	55	107	53	54	2	1	1	...	...	...
12—15	45	28	17	31	26	5	14	2	12	...	...	...
15—20	91	64	27	48	44	4	43	20	23	...	...	...
20—40	276	212	64	56	55	1	195	138	57	25	19	6
40 and over	149	90	59	3	3	...	66	69	17	60	18	42
SIKH	**8**	**7**	**1**	**5**	**5**	...	**3**	**2**	**1**	...	...	...
0—5	1	1	...	1	1	...	...	...	...	...	...	...
5—12	...	...	...	...	...	...	...	...	...	...	...	...
12—15	1	1	...	1	1	...	...	...	...	...	...	...
15—20	...	...	...	...	...	...	...	...	...	...	...	...
20—40	6	5	1	3	3	...	3	2	1	...	...	...
40 and over	...	...	...	...	...	...	...	...	...	...	...	...
B.—Others	**54,560**	**42,766**	**11,794**	**25,535**	**21,084**	**4,451**	**25,972**	**19,446**	**6,526**	**3,053**	**2,236**	**817**
0—5	4,052	2,032	2,020	4,051	2,032	2,019	1	...	1	...	...	...
5—12	4,047	2,228	1,819	3,973	2,203	1,770	74	25	49	...	...	...
12—15	1,605	1,090	515	1,312	1,002	310	290	86	204	3	2	1
15—20	4,864	3,767	1,097	3,121	2,985	136	1,703	754	949	40	28	12
20—40	32,548	27,713	4,835	12,512	12,324	188	18,599	14,140	4,459	1,437	1,249	188
40 and over	7,444	5,936	1,508	566	538	28	5,305	4,441	864	1,573	957	616
MUSALMAN	**23,693**	**19,077**	**4,616**	**11,124**	**9,464**	**1,660**	**11,299**	**8,696**	**2,603**	**1,270**	**917**	**353**
0—5	1,522	769	753	1,521	769	752	1	...	1	...	...	...
5—12	1,526	855	671	1,516	855	661	10	...	10	...	...	...
12—15	701	508	193	596	479	117	105	29	76	...	...	...
15—20	2,212	1,790	422	1,566	1,523	43	630	255	375	16	12	4
20—40	14,269	12,342	1,927	5,604	5,534	70	8,062	6,303	1,760	603	506	97
40 and over	3,463	2,813	650	321	304	17	2,491	2,110	381	651	399	252
HINDU	**19,767**	**14,934**	**4,833**	**8,191**	**6,326**	**1,865**	**10,253**	**7,596**	**2,657**	**1,323**	**952**	**371**
0—5	1,684	823	861	1,684	823	861	...	...	...	...	...	...
5—12	1,853	1,026	827	1,795	1,002	793	58	24	34	...	...	...
12—15	644	423	221	498	380	118	144	42	102	2	1	1
15—20	1,869	1,390	479	1,026	1,003	20	823	371	452	20	13	7
20—40	10,869	9,044	1,825	3,024	3,013	11	7,283	5,537	1,740	559	494	65
40 and over	2,848	2,228	620	164	162	2	1,942	1,622	320	742	444	298
SIKH	**5,037**	**4,211**	**826**	**2,029**	**1,767**	**262**	**2,667**	**2,142**	**525**	**341**	**302**	**39**
0—5	277	154	123	277	154	123	...	...	...	...	...	...
5—12	258	139	119	253	138	115	5	1	4	...	...	...
12—15	130	90	40	98	77	21	31	12	19	1	1	...
15—20	524	442	82	330	328	2	190	111	79	4	3	1
20—40	3,289	2,902	387	1,047	1,046	1	2,017	1,643	374	225	213	12
40 and over	559	484	75	24	24	...	424	375	49	111	85	26
CHRISTIAN	**5,085**	**3,941**	**1,144**	**3,758**	**3,198**	**560**	**1,253**	**705**	**548**	**74**	**38**	**36**
0—5	424	213	211	424	213	211	...	...	...	...	...	...
5—12	300	148	152	209	148	151	1	...	1	...	...	...
12—15	77	43	34	73	40	33	4	3	1	...	...	...
15—20	189	103	86	158	94	64	31	9	22	...	...	...
20—40	3,648	3,115	533	2,750	2,658	92	873	440	433	25	17	8
40 and over	447	319	128	54	45	9	344	253	91	49	21	28
OTHER MINOR RELIGIONS	**978**	**603**	**375**	**433**	**269**	**164**	**500**	**307**	**193**	**45**	**27**	**18**
0—5	145	73	72	145	73	72	...	...	...	...	...	...
5—12	110	60	50	110	60	50	...	...	...	...	...	...
12—15	53	26	27	47	26	21	6	...	6	...	...	...
15—20	70	42	28	41	34	7	29	8	21	...	...	...
20—40	473	310	163	87	73	14	361	218	143	25	19	6
40 and over	127	92	35	3	3	...	104	81	23	20	8	12

TABLE XV.

Occupation or Means of Livelihood.

This Table is divided into five Parts. Part A, which is complete in itself, deals with the occupations of the whole population, and consists (*i*) of a provincial summary, and (*ii*) of a detailed statement for the various districts and states. Part B treats of the subsidiary occupations of agriculturists who returned themselves as actual workers. A review of certain other mixed occupations is given in Part C. In Part D all occupations are classified by religion. Part E contains the results of a supplementary Industrial census which was taken on the census night.

Group No.	OCCUPATION	BALŪCHISTĀN				
		Total workers and dependants	Actual workers			Dependants
			Total		Partially agriculturists	
			Males	Females		
1	2	3	4	5	6	7
	TOTAL	**834,703**	**295,953**	**7,331**	**23,532**	**531,419**
	A—Production of raw materials	**666,661**	**219,259**	**92**	**6,609**	**447,310**
	I.—EXPLOITATION OF THE SURFACE OF THE EARTH	***664,987***	***218,030***	***85***	***6,257***	***446,872***
	1 Pasture and agriculture	***659,433***	***216,408***	***85***	***6,172***	***442,940***
	(a) Ordinary cultivation	*561,053*	*182,581*	*7*	*37*	*378,465*
1	Income from rent of agricultural land	77,649	22,524	7	...	55,118
2	Ordinary cultivators	476,868	155,068	...	...	321,800
3	Land-agents, managers of landed estates, etc.	325	145	...	37	180
4	Farm servants, field labourers	6,211	4,844	...	...	1,367
6	*(b) Growers of special products, market-gardening (fruit, flower, vegetable, vine, etc.)*	*2,310*	*1,021*	...	*162*	*1,289*
	(c) Forestry	*3,037*	*1,034*	...	*200*	*2,003*
7	Forest officers, rangers, guards, etc.	102	57	...	28	45
8	Wood-cutters; firewood collectors, etc.	2,935	977	...	172	1,958
	(d) Raising of farm stock	*93,033*	*31,772*	*78*	*5,773*	*61,183*
9	Cattle and buffalo breeders and keepers	2,086	701	74	448	1,311
10	Sheep and goat breeders	79,087	26,890	2	4,923	52,195
11	Breeders of other animals	6,448	2,052	...	256	4,396
12	Herdsmen, shepherds, goatherds, etc.	5,412	2,129	2	146	3,281
	2 Fishing and hunting	***5,554***	***1,622***	...	***85***	***3,932***
14	Fishing	5,504	1,602	...	80	3,902
15	Hunting	50	20	...	5	30
	II.—EXTRACTION OF MINERALS	***1,674***	***1,229***	***7***	***352***	***438***
	3 Mines	***1,400***	***1,149***	***7***	***350***	***244***
16	Coal mines, petroleum wells	1,395	1,146	7	348	242
17	Other mines and metallic minerals	5	3	...	2	2
	5 Salt, etc.	***274***	***80***	...	***2***	***194***
19	Rock, sea and marsh salt	273	79	...	2	194
20	Extraction of saltpetre, alum, etc.	1	1	...	...	...
	B—Preparation and supply of material substances	**95,252**	**38,952**	**887**	**4,662**	**55,413**
	III.—INDUSTRY	***37,233***	***15,074***	***833***	***1,598***	***21,326***
	6 Textiles	***2,532***	***905***	***28***	***126***	***1,599***
21	Cotton ginning, cleaning, etc.	22	16	...	...	6
22	Cotton spinning, sizing, weaving	1,203	424	5	28	774
24	Rope, twine, string	46	22	...	...	24
26	Wool carders, weavers, etc.	1,113	390	4	94	719
27	Silk spinners, weavers	6	3	...	...	3
30	Dyeing, bleaching, etc.	22	8	...	...	14
31	Other textile industries (embroideries, etc.)	120	42	19	4	59
	7 Hides, skins, hard animal materials	***207***	***71***	...	...	***136***
32	Tanners, curriers, etc.	35	14	...	...	21
33	Makers of leather articles	156	50	...	...	106
34	Furriers	16	7	...	...	9
	8 Wood	***5,227***	***1,786***	***80***	***283***	***3,361***
36	Sawyers, carpenters, turners, etc.	3,929	1,460	...	248	2,469
37	Basket and palm mat-makers, etc.	1,298	326	80	35	892
	9 Metals	***7,323***	***2,714***	...	***211***	***4,609***
38	Forging and rolling of iron, etc.	1	1	...	...	...
40	Makers of arms, guns, etc.	538	365	...	17	173
41	Other workers in iron	6,422	2,181	...	192	4,241
42	Workers in brass, copper, bell metal	208	100	...	2	106
43	Workers in other metals (tins, etc.)	154	67	...	...	87
	10 Ceramics	***722***	***271***	...	***44***	***451***
47	Potters, earthen pipe and bowl makers	598	207	...	40	391
48	Brick and tile makers	124	64	...	4	60
	11 Manufacture of chemical and analogous products	***327***	***122***	...	***47***	***205***
50	Matches and explosive materials	28	8	...	8	20
51	Ærated and mineral waters	29	28	...	6	1
52	Dyes, paint, ink	5	2	...	...	3
53	Vegetable and mineral oils	258	81	...	33	177
55	Other (soap, candles, etc.)	7	3	...	...	4
	12 Food industries	***3,844***	***1,585***	***198***	***256***	***2,061***
56	Rice pounders, huskers, flour grinders	715	179	188	41	348
57	Bakers, biscuit makers	582	383	4	35	195
58	Grain parchers, etc.	747	261	2	68	484
59	Butchers	1,033	381	3	40	649
61	Butter, cheese, ghee makers	5	1	...	...	4
63	Sweetmeat makers, etc.	668	307	1	19	360
64	Brewers, distillers	93	72	...	53	21
66	Manufacture of tobacco, opium, etc.	1	1	...	...	...

PART A—PROVINCIAL SUMMARY.

DISTRICTS					STATES					
Total workers and dependants	Actual workers			Dependants	Total workers and dependants	Actual workers			Dependants	Group No.
	Total		Partially agriculturists			Total		Partially agriculturists		
	Males	Females				Males	Females			
8	9	10	11	12	13	14	15	16	17	
414,412	**154,742**	**1,976**	**17,966**	**257,694**	**420,291**	**141,211**	**5,355**	**6,466**	**273,725**	
316,685	**101,193**	**91**	**3,127**	**215,401**	**349,976**	**118,066**	**1**	**3,482**	**231,909**	
315,277	***100,041***	***84***	***2,775***	***215,152***	***349,710***	***117,989***	***1***	***3,482***	***231,720***	
315,273	***100,038***	***84***	***2,775***	***215,151***	***344,160***	***116,370***	***1***	***3,397***	***227,789***	
272,553	*85,422*	*6*	*28*	*187,125*	*288,500*	*97,159*	*1*	*9*	*191,340*	
36,753	10,117	6	...	26,630	40,896	13,407	1	...	28,488	1
234,911	74,716	...	...	160,195	241,957	80,353	...	...	161,605	2
161	86	...	28	75	164	59	...	9	105	3
728	503	...	...	225	5,483	4,341	...	...	1,143	4
747	*547*	...	*130*	*200*	*1,563*	*474*	...	*32*	*1,089*	6
779	*303*	...	*178*	*476*	*2,258*	*731*	...	*22*	*1,527*	
87	53	...	28	34	15	4	...	...	11	7
693	250	...	150	443	2,243	727	...	22	1,516	8
41,194	*13,766*	*78*	*2,439*	*27,350*	*51,839*	*18,006*	...	*3,334*	*33,833*	
416	153	74	9	189	1,670	546	...	439	1,128	9
33,464	11,053	2	2,231	22,409	45,623	15,837	...	2,692	29,786	10
4,698	1,518	...	67	3,180	1,750	534	...	189	1,216	11
2,616	1,042	2	132	1,572	2,796	1,087	...	14	1,709	12
4	***3***	...	...	***1***	***5,550***	***1,619***	...	***85***	***3,931***	
2	2	...	...	...	5,502	1,600	...	80	3,902	14
2	1	...	...	1	48	19	...	5	29	15
1,408	***1,159***	***7***	***352***	***249***	***266***	***77***	...	...	***189***	
1,400	***1,149***	***7***	***350***	***244***	...	...	...	...	...	
1,395	1,146	7	348	242	...	...	...	...	...	16
5	3	...	2	2	...	...	...	...	...	17
8	***3***	...	***2***	***5***	***266***	***77***	...	...	***189***	
8	3	...	2	5	265	76	...	...	189	19
...	...	...	...	...	1	1	...	...	...	20
49,609	**23,471**	**522**	**2,862**	**25,616**	**45,643**	**15,461**	**365**	**1,800**	**29,797**	
18,185	***8,845***	***469***	***895***	***8,871***	***19,048***	***6,229***	***364***	***703***	***12,455***	
880	***341***	***9***	***87***	***537***	***1,652***	***564***	***26***	***39***	***1,062***	
22	16	...	...	6	...	...	...	...	...	21
6	3	...	...	3	1,197	431	5	26	771	22
19	11	...	...	8	27	11	...	...	16	24
794	297	2	87	495	319	93	2	7	234	26
...	...	...	...	...	6	3	...	...	3	27
22	8	...	...	14	...	...	...	...	...	30
17	6	...	...	11	103	36	19	4	48	31
31	***17***	...	...	***14***	***176***	***54***	...	...	***122***	
14	9	...	...	5	21	5	...	...	16	32
1	1	...	...	...	155	49	...	...	106	33
16	7	...	...	9	...	...	...	...	...	34
1,621	***689***	...	***117***	***932***	***3,606***	***1,097***	***80***	***166***	***2,429***	
1,365	602	...	117	763	2,564	858	...	131	1,706	36
256	87	...	...	169	1,042	239	80	35	723	37
3,304	***1,400***	...	***179***	***1,904***	***4,019***	***1,314***	...	***32***	***2,705***	
1	1	...	...	...	...	...	...	...	...	38
529	364	...	17	165	9	1	...	...	8	40
2,559	923	...	160	1,636	3,863	1,258	...	32	2,605	41
118	68	...	2	50	90	32	...	...	58	42
97	44	...	...	53	57	23	...	...	34	43
216	***93***	...	***21***	***123***	***506***	***178***	...	***23***	***328***	
157	53	...	17	104	441	154	...	23	287	47
59	40	...	4	19	65	24	...	...	41	48
62	***39***	...	***6***	***23***	***265***	***83***	...	***41***	***182***	
...	...	...	...	...	28	8	...	8	20	50
29	28	...	6	1	...	...	...	...	...	51
5	2	...	...	3	...	...	...	...	...	52
21	6	...	...	15	237	75	...	33	162	53
7	3	...	...	4	...	...	...	...	...	55
1,942	***1,039***	***24***	***170***	***879***	***1,903***	***546***	***174***	***86***	***1,183***	
374	161	17	41	196	341	18	171	...	152	56
503	352	3	35	148	79	31	1	...	47	57
121	57	...	11	64	626	204	2	57	420	58
566	230	3	17	333	467	151	...	23	316	59
...	...	...	...	...	5	1	...	...	4	61
286	168	1	13	117	382	139	...	6	243	63
91	70	...	53	21	3	2	...	...	...	64
1	1	...	...	...	...	...	...	...	...	66

Group No.	OCCUPATION	BALŪCHISTĀN				
		Total workers and dependants	ACTUAL WORKERS			Dependants
			TOTAL		Partially agriculturists	
			Males	Females		
1	2	3	4	5	6	7
	III.—INDUSTRY—contd.					
	13 Industries of dress and the toilet	***7,621***	***3,280***	***168***	***371***	***4,173***
67	Hat, cap, turban makers	2	1	...	...	1
68	Tailors, milliners, etc.	1,467	760	108	82	599
69	Shoe, boot, sandal makers	2,979	1,119	2	123	1,858
70	Other industries pertaining to dress	10	9	1	...	...
71	Washing, cleaning, dyeing	2,071	843	57	122	1,171
72	Barbers, hairdressers, etc.	1,077	544	...	94	533
73	Shampooers, bath houses, etc.	15	4	...	...	11
	14 Furniture industries	***100***	***41***	***1***	***1***	***58***
74	Cabinet makers, carriage painters, etc.	99	41	...	1	58
75	Upholsterers, etc.	1	...	1	...	...
	15 Building industries	***3,191***	***1,581***	***19***	***170***	***1,591***
76	Lime burners, cement workers	49	19	...	2	30
77	Excavators, wellsinkers	622	267	...	33	355
78	Stone workers, masons	1,214	590	...	41	624
79	Thatchers, building contractors, plumbers, etc.	1,306	705	19	94	582
	16 Construction of means of transport	***41***	***25***	...	***2***	***16***
80	Cart and carriage makers, wheelwrights	6	5	...	...	1
81	Saddlers, harness makers, etc.	35	20	...	2	15
	18 Industries of luxury, literature, arts, sciences	***2,039***	***813***	***2***	***56***	***1,224***
84	Printers, lithographers, etc.	88	48	1	6	39
85	Newspaper managers, editors, etc.	3	...	1	...	2
86	Bookbinders, etc.	13	9	...	...	4
87	Makers of musical instruments	8	2	...	...	6
88	Makers of watches, clocks, surgical instruments, etc.	33	10	...	...	23
89	Jewellers, etc.	1,824	701	...	45	1,123
91	Toy, kite, cage, fishing tackle, etc.	7	6	...	...	1
92	Others (non-performers in theatres, race course service, huntsmen, etc.)	63	37	...	5	26
93	***19 Industries concerned with refuse (sweepers, scavengers, etc.)***	***4,059***	***1,880***	***337***	***31***	***1,842***
	IV.—TRANSPORT	***28,756***	***12,166***	***6***	***2,371***	***16,584***
	20 Transport by water	***888***	***470***	***1***	***125***	***417***
95	Ships' officers, engineers, mariners, etc.	57	55	...	...	2
96	Employés on streams, rivers, canals	400	250	1	123	149
97	Boat-owners, boatmen, tow-men	431	165	...	2	266
	21 Transport by road	***21,785***	***7,901***	***5***	***1,134***	***13,879***
98	Employés on roads and bridges	884	438	2	48	444
99	Cart owners, coachmen, stable boys, etc.	882	485	1	60	396
100	Palki, etc., bearers and owners	6	6	...	2	...
101	Pack-animal owners and drivers	19,554	6,731	2	977	12,821
102	Porters, messengers	459	241	...	47	218
	22 Transport by rail	***4,960***	***3,307***	...	***963***	***1,653***
103	Railway employés	4,784	3,164	...	905	1,620
104	Labourers on railway construction	176	143	...	58	33
105	***23 Post office, Telegraph, Telephone services***	***1,123***	***488***	...	***149***	***635***
	V.—TRADE	***29,263***	***11,712***	***48***	***693***	***17,503***
106	***24 Bank managers, money lenders, money changers, etc.***	***719***	***254***	...	***30***	***465***
107	***25 Brokers, commercial travellers, ware-house owners and employés***	***212***	***87***	...	***8***	***125***
108	***26 Trade in textiles (piece-goods, etc.)***	***5,070***	***1,970***	***1***	***170***	***3,099***
109	***27 Trade in skins, leather, furs***	***146***	***72***	...	***2***	***74***
110	***28 Trade in wood (timber, cork, bark, etc.)***	***752***	***223***	...	***4***	***529***
111	***29 Trade in metals (machinery, knife, tools, etc.)***	***19***	***10***	...	***2***	***9***
112	***30 Trade in pottery***	***9***	***6***	...	***3***	***3***
113	***31 Trade in chemical products (drugs, petroleum, etc.)***	***890***	***341***	***1***	***66***	***548***
	32 Hotels, cafés, restaurants, etc.	***354***	***209***	...	***13***	***145***
114	Vendors of liquors, aerated waters, etc.	215	118	...	3	97
115	Owners, managers, employés of sarais, etc.	139	91	...	10	48
	33 Other trade in food stuffs	***13,037***	***5,580***	***43***	***265***	***7,414***
116	Fish dealers	283	94	...	1	189
117	Grocers, sellers of vegetable oil, salt, etc.	9,530	4,052	2	103	5,476
118	Sellers of milk, butter, ghee, poultry, eggs, etc.	510	238	30	13	242
119	Sellers of sweetmeats, sugar, etc.	7	3	...	...	4
120	Cardamom, betel-leaf, vegetables, fruit, areca-nut sellers	1,106	487	10	79	608
121	Grain and pulse dealers	918	398	...	39	520
122	Tobacco, opium, ganja, etc., sellers	138	69	1	3	68
123	Dealers in sheep and goats, etc.	364	145	...	11	219
124	Dealers in hay, grass, fodder	182	94	...	16	88

PART A—PROVINCIAL SUMMARY.

DISTRICTS					STATES					Group No.
Total workers and dependants	Actual workers — Total — Males	Actual workers — Total — Females	Actual workers — Partially agriculturists	Dependants	Total workers and dependants	Actual workers — Total — Males	Actual workers — Total — Females	Actual workers — Partially agriculturists	Dependants	
8	9	10	11	12	13	14	15	16	17	
3,895	***2,031***	***103***	***125***	***1,762***	***3,726***	***1,249***	***66***	***246***	***2,411***	
2	1	...	...	1	...	...	...	...	...	67
1,221	708	44	32	479	238	53	64	...	120	68
1,085	486	3	48	597	1,894	633	...	75	1,261	69
10	9	1	...	...	...	...	...	...	...	70
1,031	478	55	11	498	1,040	365	...	111	678	71
531	345	...	34	176	556	199	...	60	357	72
15	4	...	...	11	...	...	...	...	...	73
86	***36***	***1***	***1***	***49***	***14***	***5***	...	..	***9***	
85	36	...	1	49	14	5	...	...	9	74
1	...	1	...	...	...	...	...	...	...	75
1,690	***1,027***	***1***	***138***	***662***	***1,501***	***554***	***18***	***32***	***929***	
40	16	...	1	24	9	3	...	1	6	76
303	159	...	20	144	319	108	.	13	211	77
519	345	...	24	174	695	245	...	17	450	78
828	507	1	93	320	478	198	18	1	262	79
41	***25***	...	***2***	***16***	...	...	...	...	...	
6	5	...	...	1	...	...	...	...	...	80
35	20	...	2	15	...	...	...	...	...	81
871	***417***	***2***	***23***	***452***	***1,168***	***396***	...	***28***	***772***	
88	48	1	6	39	...	...	...	...	...	84
3	...	1	...	2	...	...	...	...	...	85
13	9	...	...	4	...	...	...	...	...	86
...	...	...	...	...	8	2	...	...	6	87
38	10	...	...	28	...	...	...	...	...	88
670	312	...	17	358	1,154	389	...	28	765	89
2	2	...	...	...	5	4	...	...	1	91
62	36	...	5	26	1	1	...	...	...	92
3,546	***1,691***	***337***	***91***	***1,518***	***513***	***189***	...	***10***	***324***	93
17,972	***8,566***	***6***	***1,507***	***9,400***	***10,784***	***3,600***	...	***864***	***7,184***	
399	***249***	***1***	***122***	***149***	***489***	***221***	...	***3***	***268***	
...	...	...	...	..	57	55	...	...	2	95
399	249	1	122	149	1	1	...	1	...	96
..	...	...	...	..	431	165	...	2	266	97
11,957	***4,681***	***5***	***314***	***7,271***	***9,828***	***3,220***	...	***820***	***6,608***	
868	428	2	48	438	21	10	...	...	11	98
872	481	1	60	390	10	4	...	...	6	99
6	6	...	2	...	...	...	...	...	...	100
9,986	3,601	2	160	6,383	9,566	3,130	...	817	6,436	101
228	165	...	44	63	231	76	...	3	155	102
4,916	***3,287***	...	***960***	***1,629***	***44***	***20***	...	***3***	***24***	
4,755	3,151	...	903	1,604	29	13	...	2	16	103
161	136	...	57	25	15	7	...	1	8	104
700	***349***	...	***111***	***351***	***423***	***139***	...	***38***	***284***	105
13,459	***6,060***	***47***	***460***	***7,345***	***15,811***	***5,652***	***1***	***933***	***10,158***	
288	***109***	...	***30***	***179***	***431***	***145***	...	...	***286***	106
115	***58***	...	***8***	***57***	***97***	***29***	...	...	***68***	107
2,540	***1,026***	***1***	***190***	***1,513***	***2,530***	***944***	...	***50***	***1,586***	108
88	***48***	...	***1***	***40***	***58***	***24***	...	***1***	***34***	109
7	***5***	...	...	***2***	***745***	***218***	...	***4***	***527***	110
19	***10***	...	***2***	***9***	...	...	...	...	...	111
9	***6***	...	***3***	***3***	...	...	...	...	...	112
519	***217***	***1***	***17***	***301***	***371***	***124***	..	***49***	***247***	113
271	***179***	...	***13***	***92***	***83***	***30***	...	...	***53***	
143	93	...	3	50	73	26	...	—	47	114
129	87	...	10	42	10	4	...	...	6	115
6,384	***3,073***	***43***	***188***	***3,268***	***6,653***	***2,507***	...	***82***	***4,146***	
8	3	...	..	5	275	91	...	1	184	116
4,525	2,133	2	103	2,390	5,005	1,919	...	...	3,086	117
403	194	20	13	179	107	44	...	...	63	118
7	3	...	...	4	...	...	...	...	...	119
544	291	10	30	243	561	196	...	40	365	120
375	198	...	13	177	543	200	...	26	343	121
105	57	1	3	47	33	12	...	...	21	122
285	100	...	5	185	129	45	...	6	84	123
182	94	...	16	88	...	...	...	...	...	124

Group No.	OCCUPATION	BALŪCHISTĀN				
		Total workers and dependants	Actual workers			Dependants
			Total		Partially agriculturists	
			Males	Females		
1	2	3	4	5	6	7
	V.—TRADE—contd.					
125	***34 Trade in clothing (ready-made) and toilet articles***	***219***	***98***	***1***	***7***	***120***
	35 Trade in furniture	***1,083***	***390***	...	***24***	***693***
126	Trade in furniture, carpets, etc.	1,046	363	...	22	683
127	Hardware sellers	37	27	...	2	10
128	***36 Trade in Building Materials***	***51***	***12***	...	...	***39***
129	***37 Trade in means of transport (dealers and hirers of transport animals, carriages, saddlery, etc.)***	***342***	***129***	...	***8***	***213***
130	***38 Trade in fuel (firewood, charcoal, coal, etc.)***	***490***	***167***	***1***	***19***	***322***
	39 Trade in articles of luxury, letters, arts, sciences	***662***	***311***	***1***	***7***	***350***
131	Dealers in jewellery, clocks, etc.	40	28	...	1	12
132	Dealers in bangles, toys, flowers, etc.	599	272	1	6	326
133	Publishers, book-sellers, stationers, etc.	23	11	...	...	12
	41 Trade of other sorts	***5,208***	***1,853***	...	***65***	***3,355***
135	Shopkeepers, otherwise unspecified	4,977	1,744	...	58	3,233
136	Pedlars, hawkers, etc.	190	89	...	5	101
137	Conjurors, acrobats, fortune tellers, etc.	11	6	...	...	5
138	Farmers of pounds, tolls, etc.	30	14	...	2	16
	C—Public administration and liberal arts	**42,194**	**26,344**	**213**	**10,266**	**15,637**
	VI.—PUBLIC FORCE	***20,397***	***16,584***	***1***	***7,778***	***3,812***
	43 Army	***18,519***	***15,302***	***1***	***7,047***	***3,216***
139	Army (Imperial)	16,899	14,515	1	6,940	2,383
140	Army (Native States)	1,620	787	...	107	833
	44 Police	***1,878***	***1,282***	...	***731***	***596***
142	Police	1,874	1,281	...	730	593
143	Village watchmen	4	1	...	1	3
	VII.—PUBLIC ADMINISTRATION	***9,996***	***5,226***	***2***	***2,495***	***4,768***
	45 Public Administration	***9,996***	***5,226***	***2***	***2,425***	***4,768***
144	Service of the State	6,504	3,762	...	2,087	2,742
145	Service of Native States	2,803	1,084	...	203	1,719
146	Municipal and other non-village service	443	242	2	75	199
147	Village officials other than watchmen	246	138	...	60	108
	VIII.—PROFESSIONS AND LIBERAL ARTS	***11,169***	***4,407***	***182***	***634***	***6,580***
	46 Religion	***6,999***	***2,523***	***55***	***311***	***4,421***
148	Priests, ministers, etc.	4,044	1,388	2	167	2,654
149	Religious mendicants, etc.	2,599	973	47	118	1,579
150	Catechists, church and mission service	48	24	6	7	18
151	Temple, burial-ground service, etc.	308	138	...	19	170
	47 Law	***233***	***72***	...	***27***	***161***
152	Lawyers, Kāzis, etc.	96	29	...	15	67
153	Petition writers, etc.	137	43	...	12	94
	48 Medicine	***867***	***413***	***79***	***9 9***	***375***
154	Medical practitioners, dentists, oculists, veterinary surgeons	392	179	4	42	209
155	Midwives, vaccinators, compounders, nurses, etc.	475	234	75	57	166
156	***49 Instruction (professors, teachers, clerks, etc.)***	***606***	***348***	***48***	***46***	***210***
	50 Letters, arts, sciences	***2,464***	***1,051***	...	***151***	***1,413***
157	Public scribes, copyists, etc.	28	19	...	4	9
158	Architects, surveyors, with employés	892	454	...	95	438
159	Authors, photographers, artists, astronomers, etc.	117	58	...	6	59
160	Music players, singers, actors, dancers	1,427	520	...	46	907
	IX.—PERSONS LIVING ON THEIR INCOME	***632***	***127***	***28***	***29***	***477***
161	***51 Persons living principally on their income (proprietors, other than of agricultural land, pensioners, etc.)***	***632***	***127***	***28***	***29***	***477***
	D—Miscellaneous	**30,596**	**11,398**	**6,139**	**1,395**	**13,059**
	X.—DOMESTIC SERVICE	***14,294***	***5,070***	***5,819***	***848***	***3,405***
	52 Domestic service	***14,294***	***5,070***	***5,819***	***848***	***3,405***
162	Cooks, water carriers, door-keepers, watchmen and other indoor servants	12,660	3,812	5,819	531	3,029
163	Private grooms, coachmen, dog boys, etc.	1,634	1,258	..	317	376
	XI.—INSUFFICIENTLY DESCRIBED OCCUPATIONS	***10,756***	***4,096***	***76***	***404***	***6,584***
	53 Indefinite occupations	***10,756***	***4,096***	***76***	***404***	***6,584***
164	Manufacturers, contractors	284	132	...	24	152
165	Cashiers, accountants, book-keepers, etc., in unspecified offices, etc.	112	60	1	6	51
166	Mechanics otherwise unspecified	1	1	...		...
167	Labourers, etc., otherwise unspecified	10,359	3,903	75	374	6,381
	XII.—UNPRODUCTIVE	***5,546***	***2,232***	***244***	***143***	***3,070***
168	***54 Inmates of jails, asylums, hospitals***	***350***	***328***	***19***	***8***	***3***
169	***55 Beggars, vagrants, prostitutes***	***5,196***	***1,904***	***225***	***135***	***3,067***

PART A.—PROVINCIAL SUMMARY.

DISTRICTS					STATES					
Total workers and dependants	Actual workers — Total — Males	Actual workers — Total — Females	Partially agriculturists	Dependants	Total workers and dependants	Actual workers — Total — Males	Actual workers — Total — Females	Partially agriculturists	Dependants	Group No.
8	9	10	11	12	13	14	15	16	17	
213	*96*	*1*	*7*	*116*	*6*	*2*	...	...	*4*	125
317	*146*	...	*10*	*171*	*766*	*244*	...	*14*	*522*	
287	120	...	8	167	759	243	...	14	516	126
30	26	...	2	4	7	1	...	...	6	127
22	*4*	...	...	*18*	*29*	*8*	...	..	*21*	128
258	*97*	...	*6*	*161*	*84*	*32*	...	*2*	*52*	129
357	*127*	...	*7*	*230*	*133*	*40*	*1*	*12*	*92*	130
512	*249*	*1*	*7*	*262*	*150*	*62*	...	..	*88*	
38	26	...	1	12	2	2	...	...	...	131
451	212	1	6	238	148	60	...	...	88	132
23	11	...	...	12	...	...	...	..	...	133
1,533	*610*	...	*46*	*923*	*3,675*	*1,243*	...	*19*	*2,432*	
1,364	522	..	30	842	3,613	1,222	...	19	2,391	135
151	76	...	5	75	39	13	...	..	26	136
9	5	...	..	4	2	1	...	...	1	137
9	7	...	2	2	21	7	...	...	14	138
31,766	**22,062**	**270**	**10,067**	**9,574**	**10,428**	**4,282**	**13**	**799**	**6,133**	
18,638	*15,667*	*1*	*7,660*	*2,970*	*1,759*	*917*	...	*118*	*842*	
16,761	*14,386*	*1*	*6,929*	*2,374*	*1,758*	*916*	...	*118*	*842*	
16,761	14,386	1	6,929	2,374	138	129	...	11	9	139
...	...	...	...	...	1,620	787	...	107	833	140
1,877	*1,281*	...	*731*	*596*	*1*	*1*	...	...	...	
1,873	1,280	...	730	593	1	1	...	...	...	142
4	1	...	1	3	...	...	...	.	.	143
6,345	*3,653*	*2*	*2,005*	*2,690*	*3,651*	*1,573*	...	*420*	*2,078*	
6,345	*3,653*	*2*	*2,005*	*2,690*	*3,651*	*1,573*	...	*420*	*2,078*	
5,645	3,266	...	1,872	2,379	859	496	...	215	363	144
19	12	...	1	7	2,784	1,072	...	202	1,712	145
443	243	2	75	198	...	...	...	..	...	146
238	133	...	57	105	8	5	...	3	3	147
6,220	*2,629*	*171*	*379*	*3,420*	*4,949*	*1,778*	*11*	*255*	*3,160*	
3,566	*1,312*	*53*	*118*	*2,201*	*3,433*	*1,211*	*2*	*193*	*2,220*	
2,219	770	2	68	1,447	1,825	618	...	99	1,207	148
1,176	448	45	37	683	1,423	525	2	81	896	149
48	24	6	7	18	...	...	...	...	...	150
123	70	...	6	53	185	68	...	13	117	151
146	*43*	...	*13*	*103*	*87*	*29*	...	*14*	*58*	
16	3	...	2	13	80	26	...	13	54	152
130	40	...	11	90	7	3	...	1	4	153
792	*386*	*70*	*94*	*336*	*75*	*27*	*9*	*5*	*39*	
349	163	4	41	182	43	16	..	1	27	154
443	223	66	53	154	32	11	9	4	12	155
534	*303*	*48*	*44*	*183*	*72*	*45*	...	*2*	*27*	156
1,182	*585*	...	*110*	*597*	*1,282*	*466*	...	*41*	*816*	
28	19	...	4	9	...	...	...	...	...	157
868	444	...	93	424	24	10	...	2	14	158
89	47	...	6	42	28	11	...	...	17	159
197	75	...	7	122	1,230	445	...	39	785	160
563	*113*	*96*	*93*	*494*	*69*	*14*	*2*	*6*	*53*	
563	*113*	*96*	*93*	*494*	*69*	*14*	*2*	*6*	*53*	161
16,352	**8,016**	**1,163**	**1,010**	**7,173**	**14,244**	**3,382**	**4,976**	**385**	**5,886**	
7,158	*4,191*	*908*	*759*	*2,059*	*7,136*	*879*	*4,911*	*89*	*1,346*	
7,158	*4,191*	*908*	*759*	*2,059*	*7,136*	*879*	*4,911*	*89*	*1,346*	
5,702	3,030	908	446	1,764	6,958	783	4,911	85	1,265	162
1,456	1,161	...	313	295	178	97	...	4	81	163
6,112	*2,552*	*38*	*210*	*3,522*	*4,644*	*1,544*	*38*	*194*	*3,062*	
6,112	*2,552*	*38*	*210*	*3,522*	*4,644*	*1,544*	*38*	*194*	*3,062*	
185	102	...	24	83	99	30	...	...	69	164
81	47	1	3	33	31	13	..	3	18	165
1	1	...	...	...	...	...	...	...	..	166
5,845	2,402	37	183	3,406	4,514	1,501	38	191	2,975	167
3,082	*1,273*	*217*	*41*	*1,592*	*2,464*	*959*	*27*	*102*	*1,478*	
302	*282*	*18*	*8*	*2*	*48*	*46*	*1*	..	*1*	168
2,780	*991*	*199*	*33*	*1,590*	*2,416*	*913*	*26*	*102*	*1,477*	169

Group No.	OCCUPATION	QUETTA-PISHIN — Actual workers — Total — Males	Females	Partially agriculturists	Dependants
1	2	3	4	5	6
	TOTAL	**50,982**	**937**	**6,054**	**75,729**
	A.—Production of raw materials	**22,559**	**68**	**410**	**53,528**
	I.—EXPLOITATION OF THE SURFACE OF THE EARTH	***22,527***	***68***	***406***	***53,514***
	1 Pasture and agriculture	***22,527***	***68***	***406***	***53,514***
	(a) Ordinary cultivation	*20,488*	*3*	*16*	*50,139*
1	Income from rent of agricultural land	2,964	3	...	9,562
2	Ordinary cultivators	17,413	...	...	40,507
3	Land-agents, managers of landed estates, etc.	59	...	16	43
4	Farm servants, field labourers	52	...	...	27
6	*(b) Growers of special products, market gardening (fruit, flower, vegetable, vine, etc.)*	*407*	...	*91*	*131*
	(c) Forestry	*215*	...	*149*	*400*
7	Forest officers, rangers, guards, etc.	18	...	9	21
8	Wood cutters; firewood collectors, etc.	197	...	140	379
	(d) Raising of farm stock	*1,417*	*65*	*150*	*2,844*
9	Cattle and buffalo breeders and keepers	87	65	6	70
10	Sheep and goat breeders	906	...	139	1,885
11	Breeders of other animals	273	...	2	656
12	Herdsmen, shepherds, goatherds, etc.	151	...	3	233
	2 Fishing and hunting	...	...	...	...
14	Fishing	...	...	...	...
15	Hunting	...	...	...	...
	II.—EXTRACTION OF MINERALS	***32***	...	***4***	***14***
	3 Mines	***30***	...	***2***	***11***
16	Coal mines, petroleum wells	28	...	...	11
17	Other mines and metallic minerals	2	...	2	...
	5 Salt, etc.	***2***	...	***2***	***3***
19	Rock, sea and marsh salt	2	...	2	3
20	Extraction of saltpetre, alum, etc.	...	...	...	...
	B.—Preparation and supply of material substances	**11,982**	**300**	**1,137**	**12,519**
	III.—INDUSTRY	***5,333***	***332***	***350***	***4,969***
	6 Textiles	***50***	***1***	...	***50***
21	Cotton ginning, cleaning, etc.	16	...	...	6
22	Cotton spinning, sizing, weaving	...	...	...	...
24	Rope, twine string	8	...	...	6
26	Wool carders, weavers, etc.	20	1	...	27
27	Silk spinners, weavers	...	...	...	...
30	Dyeing, bleaching, etc.	...	...	...	...
31	Other textile industries (embroideries, etc.)	6	...	...	11
	7 Hides, skins, hard animal materials	***17***	...	...	***14***
32	Tanners, curriers, etc.	9	...	...	5
33	Makers of leather articles	1	...	...	...
34	Furriers	7	...	...	9
	8 Wood	***302***	...	***36***	***337***
36	Sawyers, carpenters, turners, etc.	277	...	36	304
37	Basket and palm mat makers, etc.	25	...	..	33
	9 Metals	***918***	...	***42***	***971***
38	Forging and rolling of iron, etc.	1	...	...	...
40	Makers of arms, guns, etc.	357	...	17	162
41	Other workers in iron	471	...	23	752
42	Workers in brass, copper, bell metal	61	...	2	35
43	Workers in other metals (tins, etc.)	28	...	...	22
	10 Ceramics	***23***	...	***2***	***15***
47	Potters, earthen pipe and bowl makers	...	...	...	...
48	Brick and tile makers	23	...	2	15
	11 Manufacture of chemical and analogous products	***22***	...	***5***	***4***
50	Matches and explosive materials	...	...	...	...
51	Ærated and mineral waters	19	...	5	...
52	Dyes, paint, ink	...	...	...	...
53	Vegetable and mineral oils	...	...	...	...
55	Others (soap, candles, etc.)	3	...	...	4
	12 Food Industries	***703***	***5***	***134***	***562***
56	Rice pounders, huskers, flour grinders	107	2	28	101
57	Bakers, biscuit makers	245	1	25	109
58	Grain parchers, etc.	17	...	3	5
59	Butchers	170	1	15	256
61	Butter, cheese, ghee makers	...	...	...	...
63	Sweetmeat makers, etc.	94	1	10	70
64	Brewers, distillers	69	...	53	21
66	Manufacture of tobacco, opium, etc.	1	...	...	...

DETAILS BY DISTRICTS AND STATES.

LŌRALAI				ZHŌB				BŌLĀN				Group No.
Actual workers			Dependants	Actual workers			Dependants	Actual workers			Dependants	
Total		Partially agriculturists		Total		Partially agriculturists		Total		Partially agriculturists		
Males	Females			Males	Females			Males	Females			
7	8	9	10	11	12	13	14	15	16	17	18	
23,225	137	2,570	52,407	25,680	54	3,066	44,613	1,269	19	339	896	
21,662	13	487	46,336	20,912	...	804	43,158	257	...	13	480	
21,602	13	427	46,336	20,210	...	804	42,154	207	...	2	375	
21,602	13	427	46,336	20,210	...	804	42,154	207	...	2	375	
18,389	8	5	39,924	15,623	...	1	33,324	186	...	...	371	
1,403	3	...	3,694	2,777	...	...	5,748	31	...	...	111	1
16,966	...	...	36,200	12,835	...	...	27,506	151	...	...	260	2
10	...	5	16	4	...	1	4	...	...	...	...	3
11	...	...	14	7	...	...	11	4	...	...	...	4
25	...	2	14	12	...	2	6	20	...	2	4	6
20	...	8	13	16	...	...	1	...	...	...	...	
8	...	5	...	...	...	...	...	...	...	...	...	7
13	...	...	13	16	...	...	1	...	...	...	...	8
3,168	10	478	6,385	4,552	...	794	8,893	1	...	...	...	
50	9	1	88	5	...	1	6	...	...	...	...	9
2,509	...	467	5,284	4,290	...	679	8,401	...	...	...	...	10
371	...	1	656	11	...	...	19	...	...	...	...	11
238	1	9	357	246	...	114	379	1	...	...	...	12
...	...	...	...	...	...	...	...	...	...	...	...	
...	...	...	...	...	...	...	...	...	...	...	...	14
...	...	...	...	...	...	...	...	...	...	...	...	15
...	...	...	...	2	—	...	4	50	...	4	34	
...	...	...	...	1	...	...	2	50	...	4	34	
...	...	...	...	...	...	...	...	50	...	4	34	16
...	...	...	...	1	...	...	2	...	...	...	...	17
...	...	...	...	1	...	...	2	...	...	...	...	
...	...	...	...	1	...	...	2	...	...	...	...	19
...	...	...	...	...	...	...	...	...	...	...	...	20
3,161	62	396	4,508	1,411	38	227	1,949	758	6	215	394	
943	69	180	971	783	35	111	739	74	5	6	57	
88	...	21	123	184	1	60	328	...	...	...	...	
...	...	...	...	...	...	...	...	...	...	...	...	21
...	...	...	...	1	...	...	...	...	...	...	...	22
3	...	...	2	...	...	...	...	...	...	...	...	24
84	...	21	121	183	1	60	328	...	...	...	...	26
1	...	...	...	...	...	...	...	...	...	...	...	27
...	...	...	...	...	...	...	...	...	...	...	...	30
...	...	...	...	...	...	...	...	...	...	...	...	31
...	...	...	...	...	...	...	...	...	...	...	...	
...	...	...	...	...	...	...	...	...	...	...	...	32
...	...	...	...	...	...	...	...	...	...	...	...	33
...	...	...	...	...	...	...	...	...	...	...	...	34
68	...	28	77	29	...	3	1	7	...	3	4	
67	...	28	68	29	...	3	1	7	...	3	4	36
1	...	...	9	—	...	...	...	...	...	...	...	37
200	...	75	381	126	...	16	221	...	...	...	...	
...	...	...	...	...	...	...	...	...	...	...	...	38
6	...	...	3	...	...	...	...	...	...	...	...	40
189	...	75	371	128	...	16	221	...	...	...	...	41
3	...	...	5	...	...	...	...	...	...	...	...	42
2	...	...	3	3	...	...	...	...	...	...	...	43
11	...	3	7	3	...	2	3	...	...	...	...	
3	...	2	7	1	...	...	3	...	...	...	...	47
8	...	1	...	2	...	1	...	...	...	...	...	48
1	...	...	...	2	...	1	1	...	...	...	...	
...	...	...	...	...	...	...	...	...	...	...	...	50
1	...	...	...	2	...	1	1	...	...	...	...	51
...	...	...	...	...	...	...	...	...	...	...	...	52
...	...	...	...	...	...	...	...	...	...	...	...	53
...	...	...	...	...	...	...	...	...	...	...	...	55
67	6	8	49	61	...	7	46	16	1	1	18	
8	6	...	13	11	...	3	24	...	...	...	...	56
21	...	6	10	23	...	3	6	9	...	...	10	57
6	...	...	5	5	...	1	...	...	...	...	...	58
9	...	...	9	15	...	1	10	2	1	1	5	59
...	...	...	...	...	...	...	...	...	...	...	...	61
23	...	3	12	6	...	...	6	5	...	...	3	63
...	...	...	...	1	...	...	...	...	...	...	...	64
...	...	...	...	...	...	...	...	...	...	...	...	66

Group No.	OCCUPATION	CHAGAI — Actual workers — Total — Males	CHAGAI — Actual workers — Total — Females	CHAGAI — Actual workers — Partially agriculturists	CHAGAI — Dependants
1	2	19	20	21	22
	TOTAL	**5,720**	**65**	**565**	**10,559**
	A.—Production of raw materials	**4,055**	...	**169**	**8,211**
	I.—EXPLOITATION OF THE SURFACE OF THE EARTH	***4,055***	...	***169***	***8,211***
	1 Pasture and agriculture	***4,054***	...	***169***	***8,210***
	(a) Ordinary cultivation	*2,097*	...	...	*4,493*
1	Income from rent of agricultural land	674	...	...	1,577
2	Ordinary cultivators	1,371	...	...	2,823
3	Land-agents, managers of landed estates, etc.	1	...	...	4
4	Farm servants, field labourers	51	...	...	19
6	*(b) Growers of special products, market gardening (fruit, flower, vegetable, vine, etc.)*	*16*	...	*1*	*12*
	(c) Forestry	*4*	...	*1*	*2*
7	Forest officers, rangers, guards, etc.	3	...	1	1
8	Wood cutters, firewood collectors, etc.	1	...	...	1
	(d) Raising of farm stock	*1,937*	...	*167*	*3,773*
9	Cattle and buffalo breeders and keepers	3	...	1	14
10	Sheep and goat breeders	1,222	...	103	2,331
11	Breeders of other animals	594	...	62	1,276
12	Herdsmen, shepherds, goatherds, etc.	118	...	1	162
	2 Fishing and hunting	***1***	...	...	***1***
14	Fishing	...	...	...	...
15	Hunting	1	...	...	1
	II.—EXTRACTION OF MINERALS	...	...	...	...
	3 Mines	...	...	...	...
16	Coal mines, petroleum wells	...	...	...	...
17	Other mines and metallic minerals	...	...	...	...
	5 Salt, etc.	...	...	...	...
19	Rock, sea and marsh salt	...	...	...	...
20	Extraction of saltpetre, alum, etc.	...	...	...	...
	B.—Preparation and supply of material substances	**876**		**170**	**1,194**
	III.—INDUSTRY	***190***	***4***	***54***	***301***
	6 Textiles	...	...	...	***2***
21	Cotton ginning, cleaning, etc.	...	...	...	...
22	Cotton spinning, sizing, weaving	...	...	...	...
24	Rope, twine, string	...	...	...	...
26	Wool carders, weavers, etc.	...	...	...	2
27	Silk spinners, weavers	...	...	...	...
30	Dyeing, bleaching, etc.	...	...	...	...
31	Other textile industries (embroideries, etc.)	...	...	...	...
	7 Hides, skins, hard animal materials	...	...	...	...
32	Tanners, curriers, etc.	...	...	...	...
33	Makers of leather articles	...	...	...	...
34	Furriers	...	...	...	...
	8 Wood	***21***	...	***3***	***41***
36	Sawyers, carpenters, turners, etc.	21	...	3	41
37	Basket and palm mat makers, etc.	...	...	...	...
	9 Metals	***34***	...	...	***83***
38	Forging and rolling of iron, etc.	...	...	...	...
40	Makers of arms, guns, etc.	...	...	...	...
41	Other workers in iron	32	...	...	75
42	Workers in brass, copper, and bell metal	1	...	...	3
43	Workers in other metals (tins, etc.)	1	...	...	5
	10 Ceramics	...	...	...	...
47	Potters, earthen pipe and bowl makers	...	...	...	...
48	Brick and tile makers	...	...	...	...
	11 Manufacture of chemical and analogous products	...	...	...	...
50	Matches and explosive materials	...	...	...	...
51	Ærated and mineral waters	...	...	...	...
52	Dyes, paint, ink	...	...	...	...
53	Vegetable and mineral oils	...	...	...	...
55	Others (soap, candles, etc.)	...	...	...	...
	12 Food industries	***23***	***3***	***11***	***48***
56	Rice pounders, huskers, flour grinders	16	3	11	41
57	Bakers, biscuit makers	3	...	...	2
58	Grain parchers, etc.	...	...	...	...
59	Butchers	2	...	...	5
61	Butter, cheese, ghee makers	...	...	...	...
63	Sweetmeat makers, etc.	2	...	...	...
64	Brewers, distillers	...	...	...	...
66	Manufacture of tobacco, opium, etc.	...	...	...	...

DETAILS BY DISTRICTS AND STATES.

SIBÎ				KALÂT				LAS BÊLA				Group No.
Actual workers			Dependants	Actual workers			Dependants	Actual workers			Dependants	
Total		Partially agriculturists		Total		Partially agriculturists		Total		Partially agriculturists		
Males	Females			Males	Females			Males	Females			
23	24	25	26	27	28	29	30	31	32	33	34	
42,247	764	4,482	73,578	120,683	4,579	4,425	233,834	20,528	776	2,641	39,901	
32,508	10	1,234	64,750	101,469	1	2,009	199,539	16,586	...	1,473	32,370	
31,440	*3*	*890*	*64,562*	*101,404*	*1*	*2,009*	*199,350*	*16,585*	...	*1,473*	*32,370*	
31,438	*3*	*890*	*64,562*	*100,831*	*1*	*1,959*	*198,057*	*15,539*	...	*1,438*	*29,739*	
28,639	...	*6*	*58,944*	*88,090*	*1*	*9*	*173,478*	*9,139*	...	...	*17,869*	
2,269	..	...	5,943	10,992	1	..	25,334	1,415	...	...	3,154	1
25,980	...	...	52,839	73,245	...	...	147,175	7,107	...	...	14,430	2
12	...	6	8	59	...	9	105	...	...	...	..	3
378	...	...	154	3,724	...	...	864	617	.	..	278	4
60	...	*11*	*83*	*487*	...	*39*	*1,063*	*17*	...	...	*96*	6
48	...	*23*	*60*	*23*	...	*2*	*53*	*708*	...	*20*	*1,474*	
24	...	13	12	4	...	...	11	...	...	...	...	7
24	..	10	48	19	...	2	42	708	...	20	1,474	8
3,691	*3*	*850*	*5,595*	*12,331*	...	*1,916*	*23,463*	*5,675*	...	*1,418*	*10,370*	
8	...	...	11	25	...	..	34	523	...	439	1,088	9
3,126	2	843	4,518	11,041	...	1,721	20,967	4,796	...	971	8,819	10
269	...	2	573	515	...	184	1,174	19	...	5	43	11
288	1	5	423	750	...	11	1,288	337	..	3	431	12
2	...	...	...	*573*	...	*50*	*1,293*	*1,046*	...	*35*	*2,638*	
2	...	...	...	555	...	45	1,264	1,045	...	35	2,638	14
...	...	...	...	18	...	5	29	1	...	...	...	15
1,068	*7*	*344*	*197*	*76*	...	...	*189*	*1*	...	...	...	
1,068	*7*	*344*	*197*	...	...	...	..	..	...	...	...	
1,068	7	344	197	...	...	...	...	...	...	...	...	16
...	...	...	...	...	...	...	...	...	...	...	...	17
...	...	...	...	*76*	...	...	*189*	*1*	...	...	...	
...	...	...	...	76	...	...	189	...	...	...	...	19
...	...	...	...	...	...	..	...	1	...	...	...	20
5,283	48	787	5,862	12,290	275	1,683	25,301	2,272	98	197	6,496	
1,522	*41*	*194*	*1,834*	*5,393*	*274*	*614*	*10,719*	*836*	*90*	*82*	*1,736*	
19	...	*6*	*34*	*454*	*2*	*28*	*846*	*110*	*24*	*11*	*216*	
...	...	...	...	...	...	...	...	...	...	...	...	21
2	...	...	3	400	1	28	752	12	4	...	19	22
...	...	...	...	4	...	...	9	7	...	...	7	24
10	...	6	17	20	1	...	54	73	1	7	170	26
...	...	...	...	3	...	...	3	...	...	...	...	27
7	...	..	14	...	...	...	...	...	...	...	...	30
...	...	...	...	18	..	...	28	18	19	4	20	31
...	...	...	...	*54*	...	...	*122*	...	...	...	...	
...	...	...	...	5	...	..	16	...	...	...	...	32
...	...	...	...	49	...	...	106	...	...	...	...	33
...	...	...	...	...	...	...	...	...	...	...	...	34
262	...	*49*	*472*	*943*	*65*	*147*	*2,056*	*154*	*15*	*19*	*373*	
201	...	49	345	794	...	116	1,559	64	...	15	147	36
61	...	...	127	149	65	31	497	90	15	4	226	37
122	...	*46*	*248*	*1,226*	...	*26*	*2,499*	*88*	...	*6*	*206*	
...	...	...	...	...	...	...	...	...	...	...	...	39
1	...	...	.	1	...	...	8	...	...	...	...	40
108	...	46	217	1,177	...	26	2,413	81	...	6	192	41
3	...	...	7	27	...	...	50	5	...	...	8	42
10	...	...	24	21	...	...	28	2	...	...	6	43
56	...	*15*	*98*	*154*	...	*13*	*282*	*24*	...	*10*	*46*	
49	...	15	94	130	...	13	241	24	...	10	46	47
7	...	...	4	24	...	...	41	...	...	...	...	48
14	...	...	*18*	*78*	...	*41*	*170*	*5*		...	*12*	
...	...	...	...	8	...	8	20	...	...	...	...	50
6	...	...	...	...	...	...	...	...	...	...	...	51
2	...	...	3	...	...	...	...	...	...	...	...	52
6	...	...	15	70	...	33	150	5	...	...	12	53
...	..	...	...	...	...	...	...	...	...	...	...	55
169	*9*	*9*	*156*	*510*	*138*	*77*	*1,091*	*36*	*36*	*9*	*91*	
19	6	...	17	17	135	...	181	1	36	...	31	56
51	2	1	11	29	1	...	43	2	...	...	4	57
29	...	7	54	303	2	57	404	2	...	...	16	58
32	1	...	46	141	...	20	290	10	...	3	17	59
...	...	...	...	1	...	...	4	...	...	...	...	61
38	...	1	26	116	...	...	310	21	...	6	33	63
...	.	...	...	2	...	...	...	...	...	...	...	64
...	...	...	...	...	...	...	...	...	..	...	...	66

Group No.	OCCUPATION	QUETTA-PISHIN: Actual workers: Total: Males	Females	Partially agriculturists	Dependants
1	2	3	4	5	6
	III.—INDUSTRY—contd.				
	13 Industries of dress and the toilet	***1,337***	***69***	***54***	***1,101***
67	Hat, cap, turban makers	1	...	...	1
68	Tailors, milliners, etc.	542	26	20	397
69	Shoe, boot, sandal makers	258	2	11	263
70	Other industries pertaining to dress	9	1	...	...
71	Washing, cleaning, dyeing	324	40	6	356
72	Barbers, hairdressers, etc.	199	...	17	73
73	Shampooers, bath houses, etc.	4	...	...	11
	14 Furniture industries	***32***	...	***1***	***45***
74	Cabinet makers, carriage painters, etc.	32	...	1	45
75	Upholsterers, etc.	...	...	..	...
	15 Building industries	***501***	...	***47***	***395***
76	Lime burners, cement workers	16	...	1	24
77	Excavators, well-sinkers	77	...	20	64
78	Stone workers, masons	167	...	5	99
79	Thatchers, building contractors, plumbers, etc.	241	...	21	208
	16 Construction of means of transport	***14***	...	...	***9***
80	Cart and carriage makers, wheelwrights	5	...	...	1
81	Saddlers, harness makers, etc.	9	...	...	8
	18 Industries of luxury, literature, arts, sciences	***256***	***2***	***13***	***296***
84	Printers, lithographers, etc.	47	1	5	39
85	Newspaper managers, editors, etc.	...	1	...	2
86	Book binders, etc.	9	...	...	4
87	Makers of musical instruments	...	...	...	...
88	Makers of watches, clocks, surgical instruments, etc.	9	...	...	23
89	Jewellers, etc.	157	...	3	204
91	Toy, kite, cage, fishing tackle, etc.	2	...	...	...
92	Others (non-performers in theatres, race course service, huntsmen, etc.)	32	...	5	24
93	***19 Industries concerned with refuse (sweepers, scavengers, etc.)***	***1,158***	***255***	***16***	***1,170***
	IV.—TRANSPORT	***3,874***	***3***	***600***	***4,096***
	20 Transport by water	***164***	***1***	***80***	***107***
95	Ships' officers, engineers, mariners, etc.	...	...	...	...
96	Employés on streams, rivers, canals	164	1	80	107
97	Boat owners, boatmen, towmen	...	...	...	...
	21 Transport by road	***2,204***	***2***	***212***	***3,114***
98	Employés on roads and bridges	203	1	26	220
99	Cart owners, coachmen, stable boys, etc.	401	1	50	325
100	Palki, etc., bearers and owners	...	...	...	...
101	Pack-animal owners and drivers	1,468	...	95	2,524
102	Porters, messengers	132	...	41	45
	22 Transport by rail	***1,335***	...	***259***	***726***
103	Railway employés	1,263	...	226	717
104	Labourers on railway construction	72	...	33	9
105	***23 Post office, Telegraph, Telephone services***	***171***	...	***49***	***149***
	V.—TRADE	***2,775***	***34***	***187***	***3,454***
106	***24 Bank managers, money lenders, money changers, etc.***	***55***	...	***5***	***60***
107	***25 Brokers, commercial travellers, warehouse owners and employés***	***40***	...	***8***	***43***
108	***26 Trade in textiles (piece-goods, etc.)***	***534***	***1***	***20***	***1,061***
109	***27 Trade in skins, leather, furs***	***28***	...	...	***18***
110	***28 Trade in wood (timber, cork, bark, etc.)***	***3***	...	...	...
111	***29 Trade in metals (machinery, knife, tools, etc.)***	***8***	...	***2***	***7***
112	***30 Trade in pottery***	***6***	...	***3***	***3***
113	***31 Trade in chemical products (drugs, petroleum, etc.)***	***90***	***1***	***2***	***117***
	32 Hotels, cafés, restaurants, etc.	***115***	...	***2***	***75***
114	Vendors of liquors, aerated waters, etc.	67	...	2	39
115	Owners, managers, employés of sarais, etc.	48	...	...	36
	33 Other trade in food stuffs	***1,189***	***30***	***94***	***1,072***
116	Fish dealers	2	...	...	...
117	Grocers, sellers of vegetable oil, salt, etc.	508	1	36	448
118	Sellers of milk, butter, ghee, poultry, eggs, etc.	139	18	8	134
119	Sellers of sweetmeats, sugar, etc.	2	...	...	1
120	Cardamom, betel-leaf, vegetables, fruit, areca nut sellers	217	10	27	189
121	Grain and pulse dealers	136	...	7	93
122	Tobacco, opium, ganja, etc., sellers	43	1	1	38
123	Dealers in sheep and goats, etc.	66	...	4	97
124	Dealers in hay, grass fodder	69	...	11	72

DETAILS BY DISTRICTS AND STATES.

LŌṚALAI				ZHŌB				BŌLĀN				Group No.
Actual workers			Dependants	Actual workers			Dependants	Actual workers			Dependants	
Total		Partially agriculturists		Total		Partially agriculturists		Total		Partially agriculturists		
Males	Females			Males	Females			Males	Females			
7	8	9	10	11	12	13	14	15	16	17	18	
199	*25*	*11*	*98*	*137*	*4*	*12*	*69*	*10*	...	...	*8*	
...	...	...	...	...	...	...	...	...	...	...	...	67
28	15	5	14	48	2	5	24	5	...	...	1	68
36	...	3	47	31	...	6	14	1	...	...	...	69
...	...	...	...	...	...	...	...	...	...	...	...	70
87	10	1	35	31	2	...	31	2	...	...	5	71
28	...	2	2	27	...	1	...	2	...	...	2	72
...	...	...	...	...	...	...	...	...	...	...	...	73
...	...	...	...	...	...	...	...	*1*	...	...	*1*	
...	...	...	...	...	...	...	...	1	...	...	1	74
...	...	...	...	...	...	...	...	...	...	...	...	75
171	*1*	*28*	*76*	*117*	...	*7*	*30*	*5*	...	*2*	*2*	
...	...	...	...	...	...	...	...	...	...	...	...	76
54	...	...	57	27	...	...	19	...	...	...	...	77
30	...	9	6	52	...	2	5	5	...	2	2	78
87	1	19	13	38	...	5	6	...	...	...	...	79
10	...	*2*	*6*	...	...	...	...	...	...	...	...	
...	...	...	...	...	...	...	...	...	...	...	...	80
10	...	2	6	...	...	...	...	...	...	...	...	81
44	...	*7*	*42*	*17*	...	*3*	*11*	...	...	...	...	
...	...	...	...	...	...	...	...	...	...	...	...	84
...	...	...	...	...	...	...	...	...	...	...	...	85
...	...	...	...	...	...	...	...	...	...	...	...	86
...	...	...	...	...	...	...	...	...	...	...	...	87
...	...	...	...	...	...	...	...	...	...	...	...	88
44	...	7	42	17	...	3	11	...	...	...	...	89
...	...	...	...	...	...	...	...	...	...	...	...	91
...	...	...	...	...	...	...	...	...	...	...	...	92
154	*30*	*2*	*119*	*107*	*20*	*1*	*29*	*35*	*4*	...	*24*	93
1,348	...	*30*	*2,485*	*211*	*1*	*31*	*203*	*619*	...	*204*	*224*	
9	...	...	...	*1*	...	*1*	...	...	...	...	...	
...	...	...	...	...	...	...	...	...	...	...	...	95
9	...	...	...	1	...	1	...	...	...	...	...	96
...	...	...	...	...	...	...	...	...	...	...	...	97
1,311	...	*22*	*2,469*	*173*	*1*	*17*	*165*	*10*	...	*1*	*6*	
50	...	5	21	78	...	2	82	6	...	1	...	98
28	...	7	22	...	...	...	...	...	...	...	...	99
...	...	...	...	6	...	2	...	...	...	...	...	100
1,227	...	8	2,416	84	1	13	81	3	...	...	6	101
6	...	2	3	5	...	...	2	1	...	...	...	102
...	...	...	...	...	...	...	...	*604*	...	*201*	*206*	
...	...	...	...	...	...	...	...	598	...	201	206	103
...	...	...	...	...	...	...	...	6	...	...	...	104
28	...	*8*	*93*	*37*	...	*13*	*38*	*5*	...	*2*	*12*	105
870	...	*116*	*1,119*	*417*	*7*	*85*	*407*	*65*	*1*	*5*	*43*	
35	...	*18*	*64*	...	...	...	...	...	...	...	...	106
4	...	...	*4*	*1*	...	...	*3*	*1*	...	...	...	107
223	...	*33*	*254*	*105*	...	*56*	*56*	*10*	...	*2*	*14*	108
14	...	...	*17*	...	...	...	...	...	...	...	...	109
...	...	...	...	...	...	...	...	...	...	...	...	110
...	...	...	...	...	...	...	...	...	...	...	...	111
...	...	...	...	...	...	...	...	...	...	...	...	112
3	...	...	*4*	*38*	...	*15*	*69*	...	...	...	...	113
28	...	*8*	*9*	*7*	...	*2*	*2*	*3*	...	...	...	
4	...	1	3	3	...	...	2	1	...	...	...	114
24	...	7	6	4	...	2	...	2	...	...	...	115
300	...	*31*	*365*	*106*	*7*	*8*	*76*	*43*	*1*	*3*	*28*	
...	...	...	...	...	...	...	...	...	...	...	...	116
257	...	26	305	51	...	3	44	43	1	3	27	117
3	...	1	6	12	7	1	10	...	...	...	...	118
1	...	...	3	...	...	...	...	...	...	...	...	119
15	...	3	13	18	...	...	8	...	...	...	1	120
6	...	...	13	1	...	1	...	...	...	...	...	121
5	...	1	6	3	...	...	2	...	...	...	...	122
10	...	...	19	6	...	...	...	...	...	...	...	123
3	...	...	...	15	...	3	12	...	...	...	...	124

Group No.	OCCUPATION	CHĀGAI — Actual workers — Total — Males	Females	Partially agriculturists	Dependants
1	2	19	20	21	22
	III.—INDUSTRY—contd.				
	13 Industries of dress and the toilet	***19***	...	***2***	***35***
67	Hat cap, turban makers	...	...	...	...
68	Tailors, milliners, etc.	4	...	...	11
69	Shoe, boot, sandal makers	12	...	2	24
70	Other industries pertaining to dress	...	...	...	...
71	Washing, cleaning, dyeing	2	...	...	...
72	Barbers, hairdressers, etc.	1	...	...	...
73	Shampooers, bath houses, etc.	...	...	...	...
	14 Furniture industries	...	***1***	...	...
74	Cabinet makers, carriage painters, etc.	...	...	...	...
75	Upholsterers, etc.	...	1	...	...
	15 Building industries	***64***	...	***37***	***42***
76	Lime burners, cement workers	...	...	...	...
77	Excavators, well sinkers	...	...	...	...
78	Stone workers, masons	10	...	2	1
79	Thatchers, building contractors, plumbers, etc.	54	...	35	41
	16 Construction of means of transport	...	...	...	...
80	Cart and carriage makers, wheelwrights	...	...	...	...
81	Saddlers, harness makers, etc.	...	...	...	...
	18 Industries of luxury, literature, arts, sciences	***17***	...	...	***38***
84	Printers, lithographers, etc.	...	...	...	...
85	Newspaper managers, editors, etc.	...	...	...	...
86	Bookbinders, etc.	...	...	...	...
87	Makers of musical instruments	...	...	...	...
88	Makers of watches, clocks, surgical instruments, etc.	...	...	...	...
89	Jewellers, etc.	17	...	...	38
91	Toy, kite, cage, fishing tackle, etc.	...	...	...	...
92	Others (non-performers in theatres, race course service, huntsmen, etc.)	...	...	...	...
93	***19 Industries concerned with refuse (sweepers, scavengers, etc.)***	***19***	...	***1***	***12***
	IV.—TRANSPORT	***478***	..	***100***	***713***
	20 Transport by water	***3***	...	...	***5***
95	Ships' officers, engineers, mariners, etc.	...	...	...	...
96	Employés on streams, rivers, canals	3	...	...	5
97	Boat owners, boatmen, towmen	...	...	...	...
	21 Transport by road	***307***	...	***37***	***573***
98	Employés on roads and bridges	52	...	...	75
99	Cart owners, coachmen, stable boys, etc.	4	...	...	4
100	Palki, etc., bearers, and owners	...	...	...	...
101	Pack-animal owners and drivers	249	...	37	494
102	Porters, messengers	2	...	...	...
	22 Transport by rail	***99***	...	***39***	***23***
103	Railway employés	81	...	30	12
104	Labourers on railway construction	18	...	9	11
105	***23 Post office, Telegraph, Telephone services***	***69***	...	***24***	***119***
	V.—TRADE	***208***	...	***16***	***180***
106	***24 Bank managers, money lenders, money changers, etc.***	***2***	...	***1***	***1***
107	***25 Brokers, commercial travellers, warehouse owners and employés***	***3***	...	...	***1***
108	***26 Trade in textiles (piece-goods, etc.)***	***80***	...	***4***	***79***
109	***27 Trade in skins, leather, furs***	...	...	...	...
110	***28 Trade in wood (timber, cork, bark, etc.)***	...	...	...	...
111	***29 Trade in metals (machinery, knife, tools, etc.)***	...	...	...	...
112	***30 Trade in pottery***	...	...	...	...
113	***31 Trade in chemical products (drugs, petroleum, etc.)***	***1***	...	...	***2***
	32 Hotels, cafés, restaurants, etc.	...	...	...	...
114	Vendors of liquors, aerated waters, etc.	...	...	...	...
115	Owners, managers, employés of sarais, etc.	...	...	...	...
	33 Other trade in food stuffs	***98***	..	***11***	***89***
116	Fish dealers	...	...	...	...
117	Grocers, sellers of vegetable oil, salt, etc.	...	...	...	...
118	Sellers of milk, butter, ghee, poultry, eggs, etc.	76	...	10	59
119	Sellers of sweetmeats, sugar, etc.	6	...	1	...
120	Cardamom, betel-leaf, vegetables, fruit, areca-nut sellers	...	...	...	...
121	Grain and pulse dealers	5	...	...	4
122	Tobacco, opium, ganja, etc., sellers	10	...	...	14
123	Dealers in sheep and goats, etc.	...	...	...	...
124	Dealers in hay, grass, fodder	1	...	...	5

DETAILS BY DISTRICTS AND STATES.

SIBÎ				KALÂT				LAS BÊLA				Group No.
Actual workers			Dependants	Actual workers			Dependants	Actual workers			Dependants	
Total		Partially agriculturists		Total		Partially agriculturists		Total		Partially agriculturists		
Males	Females			Males	Females			Males	Females			
23	24	25	26	27	28	29	30	31	32	33	34	
399	*4*	*46*	*451*	*1,100*	*51*	*223*	*2,124*	*149*	*15*	*23*	*287*	
...	...	...	...	...	...	...	...	...	...	...	...	67
81	1	2	32	50	49	...	117	2	15	...	3	68
148	...	26	249	570	...	69	1,137	63	...	6	124	69
...	...	...	...	...	...	...	...	...	...	...	...	70
82	3	4	71	294	2	96	535	71	...	15	138	71
88	...	14	99	186	...	58	336	13	...	2	22	72
...	...	...	...	...	...	...	...	...	...	...	...	73
3	...	...	*3*	*3*	...	...	*3*	*2*	...	...	*6*	
3	...	...	3	3	...	...	3	2	...	...	6	74
..	...	..	...	...	...	...	...	...	...	...	...	75
169	...	*17*	*117*	*333*	*18*	*22*	*629*	*221*	...	*10*	*400*	
...	...	...	...	1	...	1	...	2	...	...	6	76
1	...	...	4	108	...	13	311	...	...	...	...	77
81	...	4	61	26	...	7	56	219	...	10	394	78
87	...	13	52	198	18	1	262	...	...	...	...	79
1	...	...	*1*	...	...	...	...	...	...	...	...	
...	...	...	...	...	...	...	...	...	...	...	...	80
1	...	...	1	...	...	...	...	...	...	...	...	81
83	...	*5*	*65*	*357*	...	*27*	*681*	*39*	...	*1*	*91*	
1	...	1	...	...	...	...	...	...	...	...	...	84
...	...	...	...	...	...	...	...	...	...	...	...	85
...	...	...	...	...	...	...	...	...	...	...	...	86
...	...	...	...	...	...	...	...	2	...	...	6	87
1	...	...	...	...	...	...	...	...	...	...	...	88
77	...	4	63	354	...	27	680	35	...	1	85	89
...	...	...	...	3	...	...	1	1	...	...	...	91
4	...	..	2	...	...	...	...	1	...	...	...	92
225	*28*	*1*	*171*	*181*	...	*10*	*316*	*8*	...	...	*8*	93
2,036	*2*	*542*	*1,679*	*2,904*	...	*809*	*5,683*	*696*	...	*55*	*1,501*	
72	..	*41*	*37*	*159*	...	*3*	*124*	*63*	...	...	*144*	
...	.	...	...	55	...	...	2	...	...	...	...	95
72	..	41	37	1	...	1	...	...	...	...	...	96
...	...	...	...	103	...	2	122	63	...	...	144	97
676	*2*	*25*	*951*	*2,654*	...	*784*	*5,414*	*566*	...	*36*	*1,194*	
39	1	14	35	10	...	...	11	...	...	...	...	98
48	...	3	39	4	...	...	6	...	...	...	...	99
...	...	...	...	...	...	...	...	...	...	...	...	100
570	1	7	864	2,579	...	782	5,287	551	...	35	1,149	101
19	...	1	13	61	...	2	110	15	...	1	45	102
1,249	...	*461*	*674*	*20*	...	*3*	*24*	...	...	...	...	
1,209	...	446	670	13	...	2	16	...	...	...	...	103
40	...	15		7	...	1	8	...	...	...	...	104
39	...	*15*	*17*	*71*	...	*19*	*121*	*68*	...	*19*	*163*	105
1,725	*5*	*51*	*2,149*	*4,912*	*1*	*180*	*8,899*	*740*	...	*53*	*1,959*	
17	...	*6*	*54*	*120*	...	...	*238*	*25*	..	...	*48*	106
9	...	..	*6*	*23*	...	...		*6*	...	...	*19*	107
74	...	*5*	*9*	*806*	...	*50*	*1,307*	*138*	...	...	*279*	108
6	...		*5*	*9*	...	...	*10*	*15*	...	*1*	*24*	109
2	...	...	*2*	*218*	...	*4*	*527*	...	...	...	...	110
2	...	...	*2*	...	...	...	...	...	...	...	...	111
...	...	...	...	...	...	...	...	...	...	...	...	112
85	...	...	*109*	*44*	...	...	*110*	*80*	...	*49*	*137*	113
26	...	*1*	*6*	*26*	...	...	*46*	*4*	...	...	*7*	
17	...	...	6	26	..	...	46	...	...	...	1	114
9	...	1	...	...	...	...	...	4	...	...	6	115
1,344	*5*	*36*	*1,645*	*2,080*	...	*81*	*3,465*	*27*	...	*1*	*681*	
1	...	...	5	31	...	...	66	60	...	1	118	116
1,198	...	25	1,507	1,633	...	...	2,696	286	...	...	390	117
34	5	2	29	29	...	...	41	15	...	...	22	118
...	...	...	...	...	...	...	...	...	...	...	...	119
36	...	...	28	193	...	49	361	2	...	...	4	120
45	...	5	57	142	...	26	209	58	...	...	134	121
6	...	1	1	12	...	...	21	...	...	...	...	122
17	...	1	14	40	...	6	71	5	...	...	13	123
7	...	2	4	...	...	...	...	...	...	...	...	124

Group No.	OCCUPATION	QUETTA-PISHIN: Actual workers: Total: Males	Females	Partially agriculturists	Dependants
1	2	3	4	5	6
	V.—TRADE—contd.				
125	*34 Trade in clothing (ready-made) and toilet articles*	*78*	*1*	*4*	*108*
	35 Trade in furniture	*105*	...	*7*	*86*
126	Trade in furniture, carpets, etc.	81	...	5	82
127	Hardware sellers	24	...	2	4
128	*36 Trade in building materials*	*3*	...	...	*16*
129	*37 Trade in means of transport (dealers and hirers of transport animals, carriages, saddlery, etc.).*	*64*	...	*6*	*154*
130	*38 Trade in fuel (firewood, charcoal, coal, etc.)*	*53*	...	*5*	*50*
	39 Trade in articles of luxury, letters, arts, sciences	*181*	*1*	*5*	*198*
131	Dealers in jewellery, clocks, etc.	24	...	1	12
132	Dealers in bangles, toys, flowers, etc.	148	1	4	175
133	Publishers, booksellers, stationers, etc.	9	...	...	11
	41 Trade of other sorts	*230*	...	*24*	*386*
135	Shopkeepers otherwise unspecified	204	...	23	370
136	Pedlars, hawkers, etc.	20	...	...	11
137	Conjurors, acrobats, fortune tellers, etc.	3	...	...	4
138	Farmers of pounds, tolls, etc.	3	...	1	1
	C—Public administration and liberal arts	**12,087**	**157**	**3,867**	**5,677**
	VI.—PUBLIC FORCE	*9,599*	*1*	*3,317*	*2,452*
	42 Army	*8,996*	*1*	*2,980*	*2,163*
139	Army (Imperial)	8,996	1	2,980	2,163
140	Army (Native States)	...	...	...	...
	44 Police	*596*	...	*337*	*289*
142	Police	596	...	337	289
143	Village watchmen	...	...	...	...
	VII.—PUBLIC ADMINISTRATION	*955*	...	*369*	*1,079*
	45 Public administration	*955*	...	*369*	*1,079*
144	Service of the State	706	...	287	887
145	Service of Native States	5	...	...	5
146	Municipal and other non-village service	207	...	66	167
147	Village officials other than watchmen	37	...	16	20
	VIII.—PROFESSIONS AND LIBERAL ARTS	*1,397*	*135*	*171*	*1,794*
	46 Religion	*637*	*43*	*34*	*1,029*
148	Priests, ministers, etc.	365	2	28	709
149	Religious mendicants, etc.	222	37	...	271
150	Catechists, church and mission service	10	4	4	7
151	Temple, burial ground service, etc.	40	...	2	42
	47 Law	*13*	...	*2*	*41*
152	Lawyers, Kāzis, etc.	...	...	...	...
153	Petition writers, etc.	13	...	2	41
	48 Medicine	*235*	*50*	*58*	*245*
154	Medical practitioners, dentists, oculists, veterinary surgeons	87	2	15	115
155	Midwives, vaccinators, compounders, nurses, etc.	148	48	43	130
156	*49 Instruction (professors, teachers, clerks, etc.)*	*184*	*42*	*27*	*121*
	50 Letters, arts, sciences	*328*	...	*50*	*358*
157	Public scribes, copyists, etc.	16	...	3	7
158	Architects, surveyors, with employés	258	...	40	300
159	Authors, photographers, artists, astronomers, etc.	23	...	6	43
160	Music players, singers, actors, dancers	31	...	1	8
	IX.—PERSONS LIVING ON THEIR INCOME	*93*	*21*	*10*	*352*
161	*51 Persons living principally on their income (proprietors, other than of agricultural land, pensioners, etc.)*	*93*	*21*	*10*	*352*
	D.—Miscellaneous	**4,404**	**343**	**640**	**4,005**
	X.—DOMESTIC SERVICE	*2,730*	*187*	*500*	*1,562*
	52 Domestic Service	*2,730*	*187*	*500*	*1,562*
162	Cooks, water carriers, door-keepers, watchmen and other indoor servants	2,170	187	355	1,322
163	Private grooms, coachmen, dog boys, etc.	560	...	145	240
	XI.—INSUFFICIENTLY DESCRIBED OCCUPATIONS	*1,366*	*9*	*129*	*2,122*
	53 Indefinite occupations	*1,366*	*9*	*129*	*2,122*
164	Manufacturers, contractors	58	...	11	57
165	Cashiers, accountants, book-keepers, etc., in unspecified offices, etc.	38	1	2	13
166	Mechanics otherwise unspecified	1	...	...	...
167	Labourers, etc., otherwise unspecified	1,269	8	116	2,052
	XII.—UNPRODUCTIVE	*308*	*147*	*11*	*321*
168	*54 Inmates of jails, asylums, hospitals*	*38*	*3*	*7*	*1*
169	*55 Beggars, vagrants, prostitutes*	*270*	*144*	*4*	*320*

DETAILS BY DISTRICTS AND STATES.

LŌRALAI				ZHŌB				BŌLĀN				
Actual workers			Dependants	Actual workers			Dependants	Actual workers			Dependants	Group No.
Total		Partially agriculturists		Total		Partially agriculturists		Total		Partially agriculturists		
Males	Females			Males	Females			Males	Females			
7	8	9	10	11	12	13	14	15	16	17	18	
19	...	3	5	9	...	...	...	...	...	...	...	125
6	...	...	39	9	...	1	4	...	...	...	...	
5	...	...	39	2	...	1	4	..	...	...	...	126
1	...	...	...	...	...	...	...	...	...	...	...	127
...	...	...	...	...	...	...	..	...	...	...	...	128
11	...	...	3	9	...	...	3	1	...	...	...	129
91	...	...	39	59	...	2	144	...	...	...	...	130
33	...	2	33	22	...	...	17	...	...	...	...	
...	...	...	...	...	...	...	...	...	...	...	...	131
33	...	2	33	22	...	...	17	...	...	...	...	132
...	...	..	..	...	...	...	...	...	...	...	...	133
180	...	21	283	73	...	1	38	7	...	...	1	
125	...	16	231	72	...		32	6	...	...	1	135
51	...	5	63	...	...	...	...	1	...	...	...	136
1	..	...	...	...	...	...	...	...	...	...	...	137
3	...	...	...	1	...	1	1	...	...	...	...	138
2,304	5	1,543	784	3,546	4	1,967	710	195	2	91	69	
1,494	...	1,227	115	1,971	...	990	103	148	...	75	16	
1,373	...	1,149	60	1,803	...	899	91	91	...	51	6	
1,373	..	1,142	60	1,803	...	893	21	91	...	51	6	139
...	...	...	...	...	...	...	...	...	...	...	...	140
121	...	85	55	168	...	98	83	57	...	24	10	
120	...	84	52	168	...	98	83	57	...	24	10	142
1	...	1	3	...	...	...	...	...	..	...	...	143
493	...	247	329	1,356	...	924	292	24	...	10	23	
423	...	247	329	1,356	...	924	292	24	...	10	23	
381	...	231	274	1,331	...	913	281	23	...	9	23	144
...	..	...	...	...	...	...	...	..	...	...	...	145
6	...	2	6	2	...	1	1	...	...	...	...	146
36	...	14	41	23	...	10	10	1	...	1	...	147
386	5	68	343	906	3	45	974	23	1	6	30	
176	...	21	228	90	...	14	212	6	...	1	10	
138	...	15	194	68	...	12	172	3	...	...	8	148
20	...	3	27	21	...	2	37	2	...	...	2	149
3	...	2	1	...	...	...	...	...	...	...	...	150
15	...	1	6	1	...	...	3	1	...	1	...	151
9	...	4	6	4	...	...	8	1	...	..	..	
...	...	...	..	...	...	...	...	1	...	...	...	152
9	...	4	6	4	...	...	8	...	..	...	...	153
53	4	8	22	41	3	17	8	4	1	2	14	
19	...	6	14	30	1	13	6	3	...	2	10	154
34	4	2	8	11	2	4	2	1	1	...	4	155
49	1	5	19	15	...	3	5	...	...	...	...	156
99	...	30	75	56	...	11	41	12	...	3	6	
1	...	...	..	...	...	...	...	-	...	...	...	157
75	...	30	44	56	...	11	41	12	...	3	6	158
23	...	...	31	...	...	...	...	...	...	...	...	159
...	...	...	...	...	...	...	...	...	...	...	...	160
1	...	1	4	9	1	8	41	...	1	...	...	
1	...	1	4	9	1	8	41	...	1	...	...	161
1,158	57	204	719	534	17	68	396	59	11	10	6	
733	23	178	97	193	3	25	16	15	11	1	2	
733	23	178	97	193	3	25	16	15	11	1	2	
226	23	27	60	156	3	17	15	15	11	1	2	162
507	...	151	37	37	...	8	1	...	...	...	...	163
193	10	18	366	223	3	27	156	28	...	9	...	
193	10	18	366	223	3	27	156	28	...	9	...	
13	...	1	22	4	...	...	3	13	...	7	...	164
2	...	...	2	...	...	...	...	1	...	...	...	165
...	...	...	..	...	...	...	...	...	...	...	...	166
178	10	17	343	219	3	27	154	14	...	2	...	167
232	24	8	256	118	11	16	224	16	..	...	4	
71	10	1	1	33	2	...	...	9	...	...	...	168
161	14	7	255	85	9	16	224	7	...	...	4	169

Group No.	OCCUPATION	CHĀGAI — Actual workers — Total — Males	Females	Partially agriculturists	Dependants
1	2	19	20	21	22
	V.—TRADE—contd.				
125	***34 Trade in clothing (ready-made) and toilet articles***	***2***	...	...	***3***
	35 Trade in furniture	...	...	...	...
126	Trade in furniture, carpets, etc.	...	...	...	...
127	Hardware sellers	...	...	...	...
128	***36 Trade in building material***	***1***	..	...	***2***
129	***37 Trade in means of transport (dealers and hirers of transport animals, carriages, saddlery, etc.)***	***5***	...	...	...
130	***38 Trade in fuel (firewood, charcoal, coal, etc.)***	***1***	...	...	***4***
	39 Trade in articles of luxury, letters, arts, sciences	***1***	...	...	...
131	Dealers in jewellery, clocks, etc.	...	...	...	...
132	Dealers in bangles, toys, flowers, etc.	1	...	...	...
133	Publishers, booksellers, stationers, etc.	...	...	..	...
	41 Trade of other sorts	***14***	...	...	***6***
135	Shopkeepers, otherwise unspecified	14	...	...	6
136	Pedlars, hawkers, etc.	...	...	...	...
137	Conjurors, acrobats, fortune tellers, etc.	...	...	...	...
138	Farmers of pounds, tolls, etc.	...	...	...	...
	C—Public administration and liberal arts	**447**	**2**	**212**	**577**
	VI.—PUBLIC FORCE	***55***	...	***31***	***79***
	42 Army	***28***	...	***8***	***68***
139	Army (Imperial)	28	...	8	68
140	Army (Native States)	...	...	..	...
	44 Police	***27***	...	***23***	***11***
142	Police	27	...	23	11
143	Village watchmen	...	...	...	...
	VII.—PUBLIC ADMINISTRATION	***275***	...	***150***	***303***
	45 Public administration	***275***	...	***150***	***303***
144	Service of the State	267	...	145	295
145	Service of Native States	...	...	...	...
146	Municipal and other non-village service	2	...	1	5
147	Village officials other than watchmen	6	...	4	3
	VIII.—PROFESSIONS AND LIBERAL ARTS	***116***	***1***	***31***	***195***
	46 Religion	***85***	...	***19***	***159***
148	Priests, ministers, etc.	44	...	2	96
149	Religious mendicants, etc.	39	...	17	62
150	Catechists, church and mission service	...	...	...	...
151	Temple, burial ground service, etc.	2	...	...	1
	47 Law	3	..	***3***	***14***
152	Lawyers, Kázis, etc.	2	...	2	13
153	Petition writers, etc.	1	...	1	1
	48 Medicine	***7***	***1***	***5***	***5***
154	Medical practitioners, dentists, oculists, veterinary surgeons	4	...	2	4
155	Midwives, vaccinators, compounders, nurses, etc.	3	1	3	1
156	***49 Instruction (professors, teachers, clerks, etc.)***	***4***	...	***1***	...
	50 Letters, arts, sciences	***7***	...	***3***	***17***
157	Public scribes, copyists, etc.	...	...	...	...
158	Architects, surveyors, with employés	6	...	3	
159	Authors, photographers, artists, astronomers, etc.	1	...	...	
160	Music players, singers, actors, dancers	10	...	...	13
	IX.—PERSONS LIVING ON THEIR INCOME	***1***	***1***	...	...
161	***51 Persons living principally on their income (proprietors, other than of agricultural land, pensioners, etc.)***	***1***	***1***	...	...
	D—Miscellaneous	**342**	**59**	**14**	**577**
	X.—DOMESTIC SERVICE	***70***	***58***	***10***	***122***
	52 Domestic service	***70***	***58***	***10***	***122***
162	Cooks, water carriers, door-keepers, watchmen and other indoor servants	67	58	8	118
163	Private grooms, coachmen, dog boys, etc.	3	...	2	4
	XI.—INSUFFICIENTLY DESCRIBED OCCUPATIONS	***219***	***1***	***4***	***348***
	53 Indefinite occupations	***219***	***1***	***4***	***348***
164	Manufacturers, contractors	4	...	2	2
165	Cashiers, accountants, book-keepers, etc., in unspecified offices, etc.	1	...	1	2
166	Mechanics otherwise unspecified	...	...	...	...
167	Labourers, etc., otherwise unspecified	214	1	1	344
	XII.—UNPRODUCTIVE	***53***	...	...	***107***
168	***54 Inmates of jails, asylums, hospitals***	...	...	...	...
169	***55 Beggars, vagrants, prostitutes***	***53***	...	...	***107***

DETAILS BY DISTRICTS AND STATES.

SIBĪ				KALĀT				LAS BĒLA				Group No.
Actual workers			Dependants	Actual workers			Dependants	Actual workers			Dependants	
Total		Partially agriculturists		Total		Partially agriculturists		Total		Partially agriculturists		
Males	Females			Males	Females			Males	Females			
23	24	25	26	27	28	29	30	31	32	33	34	
2	...	...	...	2	...	...	4	...	...	...	...	125
33	...	2	43	239	...	14	515	5	...	...	7	
32	..	2	43	238	...	14	509	5	...	...	7	126
1	...	..	...	1	...	...	6	...	...	...	...	127
...	...	...	...	8	...	...	91	...	...	...	...	128
7	...	...	1	30	...	2	46	2	...	...	6	129
...	...	...	...	40	1	12	22	...	...	...	...	130
12	...	...	14	39	...	...	47	23	...	...	41	
2	...	...	...	2	...	...	...	...	...	...	...	131
8	...	...	13	37	...	...	47	23	...	...	41	132
2	..	...	1	...	...	...	...	...	...	...	...	133
106	...	...	214	1,228	...	17	2,422	15	...	2	10	
101	...	...	212	1,210	...	17	2,386	12	...	2	5	135
4	...	...	2	10	...	...	21	3	...	...	5	136
1	...	...	...	1	...	...	1	...	...	...	...	137
...	...	...	...	7	...	...	14	...	...	...	...	138
3,537	**30**	**2,287**	**1,687**	**3,483**	**10**	**638**	**4,743**	**799**	**3**	**161**	**1,390**	
2,407	...	2,020	205	578	...	73	332	330	...	45	510	
2,095	...	1,856	56	577	...	73	332	330	...	45	510	
2,095	...	1,856	56	129	...	11	9	...	...	...	...	139
...	...	...	...	448	...	62	323	330	...	45	510	140
312	...	164	149	1	...	...	...	...	...	...	...	
312	...	164	149	1	...	...	...	...	...	...	...	142
...	...	...	...	...	...	...	...	...	...	...	...	143
620	2	305	671	1,362	...	359	1,624	211	...	61	454	
620	2	305	671	1,362	...	359	1,624	211	...	61	454	
558	...	287	618	495	...	315	354	1	...	...	9	144
7	...	1	2	863	...	141	1,270	209	...	61	442	145
25	2	5	20	...	...	...	...	...	...	...	...	146
30	...	12	31	4	...	3	...	1	...	...	3	147
501	26	58	784	1,533	8	201	2,762	245	3	54	398	
318	10	22	563	1,089	2	175	2,034	122	...	18	186	
152	...	11	268	585	...	97	1,163	33	...	2	4	148
144	8		284	471	2	76	846	54	...	5	50	149
11	2	1	10	...	...	...	...	...	...	...	...	150
11	...	2	1	33	...	2	26	35	...	11	91	151
13	...	4	34	25	...	13	47	4	...	1	11	
...	...	...	...	23	...	13	46	3	...	...	8	152
13	...	4	34	2	...	...	1	1	...	1	3	153
46	11	4		27	6	5	37	...	3	...	2	
20	1	3	33	16	...	1	27	...	...	...	...	154
26	10	1	9	11	6	4	10	...	3	...	2	155
51	5	8	45	43	...	2	12	2	...	...	8	156
73	...	13	100	349	...	6	625	117	...	35	191	
2	...	1	2	...	...	...	...	...	...	...	...	157
37	...	6	31	10	...	2	14	...	...	...	...	158
...	...	...	1	11	...	...	17	...	...	...	...	159
34	...	6	66	328	...	4	594	117	...	35	191	160
9	2	4	27	10	2	5	25	4	...	1	28	
9	2	4	27	10	2	5	25	4	...	1	28	161
1,519	**676**	**74**	**1,470**	**2,511**	**4,293**	**175**	**4,241**	**871**	**683**	**210**	**1,645**	
450	626	45	260	730	4,234	86	1,167	149	677	3	179	
450	626	45	260	730	4,234	86	1,167	149	677	3	179	
396	626	38	247	645	4,234	82	1,110	137	677	3	155	162
54	...	7	13	85	...	4	57	12	...	...	24	163
523	15	23	530	1,102	36	43	2,043	442	2	151	1,019	
523	15	23	530	1,102	36	43	2,043	442	2	151	1,019	
10	..	3	...	7	...	3	8	23	...	...	61	164
5	...	...	16	13	...	...	18	...	...	...	...	165
...	...	...	...	...	...	...	...	...	...	...	...	166
508	15	20	514	1,082	36	40	2,017	419	2	151	958	167
546	35	6	680	679	23	46	1,031	280	4	56	447	
131	3	...	...	28	1	...	1	18	...	...	...	168
415	32	6	680	651	22	46	1,030	262	4	56	447	169

XV.—OCCUPATION PART B.—SUBSIDIARY OCCUPATIONS OF AGRICULTURISTS (ACTUAL WORKERS ONLY).

(*N. B.*—The Table refers to males only, none of the seven female agriculturists having returned subsidiary occupations.)

Occupation	Balūchistān	Districts							States	
		Quetta-Pishin	Lōṛalai	Zhōb	Bōlān	Chāgai	Sibi: Administered area	Sibi: Mari-Bugti country	Kalāt	Las Bēla
1	2	3	4	5	6	7	8	9	10	11
I.—All Rent Receivers (non-cultivating landlords)	**22,531**	**2,967**	**1,465**	**2,777**	**31**	**674**	**2,201**	**68**	**10,993**	**1,415**
Rent Receivers who returned Subsidiary occupations	***9,439***	***984***	***739***	***1,359***	***7***	***934***	***1,166***	***46***	***4,091***	***597***
Rent payers	873	119	77	20	...	34	199	...	423	...
Agricultural labour	150	...	...	17	...	...	14	...	119	...
Stock breeding	5,247	79	420	869	...	153	817	41	2,573	295
Herdsmen	79	7	26	31	...	...	1	4	2	8
Artisans	207	...	9	11	...	...	37	...	84	66
Trade	1,092	828	91	37	5	2	7	...	105	17
Pack-animal drivers	697	60	9	16	...	13	...	...	486	113
Government employé	149	61	11	13	1	9	20	1	33	...
Priests	284	38	41	15	1	2	37	...	137	13
General labour	418	54	12	296	...	5	13	...	28	10
Mendicancy	50	5	11	14	...	2	2	...	14	2
Others	194	33	25	13	...	14	19	...	87	3
II.—All Rent Payers (actual cultivators)	**155,968**	**17,413**	**16,966**	**12,835**	**151**	**1,371**	**16,852**	**9,628**	**73,945**	**7,107**
Rent Payers who returned Subsidiary occupations	***47,979***	***9,569***	***8,150***	***7,197***	***11***	***457***	***9,916***	***6,394***	***17,734***	***1,991***
Rent receivers	861	44	32	53	...	4	7	...	716	5
Agricultural labour	519	...	...	44	...	8	11	...	456	...
Stock breeding	35,705	522	7,463	6,109	7	314	2,431	6,152	11,544	1,163
Herdsmen	322	26	105	36	2	...	4	78	52	19
Mining	247	6	3	235	...	...	2	...	1	...
Artisans	1,766	31	214	87	...	...	262	...	1,066	136
Trade	2,403	1,089	90	132	...	7	36	19	869	160
Pack-animal drivers	2,472	186	17	8	...	82	26	30	1,885	238
Government employés	190	107	30	14	2	6	17	...	14	...
Priests	446	69	67	48	...	2	19	...	224	22
General labour	1,406	459	54	446	...	16	36	28	250	115
Mendicancy	145	7	39	12	...	2	6	11	50	18
Others	791	16	36	28	...	16	57	6	587	45
III.—All Farm servants and field labourers	**4,844**	**52**	**11**	**7**	**4**	**51**	**175**	**203**	**3,724**	**617**
Farm servants, etc., who returned Subsidiary occupations	***44***	***4***	...	***2***	...	...	***4***	...	***34***	...
Rent receivers	4	4	...	...	...	...	...	...	...	...
Rent payers	8	...	...	...	...	...	4	...	4	...
Stock breeding	9	...	...	2	...	...	...	...	7	...
Pack-animal drivers	14	...	...	...	...	...	...	...	14	...
General labour	1	...	...	...	...	...	...	...	1	...
Mendicancy	2	...	...	...	...	...	...	...	2	...
Others	6	...	...	...	...	...	...	...	6	...

XV.—OCCUPATION PART C.—SHOWING CERTAIN MIXED OCCUPATIONS (ACTUAL WORKERS ONLY).

(*N.B.*—**The Table comprises males only, with the exception of two female actual workers in Sibi who returned sheep and goat breeding as their one and only occupation, and one female in Sibi and one female in Zhōb who similarly returned pack animal driving.**)

Occupation	Balūchistān	Districts: Total	Quetta-Pishin	Lōralai	Zhōb	Bōlān	Chāgai	Sibi	States: Total	Kalāt	Las Bēla
1	2	3	4	5	6	7	8	9	10	11	12
Sheep and Goat Breeding	**67,540**	**36,286**	**1,534**	**10,728**	**11,225**	**4**	**1,626**	**11,169**	**31,254**	**24,746**	**6,508**
(i) As principal occupation	*26,892*	*11,055*	*906*	*2,509*	*4,290*	...	*1,222*	*2,128*	*15,837*	*11,041*	*4,796*
Subsidiary occupations: Camel breeders	70	31	3	20	2	...	6	...	46	45	1
Subsidiary occupations: Dealers in wool	513	358	47	283	7	...	...	22	155	2	153
Subsidiary occupations: Mat makers	543	5	...	...	...	...	...	5	538	526	12
Subsidiary occupations: Pack animal drivers	645	217	109	85	1	...	13	9	428	343	85
Subsidiary occupations: Shepherds, etc.	106	26	1	16	4	...	...	5	80	76	4
Subsidiary occupations: Wood cutters	188	14	...	2	12	...	...	...	174	...	174
(ii) As subsidiary occupation	*40,648*	*25,231*	*628*	*8,219*	*6,935*	*4*	*404*	*9,041*	*15,417*	*13,705*	*1,712*
Principal occupations: Camel breeders	315	283	13	190	5	...	75	...	32	32	...
Principal occupations: Dealers in wool	2	...	...	...	...	...	...	...	2	...	2
Principal occupations: Farm servants, etc.	9	2	...	...	2	...	...	...	7	7	...
Principal occupations: Mat makers	77	3	...	...	...	...	...	3	74	73	1
Principal occupations: Pack animal drivers	786	585	29	541	...	...	15	...	201	162	39
Principal occupations: Rent payers	33,971	22,116	517	7,165	6,045	4	191	8,194	11,855	10,934	921
Principal occupations: Rent receivers	4,982	2,196	65	317	854	...	119	841	2,786	2,491	295
Principal occupations: Shepherds, etc.	36	29	4	3	15	...	4	3	7	6	1
Principal occupations: Wood cutters	470	17	...	3	14	...	...	...	463	...	459
Pack Animal Driving	**10,845**	**4,465**	**1,953**	**1,373**	**110**	**3**	**384**	**642**	**6,380**	**5,393**	**987**
(i) As principal occupation	*6,733*	*3,603*	*1,468*	*1,227*	*85*	*3*	*949*	*571*	*3,130*	*2,579*	*551*
Subsidiary occupations: Camel breeders	5	5	3	2	...	...	...	...	...	...	...
Subsidiary occupations: Sheep and goat breeders	786	585	29	541	...	...	15	...	201	162	39
(ii) As subsidiary occupation	*4,112*	*862*	*485*	*146*	*25*	...	*135*	*71*	*3,250*	*2,814*	*436*
Principal occupations: Camel breeders	284	198	130	38	...	...	27	3	86	86	...
Principal occupations: Farm servants, etc.	14	...	...	...	...	...	...	...	14	14	...
Principal occupations: Rent payers	2,472	349	186	17	8	...	83	56	2,123	1,885	238
Principal occupations: Rent receivers	697	98	60	9	16	...	12	...	599	486	113
Principal occupations: Sheep and goat breeders	645	217	109	85	1	...	13	9	428	343	85

XV.—OCCUPATION PART D.—DISTRIBUTION BY RELIGION.

Group No.	Occupation	Total	Musalmān	Hindu	Sikh	Neo-Hindu	Christian	Others
1	2	3	4	5	6	7	8	9
	TOTAL BALŪCHISTĀN	**834,703**	**782,388**	**37,862**	**8,390**	**724**	**5,085**	**254**
	A.—Production of raw materials	**666,661**	**664,815**	**1,561**	**205**	**68**	**7**	**5**
	I.—EXPLOITATION OF THE SURFACE OF THE EARTH	***664,987***	***663,333***	***1,440***	***160***	***42***	***7***	***5***
	1 Pasture and agriculture	***659,433***	***657,779***	***1,440***	***160***	***42***	***7***	***5***
	(a) Ordinary cultivation	*561,053*	*560,161*	709	*153*	*22*	3	5
1	Income from rent of agricultural land	77,649	77,214	371	57	3	2	2
2	Ordinary cultivators	476,868	476,607	246	11	1	...	3
3	Land-agents, managers of landed estates, etc.	325	230	48	37	9	1	...
4	Farm servants, field labourers	6,211	6,110	44	48	9	...	...
6	*(b) Growers of special products, market gardening (fruit, flower, vegetable, vine, etc.)*	*2,310*	*1,802*	497	...	*11*	...	...
	(c) Forestry	*3,037*	*3,014*	8	*6*	5	4	...
7	Forest officers, rangers, guards, etc.	102	79	8	6	5	4	...
8	Wood-cutters, firewood collectors, etc.	2,935	2,935	...	...	...	...	...
	(d) Raising of farm stock	*93,033*	*92,802*	226	*1*	4	...	...
9	Cattle and buffalo breeders and keepers	2,086	1,888	198	...	...	...	...
10	Sheep and goat breeders	79,087	79,087	...	...	...	...	...
11	Breeders of other animals	6,448	6,415	28	1	4	...	...
12	Herdsmen, shepherds, goatherds, etc.	5,412	5,412	...	...	...	...	...
	2 Fishing and hunting	***5,554***	***5,554***	...	...	...	...	...
14	Fishing	5,504	5,504	...	...	...	...	...
15	Hunting	50	50	...	...	...	...	...
	II.—EXTRACTION OF MINERALS	***1,674***	***1,482***	***121***	***45***	***26***	...	...
	3 Mines	***1,400***	***1,208***	***121***	***45***	***26***	...	...
16	Coal mines, petroleum wells	1,395	1,207	120	45	23	...	...
17	Other mines and metallic minerals	5	1	1	...	3	...	...
	5 Salt, etc.	***274***	***274***	...	...	...	...	...
19	Rock, sea and marsh salt	273	273	...	...	...	...	...
20	Extraction of saltpetre, alum, etc.	1	1	...	...	...	...	...
	B.—Preparation and supply of material substances	**95,252**	**63,941**	**25,796**	**4,574**	**323**	**506**	**112**
	III.—INDUSTRY	***37,233***	***29,492***	***6,303***	***1,207***	***39***	***162***	***30***
	6 Textile	***2,532***	***2,501***	***20***	***10***	...	***1***	...
21	Cotton ginning, cleaning, etc.	22	22	...	...	...	...	...
22	Cotton spinning, sizing, weaving	1,203	1,203	...	...	...	...	...
24	Rope, twine, string	46	32	14	...	...	...	...
26	Wool carders, weavers, etc.	1,113	1,112	...	...	...	1	...
27	Silk spinners, weavers	6	1	5	...	...	...	...
30	Dyeing, bleaching, etc.	22	21	1	...	...	...	...
31	Other textile industries (embroideries, etc.)	120	110	...	10	...	...	...
	7 Hides, skins and hard animal materials	***207***	***206***	***1***	...	...	...	...
32	Tanners, curriers, etc.	35	35	...	...	...	...	...
33	Makers of leather articles	156	155	1	...	...	...	...
34	Furriers	16	16	...	...	...	...	...
	8 Wood	***5,227***	***4,838***	***54***	***334***	...	***1***	...
36	Sawyers, carpenters, turners, etc.	3,920	3,564	30	334	...	1	...
37	Basket and palm mat makers, etc.	1,298	1,274	24	...	...	...	...
	9 Metals	***7,323***	***6,967***	***200***	***136***	***1***	***5***	***14***
38	Forging and rolling of iron, etc.	1	...	1	...	...	...	...
40	Makers of arms, guns, etc.	528	298	140	74	...	3	14
41	Other workers in iron	6,422	6,315	42	62	1	2	...
42	Workers in brass, copper, bell metal	208	203	5	...	...	...	...
43	Workers in other metals (tins, etc.)	154	151	3	...	...	...	...
	10 Ceramics	***722***	***698***	***24***	...	...	...	...
47	Potters, earthen pipe and bowl makers	598	598	...	...	...	...	...
48	Brick and tile makers	124	100	24	...	...	...	...
	11 Manufacture of chemical and analogous products	***327***	***287***	***39***	...	...		1
50	Matches, and explosive materials	28	28	...	...	...	...	...
51	Ærated and mineral waters	29	16	12	...	...	...	1
52	Dyes, paint, ink	5	5	...	...	...	...	...
53	Vegetable and mineral oils	258	231	27	...	...	...	...
55	Others (soap, candles, etc.)	7	7	...	...	...	...	...
	12 Food industries	***3,844***	***2,825***	***764***	***232***	***9***	***12***	***2***
56	Rice pounders, huskers, flour grinders	715	631	72	7	3	...	2
57	Bakers, biscuit makers	582	456	61	64	1	...	...
58	Grain parchers, etc.	747	678	64	5	...	...	...
59	Butchers	1,033	1,024	9	...	...	...	...
61	Butter, cheese, ghee makers	5	5	...	...	...	...	...
63	Sweetmeat makers, etc.	668	1	549	104	5	9	...
64	Brewers, distillers	93	29	9	52	...	3	...
66	Manufacture of tobacco, opium, etc.	1	1	...	...	...	...	...

XV.—OCCUPATION PART D.—DISTRIBUTION BY RELIGION.

Group No.	Occupation	Total	Musalmān	Hindu	Sikh	Neo-Hindu	Christian	Others
1	2	3	4	5	6	7	8	9
	III.—INDUSTRY—contd.							
	13 Industries of dress and the toilet	***7,621***	***6,450***	***1,011***	***118***	***16***	***26***	...
67	Hat, cap, turban makers	2	2	...	...	...	...	...
68	Tailors, milliners, etc.	1,467	1,200	69	88	3	17	...
69	Shoe, boot, sandal makers	2,979	2,728	223	19	...	9	...
70	Other industries pertaining to dress	10	...	1	...	9	...	...
71	Washing, cleaning, dyeing	2,071	1,465	600	2	4	...	...
72	Barbers, hairdressers, etc.	1,077	950	118	9	...	...	...
73	Shampooers, bath houses, etc.	15	15	...	...	...	...	...
	14 Furniture industries	***100***	***92***	***8***	...	...	...	...
74	Cabinet makers, carriage painters, etc.	99	91	8	...	...	...	...
75	Upholsterers, etc.	1	1	...	...	...	...	...
	15 Building industries	***3,191***	***2,667***	***341***	***172***	***9***	...	***2***
76	Lime burners, cement workers	40	40	...	...	...	...	...
77	Excavators, well-sinkers	622	622	...	...	...	...	...
78	Stone workers, masons	1,214	1,042	107	64	1	...	...
79	Thatchers, building contractors, plumbers, etc.	1,306	954	234	108	8	...	2
	16 Construction of means of transport	***41***	***20***	***18***	...	...	***2***	***1***
80	Cart and carriage makers, wheelwrights	6	5	1	...	...	...	...
81	Saddlers, harness makers, etc.	35	15	17	...	...	2	1
	18 Industries of luxury, literature, arts, sciences	***2,030***	***1,416***	***444***	***156***	***4***	***9***	***10***
84	Printers, lithographers, etc.	88	48	14	16	...	4	6
85	Newspaper managers, etc.	3	...	...	...	...	3	...
86	Bookbinders, etc.	13	13	...	...	...	...	...
87	Makers of musical instruments	8	8	...	...	...	...	...
88	Makers of watches, clocks, surgical instruments, etc.	33	20	6	4	...	...	3
89	Jewellers, etc.	1,824	1,280	407	134	3	...	...
91	Toy, kite, cage, fishing tackles, etc.	7	2	5	...	...	...	...
92	Others, (non-performers in theatres, race course service, huntsmen, etc.)	63	45	12	2	1	2	1
93	***19 Industries concerned with refuse (sweepers, scavengers, etc.)***	***4,059***	***595***	***3,379***	***49***	...	***106***	...
	IV.—TRANSPORT	***28,756***	***25,602***	***2,130***	***482***	***194***	***313***	***35***
	20 Transport by water	***888***	***751***	***87***	***16***	***18***	***14***	***2***
95	Ships' officers, engineers, mariners, etc.	57	42	...	...	...	13	2
96	Employés on streams, rivers, canals	400	312	53	16	18	1	...
97	Boat owners, boatmen, towmen	431	397	34	...	...	...	...
	21 Transport by road	***21,785***	***21,381***	***287***	***119***	***3***	...	***2***
98	Employés on roads and bridges	884	847	25	12	...	...	...
99	Cart owners, coachmen, stable boys, etc.	882	712	109	56	3	...	2
100	Palki, etc., bearers and owners	6	...	6	...	...	...	...
101	Pack-animal owners and drivers	19,554	19,538	11	5	...	...	...
102	Porters, messengers	459	284	136	39	...	...	...
	22 Transport by rail	***4,960***	***2,668***	***1,554***	***323***	***118***	***266***	***31***
103	Railway employés	4,784	2,511	1,535	323	118	266	31
104	Labourers on railway construction	176	157	19	...	...	...	...
105	***23 Post office, Telegraph, Telephone services***	***1,123***	***802***	***202***	***31***	***55***	***33***	...
	V.—TRADE	***29,263***	***8,847***	***17,363***	***2,885***	***90***	***31***	***47***
106	***24 Bank managers, money lenders, money changers, etc.***	***719***	***33***	***601***	***79***	***5***	***1***	...
107	***25 Brokers, commercial travellers, warehouse owners and employés.***	***212***	***35***	***159***	***18***	...	...	...
108	***26 Trade in textiles (piece-goods, etc.)***	***5,070***	***1,799***	***2,849***	***394***	***23***	***1***	***4***
109	***27 Trade in skins, leather, furs***	***146***	***146***	...	...	...	...	...
110	***28 Trade in wood (timber, cork, bark, etc.)***	***752***	***744***	***2***	***6***	...	...	...
111	***29 Trade in metals (machinery, knife, tools, etc.)***	***19***	***13***	***6***	...	...	...	...
112	***30 Trade in pottery***	***9***	***9***	...	...	...	...	...
113	***31 Trade in chemical products (drugs, petroleum etc.)***	***890***	***136***	***686***	***55***	***7***	***6***	...
	32 Hotels, cafés, restaurants, etc.	***354***	***128***	***173***	***31***	***1***	***7***	***14***
114	Vendors of liquors, ærated waters, etc.	215	39	138	30	1	...	7
115	Owners, managers, employés of sarais, etc.	139	89	35	1	...	7	7
	33 Other trade in food stuffs	***13,037***	***2,303***	***9,153***	***1,524***	***39***	***3***	***15***
116	Fish dealers	283	268	15	...	...	...	...
117	Grocers, sellers of vegetable oil, salt, etc.	9,830	218	7,994	1,287	26	3	2
118	Sellers of milk, butter, ghee, poultry, eggs, etc.	510	243	260	5	2	...	...
119	Sellers of sweetmeats, sugar, etc.	7	5	2	...	...	...	...
120	Cardamom, betel-leaf, vegetables, fruit, areca nut sellers	1,105	706	374	17	...	...	8
121	Grain and pulse dealers	918	288	452	175	1	...	2
122	Tobacco, opium, ganja, etc., sellers	138	93	38	7	...	...	
123	Dealers in sheep and goats, etc.	364	361	3	...	...	...	...
124	Dealers in hay, grass, fodder	182	121	15	33	10	...	3
125	***34 Trade in clothing (ready-made) and toilet articles***	***219***	***195***	***16***	***4***	...	***3***	***1***
	35 Trade in furniture	***1,083***	***1,033***	***35***	***11***	...	...	***4***
126	Trade in furniture, carpets, etc.	1,046	1,031	10	1	...	...	4
127	Hardware sellers	37	2	25	10	...	...	...

XV.—OCCUPATION PART D.—DISTRIBUTION BY RELIGION.

Group No.	Occupation	Total	Musalmān	Hindu	Sikh	Neo-Hindu	Christians	Others
1	2	3	4	5	6	7	8	9
	V.—TRADE—contd.							
128	***36 Trade in building materials***	***51***	***51***	..	...	...	...	...
129	***37 Trade in means of transport (dealers and hirers of transport animals, carriages, saddlery, etc.)***	***342***	***306***	***29***	***1***	***2***	...	***4***
130	***38 Trade in fuel (firewood, charcoal, coal, etc.)***	***490***	***437***	***42***	***6***	***4***	...	***1***
	39 Trade in articles of luxury, letters, arts, sciences	***662***	***331***	***292***	***24***	***5***	***10***	...
131	Dealers in jewellery, clocks, etc.	40	8	29	...	...	3	...
132	Dealers in bangles, toys, flowers, etc.	599	322	259	17	...	1	...
133	Publishers, booksellers, stationers, etc.	23	1	4	7	5	6	...
	41 Trade of other sorts	***5,908***	***1,148***	***3,320***	***739***	***4***	...	***4***
135	Shopkeepers otherwise unspecified	4,977	1,115	3,139	715	4	...	4
136	Pedlars, hawkers, etc.	190	17	168	5	...	...	...
137	Conjurors, acrobats, fortune tellers, etc.	11	11	...	...	...	...	...
138	Farmers of pounds, tolls, etc.	30	5	13	12	...	...	...
	C.—Public Administration and liberal Arts	**42,194**	**27,088**	**7,356**	**3,149**	**319**	**4,173**	**109**
	VI.—PUBLIC FORCE	***20,397***	***9,128***	***4,851***	***2,540***	***54***	***3,757***	***67***
	42 Army	***18,519***	***7,797***	***4,676***	***2,193***	***38***	***3,748***	***67***
139	Army (Imperial)	16,899	6,232	4,668	2,146	38	3,748	67
140	Army (Native States)	1,620	1,565	8	47	...	...	...
	44 Police	***1,878***	***1,331***	***175***	***347***	***16***	***9***	...
142	Police	1,874	1,327	175	347	16	9	...
143	Village watchmen	4	4	...	...	...	...	...
	VII.—Public administration	***9,996***	***8,469***	***1,025***	***256***	***145***	***81***	***20***
	45 Public administration	***9,996***	***8,469***	***1,025***	***256***	***145***	***81***	***20***
144	Service of the State	6,504	5,353	745	207	115	64	20
145	Service of Native States	2,803	2,712	83	6	1	1	...
146	Municipal and other non-village service	443	241	133	26	27	16	...
147	Village officials other than watchmen	246	163	64	17	2	...	...
	VIII.—PROFESSIONS AND LIBERAL ARTS	***11,169***	***8,972***	***1,421***	***341***	***120***	***293***	***22***
	46 Religion	***6,999***	***6,178***	***684***	***98***	...	***30***	***9***
148	Priests, ministers, etc.	4,044	3,991	20	...	...	24	9
149	Religious mendicants, etc.	2,599	2,000	548	51	...	...	...
150	Catechists, church and mission service	48	2	14	26	...	6	...
151	Temple, burial ground service, etc.	308	185	102	21	...	...	...
	47 Law	***233***	***135***	***53***	***15***	***30***	...	...
152	Lawyers, Kāzis, etc.	96	95	1	...	...	...	...
153	Petition writers, etc.	137	40	52	15	30	...	...
	48 Medicine	***867***	***350***	***255***	***69***	***17***	***163***	***13***
154	Medical practitioners, dentists, oculists, veterinary surgeons	392	152	114	36	13	64	13
155	Midwives, vaccinators, compounders, nurses, etc.	475	198	141	33	4	99	...
156	***49 Instruction (professors, teachers, clerks, etc.)***	***606***	***456***	***35***	***26***	***19***	***70***	...
	50 Letters, arts, sciences	***2,464***	***1,853***	***394***	***133***	***54***	***30***	...
157	Public scribes, copyists, etc.	28	8	19	...	1	...	...
158	Architects, surveyors with employés	892	329	350	132	53	28	...
159	Authors, photographers, artists, astronomers, etc.	117	90	24	1	...	2	...
160	Music players, singers, actors, dancers	1,427	1,426	1	...	...	...	...
	IX.—PERSONS LIVING ON THEIR INCOME	***632***	***519***	***59***	***12***	...	***42***	...
161	***51 Persons living principally on their income (proprietors, other than of agricultural land, pensioners, etc.)***	***632***	***519***	***59***	***12***	...	***42***	...
	D.—Miscellaneous	**30,506**	**26,894**	**2,889**	**462**	**14**	**399**	**28**
	X.—DOMESTIC SERVICE	***14,294***	***11,987***	***1,712***	***188***	***13***	***387***	***7***
	52 Domestic service	***14,294***	***11,987***	***1,712***	***188***	***13***	***387***	***7***
162	Cooks, water carriers, door-keepers, watchmen and other indoor servants	12,660	11,063	1,016	175	13	387	6
163	Private grooms, coachmen, dog boys, etc.	1,634	924	696	13	...	...	1
	XI.—INSUFFICIENTLY DESCRIBED OCCUPATIONS	***10,756***	***9,642***	***841***	***249***	***1***	***9***	***14***
	53 Indefinite occupations	***10,756***	***9,642***	***841***	***249***	***1***	***9***	***14***
164	Manufacturers, contractors	284	210	59	8	...	...	7
165	Cashiers, accountants, book-keepers, etc., in unspecified offices, etc.	112	28	64	3	1	9	7
166	Mechanics otherwise unspecified	1	1	...	...	...	...	...
167	Labourers, etc., otherwise unspecified	10,359	9,403	718	238	...	...	...
	XII.—UNPRODUCTIVE	***5,546***	***5,175***	***336***	***25***	...	***3***	***7***
168	***54 Inmates of jails, asylums, hospitals***	***350***	***340***	***8***	***2***	...	...	...
169	***55 Beggars, vagrants, prostitutes***	***5,196***	***4,835***	***328***	***23***	...	***3***	***7***

XV.—OCCUPATION PART E.—STATISTICS OF INDUSTRIES.

Description	Locality	Classification by number employed	Total number employed: Males	Total number employed: Females	Direction, supervision and clerical work: Europeans and Anglo-Indians, Males	Direction, supervision and clerical work: Indians, Males	Skilled workmen: Europeans and Anglo-Indians, Males	Skilled workmen: Indians, Males	Unskilled labourers: Age 14 and over, Males	Unskilled labourers: Age 14 and over, Females	Unskilled labourers: Under 14, Males	Mechanical power, if any	State of business	Owner	Manager
1	2	3	4	5	6	7	8	9	10	11	12	13	14	15	16
11 Factories, etc.	**Balūchistān**	...	**2,316**	**12**	**52**	**77**	**2**	**549**	**1,560**	**12**	**76**	...	...	...	...
Arsenal	Quetta (Quetta-Pishīn)	400 & over	537	...	37	17	...	129	338	...	16	Steam	Normal	Government	European
Brewery	Kirāni (Quetta-Pishīn)	50 to 100	83	...	1	1	...	35	46	...	...	Steam	Much slacker than usual	Company (European)	European
Briquette factory	Khōst (Sibī)	20 to 50	35	...	1	2	...	5	27	...	...	Steam	Normal	Government	European
Building workshop	Quetta (Quetta-Pishīn)	200 to 400	212	...	5	9	...	61	134	...	3	Steam	Normal	Government	European
Collieries	Mach (Bōlān)	20 to 50	49	...	...	1	...	2	44	...	2	...	Slacker than usual	Private (Pārsī)	Pārsī
	Harnai (Sibī)	20 to 50	26	...	1	1	...	1	23	...	...	...	Normal	Company (European and Indian)	European
	Shāhrig (Sibī)	50 to 100	65	...	2	6	...	2	55	...	...	...	Normal	Company (European and Indian)	European
	Khōst (Sibī)	400 & over	969	12	1	34	...	135	748	12	51	Steam	Brisker than usual	Government	European
Railway workshops	Sibī (Quetta-Pishīn)	20 to 50	40	...	1	1	...	17	21	...	...	Steam	Normal	Government	European
	Quetta (Quetta-Pishīn)	50 to 100	98	...	1	3	...	16	74	...	4	...	Normal	Government	European
	Quetta (Quetta Pishīn)	200 to 400	202	...	2	2	2	146	50	...	...	Steam and air pressure	Brisker than usual	Government	European

TABLE XVI.

Occupation by Selected Tribes and Races.

NOTE.—In the columns headed 'persons' 90 females are included as under :—

Tribe, etc.	Females included in columns										
	6	10	13	14	18	19	21	24	25	26	27
Total	***3***	***1***	***7***	***3***	***1***	***5***	***1***	***4***	***18***	***35***	***12***
Balōch	...	...	...	...	...	...	...	**1**	**1**	**3**	**2**
Khetrān	...	...	...	...	...	...	...	...	1	...	...
Rakhshānī and Naushērwānī	...	...	...	...	...	...	...	...	...	...	1
Rind (Eastern)	...	...	...	...	...	...	...	1	...	...	...
Rind (Western)	...	...	...	...	...	...	...	...	...	...	1
Sangur	...	...	...	...	...	...	...	...	...	3	...
Brāhūī	...	...	...	...	**1**	...	...	...	...	**1**	**1**
Māmasanī	...	...	...	...	1	...	...	...	...	...	...
Sarparra	...	...	...	...	...	...	...	...	...	1	...
Zagr Mēngal	...	...	...	...	...	...	...	...	...	...	1
Paṭhān	**3**	**1**	...	...	...	...	...	**1**	...	**3**	**1**
Dumar	...	...	...	...	...	...	...	...	...	...	1
Sanzarkhēl	2	1	...		...	...	...	...	...	...	...
Snaṭia	...	...	...	...	...	...	...	1	...	...	...
Panī	1	...	...	...	...	...	...	...	...	3	...
Main branch	...	...	...	...	...	...	...	...	...	*3*	...
Mūsakhēl	*1*	...	...	...	...	...	...	...	...	...	...
Lāsī	...	...		...	...	...	...	...	...	...	**1**
Angāria	...	...	...	...	...	...	...	...	...	...	1
Jaṭṭ	...	...	...	...	...	...	...	...	...	**2**	...
Others	...	...	**7**	...	...	...	...	...	...	**5**	...
Darzāda	...	...	3	...	...	...	...	...	...	4	...
Nakīb	...	...	4	...	...	...	...	...	...	...	...
Mēd	...	...	...	...	...	...	...	...	...	1	...
Miscellaneous Aliens	...	...	...	**3**	...	**5**	**1**	**2**	**17**	**21**	**7**
European	...	...	...	3	...	5	1	2	11	14	7
Anglo-Indian	...	...	...	...	...	...	...	...	6	7	...

XVI.—OCCUPATION BY

TRIBE OR RACE	POPULATION DEALT WITH				RECORDED PRINCIPAL OCCU-										
					I.—Exploitation of the surface of the soil						II.—Extraction of minerals		III.—Industries		
	Actual workers		Dependants		Income from rent of land	Cultivators of all kinds	Agents, managers of landed estates, planters, etc.	Field labourers, wood-cutters, forest guards, etc.	Raisers of live-stock, milkmen and herdsmen	Fishing and hunting	Owners, managers, clerks, etc.	Labourers	Owners, managers, clerks, etc.	Artisans and other workmen	
	Males	Females	Males	Females	Persons	Males	Males	Males	Persons	Males	Males	Persons	Persons	Males	Females
1	2	3	4	5	6	7	8	9	10	11	12	13	14	15	16
Balōch	**46,686**	**94**	**30,997**	**65,130**	**4,215**	**35,120**	**4**	**93**	**3,721**	**499**	**4**	**40**	..	**446**	**55**
(i) Eastern	*34,823*	*44*	*22,660*	*47,273*	*2,478*	*29,015*	*1*	*70*	*2,019*	*3*	*4*	*40*	..	*252*	*15*
Bugti	6,486	1	4,407	8,476	17	5,594	..	..	733	..	4	..	..	24	..
Khetrān	4,414	25	2,958	6,756	361	3,816	..	7	102	..	..	..	..	30	8
Magasi	6,134	10	3,638	7,995	29	5,549	..	..	334	..	..	1	..	60	6
Mari	7,347	1	5,161	9,724	798	5,666	1	13	664	..	..	..	..	92	..
Rind	10,442	7	6,496	14,322	1,273	8,390	..	50	186	3	..	39	..	46	1
(ii) Western	*11,863*	*50*	*8,337*	*17,357*	*1,737*	*6,105*	*3*	*23*	*1,702*	*496*	..	..	..	*194*	*40*
Bulēdī	429	..	294	617	124	221	..	..	57	10	..	..	..	3	..
Gichki	179	..	90	285	123	40	3	2	3	..	..	..	..	..	..
Rais	1,237	17	950	1,943	408	575	..	1	9	166	..	..	..	8	17
Rakhshāni and Nausherwāni	5,430	6	3,806	8,004	400	2,955	..	5	1,161	7	..	..	..	48	2
Rind	2,753	19	1,983	4,267	600	1,724	..	..	229	5	..	..	..	49	16
Sangur	1,835	8	1,214	2,741	82	590	..	15	243	308	..	..	..	91	5
Brāhūī	**56,058**	**77**	**35,456**	**73,353**	**6,862**	**29,847**	**23**	**670**	**12,108**	**104**	..	**13**	..	**360**	**48**
(i) Original nucleus	*5,047*	*22*	*3,155*	*6,642*	*414*	*2,773*	..	*61*	*1,279*	*12*	..	..	..	*23*	*12*
Gurgnāri	708	..	416	917	19	372	..	11	276	..	..	..	..	4	..
Kalandrāri	639	..	499	874	37	492	..	7	52	..	..	..	..	4	..
Kambrāri	968	5	711	1,411	72	605	..	19	127	7	..	..	..	8	1
Mirwāri	929	8	521	1,196	75	548	..	10	254	4	..	..	..	1	7
Rodēni	470	4	254	597	153	204	..	7	28	..	..	..	..	4	3
Sumālāri	1,333	5	754	1,647	58	552	..	7	542	1	..	..	..	2	1
(ii) Sarāwān	*19,087*	*18*	*11,528*	*24,737*	*4,485*	*9,387*	*5*	*246*	*1,577*	*17*	..	*6*	..	*170*	*9*
Bangulzai	3,971	6	2,406	5,212	1,192	1,812	..	60	343	..	..	..	..	8	2
Kūrd	1,167	5	761	1,543	165	753	..	5	53	17	..	3	..	12	3
Lahri	2,040	..	1,274	2,525	998	490	..	57	128	..	..	1	..	3	..
Lāngav	3,685	4	2,322	4,968	185	2,782	2	32	92	..	..	1	..	61	3
Māmashahi	1,371	..	772	1,723	318	537	..	32	113	..	..	..	..	2	..
Raisāni	697	..	396	884	122	356	2	3	20	..	..	..	..	7	..
Rustumzai	201	..	140	315	74	87	..	3	1	..	..	..	..	3	..
Sarparra	788	1	425	998	169	403	..	9	21	..	..	..	..	12	..
Sātakzai	465	..	250	563	115	307	..	1	8	..	..	..	..	1	..
Shahwāni	3,112	..	1,782	3,876	938	1,284	1	39	280	..	..	1	..	21	..
Zagr Mēngal	1,590	2	1,000	2,130	209	576	..	5	518	..	..	..	..	40	1
(iii) Jhalawān	*31,924*	*37*	*20,773*	*41,974*	*1,963*	*17,687*	*18*	*363*	*9,252*	*75*	..	*7*	..	*167*	*27*
Bizanjav	3,572	13	2,334	4,939	169	1,635	1	121	1,342	33	..	..	..	7	12
Hārūni	406	..	268	574	25	239	..	..	104	..	..	..	..	..	..
Māmasani	4,429	3	3,045	6,012	211	1,889	..	18	1,734	17	..	..	..	20	1
Mēngal	9,415	6	5,784	11,600	274	4,906	..	65	3,324	6	..	5	..	69	2
Nichāri	1,238	2	822	1,579	164	840	15	8	115	..	..	..	..	17	2
Pandrāni	664	..	451	892	253	196	..	3	182	..	..	..	..	9	..
Sājdi	1,318	13	921	1,759	72	713	..	97	370	17	..	1	..	4	10
Zahri	10,882	..	7,148	14,619	795	7,269	2	71	2,081	2	..	1	..	41	..
Pathān	**58,681**	**64**	**41,576**	**84,437**	**5,433**	**41,419**	**5**	**942**	**5,474**	..	..	**167**	**4**	**798**	**13**
Jafar	409	..	281	596	4	364	..	1	13	..	..	..	..	15	..
Kākar	33,770	40	23,121	46,637	3,498	21,875	1	223	4,320	..	..	104	3	319	9
Dumar	*2,545*	*1*	*1,722*	*3,487*	*238*	*1,557*	..	*3*	*563*	..	..	*4*	..	*13*	..
Sanzarkhel	*18,198*	*30*	*12,146*	*25,358*	*1,913*	*11,849*	..	*11*	*2,983*	..	..	*23*	*1*	*194*	*7*
Sargara	*749*	*2*	*516*	*1,076*	*35*	*558*	..	*2*	*17*	..	..	..	..	*15*	..
Snatia	*7,632*	*3*	*5,313*	*10,401*	*1,140*	*4,493*	*1*	*199*	*620*	..	..	*75*	*2*	*46*	*1*
Targhara	*4,646*	*4*	*3,424*	*6,315*	*172*	*3,418*	..	*8*	*137*	..	..	*2*	..	*51*	*1*
Kāsi	397	..	308	632	197	79	1	..	2	..	..	..	..	15	..
Lūni	852	1	644	1,319	99	685	..	1	14	..	..	..	..	9	..
Pani	8,867	11	6,378	13,419	412	6,963	1	9	794	..	..	3	1	219	3
Main branch	*2,149*	*4*	*1,347*	*3,214*	*228*	*1,351*	..	*7*	*339*	..	..	..	*1*	*99*	..
Isot	*882*	..	*633*	*1,297*	*5*	*636*	..	..	*158*	..	..	..	..	*6*	..
Mandōkhel	*1,474*	..	*1,179*	*2,291*	*24*	*1,028*	..	*2*	*236*	..	..	..	..	*61*	..
Mūsakhel	*3,740*	*6*	*2,793*	*5,663*	*110*	*3,431*	*1*	..	*59*	..	..	*3*	..	*36*	*3*
Zarkūn	*622*	*1*	*426*	*954*	*45*	*517*	..	..	*2*	..	..	..	..	*17*	..
Shirāni	2,631	3	1,907	4,011	66	2,305	..	2	51	..	..	8	..	58	1
Tarin	11,323	9	8,675	17,289	1,155	8,749	2	6	280	..	..	52	..	134	..
Abdāl Achakzai	*6,278*	*6*	*4,921*	*9,067*	*128*	*5,486*	*2*	*3*	*25*	..	..	*19*	..	*53*	..
Spin Tarin	*1,721*	*3*	*992*	*2,418*	*51*	*1,331*	..	*3*	*192*	..	..	*9*	..	*40*	..
Tor Tarin	*3,324*	..	*2,762*	*5,804*	*976*	*1,932*	..	..	*63*	..	..	*24*	..	*41*	..
Zmarai	432	..	262	534	2	399	..	..	..	..	..	..	..	24	..
Lāsi (Panj Rāj)	**9,323**	**30**	**5,534**	**12,892**	**559½**	**4,484**	..	**277**	**2,810**	**125**	..	..	..	**240**	**26**
Angaria	1,023	2	633	1,488	6	527	..	19	249	29	..	..	..	74	..
Burra	1,806	2	1,127	2,439	49	1,049	..	..	636	28	..	..	..	4	1
Jāmōt	3,351	18	1,852	4,503	177	1,325	..	74	1,492	43	..	..	..	96	17
Rūnjhā	1,689	4	999	2,411	374	970	..	86	60	7	..	..	..	58	4
Shēkh	1,454	4	923	2,051	253	613	..	98	373	18	..	..	..	8	4
Jatt	**27,039**	**16**	**15,631**	**35,711**	**684**	**21,248**	**3**	**148**	**1,214**	**6**	..	**77**	..	**2,328**	**14**
Sayyid	**6,370**	**7**	**4,638**	**10,281**	**1,430**	**3,333**	..	**12**	**424**	..	..	**8**	..	**162**	**2**
Others	**16,739**	**149**	**10,152**	**23,757**	**1,198**	**7,517**	**7**	**103**	**701**	**730**	..	**95**	**2**	**3,137**	**104**
Darzāda	3,229	97	1,986	4,945	85	2,523	6	15	22	37	..	56	..	321	66
Dēhwār	2,728	1	1,281	3,316	994	1,066	1	4	29	2	..	4	..	195	..
Gadrā	2,368	10	1,348	3,475	84	1,231	..	76	135	112	..	1	..	241	10
Jat	1,993	2	1,158	2,527	..	530	..	6	464	..	..	1	..	111	1
Khōja	119	2	66	180	..	..	..	..	..	..	..	..	..	2	2
Lōri	3,624	11	2,288	5,013	12	434	..	2	28	3	..	..	2	2,176	4
Mēd	678	12	581	1,223	..	..	..	..	16	572	..	..	..	18	11
Nakib	2,000	14	1,444	3,078	23	1,733	..	..	7	4	..	33	..	73	10
Miscellaneous Aliens	**3,147**	**85**	**299**	**802**	..	..	**1**	..	..	..	**2**	..	**16**	..	..
European	3,098	70	284	758	..	..	1	..	..	..	2	..	16	..	..
Anglo-Indian	49	15	15	44	..	..	..	..	..	..	..	..	..	..	..

SELECTED TRIBES AND RACES.

PATION OF ACTUAL WORKERS

IV.—Transport		V.—Trade	VI.—Public force		VII.—Public administration		VIII.—Arts and professions			IX.—Persons living on their income	X.—Domestic service		XI.—Labourers unspecified		XII.—Beggars, criminals and inmates of jails and asylums		Tribe or race
Owners, managers, ships' officers, etc.	Labourers, boatmen, carters, etc.		Commissioned and gazetted officers	Others	Gazetted officers	Others	Religious	Lawyers, doctors, teachers, engineers, etc.	Others								
Males	Persons	Persons	Males	Persons	Males	Males	Persons	Persons	Persons	Persons	Males	Females	Males	Females	Males	Females	
17	18	19	20	21	22	23	24	25	26	27	28	29	30	31	32	33	34
..	**1,055**	**231**	..	**53**	..	**450**	**124**	**15**	**16**	**6**	**153**	**17**	**225**	**15**	**223**	..	**Balōch**
..	*163*	*52*	..	*19*	..	*205*	*78*	*12*	*13*	*1*	*105*	*14*	*133*	*13*	*162*	..	*(i) Eastern*
..	1	6	..	..	..	3	2	..	..	..	3	..	69	1	30	..	Bugti
..	..	3	..	..	..	48	17	2	2	..	2	13	1	3	24	..	Khetrān
..	7	34	..	3	..	9	6	5	2	..	57	..	22	4	16	..	Magasi
..	22	1	..	..	..	48	..	..	1	..	2	..	3	1	36	..	Mari
..	133	8	..	16	..	97	53	5	8	1	41	1	38	4	56	..	Rind
..	*892*	*179*	..	*34*	..	*245*	*46*	*3*	*3*	*5*	*48*	*3*	*92*	*2*	*61*	..	*(ii) Western*
..	8	1	..	..	..	2	..	..	..	..	..	..	3	..	..	..	Bulēdī
..	..	1	..	..	..	2	3	..	..	1	..	..	1	..	..	..	Gichkī
..	35	12	..	5	..	7	7	..	..	..	..	..	1	..	3	..	Rais
..	477	25	..	26	..	221	27	..	..	2	10	1	49	2	23	..	Rakhshānī and Naushērwānī
..	86	14	..	3	..	11	9	3	..	2	3	2	6	..	10	..	Rind
..	286	126	..	..	..	2	..	..	3	..	35	..	32	..	25	..	Sangur
..	**2,788**	**418**	**1**	**489**	..	**947**	**153**	**37**	**30**	**11**	**210**	**12**	**744**	**4**	**246**	**10**	**Brāhūī**
..	*152*	*36*	*1*	*61*	..	*120*	*10*	..	..	*2*	*10*	*4*	*53*	*2*	*40*	*4*	*(i) Original nucleus*
..	12	1	..	..	..	9	..	..	..	..	..	..	3	..	1	..	Gurgnāri
..	2	8	..	3	..	6	..	..	..	2	..	..	8	..	18	..	Kalandrāri
..	80	16	..	5	..	9	1	..	..	..	..	2	15	..	4	2	Kambrāri
..	9	3	..	3	..	3	5	..	..	..	4	..	6	1	4	..	Mirwāri
..	19	6	..	15	..	20	3	..	..	..	2	..	6	1	3	..	Rodēnī
..	30	2	1	35	..	73	1	..	..	..	4	2	15	..	10	2	Sumalāri
..	*1,606*	*128*	..	*234*	..	*541*	*90*	*9*	*22*	*3*	*128*	*2*	*346*	*2*	*89*	*3*	*(ii) Sarāwān*
..	279	7	..	51	..	142	18	1	3	..	14	1	28	..	13	3	Bangulzai
..	72	4	..	9	..	29	5	3	..	1	5	1	27	1	4	..	Kūrd
..	195	26	..	16	..	48	14	2	4	1	7	..	48	..	12	..	Lahri
..	291	41	..	24	..	23	7	1	3	..	44	..	90	1	6	..	Lāngav
..	240	7	..	16	..	62	8	..	..	..	5	..	24	..	7	..	Māmashahī
..	71	2	..	5	..	60	12	2	1	..	24	..	7	..	3	..	Raisānī
..	4	3	..	..	..	28	1	..	..	..	2	..	..	..	..	..	Rustumzai
..	46	6	..	32	..	65	6	..	1	..	2	..	13	..	4	..	Sarparra
..	9	1	..	..	..	10	..	..	2	..	1	..	6	..	4	..	Sātakzai
..	328	22	..	45	..	42	16	..	7	..	15	..	50	..	23	..	Shahwānī
..	71	9	..	36	..	42	3	..	1	1	9	..	58	..	18	..	Zagr Mēngal
..	*1,030*	*254*	..	*194*	..	*286*	*53*	*28*	*8*	*6*	*72*	*6*	*345*	..	*117*	*3*	*(iii) Jhalawān*
..	154	50	..	7	..	6	9	..	..	..	14	..	16	..	8	1	Bizanjav
..	14	..	..	2	..	17	..	..	..	..	1	..	2	..	2	..	Hārūnī
..	232	19	..	31	..	68	6	26	..	5	24	1	86	..	44	..	Māmasānī
..	353	53	..	88	..	120	26	1	4	1	20	3	78	..	22	1	Mēngal
..	17	16	..	13	..	11	..	..	..	..	6	..	12	..	4	..	Nichārī
..	4	1	..	2	..	..	1	..	1	..	1	..	9	..	2	..	Pandrānī
..	33	10	..	..	..	..	..	..	..	..	..	2	11	..	10	1	Sājdī
..	223	105	..	51	..	64	11	1	3	..	6	..	131	..	25	..	Zahri
5	**1,155**	**458**	..	**99**	..	**1,430**	**446**	**7**	**116**	**16**	**190**	**7**	**821**	**6**	**415**	**29**	**Pathān**
..	..	3	..	..	..	4	..	1	..	..	..	..	3	..	1	..	Jafar
5	756	291	..	35	..	941	293	1	75	16	133	3	630	3	256	20	Kākar
..	*23*	*8*	..	*3*	..	*46*	*14*	..	*11*	*1*	*4*	..	*39*	..	*19*	..	*Dumar*
..	*284*	*117*	..	*15*	..	*474*	*120*	*1*	*43*	*10*	*50*	*2*	*246*	*3*	*167*	*15*	*Sanzarkhel*
..	*47*	*14*	..	..	..	*29*	*14*	..	*1*	..	*3*	..	*14*	..	..	*2*	*Sargara*
5	*244*	*70*	..	*13*	..	*325*	*91*	..	*18*	*5*	*60*	*1*	*202*	..	*24*	..	*Snatia*
..	*158*	*82*	..	*4*	..	*67*	*51*	..	*2*	..	*16*	..	*129*	..	*46*	*3*	*Targhara*
..	21	5	..	6	..	27	12	1	..	..	3	..	25	..	3	..	Kāsi
..	..	[illegible]	..	..	..	11	8	..	8	..	2	..	11	..	6	1	Lūṇi
..	36	44	..	6	..	256	32	..	13	..	8	1	8	1	66	2	Paṇi
..	*16*	*12*	..	*4*	..	*42*	*9*	..	*5*	..	*3*	*1*	*6*	..	*31*	..	*Main branch*
..	*5*	..	..	..	..	*58*	*4*	..	..	..	..	..	*1*	..	*9*	..	*Isōt*
..	*8*	*28*	..	*1*	..	*71*	*8*	..	*2*	..	*2*	..	..	..	*3*	..	*Mandokhel*
..	*7*	*4*	..	*1*	..	*59*	*8*	..	*3*	..	*3*	..	*2*	..	*14*	*2*	*Mūsakhel*
..	..	..	..	..	..	*26*	*3*	..	*3*	..	..	..	..	*1*	*9*	..	*Zarkūn*
..	7	35	..	16	..	34	10	1	6	..	3	..	14	2	20	..	Shirānī
..	334	77	..	36	..	157	90	2	19	..	41	3	130	..	59	6	Tarin
..	*207*	*48*	..	*29*	..	*94*	*43*	..	*14*	..	*35*	*2*	*75*	..	*17*	*4*	*Abdāl Achakzai*
..	*15*	*8*	..	*1*	..	*21*	*11*	..	*2*	..	*2*	*1*	*16*	..	*19*	*2*	*Spin Tarin*
..	*112*	*21*	..	*6*	..	*42*	*36*	*2*	*3*	..	*4*	..	*39*	..	*23*	..	*Tōr Tarin*
..	1	..	..	..	..	..	1	1	..	..	..	..	..	..	4	..	Zmarai
..	**147**	**34**	..	**102**	..	**65**	**19**	**4**	..	**3**	**5**	**1**	**104**	**1**	**46**	**1**	**Lāsi (Panj Raj)**
..	33	1	..	3	..	2	..	..	..	3	..	1	72	..	6	..	Angāria
..	2	1	..	6	..	7	2	..	..	..	..	..	16	..	6	1	Burrā
..	61	16	..	29	..	9	8	..	..	..	1	..	8	1	12	..	Jāmōt
..	14	12	..	49	..	41	9	4	..	..	1	..	1	..	3	..	Rūnjhā
..	37	4	..	15	..	6	..	..	..	..	3	..	7	..	19	..	Shēkh
..	**304**	**96**	..	**18**	..	**194**	**296**	**22**	**57**	**1**	**114**	..	**91**	..	**210**	..	**Jaṭṭ**
..	**102**	**156**	..	**28**	..	**122**	**542**	**16**	**13**	**10**	**12**	**4**	**59**	**1**	**1**	..	**Sayyid**
..	**929**	**413**	**1**	**237**	..	**136**	**105**	**7**	**472**	**2**	**76**	**22**	**350**	**1**	**583**	**10**	**Others**
..	37	43	..	1	..	19	33	5	6	2	6	22	12	1	7	1	Darzāda
..	40	52	1	133	..	45	40	1	13	..	21	..	36	..	51	1	Dēhwār
..	83	18	..	94	..	27	4	..	..	..	16	..	227	..	19	..	Gadrā
..	720	105	..	..	..	6	4	..	..	..	7	..	28	..	11	1	Jat
..	1	111	..	..	..	2	..	..	..	..	2	..	1	..	..	..	Khōja
..	5	17	..	7	..	8	8	..	452	..	22	..	20	..	428	7	Lōri
..	43	20	..	..	..	3	3	1	1	..	..	..	1	..	1	..	Mēd
..	..	47	..	2	..	26	13	..	..	..	2	..	25	..	16	..	Nakib
116	..	**14**	**313**	**2,599**	**18**	**8**	**9**	**50**	**38**	**16**	**3**	**29**	..	..	..	..	**Miscellaneous Aliens**
95	..	14	312	2,594	17	5	9	40	17	16	3	27	..	..	..	..	European
21	..	..	1	5	1	3	..	10	21	..	..	2	..	..	..	..	Anglo-Indian

TABLE XVII.

Territorial Distribution of the Christian Population by Sect and Race.

The term Anglo-Indian includes all persons of mixed blood formerly known as Eurasian, and is not confined to those of partly British origin.

Under the head 'Minor Protestant Denominations' are grouped one male European belonging to the Church of India, two male Indians belonging to the American Church of God Mission, and two male and two female Indians belonging to the Church of God.

One European male Theosophist and one Indian male Unitarian have been classed under 'Indefinite Beliefs.'

XVII.—TERRITORIAL DISTRIBUTION OF THE CHRISTIAN POPULATION BY SECT AND RACE.

Denominations	BALŪCHISTĀN			DISTRICTS: Quetta-Pishīn		Lōralai		Zhōb		Bōlān		Chāgai		Sibi		STATES: Kalāt		Las Bēla	
	Persons	Males	Females	Males	Females	Males	Females	Males	Females	Males	Females	Males	Females	Males	Females	Males	Females	Males	Females
1	2	3	4	5	6	7	8	9	10	11	12	13	14	15	16	17	18	19	20
All denominations	***5,085***	***3,941***	***1,144***	***3,549***	***1,015***	***58***	***13***	***154***	***14***	***14***	***12***	***6***	***3***	***111***	***81***	***45***	***6***	***4***	..
European and allied races	4,210	3,382	828	3,109	740	41	12	132	12	10	7	1	1	73	52	15	4	1	..
Anglo-Indians	123	64	59	44	39	..	1	1	..	2	3	..	..	12	16	4	..	1	..
Indians	752	495	257	396	236	17	..	21	2	2	2	5	2	26	13	26	2	2	..
Anglican Communion	**3,346**	**2,537**	**809**	**2,281**	**711**	**42**	**12**	**102**	**10**	**11**	**10**	**4**	**3**	**79**	**57**	**16**	**6**	**2**	..
European and allied races	2,870	2,270	600	2,056	529	37	11	99	9	9	7	1	1	59	39	9	4	..	..
Anglo-Indians	58	28	30	14	17	..	1	1	..	2	3	..	..	6	9	4	..	1	..
Indians	418	239	179	211	165	5	..	2	1	..	..	3	2	14	9	3	2	1	..
Baptist	**10**	**7**	**3**	**6**	**3**	..	..	**1**	..	..	..	..	..	..	..	..	..	..	..
European and allied races	10	7	3	6	3	..	..	1	..	..	..	..	..	..	..	..	..	..	..
Anglo-Indians	..	..	..	..	..	..	..	..	..	..	..	..	..	..	..	..	..	..	..
Indians	..	..	..	..	..	..	..	..	..	..	..	..	..	..	..	..	..	..	..
Congregationalist	**2**	**2**	..	**2**	..	..	..	..	..	..	..	..	..	..	..	..	..	..	..
European and allied races	2	2	..	2	..	..	..	..	..	..	..	..	..	..	..	..	..	..	..
Anglo-Indians	..	..	..	..	..	..	..	..	..	..	..	..	..	..	..	..	..	..	..
Indians	..	..	..	..	..	..	..	..	..	..	..	..	..	..	..	..	..	..	..
Lutheran	**2**	**2**	..	..	..	..	..	..	..	..	..	..	..	..	..	..	..	**2**	..
European and allied races	1	1	..	..	..	..	..	..	..	..	..	..	..	..	..	..	..	1	..
Anglo-Indians	..	..	..	..	..	..	..	..	..	..	..	..	..	..	..	..	..	..	..
Indians	1	1	..	..	..	..	..	..	..	..	..	..	..	..	..	..	..	1	..
Methodist	**191**	**137**	**54**	**128**	**51**	..	..	**4**	..	**1**	..	..	..	**4**	**3**	..	..	..	..
European and allied races	158	118	40	110	38	..	..	4	..	1	..	..	..	3	2	..	..	..	..
Anglo-Indians	4	..	4	..	3	..	..	..	..	..	..	..	..	..	1	..	..	..	..
Indians	29	19	10	18	10	..	..	..	..	..	..	..	..	1	..	..	..	..	..
Minor Prot. Denominations	**7**	**5**	**2**	**1**	..	..	..	**1**	..	..	..	..	..	**3**	**2**	..	..	..	..
European and allied races	1	1	..	1	..	..	..	..	..	..	..	..	..	..	..	..	..	..	..
Anglo-Indians	..	..	..	..	..	..	..	..	..	..	..	..	..	..	..	..	..	..	..
Indians	6	4	2	..	..	..	..	1	..	..	..	..	..	3	2	..	..	..	..
Presbyterian	**160**	**121**	**39**	**104**	**36**	**2**	**1**	**7**	**1**	..	..	..	..	**5**	**1**	**3**	..	..	..
European and allied races	139	111	28	97	27	2	1	6	..	..	..	..	..	3	..	3	..	..	..
Anglo-Indians	2	2	..	2	..	..	..	..	..	..	..	..	..	..	..	..	..	..	..
Indians	19	8	11	5	9	..	..	1	1	..	..	..	..	2	1	..	..	..	..
Roman Catholic	**1,360**	**1,125**	**235**	**1,022**	**212**	**14**	..	**39**	**3**	**2**	**2**	**2**	..	**20**	**18**	**26**	..	..	..
European and allied races	1,023	868	155	833	141	2	..	22	3	..	..	..	..	8	11	3	..	..	..
Anglo-Indians	59	34	25	28	19	..	..	..	..	..	..	..	..	6	6	..	..	..	..
Indians	278	223	55	161	52	12	..	17	..	2	2	2	..	6	1	23	..	..	..
Sect not returned	**5**	**3**	**2**	**3**	**2**	..	..	..	..	..	..	..	..	..	..	..	..	..	..
European and allied races	5	3	2	3	2	..	..	..	..	..	..	..	..	..	..	..	..	..	..
Anglo-Indians	..	..	..	..	..	..	..	..	..	..	..	..	..	..	..	..	..	..	..
Indians	..	..	..	..	..	..	..	..	..	..	..	..	..	..	..	..	..	..	..
Indefinite beliefs	**2**	**2**	..	**2**	..	..	..	..	..	..	..	..	..	..	..	..	..	..	..
European and allied races	1	1	..	1	..	..	..	..	..	..	..	..	..	..	..	..	..	..	..
Anglo-Indians	..	..	..	..	..	..	..	..	..	..	..	..	..	..	..	..	..	..	..
Indians	1	1	..	1	..	..	..	..	..	..	..	..	..	..	..	..	..	..	..

TABLE XVIII.

Europeans, Armenians and Anglo-Indians by Age.

No Armenians were returned in Balūchistān.

The term Anglo-Indian includes all persons of mixed blood formerly known as Eurasian, and is not confined to those of partly British origin.

XVIII.—EUROPEANS, ARMENIANS AND ANGLO-INDIANS BY AGE.

Race and Age	BALŪCHISTĀN			DISTRICTS												STATES			
				QUETTA-PISHĪN		LŌRALAI		ZHŌB		BŌLĀN		CHĀGAI		SIBI		KALĀT		LAS BĒLA	
	Persons	Males	Females	Males	Females	Males	Females	Males	Females	Males	Females	Males	Females	Males	Females	Males	Females	Males	Females
1	2	3	4	5	6	7	8	9	10	11	12	13	14	15	16	17	18	19	20
Total	*4,333*	*3,446*	*887*	*3,153*	*779*	*41*	*13*	*133*	*12*	*12*	*10*	*1*	*1*	*85*	*68*	*19*	*4*	*2*	..
European and Allied Races	**4,210**	**3,382**	**828**	**3,109**	**740**	**41**	**12**	**132**	**12**	**10**	**7**	**1**	**1**	**73**	**52**	**15**	**4**	**1**	..
British subjects	4,169	3,360	809	3,088	724	41	11	132	12	10	6	1	1	73	51	15	4	..	..
0—12	506	249	257	225	235	4	2	6	2	1	1	..	..	13	16	..	1	..	..
12—15	40	20	20	18	19	..	..	1	..	..	..	..	..	1	1	..	..	..	..
15—30	2,549	2,300	249	2,171	226	15	2	90	..	2	3	..	..	16	17	6	1	..	..
30—50	1,018	754	264	643	228	22	7	35	10	5	2	1	1	39	14	9	2	..	..
50 and over	56	37	19	31	16	..	..	..	..	2	..	..	..	4	3	..	..	..	..
Others	41	22	19	21	16	..	1	..	..	..	1	..	..	..	1	..	..	1	..
0—12	5	4	1	4	1	..	..	..	..	..	..	..	..	..	..	..	..	..	..
12—15	..	..	..	..	..	..	..	..	..	..	..	..	..	..	..	..	..	..	..
15—30	13	6	7	6	6	..	1	..	..	..	..	..	..	..	..	..	..	..	..
30—50	17	7	10	6	8	..	..	..	..	..	1	..	..	..	1	..	..	1	..
50 and over	6	5	1	5	1	..	..	..	..	..	..	..	..	..	..	..	..	..	..
Anglo-Indians	**123**	**64**	**59**	**44**	**39**	..	**1**	**1**	..	**2**	**3**	..	..	**12**	**16**	**4**	..	**1**	..
0—12	25	14	11	9	5	..	..	..	..	..	..	..	..	5	6	..	..	..	..
12—15	5	2	3	..	1	..	..	..	..	1	1	..	..	1	1	..	..	..	..
15—30	53	23	30	17	22	..	1	1	..	1	1	..	..	3	6	1	..	..	..
30—50	35	23	12	16	8	..	..	..	..	..	1	..	..	3	3	3	..	1	..
50 and over	5	2	3	2	3	..	..	..	..	..	..	..	..	..	..	..	..	..	..

PROVINCIAL TABLE I.

Area and Population by Political Agencies, Tahsils and other Local Areas.

In this and the following table certain main statistics are given for the administrative divisions of the various Political Agencies.

Statistics of nomadism were collected in the tribal census only; all censused in the regular areas have accordingly been assumed to be 'settled.'

I.—AREA AND POPULATION BY POLITICAL AGENCIES, TAHSILS AND OTHER LOCAL AREAS.

Political Agency, Tahsil, etc	Area (square miles)	Population												Percentage of variation, 1901-11	No. of persons per square mile, 1911
		1911									1901				
		Total			Settled		Semi-nomadic		Nomadic						
		Persons	Males	Females	Males	Females	Males	Females	Males	Females	Persons	Males	Females		
1	2	3	4	5	6	7	8	9	10	11	12	13	14	15	16
BALŪCHISTĀN	*134,638*	*834,703*	*466,419*	*368,284*	*273,528*	*208,842*	*52,457*	*44,538*	*140,434*	*114,904*	*810,746*	*445,520*	*365,226*	*+3*	*6·2*
I. Quetta-Pishin Agency	**5,220**	**127,648**	**76,467**	**51,181**	**59,853**	**37,693**	**2,767**	**2,239**	**13,847**	**11,249**	**114,087**	**68,945**	**45,142**	**+11·9**	**24·5**
Pishīn Tahsīl	3,052	53,295	28,374	24,921	23,379	20,797	1,707	1,401	3,288	2,723	51,753	28,258	23,495	+ 2·9	17·4
Chaman Subdivision	1,206	17,252	10,048	7,204	1,920	515	358	292	7,770	6,397	16,437	9,915	6,522	+ 4·9	14·3
Shōrarūd Sub Tahsīl	414	2,079	1,077	1,002	676	630	59	59	342	313	1,062	573	489	+95·7	5
Quetta Tahsīl	548	55,022	36,968	18,054	33,878	15,751	643	487	2,447	1,816	44,835	30,199	14,636	+22·7	100·4
II. Lōralai Agency	**7,525**	**80,769**	**44,923**	**35,846**	**25,090**	**18,928**	**9,679**	**8,611**	**10,154**	**8,307**	**68,332**	**38,088**	**30,244**	**+18·2**	**10.7**
Dukī Tahsīl	1,688	17,219	9,368	7,851	5,176	4,388	23	11	4,169	3,452	12,630	6,875	5,755	+36·3	10·2
Bōri Tahsīl	1,671	17,298	10,743	6,555	8,271	4,473	906	832	1,566	1,250	18,174	11,220	6,954	− 4·8	10·3
Sanjāwī Sub Tahsīl	676	7,568	4,107	3,461	2,155	1,743	1,566	1,441	386	277	6,866	3,630	3,236	+10·2	11·1
Bārkhān Tahsīl	1,309	17,970	9,618	8,352	7,064	6,304	581	483	1,973	1,565	15,125	7,989	7,136	+18·8	13·6
Mūsakhēl Tahsīl	2,181	20,714	11,087	9,627	2,424	2,020	6,603	5,844	2,060	1,763	15,537	8,374	7,163	+33·3	9·4
III. Zhōb Agency	**10,315**	**70,366**	**40,346**	**30,020**	**9,797**	**4,266**	**22,260**	**19,105**	**8,289**	**6,649**	**69,718**	**39,637**	**30,081**	**+·9**	**6·8**
Fort Sandeman Tahsīl	3,882	35,970	21,255	14,715	8,092	3,170	9,879	8,929	3,284	2,616	34,854	20,102	14,752	+ 3·2	9·2
Hindūbāgh Tahsīl	1,459	12,360	6,806	5,554	1,036	740	5,403	4,499	367	315	12,518	6,973	5,545	− 1·2	8·4
Killa Saifulla Tahsīl	2,398	17,820	9,955	7,865	570	325	6,933	5,635	2,452	1,905	18,102	10,212	7,890	− 1·5	7·4
Kākar Khurasān Sub Tahsīl	2,576	4,216	2,330	1,886	99	31	45	42	2,186	1,813	4,244	2,350	1,894	− ·6	1·6
IV. Chāgai Agency	**19,622**	**16,344**	**9,107**	**7,237**	**3,482**	**2,482**	**588**	**534**	**5,037**	**4,221**	**15,689**	**8,259**	**7,430**	**+4·2**	**·8**
Nushkī Tahsīl	2,361	8,118	4,520	3,598	3,027	2,332	582	533	911	733	10,756	5,735	5,021	−24·5	3·4
Chāgai Tahsīl	7,407	6,606	3,634	2,972	233	54	...	...	3,401	2,918	4,933	2,524	2,409	+33·9	·8
Western Sanjrānī country	9,854	1,620	953	667	222	96	6	1	725	570	...	...	...	...	·1
V. Sibi Agency	**11,193**	**117,189**	**66,846**	**50,343**	**37,740**	**26,883**	**2,378**	**1,794**	**26,728**	**21,666**	**112,344**	**63,111**	**49,233**	**+4·3**	**10·5**
Sibi Tahsīl	1,169	25,581	15,080	10,501	12,909	8,649	296	242	1,875	1,610	23,848	13,484	10,364	+ 7·2	21·8
Shāhrig Tahsīl	1,567	18,152	10,970	7,182	4,694	1,859	587	436	5,689	4,887	16,573	9,421	7,152	+ 9·5	11·6
Nasīrābād Tahsīl	827	33,977	18,810	15,167	18,527	14,942	80	69	203	156	35,713	19,885	15,828	− 4·8	41
Kōhlu Sub Tahsīl	362	4,713	2,698	2,015	787	694	44	32	1,867	1,289	1,853	1,046	807	+154·3	13
Marī country	3,392	14,109	7,823	6,286	623	473	1,338	983	5,862	4,830	15,829	9,009	6,820	−10·8	4·1
Bugṭī country	3,876	20,657	11,465	9,192	200	266	33	32	11,232	8,894	18,528	10,266	8,262	+11·4	5·3
VI. Kalāt Agency	**80,763**	**422,387**	**228,730**	**193,657**	**137,566**	**118,590**	**14,785**	**12,255**	**76,379**	**62,812**	**430,576**	**227,480**	**203,096**	**−1·9**	**5·2**
Bōlān	353	2,096	1,492	604	1,463	585	..	...	29	19	1,936	1,483	453	+ 8·2	5·9
Kalāt	73,278	359,086	194,598	164,488	116,487	100,616	14,718	12,207	63,393	51,665	372,531	196,279	176,252	− 3·6	4·9
Sarāwān	*5,230*	*63,781*	*35,082*	*28,699*	*13,073*	*10,909*	*9,481*	*7,700*	*12,528*	*10,090*	*65,549*	*36,366*	*29,183*	*− 2·6*	*12·1*
Jhalawān	*20,795*	*84,398*	*46,880*	*37,518*	*10,561*	*8,839*	*2,307*	*1,868*	*34,012*	*26,811*	*224,073*	*115,077*	*108,996*	*−62·3*	*4*
Kachhi	*4,060*	*92,759*	*50,191*	*42,568*	*48,670*	*41,344*	*426*	*349*	*1,095*	*875*	*63,367*	*34,251*	*29,116*	*+46·3*	*22·8*
Ḍōmbkī-Kahērī country[1]	*1,359*	*23,543*	*12,624*	*10,919*	*11,446*	*9,958*	*31*	*32*	*1,147*	*929*	*19,542*	*10,585*	*8,957*	*+20·4*	*17·3*
Makrān	*23,269*	*71,942*	*37,698*	*34,244*	*28,117*	*25,501*	*662*	*682*	*8,919*	*8,061*	...	...	...	...	*3*
Khārān[2]	*18,565*	*22,663*	*12,123*	*10,540*	*4,620*	*4,065*	*1,811*	*1,576*	*5,692*	*4,899*		...		...	*1·2*
Las Bēla	7,132	61,205	32,640	28,565	19,616	17,389	67	48	12,957	11,128	56,109	29,718	26,391	+ 9	8·5

[1] For certain purposes the Ḍōmbkī-Kahērī country is under the control of the Sibī Political Agency.
[2] Khārān is temporarily under the Political Agent, Chāgai.

PROVINCIAL TABLE II.

Population of Political Agencies, etc., by Religion and Education.

II.—POPULATION OF POLITICAL AGENCIES, ETC., BY RELIGION AND EDUCATION.

Political Agency, tahsil, etc	Legal status	DISTRIBUTION BY RELIGION										NO. OF LITERATES	
		MUSALMĀN		HINDU		SIKH		CHRISTIAN		OTHERS			
		Males	Females	Males	Females	Males	Females	Males	Females	Males	Females	Males	Females
1	2	3	4	5	6	7	8	9	10	11	12	13	14
BALŪCHISTĀN	......	***430,850***	***351,798***	***25,008***	***12,594***	***6,017***	***2,373***	***3,941***	***1,144***	***603***	***375***	***26,202***	***1,723***
I. Quetta-Pishin Agency	......	**60,950**	**45,752**	**9,600**	**3,644**	**1,934**	**496**	**3,549**	**1,015**	**434**	**274**	**11,484**	**1,263**
Pishin Tahsīl	British Balūchistān	27,825	24,695	426	190	95	25	3	...	25	11	797	23
Chaman Sub division	British Balūchistān	9,047	6,974	569	183	395	18	30	25	7	4	610	40
Shōrarūd Sub Tahsīl	British Balūchistān	1,071	995	6	7	...	...	...	...	...	...	16	...
Quetta Tahsīl	Agency Territory	23,007	13,088	8,599	3,264	1,444	453	3,516	990	402	259	10,061	1,200
II. Lōralai Agency	....	**41,955**	**34,800**	**2,038**	**920**	**838**	**98**	**58**	**13**	**34**	**15**	**2,083**	**83**
Dukī Tahsīl	British Balūchistān	9,064	7,643	283	200	17	3	1	...	13	5	228	13
Bōrī Tahsīl	Agency Territory	8,734	6,123	1,178	327	761	85	56	13	14	7	1,381	60
Sanjāwi Sub Tahsīl	Agency Territory	4,064	3,450	32	5	18	4	...	...	3	2	40	2
Bārkhān Tahsīl	Agency Territory	9,162	8,025	446	322	8	5	1	...	1	...	306	8
Mūsakhēl Tahsīl	Agency Territory	10,951	9,559	99	66	34	1	...	...	3	1	128	...
III. Zhōb Agency	......	**38,363**	**29,725**	**1,150**	**198**	**649**	**66**	**154**	**14**	**30**	**17**	**1,567**	**52**
Fort Sandeman Tahsīl	Agency Territory	19,383	14,449	1,096	178	597	63	154	14	25	11	1,375	46
Hindubāgh Tahsīl	Agency Territory	6,762	5,537	30	11	11	2	...	...	3	4	113	4
Killa Saifulla Tahsīl	Agency Territory	9,890	7,853	22	9	41	1	...	...	2	2	74	2
Kākaṛ Khurasān Sub Tahsīl	Agency Territory	2,328	1,886	2	...	...	...	...	...	...	...	5	...
IV. Chāgai Agency	......	**8,800**	**7,116**	**264**	**112**	**29**	**5**	**6**	**3**	**8**	**1**	**376**	**23**
Nushkī Tahsīl	Quasi-Agency Territory	4,275	3,482	221	109	19	4	2	2	3	1	263	18
Chāgai Tahsīl	Quasi-Agency Territory	3,585	2,968	38	3	4	...	4	1	3	...	87	3
Western Sanjrānī country	Quasi-Agency Territory	940	666	5	...	6	1	..	...	2	...	26	2
V. Sibī Agency	......	**60,788**	**47,685**	**5,002**	**2,313**	**861**	**207**	**111**	**81**	**84**	**57**	**3,628**	**242**
Sibī Tahsīl	British Balūchistān	11,680	9,042	2,907	1,260	352	95	84	65	57	39	1,848	160
Shāhrig Tahsīl	British Balūchistān	9,978	6,952	580	153	361	43	27	16	24	18	847	65
Nasīrābād Tahsīl	Agency Territory	17,364	14,372	1,297	726	146	69	...	...	3	..	818	17
Kōhlu Sub Tahsīl	Agency Territory	2,682	2,008	14	7	2	...	...	...	...	...	25	...
Mari country	Tribal area	7,738	6,223	85	63	...	...	...	...	...	...	22	...
Bugṭi country	Tribal area	11,346	9,088	119	104	...	..	...	.	..	.	73	...
VI. Kalāt Agency	......	**219,994**	**186,720**	**6,954**	**5,407**	**1,706**	**1,501**	**63**	**18**	**13**	**11**	**7,064**	**60**
Bōlān	Agency Territory	972	450	416	107	82	25	14	12	8	10	274	26
Kalāt	Native State	187,435	158,471	5,550	4,552	1,564	1,458	45	6	4	1	5,720	25
Sarāwān	......	*34,411*	*28,249*	*600*	*403*	*68*	*45*	*3*	*2*	...	...	*995*	*7*
Jhalawān	......	*46,491*	*37,423*	*380*	*92*	*9*	*3*	...	...	...	...	*274*	...
Kachhī	......	*45,823*	*38,566*	*3,748*	*3,428*	*616*	*572*	*4*	*2*	...	...	*2,684*	*9*
Dōmbkī-Kahērī country	......	*11,091*	*9,483*	*664*	*598*	*869*	*838*	...	...	...	...	*1,164*	*2*
Makrān	......	*37,528*	*34,230*	*126*	*11*	*2*	...	*38*	*2*	*4*	*1*	*484*	*7*
Khārān	......	*12,091*	*10,520*	*32*	*20*	...	...	...	...	...	...	*119*	...
Las Bēla	Native State	31,587	27,799	988	748	60	18	4	...	1	...	1,070	9

INDEX

INDEX.

(The references throughout are to paragraphs, not pages.)